Fortifying Your Faith

by David E. Sproule, II

Fortifying Your Faith

Copyright © 2017 by   David Sproule
4067 Leo Lane
Palm Beach Gardens, FL 33410

All rights reserved. No part of this book may be reproduced in any form without written permission from the author.

Unless otherwise indicated, all Scripture quotations are the New King James Version®. Copyright © 1982 by Thomas Nelson, Inc. Used by Permission. All rights reserved.

ISBN-10: 1981281835
ISBN-13: 978-1981281831

Preface

The Christian faith is under attack. Unfortunately, today, those attacks are not only coming from outside the Lord's church, but also from inside. There is a critical need among members of the body of Christ to have their faith fortified!

Many Christians today are struggling with their faith. There are new converts, who are trying to get their "spiritual feet underneath them." There are young people, who are trying to determine the truthfulness of what they have been taught. There are other Christians, who have been in the church for a while but have not grown as they should. There is a critical need, especially among these members of the body of Christ, to have their faith fortified!

The Lord's church desperately needs strong leaders today. Those men who may be appointed as elders in the church one day must be able to discern truth from error (Acts 20:28-30; 1 John 4:1, 6) and "be able both to exhort in sound doctrine and to refute those who contradict" (Tit. 1:9, NASB). There is a critical need, especially among these men in the body of Christ, to have their faith fortified!

These are the three main purposes for the production of this book. These are not considered merely localized needs, confined to one particular area or one particular congregation. The Christian faith is under attack everywhere. Christians are struggling with their faith everywhere. Strong leaders are needed in the church everywhere. Thus, this material was published to fortify the faith of Christians everywhere.

These 26 lessons were prepared for and presented to the Palm Beach Lakes church of Christ in West Palm Beach, Florida, over the course of an entire year. The elders wanted to have a specialized class for all of the members on Sunday afternoons that would "increase" their faith (Luke 17:5), "ground" them in the faith (Col. 1:23) and "strengthen" (i.e., fortify) their faith (Acts 14:22; 18:23). These lessons were designed for that purpose, and it is believed that they can be of great benefit to all Christians, congregations and Bible students.

Appreciation is expressed to Dan Jenkins, for his input and suggestions in the writing of these lessons. Dan and I have labored together at Palm Beach Lakes for more than 20 years, and he is a dear friend.

The word "fortify" means "to strengthen and secure," in order "to protect against attack." That is the prayer for each reader of this book—that your faith may be strengthened and secured in the Word of God, in order to protect against attack from the evil one. May all such fortifying of faith be to the glory of God!

Table of Contents

1. The Godhead 1
2. The Work of the Holy Spirit 8
3. The Inspiration of the Bible 17
4. Authority in Religion 30
5. Interpreting the Bible 37
6. The Two Covenants 67
7. The Divine Origin of the Church 76
8. The Distinct Nature of the Church 84
9. The Unique Identity of the Church 91
10. The Unity of the Church 99
11. Christians and Denominationalism 114
12. The Organization of the Church 130
13. Qualifications and Responsibilities of Elders 140
14. The Mission and Work of the Church 155
15. The Worship of the Church 164
16. The Lord's Supper 175
17. Music in the Worship of the Church 185
18. The Role of Women in the Church 198
19. The Doctrine of Salvation 207
20. The Person, Process & Purpose of Baptism 228
21. The Danger and Reality of Apostasy 246
22. Withdraw of Fellowship 260
23. The Second Coming of Christ 282
24. The Purpose and Duration of Miracles 307
25. Marriage, Divorce and Remarriage 329
26. The Christian Life 374

Lesson 1: The Godhead

I. **To Understand the Godhead, We Must Understand "God."**
   A. When one thinks of "God," it is usually "God, the Father" who is in mind.
      1. However, the term "God" is more of a description than merely a name.
      2. The word "God" emphasizes divine nature.
   B. The most frequent Hebrew word for "God" is *Elohim*.
      1. *Elohim* occurs more than 2,500 times in the Old Testament.
      2. The name *Elohim* emphasizes strength, might and the power to create and effect.
      3. *Elohim* is an apt description for the Creator and Sustainer of all things.
      4. God truly is the Supreme One!
   C. *Elohim* is a Hebrew masculine noun that is a plural form.
      1. "In the beginning God created the heavens and the earth" (Gen. 1:1).
      2. "God" is from *Elohim* and is plural. "Created" is a singular verb.
      3. *Elohim* (plural) is almost always tied to a singular verb or adjective.
      4. This is significant in a study of the Godhead.
   D. The most frequent Hebrew name for God is *Jehovah*.
      1. *Jehovah* occurs more than 6,500 times in the Old Testament.
      2. *Jehovah* (or *Yahweh*) is translated Lord, so English readers can recognize the word.
      3. The name *Jehovah* comes from a Hebrew word that means "to be" or "being."
      4. Jehovah, therefore, is "the being one, the existing one," thus, "the eternal one."
      5. This name assured the Jews of the special covenant they had with the one true God.
   E. *Jehovah* is, therefore, the Great "I AM."
      1. "And God said to Moses, 'I AM WHO I AM'" (Ex. 3:14; cf. 6:3). This is *Jehovah*.
      2. It has been noted that "I AM WHO I AM" emphasizes God's self-existence, self-sufficiency and immutability.
      3. This helps to see the significance of Jesus claiming to be "I AM" (John 8:58, 24).
   F. The Jews so revered the name *Jehovah* that they determined to never pronounce it.
      1. They would often substitute the word *Adonai* when reading the Scriptures.
      2. *Adonai*, also a plural form, means "Master," "Lord" and even "Owner."
      3. The N.T. equivalent is *kurios*, which means "Lord," "Master," "Supreme Authority."

II. **To Understand the Godhead, We Must Understand the Nature/Essence of God.**
   A. In studying the nature/essence of God, we are studying "what God is."
   B. God is Spirit (John 4:24; Luke 24:39; Rom. 1:20; John 1:18).
      1. God is not a material being (Acts 17:29).
      2. God does not have a body, although the Bible uses anthropomorphic language to speak of God in human terms, to help humans understand His nature.
   C. God is Self-Existent (John 5:26; Acts 17:25).
      1. God is the "first cause," and therefore, He is "uncaused."
      2. God is not dependent upon any outside factor for His existence.
      3. God is the "living God," who caused all things to exist (Matt. 16:16; Heb. 3:4).
      4. God "does whatever He pleases" (Psa. 115:3).
   D. God is a Person/Personality (Psa. 23; John 3:16).
      1. God is not an impersonal force or power or influence.
      2. God is described as a "Person" in human terms to emphasize to us that He is a "Personality" with "arms," "eyes," "hands," etc., who "knows," "commands," "wills," "hears," "walks," etc., and Who also possesses "joy," "love," "anger," "grief," etc.

E. God is Limitless/Infinite (1 Kgs. 8:27; Isa. 66:1; Rev. 1:4, 8).
   1. God is not limited or contained to a time, space or matter.
   2. Finite creatures cannot possibly comprehend the fullness of that which is infinite.
   3. Yet, the Infinite is interested in His finite creatures (Heb. 2:6; Matt. 10:30; Phil. 2:5-8).
F. God is Eternal (Psa. 90:1-2; 102:27; Isa. 44:6; 46:9-10; 57:15; Deut. 33:27; Jude 25).
   1. God is without beginning or end.
   2. God is not limited by time. He does not view time as we do. He is the "I Am."
   3. God is immortal (1 Tim. 1:17; 6:16).
G. God is Omnipresent (Psa. 139:7-12; Jer. 23:23-24; Acts 17:27-28).
   1. God is everywhere. He is not contained or limited by space.
   2. God sees all (Prov. 15:3; 1 Pet. 3:12; 2 Chron. 16:9).
H. God is Omnipotent (Gen. 17:1; 18:14; Rev. 19:6; Jer. 32:17; Luke 1:37; Eph. 3:20-21).
   1. God is all-powerful and all-mighty. He is able to do whatever He wills.
   2. God has unlimited power to do all things consistent with His nature and purpose.
I. God is Omniscient (Psa. 139:1-6; 147:5; Rom. 11:33-36; Job 38:3-5; Matt. 10:29-30).
   1. God is all-wise and all-knowing. He knows everything.
   2. There is nothing hidden or unknown to God (Heb. 4:12-13; Ezek. 11:5; Ecc. 12:14).
J. God is Immutable (Jas. 1:17; Mal. 3:6; Heb. 1:12; Ex. 3:14; Num. 23:19; Ecc. 3:14).
   1. God is unchangeable in His nature, His essence and His attributes.
   2. God does not increase or decrease, improve or deteriorate! He is perfect!
K. Each member of the Godhead equally retains and shares the one essence of God!

III. To Understand the Godhead, We Must Understand the Attributes/Qualities of God.
A. In studying the attributes of God, we are studying "what God does in relation to man."
   1. These are the distinguishing characteristics or inherent qualities of the divine nature.
   2. God possesses these qualities to an infinite degree—they are absolute and unchanging.
B. God is Holy (Isa. 6:1-5; Ex. 15:11; Rev. 15:4; Psa. 99:5, 9; 1 Pet. 1:15-16; Hab. 1:13).
C. God is Love (1 John 4:7-21; John 3:16; Rom. 5:8; Eph. 2:4; Rev. 1:5; Eph. 5:2).
D. God is Good (Psa. 52:1; 25:8; 100:5; 107:1-43; Mark 10:18; Nah. 1:7).
E. God is Truth (Psa. 146:5-6; Num. 23:19; Heb. 6:17-18; Tit. 1:2; John 1:17; 8:32; 17:17).
F. God is Faithful (Lam. 3:22-23; Deut. 7:9; Psa. 36:5; 89:8; 2 Tim. 2:13; 1 Cor. 1:9; 10:13).
G. God is Patient (Rom. 15:5; Psa. 114:8; Nah. 1:3; Num. 14:18; 1 Pet. 3:20; 2 Pet. 3:9).
H. God is Just (Gen. 18:25; 1 John 3:7; Isa. 45:21; Psa. 89:14; Rom. 3:26; 1 John 1:9).
I. God is Gracious and Merciful (Ex. 34:6; Psa. 136; 57:10; Rom. 3:24-26; Eph. 2:1-10).
J. God is a God of Wrath (Rom. 1:28; Psa. 95:11; Heb. 10:31; 12:29; Rom. 11:22; Rev. 19:15).
K. Each member of the Godhead equally retains and shares these attributes/qualities of God.
   1. Each of these qualities are necessary—to an infinite degree—for God to be God!

IV. To Understand the Godhead, We Must Understand That There Is One God!
A. Belief in the God of the Bible is monotheism and not polytheism.
   1. Monotheism is the belief that there is one God.
   2. Polytheism is the belief that there are numerous gods.
   3. The Biblical doctrine of the Godhead affirms monotheism and not polytheism.
B. The Bible teaches clearly, repeatedly and firmly that there is only one God!
   1. "The LORD our God, the LORD is one!" (Deut. 6:4; cf. Mark 12:29-32; Zech. 14:9).
   2. "You shall have no other gods before me" (Ex. 20:3).
   3. "...the LORD Himself is God; there is none other besides Him" (Deut. 4:35, 39; 1 Kgs. 8:60).
   4. "I, even I, am the LORD, And besides Me there is no savior" (Isa. 43:11).
   5. "There is one God" (1 Tim. 2:5), for "God is one" (Gal. 3:20; cf. Jas. 2:19).

C. There is one "God," but that is not the "name" of His personality but of His nature.
   1. To be "God" necessitates being divine in one's nature and one's quality.
   2. There exists only one divine Being possessing the one divine nature – there is only God!
   3. That divine nature is not divided but is equally retained and shared by the one God.
V. **The Bible Student Must Understand What the Bible Teaches about the Godhead.**
   A. First of all, it would be helpful to define some terms.
      1. The word "Godhead" is found three times in the Bible (in various translations).
         (a) The Greek words used in these passages (Acts 17:29; Rom. 1:20; Col. 2:9) all signify "divinity" or "deity" or "divine nature/essence."
         (b) The term as used in these passages does not immediately entail three entities.
      2. The word "Godhead" has come to be used to express the Biblical concept of the "divine nature/essence" being shared by three distinct Personalities of the Godhead.
      3. The word "trinity" is not in the Bible, but when it is properly (i.e., Biblically) defined, it also focuses on the one divine essence of the three personalities.
   B. The Bible teaches that:
      1. There are three divine (and distinct) personalities (Father, Son and Holy Spirit), who each fully share the one (i.e., the same) divine nature (see II on pages 2-3), and who exist and function in complete unity as One. (See diagram on page 6.)
      2. Each member of the Godhead is equally, distinctly and totally God (i.e., divine).
         (a) The Father is God (1 Cor. 1:3; Eph. 1:3).
            (1) But, the Father is not the Son (Mark 13:32) or the Holy Spirit (Matt. 3:16-17).
         (b) The Son is God (John 1:1-2, 14; Tit. 2:13; Heb. 1:8).
            (1) But, the Son is not the Father (Heb. 1:5) or the Holy Spirit (John 14:26).
         (c) The Holy Spirit is God (Acts 5:3-4; 1 Cor. 2:11-14).
            (1) But, the Holy Spirit is not the Father (Gal. 4:6) or the Son (John 15:26).
         (d) Each one is referred to as God, therefore, each One is divine!
            (1) Yet, each One is distinct from the others, therefore, there must be three distinct personalities in the one true Godhead (or nature of God).
         (e) Those who argue (including the Jehovah's Witnesses) that the Son and the Spirit are not divine in nature argue against the plain teaching of the Bible.
         (f) Those who argue (including the United Pentecostal Church) that the Father, the Son and the Holy Spirit are merely manifestations or names of a single divine person without any distinctions are also arguing against the plain teaching of the Bible.
      3. There is one divine nature with three distinct personalities possessing that nature.
   C. The divine plurality is taught in the Old Testament.
      1. The Old and New Testaments both emphasize the unity of the Godhead, while at the same time emphasizing the plurality of the Godhead.
         (a) The Old Testament does not make known the triune nature (but the N.T. does).
      2. The Old Testament frequently uses plural nouns with singular verbs.
         (a) "In the beginning God (plural) created (singular)" (Gen. 1:1).
         (b) "Remember now your Creator (plural) in the days of your youth" (Ecc. 12:1).
         (c) "The LORD (singular) our God (plural), the LORD (singular) is one!" (Deut. 6:4).
      3. The Old Testament frequently uses the second person plural pronoun for God.
         (a) "Then God (plural) said, 'Let **Us** make man in **Our** image, according to **Our** likeness" (Gen. 1:26; cf. 3:22).
         (b) "Come (plural), let **Us** go down and there confuse their language" (Gen. 11:7).

            (c) "I heard the voice of the Lord, saying: 'Whom shall I send, And who will go for **Us**?'" (Isa. 6:8).
        4. The Old Testament distinction of divine personalities reaches into the New Testament.
            (a) There are numerous prophecies of the Messiah applied to the Christ of the N.T.
            (b) There are numerous references to Jehovah which are applied to Christ in the N.T.
            (c) "The LORD (Jehovah) said to my Lord, 'Sit at My right hand, Till I make Your enemies Your footstool'" (Psa. 110:1). This verse emphasizes:
                (1) Distinction within the Godhead.
                (2) Communication within the Godhead.
                (3) That Jesus shares in the Godhead (divine nature).
    D. The divine plurality is taught in the New Testament.
        1. The triune nature of the Godhead is made known in the New Testament.
        2. The three persons of the Godhead are spoken of together and yet separate:
            (a) "When He had been baptized, **Jesus** came up immediately from the water; and behold, the heavens were opened to Him, and He saw **the Spirit of God** descending like a dove and alighting upon Him. And suddenly a **voice came from heaven**, saying, 'This is My beloved **Son**, in whom **I am** well pleased'" (Matt. 3:16-17).
            (b) "Go therefore and make disciples of all the nations, baptizing them in the name of **the Father** and of **the Son** and of **the Holy Spirit**" (Matt. 28:19).
            (c) "...**the Holy Spirit**, whom **the Father** will send in **My** name" (John 14:26).
            (d) "The grace of the **Lord Jesus Christ**, and the love of **God**, and the communion of **the Holy Spirit** be with you all" (2 Cor. 13:14).
            (e) "There is one body and one **Spirit**, just as you were called in one hope of your calling; one **Lord**, one faith, one baptism; one God and **Father** of all" (Eph. 4:4-6).
            (f) "...elect according to the foreknowledge of God **the Father**, in sanctification of **the Spirit**, for obedience and sprinkling of the blood of **Jesus Christ**..." (1 Pet. 1:2).
        3. There are distinctions made between the Father and the Son (1 Tim. 2:5; John 1:1; 5:22, 30; 7:16, 28; 8:16-17, 19, 38, 42, 54; 15:1; 16:27; Mark 13:32; 1 Cor. 8:6; Eph. 2:18).
        4. There are distinctions made between the Son and the Holy Spirit (Matt. 12:32; 3:16-17; John 14:16, 26; 15:26).
        5. There are distinctions made between the Father and the Holy Spirit (John 14:16, 26; 15:26; 1 Cor. 2:11-14; Gal. 4:6).
    E. The Bible teaches that each member of the Godhead is equally divine.
        1. Each is eternal: Father (Isa. 44:6; Rom. 16:26), Son (Rev. 1:17), Spirit (Heb. 9:14).
        2. Each is God: Father (1 Pet. 1:2), Son (Heb. 1:8; John 1:1), Spirit (Acts 5:3-4).
        3. Each created: Father (1 Cor. 8:6; Psa. 100:3), Son (Col. 1:16; John 1:3), Spirit (Job 33:4).
        4. Each is omnipresent: Father (Jer. 23:24), Son (Matt. 28:20), Spirit (Psa. 139:7).
    F. Our inability to fully comprehend a Bible subject does not nullify its truthfulness.
VI. The Bible Teaches That Jesus Christ Is God.
    A. The summary of the whole Bible is Jesus Christ (John 3:16; 1 Pet. 1:18-19; Gal. 3:19-25).
    B. Jesus is God.
        1. "'...They shall call His name Immanuel,' which is translated, 'God with us'" (Matt. 1:23).
        2. "...The Word was God" (John 1:1).
    C. Jesus is eternal.
        1. "Before Abraham was, I AM" (John 8:58).
        2. "In the beginning was the Word" (John 1:1).

D. Jesus is fully divine.
   1. "For in Him dwells all the fullness of the Godhead bodily" (Col. 2:9).
   2. "...with the glory which I had with You before the world was" (John 17:4-5).
E. Jesus is the Creator.
   1. "All things were made through Him, and without Him nothing was made that was made" (John 1:3).
   2. "For by Him all things were created that are in heaven and that are on earth, visible and invisible, whether thrones or dominions or principalities or powers. All things were created through Him and for Him" (Col. 1:16).
F. Jesus is Jehovah.
   1. John the Baptist prepared the way for Jehovah/Jesus (Isa. 40:3-5 + Mark 1:1-3).
   2. Jehovah/Jesus created all things (Isa. 44:24; 42:5 + Col. 1:16; John 1:3).
   3. Jehovah/Jesus is the Savior (Isa. 43:11 + Tit. 2:13).
   4. Jehovah/Jesus is the Redeemer (Isa. 43:14 + Tit. 2:13-14).
   5. Jehovah/Jesus is the first and the last (Isa. 44:6 + Rev. 1:17; 2:8).
   6. Jehovah/Jesus is God (Isa. 45:5 + John 1:1, 14; Tit. 2:13).
   7. Jehovah/Jesus is the I AM (Ex. 3:14 + John 8:58).
   8. The sacred name "Jehovah" is applied to Jesus, as well as to the Father.
   9. Jesus is not a created being (as Jehovah's Witnesses teach). He is Jehovah God!
G. Jesus is Deity.
   1. Jesus fulfilled all 332 Old Testament prophecies about the coming Messiah (Luke 24:44).
   2. Jesus was born of a virgin (Isa. 7:14; Matt. 1:20-23).
   3. Jesus worked many genuine miracles (John 10:37-38; 20:30-31; Matt. 11:3-5; Acts 2:22).
   4. Jesus forgives sins (Mark 2:1-12; Luke 7:44-50).
   5. Jesus accepts worship (Matt. 2:11; 8:2; 9:18; Mark 14:32-33; John 20:28; Rev. 5:13-14).
   6. Jesus was raised from the dead (Mt. 28; Mk. 16; Lk. 24; Jn. 20; 1 Cor. 15:3-23; Rom. 1:4).
H. Two key passages help Bible readers to know who Jesus is.
   1. John 1:1-3, 14
      (a) The Greek imperfect tense ("was") emphasizes a continuous action in the past.
      (b) Jesus was already existing "in the beginning," He was "with God" as long as God was God, and He "was God" as long as God was God. Jesus is the eternal God!
   2. Philippians 2:5-11
      (a) Jesus has always been and always will be "existing in the form of God" (2:6, ASV).
      (b) He possesses the essence of divine nature, as does the Father and the Spirit!

VII. The Bible Doctrine of the Godhead Demands a Response.
   A. As God's creation, we must acknowledge Him and believe in Him (Heb. 11:6; John 8:24).
   B. As God's creation, we must submit to Him and obey Him (Col. 3:17; Matt. 28:18-20).
   C. As God's creation, we must worship Him (Matt. 4:10; John 4:23-24; Rev. 22:9).
   D. As God's creation, we must love Him above everything else (Deut. 6:4-5; Mark 12:29-32).

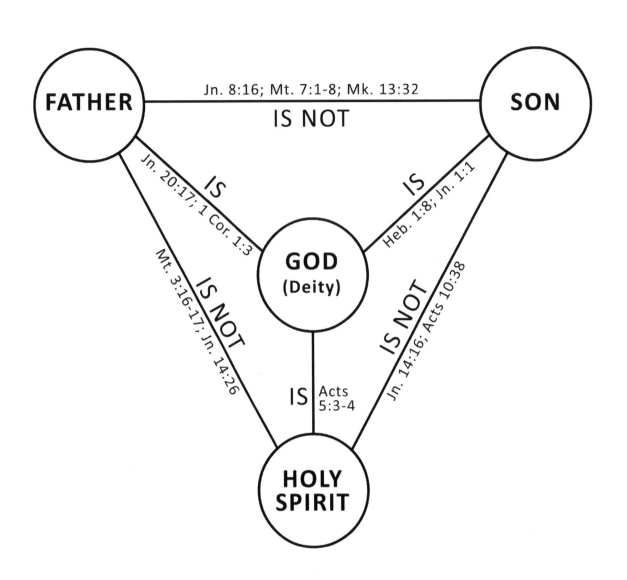

Recommended Resources

<u>Books</u>

Clarke, B.J., ed. *The Godhead: A Study of the Father, Son and Holy Spirit.* Southaven, MS: Southaven church of Christ, 1998.

Lanier, Roy H., Sr. *The Timeless Trinity for the Ceaseless Centuries.* Denver: Lanier, 1974.

Taylor, Robert R., Jr. *The Bible Doctrine of Jehovah God.* Abilene: Quality Publications, 2002.

Turner, J.J. & Edward P. Myers. *Doctrine of the Godhead.* Abilene: Quality Publications, 1985.

<u>Articles</u>

Butt, Kyle. "The Trinity." *ApologeticsPress.org.*
http://www.apologeticspress.org/APContent.aspx?category=11&article=5233

Clarke, B.J. "Jesus Christ—The Fulness of the Godhead Bodily." *Exalting Jesus Christ.* Ed. Donald W. Walker. San Antonio, TX: Shenandoah church of Christ, 1999. 38-56.

Jackson, Wayne. "The Biblical Doctrine of the Godhead." *ChristianCourier.com.*
https://www.christiancourier.com/articles/1488-biblical-doctrine-of-the-godhead-the

Jackson, Wayne. "Was Jesus the 'Son of God' Eternally?" *ChristianCourier.com.*
https://www.christiancourier.com/articles/1359-was-jesus-the-son-of-god-eternally

Jackson, Wayne. "What About the Terms 'Godhead' And 'Trinity'?" *ChristianCourier.com.*
https://www.christiancourier.com/articles/821-what-about-the-terms-godhead-and-trinity

Lyons, Eric. "The Only True God." *ApologeticsPress.org.*
http://www.apologeticspress.org/APContent.aspx?category=6&article=983

Vestal, Mike. "The Triune Nature of God." *The Godhead: A Study of the Father, Son, and Holy Spirit.* Ed. B.J. Clarke. Southaven, MS: Southaven church of Christ, 1998. 119-139.

Lesson 2: The Work of the Holy Spirit

I. **A Biblically Correct Understanding of the Holy Spirit Is Essential!**
   A. There is so much misunderstanding, misinformation and misleading about the Holy Spirit.
      1. Some view the Holy Spirit as some sort of mystical force, like a ghost or energy field.
      2. Some have created entire doctrines which demand a direct operation of the Holy Spirit upon the heart of an alien sinner, which is entirely without Biblical foundation.
      3. Some have become so confused that they avoid all study on the topic of the Spirit.
   B. Christians need to know what the Bible teaches about the Holy Spirit!
      1. There are certainly some things that we do not know and cannot know (Deut. 29:29).
      2. But, where the Bible speaks, (1) we need to learn, and (2) we need to speak.
      3. In order to be able to defend against error on this topic, we need to know the truth!
   C. We must study the truth about the Spirit, not as a reaction to error but as a desire for truth!

II. **The Holy Spirit Is a Divine Person in the Godhead!**
   A. The Holy Spirit is "a person."
      1. The personal, masculine pronouns applied to the Holy Spirit show that He is "a person."
         (a) Jesus used seven personal pronouns for the Holy Spirit in John 16:13 alone.
         (b) The Holy Spirit is not an "it" or a mystical force. He is a "He."
      2. The works of the Holy Spirit proclaim that He is "a person."
         (a) Scripture teaches that He "speaks" (John 16:13; 1 Tim. 4:1), "testifies" (John 15:26), "teaches" and "stirs the memory" (John 14:26), "guides" (John 16:13), "leads" and "forbids" (Acts 16:6-7), "searches" (1 Cor. 2:10), etc.
         (b) A "thing" or an "influence" cannot do these things. Only a person can do them.
      3. The characteristics of the Holy Spirit verify that He is "a person."
         (a) He has a "mind" (Rom. 8:27), "knowledge" (1 Cor. 2:11), "affection" (Rom. 15:30), a "will" (1 Cor. 12:11), "goodness" (Neh. 9:20), etc.
         (b) A "thing" or an "influence" cannot have these things. Only a person can.
      4. The slights and injuries that He is able to suffer proves the Holy Spirit is "a person."
         (a) He can be "grieved" (Eph. 4:30; Isa. 63:10), "lied to" (Acts 5:3), "insulted" (Heb. 10:29), "blasphemed" (Matt. 12:31-32), "resisted" (Acts 7:51), etc.
         (b) A "thing" or "influence" cannot suffer such maltreatment. Only a person can.
   B. The Holy Spirit is a "Divine" person.
      1. The attributes of the Holy Spirit show that He is a "Divine" person.
         (a) He is "eternal" (Heb. 9:14), "omniscient" (1 Cor. 2:10-11), "omnipotent" (Mic. 3:8), "omnipresent" (Psa. 139:7-12). "The Holy Spirit" (Acts 5:3) is "God" (5:4).
         (b) Who but the Divine can possess such attributes?
      2. The works of the Holy Spirit indicate that He is a "Divine" person.
         (a) The Holy Spirit was at work in creation (Gen. 1:2; Job 26:13; 33:4; Ps. 33:6; 104:30).
         (b) The Holy Spirit is at work in regeneration (John 3:5; Tit. 3:5; Rom. 8:11).
         (c) The Holy Spirit is at work in providence (Psa. 104:30; Isa. 63:10-14; Acts 16:6-7).
         (d) The Holy Spirit was at work in the revelation and inspiration of the Holy Scriptures (Eph. 3:1-7; 1 Pet. 1:10-12; 2 Pet. 1:20-21).
         (e) The Holy Spirit was the source of the miraculous, when such was being practiced (Matt. 12:28; Acts 2:1-4ff; 1 Cor. 12:4-11; Heb. 2:1-4; 1 Cor. 13:8-10).
         (f) The Holy Spirit was the "another Comforter" whom the Father sent (John 14:16).
         (g) Who but the Divine can do such works?

C. The Holy Spirit is a Divine person "in the Godhead."
   1. The Bible teaches that there is a Godhead (Acts 17:29; Rom. 1:20; Col. 2:9).
   2. The Bible teaches that the Godhead is composed of three Divine persons—the Father, the Son and the Holy Spirit (Matt. 28:19; Rom. 15:30; 2 Cor. 13:14; Eph. 4:3-6).
   3. The Bible teaches that the three persons of the Godhead are separate and distinct (John 14:26; 16:13-15; Matt. 3:13-17), and that the Spirit is equally one of the three.

III. The Holy Spirit Was at Work Among God's People Throughout the Old Testament!
A. The Bible reader is introduced to the Holy Spirit in the second verse of the Bible.
   1. "And the Spirit of God was hovering over the face of the waters" (Gen. 1:2).
B. Pharaoh recognized the Spirit working providentially in the life of Joseph (Gen. 41:38).
C. "The Spirit of God" "filled" certain men with special abilities (which they did not possess before), in order to be used by God to build His tabernacle (Ex. 31:1-11; 35:30-35).
D. "The Spirit of God" gave "word," "oracle" and "utterance" to God's prophets, to speak as inspired messengers to mankind and "instruct" them on behalf of God (Num. 24:2-9; 2 Sam. 23:2; 2 Chron. 15:1; 24:20; Neh. 9:20, 30; Ezek. 2:2; Zech. 7:12; cf. 2 Pet. 1:20-21).
E. "The Spirit of the Lord came upon" the judges as they led God's people (Judg. 3:10; 6:34; 11:29).
F. "The Spirit of the Lord" is spoken of frequently in the life of Samson, giving him strength and courage (Judg. 13:25; 14:6, 19; cf. 16:5, 19-20).
G. "The Spirit of the Lord" worked among the kings of Israel (1 Sam. 10:6, 10; 16:13-14; 2 Sam. 23:2; 1 Chron. 28:11-12).
H. Nebuchadnezzar recognized that the Spirit of God was at work in the life and the words of Daniel (Dan. 4:8-9, 18).
I. Joel prophesied of the establishment of the Lord's kingdom and of the Spirit's power-filled and abundant work in those early days of the church: "And it shall come to pass afterward That I will pour out My Spirit on all flesh" (Joel 2:38-32).
J. Since "whatever things were written before were written for our learning" (Rom. 15:4), there is much that we can learn from the O.T. about the Holy Spirit and how He operated.

IV. The Holy Spirit Was Responsible for Divine Revelation!
A. The Holy Spirit was operative in the revelation of God's Word to mankind.
   1. God's Word was revealed in words—an objective, understandable form of instruction.
   2. Note carefully that "prophecy never came by the will of man" (2 Pet. 1:21).
   3. Therefore, the words *always* came as inspired men "were moved by the Holy Spirit."
   4. David affirmed, "The Spirit of the Lord spoke by me, and His word was on my tongue" (2 Sam. 23:2; see also Acts 1:16). The words spoken were of the Holy Spirit.
   5. Jesus promised His apostles, "It will be given to you...what you should speak; for it is not you who speak, but the Spirit of your Father who speaks in you" (Mt. 10:19-20).
   6. The promises of the revelations of the Spirit in John 14-16 (to remind, bear witness, teach, guide) applied to those inspired men in the first century and not to us today.
      (a) Read through those chapters and mark every time Jesus used the word "you."
      (b) Then, know the context: Jesus is speaking to His apostles before He leaves them.
   7. God has revealed His Word and His wisdom to us "through His Spirit" (1 Cor. 2:10-13).
   8. See Lesson 3 for more on "The Inspiration of the Bible."
B. The Holy Spirit was operative in the overwhelming measure (i.e., baptism) of the Spirit.
   1. The Spirit was promised to be poured out on all flesh, Jews and Gentiles (Matt. 3:11; John 1:33-34; Joel 2:28-32; Acts 2:17-21).
   2. There are only two recorded instances of Holy Spirit baptism (Acts 2 and Acts 10).

3. In Acts 2, the apostles (Jews) were overwhelmed/baptized by the Holy Spirit:
   (a) To fulfill the promise of Jesus to His apostles (John 14:26; 16:13; Acts 1:4-5).
   (b) To empower them to perform miracles and impart miraculous gifts to Christians through the laying on of their hands (Acts 1:8; 2:3-4, 6-8; 3:6-10; 4:7-10; 8:14-19).
4. In Acts 10, the household of Cornelius (Gentiles) were baptized by the Holy Spirit:
   (a) To convince the Jews that the Gentiles had a right to salvation (10:44-48; 11:14-18).
5. Peter affirmed that these were the only two instances of Spirit baptism (Ac. 11:15-17).
6. Today there is only "one baptism" (Eph. 4:5).
   (a) Holy Spirit baptism was limited and temporary (and no longer occurring today).
   (b) Water baptism is the "one baptism," "even to the end of the age" (Matt. 28:18-20).
7. See Lesson 24 for more on the baptism of the Holy Spirit.

C. The Holy Spirit was operative in the spiritual gifts measure of the Spirit in the first century.
   1. The apostles were empowered to impart miraculous gifts to Christians through the "laying on of the apostles' hands" (Acts 8:18; 6:6; 19:6; 2 Tim. 1:6).
   2. These miraculous gifts worked "signs" which were intended to "confirm" the spoken message (Mk. 16:20; Heb. 2:3-4)—power from God proving the message was from God.
      (a) These miraculous, spiritual gifts included: the word of wisdom, the word of knowledge, faith, gifts of healings, the working of miracles, prophecy, discerning of spirits, different kinds of tongues, the interpretation of tongues (1 Cor. 12:7-12).
      (b) These gifts also aided in the building of the church, giving ordinary people supernatural gifts, so the church could function (see 1 Cor. 14).
   3. The duration of this measure of the Spirit (i.e., miraculous gifts) was limited:
      (a) It was limited to new revelations being confirmed. There are no new revelations from God today (Jude 3; 2 Pet. 1:3; 2 Tim. 3:16-17). Thus, this measure has ceased.
      (b) It was limited until the revelation of the N.T. was complete (1 Co. 13:8-13; Eph. 4:7-13). Now that the revelation of God is complete (Jude 3), this measure has ceased.
      (c) It was limited by the laying on of the apostles' hands (Acts 8:14-19). Since there are no apostles alive today (Acts 1:21-26), this measure has ceased.
   4. See Lesson 24 on "The Purpose and Duration of Miracles" for more on spiritual gifts.

D. There is NO new revelation being made to any man today by the Holy Spirit!
   1. The revelation of God is complete (Jude 3; 2 Pet. 1:3; 2 Tim. 3:16-17).
   2. No further miraculous manifestations of the Spirit are needed or will be forthcoming.
   3. Therefore, the Word of God, in our Bibles, is the final and last revelation of the Spirit!
   4. See Lesson 4 on "Authority in Religion" for more on the all-sufficiency of Scripture.

V. **The Holy Spirit Works in the Conversion of a Sinner to Christ!**
   A. Denominational churches and preachers have twisted this doctrine.
      1. John Calvin taught "Irresistible Grace," in which the Holy Spirit's operation to convict the sinner, create faith and convert him to Christ is an act that cannot be "resisted."
      2. Some denominations have followed suit in emphasizing that "the Spirit called me" or "the Spirit showed me" or "the Spirit whispered to me" to "bring me to Christ."
      3. The question we must ask and answer is: What does the Bible say?
   B. The work of the Spirit in the conversion of a sinner to Christ is to convict him of sin.
      1. One cannot be converted to Christ without being convicted of sin (Acts 2:37-38).
      2. Jesus clearly identified "conviction" as the work of the Spirit in conversion (Jn. 16:7-8).
      3. So, the question remains: How does the Spirit convict a person of sin?

C. The work of the Spirit in the **conviction** of the sinner is done through God's Word.
   1. The Word of God is the product of the Holy Spirit, which is the means by which the Spirit operates. (Read 2 Samuel 23:2; Nehemiah 9:20+30; Acts 1:16; Mark 13:11.)
   2. "The Word" (i.e., the product of the Spirit and not the direct operation of the Spirit) is what generates faith in the heart of a sinner (Rom. 10:17).
   3. The only instrument wielded by the Holy Spirit is "the sword of the Spirit, which is the word of God" (Eph. 6:17); therefore, He will not operate by another means.
   4. The first converts "were cut to the heart"…"when they heard" the Word (Acts 2:37).
   5. If the Spirit were to operate outside or in addition to God's Word, it would prove that the Word is not all-sufficient (2 Tim. 3:17), complete (2 Pet. 1:3) and final (Jude 3).
   6. See Lesson 4 on "Authority in Religion."
D. The work of the Spirit in the **conversion** of the sinner is done through God's Word.
   1. The Word might "convict" someone, but that does not mean they are "converted."
      (a) To be "converted" is a step beyond and above being "convicted."
      (b) Again, through the Word is the only means by which He will operate on a sinner.
   2. The new birth requires two elements—"water and the Spirit" (John 3:5).
      (a) "The Spirit" (John 3:5; Tit. 3:5) is shown to work through "the word" (Eph. 5:26).
      (b) One is baptized into the body "by the Spirit" (1 Co. 12:13), or "the word" (Eph. 5:26).
      (c) One is born again of "the Spirit" (John 3:5), through "the word" (1 Pet. 1:22-23).
      (d) One is "washed, sanctified…by the Spirit" through "the gospel" (1 Cor. 6:11; 4:15).
      (e) Notice how the effects of the Spirit are always tied to the effects of the Word.
   3. The emphasis of the New Testament could not be more obvious: the Holy Spirit is at work in the conversion of a sinner to Christ, but only through the Word of God.
   4. This chart below helps to emphasize how Scripture explains itself in the work of the Spirit in the conversion process.
      (a) The Holy Spirit is operative in the new birth through one's obedience the Word.
      (b) The water of baptism is operative in the new birth as sins as washed away.
      (c) Upon one's obedience to the Spirit's Word regarding water baptism, one is saved/cleansed from all sin and added to the Lord's body/kingdom.

Passage	Spirit/Word	Baptism	Result
John 3:5	"born of…**the Spirit**"	"born of **water**"	"enter the **kingdom** of God"
1 Cor. 12:13	"by one **Spirit**"	"baptized"	"into one **body**"
Eph. 5:26	"by **the word**"	"the **washing** of water"	"**cleanse**"
Titus 3:5	"renewing of **the Holy Spirit**"	"the **washing** of regeneration"	"**saved**"

E. The work of the Spirit in the conviction of the sinner is **never** directly on the heart.
   1. If the Spirit works directly on the heart of the sinner separate from the Word:
      (a) Then the Word is not all-sufficient, as it claims to be (2 Tim. 3:16-17; 2 Pet. 1:3).
      (b) Then the gospel is not the power of God unto salvation (Rom. 1:16; Jas. 1:21).
      (c) Then the preaching of the gospel is useless for conversion (1 Cor. 1:21).
      (d) Then the mission of the church has no purpose toward salvation (Mk. 16:15-16).
      (e) Then God is partial, for all do not receive the direct operation (Acts 10:34-25).

2. If the Spirit works directly on the heart of the sinner separate from the Word, then these questions must be answered:
    (a) Why is there not a single record of such taking place in the New Testament?
    (b) Why is there not a single conversion in Acts that can be accredited to the direct operation of the Holy Spirit and where the gospel had not been proclaimed?
    (c) How does that account for people who are not convicted? Is the Holy Spirit showing partiality? Or is that evidence of the Holy Spirit's failure or weakness?
    (d) Why has no Christian, or even a primitive knowledge of Jesus, ever been found in remote locales where the gospel has never reached?
    (e) What purpose do we have in going and preaching the Word?
F. The work of the Spirit in the conviction and conversion of the sinner is tied directly to the effect that the Word of God has on the sinner's heart as he learns it and responds to it.
    1. It is irresponsible and without Scriptural authority to teach more or less than that!

VI. The Holy Spirit Works in the Life of a Faithful Christian!
A. Different people respond differently to the idea of the Holy Spirit working in a Christian.
    1. Some embrace it and find joy in the thought of God taking a personal interest in them.
    2. Some go too far in thinking the Spirit talks to them, nudges them and controls them.
    3. Some avoid the idea all together and think the Spirit has nothing to do in/for them.
    4. The question we must ask and answer again is: What does the Bible say?
B. The Bible teaches that the Holy Spirit dwells in every faithful Christian.
    1. The Bible teaches that the Father dwells in us (John 14:23; 1 John 4:12-16; Eph. 4:6).
    2. The Bible teaches that the Son dwells in us (Col. 1:27; 2 Cor. 13:5; Ro. 8:10; Eph. 3:17).
    3. Should it be so hard to believe that the Bible teaches that the Spirit also dwells in us?
       (a) In actuality, God dwells in us through His Spirit (Eph. 2:22; 1 John 3:24; 4:13).
    4. The Holy Spirit is given (as a "gift") "to those who obey Him" (Acts 5:32; 2:38).
    5. The Spirit "is in" the Christian, who is "the temple of the Holy Spirit" (1 Cor. 6:19-20).
    6. "The Spirit of God dwells in" faithful Christians (stated three times in Romans 8:9-11).
    7. Read also Galatians 4:6; 2 Timothy 1:14; 1 Thessalonians 4:8; 1 John 3:24; 4:13; etc.
    8. However, in no passage does the Bible ever teach that the indwelling of God is sensory, physically perceptible or gives anyone a certain "feeling" of His presence.
       (a) Unlike the "baptism measure" and "spiritual gifts measure" of the Spirit, which
           (1) were miraculous measures limited to the first century, and
           (2) were not bestowed on every Christian, and
           (3) involved perceptible demonstrations of the Spirit's presence,
       (b) the "indwelling measure" of the Spirit is
           (1) for all Christians in all centuries (including today),
           (2) but there are no perceptible manifestations of His indwelling.
       (c) We only know that the Spirit dwells in us because the Bible tells us so.
C. The Bible teaches that the Holy Spirit's indwelling is essential for the Christian.
    1. The indwelling confirms to God that a Christian is redeemed in Christ (Eph. 1:13; 4:30).
    2. The indwelling assures that the Christian belongs to God (1 John 4:13; Rom. 8:9).
    3. The indwelling authenticates that a Christian is a child of God (Gal. 4:6; Rom. 8:14-17).
    4. The indwelling serves as a "guarantee of our inheritance" (Ep. 1:13-14; 2 Co. 1:22; 5:1-5).
    5. The indwelling should motivate us to "flee" from sin (1 Cor. 6:18-20; Rom. 8:9, 13).
    6. The indwelling is not unconditional. The Christian must remain faithful and not depart from God (Heb. 3:12; Psa. 51:10-11; Rom. 8:9b).

7. Do not misunderstand or misapply the indwelling of the Spirit. Keep these statements in the context of the fullness of N.T. revelation, including the next point.
D. The Bible teaches that the Holy Spirit's indwelling is in conjunction with His Word.
   1. The exact "how" of the Spirit's indwelling in the Christian is not revealed or known.
   2. The Spirit's indwelling must be in conjunction with the indwelling of the Word, for:
      (a) Christians are told that both are to "dwell" in and "fill" them (Eph. 5:18; Col. 3:16).
      (b) The work of the Spirit in a Christian cannot be outside of or separate from the Word, for God's Word is all-sufficient for the Christian life (2 Tim. 3:16-17; 2 Pet. 1:3).
      (c) The Spirit does not whisper in a Christian's ear or nudge him against his will.
   3. The Spirit's indwelling is not miraculous, for that age has passed (1 Cor. 13:8-13).
   4. The Spirit's working in the Christian is tied to the Word—exactly how is not known.
E. The Bible teaches that the Holy Spirit's indwelling imparts blessings to the Christian.
   1. Again, it must be emphasized that the exact manner of this working is unknown.
      (a) It must also be emphasized again the Spirit's work is connected to the Word.
      (b) It must also be emphasized that we must not venture where the Bible is silent.
      (c) It must also be emphasized that the Spirit is not some subjective, fuzzy "feeling."
   2. When God, through His Spirit (Eph. 2:22; 1 John 3:24), dwells in us:
      (a) He "transforms" us (2 Cor. 3:18), giving us "strength" (Eph. 3:16; Rom. 8:13), "love" (Rom. 5:5), "comfort" (Acts 9:31), "hope" (Rom. 15:13), "peace and joy" (Rom. 14:17), but not miraculously. This is done as we "behold" His Word (2 Cor. 3:18).
      (b) He helps us to produce and bear the "fruit of the Spirit" (Gal. 5:22-23; cf. 5:16-25).
      (c) He "helps us in our weaknesses" and "makes intercession for us," when "we do not know what we should pray for as we ought" (Rom. 8:26-27; cf. Eph. 6:18).
   3. What a reassuring comfort to know that the Lord is working in us (Phil. 2:13)!
F. The Bible often uses the figure of speech known as synecdoche.
   1. Synecdoche is figure used when a part is put for the whole or the whole for the part, or when part of an action is used to represent the entire action, or the entire action is used to represent the parts involved in the action.
      (a) We use synecdoche frequently, more than we might realize. For example:
         (1) "He asked for her hand in marriage." Did he just want to marry her hand?
         (2) "He got a new set of wheels." Did he get the rest of the car, too?
         (3) "The farmer planted his crop." Did he use a tractor, a team of mules or did he do it by hand? Synecdoche allows for any of these.
      (b) Two different sentences can describe the same action:
      "The man cut down the tree." "The sharp axe took the tree down with ease."
         (1) The first sentence affirms the action.
         (2) The second sentence identifies the manner in which the action was accomplished (or the implement that was used to carry out the task).
   2. Synecdoche is used in the Bible with reference to the work of the Holy Spirit.
      (a) The Spirit works powerfully in the conversion of men to Christ and in their spiritual growth as children of God.
         (1) How does He do that?
         (2) What implement (if any) does He use to carry out His task?
      (b) The Bible is described as "the sword of the Spirit" (Eph. 6:17).
         (1) The Word is the manner in which (or the implement used by) the Spirit to accomplish His work (like the sharp axe in the illustration above).

3. This chart visually depicts how the Spirit uses the Word.
   (a) The left column shows that the Holy Spirit works.
   (b) The right column shows that the Word is actively involved as the Spirit works.

The Holy Spirit	The Word
Witnesses/Testifies (Rom. 8:16; John 15:26)	Witnesses/Testifies (Jn. 5:39; Heb. 10:15-16)
Instructs (Neh. 9:10)	Instructs (2 Tim. 3:14-17)
Gives life (John 6:63; 2 Cor. 3:6)	Gives life (Psa. 119:50)
Teaches (John 14:26)	Teaches (John 6:45)
Convicts (John 16:8)	Convicts (Tit. 1:9)
Begets thru new birth (John 3:1-5)	Begets thru new birth (1 Pet. 1:23; 1 Cor. 4:15)
Saves (Tit. 3:5)	Saves (Jam. 1:21; Acts 11:14)
Sanctifies (1 Cor. 6:11; 1 Pet. 1:2)	Sanctifies (John 17:17)
Washes (1 Cor. 6:11)	Washes (Eph. 5:26)
Frees (Rom. 8:2)	Frees (John 8:32)
Comforts (Acts 9:31)	Comforts (1 Thess. 4:18)
Gives love (Rom. 5:5)	Gives love (1 John 2:5)
Leads (Rom. 8:14)	Leads (Psa. 119:105)
Dwells (Rom. 8:9-11)	Dwells (Col. 3:16)
Strengthens (Eph. 3:16)	Strengthens (Acts 20:32; Deut. 11:8)
Has power (Rom. 15:13)	Has power (Heb. 4:12)
Raises the dead (Rom. 8:11)	Raises the dead (John 5:28-29)

VII. Conclusion
A. There is much about the Holy Spirit and His work that we do not know!
B. We must not speak or suppose or wander into realms where God has given no revelation!
C. Nevertheless, where God has spoken, we must learn, teach and abide!
D. The Holy Spirit does not speak to us, move us or tell us what to do!
E. The Bible speaks to us, moves us and tells us what to do, for it is all-sufficient for the task!
   1. The Holy Spirit guided the Bible writers "into all truth" (John 16:13).
   2. Therefore, in the Bible, we have all the truth that the Spirit intended for us to have.
F. How encouraging to know that as a Christian, we are not alone, but God is with us!
   1. As Christians, we have a new relationship with the Father, the Son and the Holy Spirit, which the world does not have (Matt. 28:18-20).
   2. The entire Godhead is interested in us and is "for us" (Rom. 8:26, 31, 34).
G. When it comes to the work of the Holy Spirit, may God help us to:
   1. Speak only where the Bible speaks, and
   2. Live humbly and faithfully as "the temple of the Holy Spirit" (1 Cor. 6:19-20).

Recommended Resources

Books

Nichols, Gus. *Lectures on the Holy Spirit.* Plainview, TX: Nichols Bros. Publishing, 1967.

Sweeney, Z.T. *The Spirit and the Word.* Nashville: Gospel Advocate, nd.

Taylor, Robert R., Jr. *The Bible Doctrine of the Holy Spirit.* Abilene: Quality Publications, 1996.

Winkler, Wendell. *The Holy Spirit: Questions Often Asked.* Tuscaloosa, AL: Winkler Publications, 2005.

Winkler, Wendell, ed. *"What Do You Know About the Holy Spirit?" (Fort Worth Lectures).* Montgomery, AL: Winkler Publication, 1980.

Articles

Boren, Maxie B. "Your Body Is the Temple of the Holy Spirit." *"What Do You Know About the Holy Spirit?" (Fort Worth Lectures).* Ed. Wendell Winkler. Montgomery, AL: Winkler Publication, 1980. 91-99.

Deaver, Roy. "Romans 8 and the Holy Spirit." *"What Do You Know About the Holy Spirit?" (Fort Worth Lectures).* Ed. Wendell Winkler. Montgomery, AL: Winkler Publication, 1980. 243-249.

Duncan, Bobby. "He Shall Baptize You with the Holy Ghost and with Fire." *"What Do You Know About the Holy Spirit?" (Fort Worth Lectures).* Ed. Wendell Winkler. Montgomery, AL: Winkler Publication, 1980. 124-134.

Jackson, Wayne. "False Ideas about the Holy Spirit." *ChristianCourier.com*.
https://www.christiancourier.com/articles/29-false-ideas-about-the-holy-spirit

---. "Is Holy Spirit Baptism Available Today?" *ChristianCourier.com*.
https://www.christiancourier.com/articles/519-is-holy-spirit-baptism-available-today

---. "What Do You Know About the Holy Spirit?" *ChristianCourier.com*.
https://www.christiancourier.com/articles/1545-what-do-you-know-about-the-holy-spirit

Marlin, J.T. "How Did, or Does, God Work Through the Holy Spirit?" *Questions Men Ask About God (Fort Worth Lectures).* Ed. Eddie Whitten. Bedford, TX: Christian Supply Center, 1987. 266-274.

McCord, Hugo. "The Indwelling of the Holy Spirit and the Christian." *"What Do You Know About the Holy Spirit?" (Fort Worth Lectures).* Ed. Wendell Winkler. Montgomery, AL: Winkler Publication, 1980. 352-356.

Meadows, James. "The Holy Spirit and Cornelius." *"What Do You Know About the Holy Spirit?" (Fort Worth Lectures).* Ed. Wendell Winkler. Montgomery, AL: Winkler Publication, 1980. 318-327.

Music, Goebel. "The Personality, Individuality, Attributes, Deity and Names of the Holy Spirit." *"What Do You Know About the Holy Spirit?" (Fort Worth Lectures).* Ed. Wendell Winkler. Montgomery, AL: Winkler Publication, 1980. 7-17.

Turner, Rex A. "The Holy Spirit and Conversion." *"What Do You Know About the Holy Spirit?" (Fort Worth Lectures).* Ed. Wendell Winkler. Montgomery, AL: Winkler Publication, 1980. 106-115.

Waddey, John. "For As Many As Are Led By the Spirit of God, They Are the Sons of God." *"What Do You Know About the Holy Spirit?" (Fort Worth Lectures).* Ed. Wendell Winkler. Montgomery, AL: Winkler Publication, 1980. 267-272.

Watkins, James W. "The Holy Spirit and the Word." *"What Do You Know About the Holy Spirit?" (Fort Worth Lectures).* Ed. Wendell Winkler. Montgomery, AL: Winkler Publication, 1980. 164-168.

Young, Frank D. "The Measures of the Spirit." *"What Do You Know About the Holy Spirit?" (Fort Worth Lectures).* Ed. Wendell Winkler. Montgomery, AL: Winkler Publication, 1980. 58-64.

Lesson 3: The Inspiration of the Bible

I. **In an Age of Skepticism, the Bible Reader Can Have Confidence in the Bible.**
   A. We are living in an age of great skepticism, agnosticism and atheism.
   B. In many places (especially in schools), a deliberate effort is being made to destroy faith in the Bible as the Word of God.
   C. At the same time, there are other books that claim to be inspired and call for followers.
      1. The Hindus have the Vedas and the Bhagavad Gita.
      2. The Buddhists have the Tipitaka.
      3. The Muslims have the Koran.
      4. The Mormons have the Book of Mormon.
   D. In a sea of confusion, the Bible reader can have absolute confidence that the 66 books of the Bible (and no other religious volume) are inspired by the God of heaven.

II. **It Is Important to Understand the Definitions of Revelation and Inspiration.**
   A. The word "revelation" means an "uncovering" of something previously unknown to man.
   B. **Revelation** is God's revealing of Himself to mankind.
      1. God wants man to come to know Him and even have a relationship with Him.
   C. There are two types of revelation:
      1. There is **general revelation**, which is a "natural" revelation.
         (a) This is God revealing Himself to mankind through His creation.
         (b) Through creation, God has revealed Himself to all peoples at all times in all places.
         (c) "He did not leave Himself without witness…" (Acts 14:17).
         (d) "The heavens declare the glory of God…" (Psa. 19:1).
         (e) His creation reveals "His eternal power and divine nature" (Rom. 1:19-20).
         (f) By itself, general revelation is not sufficient to bring mankind into a saving relationship with God.
      2. There is **special revelation**, which is a "supernatural" revelation.
         (a) This is God revealing Himself to mankind through the Bible.
            (1) While in Biblical times God revealed Himself to mankind through direct appearances, direct communications and miraculous events, those were temporary means of revelation—only for a specific time, people and purpose.
            (2) The Bible is the one permanent revelation of God to man.
         (b) The purpose of special revelation is to give mankind a deeper knowledge of God and His eternal plan, and to bring people into a saving relationship with God.
   D. **Inspiration** is God's working directly through select men to write the very words of God without error or omission.
      1. "Inspiration" comes from the Greek word *theopneustos,* which literally means "God-breathed."
      2. "Inspiration is that mysterious process by which the divine causality worked through the human prophets without destroying their individual personalities and styles to produce divinely authoritative and inerrant writings" (Geisler & Nix, *A General Introduction to the Bible,* p. 39).
      3. Inspiration is "that inexplicable power which the Divine Spirit put forth of old on the authors of holy Scripture, in order to their guidance even in the employment of the words they used, and to preserve them alike from all error and from all omission" (L. Glaussen, *Theopneustia—The Plenary Inspiration of the Holy Scriptures,* p. 34).

4. "The original documents of the Bible were written by men, who, though permitted the exercise of their own personalities and literary talents, yet wrote under the control and guidance of the Spirit of God, the result being in every word of the original documents a perfect and errorless recording of the exact message which God desired to give to man" (Frank E. Gaebelein, *The Meaning of Inspiration*, p. 9).
   E. Biblical inspiration is verbal inspiration—the authors, being directly under divine influence, infallibly recorded the God-given (i.e., God-breathed) words.
   F. God moved men to write exactly what He wanted written, in order to communicate clearly the knowledge of His saving grace to all people.
III. **The Bible Claims Verbal Inspiration Throughout Its Pages.**
   A. There are three key passages to know regarding the Bible's inspiration.
      1. The Bible teaches that it is God-breathed in **2 Timothy 3:16-17**.
         (a) "ALL" Scripture is "breathed of God," having originated in and coming from Him.
            (1) This includes both the Old Testament and the New Testament (cf. 1 Tim. 5:18).
            (2) No part of Scripture is exempt. This includes every word.
         (b) "Scripture" (from the Greek word *graphe*) focuses on that which is written.
         (c) "Inspired" focuses on the very words themselves as being God-breathed.
            (1) It did not matter if the writers were fallible men.
            (2) Inspiration assured the infallibility and inerrancy of the writings.
         (d) Every Scripture is "profitable" for fulfilling God's purpose and producing God's intended results.
      2. The Bible teaches that it is the product of the Holy Spirit of God in **2 Peter 1:20-21**.
         (a) No part of God's inspired Scripture ever "came by the will of man."
         (b) In fact, Bible writers often did not fully understand what they were writing, therefore, the ideas could not have been their own (1 Pet. 1:10-12).
         (c) The Holy Spirit "moved" (i.e., "carried along" or "bore along") the writers.
         (d) The writers were not permitted to set forth their own ideas or "interpretation."
         (e) Spirit-moved writers recorded God-breathed writings. That's inspiration!
      3. The Bible teaches that it is the revelation of the mind of God in **1 Corinthians 2:10-13**.
         (a) Only the Spirit of God knows the thoughts and the mind of God.
         (b) The Bible writers received the Spirit of God in order to write the thoughts of God.
         (c) The very words of the Bible are the mind of God revealed to inspired writers.
         (d) Inspired writers were "combining spiritual things with spiritual words" (2:13, ASV).
         (e) The Bible reader can have confidence that every word he reads is directly from God.
      4. These passages emphasize the verbal (i.e., "word") inspiration of the Bible—it is directly from God and not from human wisdom.
         (a) Both testaments are inspired.
         (b) Every book is inspired.
         (c) Every chapter is inspired.
         (d) Every verse is inspired.
         (e) Every sentence is inspired.
         (f) Every phrase is inspired.
         (g) Every word is inspired.
         (h) Every part of every word is inspired.
   B. The Old Testament claims verbal inspiration.
      1. More than 3,800 times, Old Testament writers emphasized that the origin of their words was God Himself.

(a) They used expressions like: "The Lord says," "Thus says the Lord," "The word of God came saying."
2. Moses understood that he was writing the commandments of the Lord (Ex. 17:14; 34:27; Num. 33:2).
3. The expression, "The Lord spoke to Moses," is found 103 times in the Pentateuch.
4. David said, "The Spirit of the Lord spoke by me, and His word was on my tongue" (2 Sam. 23:2). (Note that it was not thoughts or concepts but actual words given to him.)
5. God said to Isaiah, "I have put My words in your mouth" (Isa. 51:16).
6. God said to Jeremiah, "I have put My words in your mouth" (Jer. 1:9).
7. God said to Ezekiel, "I will open your mouth, and you shall say to them, 'Thus says the Lord God" (Ezek. 3:27).
8. God "instructed" and "testified" through His prophets (Neh. 9:20, 30).
9. It is affirmed 175 times in Psalm 119 that Scriptures are the Word of God.

C. The New Testament claims verbal inspiration.
1. Jesus affirmed that "every word" of the Bible was perfectly "written" by God to fulfill His purposes (Matt. 4:1-11; 5:17-18).
2. Jesus affirmed that the smallest parts of the Bible ("jot"=smallest Hebrew letter, "tittle"=small stroke on letters) were evidence from God (Matt. 5:17-18).
3. Jesus affirmed that the Old Testament "was spoken to you by God," and argued that even the grammar (specifically, the verb tense) was inspired of God (Matt. 22:31-32).
   (a) The truth that God is the "God of the living" is established by the present tense, "I am," in Exodus 3:6. God chose the specific tense of a verb to teach His truth.
4. Jesus affirmed that the words He spoke came from the Father (John 12:49-50; 17:8).
5. Jesus promised His apostles that the Holy Spirit would give them words from the Father:
   (a) To speak a message and deliver a defense (Luke 12:11-12).
   (b) To remind them of "all things" that Jesus ever taught them (John 14:25-26).
   (c) To guide them into "all truth" (John 16:13).
       (1) This statement provides authenticity to all other New Testament books.
       (2) "Truth" is not just found in the "red letters" of the Bible.
       (3) "All truth" is found in every page of the Bible.
       (4) And, NO truth is found anywhere else other than the Bible.
6. The New Testament writers, like Old Testament writers, were conscious of inspiration.
   (a) Peter affirmed that what he was writing was from "the Holy Spirit" (2 Pet. 1:20-21).
   (b) Paul affirmed that his words were from God on several occasions:
       (1) "I received from the Lord that which I also delivered to you" (1 Cor. 11:23).
       (2) "For this we say to you by the word of the Lord" (1 Thess. 4:15).
       (3) "For I neither received it from man, nor was I taught it, but it came through the revelation of Jesus Christ" (Gal. 1:12).
       (4) "...when you received the word of God which you heard from us, you welcomed it not as the word of men, but as it is in truth, the word of God" (1 Thess. 2:13).
       (5) "...things which I write to you are the commandments of the Lord" (1 Cor. 14:37).
       (6) "...we speak, not in words which man's wisdom teacheth, but which the Spirit teacheth; combining spiritual things with spiritual words" (1 Cor. 2:11-13, ASV).
   (c) New Testament writers considered one another's writings to be inspired.
       (1) Paul quoted from Deuteronomy 25:4 and Luke 10:7, and he classified both passages as "Scripture" (1 Tim. 5:18).
       (2) Peter classified Paul's writings with "the rest of the Scriptures" (2 Pet. 3:15-16).

D. **The Bible is verbally and completely inspired by God.**
   1. We can know unequivocally that every word and every part of the Bible is from God.
   2. The smallest parts of the Bible have been inspired and preserved by God (Matt. 5:17-18).
   3. The tenses of the verbs were inspired of God (Matt. 22:31-32; John 8:58).
   4. Whether a word was singular or plural was inspired of God (Gal. 3:16; cf. Gen. 22:18).
      (a) Paul made an argument based upon "Seed" being singular in God's promise.
      (b) God chose the specific number of that word to teach His truth.

IV. **There Are Many False Theories Regarding the Bible's Inspiration.**
   A. Natural Inspiration – the Bible is not from God.
      1. Some have falsely claimed that the writers were "inspired" in the same way that modern-day authors, painters and artists get "inspired" to produce great works.
      2. This "theory" cannot adequately explain the marvel of the Bible!
   B. Partial Inspiration – some parts of the Bible may be from God.
      1. In an effort to minimize the all-authoritative nature of Scripture, some have claimed that not "all" of Scripture is "authoritative," but only parts of it are.
      2. Some claim "The Thoughts of the Bible" are inspired but not the exact words, as God provided the writers with a general thought and allowed them to express it in their own words, however they chose.
         (a) This "theory" imagines that thoughts (specifically, the mind of God) can be conveyed without specific words to express those thoughts. If God inspired the "thoughts" of the Bible, He inspired the very "words."
      3. Some claim "The Moral Teachings of the Bible" are inspired but the rest of Scripture that conveys general knowledge of humanity already known is not given by God.
         (a) This "theory" imagines the writer going in and out of inspiration, and it concedes that some parts could contain errors (if the writer got a number, place or event wrong) and misleading language, and it is left up to the reader to determine which parts are "from God" (and accurate), and which part are "from man" (and could contain false ideas or information).
      4. Some claim "The Non-Miraculous Portions and Spiritual Teachings of the Bible" are inspired but the miraculous accounts are mere superstition or hyperbole.
         (a) This "theory," which seeks to "demythologize" the Bible, imagines that God could inspire ordinary men to write an obviously God-breathed book to draw the world to Him, but that same God could not empower ordinary men to perform miraculous acts to draw the world to Him.
      5. The "Partial Inspiration" adherents believe the Bible "contains" the Word of God, but they do not believe that all of Scripture is given by the inspiration of God.
         (a) This view grants man with power over infinite truth rather than under it.
         (b) This view removes Scripture as authoritative, as it gives that authority to man.
         (c) There can be nothing less than "full and complete inspiration" of the Bible. If there is, then the Bible is proven to be a falsified document and must be avoided.
   C. Encounter Inspiration – the Bible "becomes" God's Word when it "inspires" a reader.
      1. Some have falsely claimed that Scripture, while a humanly-devised document, is God's means of communication, but it only "becomes" inspired when an individual reader "encounters" God in it and is "inspired" to action.
      2. This "theory" lets man decide which portions of Scripture are "inspired" and which are not. Scripture is nothing more than a subjective standard with man as the authority.

D. Summary:
   1. It is not that the Bible "CONTAINS" the Word of God.
   2. It is not that the Bible "BECOMES" the Word of God.
   3. It is that the Bible "IS" the Word of God.
E. The exact "how" of inspiration (i.e., "how" the Holy Spirit guided the Biblical writers to produce a work that is entirely from God but still bears some marks of the individuals writer's personalities) is unknown.
   1. However, any theory of inspiration that alleges that the writers themselves, unaided by the Holy Spirit, selected the words of divine revelation contradicts the Scriptures rather than explains them.
   2. Any theory that does not guarantee absolute accuracy of the substance (the thoughts) and the form (the words) cannot be accepted as the correct one.

V. **There Is an Abundance of Evidence to Prove That the Bible Is Inspired of God.**
   A. It should not surprise the Bible reader that the Bible claims to be inspired of God.
      1. It also should not surprise the reader how prevalent the writers made that declaration.
      2. However, other human documents have alleged to be inspired (like the Book of Mormon).
      3. So, beyond the claim of inspiration, there must be actual and sufficient evidence.
      4. When it comes to the Bible, the evidence of God's inspiration is overwhelming.
   B. The **"Unity of the Biblical Record"** is evidence for the Bible's inspiration.
      1. The unity of the Bible's **penmen** is inexplicable on a human level. It must be divine.
         (a) The Bible was penned over a period of about 1,600 years...
         (b) By about 40 different men...
         (c) From vastly different backgrounds (ex: shepherd, fisherman, physician, king, etc.)...
         (d) In three different languages (Hebrew, Aramaic and Greek)...
         (e) From two continents (Europe and Asia)...
         (f) Covering diverse topics (ex: God, creation, man, sin, salvation, church, eternity, etc.)...
         (g) Interweaving details about history, geography, biography, medicine, etc....
         (h) Yet, there are no disagreements, inconsistencies or errors within their writings.
         (i) "The Bible exhibits such astounding harmony, such consistent flow, and such unparalleled unity that it defies any purely naturalistic explanation" (Bert Thompson, *In Defense of the Bible's Inspiration,* p. 29).
      2. The unity of the Bible's **theme** is inexplicable on a human level. It must be divine.
         (a) From beginning to end, the general theme of the Bible is absolutely consistent:
            (1) The fall of man
            (2) The problem of sin
            (3) God's redemptive plan
            (4) The coming Messiah and Savior
            (5) The sacrificial death of Jesus Christ
            (6) The establishment of the church
            (7) The victory of God's people and God's plan
         (b) Consider again how such diverse penmen could produce such a united theme, without deviating from it or altering it one iota. There is no reasonable explanation other than God!
      3. The unity of the Bible's **doctrine** is inexplicable on a human level. It must be divine.
         (a) No single Bible penmen ever strays from the unified doctrine in the Bible, on matters such as (but not limited to):
            (1) The triune nature of the Godhead

           (2) 6-day creation of the universe and all things of the Earth
           (3) Sin as a personal choice of an accountable person
           (4) The essentiality of blood for man's atonement
           (5) Faith and obedience required for man's atonement
           (6) Earthly and eternal consequences (i.e., punishment) for sin
        (b) Consider again how such diverse penmen could produce such united doctrine, without deviating from it or altering it one iota. There is no reasonable explanation other than God!
    4. The unity of the Bible's **details** is inexplicable on a human level. It must be divine.
        (a) While recording a period of history covering thousands of years, there is remarkable and precise harmony on the details of this history.
        (b) There is agreement among the penmen as to WHAT happened, WHEN it happened, WHERE it happened and WHO was there and speaking.
        (c) Consider again how such diverse penmen could produce such united details. There is no reasonable explanation other than God!
    5. The unity of the Bible's **structure** is inexplicable on a human level. It must be divine.
        (a) The Bible can be divided into three major sections, defined by three sentences:
           (1) Someone is coming! (Genesis thru Malachi)
           (2) Someone is here! (Matthew thru John)
           (3) Someone is coming again! (Acts thru Revelation)
        (b) That someone, of course, is Jesus Christ!
        (c) Astoundingly, that structure is upheld without a single exception or slip-up.
           (1) No penmen in any of those three major sections ever mistakenly breaks theme and writes outside his intended section.
        (d) Consider again how such diverse penmen could produce such united structure without deviating from it or altering it one iota. There is no reasonable explanation other than God!
C. The **"Factual Accuracy of the Biblical Record"** is evidence for the Bible's inspiration.
    1. If the Bible was a human production, one would expect to find numerous flaws.
    2. If the Bible was a divine production, one would expect to find no flaws in its accuracy.
    3. A careful reader of the Bible will find meticulous accuracy, proving its divine origin.
    4. The historical and geographical details of the Bible exhibit a flawless accuracy that is inexplicable on a human level.
        (a) The Bible indicates that Moses wrote the Pentateuch (Ex. 17:14; Deut. 31:24; Josh. 1:7; Mark 12:26), which has been confirmed by numerous historians.
           (1) For a period of time, critics scoffed at and denied Mosaic authorship.
           (2) Once again, critics were proven wrong and the Bible was proven accurate!
        (b) The Bible mentions that Sargon was a king of Assyria (Isa. 20:1), which was confirmed by archaeologists in the 19th century.
           (1) For a period of time, critics scoffed at and denied anyone named Sargon was king of Assyria.
           (2) Once again, critics were proven wrong and the Bible was proven accurate!
        (c) The Bible mentions a people called the Hittites (Deut. 7:1; Josh. 1:4; 2 Kgs. 7:6), and evidence was discovered in the 19th century to their existence.
           (1) For a period of time, critics scoffed at and denied the Hittites ever existed.
           (2) Once again, critics were proven wrong and the Bible was proven accurate!

(d) The Bible mentions that the Israelites, while enslaved in Egypt, were forced to make bricks for building Pharaoh's cities—first with straw, then without straw.
  (1) Excavations in the late 19th and early 20th centuries found one of Pharaoh's cities that had straw-filled bricks on the lower levels but no straw on the upper.
  (2) Even down to this minute detail, the Bible has been found to be accurate.
(e) The listing of Biblical accuracies (that have no human explanation) is unending.
5. Many so-called scholars and skeptics have tried (unsuccessfully) to discredit the Bible.
  (a) One famous archaeologist was Sir William Ramsay, who was determined to disprove the historical and geographical accuracy of the book of Acts.
    (1) After years of research and archaeological digs, searching for "truth" in the land, Ramsay reversed his position and said that he found "truth" in Acts.
    (2) Ramsay concluded that the book of Acts was historically accurate and that Luke was "a historian of the first rank" *(The Bearing of Recent Discovery on the Trustworthiness of the New Testament,* p. 222).
  (b) Wayne Jackson noted, "In Acts, Luke mentions thirty-two countries, fifty-four cities, and nine Mediterranean islands. He also mentions ninety-five persons, sixty-two of which are not named elsewhere in the New Testament. And his references, where checkable, are always correct. This is truly remarkable, in view of the fact that the political/territorial situation of his day was in a state of almost constant flux" *(Surveying the Evidence,* p. 128).
6. Archaeologist Nelson Glueck wrote, "It may be stated categorically that no archaeological discovery has ever controverted a Biblical reference. Scores of archaeological findings have been made which confirm in clear outline or exact detail historical statements in the Bible" *(Rivers in the Desert,* p. 31).
7. When one starts to compile all of the details that the Bible had precisely accurate centuries ago, the honest investigator is forced to agree with J.W. McGarvey: "How could they [the Bible writers] have done what learned and careful men of their own age and of subsequent ages have failed to do, unless they were guided, as they claim to have been, by wisdom from on high?" *(Lands of the Bible,* p. 386).

D. The **"Fulfilled Prophecy of the Biblical Record"** is evidence for the Bible's inspiration.
  1. Predictive prophecy is one of the strongest proofs of divine inspiration.
    (a) The Bible itself speaks of the significance of being able to prophesy actual future events (Deut. 18:20-22; Isa. 41:22), a feat which is far beyond human ability.
    (b) Obviously, man is unable to see or foretell the future, so if there are actual historical events that are written in Scripture hundreds of years in advance, this would prove to be some of the most convincing evidence for inspiration.
    (c) It is one thing to make a prediction about the future, but for that prediction (and hundreds of other predictions) to actually come true demands careful attention.
    (d) The Bible (specifically the Old Testament) contains prophecies about nations, individuals and about the coming Messiah Himself.
  2. In order to determine the validity of a predictive prophecy, certain criteria must be met:
    (a) The prophecy must be specific and detailed!
      (1) Valid prophecy is not vague generalities!
    (b) The prophecy must have sufficient timing between the prophecy and its fulfillment!
      (1) Valid prophecy cannot be influenced by the prophet himself to be fulfilled.
      (2) Valid prophecy cannot be perceived as a good guess of a not-too-distant event.
    (c) The prophecy must have a precise, unmistakable fulfillment!

(1) Valid prophecy does not have a "high degree of probability" that it was fulfilled.
3. The Bible presents numerous prophecies about **nations**, especially regarding the Jews.
   (a) The Bible prophesied the long history and destiny of the Israelite nation in Deuteronomy 28:47-68.
   (b) The Bible prophesied that Assyria would conquer Israel (Isa. 10:5-6; 2 Kgs. 17:24).
   (c) The Bible prophesied that Assyria would also fall (Isa. 10:12, 24-25; 2 Kgs. 18:13).
   (d) The Bible prophesied that Babylon would conquer Judah (Jer. 25:9-12; 2 Chr. 36:21).
   (e) The Bible prophesied that Babylon would also fall (Isa. 13:17-22; Dan. 5:28).
   (f) The Bible prophesied the destruction of the city of Tyre in amazing detail (Ezek. 26).
4. The Bible presents numerous prophecies about **individuals**.
   (a) The Bible prophesied that Sennacherib would not take Jerusalem, but would return the way he came and die by the sword (2 Kgs. 19:32-37; 19:7; Isa. 37:37-38).
   (b) The Bible prophesied of Josiah (by name) and his work, 300 hundred years before he even ascended to the throne (1 Kgs. 13:2; 2 Kgs. 23:15-16).
   (c) The Bible prophesied of Cyrus (by name) and his work, almost 200 years before he began to reign (Isa. 44:28-45:1; 2 Chron. 36:22-23).
5. The Old Testament presents **332 prophecies about the coming Messiah**.
   (a) When Jesus lived on this earth, He acknowledged these prophecies and fulfilled every one of them (Luke 4:17-21; 24:44; John 5:39; etc.). Wayne Jackson divides these prophecies into the following categories *(Fortify, p. 67-69)*:
   (b) The lineage of Christ was prophesied.
      (1) Christ would be the seed of woman (Gen. 3:15; Gal. 4:4).
      (2) Christ would be the seed of Abraham (Gen. 22:18; Gal. 3:16).
      (3) Christ would be the seed of Isaac (Gen. 26:4; Matt. 1:2).
      (4) Christ would be the seed of Jacob (Gen. 28:14; Luke 3:34).
      (5) Christ would be the seed of David (2 Sam. 7:12-14; Heb. 1:5).
      (6) Christ would be heir to the throne of David (Isa. 9:7; Matt. 1:1).
      (7) Christ would be a descendant of the tribe of Judah (Gen. 49:10; Heb. 7:14).
   (c) The birth of Christ (and events connected with it) was prophesied.
      (1) Christ would be born of a virgin (Isa. 7:14; Matt. 1:18-22).
      (2) Christ would be born in Bethlehem of Judah (Mic. 5:2; Matt. 2:1).
      (3) Infants would be killed in connection with His birth (Jer. 31:15; Matt. 2:16-18).
      (4) His family would flee to Egypt and then return (Hos. 11:1; Matt. 2:14).
      (5) Christ would come during the Roman empire (Dan. 2:44; 9:25; Luke 2:1-2).
   (d) The nature and character of Christ was prophesied.
      (1) Christ would be both divine and human (Mic. 5:2; Zech. 13:7; John 1:1, 14).
      (2) Christ would possess supernatural wisdom (Is. 11:1-5; Mt. 9:4; 12:25; Jn. 2:24-25).
      (3) Christ would be gentle & compassionate with mankind (Is. 42:1-4; Mt. 12:15-21).
      (4) Christ would flawlessly obey God (Psa. 40:8; Heb. 10:5-7).
      (5) Christ would be a righteous servant (Isa. 53:11; John 8:29; 2 Cor. 5:21).
   (e) The ministry of Christ was prophesied.
      (1) Christ would be preceded by a forerunner (Isa. 40:3-5; Mal. 4:5-6; Matt. 3:3).
      (2) Christ would work miracles (Isa. 35:5-6; John 3:2; 20:30-31).
      (3) Christ would preach to the poor and heal the sick (Isa. 61:1-3; Luke 4:17-20).
      (4) Christ would minister in Galilee (Isa. 9:1-2; Matt. 4:12-17).
      (5) Christ would teach in parables (Psa. 78:2; Matt. 13:34-35).
      (6) Christ would be a prophet like Moses (Deut. 18:15-19; Jn. 6:14; Acts 3:22-23).

                (7) Christ would be a priest like Melchizedek (Psa. 110:4; Heb. 6:20).
        (f) The death and resurrection of Christ (and surrounding events) were prophesied.
                (1) Christ would be rejected by the Jews (Isa. 53:3; John 1:11).
                (2) Christ would be betrayed by a friend (Psa. 41:9; Mark 14:10).
                (3) Christ would be betrayed for 30 pieces of silver (Zech. 11:12; Matt. 26:15).
                (4) Christ would be spit upon and beaten (Isa. 50:6; Matt. 26:67-68).
                (5) Christ would be silent when accused (Isa. 53:7; Matt. 26:62-64).
                (6) Christ would have His hands and feet pierced (Psa. 22:16; Lk. 24:39; Jn. 20:27).
                (7) Christ would have none of His bones broken (Psa. 34:20; Ex. 12:46 Jn. 19:33).
                (8) Christ would be given vinegar to drink (Psa. 69:21; Matt. 27:34).
                (9) Christ would have His garments gambled away (Psa. 22:18; Mark 15:24).
                (10) Christ would be buried with the rich (Isa. 53:9; Matt. 27:57-60).
                (11) Christ would be raised from the dead (Psa. 16:10; Matt. 28:1-9).
                (12) Christ would ascend into heaven (Psa. 110:1; Matt. 26:64; Acts 1:9-11).
        (g) To understand the magnitude of one man fulfilling 332 prophecies, Josh McDowell, in *Evidence That Demands a Verdict* (p. 167), cited the research from a mathematician Peter Stoner:
                (1) The following probabilities are taken from Peter Stoner in *Science Speaks* (Moody Press, 1963) to show that coincidence is ruled out by the science of probability. Stoner says that by using the modern science of probability in reference to eight prophecies, "We find that the chance that any man might have lived down to the present time and fulfilled all eight prophecies is 1 in 10^{17}." That would be 1 in 100,000,000,000,000,000.
                (2) In order to help us comprehend this staggering probability, Stoner illustrates it by supposing that "we take 10^{17} silver dollars and lay them on the face of Texas. They will cover all of the state two feet deep. Now mark one of these silver dollars and stir the whole mass thoroughly, all over the state. Blindfold a man and tell him that he can travel as far as he wishes, but he must pick up one silver dollar and say that this is the right one. What chance would he have of getting the right one? Just the same chance that the prophets would have had of writing these eight prophecies and having them all come true in any one man."
                (3) Stoner considers 48 prophecies and says, "We find the chance that any one man fulfilled all 48 prophecies to be 1 in 10^{157}.
                (4) "This is a really large number and it represents an extremely small chance. Let us try to visualize it. The silver dollar, which we have been using, is entirely too large. We must select a smaller object. The electron is about as small as an object as we know of. It is so small that it will take 2.5 times 10^{15} of them laid side by side to make a line, single file, one inch long. If we were going to count the electrons in this line one inch long, and counted 250 each minute, and if we counted day and night, it would take us 19,000,000 years to count just the one-inch line of electrons. If we had a cubic inch of these electrons and we tried to count them it would take us, counting steadily 250 each minute, 19,000,000 times 19,000,000 times 19,000,000 years or 6.9 times 10^{21} years.
                (5) With this introduction, let us go back to our chance in 10^{157}. Let us suppose that we are taking this number of electrons, marking one, and thoroughly

stirring it into the whole mass, then blindfolding a man and letting him try to find the right one. What chance has he of finding the right one? What kind of pile will this number of electrons make? They make an inconceivably large volume."
- (6) Such is the chance of any one man fulfilling 48 prophecies.
- (h) And Jesus fulfilled not just 8 or 48 prophecies! Jesus fulfilled 332 prophecies!
- (i) To understand the magnitude of one man fulfilling 332 prophecies, Hugo McCord wrote about "The law of probability" in *From Heaven or From Men* (p. 47-48):
  - (1) If only fifty prophecies about Jesus had been made, assuming an equal chance for their happening or not happening, the law of probability against all fifty's being fulfilled "is that of the fiftieth power of two to unity; that is the probability is greater than *eleven hundred and twenty-five millions to one* that all of these circumstances do turn up." Then to assume that the fifty events would happen contemporaneously "surpasses the power of numbers to express correctly the immense improbability of its taking place."
  - (2) The previous paragraph deals with the law of probability as regards inanimate objects. It does not consider the will and acts of free agents for and against God, namely: "passions of multitudes, the ambition of princes, the studies of the wise, the craft of the wicked, the wars, the revolutions, and the varied destinies of nations."
  - (3) If only one hundred prophecies had been made, the chance that they would happen to one man is less than all the drops of water if the world were completely water.
  - (4) But not fifty, nor one hundred, but three hundred thirty-two prophecies of Christ had been counted...
  - (5) That Jesus fulfilled the prophecies is generally admitted. The only way to deny His claim is to assert that the prophecies were written after Jesus came. But this assertion is disproved even by infidels. An odd turn has come about by which Jewish infidels strongly attest to the antiquity and textual accuracy of the Old Testament books.

E. The **"Scientific Foreknowledge of the Biblical Record"** is evidence for the Bible's inspiration.
  1. One of the very exciting proofs of the Bible's inspiration is to read scientific truths tucked within the pages of the Bible that man did not "discover" for centuries (and many of them were only "discovered" in the last 200-300 years).
  2. It is obvious that the penman who wrote these scientific truths in the Bible could not have known them on their own or by any natural means, which leaves only one plausible explanation for how they got there—the Bible is inspired of God!
  3. Wayne Jackson and Bert Thompson have classified these truths in these categories:
  (a) The Bible presents scientific foreknowledge in the field of **astronomy**.
    (1) The earth is spherical in shape (Isa. 40:22; Prov. 8:27).
    (2) The earth is suspended in space "on nothing" (Job 26:7).
    (3) The sun has its own "circuit" or orbit through space (Psa. 19:5-6).
    (4) The stars cannot be counted (Jer. 33:22; Gen. 15:5; 22:17).
  (b) The Bible presents scientific foreknowledge in the field of **oceanography**.
    (1) There is a water cycle over the earth (Ecc. 1:7; 11:3; Job 36:27-28; Amos 9:6).
    (2) There are "paths" or currents in the seas (Psa. 8:8).
    (3) There are vast "recesses" (trenches) in the ocean floors (Job 38:16; 2 Sam. 22:16).

                (4) There are fresh water springs in the ocean (Job 38:16; Gen. 7:11).
            (b) The Bible presents scientific foreknowledge in the field of **physics**.
                (1) Creation is finished; no matter or energy is currently being created (Gen. 2:1).
                (2) The Earth is wearing out like a garment (Psa. 102:26; Isa. 51:6; Heb. 1:11).
                (3) Light travels in a path (or a "way") (Job 38:19, 24).
            (c) The Bible presents scientific foreknowledge in the field of **biology**.
                (1) Living things reproduce "after their kind" (Gen. 1:11, 12, 21, 24).
                (2) Life does not and is not spontaneously generated (Acts 17:25).
                (3) All peoples are from one common blood (Acts 17:26).
                (4) There are four "fleshes" with different biochemical structures (1 Cor. 15:39).
            (d) The Bible presents scientific foreknowledge in the field of **medicine**.
                (1) Life is in the blood (Lev. 17:11-14).
                (2) Animals that have died naturally should not be eaten (Lev. 17:15).
                (3) Sanitation laws regarding human waste are for man's own good (Deut. 23:12-14).
                (4) The eighth day is the perfect day to circumcise a baby boy (Gen. 17:12).
        2. The question that must be asked is, "How did these writers know these intricate details of the earth and science thousands of years before they were 'discovered'?"
            (a) The answer should be obvious: God put those scientific truths in the Bible to prove that "all Scripture is given by the inspiration of God" (2 Tim. 3:16-17)!
            (b) The Bible is not the product of man! It is clearly the product of an infinite God!
VI. Conclusion
   A. How exciting it is to know that we hold in our hands the very words of God!
      1. The Almighty, Infinite, Loving God revealed Himself to mankind!
      2. He chose to reveal His mind and His will to His special creation!
      3. He revealed Himself in direct, clear, understandable terms!
      4. He did not leave us without witness or without direction in this life!
   B. The evidence for the verbal, plenary inspiration of the Bible is overwhelming!
      1. No other book in human history has the perfect unity that the Bible has!
      2. No other book in human history has the factual accuracy that the Bible has!
      3. No other book in human history has the fulfilled prophecy that the Bible has!
      4. No other book in human history has the scientific foreknowledge that the Bible has!
      5. To claim that the Bible is anything but the divinely revealed Word of the Almighty God of heaven is to ignore the abundance of clear evidence.
   C. What a blessing to know that "All Scripture is given by inspiration of God, and is profitable for doctrine, for reproof, for correction, for instruction in righteousness, that the man of God may be complete, thoroughly equipped for every good work" (2 Tim. 3:16-17).
      1. No human wisdom did or could have produced such a marvelous book!
      2. It gives us great assurance and confidence to know that *every* part of *every* letter of *every* word of *every* phrase of *every* sentence of *every* verse of *every* chapter of *every* book of *both* testaments was "breathed by God"!
      3. "How precious is the Book divine, by inspiration given!" (Lloyd O. Sanderson, 1935).

Recommended Resources

Books

Butt, Kyle. *Behold! The Word of God.* Montgomery: Apologetics Press, 2007.

Geisler, Norman L. and William E. Nix. *A General Introduction to the Bible.* Chicago: Moody, 1986.

Jackson, Wayne. *Fortify Your Faith.* Stockton, CA: Christian Courier, 1974.

Jackson, Wayne. *The Bible & Science.* Stockton, CA: Christian Courier, 2000.

Jackson, Wayne, Eric Lyons and Kyle Butt. *Surveying the Evidence.* Montgomery: Apologetics Press, 2008.

Jividen, Jimmy. *Inspiration and Authority of the Scriptures.* Nashville: Gospel Advocate, 2005.

Laws, Jim, ed. *The Inspiration of the Bible (Spiritual Sword Lectureship).* Memphis: Getwell church of Christ, 1996.

Lyons, Eric. *The Anvil Rings: Volumes 1 & 2.* Montgomery: Apologetics Press, 2003.

McCord, Hugo. *From Heaven or From Men?* Austin: Firm Foundation, 1964.

McDowell, Josh. *Evidence That Demands a Verdict.* San Bernardino, CA: Here's Life Publishers, 1979.

Thompson, Bert. *In Defense of the Bible's Inspiration.* Montgomery: Apologetics Press, 2003.

Articles

Brownlow, Leroy. "Because It Believes All the Bible to Be the Inspired Word of God." *Why I Am a Member of the Church of Christ.* Fort Worth: Brownlow Publishing, 1973. 51-59.

Butt, Kyle. "Scientific Foreknowledge and Medical Acumen of the Bible." *ApologeticsPress.org* http://apologeticspress.org/APContent.aspx?category=13&article=2024

Butt, Kyle. "The Unity of the Bible." *ApologeticsPress.org* http://apologeticspress.org/APContent.aspx?category=13&article=2151

Goodpasture, B.C. "The Inspiration of the Bible." *The Church Faces Liberalism (Freed-Hardeman College Lectureship).* Ed. Thomas B. Warren. Nashville: Gospel Advocate, 1970. 53-68.

Jackson, Jason. "What Is Bible 'Inspiration'"? *ChristianCourier.com* https://www.christiancourier.com/articles/1158-what-is-bible-inspiration

Jackson, Wayne. "The Holy Scriptures—Verbally Inspired." *ApologeticsPress.org* http://apologeticspress.org/APContent.aspx?category=13&article=5174

Lyons, Eric. "3 Good Reasons to Believe the Bible Is from God." *ApologeticsPress.org* http://apologeticspress.org/APContent.aspx?category=13&article=5089

Lyons, Eric and Dave Miller. "Biblical Inerrancy." *ApologeticsPress.org*
http://apologeticspress.org/APContent.aspx?category=13&article=472

Major, Trevor. "The Fall of Tyre." *ApologeticsPress.org*
http://apologeticspress.org/APContent.aspx?category=13&article=848

McCord, Hugo. "Prophecy." *From Heaven or From Men?* Austin: Firm Foundation, 1964.

Miller, Dave. "The Nature of Bible Inspiration." *ApologeticsPress.org*
http://apologeticspress.org/APContent.aspx?category=13&article=5012

Sanders, Ed. "An Exegetical Study of 1 Corinthians 2:9-16—'Spiritual Things with Spiritual Words.'" *"What Do You Know About the Holy Spirit?" (Fort Worth Lectures).* Ed. Wendell Winkler. Montgomery, AL: Winkler Publication, 1980. 261-266.

Thompson Bert. "Why the Eighth Day?" *ApologeticsPress.org*
http://apologeticspress.org/APContent.aspx?category=13&article=834

Veil, Robert C. "How I Would Prove to a Jury That the Bible Is True." *ApologeticsPress.org*
http://apologeticspress.org/APContent.aspx?category=13&article=1163

Periodicals

The Spiritual Sword. April 1970. "The Inspiration of the Bible."

Lesson 4: Authority in Religion

I. **Authority Is Necessary in All Matters of Life!**
   A. Having authority is a necessity of life – in a home, school, nation, religion, etc.
      1. Authority is "the right to command and enforce obedience; the power to give orders."
      2. While some individuals may reject or despise authority, that does not diminish the need for authority in all matters of life. In fact, it may intensify the need.
   B. Authority makes the difference between harmonious unity and chaotic confusion.
      1. Imagine the stock exchange without an authoritative standard of currency.
      2. Imagine the produce market without an authoritative standard of weights.
      3. Imagine the lumber yard without an authoritative standard of measurements.
      4. Imagine the football field without an authoritative standard of rules.
      5. Imagine the military unit without an authoritative standard of regulations.
      6. Imagine the highway without an authoritative standard of laws.
   C. Nowhere else is authority as essential as it is in religion.
      1. An objective standard is absolutely crucial when it comes to our eternal salvation!
      2. Without authority in religion, then division, chaos and confusion will exist.
      3. The condition of the religious world today reflects a lack of following a standard.
      4. Religious unity is only possible by submitting to the same standard of authority.
      5. It is imperative that we find and follow that standard of authority.
   D. Jesus taught that there are only two sources of authority (Matt 21:23-27).
      1. One source of authority is from Heaven, the other is from Men.
      2. That which is authorized by heaven must be believed and obeyed.
      3. That which is authorized merely by men must be rejected and not obeyed.
      4. It is imperative that we differentiate between the two and yield to heaven's authority.
      5. While two sources of authority exist, they cannot co-exist within Christianity!
         (a) Most who adhere to religious error will claim, "But we are following the Bible!"
         (b) Any time individuals bring human sources of authority into the church:
            (1) They "leave the commandment of God" and "make void" His word (Mark 7:6-13).
            (2) They violate the authority of heaven (Matt. 21:23-27)!
      6. It is essential to closely examine and validate all authority within one's religion to ensure:
         (a) That one is NOT following a man-made authority!
         (b) That one is ONLY following heaven's authority!

II. **Man Has Failed in Many Attempts to Identify His Own Authority in Religion!**
   A. Man has sought "externally" for an adequate source of authority:
      1. Follow the majority (Ex. 23:2; Gen. 6:5-13; 1 Sam. 8:4-8; Matt. 7:13-14).
      2. Follow a group of men—church councils, synods, conferences, associations (Gal. 1:9).
      3. Follow a man—like the Pope or a favorite preacher (Eph. 1:22-23; Gal. 1:6-9).
      4. Follow human traditions/commandments of men (cf. Mt. 15:3-9; Mk. 7:1-13; Col. 2:8).
      5. Follow human creeds—confessions of faith, manuals and church disciplines (Gal. 1:9).
      6. Follow the religious beliefs and practices of our ancestors (Phil. 3:3-14; Matt. 10:37).
      7. There is no adequate human external source of authority in religion.
      8. Man always has and always will fail when he seeks a human authority in religion!
   B. Man has sought "internally" for an adequate source of authority:
      1. Personal feelings (Prov. 14:12; 28:26; Jer. 10:23).
      2. Individual conscience & sincerity (Acts 23:1; 26:9-11; 1 Tim. 1:13-16; 4:2; Mt. 7:21-23).
      3. Human wisdom & reasoning (Isa. 55:8-9; 1 Cor. 1:18-29; 2 Kgs. 5:11; 2 Sam. 6:3-7).

4. Direct (modern-day) revelation from God (2 Pet. 2:1; 1 John 4:1; Jude 3).
5. There is no adequate human internal source of authority in religion.
6. Man always has and always will fail when he seeks a human authority in religion!
C. Neither man nor any of his devices are an adequate authority in religion.
1. "There is a way that seems right to a man, but its end is the way of death" (Pro. 14:12).
2. "...It is not in man who walks to direct his own steps" (Jer. 10:23).
3. Man's ways and devices lead him "far from God," not toward Him (Matt. 15:8-9).
4. For Jesus taught, "If the blind leads the blind, both will fall into a ditch" (Matt. 15:14).

III. Christ Alone Has All Authority in Religious Matters!
A. The only authority in religion is the authority of Heaven, of God Himself!!!
1. That is precisely why Jesus asked, "From heaven or from men?" (Matt. 21:23-27).
2. "God made the world and everything in it...He is Lord of heaven and earth" (Ac. 17:24).
3. All authority inherently resides in God the Father (Gen. 1-3; Rom. 9:8-24).
4. God has spoken His Word through His Son (Heb. 1:1-2).
B. All authority was given by the Father unto Christ!
1. Christ has all authority in heaven and on earth (Matt. 28:18).
2. Christ is the head/authority over all, including His church (Eph. 1:20-23; Col. 1:18).
3. Christ is to be heard in all things and over all persons (Matt. 17:1-5; Acts 3:22-23).
4. Consequences are assured upon those who do not heed His words (Acts 3:22-23).
5. Those who heard Christ speak recognized His inherent authority (Matt. 7:28-29).
C. Christ's authority resides in His Word!
1. The authoritative words He spoke were from the Father (Heb. 1:1-2).
   (a) "For I have not spoken on My own authority; but the Father who sent Me gave Me a command, what I should say and what I should speak" (John 12:49).
   (b) "Whatever I speak, just as the Father has told Me, so I speak" (John 12:50).
2. The authoritative words He spoke will judge all mankind (John 12:48).
   (a) "...The word that I have spoken will judge him in the last day."
3. When we understand where all authority resides, we know also where it is not.
   (a) It is not in man or in man-made religion (see II, A and II, B above).
D. Christ delivered His all-authoritative Word to His apostles through the Holy Spirit!
1. While with His apostles, He gave them the words of the Father (John 17:8, 14).
2. When Jesus left the earth, He sent the Holy Spirit to the apostles. The Spirit:
   (a) Would "teach [the apostles] all things" (John 14:26).
   (b) Would "bring to [the apostles'] remembrance all things [Jesus] said" (14:26).
   (c) Would "guide [the apostles] into all truth" (John 16:13, 7-15).
   (d) Would "speak" through the apostles (Mark 13:11).
   (e) Like Christ, would speak only the words and will of the Father (John 16:13).
3. When the all-authoritative Christ left this earth, His all-authoritative Word was left to select men, as they were directed by the Holy Spirit.
E. The apostles spoke and wrote by inspiration of the Holy Spirit!
1. The writings of the Old Testament and New Testament:
   (a) Never came by "any private interpretation" of the writer (2 Pet. 1:20).
   (b) Never "came by the will of man" (2 Pet. 1:21).
   (c) Were the result of inspired men being "moved by the Holy Spirit" (2 Pet. 1:21).
   (d) Were the result of "the inspiration of God" (i.e., "God-breathed") (2 Tim. 3:16).
   (e) Are "the Word of God" and not "the word of men" (1 Thess. 2:13).
   (f) Are "the commandments of the Lord" and not man (1 Cor. 14:37).

2. The inspired writings reveal to us the mind and will of God (1 Cor. 2:11-13).
3. Scripture was given so that all mankind in the centuries to come might have the inspired writers' understanding of the will of God (Eph. 3:3-5).
F. Thus, the very authority of God is inherent in the words of the Bible!
   1. The inspired words are preserved in the Bible, providing us with Heaven's authority.
   2. Follow the "Chain of Authority," as outlined in points A through F and illustrated below:
      (a) The <u>same</u> word that the Father gave to the Son and that the Holy Spirit received and gave to the apostles is the <u>same</u> word that is written in the Bible!
      (b) The Bible is God's Word!
   3. The Bible alone is the true objective standard in religious matters today.
   4. God authorizes only the teachings and practices found in the New Testament.
   5. Any teaching or practice foreign or contrary to the N.T. is not authorized by God.
   6. Our utmost attention must be given to learning and following His authoritative Word!
      (a) Teaching or practicing less than the Bible is too little!
      (b) Teaching or practicing more than the Bible is too much!

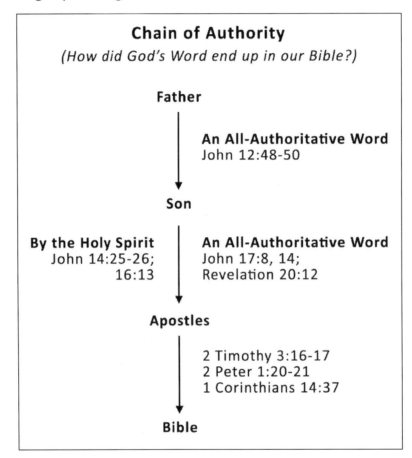

G. God's written word is the only authority that can prepare us for judgment and eternity!
   1. On the day of judgment, every person will stand before Christ (Ro. 14:10; 2 Cor. 5:10).
   2. On the day of judgment, Christ Himself will be the Judge of all (Acts 17:30-31).
   3. Christ will use His Word to judge all mankind on the last day (John 12:48).
   4. Each one will be "judged according to their works" by the words of Christ (Rev. 20:12).
   5. No human standard will be present on the day of judgment.
   6. No human standard will determine man's eternal destiny.
   7. Only Christ's all-authoritative Word will judge and determine eternal destinies.

IV. The All-Authoritative Word of God Is All-Sufficient and All-Delivered!
A. God's Word is all-sufficient – it is complete and lacking in nothing.
 1. "All Scripture is given by the inspiration of God" (2 Tim. 3:16).
 2. With it, man is "complete, thoroughly equipped for every good work" (2 Tim. 3:16-17).
 3. With it, man has "all things that pertain to life and godliness" (2 Pet. 1:3).
 4. All of these things were written and completed in the first century. The Word of God that we have today in the Bible has long been complete and lacking in nothing!
 5. To impugn the all-sufficiency of Scripture would be to impugn the wisdom of God.
B. God's Word is all-delivered – it has all been given and there is nothing else to be given.
 1. Jesus promised that the Holy Spirit would guide His apostles into "all truth" (Jn. 16:13).
 2. Jude affirmed that God's will had been "once for all delivered to the saints" (Jude 3).
 3. Jude used the past tense to emphasize that the revealed will of God was all finalized and completely given in the first century, with nothing more to be added later.
 4. No further revelation has been, will be or even needs to be given. It is final!
 5. To claim direct revelation today is to charge God with lying and falsehood!
C. God's Word is all that is needed to preach the fullness of the gospel!
 1. There is "not another" gospel, except one that has been "perverted" (Gal. 1:6-7).
 2. There is not "any other gospel" that can be or should be preached (Gal. 1:8-9).
 3. For anyone who preaches anything more, less or different than the revealed gospel, God has pronounced a curse: "Let him be accursed" (Gal. 1:8-9).
D. God's Word is "the perfect law of liberty" (Jas. 1:25).
 1. The word "perfect" emphasizes that it is without defect and all-sufficient to accomplish its purpose.
 2. God's "perfect law" requires man's compliance and not defiance (Jas. 1:21-25).
E. God's Word supplies man with "the whole counsel of God" (Acts 20:27; cf. 2 Pet. 1:3; 2 Tim. 3:14-17) on matters, such as:
 1. Understanding the revelation of God (Eph. 3:3-5; Rom. 16:25-26).
 2. Believing in Jesus as the Son of God (John 20:30-31).
 3. Growing in the grace and knowledge of Jesus Christ (2 Pet. 1:5-11).
 4. Finding strength and advocacy to overcome sin (1 John 2:1).
 5. Finding true joy in fellowship with God the Father and Jesus Christ (1 John 1:3-4).
 6. Learning about the nature of God, which provides comfort and hope (Rom. 15:4).
 7. Ministering to the saints, especially in time of need (2 Cor. 9:1ff).
 8. Defending and standing firm in the faith (John 8:31-32; 2 Th. 2:15; Tit. 1:9; 2 Jn. 6-11).
 9. Properly conducting oneself in the church of the living God (1 Tim. 3:15).
 10. Confidently securing eternal life in His name (John 20:30-31; 1 John 5:13).
F. God is omniscient (all-knowing) and omnipotent (all-powerful).
 1. He has both the knowledge and the power to deliver a written revelation that is all-sufficient to accomplish His purpose (Isa. 55:8-11).
 2. To suggest otherwise is impugn the wisdom and the power of God!

V. Man's Only Proper Response Is to Respect and Obey the All-Authoritative Word!
A. We must accept God's will completely (Luke 10:16; John 12:48).
B. We must, like the Bereans, "search the Scriptures" as our standard (Acts 17:11).
C. We must do all things by the name/authority of Christ (Col. 3:17).
 1. To do something "by the name of" another is to do it "by the power of" or "by the authority of" that person.

(a) Peter and John were asked, "By what power or by what name have you done this?" (Acts 4:7). In other words, "Who gave you the right?" That's a critical question.
(b) Peter replied, "By the name (i.e., authority) of Jesus Christ..." (Acts 4:10). That's the essential answer that we must be able to give—not just by speaking those words but by actually having the authority of Christ for what we do.
2. What if religious groups were asked today, "By what authority do you do this?"
3. If we cannot point to clear, divine, New Testament authority for what we are teaching and what we are practicing, then we are operating outside the authority of Christ. That's why Paul said, "And **whatever** you do in word or deed, do **all** in the name of the Lord Jesus, giving thanks to God the Father through Him" (Col. 3:17).
D. We must recognize that "there is no other name under heaven given among men by which we must be saved" (Acts 4:12).
E. We must "walk by faith," by walking according to His Word (2 Cor. 5:7; Rom. 10:17).
F. We must demonstrate our love for Him by keeping His commandments (John 14:15).
G. We must not add to or subtract from God's Word (Deut. 4:2; 12:32; Rev. 22:18-19).
1. "God will add" eternal punishment to those who add to His word (Rev. 22:18).
2. "God shall take away" eternal reward from those who take away from His Word (22:19).
H. We must not modify, substitute or pervert the will of God (Gal. 1:6-9; Matt. 15:3, 9).
1. Neither the apostles nor the angels had the authority to change any part of God's Word (Gal. 1:8)! What mortal today can have such a right (1:9)?
2. Those who elevate their own doctrines, ideas and traditions above God's Word:
(a) "Lay aside the commandment of God" (Mark 7:8).
(b) "Reject the commandment of God" (Mark 7:9).
(c) "Make the word of God of no effect" (Mark 7:13).
3. As a consequence, "Every plant which [the] heavenly Father has not planted will be uprooted" (Matt. 15:13).
I. We must not go beyond that which is written (1 Cor. 4:6).
1. "Whoever transgresses [goes too far, NASB] and does not abide in the doctrine of Christ does not have God" (2 John 9).
J. We must not speak beyond that which is written (1 Pet. 4:11).
K. We must hear Christ's Words and prepare for judgment (Matt. 17:5; John 12:48).
L. We must respect and obey God's Word to enter heaven (Matt. 7:21-27; Heb. 5:9).
1. Jesus' words in Matthew 7:21 are key: "Not everyone who says to Me, 'Lord, Lord,' shall enter the kingdom of heaven, but he who does the will of My Father in heaven."

VI. God Will Not Tolerate That Which Is Unauthorized!
A. Whatever is not authorized by God is not acceptable to God, even if "intended to be."
1. Cain's worship (surely intended to be acceptable) was not acceptable to God (Gen. 4).
2. Israel's worship was not acceptable to God (Mal. 1:6-9).
3. The worship of the Pharisees and scribes was not acceptable to God (Matt. 15:7-9).
4. Uzzah's "well-intentioned" touching of the Ark was not acceptable (2 Sam. 6:3-7).
5. Moses' striking of the rock rather than speaking was not acceptable (Num. 20:7-12).
6. Saul lost his kingdom because of worship that was not acceptable (1 Sam. 13, 15).
7. When men do not respect and obey God's authority, disastrous consequences await.
B. The Bible often uses the word "strange" in the sense of "not authorized by God."
1. Nadab and Abihu offered "strange" fire, not authorized by God (Lev. 10:1-3).
2. "King Solomon loved many strange women," not authorized by God (1 Kgs. 11:1).
3. Israel did evil against God "in marrying strange women," not authorized (Neh. 13:27).

      4. Sodom & Gomorrah had "gone after strange flesh," not authorized by God (Jude 7).
      5. We are warned about being "carried about with…strange doctrines" (Heb. 13:9).
      6. When men pursue that which is "strange" to God's authority, destruction awaits.
  C. Eternal condemnation awaits anyone who disregards the authority of God's Word.
      1. "And then I will declare to them, I never knew you; depart from Me, you who practice lawlessness!'" (Matt. 7:23).
      2. "These shall be punished with everlasting destruction from the presence of the Lord and from the glory of His power" (2 Thess. 1:8-9).

VII. Conclusion
  A. Man must recognize his own inferiority before God (Isa. 55:8-9; Jer. 10:23).
  B. Man must look to Christ and His Word for authority in all religious matters (Col. 3:17).
  C. Man must learn to "Speak where the Bible speaks" (1 Pet. 4:11).
      1. Man must learn to "Be silent where the Bible is silent."
      2. Man must learn to "Call Bible things by Bible names."
      3. Man must learn to "Do Bible things in Bible ways."
      4. For the Bible alone is our standard in all things!
  D. Man must live his life and prepare for the day of judgment by realizing that:
      1. Jesus respected God's authority, limited Himself to it and obeyed (Jn. 6:38; 12:49-50).
      2. The Holy Spirit respected God's authority, limited Himself to it and obeyed (Jn. 16:13).
      3. The apostles were to respect God's authority, limit themselves to it and obey (Gal. 1:8).
      4. The angels were to respect God's authority, limit themselves to it and obey (Gal. 1:8).
      5. Therefore, we all must respect God's authority, limit ourselves to it and obey (Mt. 7:21).
  E. There are only two possible sources of authority (Matt 21:23-27).
      1. One source of authority is from Heaven, the other is from Men.
      2. That which is authorized by heaven must be believed and obeyed.
      3. That which is authorized merely by men must be rejected and not obeyed.
      4. "We must obey God rather than men" (Acts 5:29).

Recommended Resources

Books

Jividen, Jimmy. *Inspiration and Authority of the Scriptures.* Nashville: Gospel Advocate, 2005.

McDade, Gary, ed. *The All-Sufficiency of the Bible (Spiritual Sword Lectureship).* Memphis: Getwell church of Christ, 2000.

McDade, Gary, ed. *The Authority of the Bible (Spiritual Sword Lectureship).* Memphis: Getwell church of Christ, 2002.

Articles

Camp, Franklin. "The Authority of the Scriptures." *The Spiritual Sword, "Bible Authority" (Vol. 21, Num. 3).* Memphis: Getwell church of Christ, April 1990. 3-6.

Gardner, E. Claude. "The New Testament Is Her Only Standard of Authority." *Introducing the Church of Christ.* Ed. Alvin Jennings. Fort Worth: Star Bible Publications, 1981. 38-41.

Highers, Alan. "The Authority of the Bible." *The Inspiration of the Bible (Spiritual Sword Lectureship).* Ed. Jim Laws. Memphis: Getwell church of Christ, 1996. 237-251.

Highers, Alan. "The Bible—None Like It in Religious Authority." *The Bible—None Like It (Memphis School of Preaching Lectureship).* Ed. Curtis A. Cates. Memphis: MSOP, 1989. 114-123.

Jividen, Jimmy. "The Authority of the Scriptures." *Inspiration and Authority of the Scriptures.* Nashville: Gospel Advoate, 2005. 55-64.

Laws, Jim. "The Delegation of Divine Authority." *The Spiritual Sword, "Bible Authority" (Vol. 21, Num. 3).* Memphis: Getwell church of Christ, April 1990. 10-14.

Liddell, Bobby. "Why Should I Believe That the Bible Is Absolute Truth?" *Why Should I Believe the Bible? (POWER Lectures).* Ed. B.J. Clarkes. Southaven, MS: Southaven church of Christ, 2005. 568-584.

McNutt, J.A. "In Her Faith and Practice No Tradition of Man Is Accepted As Binding." *Introducing the Church of Christ.* Ed. Alvin Jennings. Fort Worth: Star Bible Publications, 1981. 237-241.

White, Charles. "The Completeness of the Bible." *The Inspiration of the Bible (Spiritual Sword Lectureship).* Ed. Jim Laws. Memphis: Getwell church of Christ, 1996. 252-264.

Winkler, Wendell. "By What Authority?" *The Authority of the Bible (Spiritual Sword Lectureship).* Ed. Gary McDade. Memphis: Getwell church of Christ, 2002.469-477.

Woods, Guy N. "The Necessity of Bible Authority." *Ethics for Daily Living (Freed-Hardeman College Lectures).* Ed. Winford Claiborne. Henderson, TN: Freed-Hardeman College, 1986. 370-377.

Periodicals

The Spiritual Sword. October 1973. "The Authority of the Scriptures."

The Spiritual Sword. April 1990. "Bible Authority."

Lesson 5: Interpreting the Bible

I. **The Bible Is Inspired of God, and God Expects Man to Interpret It Properly.**
   A. The Bible is a supernatural revelation from God.
      1. It is inspired and therefore infallible (2 Tim. 3:16-17; 2 Pet. 1:20-21).
      2. It is authoritative (1 Cor. 4:6; 14:37; 2 John 9-11; 1 Thess. 2:13).
      3. It is all-sufficient (2 Tim. 3:16-17; 2 Pet. 1:3).
      4. It has been delivered once for all (Jude 3; John 16:12-13; Acts 20:27).
      5. It is enduring and unbreakable (Matt. 24:35; 1 Pet. 1:23-25; John 10:35).
      6. It is absolute truth (John 8:31-32, 44-46; 14:6; 17:17-19).
      7. It is not to be:
         (a) Added to (Rev. 22:18).
         (b) Subtracted from (Rev. 22:19).
         (c) Modified (Gal. 1:6-9).
      8. It can be understood (John 8:31-32; Luke 1:1-4; Eph. 3:3; 5:17; 2 Pet. 1:12-21; Deut. 30:11-14; 31:9-13; 2 Cor. 1:13; 1 John 2:21).
      9. It can be understood correctly (John 8:32; 2 Tim. 2:15; Gal. 1:7; 2 Pet. 3:16).
      10. It can be understood alike (Gal. 1:6-9; Eph. 4:4-5; 1 Cor. 1:10).
      11. It is "reasonable" (Isa. 1:18; Acts 17:1-3; 19:8-10; 24:25; 26:25).
      12. It is relevant to our lives today (Psa. 119:9-11; Matt. 4:4).
      13. Some things have not been revealed to us to know in this life (Deut. 29:29).
   B. God expects man to interpret the Bible properly (i.e., in the way that He intended).
      1. Since there is one God, who gave one book, to last for all time, to save all people, and to do so in the same way, how many different acceptable ways would He give to interpret that one book? Would He expect man to interpret it differently or the same?
      2. Second Timothy 2:15 is God's key to interpreting God's Word in God's way.
         (a) Interpreting the Bible in the way that God intended it to be interpreted:
            (1) Requires that one (having been commanded) **"give diligence"** (ASV).
            (2) Provides the only way to present oneself **"approved unto God"** (ASV).
            (3) Guarantees one **"as a workman who does not need to be ashamed"** (NASB).
            (4) Is achieved exclusively by **"handling aright the word of truth"** (ASV).
         (b) The last phrase is key: God's word must be handled aright!

II. **There Are Some Basic Principles for Properly Interpreting and Understanding the Bible.**
   A. Study the **content** of each individual passage.
      1. Define words.
      2. Observe grammatical relationships.
      3. Note seemingly insignificant words ("and," "so," "for," etc.).
      4. Note the relation of one sentence to another.
      5. Recognize figures of speech.
   B. Study the **context** of each individual passage.
      1. The Literary Context
         (a) Who is writing the passage?
         (b) To whom is the author writing?
         (c) When was the passage written?
         (d) What kind of literature is being used?
      2. The Immediate Context
         (a) The specific sentence

            (b) The immediate context—the verses before and after
                (1) Remember your ABC's – Read verses **A**FTER, **B**EFORE, looking at **C**ONTEXT.
            (c) The remote context—the chapter and surrounding chapters
        3. The Specific Book Context
            (a) How does this passage fit into the scope of the entire book?
            (b) How are the words and phrases in this passage used elsewhere in the book?
            (c) What was the author's intent and purpose in writing?
            (d) What circumstance(s) may have prompted the writing?
        4. The Specific Author Context
            (a) How does this passage fit into the style of this author?
            (b) How are the words and phrases in this passage used elsewhere by this author?
        5. The Parallel Passage Context
            (a) Are there passages that parallel the teaching of these verses?
            (b) What light do the parallel passages shed on these verses?
        6. The Biblical Context
            (a) No two passages of Scripture will conflict or contradict one another.
            (b) No doctrine can be true if it is opposed to any clear statement of God's Word.
            (c) How does this passage harmonize with the teaching of the rest of Scripture?
            (d) How does the rest of Scripture shed light on this passage?
        7. The Historical-Cultural Context
            (a) What are the historical and cultural circumstances that bear on this passage?
            (b) Are there any geographical considerations that might bear on this passage?
            (c) Are there any political factors that might bear on this passage?
            (d) What would this message mean to its original recipients?
        8. Keeping a passage in its context is absolutely critical to sound Biblical interpretation.
    C. Gather **all the relevant** Scriptural evidence on any Biblical subject.
        1. There is a difference between a true statement and the whole truth of a matter.
            (a) To know what the Bible teaches on a matter, all that the Bible teaches must be gathered.
            (b) It is not "some" of the Bible that is true. "The sum of thy word is truth" (Psa. 119:160).
            (c) One may be able to quote or cite a Bible verse on a subject, and any Bible verse would be a "true statement" (within its given context).
            (d) But, one must gather all Bible verses on a subject to know the "whole truth of the matter" (i.e., the truth that God intended for man to know).
            (e) Quoting one verse does not give the full/complete picture of Biblical truth on a matter, and it may, in fact, lead one into error rather than into "the truth, the whole truth and nothing but the truth."
        2. This step will likely require time, research and the use of study tools.
            (a) Make sure to gather **all** the evidence on the subject matter being studied.
            (b) Make sure the evidence gathered is **relevant** to the subject matter being studied.
        3. Let the Bible explain itself.
            (a) The Bible is indeed its own best interpreter.
            (b) A plain, clear passage should always be used to make the difficult, obscure passages clear.
            (c) A difficult passage never denies or contradicts the plain teaching of the Scripture.
    D. **Handle** the gathered evidence **correctly**.

1. Exegesis must come first.
   (a) Exegesis means "to lead out of," by bringing out the meaning of any writing.
   (b) The careful interpreter is led to his conclusions by following the text. He asks: "What did the Biblical author mean?"
      (1) "What did he say?"
      (2) "Why did he say it?"
      (3) "What did he intend his original readers to understand?"
2. Eisegesis must be avoided.
   (a) Eisegesis means "to lead into," by injecting one's own ideas into the text.
   (b) This approach reads into the passage something that was not originally there, making the Bible mean whatever the "interpreter" wants.
   (c) This approach mishandles the text in an effort to "prove" a point.
3. Hermeneutics (the interpretation) must come second.
   (a) Hermeneutics is the science of interpretation.
   (b) Answering, "What does it mean 'here and now'?"
   (c) Keep in mind that any passage, *when examined in context,* will have one correct interpretation, not several. (See II, B.)
      (1) When context is ignored, it is easy to assign a variety of meanings to a statement.
   (d) Be *careful not to confuse interpretation and application.*
      (1) While a statement can have many applications, it has only one interpretation when properly understood in its context.
   (e) The notion that each statement has a single meaning makes sense when you remember that the interpreter's task is to grasp the mind of the writer.
      (1) Every communication involves two minds: the mind of the sender (writer/speaker) and the mind of the receiver (reader/listener).
   (f) When we are interpreting a Biblical passage, we are dealing with truth and meaning.
      (1) Truth is not subjective.
      (2) When truth exists in the mind of a writer, and that writer expresses that truth in a statement, that statement (the full statement, including the context) objectively contains a particular meaning.
   (g) Don't confuse meaning and meaningfulness.
      (1) Truth is objective.
      (2) The search is not for *a* meaning. Rather, the search is for *the* meaning.
4. To handle aright the word of truth (2 Tim. 2:15):
   (a) Do not add to what is revealed (Deut. 4:2; 5:32; 12:32; Prov. 30:6; Rev. 22:18).
   (b) Do not take away from what is revealed (Deut. 4:2; 5:32; 12:32; 2 Jn. 9; Rev. 22:18).
   (c) Stay within the teaching and observe the teaching carefully, completely, lovingly and accurately (2 Tim. 2:15; John 8:31; 1 Cor. 4:6).
   (d) Realize that specific commands exclude substitutes and additions. We must do all that God commands us to do (Matt. 28:19-20).
   (e) Respect the authority of the Scriptures (Matt. 28:18-20; Col. 3:17). (See Lesson 4.)

E. To fail to follow these steps: (1) studying the content, (2) studying the context, (3) gathering all the relevant Scriptural evidence, and (4) handling the gathered evidence correctly,
   1. Means the Bible can be made to mean whatever.
      (a) It is totally subjective.
      (b) No interpretation is right or wrong.
      (c) Anything goes.

F. Then, **apply** the message of the Bible to your life.
   1. Respond to the passage with our hearts and lives.
   2. Here are some questions that will help us apply Scriptures to our lives:
      (a) Does this command something I'm not doing?
      (b) Does this suggest a change in my behavior?
      (c) Does this reflect a spirit or an attitude I'm not manifesting?
      (d) Does this confirm a belief I already hold?
      (e) Does this suggest further study or a change in my beliefs?
      (f) Have I accepted this promise and trusted God to fulfill it?
      (g) Have I seen this promise fulfilled in my life?
      (h) How would it change matters if everyone obeyed this command?
      (i) What would Jesus do in my place?
G. The proof that we need to follow this pattern and these principles of proper Biblical interpretation is found in the example of Jesus Himself in Matthew 4:1-11.

III. Significant Distinctions Must Be Made to Properly Interpret and Understand the Bible.
A. We must distinguish between the Patriarchal, Mosaic/Jewish and Christian Ages.
   1. There are certain eternal principles that are common in each dispensation.
   2. There are certain requirements of God that differ in each dispensation.
   3. There are certain specifics of Christianity not found in the Patriarchal or Jewish Ages.
B. We must distinguish between the Old Testament and the New Testament.
   1. They were designated as two different covenants (2 Cor. 3:6,14; Heb. 8:13; 9:1,15,18; 10:9).
   2. They were delivered through two different mediators (Heb. 1:1-2; 8:6; 9:15; 12:24).
   3. The nature of the two covenants differs tremendously (2 Cor. 3:3-11; Heb. 8-10).
   4. They have two very different sacrificial systems (Heb. 7:12-14,24-26; 9:14-28; 10:4,10-11).
   5. They have two very different remedies for sin (Heb. 7:19,25; 8:12; 9:9,13-14; 10:1-4,11,14).
   6. They represent two different covenants for two different peoples (Deut. 5:2-3; Eph. 2:11-13; Mark 16:15; Col. 1:5; John 3:3-5).
   7. They have two very different purposes (Gal. 3:19-25; Rom. 8:2; Heb. 8:12).
   8. They have two very different durations (2 Cor. 3:11, 14; Heb. 8:13; 10:9; 13:20; Eph. 2:14-15; Rev. 14:6).
   9. See Lesson 6 for more on the difference between "The Two Covenants."
C. We must distinguish between the merely reported and the authorized.
   1. There's a difference between "essentials" and "incidentals"
      (a) In Acts 16:9-12, Paul traveled by ship (incidental) to preach the gospel (essential).
      (b) In Acts 20:7-9, the church met on 3rd floor (incidental) to worship God (essential).
D. We must distinguish between circumstance and condition.
   1. Circumstances surrounding conversions vary.
      (a) It could be by a riverside on the Sabbath or outside a prison at midnight (Acts 16).
      (b) Circumstances surrounding conversions vary and are "incidental" in nature.
   2. Conditions of conversion do not vary.
      (a) Every conversion involves preaching, hearing, believing, repenting, confessing and baptism (all essential for salvation).
      (b) Conditions for conversion do not vary and are "essential" in nature.
E. We must distinguish between the temporary and the permanent.
   1. Some elements in the early church were necessary yet temporary:
      (a) Miracles (Mark 16:20; Heb. 2:3-4; Acts 2:4).
      (b) Imparting miraculous gifts (Acts 8:14-20; 19:1-6; 2 Cor. 12:12).

- (c) Prophesying (1 Cor. 12:10; 13:8-13; 14:29-31).
- (d) Spiritual/Miraculous gifts (1 Cor. 13:8-13; 9:2; Eph. 4:11-13; 2 Tim. 1:6).
- (e) They were necessary for the infant church but never intended to be a permanent part of Christianity. (See Lesson on "The Purpose and Duration of Miracles.")
2. Many elements in the early church were intended to be permanent:
   - (a) The esteem for the New Testament as God's authorized will for man (Col. 3:17).
   - (b) The Great Commission, preaching the gospel to every creation (Matt. 28:18-20).
   - (c) The gospel plan of salvation (Mark 16:16; Acts 2:38-47).
   - (d) The specified worship on every first day of the week (Acts 2:42; 1 Cor. 16:1-2).
   - (e) The central place of the church in the lives of every Christian (Matt. 6:33).
3. See VIII, C, D, E, F on pages 50-52 for more.

F. We must distinguish between faith and opinion.
   1. It is dangerous to treat the faith as an opinion, likewise it is dangerous to treat an opinion as the faith.
   2. It is dangerous to treat the revealed as if unrevealed, and likewise the unrevealed as if revealed.
   3. There is and must be a distinct difference between faith (God's revealed will) and opinion (man's thoughts).
   4. Failing to distinguish between faith (God's say so) and opinion (man's think so) is the source of religious division.
   5. We must never arrogantly treat our opinions as divine revelation or lower God's Word to the level of human thoughts (cf. Isa. 55:8-9).
   6. Example of differences of opinion: Paul and Barnabas regarding John Mark (Acts 15:36-41).
      - (a) They did not disagree over a matter of faith (they were united).
      - (b) They disagreed over a matter of opinion (parted company).
      - (c) But, they were still brothers; Paul later wrote 1 Corinthians 9:6 and 2 Timothy 4:11.
   7. Summary:
      - (a) In matters of faith   -   There must be Unity!
      - (b) In matters of opinion -   There must be Liberty!
      - (c) In all things   -   There must be Love!

G. We must distinguish between custom and law.
   1. Law is binding, custom is not. There may be principles taught by customs without binding the custom.
      - (a) Examples of customs include: Circumcision, Foot washing, Fasting, Head covering.
   2. We must be careful not to bind customs.
   3. We must be careful concerning stumbling blocks.
   4. Some things in God's Word may be permitted but not required.

IV. Rational Reasoning Is Required for Properly Interpreting and Understanding the Bible.
A. Every student of the Bible functions as either rational or irrational.
   1. To be rational is to:
      - (a) Gather all the relevant evidence.
      - (b) Draw only such conclusions as are warranted by the evidence.
      - (c) Say, "My conclusions cannot outrun the evidence."
      - (d) Know that faith does not outrun or extend beyond the relevant evidence in God's Word.
   2. To be irrational is to:

(a) Reject the proper roles of evidence, reason and conclusion.
(b) Draw conclusions for which one does not have adequate evidence.
(c) Hold that faith must involve the acceptance of some inadequately supported conclusion by some "leap in the dark" beyond the evidence.
(d) Reject the Bible and deny that the Bible is the authoritative Word of God.
3. There is not one thing which God expects men to hold as a constituent element of their faith except that for which He has provided adequate evidence.
  (a) If faith is a "leap in the dark," one would have as much grounds for "leaping" into Buddhism, Islam, Agnosticism or Atheism as he would for "leaping" into Christianity.
  (b) Such an irrational view of faith amounts to a rejection of Christianity, denying that one can know that Christianity is the one true religion of the one true God.
B. The Bible demands that men be rational.
  1. The Bible plainly teaches that we *can* prove and therefore know:
    (a) That God exists.
    (b) That the Bible is the Word of God.
    (c) That Jesus Christ is the Son of God.
    (d) That, to be saved, one must believe in, love and obey Jesus Christ.
  2. Men must recognize the proper role of reason in connection with Biblical evidence.
    (a) The Bible not only demands that men reason but that they reason correctly in their study of the evidence which God has given them.
      (1) Men must be diligent in their search for and learning of the evidence (2 Tim. 2:15).
      (2) Men must prove (put to the test, examine) all things (1 Thess. 5:21).
      (3) Men must search the Scriptures to see if what men teach is true (Acts 17:11).
      (4) Men must be prepared to give a defense to those who ask for a reasoned defense (1 Pet. 3:15).
    (b) After gathering the evidence, men must hold only to that which is true (1 Thess. 5:21; Acts 17:11; 1 Pet. 3:15).
  3. Jesus is our perfect example of approaching the Bible rationally and providing a reasoned defense thereof (Matt. 4:1-11).
C. Christianity is a religion of rational reasoning based upon Biblical authority.

V. **The Necessity for Authority in Religious Matters (And Knowing How the Bible Authorizes) Cannot Be Overemphasized!**
  A. It is imperative that we be concerned about Bible authority and how to ascertain it.
    1. Unless we know how God (or the Bible) authorizes, we cannot be sure about anything we do or say in the realm of religion.
    2. We must answer, "Is what we are doing from heaven or from men?" (cf. Mt. 21:23-27).
  B. Authority (an objective standard) is absolutely necessary in religious matters.
    1. There is an obvious need for an objective standard in ordinary affairs.
      (a) If no objective standards were recognized, there would be chaos in ordinary affairs of everyday life.
      (b) In order to have an orderly, rather than chaotic society, we have need for objective standards in our daily lives to ascertain taxes on houses, weight of produce, length of lumber, postage on letters, scores of games, etc., etc.
    2. In the same way, an objective standard is absolutely crucial to properly answering questions which pertain to man's salvation from sin.
      (a) Men do not merely need answers to religious questions; they need the right answers!
      (b) Jesus did not come into the world to make men religious (many already were);

He came that men might be right religiously (Matt. 7:21-23)!
3. God has made it abundantly clear that the only belief or action (in religion) which is acceptable to Him is that which is **authorized** by His word.
    (a) "Whatever you do in word or deed, do all in the name of the Lord Jesus" (Col. 3:17).
        (1) "In the name of the Lord" means "by the authority of the Lord, as the Lord has authorized" (cf. Acts 4:7-10).
        (2) In matters of religious faith and practice, God never accepts that which is believed or done by mere human authority.
    (b) "Whoever goes too far and does not abide in the doctrine of Christ does not have God" (2 John 9).
        (1) One who does that which is not authorized by the teaching of Christ in His New Testament sins in so doing and does not have God's approval.
    (c) Christians are obligated and privileged to "walk by faith" (2 Cor. 5:7).
        (1) That is our standard.
        (2) "Faith comes by hearing, and hearing by the word of God" (Rom. 10:17).
        (3) "Without faith it is impossible to please Him" (Heb. 11:6).
        (4) Thus, we must walk by the Word of God in order to please God.
        (5) No one's faith can "out-run" his knowledge of the Word of God.
C. The Bible is the true (and only) standard, as the authority it possesses comes ultimately from the all-authoritative God. Understanding the chain of authority is vital.
    1. All authority inherently resides in God the Father (Gen. 1-3; Rom. 9:8-24).
    2. God gave all authority unto the Son, Jesus Christ (Matt. 28:18-20).
    3. Christ sent the Holy Spirit to guide the apostles (John 16:13; 14:26).
    4. The Holy Spirit guided the apostles and prophets in writing every word of the Bible (2 Pet. 1:20-21; Eph. 3:5).
    5. Thus, the very authority of God is inherent in the words of the Bible (1 Thess. 2:13; 1 Cor. 14:37).
    6. The Bible, and the Bible alone, is the true objective standard that provides the only right answers to religious questions.
D. The New Testament is the Divine pattern for us today.
    1. In Genesis 6, Noah was given a pattern for the ark.
        (a) "Thus Noah did; according to all that God commanded him, so he did" (Gen. 6:22).
    2. In Exodus 25, Moses was given a pattern for the tabernacle.
        (a) "See to it that you make them according to the pattern" (Ex. 25:40; cf. Heb. 8:5).
        (b) "Thus Moses did; according to all that the Lord had commanded him, so he did" (Ex. 40:16).
    3. In the New Testament, God has given mankind the pattern for building his life.
        (a) "Hold fast the pattern of sound words" (2 Tim. 1:13-14).
        (b) We have the pattern for Christian character.
        (c) We have the pattern for the church.
        (d) As with all of God's patterns, we are obligated and privileged to build according to the divine pattern.
    4. The pattern nature of the New Testament is inherent in the very fact that it is the Lord's New Testament (cf. Matt. 26:28; Heb. 9:15; Gal. 3:15).
        (a) A testament is something which is to be taken seriously.
        (b) It is not to be changed or disregarded.
    5. The fact that the New Testament is designed to be our pattern is emphatically

declared in numerous passages (2 John 9; 1 Cor. 4:6; Gal. 1:6-9; Rev. 22:18-19).
    6. God expects us to walk according to and to live in harmony with the divine pattern (Matt. 28:20; Eph. 5:11; 2 John 10; John 14:15; 15:14; 1 John 5:3).
E. God will not tolerate that which is not authorized.
    1. Whatever is not authorized by God is not acceptable to God, even if it is "intended to be" acceptable.
        (a) Cain's worship (surely intended to be acceptable) was not acceptable to God (Gen. 4:2-5).
        (b) Israel's worship (surely intended to be acceptable) was not acceptable to God (Mal. 1:6-9).
        (c) The worship of the Pharisees and scribes (surely intended to be acceptable) was not acceptable to God (Matt. 15:7-9).
    2. The Bible often uses the word "strange" in the sense of "not acceptable because not authorized."
        (a) Nadab and Abihu "offered strange/profane fire before the Lord, which He had not commanded them" (Lev. 10:1-2).
        (b) "King Solomon loved many strange women" (1 Kgs. 11:1).
        (c) Israel also did "this great evil, to transgress against our God in marrying strange/pagan wives" (Neh. 13:27).
        (d) Sodom and Gomorrah had "gone after strange flesh" (Jude 7).
        (e) We are warned about being "carried about with various and strange doctrines" (Heb. 13:9).
F. We must know how God does not authorize.
    1. To stand faithfully on the mountain top of Bible authority, we must know:
        (a) How God does authorize.
        (b) How God does not authorize.
    2. God does not authorize upon the basis of:
        (a) My personal likes or dislikes (Prov. 14:12; Jer. 10:23).
        (b) What pleases me (John 8:29).
        (c) Erroneous conclusions that I may reach (2 Kgs. 5:11).
        (d) My opinion or the opinions of others (2 Pet. 1:20).
        (e) What is popular (Matt. 7:13-14; 1 Sam. 8:4-8).
        (f) The consensus or thinking of the majority (Matt. 7:13-14).
        (g) What a well-known or highly respected brother says (Gal. 1:6-9).
        (h) Human traditions or creeds (Matt. 15:9; Col. 2:8; Gal. 1:8).
        (i) My inability to "see any harm in it" (2 Sam. 6:3-7).
        (j) Long-standing practices or "what we've always done/believed" (Josh. 5:2-9).
        (k) What I feel in my heart (Acts 23:1; 1 Tim. 1:15; Prov. 28:26; 30:20).
        (l) Experiences that I have had (Phil. 3:4-15).
        (m) My sincere claim, "I'm doing this in God's name" (Matt. 7:21-23).
        (n) The Law of the Old Testament (Gal. 3:19-25; Col. 2:14).
    3. Remember: whatever is not authorized by God is not acceptable to God.
G. We must stand on authorized Bible truth and avoid the destructiveness of extremes.
    1. Bible truth is our only standard of authority (Col. 3:17; 1 Cor. 4:6; Rev. 22:18-19; John 8:31-32).
        (a) Man's tendency is to react from one extreme to an opposite extreme.
        (b) Extremes breed extremes.

- (c) Truth lies between extremes.
 2. To one extreme, man "adds" his will to God's will.
    - (a) He makes laws that God did not make.
    - (b) He treats matters of opinion as matters of faith.
    - (c) He seeks to bind where God has not bound.
 3. To another extreme, man "takes away" from God's will.
    - (a) He disregards laws that God did make.
    - (b) He treats matters of faith as matters of opinion.
    - (c) He seeks to loose where God has bound.
 4. In backing away from one extreme, individuals often fall into the other extreme.
    - (a) We must be exceedingly careful to stay on the mountain top of Bible authority.
    - (b) We must not fall off this sacred mountain of Bible truth to either extreme. There is destruction and death on both sides!
 5. In our postmodern culture, new "standards" or "extremes" are being set.
    - (a) Postmodern man dismisses God's authority and is unwilling to make any judgments.
    - (b) Postmodern man treats matters of faith and opinion as relative—there are no absolutes.
    - (c) Postmodern man is tolerant of all views, unwilling to judge any view and sets each man as his own authority.

H. God demands Biblical authority for a Christian's work and worship.
 1. The Scriptures teach that in Christian work and worship we must do only that which is authorized by the Word of God.
 2. It is possible for human beings to ascertain that which is authorized by the Word of God.
 3. It is possible for human beings to practice in Christian work and worship only that which is authorized by the Word of God.
 4. How does a Christian ascertain Scriptural authority for his actions and attitudes? That is the focus of this lesson.

I. Unless we know how God (or the Bible) authorizes, we cannot be sure about anything we do or say in the realm of religion.
 1. If I <u>can</u> do certain things, and if I <u>must</u> do certain things, how can I *know* that I can and how can I *know* that I must?
 2. If I <u>cannot</u> do certain things, and if I <u>must not</u> do certain things, how can I *know* that I cannot or must not?
 3. How do we decide? How do we ascertain Bible authority for matters today?

J. The Word of God authorizes, as one might expect, in the exact way that humans authorize certain actions in their communications with one another—through direct statement, implication, expediency and accounts of approved action.
 1. In order to know if any portion of Scripture (any verse, any statement, any action) is binding on us today, the diligent Bible student must:
    - (a) Use the inductive process: Gather all the relevant evidence to the Biblical question being studied.
      - (1) Study "the total context": the specific statement, the immediate context and the remote context.
    - (b) Use the deductive process: Draw only such conclusions as are warranted by the totality of that evidence.
      - (1) This is done by the correct use of logic (the principles of valid reasoning) in handling the total evidence.

VI. The Bible Authorizes By Direct Statement.
A. To say the Bible authorizes by direct statement is to say the Bible says something and teaches it explicitly! God comes right out and says some things explicitly!
B. Direct Statements include:
1. Imperative Statements (which command or give directions in an authoritative manner).
   (a) Mark 16:15 – Preaching the gospel to every creature is a command of God.
   (b) Acts 2:38 – Repenting and being baptized is a command of God.
2. Declarative Statements (which state that something is or is not the case).
   (a) Mark 16:16 – Salvation comes only after a person both believes and is baptized.
   (b) John 20:30-31 – Believing that Jesus is the Christ is essential to life in His name.
   (c) James 2:24-26 – Faith and works are both equally necessary for salvation.
   (d) Galatians 3:26-27 – Sons of God have, through faith, been baptized into Him.
3. Interrogative Statements (which ask a question, sometimes to give information).
   (a) 1 Corinthians 1:13 – Christ is not divided and no one else can save.
   (b) Acts 10:47 – Gentiles were subjects for baptism, the element of which is water.
   (c) Romans 10:13-14 – Believing and calling on His name are essential to be saved.
   (d) Romans 6:3 – Men are baptized into Christ and into His death.
4. Hortatory Statements (which express a strong wish or desire).
   (a) Romans 5:20-6:1 – God forbid that any would sin more to get more grace.
   (b) Romans 15:5-6 – May all Christians be of the same mind—the mind of Christ.
   (c) 1 Thess. 3:11-12 – May every Christian love each other and all men as well.
   (d) Hebrews 6:1 – May each Christian grow in Christ and go on to maturity.
5. Conditional Statements (which contain two clauses: the condition and the consequence).
   (a) Romans 7:2-3 – Only certain persons are free to marry (those never married, or whose spouse died, or the innocent spouse of an adulterous mate).
   (b) 1 Corinthians 15:12-20 – Christ's resurrection guarantees a general resurrection.
   (c) Romans 8:12-13 – If a Christian lives according to the flesh he will die spiritually.
   (d) John 3:3-5 – Baptism is essential to entering the kingdom of God (being saved).

VII. The Bible Authorizes By Implication.
A. Everything that the Bible teaches it teaches either explicitly or implicitly.
1. Any set of statements, no matter who makes them, imply other statements.
   (a) God has given a set of statements which form the explicit statements of the Bible. The explicit statements in turn imply statements.
   (b) Thus, God says everything which He says explicitly in the Bible, and additionally He says everything which is implied in what He says explicitly. The implicit statements are actually "said" in the explicit statements.
2. That which the Bible teaches implicitly is just as true, just as binding and just as authoritative as that which it teaches explicitly. These are logical conclusions that must be drawn!
3. The authority inherent in that which is implied relies not on one's ability to reason correctly regarding an explicit statement, but on the fact that GOD HAS IMPLIED IT!
4. As one can be absolutely certain that the explicit statements of the Bible are true, he can be just as certain that what those explicit statements imply are true.
B. There is a vast difference between "implication" and "assumption." We must be careful to distinguish what a text actually says and implies from what "we want it to say."
1. Implication is not mere assertion, personal interpretation or wishful thinking.
2. Implication is a logical relationship among terms of a proposition.

3. In implication, conclusions are necessitated and cannot be avoided given the set premises.
4. We must stay within what a text teaches and authorizes and not conjecture or assume things that are not within Scripture.

C. To say that the Bible authorizes by implication is to say that it is impossible for direct (explicit) statements to be true and yet the implied statements to be false.
1. Consider these modern illustrations to understand the authority and certainty that implication carries (just as much as the explicit statements):
   (a) Illustration #1:
      (1) Explicitly True: "Bill is taller than Jack."
      (2) Explicitly True: "Jack is taller than John."
      (3) Implicitly True: Bill is taller than John.
      (4) The implicit is just as certain and true as the explicit.
   (b) Illustration #2:
      (1) Explicitly True: "This square has one side 6 inches long."
      (2) Implicitly True: There are 3 other sides each 6 inches long.
      (3) Implicitly True: The perimeter of the square is 24 inches.
      (4) Implicitly True: The area of the square is 36 inches.
      (5) Implicitly True: There are 4 right angles.
      (6) The implied statements are equally as true as the explicit statement, and the implied statements are actually "stated" in the explicit statement.
2. Consider these Scriptural illustrations of implication that were used and expected to be understood:
   (a) Jesus taught by implication (Matt. 22:29-32).
      (1) Explicitly stated: "God said, 'I am the God of Abraham, the God of Isaac, and the God of Jacob.'"
      (2) Explicitly stated: "God is not the God of the dead, but of the living."
      (3) Implicitly stated: "Abraham, Isaac and Jacob were somewhere, living. There is life after death."
      (4) The Sadducees were obligated to imply (but not necessarily admit) that Abraham, Isaac and Jacob were alive. Their Scriptures taught this (Ex. 3:6)!
      (5) Their failure to reason correctly was equated by Jesus with their failure to know the Scriptures.
      (6) They were in error because of their failure to appreciate that which was implied by God in His Word.
   (b) Paul taught by implication (1 Cor. 15:12-18).
      (1) Explicitly stated: "If there is no resurrection of the dead, then Christ is not risen."
      (2) Explicitly stated: "If Christ is not risen, then…your faith is also empty."
      (3) Explicitly stated: "He did not raise up—if in fact the dead do not rise."
      (4) Explicitly stated: "For if the dead do not rise, then Christ is not risen."
      (5) Explicitly stated: "If Christ is not risen, your faith is futile."
      (6) Implicitly stated: My faith is not empty or futile, therefore, Christ is risen!
      (7) Implicitly stated: Christ was raised, therefore, all will be raised!
   (c) God expects us to use logical reasoning skills and understand what His explicit statements imply. For example:
      (1) Genesis 13:1 states explicitly: "Then Abram went up from Egypt, he and his wife and all that he had, and Lot with him, to the South."

(2) The Bible never says explicitly that Lot went down to Egypt.
(3) However, logical reasoning skills demand the implicit truth (that Lot did go down to Egypt) based upon the explicit statement (that Lot went up from Egypt).

D. Notice a few truths that the Bible teaches implicitly (some may also be taught explicitly):
1. First of all, implication is really the only way the Bible authorizes itself to be personally applied to any person living today.
   (a) Where do you find your name in the text? Where does the Bible say, "[Your name], be faithful until death and I will give you a crown of life"?
   (b) As no Scripture can technically be said to have been spoken directly or explicitly to any person now living, all authorized instructions are applied through principles of implication.
2. Implication teaches and authorizes that baptism is by immersion in water.
   (a) When Jesus was baptized, He "came up from the water" (Matt. 3:16).
   (b) Implied: Jesus went down into the water.
   (c) When Philip baptized the eunuch, they both "went down into the water, and he baptized him," and then "they came up out of the water" (Acts 8:38-39).
   (d) Implied: Therefore, baptism is by immersion.
3. Implication teaches and authorizes that Saul repented of his sins.
   (a) No person can become a Christian without repenting of sins (Lk. 13:3; Acts 17:30).
   (b) Saul of Tarsus did become a Christian (1 Tim. 1:12-15).
   (c) Scripture does not explicitly state that Saul of Tarsus repented.
   (d) Implied: Therefore, Saul, in becoming a Christian, did repent of his sins.
4. Implication teaches and authorizes that you, the reader, must repent of your sins.
   (a) "God...now commands all men everywhere to repent" (Acts 17:30).
   (b) Your name is not in that verse, but you are a member of mankind somewhere.
   (c) Implied: Therefore, you must repent.
5. Implication teaches and authorizes that Saul was not saved before he was baptized.
   (a) After praying and fasting for three days (Acts 9:9), Saul was told, "Wash away your sins" (Acts 22:16).
   (b) Implied: Saul still had his sins. He was not saved yet.
   (c) Saul was commanded, "Arise and be baptized, and wash away your sins, calling on the name of the Lord" (Acts 22:16).
   (d) Implied: Therefore, Saul, because he had not yet been baptized, was still lost in his sins.
6. Implication teaches and authorizes that baptism is absolutely essential to salvation.
   (a) The explicit teaching of Galatians 3:26-27 implies that if one is not baptized:
      (1) He is not a son of God (and, thus, remains a child of the devil).
      (2) He is not in Christ (where salvation is, 2 Tim. 2:10).
      (3) He is not clothed with Christ (and, thus, is still clothed with the "filthy rags" of his own sins).
   (b) The explicit teaching of 1 Corinthians 1:13 implies that in order to truly belong to Christ (or Paul or Cephas or Apollos), two things are essential:
      (1) Christ must have been crucified for you!
      (2) You must have been baptized in the name of Christ!
7. Implication teaches and authorizes partaking of the Lord's Supper every Sunday.
   (a) The central purpose of the Sunday assembly of the church is the Lord's Supper (Acts 20:7).

(b) The N.T. church met together every first day of the week (1 Cor. 16:1-2).
(c) Implied: Therefore, the early church observed the Lord's Supper every Sunday when they assembled to worship, and so should we.
8. Implication teaches and authorizes that the Sabbath observance has been taken away.
    (a) The Sabbath observance was first commanded in the Law of Moses, specifically in the Ten Commandments portion of the old covenant (Ex. 20:8; 34:28; Deut. 4:13).
    (b) When Jesus died on the cross, He "wiped out the handwriting of requirements… having nailed it to the cross" (Col. 2:14). We are no longer under (or bound) by any portion of that old covenant (Gal. 3:19-25), for Jesus is the Mediator of a new covenant, which is not according to the old (Heb. 8:8-13; 9:15).
    (c) Implied: Therefore, the observance of the Sabbath Day was "taken away," along with the rest of the old law (cf. Rom. 7:1-7; Col. 2:14-17; Neh. 9:13-14).
9. Implication teaches and authorizes that only men may serve as elders in the church.
    (a) Among the qualifications that God gives for "bishops/elders" in 1 Timothy 3:1-7 and Titus 1:5-9 is that he must be "the husband of one wife."
    (b) Only men (not women) can be husbands.
    (c) Implied: Therefore, only men can be elders in the church.
E. One can be absolutely certain that the Bible's implicit teachings are just as true, just as binding and just as authoritative as its explicit teaching, for God is the one who gave the explicit statements, along with their implications.

VIII. The Bible Authorizes By Accounts of Approved Action.
A. An "account of action" is the description of what some individual or group did (or said).
    1. Accounts of action can be used to prove a thing to be essential when:
        (a) Correct logic is used (the principles of valid reasoning).
        (b) The total context is examined (the specific statement, the immediate context and the remote context).
        (c) Only such conclusions as are warranted by the total context are drawn.
B. While the law of the Old Testament has been repealed and is no longer in force, there are principles set forth in the O.T. that are binding on and applicable to men living today.
    1. If such were not the case, the O.T. would be of no value at all to men living today.
        (a) But, all Scripture is "profitable for doctrine" (2 Tim. 3:16-17).
        (b) Messages to Christians in the New Testament instruct them to learn from what happened to people during the Old Testament period.
    2. That the principles of the Old Testament are binding on men living today can be seen in:
        (a) The infinite nature of God.
            (1) God is omniscient, omnipotent and immutable.
            (2) Thus, whatever He has required at any time is, in its basic essence, required of all men during every covenant age (such as faith and obedience).
        (b) The specific instructions to that effect in the New Testament.
            (1) Romans 15:4 – The principles involved in God's dealings with men would outlive the Law.
            (2) 1 Corinthians 10:6, 11 – Certain actions are prohibited to men in all ages.
            (3) Hebrews 11:1-12:1 – It is essential for men living today to act "by faith."
            (4) Luke 17:32 – When God gives instructions that a thing is to be done, it must be done.
            (5) 2 Peter 2:4-11 – If God did not spare others when they sinned, then He will not spare you when you sin.

(c) The principle involved in the various accounts of actions themselves.
  (1) Adam & Eve (Gen. 2-3) – Men must obey God's instructions.
  (2) Cain & Abel (Gen. 4:3-5) – We must have proper authority.
  (3) Noah & the Ark (Gen. 6-9) – God demands faithful obedience to His instructions. When God gives generic authority in a matter, men are free to exercise some liberty, but when God specifies certain details, men must be obedient to the obligations of those details.
  (4) Abraham Offering Isaac (Gen. 22:1-14; Heb. 11:17-19) – Men must be fully persuaded that God is able to do what He says He will do.
  (5) Nadab & Abihu (Lev. 10:1-2) – Men are to do only that which God has authorized.
  (6) David & the New Cart (1 Chron. 15:1-15) – Men must do in religion only what is authorized by God.
  (7) The Young Prophet (1 Kgs. 13:1-32) – While sincerity is necessary, it is not sufficient in obedience to God.
C. Actions in the New Testament can be classified <u>generally</u> in two ways:
  1. Action which is acceptable to God.
    (a) In other words, action which is authorized by God's Word.
    (b) Acceptable/Authorized actions may be sub-classified into:
      (1) Action which is obligatory (i.e., must be done to be pleasing to God).
      (2) Action which is optional (i.e., may exercise freedom of choice).
  2. Action which is not acceptable to God.
    (a) In other words, action which is not authorized by God's Word.
    (b) Unacceptable/Unauthorized actions may be sub-classified into:
      (1) Action which is explicitly forbidden.
      (2) Action which is implicitly forbidden (because not authorized by God).
      (3) The forbidding of what God's Word allows.
      (4) The binding of what God's Word has not taught to be essential.
D. Actions in the New Testament can be classified <u>specifically</u> in these five ways:
  1. Action which was permanently sinful – in other words, action which was sinful for New Testament characters and which is sinful for men living today.
    (a) Betraying Jesus (Matt. 26:47-49 + Rom. 1:29; Acts 1:18)
    (b) Denying Jesus (Matt. 26:69-75 + 2 Tim. 1:8; Titus 1:16; 2 Pet. 2:1; Jude 4)
    (c) Showing partiality (Gal. 2:12 + Acts 10:34; Jas. 2:1-6; Rom. 2:11)
    (d) Loving this world (2 Tim. 4:10 + 1 John 2:15-17; 1 Cor. 16:22; Luke 14:26-33)
    (e) Tolerating false teachers/doctrines (Rev. 2:14-15 + Rom. 16:17-18; 1 John 4:1; Matt. 7:15-23)
  2. Action which was optional and temporary – in other words, action which was optional for New Testament characters and which is not optional for men living today.
    (a) Preaching to Jews only (Acts 2-11 + Acts 10:27-28; Mark 16:15; John 3:16)
    (b) Participating in some of the Jewish sacrifices (Acts 21:23-30 + Eph. 2:13-16; Heb. 9:11-10:4)
  3. Action which was optional and permanent – in other words, action which was optional for New Testament characters and which is also optional for men living today.
    (a) Choosing the means of travel to preach (Acts 13:4 + Mark 16:15)
    (b) Eating the Lord's Supper in an upper room (Acts 20:7-8)
    (c) Giving beyond one's ability to give (2 Cor. 8:2-3 + 1 Cor. 16:2; 2 Cor. 9:7)

- (d) Selling possessions and putting it into the common treasury for those in need (Acts 2:43-46; 4:32-36 + 1 Cor. 16:1-2)
- (e) One church sending assistance to another church in order to render spiritual benefit (Acts 15:22-32)
- (f) A preacher working to support himself while he preaches (Acts 18:3; 20:34 + 1 Cor. 9:1-18)
- (g) Kneeling as a posture of prayer (Acts 20:36 + Acts 9:40; 21:5; Luke 22:41)

4. Action which was obligatory and temporary – in other words, action which was obligatory for New Testament characters but is not obligatory for men living today.
    - (a) The power and use of miraculous gifts and signs to confirm the message being preached (Acts 8:4-8 + Mark 16:17-20; Heb. 2:1-4; 1 Cor. 13:8-10; Jas. 1:25)
    - (b) Desiring and possessions spiritual gifts (1 Cor. 14:1 + 1 Cor. 13:8-10; Eph. 4:7-14)

5. Action which was obligatory and permanent – in other words, action which was obligatory upon N.T. characters and which is also obligatory upon men living today.
    - (a) Christians gathering together in an assembly to partake of the Lord's Supper every first day of the week (Acts 20:7 + 1 Cor. 11:20; 16:1-2)
        - (1) The early Christians were obligated to assemble at a specified time (Heb. 10:25).
        - (2) The early Christians were obligated (ordered) to contribute of their means every first day of the week while the church was assembled (1 Cor. 16:1-2; 4:17).
        - (3) A basic purpose of the assembling ("coming together") on the first day of the week was "to" (the infinitive of purpose is found in both passages) eat the Lord's Supper (Acts 20:7 + 1 Cor. 11:20).
        - (4) Therefore, the early church was under obligation to eat the Lord's Supper on every first day of the week and only on the first day of the week (since there is no Biblical authority for any other day of the week, Col. 3:17; 2 John 9-11; 1 Cor. 4:6).
        - (5) Consider this: if no such requirement exists, then (a) he who meets does not obey anything, and (b) he who stays away does not disobey the will of Christ.
    - (b) Christians obeying God's law when civil law or "religious law" contradict it (Acts 5:28-29 + Dan. 3:1-30; Acts 21:13; Luke 14:26-33; Rev. 2:10)
    - (c) Preaching the necessity of baptism for salvation while preaching Jesus (Acts 8:35-39 + Mark 16:15-16; Acts 2:36-38; 16:30-34)
    - (d) Baptizing for the remission of sins (Every account of conversion in the book of Acts + Mark 16:16; 1 Pet. 3:21)
    - (e) Using water as the element of baptism (Acts 8:26-40 + Acts 10:47-48; Eph. 5:26; John 3:5)
    - (f) Disciples of Christ going everywhere preaching the Word (Acts 8:4 + Mark 16:15)
    - (g) Searching the Scriptures to see if what is taught is true (Acts 17:11 + 1 John 4:1; Rom. 16:17-18)

E. Only the actions which were optional-and-permanent and/or obligatory-and-permanent have any relationship to present-day Christianity.
   1. When we find in the New Testament the account of an action:
      - (a) Which was manifestly right within itself,
      - (b) Which was either optional or obligatory,
      - (c) And, which related to a permanent element of Christianity,
   2. Then, we have authority for imitating that action.

F. How can we know when an account of action is approved of God and a permanent

element of Christianity?
1. Study the account itself, the immediate context and remote context.
2. Look for an underlying command or Divine approval.
3. Look for the doctrinal significance of the account.
4. Apply the rules of sound Biblical interpretation and the principles of logic by gathering the totality of Bible teaching on the matter, handling it aright and drawing only such conclusions demanded by the evidence.

IX. The Bible Authorizes By Expediency.
A. In order to carry out the Christian's obligations from direct statements, implication and accounts of approved action, there is the area of expediency.
1. No propositional revelation can be exhaustive to cover every detail of every area of special revelation.
   (a) The document would be too large.
   (b) The details would be inexplicable to certain people in certain eras.
2. Every obligation that God ever gave involved expediency; therefore, expedients themselves are authorized by God. Expedients are implied in the obligation.
   (a) It is true that, when God gave obligations to be carried out, He did say *how* to carry it out, and yet that He did *not say how*.
   (b) For example: God *did* tell Noah *how* to build the ark, and yet one could say that God *did not* tell Noah *how* to build the ark.
      (1) The command "Go build an ark of gopher wood" left an endless number of expedient decisions to Noah's discretion.
3. Expediency involves human judgment.
   (a) When God specifies obligations for Christians and congregations but He does not specify all the details *how* to carry it out, then we are authorized to involve human judgment to find the most beneficial means of accomplishing that action.
   (b) It is wrong to loose where God has bound, and it is equally wrong to bind where God has not bound. Every expedient has been and must be authorized by God.
   (c) According to God's plan, elders are given and must carry the burdens of authority in the area of expediency. They carry out the laws that God has made and make judgments in the area of expediency. Elders have a right to make these decisions, and they have a right to expect the congregation's compliance (Heb. 13:7, 17).
4. As a Christian seeks to carry out obligations or options (not forbidden by God), an expedient is that which:
   (a) Expedites, aids, assists, helps, profits or benefits in carrying out God's instructions.
   (b) Is inherently advantageous in carrying it out.
   (c) Is in harmony with the Scriptures.
5. Where there is no obligation, there is no expediency.
   (a) One cannot seek to justify something simply by calling it an "expedient."
   (b) Expediency is not a license to perform unauthorized actions but only to expedite or aid what has already been authorized.
   (c) A true expedient, as Scripture would define expediency, is Divinely authorized for the carrying out of God-given obligations.
6. Using that which inherently serves as an aid to carrying out God's will is logically and necessarily authorized in the original command or requirement (provided it is not prohibited elsewhere in Scripture).

- (a) Thus, by using an expedient, we perform only the required action and not something different from what is authorized.
- (b) It is incorrect to suggest that expedients do not fall under the umbrella of Biblical authority. They most certainly do! God, through implication, authorizes the expedient.

B. We must follow some logical criteria in choosing expedients.
  1. Expedients are essential to carry out authorized actions.
     - (a) Example: The command to assemble makes a place and time essential.
  2. The type of expedient is optional.
     - (a) Example: A church can assemble in a tent, on a beach, in a building, etc. The church can rent, buy or meet in a member's home.
  3. Expedients do not and must not add to authorized actions (see C below).
     - (a) There's a difference between "benefitting" and "adding."
     - (b) Expedients do not add to the commands and practices of the New Testament.
  4. Expedients must be lawful and prove advantageous to authorized actions (Col. 3:17).
     - (a) What we do must be authorized (acceptable) by God.
     - (b) That which is not authorized is unlawful and thus sinful.
     - (c) Example: We are to baptize in water; therefore, it could be in a lake, pool, baptistry, etc. But, a font utilized for sprinkling babies is not advantageous (or expedient) in fulfilling God's authorized action of immersion.
  5. Expedients must truly be beneficial (1 Cor. 6:12; 10:23).
     - (a) Even if something is "lawful," it may not be "helpful."
     - (b) An expedient can be abused to the point that it becomes more of a hindrance than a help.
     - (c) Expedients do not necessarily work for every church, in every place, in every period of time.
  6. Expedients must not be enslaving (1 Cor. 6:12).
     - (a) Some traditions fall into this area. Most traditions begin as expedients, which men presumptuously make binding as a necessary practice.
     - (b) Man-made traditions must not be allowed to become as sacred as God's law.
     - (c) Example: Must we forever keep songbooks in the pews? Must we forever put fly-nets over the Lord's Supper trays?
  7. Expedients must be edifying (1 Cor. 10:23; 14:26).
     - (a) Expedients must not make anything confusing. God is not the author of confusion (1 Cor. 14:33).
     - (b) Freedom in expediency is not a license to cause a stumbling block (Rom. 14:13-21).
     - (c) Example: The order of worship is an expedient but should not be confusing.
  8. Expedients must be to the glory of God (1 Cor. 10:31-33).
     - (a) Some people focus the glory on themselves rather than on God.
     - (b) Anything that takes the focus off of God, His glory and His will is an effort in the wrong direction.
     - (c) Any expedient that robs God of glory ought to be abandoned.
  9. Expedients must be done in love (1 Cor. 16:14).
     - (a) Christians are not to seek their own good but the good of others (1 Cor. 10:24).
     - (b) Christians are to pursue love (1 Cor. 13:1; 1 Tim. 6:11).

C. There is a difference between an "expedient" (an aid) and an "addition."
  1. Anything which is not authorized by Scripture, but is nonetheless employed, is an addition.

(a) Additions go beyond the command and make new kinds of actions.
2. A true aid, an expedient, is authorized by the Scriptures.
   (a) Expedients act only in the realm of the lawful. If an act is not lawful, it cannot have aids or expedients to help it do its work to the pleasing of God.
   (b) Expediency can never authorize new and different instructions.
3. Here are some examples to illustrate the difference between an aid and an addition:
   (a) We are commanded, "Go into all the world and preach the gospel" (Mark 16:15).
      (1) We can go by WALKING; we could go by RIDING (two different ways of going).
      (2) These two options have a direct relationship to the obligation ("Go") but no particular relationship to each other. Walking is not an aid (expedient) to riding, and riding is not an expedient to walking.
      (3) A walking stick, used while walking, would be an expedient (aid).
   (b) Consider this simple illustration in the area of perception.
      (1) We perceive by HEARING and by SEEING (two different ways of perceiving).
      (2) Hearing is not an expedient to seeing, nor seeing to hearing.
      (3) These are definite, distinct, different ways of perceiving – i.e., they are co-ordinates.
      (4) Either one can be done without the other.
      (5) Eyeglasses would be an expedient (aid) to seeing.
      (6) A hearing aid would be an expedient (aid) to hearing.
   (c) What about "making music" in worship to God?
      (1) We can make music by SINGING; we can make music by PLAYING.
      (2) Singing and mechanical instruments are two different ways of making music – i.e., they are co-ordinates.
      (3) Either one can be done without the other.
      (4) Singing is not an expedient (aid) to playing.
      (5) Playing is not an expedient (aid) to singing.
      (6) The songbook is an expedient (aid) to singing.
      (7) Having someone lead the congregation is an expedient (aid) to singing.
      (8) When we use the songbook in our singing, we are JUST SINGING. We are NOT singing AND doing something else.
      (9) Mechanical instruments are not a method of singing or an expedient of the command to sing. Rather, it is an addition of another kind of music to that which is authorized in the New Testament.
      (10) When God commands us in the New Testament to sing in worship to Him, to play an instrument is to ADD to His Word.
4. As long as the method being used is truly aiding us to the very thing commanded, without adding to it or taking from it, the method is Scriptural. But there can be no Scriptural method for doing an unscriptural thing.
5. See the difference between expedients and additions (in chart form on the next page):

Bible Instruction	Expedient: Lawful & Authorized Action Which Helps Fulfill the Instruction	Addition: Unlawful & Unauthorized Action Which Changes the Instruction
Noah's Ark	Tools to cut wood, join wood, spread pitch	Different size, different woods, different doors
Great Commission	Traveling by foot, boat, car, plane with printed Bibles	Different message, different doctrines
Lord's Supper	Trays (type, number), cups (type, number)	Different elements, different day, different frequency
Be Baptized	Baptistry, river, lake, pool, ocean, garments	Different mode/action (i.e., sprinkling, pouring water)
Sing in Worship	Songbook, pitch pipe, tuning fork, song leader, projector	Different kind of music (i.e., instrumental and not vocal)

   D. Expediency increases the practicality, endurance and far-reaching application of God's revelation.
      1. Expedients allow for the perpetual relevancy of and practical obedience to the gospel as we pass through time.
      2. It is through expediency that we have and can defend:
         (a) Church buildings
         (b) Sunday service times
         (c) Baptistries
         (d) Teaching in simultaneous Bible classes for adults and children
         (e) Songbooks
         (f) Song leaders
         (g) Invitation songs
         (h) Individual, disposable communion cups
         (i) Tables, trays and contribution baskets
         (j) Bulletins, radio programs, TV programs, periodicals, etc.
         (k) White boards, PowerPoint projectors, etc.
         (l) Brooms, dust pans, vacuum cleaners, cleaning supplies, etc.
         (m) Sound systems, video recordings, webcasts, etc.
         (n) Copiers, printers, computers, etc.
      3. If and when and to the extent that God does specify the HOW in connection with the carrying out of any obligation, that HOW becomes just as binding as the obligation itself. But if and when and to the extent that God does NOT SPECIFY THE HOW, then the manner and method are left to the realm of human judgment, the realm of expediency.
X. **Understanding Generic and Specific Authority Is Crucial in Biblical Interpretation.**
   A. God's instructions authorize through both generic authority and specific authority.
      1. Virtually every authorized command in the Bible has both general and specific elements.
         (a) Specific commands set forth the specific manner in which God's ordinances are to be implemented.
            (1) They must be obeyed without addition, subtraction or substitution.
            (2) This means there is uniformity as all obey the same commands.
            (3) The specific element of the command rules out all other specifics.

(b) Generic commands set forth the general manner in which God's ordinances are to be implemented, leaving the specifics to the judgment of the individual.
    (1) Generic authority authorizes anything that falls within the general instruction.
    (2) The generic element gives liberty, where there may be a diversity of practice.
    (3) But, no liberty from a general instruction can violate another of God's commands.
2. Sometimes God gives very specific instructions, and sometimes He gives general instructions, leaving the details to our best judgment.
    (a) This difference is key in successfully determining authority for all things.
    (b) No man has the authority to bind where God has not bound or to loose where God has not loosed!
    (c) It is important to remember that it is not necessary to always have specific authority for something if it has been authorized through generic commands.

B. Generic authority and specific authority determine the inclusive and exclusive nature of the commands.
    1. Generic commands are both inclusive and exclusive.
        (a) Parent to Child: "Go and put on your shoes."
            (1) GENERIC (ANY shoes) and INCLUSIVE (sneakers, loafers, platform, tap, etc.).
            (2) GENERIC (ANY shoes) and EXCLUSIVE (hats, earmuffs, skates, waders, etc.).
        (b) Physician to Pharmacist: "Give the patient an antibiotic."
            (1) GENERIC (ANY antibiotic, dosage, frequency) and INCLUSIVE (penicillin, amoxicillin, 250mg, 500mg, b.i.d., t.i.d., etc.).
            (2) GENERIC (ANY antibiotic) and EXCLUSIVE (antacids, laxatives, steroids, etc.).
    2. Specific commands are both inclusive and exclusive.
        (a) Parent to Child: "Go and put on your black dress shoes."
            (1) SPECIFIC (black dress shoes) and INCLUSIVE (ANY black dress shoes in closet).
            (2) SPECIFIC (black dress shoes) and EXCLUSIVE (ALL other shoes).
            (3) The very thing that the Generic Command included (i.e., any type of shoe) is that which the Specific Command excludes.
            (4) By specifying the type of shoe, the parent automatically (without saying another word) excludes every other type of shoe. A thing does not have to be specifically forbidden to be unauthorized.
        (b) Physician to Pharmacist: "Give the patient 250mg of tetracycline b.i.d."
            (1) SPECIFIC (tetracycline) and INCLUSIVE (ANY brand or generic).
            (2) SPECIFIC (tetracycline) and EXCLUSIVE (ALL other drugs, dosages and frequencies).
            (3) The very thing that the Generic Command included (i.e., any type of antibiotic, dosage, frequency) is that which the Specific Command excludes.
            (4) By specifying the type of antibiotic, the physician automatically (without saying another word) excludes every other type of antibiotic. A thing does not have to be specifically forbidden to be unauthorized.

C. God utilized Generic Authority and Specific Authority in the commands of the Bible.
    1. God told Noah, "Make yourself an ark of gopherwood; make rooms in the ark..." (Gen. 6:14-16).
        (a) GENERIC Commands
            (1) "Make" is INCLUSIVE (ANY tools: hammer, saw, etc.) and EXCLUSIVE (buying an ark).

(2) "Make rooms" is INCLUSIVE (ANY number of rooms, ANY size rooms, etc.) and EXCLUSIVE (one big open space).
- (b) SPECIFIC Commands
  - (1) "Gopherwood" is INCLUSIVE (ANY board lengths, etc.) and EXCLUSIVE (ALL other kinds of wood, etc.).
  - (2) By specifying the type of wood, God automatically (without saying another word) excluded every other type of wood. A thing does not have to be specifically forbidden to be unauthorized.
  - (3) "300 x 50 x 30" is INCLUSIVE (ANY preparations clearing land for space, building scaffolding, etc.) and EXCLUSIVE (ALL other dimensions or ratios).
- (c) God's commands were to be obeyed.
  - (1) Noah had no right to add to what God had spoken.
  - (2) Noah had no right to take from what God had spoken.
  - (3) If Noah had disobeyed the commands of God (ex: including that which God had excluded), he would have sinned against, displeased and separated himself from the Lord.
2. God told Israel, "Your lamb shall be without blemish, a male of the first year" (Ex. 12:5).
   - (a) SPECIFIC Commands
     - (1) "A lamb" is INCLUSIVE (ANY qualified sheep or goat) and EXCLUSIVE (ALL other kinds of animals).
     - (2) "A male" is INCLUSIVE (ANY qualified male) and EXCLUSIVE (ALL females).
     - (3) By specifying the gender of the lamb, God automatically (without saying another word) excluded all females. A thing does not have to be specifically forbidden to be unauthorized.
3. Jesus told His disciples, "Go therefore and make disciples of all the nations, baptizing them in the name of the Father and of the Son and of the Holy Spirit, teaching them to observe all things that I have commanded you..." (Matt. 28:19-20).
   - (a) GENERIC Commands
     - (1) "Go" is INCLUSIVE (ANY means of travel: walking, riding, flying, sailing, etc.) and EXCLUSIVE (always staying in comfort zone).
     - (2) "All the nations" is INCLUSIVE (ANY nation: America, Paraguay, Chad, etc.) and EXCLUSIVE (limiting to wealthy nations).
   - (b) SPECIFIC Commands
     - (1) "Make disciples by baptizing" is INCLUSIVE (the exact method of making disciples requires baptism) and EXCLUSIVE (promising "discipleship" through any other means).
     - (2) "Baptizing them" is INCLUSIVE (need water in lake, pond, ocean, baptistry, etc.) and EXCLUSIVE (sprinkling, pouring, etc.).
     - (3) "Teaching them" is INCLUSIVE (sermons, classes, radio, TV, projectors, handouts, etc.) and EXCLUSIVE (ALL man-made doctrines).
D. We must properly understand God's use of Generic Authority and Specific Authority in the commands of the Bible.
  1. God commands Christians to partake of the Lord's Supper with unleavened bread and fruit of the vine every Sunday in their "come together" assembly (Matt. 26:26-29; Acts 20:7; 1 Cor. 11:17-26; 16:1-2; Heb. 10:25).
     - (a) GENERIC Commands

(1) "Assembling together" is INCLUSIVE (ANY building, tent, home, beach, owned, rented, etc.) and EXCLUSIVE (forsaking the assembly).
- (b) SPECIFIC Commands
  - (1) "Unleavened bread and fruit of the vine" is INCLUSIVE (wheat flour, rye flour, matzo crackers, white grape juice, etc.) and EXCLUSIVE (ALL other kinds of "food": cheese, meat, apples, soda, tea, etc.).
  - (2) By specifying the "food" in the communion, God automatically (without saying another word) excluded every other type of "food."
  - (3) "Every first day of the week" is INCLUSIVE (ANY time on Sunday: 6:00 a.m., 6:00 p.m., etc.) and EXCLUSIVE (ALL other days or frequencies).
- (c) God's commands are to be obeyed.
  - (1) We have no right to add to what God has spoken.
  - (2) We have no right to take from what God has spoken.
  - (3) If we disobey the commands of God (ex: including that which God had excluded), we sin against, displease and separate ourselves from the Lord.
2. God commands Christians, "Speaking to one another [teaching and admonishing one another, Col. 3:16] in psalms and hymns and spiritual songs, singing [with grace in your hearts, Col. 3:16] and making melody in your heart to the Lord" (Eph. 5:19).
    - (a) SPECIFIC Commands
      - (1) "Singing" is INCLUSIVE (words, tunes, pitch, 4-part harmony, 4/4 time, number of songs, etc.) and EXCLUSIVE (ALL other kinds of music).
      - (2) "Making melody in your heart to the Lord" is INCLUSIVE (each individual singer's heart) and EXCLUSIVE (ALL other kinds of melody makers: harps, guitars, etc.). Playing a mechanical instrument of music is not a "method" or a "type" of singing. It is an addition of another kind of music to what God plainly authorized.
      - (3) By specifying the "music" in Christian worship, God automatically (without saying another word) excluded every other type of "music." A thing does not have to be specifically forbidden to be unauthorized. God did not authorize instrumental music in worship as an option by neglecting to say (in so many words), "Thou shalt not use instrumental music in worship." Just like the examples above (shoes, prescriptions, wood for the ark, etc.), when the spoken words specify a particular item/action in a category, all other items/actions in that category are automatically excluded.
    - (b) We are authorized to worship God through singing to one another but not with mechanical instruments of music.
      - (1) If God had spoken in GENERIC terms and said, "Make music," then any kind of music would have been authorized. We could sing, we could play, we could sing and play at the same time.
      - (2) However, God did NOT speak in GENERIC terms. God SPECIFIED the type of music, thus, in His choice of those words, He authorized only singing and forbade playing.
      - (3) There is no Scriptural way to do an unscriptural thing.
- E. We must examine every command and direct statement to Christians in the New Testament carefully.
  1. We need to ask, "What is specifically authorized?"
     - (a) "What is included?"

- (b) "What is excluded?"
- 2. We need to ask, "What is generically authorized?"
  - (a) "What is included?"
  - (b) "What is excluded?"
- 3. We need to be thankful for the gracious gift of God's Word!
  - (a) We need to be thankful for the specificity He provides.
  - (b) We need to be thankful for the options He may give us.
- 4. We need to be content to respect God's wisdom and authority when He has not given us any options (or very few) in a particular area.

XI. **Understanding and Respecting "The Silence of the Scriptures" Is Crucial in Biblical Interpretation.**
  A. There are some matters about which it could be stated that the Bible is "silent."
  1. What does "silence of the Scriptures" mean? What is that talking about?
     - (a) This is not regarding trivial matters (like having a Pez dispenser).
     - (b) This is not regarding expedient matters (like having stripes on church parking lot).
  2. "Silence" has reference to religious teachings or practices of which the Lord did not speak.
  3. Some advocate that if a teaching or practice is not explicitly forbidden in Scripture then it is permissible to practice.
     - (a) They argue that silence in Scripture is a "permissive silence," as if God said, "It's ok, go ahead and do it. You have My permission."
     - (b) Advocates suggest, "God didn't say 'not to' do it, so it must be ok." Or they say, "Where is the verse that says, 'Thou shalt not do that'?" In their minds, God is indifferent because, as they claim, "He doesn't say anything about it."
  4. Others hold that if some teaching or practice is not authorized in Scripture (explicitly or implicitly) then it is not permissible to practice.
     - (a) The argument is that silence in Scripture is a "prohibitive silence," as if God said, "It is not authorized. Do not do it."
     - (b) The truth is, as this study shall show, that God's silence restricts and limits our teaching and practice in religious matters, as we have no authority to teach or practice outside or beyond Divine revelation.
  5. We must have a "Thus saith the Lord"! If God didn't say it, how can we do it?
     - (a) What the Bible affirms, we must believe!
     - (b) What the Bible commands, we must obey!
     - (c) What the Bible prohibits, we must avoid!
     - (d) Where the Bible speaks, we must act and practice!
     - (e) Where the Bible is silent, we must not act or practice!
  6. It is vital that Bible students understand when (and why) God has been silent and respect His silence in the way in which He intended.
  B. Remember these vital truths.
  1. The Bible is the complete, final and all-sufficient will of God (2 Tim. 3:16-17; 2 Pet. 1:3; Jude 3).
     - (a) "Complete" means nothing is to be added or taken from it (Rev. 22:18-19).
     - (b) "Final" means that God is finished with His revelation and man has no right to go beyond it (1 Cor. 4:6; 2 John 9-11).
     - (c) "All-sufficient" means it does not lack a single thing we need and requires no modification (Gal. 1:6-9).

2. The New Testament is God's all-authoritative Word for all people in all places for all time (1 Cor. 14:37; 2 John 9-11; 1 Thess. 2:13; Matt. 24:35).
   (a) It is not by mere happenstance, accident or even coincidence that we "have what we have" in the Scriptures.
   (b) God said what He had to say, He said all that He had to say, and He did not forget to say something He intended to or should have said.
   (c) The Holy Spirit guided Bible writers to reveal the mind of God to mankind (2 Pet. 1:20-21; 1 Cor. 2:11-14) – the same Holy Spirit whom Jesus said would "guide [them] into all truth" (John 16:12-13).
   (d) The Holy Spirit either did guide Bible writers into ALL truth about ALL things for ALL time (as John 16:12-13 teaches), or He didn't.
3. For men to speak, act, practice, innovate or promote religious teachings and practices of which God purposefully was "silent" is for men to presume to take the place of God Himself.
   (a) Such presumption denies that Scripture is the complete, final and all-sufficient will of God.
   (b) Such presumption insinuates that God failed to adequately provide for the needs and work of the church.
C. All responsible adults understand "silence" as a basic principle of authority (in everyday life) without any problem at all.
   1. A teacher assigns a research paper and specifies a due date.
      (a) Imagine a student turns in a paper one week late and says: "She didn't say that I couldn't turn it in a week later. Where in the instructions did she say, 'You may not turn it in one week late'?"
      (b) When the teacher specified the date, she didn't have to say another word about any other date!
   2. A parent sends a child to the store to buy milk and bread.
      (a) Imagine the child comes home with milk, bread, pretzel M&M's and a Coke and says: "Mom didn't say that I couldn't buy pretzel M&M's and a Coke. Where in her instructions did she say, 'You may not buy pretzel M&M's and a Coke'?"
      (b) When the mother specified the items to buy, she didn't have to say another word about any other product!
   3. A man orders a single book from an online distributor.
      (a) Imagine the distributor ships five cases of that book to the man, charges his credit card for the five cases and says: "The man didn't say not to ship and charge for five cases. Where in his order did he say, 'You may not ship and charge for five cases'?"
      (b) When the customer specified and authorized the purchase of that single item, he didn't have to say another word about any other product or quantity!
   4. A 10-year-old boy gets up from a restaurant table and goes to the restroom.
      (a) Imagine the boy goes into the Ladies' Restroom and says: "The sign on the door didn't say that men or boys were not allowed. Where on the sign did it say, 'No boys or men allowed'?"
      (b) When the sign specified the gender permitted to enter, it didn't have to say another word about any other gender!

5. A music tutor says to her student, "Sing the National Anthem."
   (a) Imagine the student picks up her violin and begins to play the National Anthem and says: "The tutor didn't say not to play the National Anthem. Where in her instructions did she say, 'Do not play the song'?"
   (b) When the tutor specified singing, she didn't have to say another word about any other type of music!
D. The Old Testament makes arguments from the silence of the Scriptures. That is, the Bible makes arguments based on things that the Scriptures *did not say*.
   1. Nadab and Abihu offered "strange fire" (Lev. 10:1-2).
      (a) The word "strange" means that for which there is no authority – translated "unauthorized" in ESV.
      (b) God specified the source from which they were to obtain the fire – "from off the altar" (Lev. 16:12; Num. 16:46).
      (c) Apparently, Nadab and Abihu took fire from another source, "which He had not commanded them" (Lev. 10:1).
      (d) The Lord had specified the source and was silent regarding any other source.
      (e) By getting fire from another source, "which He had not commanded them," they violated the will of God and provoked severe punishment.
      (f) What if Nadab and Abihu said, "But Moses never said we couldn't use that other source. Where is the verse that says, 'Thou shalt not use that source'"?
      (g) Conclusion: To act in a realm where the Lord is silent is prohibitive and sinful.
   2. David expressed a keen understanding of God's silence in regard to transporting the ark of the covenant (1 Chron. 15:1-24).
      (a) Unfortunately, David did not always properly act upon the silence of the Scriptures.
         (1) The ark of the covenant was to be carried by poles placed into rings on the side of the ark (Ex. 25:12-14).
         (2) In spite of this, David had the ark transported on a "new cart" (1 Chron. 13:7).
         (3) God specified carrying by poles and was silent regarding any other means.
         (4) By moving the ark on a cart, of which the Lord had said nothing, they violated the will of God, and the Lord "broke out against" them, because they "did not seek Him according to the rule" (1 Chron. 15:13).
         (5) What if David (and Uzzah) said, "But the law of Moses never said we couldn't use a cart. Where is the verse that says, 'Thou shalt not use a cart'"?
         (6) Conclusion: To act in a realm where the Lord is silent is prohibitive and sinful.
      (b) In regard to the tribe to carry the ark, David keenly interpreted God's silence.
         (1) Moses said, "The Lord separated the tribe of Levi to bear the ark of the covenant" (Deut. 10:8).
         (2) God specified the Levites as the ones authorized to carry the ark and was silent regarding any other tribes.
         (3) Notice how David properly interpreted God's silence: "No one may carry the ark of God but the Levites, for the Lord has chosen them..." (1 Chron. 15:2).
         (4) While the Lord was silent regarding any other tribe, David understood that His silence was prohibitive of any other tribe – "No one may carry...but the Levites."
         (5) What if the Israelites had said, "But the law of Moses never said the tribe of Gad couldn't carry it. Where is the verse that says, 'Gad shalt not carry'"?
         (6) Conclusion: To act in a realm where the Lord is silent is prohibitive and sinful.

3. Jeremiah revealed God's evaluation of His silence (Jer. 7:28-31).
   (a) In the Ten Commandments, God had commanded, "You shall have no other gods before Me" (Ex. 20:3).
   (b) Here is God's own commentary on that command when His people disobeyed it: "The Lord has rejected and forsaken the generation of His wrath. For the children of Judah have done evil in My sight...to burn their sons and their daughters in the fire, which I did not command, nor did it come into My heart" (Jer. 7:29-31).
   (c) It is true that God had strictly commanded them not to worship other gods/idols.
   (d) The reason He gives (in Jeremiah 7) for His strict prohibition and severe punishment was because "I did not command, nor did it come into My heart."
   (e) We learn from this that conduct which the Lord explicitly forbids (prohibits) is equivalent to (in the same class as) conduct which is unauthorized (i.e., not commanded).
   (f) Conclusion: To act in a realm where the Lord is silent is prohibitive and sinful.

E. The New Testament makes arguments regarding Jesus from the silence of the Scriptures. That is, the Bible makes arguments based on things that the Scriptures *did not say*.
   1. The superiority of Jesus over angels is argued from silence (Heb. 1:4-5, 13).
      (a) Angels had a significant role in the giving of the Old Covenant (Acts 7:53; Gal. 3:19), and thus, the Jews held them in very high regard.
      (b) To show the superiority of Jesus over angels, the inspired writer made an argument based on something the Bible did NOT say.
      (c) "For to which of the angels did He ever say: 'You are My Son, Today I have begotten You'? And again: 'I will be to Him a Father, And He shall be to Me a Son'?" (Heb. 1:5; Psa. 2:7; 2 Sam. 7:14).
      (d) "But to which of the angels has He ever said: 'Sit at My right hand, Till I make Your enemies Your footstool'?" (Heb. 1:13; Psa. 110:1).
      (e) These statements were specifically made to/about Jesus and never to any angel.
      (f) There was absolutely no authority for the Jews to hold up angels as being equal or superior to Jesus Christ, and God based His argument upon something that the Scriptures did not say (upon the silence of the Scriptures).
   2. The superiority of Jesus as High Priest and the necessity of the change of the law is argued from silence (Heb. 7:11-15).
      (a) Under the Aaronic priesthood of the Old Testament, God specified that the priests were to come out of the tribe of Levi.
      (b) Jesus could not serve as a priest on earth (Heb. 8:4), because He was of the tribe of Judah and not the priestly tribe of Levi (Heb. 7:14).
      (c) Look carefully at Hebrews 7:14 – "For it is evident that our Lord arose from Judah, of which tribe **Moses spoke nothing** concerning priesthood."
         (1) What did Moses say about priests coming from Judah? Nothing! He was silent!
      (d) Moses' silence regarding the priesthood and Judah was not a permissible silence!
         (1) When God specified the tribe of Levi and was silent regarding the other tribes, He automatically excluded and prohibited the other tribes from the priesthood by His silence.
         (2) God did not have to say, "Not Judah, not Gad, not Reuben, etc."!
         (3) Jesus could not argue, "Moses never said that someone from Judah couldn't be a priest. Where is the verse that says, 'Judah shalt not serve as priest'?"

- (e) The silence of the law was prohibitive. There was no authority for one (including Jesus) from the tribe of Judah (or any other tribe than Levi) to serve as a priest.
    - (1) The only way for Christ to serve as High Priest was to change the law.
    - (2) Therefore, Christ is a better High Priest, authorized by a better covenant.
- (f) God is the one who argues in Hebrews 7 that His silence is prohibitive.
- (g) Conclusion: To act in a realm where the Lord is silent is prohibitive and sinful. Either that or you have to change the law of God (which Jesus did in bringing the New Covenant through His death). No man has any right to change God's law!

F. Apply this basic principle of Biblical authority to the question of using mechanical instruments of music in New Testament worship today.
1. Many argue today, based upon an improper understanding and application of "the silence of the Scriptures," that mechanical instruments of music are acceptable in worship. They make claims like:
    - (a) "The Bible doesn't say not to play an instrument! Therefore, it must be ok with God."
    - (b) "Where is the verse that says, 'Do not play a mechanical instrument in worship'?"
    - (c) "This cannot be that big of a deal to God if He didn't see fit to talk about it!"
2. If that line of argumentation would provide justification for instruments in worship, would it not equally provide justification for other forms of worship of which the Lord was silent? Such as:
    - (a) Baptizing infants
    - (b) Worshiping saints
    - (c) Praying to Mary
    - (d) Counting beads
    - (e) Burning incense
    - (f) Offering animal sacrifices
    - (g) Lighting candles for the dead
    - (h) The truth is that the Bible is silent about these matters (and equally as silent about instrumental music), and therefore they are unauthorized.
3. Every New Testament verse that makes reference to music in New Testament worship always specifies singing.
    - (a) There is NO New Testament verse that makes reference to any mechanical instruments of music in worship. The N.T. is completely silent in this regard.
    - (b) Was this silence on God's part intentional or accidental? Does this silence on God's part denote "Divine" indifference to the matter, meaning that God does not care whether or not an instrument is used?
4. For God to specify singing is for God to authorize singing.
    - (a) Anything the church may do or use in obeying this command is included in the command, as long as it does not add to or subtract from God's Word
    - (b) When the church uses a songbook, it is still singing (and only singing).
    - (c) When the church uses a PowerPoint projector, it is still singing (and only singing).
5. For God to remain silent about mechanical instruments is for God to offer no Divine authority for mechanical instruments in worship.
    - (a) It is human presumption to suggest any Divine approval for instruments in New Testament worship when God Himself did not give such approval.
    - (b) When the church adds instrumental music, it has added to the singing, thereby adding to the command by bringing in a different kind of music (i.e., playing).

- (c) Bringing in a different kind of music than that which is authorized is bringing in that which is unauthorized.
- 6. The music that God authorizes in N.T. worship (i.e., singing) involves "speaking," "singing," "making melody in the heart," "giving thanks," "teaching," "admonishing," "praise," "declare/tell/proclaim," etc. (Eph. 5:19-20; Col. 3:16; Heb. 2:12; 13:15).
  - (a) All of these can be uniquely accomplished in singing.
  - (b) None of these can be fulfilled with instruments of music.
  - (c) Thus, instruments are additions to God's Word by going beyond His specified instructions and doing something different than what He authorized.
- 7. Conclusion: To act in a realm where the Lord is silent is prohibitive and sinful.
- G. We have NO RIGHT to go beyond that which is written!
  1. God has given us an objective standard of truth – His Word!
     - (a) In 2 John 9, that objective standard is called "the doctrine of Christ."
     - (b) The teaching and practice of the church is limited to and restricted by that Divine revelation.
  2. There are severe consequences for transgressing, going too far or going beyond "the doctrine of Christ" into the realm silence.
     - (a) Silence is an unauthorized realm, having been prohibited by God.
     - (b) To venture into the realm of God's silence (i.e., teaching and practicing therein) with the notion that "God didn't say NOT to" is to "have not God" (2 John 9).
  3. We must have God's authority for all that we teach or do in religious matters (Col. 3:17).
     - (a) We must faithfully and persistently abide in the doctrine of Christ (2 John 9; John 8:31-32; 15:1-10), without thinking beyond (1 Cor. 4:6), speaking beyond (1 Pet. 4:11) or going beyond (2 John 9; 1 Cor. 1:10) His Word.
     - (b) The church must stop practicing where the Bible stops teaching!
  4. Since Jesus Himself was not willing to act on His own authority and presumptuously go beyond the Father's will (John 4:34; 5:19, 30, 36; 6:38; 7:16-18; 8:26-32; 10:18; 12:48-50; 14:10, 31), and since the Holy Spirit was not willing to act on His own authority and presumptuously go beyond the Father's will (John 14:26; 16:12-15), what makes any man so daringly presumptuous to act on his own authority and go beyond the Father's will (something Jesus never dared or wanted to do)?
  5. We must respect the Biblical principle of silence!
  6. We must not speak (or act) where God has not spoken!

XII. Conclusion
- A. For one to interpret the Bible God's Way, he must:
  1. Keep every passage in its context.
  2. Diligently gather all the relevant Scriptural evidence.
  3. Handle the gathered evidence accurately.
  4. Let the passage "lead out" the meaning.
  5. Avoid letting a meaning "lead into" a passage.
  6. Expect and respect the authority of God's Word.
  7. Understand how the Bible authorizes for men today.
  8. Carefully stand within the boundaries of God's authority.
- B. May God help us to be diligent and faithful students of His Word, "handling aright the word of truth" (2 Tim. 2:15), that we may be prepared to stand before our Judge and give an account for how we have lived according to His standard (Rom. 14:12; 2 Cor. 5:10; John 12:48; Rev. 20:12; Matt. 7:21-23).

Sources Particularly Helpful and Used Extensively in the Development of This Lesson:

Deaver, Roy C. *Ascertaining Bible Authority.* Austin, TX: Firm Foundation, 1987

Hightower, Terry M., ed. *Rightly Dividing the Word (Volume 1—General Hermeneutics).* Moore, OK: National Christian Press, 1993.

Lipe, David L. *Interpreting the Bible & Instrumental Music.* Henderson, TN: Freed-Hardeman University, 1991.

Warren, Thomas B. *When Is an "Example" Binding?* Moore, OK: National Christian, 1975.

Other Recommended Resources (in addition to the ones listed above)

Books

Dungan, D.R. *Hermeneutics.* Delight, AR: Gospel Light, nd.

Lockhart, Clinton. *Principles of Interpretation.* Delight, AR: Gospel Light, 1915.

Miller, Dave. *Piloting the Strait.* Pulaski, TN: Sain Publications, 1996.

Sanders, Philip. *Let All the Earth Keep Silence.* Fort Worth: Star Bible, 2005.

Thomas, J.D. *Harmonizing Hermeneutics.* Nashville: Gospel Advocate, 1991.

Warren, Thomas B. *Logic and the Bible.* Jonesboro, AR: National Christian, 1982.

Articles

Camp, Robert. "Binding By Implication." *The Spiritual Sword* July 1970: 48-50.

Deaver, Roy. "A Look at Eternal Principles and Certain Specifics." *Rightly Dividing the Word (Volume 1: General Hermeneutics).* Ed. Terry M. Hightower. Moore, OK: National Christian, 1993. 291-295.

---. "Ascertaining Bible Authority." *Rightly Dividing the Word (Volume 1: General Hermeneutics).* Ed. Terry M. Hightower. Moore, OK: National Christian, 1993. 209-231.

---. "Ascertaining Bible Authority." *The Church of Christ (Freed-Hardeman College Lectures).* Ed. Thomas B. Warren. Nashville: Gospel Advocate, 1971. 90-102.

---. "The Effect of Approved Example." *The Spiritual Sword* April 1990: 20-24.

Fulford, Hugh. "Determining Bible Authority." *The Authority of the Bible (Spiritual Sword Lectureship).* Ed. Gary McDade. Memphis, TN: Getwell church of Christ, 2002. 199-209.

Gilmore, Ralph. "The First Principles of Hermeneutics." *Settled in Heaven (Freed-Hardeman University Lectureship).* Ed. David Lipe. Henderson, TN: Freed-Hardeman University, 1996. 153-160.

Highers, Alan E. "What Do We Mean By Silence?" *The Spiritual Sword* Oct. 2006: 1-3

Jackson, Wayne. "Aid or Addition—What Is the Difference?" *ChristianCourier.com* https://www.christiancourier.com/articles/196-aid-or-addition-what-is-the-difference

---. "The 'Silence' of the Scriptures: Permissive or Prohibitive?" *Christian Courier.com* https://www.christiancourier.com/articles/128-silence-of-the-scriptures-permissive-or-prohibitive-the

McDade, Gary. "The Case of Nadab and Abihu." *The Spiritual Sword* Oct. 2006: 12-16.

McWhorter, Don. "Respecting the 'Silence of the Scriptures.'" *Respect for God's Word (South Florida Lectureship)*. Ed. David Sproule. Palm Beach Gardens, FL: Palm Beach Lakes church of Christ, 2005. 142-156.

Miller, Dave. "Hermeneutical Principles in the Old Testament." *ApologeticsPress.org* https://www.apologeticspress.org/APContent.aspx?category=11&article=967&topic=75

---. "Jesus' Hermeneutical Principles." *ApologeticsPress.org* http://www.apologeticspress.org/APContent.aspx?category=11&article=2307&topic=379

---. "Respecting the Pattern of God's Word." *Respect for God's Word (South Florida Lectureship)*. Ed. David Sproule. Palm Beach Gardens, FL: Palm Beach Lakes church of Christ, 2005. 190-200.

Music, Goebel. "The Pattern—And God Has Always Had One." *Behold the Pattern.* Colleyville, TX: Goebel Music Publications, 1991. 46-73.

Nichols, Flavil H.. "Rightly Dividing the Word." *The Bible—None Like It (Memphis School of Preaching Lectureship)*. Ed. Curtis A. Cates. Memphis: MSOP, 1989. 133-143.

Nichols, Gus. "Divine Authority in Religion." *The Christian and Authority (Fort Worth Christian College Lectures)*. Ed. Foy Kirkpatrick. Fort Worth: Fort Worth Christian College, 1969. 245-261.

Sanders, Philip. "Do the Scriptures Teach By Silence?" *The Spiritual Sword* Oct. 2006: 4-8.

---. "The Significance of Silence." *The Spiritual Sword* July 2014: 12-15.

Wallace, G.K. "When Is An Example Binding?" *The Church Faces Liberalism (Freed-Hardeman College Lectures)*. Ed. Thomas B. Warren. Nashville: Gospel Advocate, 1970. 269-275.

Warren, Thomas B. "The Bible Is God's Law of Authority." *Rightly Dividing the Word (Volume 1: General Hermeneutics)*. Ed. Terry M. Hightower. Moore, OK: National Christian, 1993. 170-194.

Winkler, Wendell. "By What Authority?" *The Authority of the Bible (Spiritual Sword Lectureship)*. Ed. Gary McDade. Memphis, TN: Getwell church of Christ, 2002. 469-477.

Periodicals

The Spiritual Sword. April 1990. "Bible Authority."

The Spiritual Sword. October 2006. "The Silence of the Scriptures."

The Spiritual Sword. July 2014. "A Handy Guide to Understanding the Bible."

Lesson 6: The Two Covenants

I. **The Bible Is Divided into Two Covenants.**
   A. A covenant is an agreement between two parties.
      1. The agreement involves specified conditions and promised benefits.
      2. Once accepted, both parties are obligated to fulfill their stated requirements.
   B. In the Bible, God established covenants.
      1. As for God, He was the one who set the conditions/terms of the covenants.
      2. As for man, he could accept or reject the terms set out by God (but not alter them).
      3. God is the one to make the demands; man is the one to submit and follow them.
      4. God cannot (and does not) break His side of the agreement.
      5. Man must fulfill his side of the covenant, in order to receive the promised benefits.
   C. The Bible contains two main covenants (or testaments) that God made: an old covenant and a new covenant.
      1. The Old Covenant was made between God and a nation (Israel).
      2. The New Covenant was/is made between God and individuals (Christians).
      3. True to the word "covenant," each covenant had specified conditions and promised benefits.
   D. A major key to Bible study is understanding and applying the proper distinction between "The Old Testament" and "The New Testament."
      1. Failing to make that distinction has led to much religious confusion today.
      2. Failing to make that distinction has led and will lead many souls to be lost.
      3. God makes a distinction between the Old and the New, and we must follow it.

II. **God Established the First Covenant.**
   A. The first covenant was made by God with the Israelites.
      1. "I have made a covenant with you and with Israel" (Ex. 34:27).
   B. The first covenant was made by God with the Israelites when they came out of Egypt.
      1. "…After the children of Israel had gone out of the land of Egypt…the Lord called to him from the mountain, saying, '…Now therefore, if you will indeed obey My voice and keep My covenant, then you shall be a special treasure to Me above all people…And you shall be to Me a kingdom of priests and a holy nation.'…Then all the people answered together and said, 'All that the Lord has spoken we will do'" (Ex. 19:1-8; cf. 24:1-8).
   C. The first covenant was made by God with the Israelites at Mt. Sinai.
      1. "So He declared to you His covenant which He commanded you to perform" (Deut. 4:13).
      2. "The Lord our God made a covenant with us in Horeb" (Deut. 5:2).
      3. God came down "on Mount Sinai, and spoke with them from heaven, and gave them just ordinances and true laws, good statutes and commandments" (Neh. 9:13).
   D. The first covenant was made by God with the Israelites and only with the Israelites.
      1. It was a national law, which did not include any other nation but the Jews.
      2. "And God spoke all these words, saying: 'I am the Lord your God, who brought you out of the land of Egypt, out of the house of bondage'" (Ex. 20:1-2).
      3. "…It is a sign between Me and you throughout your generations…It is a sign between Me and the children of Israel forever" (Ex. 31:12-17).
      4. "For what great nation is there that has God so near to it…? And what great nation is there that has such statutes and righteous judgments…?" (Deut. 4:7-8).

III. God Intended the First Covenant to Be Temporary.
   A. As a national law and covenant, limited only to the Jews, it should have been obvious that it was only temporary.
      1. For, God had made a covenant with Abraham, promising, "In your seed all the nations of the earth shall be blessed" (Gen. 22:18).
      2. God promised to make Abraham "a great nation" (Gen. 12:1-3), and so He did with the Israelite nation. (God changed the name of Abraham's grandson, Jacob, to Israel.)
      3. But, His ultimate promise was a blessing to "all the families (or nations) of the earth" (Gen. 12:3; 22:18). This could not be and was not fulfilled in the single nation of Israel.
      4. God had a much grander plan than just one nation. His eternal plan was for all nations. Judaism could not (and did not) fulfill God's eternal plan, and the Jews themselves should have been the first to know and to affirm that truth.
   B. God foretold through Jeremiah that He would establish a new covenant.
      1. "Behold, the days are coming, says the Lord, when I will make a new covenant with the house of Israel and with the house of Judah—not according to the covenant that I made with their fathers in the day that I took them by the hand to lead them out of the land of Egypt, My covenant which they broke, though I was a husband to them, says the Lord" (Jer. 31:31-32). In these verses, it is affirmed:
         (a) God made a covenant with Israel when He brought them out of Egypt.
         (b) The time would come when He would make a new covenant.
         (c) The new covenant would not be the same covenant as the first one He made.
      2. The Hebrews writer quoted this passage in Hebrews 8:6-13 to show:
         (a) The new covenant was "a better covenant…established on better promises" (8:6).
         (b) The covenant with Israel was the "first covenant" (8:7), which implies a second.
         (c) The "new covenant…made the first obsolete…ready to vanish away" (8:13).
      3. The Divine plan for a "new covenant" indicated the "first covenant" was temporary.
   C. More than 1,000 years before Jeremiah, God had foretold of Judah's role in His plan.
      1. "The scepter shall not depart from Judah, Nor a lawgiver from between his feet, Until Shiloh comes; And to Him shall be the obedience of the people" (Gen. 49:10).
      2. The Messiah (Christ) would come through the tribe of Judah, the kingly tribe.
         (a) However, the Messiah (Christ) would come as a priest (Zech. 6:13).
            (1) Christ would "sit and rule on His throne" as King, and at the same time He would "be a priest on His throne."
            (2) The King from Judah would be the Priest from Judah—simultaneously.
         (b) But, the priests of the covenant with Israel came from Levi (Num. 3:6-8).
      3. Therefore, "For the priesthood being changed, of necessity there is also a change of the law" (Heb. 7:12).
         (a) Jesus could not be a priest on the earth, being from the tribe of Judah (Heb. 8:4).
         (b) Therefore, for the Messiah (from the tribe of Judah) to serve as priest, it required a change of the covenant.
         (c) For Jesus to be our "merciful and faithful High Priest" today (Heb. 2:17-18), we cannot be bound by (or seek to go back to) that old covenant.
      4. The change of priesthood required a change of law, emphasizing that the first covenant was designed to be temporary (Heb. 7:11-12, 19; 9:11; 10:1).
   D. God's original design for the first covenant was for it to be temporary, "till the Seed should come to whom the promise was made" (Gal. 3:19), and that Seed is "Christ" (Gal. 3:16).

1. The word "till" in Galatians 3:19 is an adverb of time:
   (a) Emphasizing the temporary nature of the covenant, and
   (b) Specifying the moment at which it would be fulfilled and removed.
2. That first covenant was:
   (a) "Added because of transgressions" (Gal. 3:19).
   (b) Given that sin "might appear sin" and "exceedingly sinful" (Rom. 7:13).
   (c) Designed to bring about fulfillment of the promise to Abraham (Gal. 3:16-19).
   (d) Purposed to be the "tutor to bring us to Christ" (Gal. 3:24).
   (e) "A shadow of the good things to come" (Heb. 10:1).
   (f) Designed to impress upon man His need for a Savior and a sacrificial atonement for sin (Heb. 9:11-14; 10:1-10).
   E. When a covenant has fulfilled its purpose, it is "ready to disappear" (Heb. 8:13, NASB).
IV. **God Intentionally Limited the Power and Effectuality of the First Covenant.**
   A. God affirmed that "it was weak through the flesh" (Rom. 8:3), and that it was annulled "because of its weakness" (Heb. 7:18) and because it was not "faultless" (Heb. 8:7).
      1. That does not mean that God was weak or ineffectual in making such a covenant.
      2. Nor does it mean that God messed up the first covenant but got it right on the second.
      3. The design of the first covenant was exactly what God intended, in order to prepare all of mankind for the "better" and "everlasting covenant" (Heb. 8:6; 13:20).
   B. It was intentionally limited/weak/faulty in that:
      1. It was made with only one nation (Ex. 19:1-8; Deut. 5:1-6).
      2. It could not remove sin (Heb. 9:12-14; 10:1-4).
         (a) "Without shedding of blood there is no remission" (Heb. 9:22).
      3. It could not justify (Gal. 3:11; Acts 13:39), give righteousness (2:21) or give life (3:21).
      4. It could not make one perfect (Heb. 7:19).
      5. It required perfect obedience, but no one could keep the law perfectly (Gal. 3:10).
   C. If the first had been perfect, then there would have been no need for the second or for the Savior, Redeemer and Sacrificial Lamb of the second (Heb. 8:7).
   D. God knew what He was doing!
V. **God Removed the First Covenant Himself, in Order to Establish the Second.**
   A. God promised that He was going to make a new covenant (Jer. 31:31-34).
      1. The old had to be annulled, in order to bring in the new (Matt. 26:28; Heb. 7:18-25).
   B. The old covenant was intended to last "till the Seed should come to whom the promise was made" (Gal. 3:19), and that Seed "is Christ" (Gal. 3:16).
      1. Therefore, the coming of Christ signaled the ending of the old covenant.
   C. Jesus declared that He came to "fulfill" the covenant that God made with Israel, and that it would "pass" when "all [the law] is fulfilled" (Matt. 5:17-18).
      1. As He died, Jesus declared, "It is finished" (John 19:30).
      2. After His death and resurrection, Jesus then declared that all things had been "fulfilled" (Luke 24:44).
      3. If all the covenant had been fulfilled, then the covenant was to pass away.
   D. The N.T. makes it clear that the first covenant was "taken away in Christ" (2 Cor. 3:14).
      1. Three times in this same passage of 2 Corinthians 3 it is affirmed that the first covenant "was passing away" (3:7, 11, 13).
      2. The first covenant "was glorious" (3:7, 11), but the second "is much more glorious" (11).
   E. The removal of the covenant took place in the death of Christ on the cross.

1. He "has broken down the middle wall of separation, having abolished in His flesh the enmity, that is, the law of commandments contained in ordinances...through the cross, thereby putting to death the enmity" (Eph. 2:14-16).
2. He "wiped out the handwriting of requirements that was against us, which was contrary to us. And He has taken it out of the way, having nailed it to the cross" (Col. 2:14).
3. The death of the Messiah (the Lamb of God) on the cross was the dividing line between the first and second covenants. (See VI, A.)

F. The stated purpose (Gal. 3:19) of the law was "to bring us to Christ, that we might be justified by faith" (Gal. 3:24)
1. "The faith has come" (Gal. 3:25).
2. Therefore, "we are no longer under" the law (Gal. 3:25), for it has passed, having fulfilled its purpose.

G. The removal of the covenant included the Ten Commandments.
1. Some have tried to divide the O.T. into a "moral law" and "ceremonial law."
   (a) They want, essentially, the Ten Commandments to be the "moral law," and the rest of the Old Testament to be the "ceremonial law."
   (b) Then, they claim that the "ceremonial law" (with the animal sacrifices, feast days, etc.) was taken away by Christ, but the "moral law" is still binding.
   (c) They want the Ten Commandments, including the Sabbath, still in effect today.
2. The Ten Commandments were part of the covenant that God made with Israel at Mt. Sinai.
   (a) The "covenant" that God made with Moses "and with Israel" included "the words of the covenant, the Ten Commandments" (Ex. 34:27-28; cf. Deut. 9:9-11).
   (b) God "declared to [Israel] His covenant which He commanded [them] to perform, the Ten Commandments" (Deut. 4:13).
   (c) When "the ark of the covenant" (pay close attention to that name) was brought into the newly-constructed temple, it was stated that, "Nothing was in the ark except the two tablets of stone which Moses put there at Horeb, when the Lord made a covenant with the children of Israel, when they came out of the land of Egypt" (1 Kgs. 8:9). Then, Solomon exclaimed regarding this temple, "And there I have made a place for the ark, in which is the covenant of the Lord which He made with our fathers, when He brought them out of the land of Egypt" (8:21). Notice that "the covenant" and the Ten Commandments are referred to interchangeably.
3. The Ten Commandments, along with all the O.T. law, were abrogated in Christ.
   (a) In Romans 7, Paul emphasized that:
      (1) We are "released from"..."free from"..."dead to"..."delivered from"...
      (2) The part of the law which included, "You shall not covet" (Rom. 7:1-7)—i.e., the Ten Commandments.
      (3) We have been delivered from the law in order to be joined to Christ (7:4).
      (4) Paul emphasizes that a Christian cannot be under the law of Christ (i.e., joined to Christ) and under the Ten Commandments at the same time.
   (b) In Colossians 2, Paul emphasized that:
      (1) Since God has "wiped out"..."taken out of the way"....and "nailed to the cross"
      (2) The part of the law that included the "Sabbaths" (2:14-17)—i.e., the Ten Commandments,
      (3) We are no longer subject to that law.

                (c) In 2 Corinthians 3, Paul emphasized that:
                    (1) The law that was "written and engraved on stones" —i.e., the Ten Commandments,
                    (2) "Was passing away" (3:3-18),
                    (3) And we are no longer under any portion of that law.
            4. The removal of the first covenant emphasizes that no part was "brought over."
                (a) It is sometimes stated that certain parts of the old were "brought over" into the new.
                    (1) That terminology is common when N.T. Christians discuss the Ten Commandments, for it is often stated that "nine of the ten were brought over into the new."
                    (2) That terminology has led to confusion and error.
                (b) The Lord did not leave some of the Old Testament law and remove the rest.
                (c) He removed all of the first and established a brand new covenant in the second.
                (d) Similarities between the covenants might be expected (as they are from the same God), but the "new" covenant truly is "new" and should not be viewed or treated as a revision, a conglomeration, or "the best of" the first.
        H. The laws of the Mosaic Covenant stand or fall together.
            1. If one goes back to the Old Testament and seeks authority to bring over just one part of that law, "he is under obligation" (debtor) "to keep the whole law" (Gal. 5:3).
            2. But the Christian is not under obligation to keep any part of that old law (Rom. 7:1-7)!
        I. There are entire books in the New Testament that have as a part of their overriding theme the abrogation of the Old Testament (including Romans, Galatians and Hebrews).
            1. These books clearly teach that the old covenant has been removed.
            2. It is not possible for us to still be under any portion of the old law (including the Ten Commandments) and for these books of the New Testament to be valid and binding.
        J. See page 170 of Lesson 15 for more on the removal of the Sabbath as a day of worship.
VI. **God Established the Second Covenant.**
    A. At the same moment the first was removed (in the death of Christ on the cross, Eph. 2), God's second covenant came in force.
        1. "He is the Mediator of the new covenant, by means of death" (Heb. 9:15).
        2. "For where there is a testament, there must also of necessity be the death of the testator. For a testament is in force after men are dead, since it has no power at all while the testator lives" (Heb. 9:16-17).
        3. Jesus tied the shedding of His blood with "the new covenant" (Matt. 26:28).
        4. Christ's will became effective upon His death; and when Christ's will went into effect, the law ended.
    B. The first had to be removed for the second to be established.
        1. Jesus is the "Mediator of a better covenant" (Heb. 8:6).
        2. "He takes away the first that He may establish the second" (Heb. 10:9-10).
        3. Establishing the second covenant required removing the first.
        4. The two covenants could not be in force at the same time.
            (a) The "first" had to be cancelled before the "second" could become operative (10:9).
            (b) The "old" had to pass away before the "new" could take effect (Heb. 8:8-13).
            (c) The two covenants could not be binding simultaneously, as such is likened to being married to two people simultaneously and thus committing "adultery" (Rom. 7:1-4).
        5. One could not (in the first century) follow both testaments as authoritative law.
        6. One cannot (today) follow both testaments as authoritative law.
    C. The Bible pinpoints the "beginning" of the New Testament law by using that very word.

1. The preaching of the full gospel of Jesus Christ (i.e., the New Testament)—which included teaching men to "observe all things" that Jesus had commanded (Matt. 28:20)—was to commence, "beginning at Jerusalem" (Luke 24:47).
2. Peter looked back at the preaching of the full gospel of Jesus Christ on the day of Pentecost as "the beginning" (Acts 11:15).

D. The second covenant, the New Testament:
1. Is the fulfillment of the promise made to Abraham (Gen. 12:1-3; 22:18; Gal. 3:13-24).
2. Is for all people (Acts 3:25; Mark 16:15-16; Luke 24:44-47; Heb. 2:9).
3. Is effected by the blood of Jesus (Heb. 5:8-9; 9:12-28; 10:1-4, 29; Matt. 26:28).
4. Completely removes sin (Heb. 8:12; 9:25; Col. 2:11; Rev. 1:5).
5. Sanctifies and justifies (Heb. 9:13-14; 10:10-14, 29; 13:12; Rom. 10:9; Gal. 3:24).
6. Gives life and makes perfect (Rom. 8:2; Heb. 9:11; 10:14).
7. Places the faithful in a spiritual condition where "there is no condemnation" (Rom. 8:1).
8. Provides the fullness of God's grace and truth (John 1:17, 14).
9. Is founded upon and sustained by a living Mediator (1 Tim. 2:5; Heb. 4:14; 7:25).
10. Promises eternal life (Heb. 8:6; 1 John 2:25; 5:13).
11. Is to last until the end of time (Heb. 13:20; Rev. 14:6).
12. See the chart on page 74 for a "Contrast of the Two Covenants."

VII. While Christians Are Not Under the Old Covenant, It Still Has Great Value to Us.
A. The Old Testament is no longer binding today, but that does not mean it is worthless.
B. Jesus and the New Testament writers must have seen its value, for they all used it.
C. We have the Old Testament "for our learning" and "admonition" (Rom. 15:4; 1 Cor. 10:11).
1. We learn about the origin of all things, including man and the universe (Gen. 1:1-31).
2. We learn about the nature of God and man's need for a Savior (Gen. 1-3; Isa. 53; Psa. 23).
3. We learn about the deity of Jesus (Acts 2:22-36; 3:13-26; 10:43; 17:3; Luke 24:27, 44).
4. We learn about the church (2 Sam. 7:11-16; Isa. 2:1-4; Dan. 2:44; Micah 4:1-5).
5. We learn about man's purpose to bring "glory" to His Creator (Isa. 43:7).
6. We learn about God's expectations for obedience (1 Sam. 5:22; Ecc. 12:13; Heb. 11).
7. We learn about the devastating consequences of sin (Gen. 3:1-24; 2 Sam. 12:13-14).
8. We learn about the gift of God's grace/favor (Gen. 6:8; Ex. 33:12-23; Psalm 51).
9. We are presented with a shadow of Christianity (Col. 2:16-17; Heb. 8:5; 10:1).
10. We see Jesus as the scapegoat, the Passover lamb, the high priest, the brass serpent.
11. We read background on people like Abraham, Elijah, Moses, David, Job, Naaman, etc.
12. We read background on events like Lot's wife, Esau's birthright, Elijah's praying, etc.
13. We read background on days like the Passover, Pentecost, Sabbath, etc.
14. We connect Noah's flood to baptism, Jonah to the resurrection, Canaan to heaven, etc.
15. We gain foundational knowledge on sin, faith, righteousness, holiness, prayer, etc.
16. We gain insight into the heart of God and His longings for the heart of man.
17. We come to know God more personally and deeply.

D. Much of the New Testament is better understood with a knowledge of the Old Testament.
E. It has been said, "The Old Testament is the New Testament concealed, and the New Testament is the Old Testament revealed."

VIII. Conclusion
A. The careful Bible student must recognize the distinction that God makes between the Old Testament and the New Testament. (See III, B on page 40.)
B. Some denominational errors have originated and lingered in the improper usage and reliance on Old Testament law for justification of doctrines and practices.

C. The Old Testament is no longer a binding law on us today.
D. The Old Testament was removed at the same time that the New Testament began.
E. To attempt to be justified by the Old Testament today is to "fall from grace" (Gal. 5:4).
F. The New Testament beautifully reveals God's full plan for man's redemption through the sacrificial gift of His Son and the message of His gospel.

A Contrast of Two Covenants

The Old Covenant	The New Covenant
1. The letter, killeth (2 Cor. 3:6)	1. The Spirit, giveth life (2 Cor. 3:6; Rom. 8:2)
2. Ministration of death (2 Cor. 3:7)	2. Ministration of the spirit (2 Cor. 3:8)
3. Ministration of condemnation (2 Cor. 3:9)	3. Ministration of righteousness (2 Cor. 3:9)
4. Written on tablets of stones (2 Cor. 3:3-7)	4. Written on tablet of the heart (2 Cor. 3:3; Heb. 8:10)
5. Glorious, done away (2 Cor. 3:11)	5. More glorious, remaineth (2 Cor. 3:11)
6. Veil upon their heart (2 Cor. 3:14)	6. Veil done away in Christ (2 Cor. 3:14)
7. The Old Testament (2 Cor. 3:14)	7. The New Testament (2 Cor. 3:6)
8. Spoken unto the fathers by the prophets (Heb. 8:8-9)	8. Spoken unto us by His Son (Heb. 1:1-2)
9. Priesthood of men (Heb. 7:11)	9. Priesthood of Christ (Heb. 7:28)
10. Changeable priesthood (Heb. 7:12)	10. Unchangeable priesthood (Heb. 7:24)
11. Imperfect priesthood (Heb. 7:12)	11. Perfect priest (Heb. 7:26)
12. Priests of the tribe of Levi (Heb. 7:5)	12. Christ of the tribe of Judah (Heb. 7:14)
13. Priesthood changed (Heb. 7:12)	13. The law changed (Heb. 7:12)
14. Made nothing perfect (Heb. 7:19)	14. Makes all things perfect (Heb. 10:14)
15. Priests without an oath, during the law (Heb. 7:21)	15. Christ, a priest by an oath, since the law (Heb. 7:28)
16. Founded upon promises (Heb. 8:6)	16. Founded upon better promises (Heb. 8:6)
17. Was not perfect (Heb. 8:8)	17. The perfect law (Jas. 1:25)
18. Shadow of good things (Heb. 9:1-9)	18. The substance (Heb. 10:1)
19. Purged the flesh, not conscience (Heb. 9:9, 13)	19. Purges the conscience (Heb. 9:14)
20. Lasted only until *reformed* by Christ (Heb. 9:19)	20. Given to last till the end of time (Heb. 13:20)
21. Dedicated by blood of animals (Heb. 9:19; 10:4)	21. Dedicated by blood of Christ (Heb. 9:14)
22. No forgiveness; sins remembered yearly (Heb. 10:3)	22. Sins and iniquities remembered no more (Heb. 8:12)
23. Could never make any man perfect (Heb. 10:1)	23. Makes man absolutely perfect (Heb. 9:11)
24. Many offerings made often (Heb. 10:11)	24. Christ offered once for all (Heb. 9:28)
25. Cannot take away sins (Heb. 10:11)	25. Saves to the uttermost (Heb. 7:25)
26. The old way (Heb. 9:19-23)	26. The new and living way (Heb. 10:20)
27. Tabernacle made with hands (Heb. 9:24)	27. Tabernacle made without hands (Heb. 9:11)
28. For one nation – the Jews (Deut. 5:2-3)	28. For all nations (Matt. 28:19)
29. Was the first covenant (Heb. 8:7)	29. Is the second covenant (Heb. 8:7)
30. Was the old covenant (Heb. 8:13)	30. Is the new covenant (Heb. 8:13)
31. He taketh away the first (Heb. 8:13)	31. That He may establish the second (Heb. 10:9)
32. Law in the flesh (Gen. 17:13)	32. Law in mind and heart (Heb. 8:10)
33. Circumcision in flesh (Eph. 2:11)	33. Circumcision in heart (Rom. 2:29)
34. Circumcision with hands (Eph. 2:11)	34. Circumcision without hands (Col. 2:11)
35. Abolished in the flesh of Christ (Eph. 2:14-15)	35. Brought to light in His resurrection (Rom. 1:4)
36. Kept its subjects under a curse (Gal. 3:10)	36. Redeems men from the curse (Gal. 3:13)
37. Could never justify any man (Gal. 3:11; 5:4)	37. Can justify all men (Gal. 3:24)
38. Didn't give inheritance (Gal. 3:18)	38. Gives inheritance (Acts 20:32)
39. Was to last only until Christ (Gal. 3:19)	39. Is to continue everlastingly (Rev. 14:6)
40. Could not make alive – give life (Gal. 3:21)	40. The "Law of the Spirit of life" (Rom. 8:2)
41. Only a Jewish schoolmaster till Christ (Gal. 3:24)	41. No longer under the schoolmaster (Gal. 3:25)
42. Yoke of bondage (Gal. 5:1)	42. Liberty – made free (Gal. 5:1)
43. Was blotted out – nailed to the cross (Col. 2:14)	43. An eternal covenant (Heb. 13:20)

The Old made Jews   *The New makes Christians*

Recommended Resources

<u>Books</u>

Clarke, B.J., ed. *The Two Covenants (POWER Lectures)*. Southaven, MS: Southaven church of Christ, 1996.

Johnson, Ashley S. *The Two Covenants.* Hollywood, CA: Old Paths Book Club, 1949.

<u>Articles</u>

Brownlow, Leroy. "Because It Believes the Bible Is a Book to Be Rightly Divided." *Why I Am a Member of the Church of Christ.* Fort Worth: Brownlow Publishing, 1973. 60-69.

Camp, Franklin. "Covenants: Old and New." *Everyday Christianity (Freed-Hardeman College Lectures).* Ed. Winford Claiborne. Henderson, TN: Freed-Hardeman College, 1984. 35-47.

Jackson, Wayne. "Did Christ Abolish the Law of Moses?" *www.ChristianCourier.com*
https://www.christiancourier.com/articles/485-did-christ-abolish-the-law-of-moses

---. "Is the Abolition of the Ten Commandments Ridiculous?" *www.ChristianCourier.com*
https://www.christiancourier.com/articles/658-is-the-abolition-of-the-ten-commandments-ridiculous

---. "Should Christians Keep the Sabbath?" *www.ChristianCourier.com*
https://www.christiancourier.com/articles/314-should-christians-keep-the-sabbath

---. "The Last Will and Testament of Jesus Christ." *www.ChristianCourier.com*
https://www.christiancourier.com/articles/739-last-will-and-testament-of-jesus-christ-the

---. "The Value of the Old Testament for Today." *www.ChristianCourier.com*
https://www.christiancourier.com/articles/659-value-of-the-old-testament-for-today-the

Jenkins, Dan. "Written for Our Admonition." *Written for Our Admonition (South Florida Lectureship).* Ed. David Sproule. Palm Beach Gardens, FL: Palm Beach Lakes church of Christ, 2003. 39-61.

Meadows, James. "Questions and Answers About the Sabbath." *Jesus Christ: The Son of God (Freed-Hardeman College Lectures).* Ed. William Woodson. Nashville: Gospel Advocate, 1973. 327-336.

Wharton, Edward C. "The Distinctive Nature of the New Covenant." *The Church of Christ.* Nashville: Gospel Advocate, 1997. 23-37

Woodson, William. "The Old Testament Is for Her Learning, But Not Her Law." *Introducing the Church of Christ.* Ed. Alvin Jennings. Fort Worth: Star Bible, 1981. 42-45.

Young, Frank D. "The Bible: Contrasts of the Two Covenants." *A Plea for Fundamentals (Freed-Hardeman College Lectures).* Ed. William Woodson. Henderson, TN: Freed-Hardeman College, 1977. 19-23.

Lesson 7: The Divine Origin of the Church

I. **Having Knowledge about the Origin of Anything Is Desired and Important.**
   A. When we meet someone, we like to know, "Where are you from?"
   B. When we buy a product, we may want to know, "Was this made in the U.S.A.?"
   C. When we buy produce, we may want to know, "Was this grown locally?"
   D. We want to know about the origin, because that usually provides very helpful information about the thing being studied or considered.
   E. Knowing "where someone/something came from" will usually tell us volumes; in fact, it will often tell us all that we need to know.

II. **Knowing the Origin of the Church Will Help Us to Understand It Tremendously.**
   A. "Where did the church come from? When did it start? Who started it?"
      1. These are questions that need answers, if we are going to understand the church and make a proper evaluation of it.
   B. There is great confusion today about the church, and much of it stems from:
      1. A lack of knowledge about the Divine origin of the church.
      2. A lack of knowledge about the Divine nature of the church.
      3. A lack of knowledge about the Divine identity of the church.
      4. A lack of knowledge about the Divine unity of the church.
      5. Years of exposure to man-made religion, with no concept of anything else.
      6. Assumption that denominationalism is "the norm."
      7. These matters will be addressed in these next several lessons.
   C. Was man responsible for the establishment and beginning of the church?
      1. If so, we ought to look to man for direction and authority for the church.
      2. If so, then the church can be nothing more than a glorified social club or association.
      3. If so, then the church could take on whatever form or look that man desired.
   D. Was God responsible for the establishment and beginning of the church?
      1. If so, then the church is among the greatest institutions ever created.
      2. If so, then man would be foolish to dismiss the church as insignificant or unnecessary.
      3. If so, then we must investigate the church and give it our utmost attention.
   E. Since we read about the church in the Bible, then the Bible is our sole source of information and direction.

III. **The Church of the Bible Was <u>Purposed</u> in the Mind of God from Eternity.**
   A. The Bible teaches that the church was "in accordance with the eternal purpose which [God] carried out in Christ Jesus our Lord" (Eph. 3:10-11, NASB).
      1. The church was a part of God's "purpose" from before the ages of time.
      2. "Before the mountains were brought forth, Or ever You had formed the earth and the world, Even from everlasting to everlasting, You are God" (Psa. 90:2).
      3. That's "when" God purposed the church—before creation.
      4. Think about the significance of God having and executing an eternal plan, which included the church that we read about in the Bible.
   B. We need to understand that God had a plan/purpose in place "from everlasting."
      1. The church was part of His eternal plan.
      2. God planned/purposed for man to have the opportunity to be "in Christ," and He planned for this "before the foundation of the world" (Eph. 1:4).
      3. God planned/purposed to save and extend grace "to us in Christ Jesus," and He planned for this "before time began" (2 Tim. 1:9).

4. God planned/purposed to redeem us "with the precious blood of Christ," and He "foreordained" this "before the foundation of the world" (1 Pet. 1:18-20; Rev. 13:8).
   5. In like manner, the church was integral to God's eternal saving plan (Eph. 3:10-11).
   C. The church was not a last-minute thought, addition or change to the unfolding of God's plan through the progression of time.
   1. The church was not established because the Jews rejected God's kingdom.
   2. The church was not established as a "parenthesis," until Jesus would return to establish His kingdom.
   3. The church was not established by man.
   D. The church was established according to the eternal purpose of God!
   1. This foundational point is extremely significant!
IV. **The Church of the Bible Was <u>Prophesied</u> in the Old Testament.**
   A. The prophet Daniel foretold the establishment of God's church.
   1. By "the God in heaven," Daniel interpreted a dream of King Nebuchadnezzar (Dan. 2).
      (a) Nebuchadnezzar's dream was of an image, whose:
         (1) Head was of fine gold,
         (2) Its chest and arms of silver,
         (3) Its belly and thighs of bronze,
         (4) Its legs of iron, its feet partly of iron and partly of clay (2:32-33).
      (b) Nebuchadnezzar saw:
         (1) A stone was cut out without hands,
         (2) The stone struck the image on its feet of iron and clay, and broke them in pieces,
         (3) The iron, the clay, the bronze, the silver, and the gold were crushed together, and became like chaff and the wind carried them away with no trace left,
         (4) The stone that struck the image became a great mountain and filled the whole earth (2:34-35).
   2. The interpretation of the dream foretold of four successive world empires:
      (a) The head of gold   = The Babylonian Empire (606-539 B.C.)
      (b) The chest and arms of silver = The Medo-Persian Empire (539-331 B.C.)
      (c) The belly and thighs of bronze = The Greek Empire (331-146 B.C.)
      (d) The legs of iron & feet mixed with clay = The Roman Empire (146 B.C. – A.D. 476)

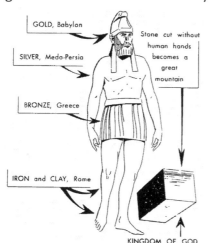

Source:
Paul T. Brown, *Bible Study Textbook Series: Daniel*.
(College Press, 1982, p. 87)
James E. Smith, *The Major Prophets*.
(College Press, 1992, p. 543)

   3. In pointing toward this last (fourth) empire, Daniel prophesied about the church, the stone which would become a great mountain and fill the whole earth:

"And in the days of these kings the God of heaven will set up a kingdom which shall never be destroyed; and the kingdom shall not be left to other people; it shall break in pieces and consume all these kingdoms, and it shall stand forever" (Dan. 2:44).
   4. Here is a very clear and descriptive prophecy about the establishment of the church. The prophecy pinpointed:
      (a) The timeframe of the coming of the church = the days of the Roman Empire.
      (b) The origin of the church = not made with human hands but by the God of heaven.
      (c) The nature of the church = an eternal institution consisting of all peoples.
      (d) The heavenly view of the church = God's unconquerable kingdom.
   5. The New Testament church is the fulfillment of God's Old Testament prophecies about His coming "kingdom," as the church is His "kingdom" (Matt. 16:18-19).
  B. The prophet Isaiah foretold the establishment of God's church.
   1. Isaiah wrote and spoke to a degenerate people who were turning away from God and who would soon find themselves away from God.
   2. But, Isaiah, the Messianic prophet, pointed to better and brighter days ahead for Israel and for all mankind.
   3. In pointing toward those better days, Isaiah prophesied about the church: "Now it shall come to pass in the latter days That the mountain of the Lord's house Shall be established on the top of the mountains, And shall be exalted above the hills; And all nations shall flow to it. Many people shall come and say, 'Come, and let us go up to the mountain of the Lord, To the house of the God of Jacob; He will teach us His ways, And we shall walk in His paths.' For out of Zion shall go forth the law, And the word of the Lord from Jerusalem" (Isa. 2:2-3; cf. Micah 4:1-3).
   4. Here is a very clear and descriptive prophecy about the establishment of the church. The prophecy pinpointed:
      (a) The timeframe of the coming of the church = the latter days.
         (1) Peter identified the events on Pentecost in Acts 2 as being in "the last days" (Acts 2:16-21 + Joel 2:28-32; cf. Heb. 1:1-2).
      (b) The origin of the church = "the Lord's house," following "His ways" and "His paths."
      (c) The heavenly view of the church = God's exalted house.
      (d) The composition of the church = all nations.
      (e) The location of its beginning = Jerusalem/Zion.
   5. The New Testament church is the fulfillment of God's Old Testament prophecies about His coming "house," as the church is His "house" (1 Tim. 3:15).
  C. Multiple prophecies are made in the Old Testament regarding the establishment of the church, usually referring to it as a "house" and a "kingdom" (see 2 Samuel 7:12-16).

V. The Church of the Bible Was <u>Prepared for</u> in the Early Days of the New Testament.
  A. John the Baptist, the forerunner of Christ who was sent to prepare the way of the Lord, went about preaching, "Repent, for the kingdom of heaven is at hand!" (Matt. 3:2).
  B. When Jesus started His ministry, He went about preaching, "Repent, for the kingdom of heaven is at hand" (Matt. 4:17).
   1. Jesus told the people, "The time is fulfilled" (Mark 1:14-15).
   2. The "time" for the establishment of the prophesied kingdom had come.
  C. When Jesus sent His twelve apostles out to the "lost sheep of the house of Israel," He told them to preach, "The kingdom of heaven is at hand" (Matt. 10:6-7).
  D. When Jesus sent seventy disciples out, He told them to preach, "The kingdom of God has come near to you" (Luke 10:9-11).

E. The message being preached during the life and ministry of Jesus was preparing people for the imminent ("at hand") coming of the long-awaited church/kingdom.
   1. Jesus went about "preaching the gospel of the kingdom" (Matt. 4:23; 9:35; 13:19).
   2. Jesus taught numerous parables about "the mysteries of the kingdom" (Matt. 13:11):
      (a) "The kingdom of heaven is like a man who sowed seed" (Matt. 13:24).
      (b) "The kingdom of heaven is like a mustard seed" (Matt. 13:31).
      (c) "The kingdom of heaven is like leaven" (Matt. 13:33).
      (d) "The kingdom of heaven is like treasure hidden in a field" (Matt. 13:44).
      (e) "The kingdom of heaven is like a merchant seeking beautiful pearls" (Mt. 13:45).
      (f) "The kingdom of heaven is like a dragnet" (Matt. 13:47).
      (g) "The kingdom of heaven is like a landowner" (Matt. 20:1).
      (h) "The kingdom of heaven shall be likened to ten virgins" (Matt. 25:1).
      (i) "The kingdom of heaven is like a man traveling to a far country" (Matt. 25:14).
   3. These parables described the nature of this kingdom/church that was coming.
F. Jesus made every preparation necessary for the establishment of His kingdom.
   1. This eternal plan of God would not be thwarted by any human effort or distraction.
   2. After hearing John the Baptist and Jesus, the people should have been ready for the kingdom of God.

VI. The Church of the Bible Was <u>Promised</u> Specifically and Clearly By Jesus Christ.
   A. The first time we ever read the word "church" in the Bible is in Matthew 16, and it is coming from the lips of Jesus. Isn't that fitting, that He spoke the word first?
      1. Peter made the great confession about the deity of Jesus (which was a revealed truth from heaven): "You are the Christ, the Son of the living God" (Matt. 16:16).
      2. Jesus then announced: "...On this rock I will build My church, and the gates of Hades shall not prevail against it" (Matt. 16:18).
         (a) The church had not yet been established—it was still future.
         (b) The church would not be established by man—it would be built by Jesus.
         (c) The church would not be founded upon a man—it would be founded upon the bedrock truth of the deity of Jesus.
            (1) The church was NOT founded upon Peter.
            (2) Jesus NEVER said or even suggested that His church would be built upon Peter.
            (3) Jesus used two different Greek words for "Peter" and "rock":
               (i) "Peter" – *petros,* masculine, meaning "small stone, fragment"
               (ii) "Rock" – *petra*, feminine, meaning "massive, boulder-like bedrock"
         (d) The church would not find its origin or existence in man—it would be Jesus' church (notice the personal possessive pronoun "My").
         (e) The church would not be a temporary institution—nothing would overpower it.
      3. Jesus added that He would provide the "keys of the kingdom of heaven" (i.e., the means of entrance).
         (a) Jesus alone could and would provide the means of entrance into the kingdom.
         (b) When Jesus spoke of "entering" His kingdom, He clearly taught that:
            (1) It would require doing the will of His Father in heaven (Matt. 7:21).
            (2) It would require humility and transformation of life (Matt. 18:3).
            (3) It would require being baptized (John 3:3-7).
         (c) Can you imagine there being some other entrance than the one Jesus opened?
      4. Notice that Jesus used the terms "church" and "kingdom" interchangeably in Matthew 16:18-19. This is significant to understand the words are synonymous.

B. Just a short time later, after His promise in Matthew 16:18, Jesus made a promise to those living in His day.
   1. "Assuredly, I say to you that there are some standing here who will not taste death till they see the kingdom of God present with power" (Mark 9:1; cf. Matt. 16:28).
   2. Jesus not only promised to build His church, He promised to build His church/kingdom in the lifetime of those hearing His words.
      (a) It was not something thousands of years away; it was coming in that generation.
      (b) Do we believe Jesus? Do we believe that He knew what He was talking about? Do we believe that He can and did keep His promise?
   3. The nature of its coming was to be powerful—something that would be evident to all.
C. Cross-reference these promises of Jesus below and you'll see how He pinpointed the establishment of His church, using the keyword "power" to tie them all together:
   1. That generation would "see the **kingdom** of God **present with power**" (Mark 9:1).
   2. Jesus promised the apostles: "Behold, I send the Promise of My Father upon you; but tarry in the city of **Jerusalem** until you are **endued with power from on high**" (Luke 24:49).
   3. Jesus promised the apostles: "But you shall receive **power when the Holy Spirit has come upon you**" (Acts 1:8).
   4. Summary of these verses:
      (a) The kingdom would come (be present) →
      (b) With power →
      (c) From on high →
      (d) When the Holy Spirit comes →
      (e) On the apostles →
      (f) In Jerusalem.
   5. This is fundamentally and critically significant! And, Jesus promised in Acts 1:5 that this was going to happen "not many days from now."

VII. The Church of the Bible Was Purchased By Jesus Christ!
A. Christ did not merely make promises and set events on a course to ensure the establishment of the church. Christ took matters into His own hands to guarantee it.
B. The Bible makes a compelling statement about Jesus' personal investment in the church: "...He purchased [the church of God] with His own blood" (Acts 20:28).
   1. Blood has always had a significant role in the work of God for man's redemption.
      (a) Blood was required over the Jews' doorposts to save their firstborn (Ex. 12).
      (b) Blood was required from the sin offering to secure atonement for all (Lev. 16).
      (c) Truly, in more ways than one, "life is in the blood" (Lev. 17:11).
   2. In like manner, and to a much greater extent, the blood of Christ was necessary to "redeem" the lost from the power of Satan and sin.
      (a) "Without shedding of blood there is no remission" (Heb. 9:22).
      (b) "In Him we have redemption through His blood, the forgiveness of sins" (Eph. 1:7).
      (c) "You were...redeemed...with the precious blood of Christ, as of a lamb without blemish and without spot" (1 Pet. 1:18-19).
      (d) The redeemed are the blood bought (1 Cor. 6:19-20) and blood washed (Rev. 7:14).
   3. The blood of Christ continues to be necessary to "cleanse us from all" sin (1 Jn. 1:7, 9).
C. The power of the blood of Jesus saves the sinner and purchases the church.
   1. The blood of Jesus saves the individual sinner from his sins (Rev. 1:5).

2. Then, those saved by the blood of Jesus are added together to the body of the saved (Acts 2:41, 47), which is the church "purchased with His own blood" (Acts 20:28).
3. Jesus loved the church so much that He "gave Himself for her" (Eph. 5:25). He is the "Savior of the body" (Eph. 5:23), which is the church (Eph. 1:22-23).
4. One cannot separate (1) salvation through Christ and (2) the church of Christ! They are inseparably linked together by His precious blood!

D. No ordinary man could have established this church! Only deity could do that!

E. By means of purchase, the church belongs to Jesus Christ!

VIII. The Church of the Bible Was <u>Established</u> on the Day of Pentecost in Acts 2.

A. Acts chapter 2 describes the events that took place on the first Pentecost after the resurrection and ascension of Jesus. "When the Day of Pentecost had fully come" (2:1).

B. Notice some key details about the events of Acts 2:
1. Where the events of Acts 2 took place: Jerusalem (Acts 2:5).
2. Upon whom the events at the beginning of Acts 2 befell: The apostles ("they" in 2:1 + "apostles" in 1:26).
3. Who came in the events of Acts 2: "They were filled with the Holy Spirit" (2:4, 17).
4. From where the Holy Spirit came in the events of Acts 2: "From heaven" (2:2).
5. What power was evident in the events of Acts 2: the apostles "began to speak with other tongues, as the Spirit gave them utterance" (2:4).

C. Look at the series of events (marked with arrows) in the summary on page 80 (VI, C, 4).
1. This series summarized Jesus' promises regarding His kingdom.
2. Now, take what we just noticed about the events in Acts 2 and reverse the arrows.
3. When you do that, what must have happened in Acts 2? What must have been established in Acts 2? What must have been "present" (cf. Mark 9:1) on that day?

D. Summary of events in Acts 2:
1. In Jerusalem →
2. On the apostles →
3. The Holy Spirit came →
4. From on high →
5. With Power →
6. The kingdom came (was "present").

E. This conclusion is inescapable.
1. The kingdom of God's eternal purpose was established in Acts 2.
2. The kingdom of Old Testament prophecy was established in Acts 2.
3. The kingdom of preparation (through the preaching of John and Jesus) was established in Acts 2.
4. The kingdom and the church are the very same entities!

F. The last verse of Acts 2 affirms the establishment of the church on that day: "And the Lord added to the church daily those who were being saved" (2:47, NKJV).
1. Those who obeyed the gospel and were "baptized" were saved (2:38).
2. The saved were "added" (2:41) "to the church" (2:47).
3. Until this day, every statement about or in reference to the church/kingdom was always pointing forward to a future reality (incl. Mark 15:43; Luke 22:18, 29-30).
4. Acts 2:47 is the first time that the church/kingdom is spoken of as a present reality.
5. Acts 5:11 also confirms that the church had come into existence in Jerusalem.
6. This was the culminating event in the eternal scheme of God!

- G. The events of Acts 2 are viewed in the Bible as "the beginning":
  1. Peter referred to that day and its events as "the beginning" (Acts 11:15).
  2. Jesus had foretold that the events of that day would be the "beginning" (Lk. 24:47).
  3. It was the beginning of the preaching of the gospel in its entirety (Acts 2:22-36).
  4. It was the beginning of the preaching of the gospel to "all nations" (Luke 24:47+Acts 1:5; cf. Matt. 28:19; Mark 16:15).
  5. It was the beginning of the preaching of God's plan of salvation and the remission of sins (Luke 24:47+Acts 2:38).
  6. It was the beginning of the new covenant in the Christian age (Heb. 8:7-13; 9:11-17; 10:15-18).
  7. It was the beginning of the church (Acts 2:40-47).
- H. After the events of Acts 2, every statement about or in reference to the church/kingdom was made about an institution that was already in existence.
  1. Before Acts 2, the church/kingdom was always spoken of as yet in the future.
  2. After Acts 2, the church/kingdom was always spoken of as being in existence.
     - (a) "Great fear came upon all the church" (Acts 5:11).
     - (b) "A great persecution arose against the church" (Acts 8:1).
     - (c) "When they had appointed elders in every church" (Acts 14:23).
     - (d) "He has…conveyed us into the kingdom" (Col. 1:13; cf. Heb. 12:28).
     - (e) "I, John, both your brother and companion in the…kingdom" (Rev. 1:9).

IX. Conclusion
- A. The church of the Bible is NOT of human origin! It is of Divine origin!
  1. In reality, that is all I need to know.
  2. That is enough to recognize that it must have my utmost attention.
- B. The church was purposed, prophesied, prepared for, promised and purchased by God!
- C. The church was established in Acts 2, as an integral fulfillment of God's eternal plan.
- D. His church, which is still in existence today, must be an integral part of my eternal plan!

Recommended Resources

Books

Baxter, Batsell Barrett. *The Family of God.* Nashville: Gospel Advocate, 1980.

Brownlow, Leroy. *Why I Am a Member of the Church of Christ.* Fort Worth: Brownlow Publishing, 1973.

Jennings, Alvin, ed. *Introducing the Church of Christ.* Fort Worth: Star Bible, 1981.

Miller, Dave. *What the Bible Says about the Church of Christ.* Montgomery, AL: Apologetics Press, 2007.

Wharton, Edward C. *The Church of Christ.* Nashville: Gospel Advocate, 1997.

Articles

Cogdill, Roy E. "The Origin of the Church." *New Testament Church.* Fairmount, IN: Truth Magazine Bookstore, 1982. 16-18.

Cotham, Perry B. "The Church of Christ—Established Almost Two Thousand Years Ago." *The Church of Christ (Freed-Hardeman College Lectures).* Ed. Thomas B. Warren. Nashville: Gospel Advocate, 1971. 41-55.

Durley, LeRoy R. "The Church Was Predicted By the Prophets." *Introducing the Church of Christ.* Ed. Alvin Jennings. Fort Worth: Star Bible, 1981. 7-11.

Ferguson, Everett. "The Establishment of the Church." *The New Testament Church.* Abilene, TX: Biblical Research Press, 1968. 13-18.

Jackson, Jason. "How Can the Church Be the Fulfillment of Daniel 2:44? *ChristianCourier.com*
https://www.christiancourier.com/articles/1243-how-can-the-church-be-the-fulfillment-of-daniel-2-44

Jackson, Wayne. "Isaiah's Prophecy of the Church." *ChristianCourier.com*
https://www.christiancourier.com/articles/430-isaiahs-prophecy-of-the-church

---. "The Establishment of the Church." *ChristianCourier.com*
https://www.christiancourier.com/articles/237-establishment-of-the-church-of-christ-the

McCord, Hugo. "The Church of Christ—Seen By the Prophets and Prepared for By John." *The Church of Christ (Freed-Hardeman College Lectures).* Ed. Thomas B. Warren. Nashville: Gospel Advocate, 1971. 35-40.

Wharton, Edward C. "The Establishment of the Church." *The Church of Christ.* Nashville: Gospel Advocate, 1997. 55-61.

Periodicals

The Spiritual Sword. July 2000. "Acts, Chapter Two."

Lesson 8: The Distinct Nature of the Church

I. **The "Church" Is a Significant New Testament Doctrine.**
   A. The English word "church" is found over 100 times in the New Testament.
      1. The word's first occurrence is in Matthew 16:18.
      2. The word is not found in the Old Testament (although it is spoken of in other terms).
   B. Yet, the concept of the church is widely misunderstood today.
      1. People talk about "my church" or "your church" or "that church down the road."
      2. People often mistake the church for the material building or the physical location.
      3. People sometimes reduce the church to merely being some religious organization.
   C. To understand the true nature and significance of the church, we must study what the Bible says about it.

II. **The Definition of the Church Will Help in Understanding Its Nature.**
   A. "Church" comes from the Greek word *ekklesia.*
      1. *Ekklesia* is a compound Greek word: *ek* = out of, *kaleo* = to call.
      2. Thus, the church, by definition, is "the called out" or "the called out ones."
   B. The church is made up of ones who have been:
      1. ..."called out of darkness into His marvelous light" (1 Pet. 2:9).
      2. ...turned "from darkness to light, and from the power of Satan to God" (Acts 26:18).
      3. ..."delivered...from the power of darkness and conveyed...into the kingdom" (Col. 1:13).
   C. That deliverance from "darkness" to "light" was God's eternal plan (cf. Isa. 9:1-7).
      1. "Darkness" represents being lost and living in unrighteousness (Prov. 4:19; 1 Jn. 1:6).
      2. "Light" represents being in the presence of God, for He is "light" (1 Jn. 1:5; 1 Th. 5:5).
      3. Therefore, one must be in the "light" (i.e., in the church) to be in God's presence.
         (a) That is precisely what is described in Colossians 1:12-14.
         (b) There is an "inheritance" that belongs to "the saints in the light" (1:12).
         (c) This inheritance belongs to those who:
             (1) "Have redemption through His blood, the forgiveness of sins" (1:14).
             (2) Have been "delivered...from the power of darkness" of sin (1:13).
             (3) Have been "conveyed...into the kingdom" (1:13), which is His church.
         (d) This passage also clearly affirms that the church/kingdom was in existence and growing in the first century.
   D. Those in the church have been "called out" by the gospel (2 Thess. 2:14).
      1. There is no other calling or other method by which one finds or enters the church than by the gospel.
      2. Of course, to be "called out," one must respond to the calling of the gospel. To ignore the calling of the gospel leaves one in darkness (and outside the church).

III. **The Composition of the Church (Specified in the N.T.) Will Help in Understanding Its Nature.**
   A. The church is composed of all those who have been saved.
      1. The "saved" are "added" by "the Lord" "to the church" (Acts 2:47).
         (a) Therefore, when one follows the Lord's plan of salvation (which requires "repent and let everyone of you be baptized," 2:38), the newly saved person becomes a part of the church immediately.
      2. Only those in the church are saved, for Jesus "is the Savior of the body" (Eph. 5:23).
         (a) Obviously, Jesus is the Savior of those who are saved.
         (b) But this passage affirms that He is the Savior of the church/body (1:22-23).
         (c) Therefore, one must be in the church/body to be saved by Jesus.

- 84 -

3. People in the church are saved people, and saved people are in the church.
B. The church is composed of all those who have been sanctified.
   1. "To the church of God which is at Corinth, to those who are sanctified in Christ Jesus, called to be saints" (1 Cor. 1:2).
   2. People in the church are sanctified (i.e., set apart) in and by Christ when they obey the gospel (1 Cor. 6:11), and the sanctified people are in the church.
   3. The identity of the person who has been "sanctified" is designated as a "saint." Saints are ones who have been set apart by God, and they make up the church.
   4. Only those who are in the church are sanctified by Christ.
C. The church is composed of all those who have been reconciled to God.
   1. At one time, all of mankind has been "without Christ...having no hope" (Eph. 2:12).
      (a) While this verse specifically referred to Gentiles, it is true that without Christ all people (Jews and Gentiles) have "no hope."
   2. But, because of "the blood of Christ," one finds hope "in Christ Jesus" (2:13)
   3. And, because of "the cross" of Christ, all can be "reconciled" to God (2:16).
   4. Note carefully that this reconciliation is "in one body" (i.e., the church) (2:16).
   5. Through the blood of Christ, one is reconciled back to God in His church.
   6. Only those who are in the church are reconciled to God.
D. The church, therefore, is composed of the "saved," the "sanctified," and the "reconciled."
   1. All those who are saved, sanctified and reconciled are in His church.
   2. Only those in the church have been saved, sanctified and reconciled.

IV. The Depictions Used for the Church in the N.T. Will Help in Understanding Its Nature.
A. The Bible uses various terms, depictions, images or figures to describe the church.
   1. The Lord's church is unlike anything else on this earth, therefore, the Lord utilized vivid pictures from daily living to help man understand and appreciate His church.
   2. By using words and concepts with which man is very familiar, God is able to convey the multifaceted nature of His church from a number of different angles.
   3. He also helps us to see how important His church is to Him.
B. The church is depicted in the New Testament as **a body** –
   "the body of Christ" (1 Cor. 12:27).
   1. The spiritual body of the church is compared with the physical body of man.
      (a) As the physical body is composed of many parts, so is the spiritual body made up of many members (1 Cor. 12:14).
      (b) As the various parts of the physical body all work together harmoniously for the good of the whole body, so should the spiritual body function (1 Cor. 12:15-17).
      (c) While there are many parts to the body, there is just one body (1 Cor. 12:20).
      (d) While the various parts of the body are different and have different functions, each part is essential to the body—which is true of the physical body and the spiritual body (1 Cor. 12:21-25).
      (e) As the parts of the physical body care for each other, so should the members of the spiritual body, the church (1 Cor. 12:25-27).
   2. Christ "is the head of the body, the church" (Col. 1:18; cf. Eph. 1:22-23; 5:23). The terms "body" and "church" are used interchangeably/synonymously in the N.T.
   3. As there is one head, "there is one body" (Eph. 4:4).
      (a) Can you envision Jesus, as the one head, having more than one body?
      (b) Jesus has only one body (i.e., one church).
   4. The emphasis of the body is upon the unity inherent within a body.

C. The church is depicted in the New Testament as **a family** –
"the household of God" (1 Tim. 3:15).
1. "The household of God" is a depiction of the church as "the family of God."
    (a) In Acts 16:31-34, we read of the conversion of the jailer and "his household."
    (b) As "his household" was his family, "the household of God" is God's family.
2. Those in God's family:
    (a) Have been "begotten" by Him (1 Pet. 1:3).
    (b) Are part of God's "whole family in heaven and earth" (Eph. 3:14-15).
    (c) Are God's "sons and daughters" (2 Cor. 6:18; cf. Gal. 3:26-27; 1 John 3:1-2).
    (d) Are "children of God…heirs of God and joint heirs with Christ" (Rom. 8:16-17).
    (e) Are brothers and sisters in Christ (1 Cor. 16:20; Acts 15:36; Jas. 2:15).
3. God, as the one Father, has only one family, which should be united together in their bond and in their working together for the Father (Eph. 4:13-16).
    (a) Can you envision God, as the one Father, having more than one family?
    (b) God has only one family (i.e., one church).
4. The emphasis of the family is upon the close-knit bond inherent within a family.

D. The church is depicted in the New Testament as **a kingdom** –
"the kingdom of God" (Acts 1:3), "the kingdom of the Son of His love" (Col. 1:13), "the kingdom of heaven" (Matt. 3:2; 4:17; 10:7; 13:31; 18:3).
1. Jesus identified the church as a kingdom, when He promised to build His church and then give the keys to the kingdom (Matt. 16:18-19), using the terms synonymously.
2. Christ is the king of His one kingdom (Rev. 19:16; 1:5), which is a spiritual or heavenly kingdom (John 18:36; Phil. 3:20).
3. The kingdom is made up of people/citizens on this earth (who are "fellow citizens," Eph. 2:19), but its Ruler and its laws are from heaven (cf. Matt. 21:25)!
4. The many parables that Jesus taught about "the kingdom of heaven" (see Matt. 13, et al.) were intended to describe for us the nature of His church.
5. Christ, as King of kings, has only one kingdom.
    (a) Can you envision Christ, as the one king, having more than one kingdom?
    (b) Christ has only one kingdom (i.e., one church).
6. The emphasis of the kingdom is upon the rule of law, government and obedient citizens inherent within a kingdom.

E. The church is depicted in the New Testament as **a bride** –
"to present you as a pure virgin to Christ" (2 Cor. 11:2).
1. The Bible likens the relationship between Christ and His church to the relationship between a husband and his wife/bride (Eph. 5:22-33).
    (a) "For the husband is head of the wife, as also Christ is head of the church" (5:23).
    (b) "Christ…loved the church and gave Himself for her" (5:25).
    (c) The church is to be "a pure virgin" (2 Cor. 11:2), "not having spot or wrinkle or any such thing, but that she should be holy and without blemish" (Eph. 5:27).
    (d) The church is "married" to Christ (Rom. 7:4; cf. Rev. 22:17).
    (e) Christ is often called "the bridegroom" (Matt. 25:1-11; John 3:29).
    (f) In the O.T., Israel was depicted as Jehovah's "wife" (Jer. 3:20; Ezek. 16:32; Hosea).
2. Christ, as the bridegroom, has only one bride.
    (a) Can you envision Christ, as the bridegroom, having more than one bride?
    (b) Christ has only one bride (i.e., one church).
3. The emphasis of the bride is upon the intimate faithfulness inherent within a bride.

F. The church is depicted in the New Testament as **a temple** –
"the temple of God" (1 Cor. 3:16-17).
   1. Individually, Christians are "the temple of the Holy Spirit" (1 Cor. 6:19-20), and collectively, the church as a whole is "the temple of God" (1 Cor. 3:16-17).
   2. Peter describes this aspect of the church as being "a spiritual house," in which "a holy priesthood" (all Christians are priests) "offer up spiritual sacrifices acceptable to God" (1 Pet. 2:5; cf. 2:9; Rev. 1:5-6; 5:10).
   3. The church is "a holy temple in the Lord" (Eph. 2:21), "built together for a dwelling place of God in the Spirit" (Eph. 2:22).
   4. The emphasis of the temple is upon the worship(ers) inherent within a temple.
      (a) The church is a worshiping society.
      (b) The church is not the building but the people (the worshipers).
G. The church is depicted in the New Testament as **a vineyard** –
"work today in my vineyard" (Matt. 21:28).
   1. In His parables which depicted the nature of His kingdom, Jesus likened His kingdom to a vineyard and the members of His kingdom to laborers (Matt. 20:1-16; 21:28-44).
   2. Vineyards require hard labor, which is likely the imagery behind 1 Corinthians 15:58, "…be steadfast, immovable, always abounding in the work of the Lord, knowing that your labor is not in vain in the Lord."
   3. The emphasis of the vineyard is upon the hard work inherent within a vineyard.
H. The church is depicted in the New Testament as **a flock** –
"the flock of God" (1 Pet. 5:2).
   1. In God's flock, Christians are the sheep and Jesus is the Shepherd (1 Pet. 2:25; John 10).
   2. Sheep have a tendency to "stray" (Matt. 18:12-13; Isa. 53:6), which illustrates deeply the need for the "Good Shepherd" and following His voice (John 10).
   3. Jesus emphasized that there is "one flock and one shepherd" (John 10:16).
   4. There is a tender relationship that exists between a shepherd and his sheep (Psa. 23).
   5. The emphasis of the flock is upon the following inherently necessary within a flock.
I. The church is depicted in the New Testament as **an army** –
"endure hardship as a good soldier of Jesus Christ" (2 Tim. 2:3).
   1. The church is engaged in a "war," but not a fleshly war with "carnal weapons" (2 Cor. 10:3-6), but against "spiritual hosts of wickedness" led by "the devil" (Eph. 6:11-12).
   2. Righteousness is always at constant odds with evil, and our "adversary the devil" would like nothing better than to destroy us (1 Pet. 5:8).
   3. As soldiers in the Lord's army (2 Tim. 2:3-4), we must "put on the whole armor of God" and stand in His strength for battle (Eph. 6:10-18).
   4. The emphasis on the army is upon defending against attacks and staying on target.
J. How beautifully depicted is the church of our Lord, so expressively described as:
   1. A body
   2. A family
   3. A kingdom
   4. A bride
   5. A temple
   6. A vineyard
   7. A flock
   8. An army
   9. By using these metaphors, God helps us to understand the nature of His church.

V. **The Sense in Which the Word "Church" Is Used Will Help in Understanding Its Nature.**
   A. The word "church" is used in a universal sense in the New Testament.
      1. Jesus promised, "I will build my church" (Matt. 16:18).
      2. Jesus "purchased the church with His own blood" (Acts 20:28).
      3. Jesus "is head of the church" and "gave Himself" for the church (Eph. 5:23, 25).
      4. "The churches of Christ greet you" (Rom. 16:16).
      5. In verses like these, "church" is used in a universal, global, continual sense, to embrace all saved persons in the church from the first century until the end of time. Used in the plural simply represents all congregations of the church of Christ.
   B. The word "church" is used in a local sense in the New Testament.
      1. "In the church that was at Antioch" (Acts 13:1).
      2. "When they had appointed elders in every church" (Acts 14:23).
      3. "He sent to Ephesus and called for the elders of the church" (Acts 20:17).
      4. "Likewise greet the church that is in their house" (Rom. 16:5).
      5. "To the church of God which is at Corinth" (1 Cor. 1:2).
      6. In verses like these, "church" is used in a local sense of those Christians in a specific locality, community or city. The word "congregation" could often be understood.
   C. The word "church" or "churches" is used in a regional/provincial sense in the N.T.
      1. "The churches throughout all Judea, Galilee, and Samaria had peace" (Acts 9:31).
      2. "The churches of Asia greet you" (1 Cor. 16:19).
      3. "The grace of God bestowed on the churches of Macedonia" (2 Cor. 8:1).
      4. "To the churches of Galatia" (Gal. 1:2).
      5. "John, to the seven churches which are in Asia" (Rev. 1:4).
      6. "The churches of Christ greet you" (Rom. 16:16).
      7. In verses like these, "churches" is used regionally or provincially of multiple congregations within a given area, which are all part of the one church.
      8. The word "congregations" could be understood as a synonym.

VI. **Knowing the Destiny of the Church Will Help in Understanding Its Essential Nature.**
   A. The church is made up of the saved (Acts 2:47; cf. John 3:3-5), and only the saved will enter heaven (Rev. 21:27).
      1. God never discusses or even considers those who are "saved" separately from those who are in His "church."
      2. What should that tell us about the essential nature of His church?
   B. Jesus is not only the "head of the church," "He is the Savior of the body" (Eph. 5:23).
      1. Could one ever successfully argue (in light of this verse) that salvation could be found outside of Christ's body/church?
   C. At the end of time, Jesus will "[deliver] the kingdom to God the Father" (1 Cor. 15:24).
      1. Is there anyone willing to argue that those who are outside of Christ's kingdom/church will also be delivered to the Father in heaven?
   D. The following conclusions from these Bible truths are inescapable:
      1. The church/body/kingdom is made up of the saved, therefore, one must be in the church/body/kingdom in order to be saved.
      2. The eternal destiny of the church/body/kingdom is heaven, therefore, one must be in the church/body/kingdom to go to heaven.
   E. The eternal destiny of the church demands that it have an essential place in our lives today.

VII. Conclusion
- A. The church is God's called out people, who have obeyed the gospel in order to be saved.
- B. The Lord gives us so many angles from which to view His church. And from every vantage point, the Lord's description is of a beautiful, unique, essential institution.
- C. The Lord only has one place for His saved, sanctified, reconciled people—in His church!
    1. And the Lord Himself is the one who places the saved in His church!
- D. There is only one church! This is emphasized in the fact that the Lord has only:
    1. One body!
    2. One family!
    3. One kingdom!
    4. One bride!
    5. One temple!
    6. One vineyard!
    7. One flock!
    8. One army!
- E. I must be in His church to be saved and to go to heaven!

Recommended Resources

<u>Books</u>

Brownlow, Leroy. *Why I Am a Member of the Church of Christ.* Fort Worth: Brownlow Publishing, 1973.

Cloer, Eddie. *God's Design for "The Church."* Searcy, AR: Resource Publications, 1993.

---. *What Is "The Church"?* Searcy, AR: Resource Publications, 1993.

Jennings, Alvin, ed.. *Introducing the Church of Christ.* Fort Worth: Star Bible, 1981.

Wharton, Edward C. *The Church of Christ.* Nashville: Gospel Advocate, 1997.

Winkler, Wendell. *The Church Everybody Is Asking About.* Tuscaloosa, AL: Winkler Publications, 1988.

<u>Articles</u>

Boren, Maxie B. "The Church Is Described By Many Figures." *Introducing the Church of Christ.* Ed. Alvin Jennings. Fort Worth: Star Bible, 1981. 32-37.

Brownlow, Leroy. "Because Salvation Is in Christ's Church." *Why I Am a Member of the Church of Christ.* Fort Worth: Brownlow Publishing, 1973. 186-192.

Cloer, Eddie. "The Divine Designations of the Church." *What Is "The Church"?* Searcy, AR: Resource Publications, 1993. 97-115.

Cogdill, Roy E. "The Nature of the Church." *New Testament Church.* Fairmount, IN: Truth Magazine Bookstore, 1982. 1-14.

Connally, Andrew M. "The Church of Christ—Essential." *The Church of Christ (Freed-Hardeman College Lectures).* Ed. Thomas B. Warren. Nashville: Gospel Advocate, 1971. 67-74.

Crawford, Doyle. "Christ's Church Is Essential to Salvation." *Introducing the Church of Christ.* Ed. Alvin Jennings. Fort Worth: Star Bible, 1981. 233-236.

Ferguson, Everett. "Images of the Church." *The New Testament Church.* Abilene, TX: Biblical Research Press, 1968. 25-30.

Jackson, Jason. "What Is the Church of Christ?" *ChristianCourier.com*
https://www.christiancourier.com/articles/1205-what-is-the-church-of-christ

Winkler, Wendell. "Do Members of the Church of Christ Believe That Every Person Who Is Not a Member of the Church of Christ Is Going to Hell?" *The Church Everybody Is Asking About.* Tuscaloosa, AL: Winkler Publications, 1988. 92-99.

<u>Periodicals</u>

The Spiritual Sword. July 1970. "The Church in the New Testament."

Lesson 9: The Unique Identity of the Church

I. **There Is Only One Church.**
   A. Understanding the unique identity of the church begins with understanding the singular nature of the church. The church is "unique" because **there is only one!**
      1. Jesus taught that there is only one church (Matt. 16:18).
         (a) Jesus promised to build His church, and He used the singular form of the word.
         (b) Jesus did not say anything about "churches" (plural) – only "church" (singular).
      2. Paul taught that there is only one church.
         (a) In 1 Corinthians 12, Paul taught that we are in "one body" (12:13, 20).
         (b) In Ephesians 4, Paul plainly stated, "There is one body" (4:4).
         (c) "The body" is the same as "the church" (Eph. 1:22-23; Col. 1:18), therefore, there is only one church.
   B. The unity required by Christ for His church demands that there is only one church.
      1. All Christians are to be united in one body, which is the church of our Lord.
      2. Jesus prayed that Christians "all may be one, as You, Father, are in Me, and I in You; that they also may be one in Us" (John 17:20-21). That kind of unity can only be fulfilled in one church (not dozens, hundreds or thousands).
      3. The Holy Spirit begged Christians to "all speak the same thing, and that there be no divisions among you, but that you be perfectly joined together in the same mind and in the same judgment" (1 Cor. 1:10). That kind of unity demands one church.
   C. There is no such thing in the New Testament or in the mind of God as "joining the church of your choice."
      1. The Lord only has one church.
      2. The Lord adds those who are saved to His church (Acts 2:47).
      3. One must, therefore, search and identify the only church of the Lord's choice.
   D. Denominationalism did not exist in the first century or in New Testament times.
      1. When the Lord established His church, there was only one church—His church.
      2. There were no denominations to "choose from" or to complicate the matter.
      3. The church of the New Testament is pre-denominational, existing centuries before man-made denominations ever came on the scene.
      4. All Christians were members of the same church—the one New Testament church.
      5. Today, people have grown so accustomed to viewing the church (or any church) as a denomination and thinking in denominational terms that it is very difficult to distance oneself from that mindset and think in purely New Testament terms.
         (a) However, such must be done in order to search for and identify the Lord's church.
         (b) Finding the church of the New Testament requires disconnecting our minds from man-made religious philosophy and connecting our minds to God's plan.
      6. When Jesus promised to build His church (Matt. 16:18) and when Jesus purchased the church with His own blood (Acts 20:28), He did not build, purchase, desire or intend for denominations. He built and purchased one church—His church.
   E. The goal of every serious Bible student must be to:
      1. Go back to the Bible and read and study about the church in the New Testament.
      2. With the identifying marks of the church from the New Testament, search for it diligently in the surrounding community and become a part of it.
      3. Restore the New Testament church (with all of its identifying marks from the New Testament) and be the church that Jesus loved and died for on the cross.

II. **There Are Definite Identifying Marks of the One True Church in the New Testament.**
   A. The only way to identify the one church of the New Testament today is to:
      1. Study the New Testament carefully and read about the church.
      2. Trust the Bible alone to provide a guide, a pattern and a model for the church.
      3. Find the identifying marks of the church in the New Testament. Here are just a few:
   B. **Identifying Mark: The church was founded by Christ.**
      1. Jesus built the church of the New Testament (Matt. 16:18).
      2. Jesus purchased the church of the New Testament (Acts 20:28).
      3. Jesus is the head of the church of the New Testament (Eph. 5:23; 1:22-23; Col. 1:18).
      4. Jesus is the lawgiver of the church of the New Testament (John 12:48; Acts 2:36).
      5. If a "church" today has a different founder, it is not the one true church of the N.T.
   C. **Identifying Mark: The church was founded upon Christ.**
      1. Jesus is the foundation upon which the church was "laid" (1 Cor. 3:11). There is "no other foundation" that "anyone" can lay for the church! Christ alone is the foundation!
      2. Jesus is the chief cornerstone upon which the church was established (Eph. 2:20).
      3. Jesus' deity is the rock upon which the church was built (Matt. 16:16-18).
      4. If a "church" today has a different foundation, it is not the one true church of the N.T.
   D. **Identifying Mark: The church was established in Jerusalem.**
      1. It was prophesied the church would be established in Jerusalem (Isa. 2:2-4; Zech. 1:16).
      2. Jesus instructed His disciples to begin His work in Jerusalem (Luke 24:46-53; Acts 1:8).
      3. The church came into existence in the city of Jerusalem in Acts 2 (2:1-5, 47).
      4. If a "church" today was started in a different place, it is not the one true church of the New Testament.
   E. **Identifying Mark: The church was established on the first Pentecost after the resurrection of Christ (~ A.D. 33).**
      1. It was prophesied that the church would be established in Roman days (Dan. 2:44).
      2. It was prophesied that the church would be established in "the latter days" (Isa. 2:2).
         (a) Joel prophesied that the Spirit would be poured out in "the last days" (Joel 2:28-32).
         (b) On the day of Pentecost (in Acts 2), Peter affirmed that the events taking place that day were "the last days" "spoken by the prophet Joel" (Acts 2:16-21).
         (c) The "last days" depicts the final dispensation of time, i.e., the Christian age.
      3. Jesus promised that the church would begin in the lifetime of His hearers (Mark 9:1).
         (a) See Lesson 7 for a detailed analysis of the timing of the kingdom's establishment.
      4. The church came into existence on the day of Pentecost in Acts 2 (2:1-4, 47).
      5. If a "church" today was started at a different time, it is not the one true church.
   F. **Identifying Mark: The church wears the name of its Founder, Owner and Savior.**
      1. There are several designations for the church found in the New Testament:
         (a) "the church" (Eph. 3:10; Col. 1:18)
         (b) "the body of Christ" (Eph. 4:12; 1 Cor. 12:27)
         (c) "the church of God" (1 Cor. 1:2; 11:16; 15:9; 1 Tim. 3:5; 1 Thess. 2:14)
         (d) "the church of the living God" (1 Tim. 3:15)
         (e) "the church of the Lord" (Acts 20:28)
         (f) "churches of Christ" (Rom. 16:16)
         (g) "the kingdom of heaven" (Matt. 13:44; 16:19)
         (h) "the kingdom of God" (Mark 1:4; 9:1; Luke 10:9; Acts 1:3; 8:12)
         (i) "the kingdom of the Son of His love" (Col. 1:13)
         (j) "the house of God" (1 Tim. 3:15; Eph. 2:19)

- (k) Compare these Scriptural designations for the church with the designations that you see today, many of which:
  - (1) Do not contain the word "church" or "God" or "Christ."
  - (2) Are not found anywhere in the New Testament.
- (l) These Scriptural expressions and designations for the church are not "proper names" or "titles" but marks of ownership.
  - (1) The church BELONGS to Christ, by right of purchase, and not any man or men. Therefore, it should bear His name, as His faithful possession!
  - (2) The church BELONGS to Christ, by right of marriage, and not any man or men. Therefore, it should wear His name, as His faithful bride!
- (m) If a "church" today wears a different name than one found in the N.T. (i.e., wears a man-made name), it is not the one true church of the New Testament.

2. There are several designations for the members of the church found in the N.T.:
   - (a) "believers" (Acts 5:14; 1 Tim. 4:12)
   - (b) "disciples" (Acts 6:1; 11:26; 19:30; 20:7)
   - (c) "saints" (Rom. 1:7; 1 Cor. 1:2; Acts 9:13; Phil. 1:1)
   - (d) "members" (1 Cor. 12:27; Eph. 2:19; 4:25)
   - (e) "sons of God" (1 John 3:1-2; Gal. 3:26; Rom. 8:14-17)
   - (f) "brethren" (1 Cor. 15:6; Jas. 1:2; 2 Pet. 1:10)
   - (g) "priests" (1 Pet. 2:5, 9; Rev. 1:6; 5:10)
   - (h) "Christians" (Acts 11:26; 26:28; 1 Pet. 4:16)
   - (i) New Testament Christians did not wear hyphenated names to designate what "kind" of Christian they were or the "kind" of church to which they belonged.
   - (j) If a "church" today has members that wear different names other than one found in the New Testament, it is not the one true church of the New Testament.
3. There is definitely something in a name – especially when that name is Christ!

G. **Identifying Mark: The church follows only one law system, doctrine, creed, discipline.**
   1. Man-made religions follow man-made doctrines from man-made creeds. Thus, the religions vary because the doctrines vary because the creeds vary.
   2. The one true church of the New Testament has only one law system, only one doctrine and only one creed that it follows – the New Testament (2 Tim. 3:16-17)!
   3. Since Christ is the head of the church (Eph. 5:23), and since He is Lord (Acts 2:36), and since His word is the all-authoritative standard of judgment (John 12:48), it follows that His word alone governs the teaching and practice of His church.
      - (a) The Bible is verbally inspired (2 Tim. 3:16-17; 2 Pet. 1:20-21; 1 Cor. 2:9-13), inerrant (Psa. 19:7; Jas. 1:25; 1 Pet. 1:22-25) and all-sufficient (2 Pet. 1:3; Jude 3).
      - (b) The Bible is not to be added to, taken from or modified in any way (Gal. 1:6-9; Rev. 22:18-19; 2 John 9-11).
      - (c) The Bible alone makes us complete and thoroughly equips us for every good work (2 Tim. 3:17).
   4. Therefore, the one true church will "hear" Christ and only Him (Matt. 17:5).
      - (a) The one true church will "continue steadfastly in the apostles' doctrine" (Ac. 2:42).
      - (b) The one true church will only "speak as the oracles of God" (1 Pet. 4:11).
      - (c) The one true church will do all and say all by the authority of Christ (Col. 3:17).
   5. Church manuals, creeds and disciplines are a direct violation of Scripture.
      - (a) If a church creed teaches more than the N.T., then it teaches too much.
      - (b) If a church creed teaches less than the N.T., then it teaches too little.

- (c) If a church creed teaches different from the N.T., then it teaches error.
- (d) If a church creed teaches the same as the N.T., then it is not needed. We have the Bible!
6. Simply stated, the apostle John instructed, "Whoever transgresses and does not abide in the doctrine of Christ does not have God. He who abides in the doctrine of Christ has both the Father and the Son. If anyone comes to you and does not bring this doctrine, do not receive him into your house nor greet him; for he who greets him shares in his evil deeds" (2 John 9-11).
    - (a) There exists "the" (singular) "doctrine of Christ."
    - (b) It is man's responsibility to "abide" within it, remaining faithful to its teaching.
    - (c) Anyone who chooses not to remain within Christ's doctrine forfeits his relationship (or potential relationship) with God.
    - (d) Those who do remain faithful to its teaching must be on guard against those who do not—watching for them, avoiding them and never lending approval to them.
7. If a "church" today uses or follows any law system, doctrine, creed or discipline other than the New Testament, it is not the one true church.

H. **Identifying Mark: The church is organized according to Scriptural guidelines.**
1. The church has only one head – Christ (Eph. 1:22-23; 5:23; Col. 1:18), not a man.
2. The church has no earthly headquarters, but only the one in heaven (1 Pet. 3:22).
3. Congregations of the church are autonomous (i.e., independent) (Acts 14:23; 20:28).
4. Mature congregations are to have a plurality of qualified men who:
    - (a) Oversee the work of the church, called elders (Acts 14:23; 1 Pet. 5:2).
    - (b) Serve in special capacities in the church, called deacons (1 Tim. 3:8-13; Phil. 1:1).
5. Congregations are to have evangelists to preach the gospel (2 Tim. 4:2-5; Eph. 4:11).
6. An entire lesson will focus on this identifying mark later in this series.
7. These guidelines were not merely "a way to do it," but they are "God's way to do it."
8. If a "church" today has a different organizational structure than the one plainly detailed in the New Testament, it is not the one true church.

I. **Identifying Mark: The church worships as authorized by the New Testament.**
1. The church follows a standard of worship—God's standard, not man's (John 4:23-24).
2. The church worships on the first day of the week (Acts 20:7; 1 Cor. 11:20; 16:1-2).
3. The church worships through partaking of the Lord's Supper (Acts 20:7; 1 Cor. 11:17-34).
4. The church worships through prayer (Acts 2:42; 1 Cor. 14:15; 1 Thess. 5:17).
5. The church worships through congregational singing (Eph. 5:19; Col. 3:16; Heb. 13:15).
6. The church worships through giving as personally prospered (1 Cor. 16:1-2; 2 Cor. 8-9).
7. The church worships through preaching of the gospel (Acts 2:42; 20:7; 2 Tim. 4:2).
8. An entire lesson will focus on this identifying mark later in this series.
9. If a "church" today worships in ways (in any way) not authorized in the New Testament, it is not the one true church.

J. **Identifying Mark: The church has clear, universal and Scriptural terms of entrance.**
1. One enters the church today in the very same way one entered the church in the N.T.
2. Believers (Acts 16:31) who repent (Acts 2:38) and confess their faith (Rom. 10:9-10) are baptized into Christ (Gal. 3:27) to obtain the forgiveness of sins (Acts 2:38; 22:16).
3. These are God's terms of entrance for all people of every nation (Acts 10:34-35; 8:12).
4. Immersion into water is the culminating step that places one:
    - (a) Into Christ (Gal. 3:27; Rom. 6:3).
    - (b) Into the church of Christ (Acts 2:41-47+5:11).

                (c) Into the body of Christ (1 Cor. 12:13).
                (d) Into the family of God (Gal. 3:26-27).
                (e) Into the kingdom of God (John 3:3-5).
            5. Salvation is found only in Christ, in His church, in His body, in His family, in His kingdom (2 Tim. 2:10; Acts 2:47). One cannot be saved outside of Christ.
                (a) Terms of entrance matter because one must be in Christ and in the Lord's church to be saved (Acts 2:38-47) and to go to heaven.
                (b) At the end of time, Jesus will deliver those in His kingdom/church/body to the Father in heaven (1 Cor. 15:24; Eph. 5:23-27).
                (c) "The gift of God is eternal life" (Rom. 6:23)! Where? In Christ! In His church!
            6. An entire lesson will focus on this identifying mark later in this series.
            7. If a "church" today teaches or practices different terms of entrance than those plainly taught and practiced in the New Testament, it is not the one true church.
        K. The New Testament church (the one purposed, promised, purchased and established by deity) has obvious identifying marks, which set it apart as the one true church. How many "churches" (using that word very loosely, as commonly used in our day and not necessarily Scripturally used) that exist today do not bear these marks?
            1. The New Testament church was founded by Christ.
                (a) How many "churches" today were founded by men?
            2. The New Testament church was founded upon Christ.
                (a) How many "churches" today had some other foundation?
            3. The New Testament church was established in Jerusalem.
                (a) How many "churches" today were founded in some other city?
            4. The New Testament church was established on the first Pentecost after Jesus' resurrection.
                (a) How many "churches" today were founded on another date, much later than A.D. 33?
            5. The New Testament church wears the name of its Founder, Owner and Savior.
                (a) How many "churches" today wear a name not even found in Scripture?
            6. The New Testament church follows only one law system—the New Testament.
                (a) How many "churches" today follow their own creed, manual or discipline?
            7. The New Testament church is organized according to Scriptural guidelines.
                (a) How many "churches" today have their own organizational structure?
            8. The New Testament church worships as authorized by the New Testament.
                (a) How many "churches" today worship in unauthorized ways?
            9. The New Testament church follows Scriptural terms of entrance.
                (a) How many "churches" today have terms of entrance not found in Scripture?
            10. The identifying marks of the New Testament church are critical!
III. **The Church of the New Testament Can Be Planted and Identified Identically in Any Age.**
    A. The Lord designed His church to be universal and identical in every age and every land.
    B. The Lord's church (as described and identified in the New Testament) can be planted in any culture today where the gospel is preached.
        1. The gospel is designated by Jesus as "the word of the kingdom" (Matt. 13:19).
        2. In that same context, "the word of the kingdom" (remembering that the kingdom and the church are the same) is called "the seed" (Luke 8:11).
            (a) Think about the nature of a seed.
            (b) Every seed produces after its kind (Gen. 1:11-12).

        (c) No matter where and when a seed is planted, it will yield the very same product.
    3. Wherever and whenever the seed of the kingdom is planted, it produces a kingdom/church that is identical in every respect to the kingdom/church that was established in the first century and that we read about in the pages of the New Testament.
        (a) The same seed will always produce the same church, with the same identifying marks.
        (b) If there are different "churches" that have different identifying marks, then those churches were not conceived by and are not true to the seed.
C. The Lord's church can be found and can be identified by going back to the seed (i.e., the Word of God) and ensuring that the final product is not that of man but that of Christ.
D. It is truly sobering to remember the words of Jesus, "Every plant which My heavenly Father has not planted will be uprooted" (Matt. 15:13).

IV. **Conclusion**
A. With thousands of man-made denominations in existence today, it can be challenging to:
    1. Identify the one true church.
    2. Think outside the denominational structure, terminology and mindset.
    3. Realize that denominations are not according to God's plan.
B. The church that Jesus purchased and established in the New Testament still exists today.
    1. Daniel prophesied that it "shall never be destroyed...it shall stand forever" (2:44).
    2. Jesus promised that "the gates of Hades shall not prevail against it" (Matt. 16:18).
    3. The Hebrews' writer assured that it "cannot be shaken" (12:28).
    4. Once established (in Acts 2), it would (and will) always exist on this earth.
C. Since the church still exists today, we must search for it and identify it.
    1. The only way to identify the N.T. church is to use its identifying marks in the N.T.
    2. These marks are not "optional" or "interesting" or "nice." They are essential!
    3. If a "church" does not possess the Scriptural identifying marks in this lesson (and others outlined in the New Testament but not included here), it is not the one true church of the New Testament.
    4. Do not settle for something that you think is "close." His true church still exists!
D. The church is a divine institution with a unique identity—there is only one.
    1. The church is the most glorious institution on earth, because it belongs to Christ!
    2. As there is no salvation outside of His one church, let us obey His terms of entrance!

Recommended Resources

Books

Baxter, Batsell Barrett. *The Family of God.* Nashville: Gospel Advocate, 1980.

Brownlow, Leroy. *Why I Am a Member of the Church of Christ.* Fort Worth: Brownlow Publishing, 1973.

Jennings, Alvin, ed. *Introducing the Church of Christ.* Fort Worth: Star Bible, 1981.

Miller, Dave. *What the Bible Says about the Church of Christ.* Montgomery, AL: Apologetics Press, 2007.

Wharton, Edward C. *The Church of Christ.* Nashville: Gospel Advocate, 1997.

Winkler, Wendell. *The Church Everybody Is Asking About.* Tuscaloosa, AL: Winkler Publications, 1988.

Articles

Barr, B.J. "She Wears Only Biblical Names." *Introducing the Church of Christ.* Ed. Alvin Jennings. Fort Worth: Star Bible, 1981. 91-95.

Brownlow, Leroy. "Because It Was Founded By the Scriptural Builder—Christ." *Why I Am a Member of the Church of Christ.* Fort Worth: Brownlow Publishing, 1973. 7-9.

---. "Because It Was Founded on the Scriptural Foundation." *Why I Am a Member of the Church of Christ.* Fort Worth: Brownlow Publishing, 1973. 10-12.

---. "Because It Was Founded at the Scriptural Place—Jerusalem." *Why I Am a Member of the Church of Christ.* Fort Worth: Brownlow Publishing, 1973. 13-19.

---. "Because It Was Founded at the Scriptural Time." *Why I Am a Member of the Church of Christ.* Fort Worth: Brownlow Publishing, 1973. 20-21.

---. "Because Christ Is the Founder of Only One Church—His Church." *Why I Am a Member of the Church of Christ.* Fort Worth: Brownlow Publishing, 1973. 22-27.

---. "Because It Is Scriptural in Name." *Why I Am a Member of the Church of Christ.* Fort Worth: Brownlow Publishing, 1973. 28-37.

Cogdill, Roy E. "The Identity of the Church." *New Testament Church.* Fairmount, IN: Truth Magazine Bookstore, 1982. 67-80.

Cope, James R. "The One True Church." Cedar Park, TX: Cope Publishers, nd.

Edwards, Earl. "The Fruit of Respecting His Pattern: The Restored Church." *Respect for God's Word (South Florida Lectureship).* Ed. David Sproule. Palm Beach Gardens, FL: Palm Beach Lakes church of Christ, 2005. 61-74.

Fulford, Hugh. "The Church Was Founded By Jesus and On Him." *Introducing the Church of Christ.* Ed. Alvin Jennings. Fort Worth: Star Bible, 1981. 12-15.

Jackson, Wayne. "Identifying the Church of the New Testament." *ChristianCourier.com* https://www.christiancourier.com/articles/470-identifying-the-church-of-the-new-testament

Jones, David B. "Bible Authority for the Identity of the Church." *The Authority of the Bible (Spiritual Sword Lectureship).* Ed. Gary McDade. Memphis: Getwell church of Christ, 2002. 241-257.

Miller, Dave. "The Unique Church." *ApologeticsPress.org* http://apologeticspress.org/APContent.aspx?category=11&article=1190&topic=81

Winkler, Wendell. "Is the Church of Christ a Denomination?" *The Church Everybody Is Asking About.* Tuscaloosa, AL: Winkler Publications, 1988. 24-31.

Winters, Howard. "She Has Jesus As Her Only Head." *Introducing the Church of Christ.* Ed. Alvin Jennings. Fort Worth: Star Bible, 1981. 28-31.

Periodicals

The Spiritual Sword. April 1993. "The Church That Jesus Built."

The Spiritual Sword. October 1999. "Identity of the Church."

Lesson 10: The Unity of the Church

I. **The Bible's Emphasis on the Singularity of the Church Emphasizes Its Unity.**
   A. The Bible clearly and emphatically teaches that there is "one" church.
      1. Everything relating Jesus to His church emphasizes its singularity!
         (a) Jesus promised to build "His church" (Matt. 16:18). How many? One!
         (b) Jesus purchased "the church" with His blood (Acts 20:28). How many? One!
         (c) Jesus is the foundation of "the church" (1 Cor. 3:11). How many? One!
         (d) Jesus is the head of "the church" (Eph. 5:23). How many? One!
      2. In the New Testament, the church is frequently <u>designated</u> as "the body."
         (a) In an extended passage, 1 Corinthians 12 depicts the church as the body.
            (1) "God composed the body, having given greater honor to that part which lacks it, that there should be no schism in the body" (12:24-25).
            (2) "Now you are the body of Christ, and members individually" (12:27).
         (b) Ephesians 4 clearly identifies the church as the body.
            (1) Christ organized the church "for the equipping of the saints for the work of ministry, for the edifying of the body of Christ" (4:12).
            (2) "Christ—from whom the whole body, joined and knit together by what every joint supplies, according to the effective working by which every part does its share, causes growth of the body for the edifying of itself in love" (4:15b-16).
         (c) The Bible frequently refers to the church as the body.
      3. In the New Testament, the church is frequently <u>equated</u> with "the body."
         (a) Christ "is the head of the body, the church" (Col. 1:18, 24).
         (b) Christ is "head over all things to the church, which is His body" (Eph. 1:22-23).
         (c) "Christ is head of the church; and He is the Savior of the body" (Eph. 5:23).
         (d) The Bible frequently uses the words "church" and "body" synonymously.
      4. In the New Testament, there is <u>only one</u> church/body.
         (a) Knowing that the church is the body of Christ, one finds great emphasis on the "one church" in the New Testament.
         (b) "There is **one body/church**" (Eph. 4:4).
         (c) "For as we have many members in **one body/church**..." (Rom. 12:4).
         (d) "So we, being many, are **one body/church** in Christ" (Rom. 12:5).
         (e) "As **the body/church is one** and has many members, but all the members of that **one body/church**, being many, are **one body/church**, so also is Christ" (1 Cor. 12:12).
         (f) "For by one Spirit we were all baptized into **one body/church**" (1 Cor. 12:13).
         (g) "But now indeed there are many members, yet **one body/church**" (1 Cor. 12:20).
         (h) "That He might reconcile them both to God in **one body/church**" (Eph. 2:16).
         (i) "...to which also you were called in **one body/church**" (Col. 3:15).
      5. The singularity of His one church emphasizes the unity that Christ expects it to have.
   B. The designations for the church in the New Testament emphasize its singularity.
      1. The church is the body of Christ (Eph. 1:22-23).
         (a) The body has one Head (Christ)!
         (b) How many "bodies" does the one Head have? One!
      2. The church is the family of God (1 Tim. 3:15).
         (a) The family has one Father (God)!
         (b) How many "families" does the one Father have? One!
         (c) Consider: "A house divided against a house falls" (Luke 11:17).

3. The church is the kingdom of Christ (Col. 1:13).
   (a) The kingdom has one King (Christ)!
   (b) How many "kingdoms" does the one King have? One!
   (c) Consider: "Every kingdom divided against itself is brought to desolation" (Lk. 11:17).
4. The church is the bride of Christ (2 Cor. 11:2; Rom. 7:1-4).
   (a) The bride has one Bridegroom (Christ)!
   (b) How many "brides" does the one Bridegroom have? One!
5. The church is the flock of God (1 Pet. 5:2).
   (a) The flock has "one Shepherd" (Christ) (John 10:16)!
   (b) How many "flocks" does the one Shepherd have? "One" (John 10:16)!
6. The singularity of His one body, one family, one kingdom, one bride and one flock emphasizes the unity that Christ expects it to have.

II. **The Bible Emphasizes Repeatedly the Supreme Importance of Unity Among God's People.**
  A. There is unity among the Godhead.
   1. While there are three distinct personalities, each share the same divine nature, and each exist and function in complete unity as One.
   2. The unity of the Godhead is seen in:
      (a) The creation of the world (Gen. 1:1 + Col. 1:16 + Job 33:4).
      (b) The revelation of Scripture (2 Tim. 3:16 + 1 Pet. 1:11 + 2 Pet. 1:21).
      (c) The salvation of mankind (John 3:16 + Tit. 2:13-14 + John 3:5).
   3. The unity of the Godhead is used as a model for the unity of God's people.
      (a) "...that they all may be one, **as** You, Father, are in Me, and I in You" (John 17:21).
      (b) True unity originated with God! "The Lord our God, Lord is one!" (Deut. 6:4)
  B. The Old Testament emphasized how unity was to be desired and praised.
   1. "Abram said to Lot, 'Please let there be no strife between you and me, and between my herdsmen and your herdsmen; for we are brethren'" (Gen. 13:8).
      (a) "Brethren" should strive for "unity" and seek to avoid "strife."
   2. "Behold, how good and how pleasant it is For brethren to dwell together in unity!" (Psa. 133:1).
      (a) While some things are good but not pleasant or pleasant but not good, "unity" among "brethren" is both good and pleasant.
      (b) When brethren "dwell together in unity," it is simultaneously beneficial and enjoyable.
   3. In a period of spiritual darkness for God's people, when they had "hewn themselves" "broken cisterns that can hold no water" (Jer. 2:13)—a reference to religious division among the Israelites—God pleaded with His people, "Stand in the ways and see, and ask for the old paths, where the good way is, and walk in it" (6:16).
   4. God has always wanted His people to strive for unity!
  C. The Lord prayed for unity (John 17:20-23).
   1. Just hours before His betrayal and crucifixion, Jesus was praying in John 17.
   2. Of utmost importance to Him and deeply imbedded in His soul was the matter of unity.
   3. The focus of this part of Jesus' prayer was that "all [His people] may be one."
      (a) Imagine if Jesus had prayed that all His people might be "two" or "three" or "four hundred." How would that have sounded? Would that make sense?
      (b) The fact that He prayed that they might be "one" is instructional and critical!

4. The scope of this part of Jesus' prayer was "for those who will believe in Me."
   (a) Christ looked down through time and saw all who would be obedient to His Word, and His dying prayer for them was that they might be united.
   (b) He was not praying only for the apostles. He did that specifically in verses 6-19, and then stated, "I do not pray for these alone" in verse 20.
   (c) His prayer was for all who would believe in Him through the words of the apostles.
5. The nature of the unity for which Jesus prayed is found in the word "as."
   (a) "That they all may be one, **as** You, Father, are in Me, and I in You; that they also may be one."
   (b) The unity of the Godhead is the model for the unity of God's people.
   (c) Jesus had taught:
       (1) "I and My Father are one" (John 10:30).
       (2) "I always do those things that please Him" (John 8:29).
   (d) When division is found between the three members of the Godhead, then believers will have found justification for division among God's people.
6. The location of the unity for which Jesus prayed is "in Us."
   (a) True unity cannot exist outside of God or outside of Christ.
   (b) True unity can only exist within a proper relationship with the Godhead.
7. The intended fruit of the unity for which Jesus prayed was to impact the world.
   (a) "...that the world may believe that You sent Me."
   (b) When unity exists among God's people, it can lead to faith and fidelity.
   (c) When disunity and division exists among God's people, it leads to infidelity.
   (d) Look at the faithless condition of our world, then look at the religious division that permeates this globe. Does the second condition (i.e., religious division and denominationalism) have anything to do with the first (i.e., rampant infidelity)?
   (e) Unity among God's people is an effective tool against disbelief in the world.
8. Did Jesus pray for "one" and then establish multiple churches, thus creating division?
   (a) To ask is to answer! He did not pray for or establish more than "one" church, nor does He approve of such!
   (b) Jesus' dying prayer was (and is) a sharp censure against a plurality of churches!
9. Are we working toward the unity for which Christ prayed?

D. The Lord demands unity (1 Cor. 1:10).
   1. Paul makes it clear that the command is based upon the authority/name of Christ!
   2. The authority of Christ calls for His people to:
      (a) "All speak the same thing."
         (1) While men may claim it cannot be done, God demands that it can...and it must!
         (2) To "speak the same thing" can only happen by going back to the "same" source – the name/authority of Christ (cf. Col. 3:17).
         (3) True unity is founded upon God's Word and the New Testament pattern!
      (b) Have "no divisions among" them.
         (1) The Lord did not approve of "one" division or "two" divisions or "four hundred" divisions.
         (2) The Lord requires that there be "no divisions."
      (c) "Be perfectly joined together."
         (1) Be one as the Father and the Son are one!
      (d) "Be perfectly joined together in the same mind."
         (1) Be united in the mind of Christ (cf. Phil. 2:5).

                (e) "Be perfectly joined together in the same judgment."
                    (1) Be united in the same purpose and intentions.
            3. A similar admonition is found in Philippians 2:2, where Christians are called to be "like-minded, having the same love, being of one accord, of one mind."
            4. Religious division is contrary to the desire and the authority of Christ!
    E. The Lord died for unity (Eph. 2:13-22).
        1. The effectual action emphasized in this passage is the death of Christ:
            (a) "The blood of Christ" (2:13).
            (b) "In His flesh" (2:15).
            (c) "Through the cross" (2:16).
        2. The effectual result of the death of Christ is the unity of believers in Christ.
            (a) The only place where unity is possible is "in Christ Jesus" (2:13).
                (1) "There is neither Jew nor Greek, there is neither slave nor free, there is neither male nor female; for you are all one **in Christ Jesus**" (Gal. 3:28).
            (b) "In Christ," there is no longer "two" but "one."
                (1) "...**one** new man from the **two**" (2:15).
                (2) The "wall of **separation**" has been "broken down" (2:14).
                (3) "The **enmity**" has been "abolished" and "put to death" (2:15-16).
                (4) Those who were "afar off" and those "who were near" "**both** have access by **one** Spirit to the Father" "**through** Christ" (2:17-18).
            (c) "In Christ," there is to be unity of all believers in one body.
                (1) Christ "made both **one**" (2:14).
                (2) Christ "create[d] in Himself **one** new man" (2:15).
                (3) Christ "reconcile[d] them both to God in **one** body" (2:16).
            (d) "In Christ," true unity involves "togetherness."
                (1) Those once separated are "being joined **together**" (2:21).
                (2) Those once separated are "being built **together**" (2:22).
                (3) Those once separated are "**fellow** citizens with the saints" (2:19).
        3. The effectual result of the unity of all believers is:
            (a) Together having "...access by one Spirit to the Father" (2:18).
            (b) "Growing into a holy temple in the Lord" (2:21).
            (c) Becoming "a dwelling place of God in the Spirit" (2:22).
        4. Disunity among believers goes against the sacrificial, loving death of our Savior!
    F. The Lord planned for unity (Eph. 4:1-6).
        1. "There is **one body** and **one Spirit**, just as you were called in **one hope** of your calling; **one Lord, one faith, one baptism; one God** and Father of all, who is above all, and through all, and in you all."
        2. This point and this passage are further studied on page 110.
    G. The early church enjoyed and exemplified unity.
        1. "Now all who believed were together, and had all things in common...So continuing daily with one accord in the temple, and breaking bread from house to house, they ate their food with gladness and simplicity of heart, praising God and having favor with all the people" (Acts 2:44-47).
        2. "Now the multitude of those who believed were of one heart and one soul; neither did anyone say that any of the things he possessed was his own, but they had all things in common...And great grace was upon them all" (Acts 4:32-33).

3. The unity of the church in those early days:
   (a) Opened doors for evangelism.
   (b) Strengthened brethren in their faith.
   (c) Prompted selfless service within the church.
   (d) Encouraged brethren in the midst of trials and persecutions.
4. The Lord's church today can experience those same benefits of being united in Christ!
H. Unity among God's people is not merely a "wish" or a "dream" or a "best-case scenario."
   1. It is more than just something to be desired!
   2. Unity among God's people is absolutely necessary to be pleasing to God!

III. **The Religious World Is Anything But United Today.**
  A. It is hard to pinpoint an exact number, as the definitions of terms vary so widely. But, one can fairly and conservatively approximate that there are:
    1. Thousands of religious groups in the world today.
    2. Thousands of denominational (so-called "Christian") groups in the world today.
  B. Each of these denominations:
    1. Wears a different name than other denominations.
    2. Organizes itself in some way different than other denominations.
    3. Believes, teaches and practices some doctrine different than other denominations.
    4. Must have something that sets it apart from other denominations, otherwise, it would have no purpose to exist separate from some other denomination.
    5. Has contributed to creating a world of confusion when it comes to Christianity.
  C. By definition, a denomination indicates separating into various divisions by name.
    1. Religiously, a denomination is "a religious body or sect that subscribes to a particular set of doctrinal tenets and is set apart from other religious groups by its name and human creed" (Wayne Jackson, *Bible Words and Theological Terms,* p. 42).
  D. Therefore, by definition, denominationalism is the absolute antithesis of unity.
    1. There can be no such thing as united division.
    2. There can be no such thing as "Christian union" that resists "unity in Christ."
  E. Denominations make claims like:
    1. "We can't all see the Bible alike, so divisions are a natural result."
    2. "Let's not focus on our differences but on common ground that we can find."
    3. "One church is as good as another. Who can say which one is right?"
    4. "Go to the church of your choice, but go to church."
    5. "We are just on different roads to the same place—heaven."
    6. "All the churches just make up the one church anyway."
  F. Can denominationalism be defended? Is there anything wrong with denominationalism? Should Christians today be overly concerned with the unity of the church?
     Is unity of Christians really that big of a deal? Is unity even possible?
     Is division (as represented in present-day denominationalism) acceptable to God?

IV. **The Causes of Division and Disunity Are Numerous and Diverse.**
  A. Each denomination has arisen under different circumstances and for different reasons.
    1. While we cannot examine (or perhaps even know) every circumstance and every reason, it would behoove us to understand generally what has led to division.
    2. Understanding some causes of division can help us to be more circumspect and to be more focused in our efforts for unity in Christ.
    3. Generally speaking, here are some causes for the religious division spreading today.

B. Division results from a de-emphasis on doctrine as "not all that important."
   1. The mistaken belief that "We can't all see the Bible alike" has led many to avoid taking a stand on certain (or sometimes, any) matters of doctrine.
   2. However, de-emphasizing doctrine runs counter to the entire New Testament.
      (a) Jesus said, "You shall know **the truth**, and **the truth** shall make you free" (Jn. 8:32).
      (b) Timothy was warned, "Take heed...to **the doctrine**" (1 Tim. 4:16).
      (c) John denounced those who would transgress "**the doctrine** of Christ" (2 John 9).
      (d) Christians are warned not to "pervert **the gospel** of Christ" (Gal. 1:6-9).
      (e) Christians are to recognize when someone is teaching "contrary to **the doctrine** which you learned" (Rom. 16:17).
   3. As unthinkable as it might be, the Lord warned that this would happen:
      (a) "...Some will depart from **the faith**..." (1 Tim. 4:1).
      (b) "...They will not endure **the sound doctrine**...and will turn away their ears from **the truth**, and turn aside unto fables" (2 Tim. 4:3-4, ASV).
   4. When man de-emphasizes doctrine, it leads to division, because God places a strong emphasis on holding true to "the doctrine" of Christ and the New Testament.
   5. When man departs from the divine pattern, it leads to division.
C. Division results from an over-emphasis on manmade doctrines and traditions.
   1. Although Scripture warns against "adding to" or "taking from" the Word of God (Rev. 22:18-19), that is precisely what has led to the religious division prevailing today.
   2. As unthinkable as it might be, the Lord warned that this would happen:
      (a) "They will heap up for themselves teachers" (2 Tim. 4:1-4).
      (b) "Men will rise up, speaking perverse things" (Acts 20:29-31).
      (c) "If anyone preaches any other gospel to you..." (Gal. 1:6-9).
      (d) "...giving heed to deceiving spirits and doctrines of demons" (1 Tim. 4:1-3).
      (e) "...giving heed to...commandments of men who turn from the truth" (Tit. 1:14).
      (f) "...why...do you subject yourselves to regulations—according to the commandments and doctrines of men?" (Col. 2:18-20).
   3. The Lord warned about following and honoring men rather than Christ, which leads to division.
      (a) In Corinth, different ones were saying, "'I am of Paul,' or 'I am of Apollos,' or 'I am of Cephas,' or 'I am of Christ'" (1 Cor. 1:12).
      (b) We cannot wear other names while attempting to serve Christ (1 Cor. 1:13-14).
      (c) The apostles spoke plainly, "We must obey God rather than men" (Acts 5:29).
   4. Jesus readily identified and condemned those who would elevate their own teachings and traditions above the doctrine of Christ, which leads to division.
      (a) Jesus asked, "Why do you also transgress the commandment of God because of your tradition?" (Matt. 15:3).
      (b) "These people draw near to Me with their mouth, And honor Me with their lips, But their heart is far from Me. And in vain they worship Me, Teaching as doctrines the commandments of men" (Matt. 15:8-9).
   5. When man advances his own doctrines over the doctrine of Christ, division will result!
   6. When man makes (and imposes) laws where God has made no laws, division will result!
   7. When man permits that which God does not authorize, division will result!
   8. When man seeks to follow the traditions of his ancestors rather than the doctrine of Christ, division will result!

9. When man holds to the teachings of certain preachers or scholars rather than the doctrine of Christ, division will result!
10. When man strives to emulate the ways of the "big, successful churches" rather than the doctrine of Christ, division will result!
11. When man is more interested in "how he sees things" rather than how Christ "sees things," division will result!

D. Division results, fundamentally, every time that the authority of Christ is rejected!
   1. When one rejects the doctrine of Christ, the gospel of Christ, the word of Christ, the pattern of Christ, the authority of Christ – unity in Christ is completely forfeited!

V. **As Equally As Unity Is Commanded on God's People, the Bible Strongly Condemns Division!**
   A. By specifically emphasizing unity, division (by implication) is condemned.
      1. However, God does more than imply the sinfulness of division, He explicitly states it!
      2. In Scripture, God makes it abundantly clear that His people must not be divided!
   B. God hates division and those who cause it!
      1. "…The Lord hates…one who sows discord among brethren" (Prov. 6:16-19).
   C. God condemns division within the church!
      1. "…that there be no divisions among you" (1 Cor. 1:10).
   D. God identifies division as a result of carnal, fleshly desires and lifestyles.
      1. "And I, brethren, could not speak to you as to spiritual people but as to carnal, as to babes in Christ. I fed you with milk and not with solid food; for until now you were not able to receive it, and even now you are still not able; for you are still carnal. For where there are envy, strife, and divisions among you, are you not carnal and behaving like mere men?" (1 Cor. 3:1-3).
   E. God warns of the destructiveness of division.
      1. "If a kingdom is divided against itself, that kingdom cannot stand. And if a house is divided against itself, that house cannot stand" (Mark 3:24-25).
   F. God identifies divisiveness as a work of the flesh which will cost a man his soul.
      1. "Now the works of the flesh are evident: …enmity, strife, jealousy, fits of anger, rivalries, dissensions, divisions… I warn you, as I warned you before, that those who do such things will not inherit the kingdom of God" (Gal. 5:19-21, ESV).
   G. God proclaims that division is contrary to the doctrine of Christ, and He commands that those who cause divisions contrary to the gospel are to be avoided.
      1. "Now I urge you, brethren, note those who cause divisions and offenses, contrary to the doctrine which you learned, and avoid them. For those who are such do not serve our Lord Jesus Christ, but their own belly, and by smooth words and flattering speech deceive the hearts of the simple" (Rom. 16:17-18).
   H. God commands Christians not to show any approval to those who would cause division.
      1. "Whoever transgresses and does not abide in the doctrine of Christ does not have God. He who abides in the doctrine of Christ has both the Father and the Son. If anyone comes to you and does not bring this doctrine, do not receive him into your house nor greet him; for he who greets him shares in his evil deeds" (2 John 9-11).
   I. God directs Christians to avoid those who would bring division.
      1. "Reject a divisive man after the first and second admonition, knowing that such a person is warped and sinning, being self-condemned" (Tit. 3:10-11).
   J. God specifically teaches that CHRIST IS NOT DIVIDED!
      1. "For it has been declared to me concerning you, my brethren, by those of Chloe's household, that there are contentions among you. Now I say this, that each of you

says, 'I am of Paul,' or 'I am of Apollos,' or 'I am of Cephas,' or 'I am of Christ.' Is Christ divided? Was Paul crucified for you? Or were you baptized in the name of Paul?" (1 Cor. 1:11-13).
	K. God is not the author of confusion! Where there is religious confusion and division, God is not the cause and God is not pleased!
		1. "God is not the author of confusion but of peace, as in all the churches" (1 Cor. 14:33).
	L. Man (especially children of God) must learn and deeply appreciate:
		1. The seriousness and the sinfulness of division!
		2. The extreme importance of unity among God's people!
	M. With the clarity and the force of God's condemnation of division among His people, how can anyone seek to justify or tolerate disunity and denominationalism?
VI. **The Bible Warns Against False Doctrine and False Teachers.**
	A. To call someone a "false teacher" today is not popular, but the Lord repeatedly warned against and rejected false teachers.
	B. To call a teaching a "false doctrine" today is not popular, but the Lord repeatedly warned against and condemned false doctrines.
	C. Consider this for a moment: If God repeatedly warned against and condemned false teachers and false doctrines:
		1. Then true doctrine and true teachers must exist and be readily identifiable.
		2. Then there must be a clear, sharp line of distinction between truth and error.
		3. Then God's people must not seek to blur the line between truth and error.
		4. Then true unity can only prevail when God's people heed His warnings, stand for truth, reject error and follow His ways rather than man's.
	D. The Bible warns against (list compiled by Warren 241-242):
		1. "False prophets" (Matt. 24:24-26).
		2. "Grievous wolves" who speak "perverse things" (Acts 20:29-30).
		3. "False apostles" (2 Cor. 11:13-15).
		4. Those who, "by the trickery of men, in the cunning craftiness," seek to carry men about "with every wind of doctrine" by "deceitful plotting" (Eph. 4:14).
		5. Those who "pervert the gospel" (Gal. 1:6-9).
		6. "False prophets" who "secretly bring in destructive heresies" (2 Pet. 2:1).
		7. Those who teach the "doctrines of demons" (1 Tim. 4:1-5).
		8. Those who teach the "fables" (2 Tim. 4:1-5).
		9. "False prophets, who come to you in sheep's clothing, but inwardly they are ravenous wolves" (Matt. 7:15).
		10. "False apostles, deceitful workers," who try to make themselves appear to be "apostles of Christ," but who are really "ministers" of Satan (2 Cor. 11:13-15).
		11. Those who do not "walk by the same rule" (the gospel), for "they are the enemies of the cross of Christ: whose end is destruction" (Phil. 3:15-19).
		12. "False brethren secretly brought in (who came in by stealth)" (Gal. 2:4).
		13. "Many false prophets have gone out into the world" (1 John 4:1).
	E. Therefore, the Bible teaches and commands God's people:
		1. To not "bear those who are evil," but to test "those who say they are apostles and are not" (Rev. 2:2).
		2. To "stand fast in the faith" (1 Cor. 16:13).
		3. To "contend earnestly for the faith" (Jude 3).
		4. To be "set for the defense of the gospel" (Phil. 1:16).

5. To "always be ready to give a defense" concerning the hope we have (1 Pet. 3:15).
6. To "know the truth" and to "walk in the truth" (John 8:32; 2 John 1-4).
7. To demand and to teach "the whole counsel of God" (Acts 20:27).
8. To "test" every religious teacher, in light of the Scriptures, to see "whether they are of God" (1 John 4:1; Acts 17:11), because many such teachers are false teachers.
9. "Mark" and "avoid" those who teach false doctrines, causing divisions (Rom. 16:17).

F. True unity can only exist where truth reigns supreme!
1. Unity cannot exist on the basis of error, for error contradicts itself and has no unity.
2. One may attempt to have "union" with false teachers, but that is not Bible "unity."
3. Bible unity demands adherence to the truth of God and rejection of every false way.

VII. The Bible Reveals God's Plan for Unity and Teaches How to Successfully Attain It.
A. Human attempts at unity, apart from God's plan, always have and always will fail.
1. Most religious men desire unity, but their attempts at achieving it through unauthorized means have never been (and never will be) successful.
2. Man has attempted unity by setting up a human as the "Head of the Church."
   (a) But Christ is the only head of the church (Col. 1:18).
   (b) And Christ is the One who has all authority (Matt. 28:18).
   (c) Unity can only be achieved by laying aside any human head of the church and turning to Christ!
3. Man has attempted unity by writing out his own "Church Creeds."
   (a) Rather than promote unity, human creeds promote division.
   (b) When one religious group has their "Church Creed," and another their "Church Manual," and another their "Church Discipline," and another their "Confession of Faith," and another their "Catechism," division will be created and will prevail.
   (c) God's Word is the only authoritative source of truth for man today (Col. 3:17).
   (d) Unity can only be achieved by laying aside any human creed for the church and turning to God's Word!
4. Man has attempted unity by seeking justification for disunity in Scripture.
   (a) Despite God's clear call to believe the same thing (John 17:20-21; Eph. 4:5), teach the same thing (1 Cor. 1:10; 2 John 9) and practice the same thing (1 Cor. 4:6; Col. 3:17), there are those who still attempt to justify the existence of modern-day denominationalism (disunity) through erroneous use of Biblical text.
   (b) For example, some have tried to teach that denominational churches are the "branches" in John 15:1-8.
      (1) But, the "branches" are those who are "in" Christ (15:2, 4, 5, 6, 7). Only those who have followed God's plan of salvation and have been immersed "for the remission of sins" (Acts 2:38) are ones who have been "baptized into Christ" (Rom. 6:3; Gal. 3:27) and are "in Christ." Those are the "branches."
      (2) The "branches" are those who have the "words" of Christ "abiding" in them" (15:7). One cannot have the words of Christ abiding in him and be consistently disobedient to those words (in a man-made denomination) at the same time.
      (3) The "branches" are those who "abide in Christ." Only those who "abide in the word of Christ" (John 8:31) can "abide in Christ."
      (4) Here's the key in John 15 that proves the "branches" are not denominations. Jesus explicitly states that the "branches" are individual Christians.
         (i) "**You** are the branches" (15:5)! Jesus was NOT talking to denominational churches in John 15. The "you" was/is His disciples.

(ii) **You** will be my disciples" (15:8)! The "branches" are Jesus' individual "disciples"! Disciples are those who have been baptized into Christ (Matt. 28:19) and are faithfully abiding in and obeying His Word (John 8:31-32).
- (c) In another example, some have tried to teach denominational churches are the "members" of the "one body" in 1 Corinthians 12:12-27.
  - (1) But, the "members" of the "one body" are those who have been immersed "for the remission of sins" (Acts 2:38), having been "baptized into one body" (1 Cor. 12:13). Only these are "members" of the "one body."
  - (2) This very context condemns division of "the one body," teaching that "God composed the body...so that there may be no division in the body" (12:24-25). Denominationalism, by definition, is division; therefore, this passage cannot possibly be justifying or defending religious division.
  - (3) Here's the key in 1 Corinthians 12 that proves the "members" are not denominations. Paul explicitly states that the "members" are "**individually** members" of "the body of Christ" (12:27). The focus is on individual Christians.
- (d) Unity can only be achieved by laying aside failed justifications for unity and accepting that unity cannot be found in denominational churches!
5. Man has attempted unity by ignoring and tolerating differing doctrines, compromising and "agreeing to disagree."
   - (a) In order to remove barriers to unity, some have sought a "lowest common denominator" of agreement (i.e., some basic common ground), and then deemed other "doctrinal" differences as merely differences of "opinion."
   - (b) They make statements like:
     - (1) "Who can know for sure who is right and who is wrong?"
     - (2) "Who has the right to tell someone else that his doctrine is wrong?"
     - (3) "Differences in doctrine can be a good thing. It opens the door to more people."
     - (4) "One should be free to believe and practice whatever he feels is right in his heart."
     - (5) "We are all serving the same God, reading the same Bible. That's all that matters."
   - (c) But, unity at the expense of truth is (1) not unity and (2) not worth seeking.
   - (d) True unity is based upon true doctrine, not upon ignoring true doctrine.
   - (e) Paul directly addressed this type of "unity" and outright condemned it.
     - (1) "I marvel that you are turning away so soon from Him who called you in the grace of Christ, to a different gospel, which is not another; but there are some who trouble you and want to pervert the gospel of Christ. But even if we, or an angel from heaven, preach any other gospel to you than what we have preached to you, let him be accursed. As we have said before, so now I say again, if anyone preaches any other gospel to you than what you have received, let him be accursed" (Gal. 1:6-9).
   - (f) Unity can only be achieved by laying aside manmade doctrines and truly turning to unity of doctrine and practice as found in Scripture!
B. God's desire for unity does not mean that He approves of all unity.
  1. There is some unity which God condemns—specifically any unity with sin or error.
  2. There is actually some division which God expects—division from sin and error.
  3. Christians are instructed:

(a) "Come out from among them and be separate" (2 Cor. 6:17).
(b) "Have no fellowship with the unfruitful works of darkness, but rather expose them" (Eph. 5:11).
(c) "Not to keep company with anyone named a brother, who is sexually immoral, or covetous, or an idolater, or a reviler, or a drunkard, or an extortioner" (1 Cor. 5:11).
(d) "If anyone teaches otherwise and does not consent to wholesome words, even the words of our Lord Jesus Christ, and to the doctrine which accords with godliness...From such withdraw yourself" (1 Tim. 6:3-5).
4. God is not interested in unity at any price!

C. God's plan for unity requires (#1): Being "in Christ."
1. Carefully note where Jesus, in His prayer, said true unity exists: "...that they all may be one...that they also may be one **in Us**" (John 17:20-21).
2. One must first be "in Christ" in order to experience the unity approved by God.
3. One enters "into Christ" by being "baptized into Christ" (Rom. 6:3; Gal. 3:27).
4. When two people—whoever they are, wherever they live, whenever they live—both follow God's plan of salvation and are baptized "into Christ" "for the remission of sins" (Acts 2:38), those two people are both:
(a) "Baptized into one body" (1 Cor. 12:13).
(b) "Reconcile(d)...to God in one body" (Eph. 2:16).
(c) "Added" by God to His church (Acts 2:47).
(d) Equally in the family of God (Gal. 3:26-27; John 3:3-5).
(e) In unity with God.
(f) In unity with each other.
5. Only when one has been Scripturally reconciled to God is he then reconciled with fellow believers (Eph. 2:13-22).
6. If one does not follow God's plan of salvation and is not baptized "into Christ" "for the remission of sins," then he is not (and cannot be) in unity with God or in unity with other Christians.

D. God's plan for unity requires (#2): Faithfully walking in the light.
1. Once united with Christ and fellow believers, that unity must be maintained.
(a) It is maintained by "walking in the light" of the gospel of Christ (1 John 1:7).
(b) It is maintained by "being like-minded, having the same love, being of one accord, of one mind," doing "nothing...through selfish ambition or conceit, but in lowliness of mind...esteem[ing] others better than" self (Phil. 2:2-3).
(c) It is maintained by living and practicing agape love (1 Cor. 13:4-7).
(d) It is maintained by "abounding in the work of the Lord" (1 Cor. 15:58).
2. John wrote, "We say that we have fellowship with Him, and walk in darkness, we lie and do not practice the truth. But if we walk in the light as He is in the light, we have fellowship with one another, and the blood of Jesus Christ His Son cleanses us from all sin" (1 John 1:6-7).
3. When we walk in harmony with God's Word, we maintain unity with God and with other baptized believers.
4. But, sin (walking in darkness) separates us from God (Isa. 59:1-2).
5. If a child of God so chooses to walk (not in the light) in the darkness of sin, he severs himself from his unity with God (cf. Gal. 5:4), and therefore, severs himself from his acceptable unity with fellow believers.

E. God's plan for unity requires (#3): Speaking the same thing—the doctrine of Christ.
1. The early church "continued steadfastly in the apostles' doctrine" (Acts 2:42).
2. God's Word is the only basis for unity, for it is the only authority that binds Christians together in the one faith and one practice that are acceptable to God!
   (a) The major cause of division today is primarily a doctrinal one.
   (b) It is impossible for ones holding differing creeds and doctrines to be united.
   (c) True unity requires eliminating human doctrines and uniting on Biblical doctrines.
3. Only by "speaking the same thing" can we truly have "no divisions" (1 Cor. 1:10).
4. Only through Christ and His word can we attain the unity for which He prayed.
5. By inspiration of the Holy Spirit, Paul pleaded with Christians "to keep the unity of the Spirit in the bond of peace" (Eph. 4:3). He then gave a seven-point platform for maintaining unity (4:4-6). (A specific note of unity is included with each of the seven points below. This has been a common way to emphasize the unity inherent within each point, but it is unknown who first suggested these explanations.)
   (a) "There is one body" – Unity of Organization.
      (1) Christ is the head of one church (cf. 1:22-23; Col. 1:18; 1 Cor. 12:20).
   (b) "There is one Spirit" – Unity of Life/Guidance.
      (1) Christ sent the Holy Spirit to give direction and guidance for life, and it is in the Bible where the Spirit has revealed "all things that pertain to life and godliness" (2 Pet. 1:3; cf. John 14:26; 16:13; Jude 3).
   (c) "There is one hope" – Unity of Expectation/Desire/Purpose.
      (1) "Christ in you" is the "hope of glory" (Col. 1:27); thus, our hope of heaven is our sure and steadfast "anchor of the soul" (Heb. 6:19), because Christ has entered there first that we might follow Him.
   (d) "There is one Lord" – Unity of Authority.
      (1) Christ has "all authority" (Matt. 28:18) and is "Lord of all" (Acts 10:36). True unity is possible because there is only one authority and not a diversity of authorities (which would lead to division).
      (2) It has been noted by some that in this seven-point platform for unity, Christ (i.e., "one Lord") is right in the center of the list, infused in the entire list.
   (e) "There is one faith" – Unity of Message.
      (1) Christ has only one message, and it is that one message which makes us "complete" (2 Tim. 3:16-17), which we must "speak" (1 Cor. 1:10), and for which we must "contend earnestly" (Jude 3).
      (2) "The faith" is "the gospel" (Gal. 1:11+23), of which there is only one (Gal. 1:6-9).
      (3) Many faiths cannot produce unity but only division. One faith produces unity.
   (f) "There is one baptism" – Unity of Practice.
      (1) Christ taught that baptism is essential for being "saved" (Mark 16:16) and to "enter the kingdom" (John 3:5).
      (2) The baptism of the New Testament is an immersion/burial (Rom. 6:4; Col. 2:12); "into the name of the Father, the Son and the Holy Spirit" (Matt. 28:19); "for the remission of sins" (Acts 2:38); as the only means of getting "into Christ" (Rom. 6:3; Gal. 3:27).
   (g) "There is one God" – Unity of Worship.
      (1) Christ taught that there is only one God (Mark 12:29; John 17:3) and only one way to acceptably worship Him (John 4:24), and that acceptable worship is

                    tied to "truth" (John 17:17). There cannot be many ways to worship when there is only one God to (i.e., one object of) worship and only one "truth."
                (h) In order to "keep the unity of the Spirit in the bond of peace" (Eph. 4:3), we must:
                    (1) Teach and hold fast to this seven-point platform for unity.
                    (2) "Walk worthy of the calling" of Christ (4:1).
                    (3) Have a spirit of "all lowliness and gentleness, with longsuffering" (4:2).
        6. For true unity to be established, to exist and to prevail:
            (a) We must speak the same thing (1 Cor. 1:10).
            (b) Teach the same thing in every place (1 Cor. 4:17; 7:17).
            (c) Sow the same seed (Luke 8:11).
    F. Scriptural unity necessitates:
        1. Complete acceptance and adherence to the truths taught in Scripture.
        2. Complete abandonment of every teaching and practice not authorized in Scripture.
        3. Complete rejection of every unscriptural name, creed, doctrine, form of worship and church government.
        4. Giving up human doctrines and "churches" and uniting on the doctrines and church of the Bible.
        5. Recognizing that Scriptural unity is not a union of or a union with false teaching.

VIII. God Is Deeply Concerned about the Unity of His Church!
    A. Division is not of God.
        1. Division brings ruin (Matt. 12:25), destroys peace (Jas. 3:14-17), displeases God (Prov. 6:16-19) and stands in the way of people obeying Christ (Rom. 16:17).
        2. Unity is not possible when we do not know God's Word, accept God's Word, respect God's Word, obey God's Word, teach God's Word and defend God's Word.
    B. Unity is possible!
        1. It requires going back to the Bible—back before all of the departures and perversions.
        2. It requires speaking the same thing—speaking where the Bible speaks.
        3. It requires being of one mind toward one another—as guided by Scripture.
        4. It requires submitting to Christ and His will—obeying Him rather than man.
    C. Jesus prayed for unity.
        1. Are we praying for unity, as desired and depicted by Him?
        2. After praying for it, are we striving for it, in order to answer that prayer?
    D. God is deeply concerned about the unity of His church! Are you?

Recommended Resources

Books

Brownlow, Leroy. *Why I Am a Member of the Church of Christ.* Fort Worth: Brownlow Publishing, 1973.

Cloer, Eddie. *What Is "The Church"?* Searcy, AR: Resource Publications, 1993.

Jennings, Alvin, ed. *Introducing the Church of Christ.* Fort Worth: Star Bible, 1981.

Winkler, Wendell. *The Church Everybody Is Asking About.* Tuscaloosa, AL: Winkler Publications, 1988.

Articles

Bailey, George W. "God's Plea for Unity—Ephesians 4." *The Church and Fellowship (Freed-Hardeman College Lectures).* Ed. William Woodson. Henderson, TN: Freed-Hardeman College, 1974. 328-334.

Bradley, C.W. "Unity: Importance of Unity." *Freedom: Heritage, Accomplishments, and Prospects in Christ (Freed-Hardeman College Lectures).* Ed. William Woodson. Henderson, TN: Freed-Hardeman College, 1976. 375-377.

---. "Unity: Causes of Disunity." *Freedom: Heritage, Accomplishments, and Prospects in Christ (Freed-Hardeman College Lectures).* Ed. William Woodson. Henderson, TN: Freed-Hardeman College, 1976. 378-380.

---. "Unity: Some Human Approaches to Unity." *Freedom: Heritage, Accomplishments, and Prospects in Christ (Freed-Hardeman College Lectures).* Ed. William Woodson. Henderson, TN: Freed-Hardeman College, 1976. 381-383.

---. "Unity: The Divine Plan for Unity." *Freedom: Heritage, Accomplishments, and Prospects in Christ (Freed-Hardeman College Lectures).* Ed. William Woodson. Henderson, TN: Freed-Hardeman College, 1976. 384-386.

Cloer, Eddie. "The Unity of the Church." *What Is "The Church"?* Searcy, AR: Resource Publications, 1993. 147-157.

Cogdill, Roy E. "Unity." *New Testament Church.* Fairmount, IN: Truth Magazine Bookstore, 1982. 55-64.

Highers, Alan E. "Foundations of the Unity of All Believers." *The Foundations (Spiritual Sword Lectureship).* Ed. Gary McDade. Memphis: Getwell church of Christ, 2004. 407-419.

Jackson, Wayne. "A Divine Platform for Unity." *ChristianCourier.com* https://www.christiancourier.com/articles/546-divine-platform-for-christian-unity-a

Robinson, Garland. "For Providing the Unity Which Christ Demands." *The All-Sufficiency of the Bible. (Spiritual Sword Lectureship).* Ed. Gary McDade. Memphis: Getwell church of Christ, 2000. 379-393.

Warren, Thomas B. "The Bases of Fellowship." *The Church and Fellowship (Freed-Hardeman College Lectures).* Ed. William Woodson. Henderson, TN: Freed-Hardeman College, 1974. 32-42.

---."The Church of Christ—Its Unity." *The Church of Christ (Freed-Hardeman College Lectures).* Ed. Thomas B. Warren. Nashville: Gospel Advocate, 1971. 237-249.

Winkler, Wendell. "Do Members of the Church of Christ Believe There Is Only One Church? If So, How Do you Know When You Find It?" *The Church Everybody Is Asking About.* Tuscaloosa, AL: Winkler Publications, 1988. 35-41.

Periodicals

The Spiritual Sword. July 1981. "The Unity Which Christ Demands."

Lesson 11: Christians and Denominationalism

I. **This Subject Must Be Approached Both Carefully and Biblically.**
   A. The subject of denominationalism is one that demands great care when addressing.
      1. Denominationalism is deeply engrained and normalized in the world today.
         (a) The view of some: "My church is a part of me. No one has a right to question what we teach or what we practice."
         (b) The view of some: "As there are different schools for different needs and different stores for different needs, there are different churches for different needs."
      2. To question anything about denominationalism, in some minds, is to question something as foundationally accepted as "red means stop" and "green means go."
      3. This is a subject that requires great care and humility.
   B. The subject of denominationalism is one that demands Biblical truth when addressing.
      1. There is no subject within religion that should not be approached first and foremost with the question, "What does the Bible say?"
      2. The Bible is our only standard of authority in everything we say and do (Col. 3:17).
      3. The Bible teaches us to put "all things" to the "test" (1 Thess. 5:21-22).
      4. "All things" would certainly include even present-day denominationalism.
      5. This is a subject that requires an open Bible.
   C. The intent of this study is to be careful in its wording and its approach, but it is the duty of all Bible students to be devoted entirely to a "Thus saith the Lord."
   D. The design of this study is to answer some key questions relating to denominationalism.

II. **What Are Denominations?**
   A. The word "denomination" is defined <u>generally</u> as:
      1. "A name or designation, especially one for a class of things."
      2. "A class or kind of persons or things distinguished by a specific name."
      3. "The act of naming or designating a person or thing" (dictionary.com).
   B. The word "denomination" is defined <u>religiously</u> as:
      1. "A large group of religious congregations united under a common faith and name, usually organized under a single administrative and legal hierarchy" (American Heritage College Dictionary).
      2. "A religious group whose beliefs differ in some ways from other groups in the same religion" (Cambridge Dictionary).
      3. "A section of the Christian religion with its own beliefs and practices" (Macmillan Dictionary).
      4. "A religious body or sect that subscribes to a particular set of doctrinal tenants and is set apart from other religious groups by its name and human creed" (Wayne Jackson, *Bible Words and Theological Terms,* p. 42).
   C. In its <u>general</u> meaning, "denomination" indicates separating or dividing by name into various groups or sections. (This is often used of separating different currency values.)
      1. Separating.   Dividing.   Sect-ions.   Different names and values.
   D. In its <u>religious</u> meaning, "denomination" indicates separating or dividing by name into various religious groups or sections, based upon differing beliefs and practices.
      1. Separating.   Dividing.   Sect-ions.   Different beliefs and practices.
   E. Thus far, we are merely trying to define and understand the term.
      1. Question: Does this sound like a Biblical term or Biblical concept?
      2. Question: What do you suppose the Bible might teach about denominationalism?

III. Where Did Denominations Originate?
A. Consider this thought for a moment (to be developed more fully in subsequent points):
1. There were no denominations in the pages of the New Testament.
2. There were no denominations in the beginning of the church in the first century.
3. Therefore, denominations must have come along later.
4. Just let that thought rest in your mind for a moment.
B. The Catholic church was established in the early seventh century (around 606 A.D.), almost 600 years after the establishment of the church in the New Testament.
1. Man began to put greater trust in their fellow man, especially in a church hierarchy.
2. Human wisdom wanted a hierarchy to determine the doctrines of the church.
3. Men (humans) were elevated to positions of universal rule over the church.
C. Protestant denominations began to be established in the early sixteenth century, almost 1,500 years after the establishment of the church in the New Testament.
1. A Roman Catholic priest named Martin Luther nailed his "Ninety-Five Theses" against the door of the Catholic church in Germany in 1517. This began what would be called the "Protestant Reformation." All protestant denominations began after this time.
2. Reformers ("protesting" against the Catholic church) began looking for ways to "reform" man's belief systems, which led to various "denominations."
   (a) Thus, the Catholic church is a little more than 1,400 years old.
   (b) The oldest protestant denomination is only 500 years old.
   (c) Think about that, compared to the church which began 2,000 years ago.
3. Protestant efforts led to the establishment and founding of:
   (a) The Lutheran Church by Martin Luther in Germany in 1520.
   (b) The Episcopal Church (Church of England) by Henry VIII in England in 1534.
   (c) The Presbyterian Church by John Knox (influenced by Calvin) in Scotland in 1560.
   (d) The Baptist Church by John Smyth in Holland in 1607.
   (e) The Methodist Church by John Wesley in England in 1738.
   (f) The Mormon Church by Joseph Smith in America 1830.
   (g) The Seventh-Day Adventist Church by Ellen G. White in America in 1863.
   (h) Many other denominations, too numerous to list here.
4. Denominations were named in various ways.
   (a) Some denominations are named after their founder.
      (1) Lutherans are named after Martin Luther.
      (2) Wesleyans are named after John Wesley.
   (b) Some denominations are named after certain doctrines that they emphasize.
      (1) Baptists are named for practicing baptism/immersion.
      (2) Presbyterians are named for the Greek word for elder.
      (3) Episcopalians are named for the Greek word for bishop.
      (4) Seventh-Day Adventists are named for the Sabbath and the second coming.
   (c) Some denominations are named with emphasis on a particular concept.
      (1) "Methodists." "Congregational." "United." "Alliance." "Fellowship."
      (2) "Reformed." "Free Will." "Missionary." "Evangelical." "Assemblies."
      (3) "Apostolic." "Pentecostal." "Metropolitan." "Community."
   (d) Some, noticeably, de-emphasize the word "church" and even the word "Christ."
   (e) Sincere Bible students should ask, "Are any of these names in the Bible?"

D. Hundreds, if not thousands, of denominations have been formed in the last 500 years.
   1. The origin of each denomination since Pentecost is exactly the same: human.
   2. Denominations are the result of man dividing from one group and making a new "church" because of some doctrinal difference or personality conflict.
   3. Sincere Bible students should take the identifying marks of the New Testament church (see pages 92-95 in Lesson 9) and compare those marks with modern-day denominations. Each denomination will be found wanting in one or more areas.
E. Consider the definition of "denomination" again:
   1. Separating or dividing by name into various religious groups or sections, based upon differing beliefs and practices.
      (a) *Separating. Dividing. Sect-ions. Different beliefs and practices.*
   2. Now, instead of finding only "one" church, man has created thousands.
   3. Does this sound like a Biblical concept? Do you suppose that God approves of this?
   4. What do you suppose the Bible might teach about denominationalism?

IV. Are Denominations Acceptable to God?
A. The Lord prophesied of HIS coming church for centuries (Isa. 2:2-3; Dan. 2:44).
B. The Lord promised to build HIS church (Matt. 16:18; Mark 9:1).
C. The Lord established HIS church on Pentecost in A.D. 33 (Mark 9:1; Acts 1:8; 2:41, 47).
D. The Lord clearly affirmed that He has ONE church (Eph. 4:4; 1:22-23; 5:23; 2:16).
E. The Lord revealed His eternal plan (called "the mystery") that all believers (including Jews and Gentiles) would be in "the SAME body," HIS church (Eph. 3:3-6).
F. Sadly, the Lord predicted an apostasy from HIS truth and from HIS church (Acts 20:29-30; 2 Thess. 2:1-4; 1 Tim. 4:1-3; 2 Tim. 4:3-4). Note the Lord's severe, disapproving language:
   1. "Savage wolves will come in among you, not sparing the flock" (Acts 20:29).
   2. "Speaking perverse things" (Acts 20:30).
   3. "Now the Spirit expressly says that…some will depart from the faith" (1 Tim. 4:1).
   4. "Giving heed to deceiving spirits and doctrines of demons" (1 Tim. 4:1).
   5. "Speaking lies in hypocrisy" (1 Tim. 4:2).
   6. "Because they have itching ears, they will heap up for themselves teachers" (2 Tim. 4:3).
   7. "They will turn their ears away from the truth, and be turned aside to fables" (2 Tim. 4:4).
G. As one surveys the modern scene of denominational divisions and multiple "churches," he must come to realize that such is entirely inconsistent with God's original plan!
   1. On the day of Pentecost in Acts 2, when the church was established, there was not a single denomination in existence. Let that sink in! No denominations existed at all!
   2. In the first century, no one belonged to a denomination. There were none to "join"!
   3. God's plan was for "one body/church" (Eph. 4:4; 1:22-23). That is acceptable to Him!
   4. Denominationalism was predicted by God, and at the same time, condemned by God.
H. Denominationalism is unacceptable to God because it violates Jesus' prayer for unity (John 17:20-23).
   1. Jesus did not condone "agreeing to disagree."
   2. Jesus desired all believers to be one in Him.
   3. Jesus paralleled the acceptable unity that is to exist among His people with the unity of the Godhead.
I. Denominationalism is unacceptable to God because it violates the Holy Spirit's command for unity (1 Cor. 1:10).
   1. The Spirit did not condone varying creeds and doctrines peculiar to each denomination.
   2. The Spirit called for zero divisions and all the "same" doctrines.

3. The Spirit left no room for a single denomination.
4. In fact, there is condemnation two verses later toward those who were "denominating" themselves, saying, "'I am of Paul,' or 'I am of Apollos,' or 'I am of Cephas,' or 'I am of Christ'" (1:11-13).

J. Denominationalism is unacceptable to God because it violates God's nature (1 Cor. 14:33).
   1. God did not condone "joining the church of your choice."
   2. "God is not the author of confusion."
   3. God did not create "choices" (and therefore, "confusion") between "churches." That is (and would be) against His nature.
   4. The "choices" and "confusion" were authored by man.

K. Denominationalism is unacceptable to God because it produces unbelievers (John 17:21).
   1. Unity among believers produces other believers.
   2. The inverse must also be true: Division among believers produces unbelievers.
   3. That is precisely what Jesus was saying.

L. Denominationalism is unacceptable to God because it teaches doctrines that are contrary to the teaching of the New Testament (Gal. 1:6-9).
   1. God never approved of the existence of multiple humanly-devised doctrines being espoused by multiple humanly-devised "churches."
   2. Paul warned about "turning away" from Christ and His gospel to a "perverted" gospel, and he then announced the severe consequences of espousing doctrines that are foreign to the New Testament:
      (a) "But even if we, or an angel from heaven, preach any other gospel to you than what we have preached to you, let him be accursed. As we have said before, so now I say again, if anyone preaches any other gospel to you than what you have received, let him be accursed" (Gal. 1:9).
      (b) No angel or apostle could teach another doctrine!
      (c) No angel or apostle could begin a denomination!
      (d) Nor can or should "any man" then or now!
   3. Yet, even a cursory examination of denominationalism reveals that different groups are teaching different things about:
      (a) How to be saved.
      (b) How to worship.
      (c) How many churches should exist.
      (d) What name the church should wear.
      (e) Where the church's headquarters is located.
      (f) What church creed should be followed.
      (g) How one becomes a part of the church.
      (h) What relationship (if any) salvation and the church have.
      (i) How the church should be organized and function.
      (j) Who is going to heaven.
   4. These are not inconsequential matters. These are of the utmost, eternal consequence.
   5. The mere existence of varying doctrines does not somehow justify them.
      (a) Leaders of various denominations have been known to offer praise to God that there are different churches with different doctrines and different practices, so that folks who are searching can find one that fits them and suits their taste.
      (b) Scripture plainly reveals that such is NOT God's evaluation of these varying churches with their varying doctrines and varying practices!

(c) Wayne Jackson asks, "How can it possibly be a righteous situation when people affirm that **mutually exclusive** propositions are **equally acceptable**?"
6. When Paul warned of "turning away" from the gospel to "a different gospel," he stated that it is "not another" gospel (Gal. 1:6-7).
    (a) There is not "another" gospel, as if we have a right to pick and choose.
    (b) There is one gospel, i.e., one faith (Gal. 1:11+23; Phil. 1:27; Eph. 4:5).
    (c) The one gospel does not teach varying doctrines fit to each denomination.
7. The Lord never approved different doctrines or different churches.
M. Consider this simple point: the word "denomination" is not found in the Bible.
    1. Not only is the word not there, one will not find any denomination in the Bible.
    2. That alone should cause serious reflection and examination.
N. Consider the definition of "denomination" again:
    1. Separating or dividing by name into various religious groups or sections, based upon differing beliefs and practices.
        (a) *Separating.   Dividing.   Sect-ions.   Different beliefs and practices.*
    2. This is in no way acceptable to God!
    3. There is not one bit of support for denominationalism anywhere in Scripture.

V. Are There Faithful Christians in Denominations?
A. The fact has been established that there were no denominations in the first century.
    1. That fact should cause great pause and serious contemplation.
    2. There were no denominations because such were not a part of God's acceptable plan.
    3. Can a faithful Christian be found in something that is not found in the Bible?
B. Defining terms is helpful and even vital in answering a Bible question like this one. The key term to properly define is the word "Christian."
    1. People have many different ideas of what a "Christian" is.
        (a) "A Christian is someone who goes to church."
        (b) "A Christian is someone who lives a good, moral life."
        (c) "A Christian is someone who helps, serves and does good to his fellow man."
        (d) "A Christian is someone who believes in Jesus."
        (e) "A Christian is someone who is trying to live different than the rest of the world."
    2. The word "Christian" is found three times in the New Testament.
        (a) "The disciples were first called Christians in Antioch" (Acts 11:26).
            One must be a true disciple of Christ for God to call him/her a "Christian."
        (b) "Agrippa said to Paul, 'You almost persuade me to become a Christian'" (Ac. 26:28).
            There is something required (i.e., steps to take) in order to "become a Christian."
        (c) "If anyone suffers as a Christian, he is…to glorify God in this name" (1 Pet. 4:16).
            A "Christian" wears the "name" of Christ and must live faithfully to that name.
    3. A "Christ-ian" is one who is "of or belongs to" Christ. (Compare the word "Floridian.")
        (a) Thus, the question must be answered, "How can one be 'of or belong to' Christ?"
        (b) One must be "in Christ" and "put on Christ" to be "of Christ" and "belong to" Christ.
        (c) Scripture tells us very plainly when that takes place.
            (1) "For you are all sons of God **through faith** in Christ Jesus. For as many of you as were **baptized into Christ** have **put on Christ**" (Gal. 3:26-27).
            (2) "Or do you not know that as many of us as were **baptized into Christ Jesus** were baptized into His death? Therefore we were buried with Him through baptism into death, that just as Christ was raised from the dead by the glory of the Father, even so we also should walk in newness of life" (Rom. 6:3-4).

(3) The only way "into Christ" is being "baptized into Christ"! Only then can one be "of Christ" and "belong to" Christ (i.e., only then is one a "Christian").
   (d) This is in perfect harmony with the Great Commission of Jesus.
      (1) "He who **believes and is baptized** will be saved" (Mark 16:16).
         (i) When one "believes and is baptized," he/she becomes a Christian.
      (2) "Make disciples of all the nations, **baptizing them** in the name of the Father and of the Son and of the Holy Spirit" (Matt. 28:19).
         (i) The Greek participle "baptizing" indicates how one is made a "disciple."
         (ii) One is made a disciple by being baptized (after he has been taught and believes the gospel, cf. Mark 16:15-16; Rom. 10:14-17).
         (iii) When one becomes a "disciple" by means of Bible baptism, he/she becomes a "Christian" (a "disciple" is a "Christian," Acts 11:26), having taken the proper steps to "become a Christian" (Acts 26:28).
C. The very way that one becomes a "Christ-ian" (belonging to Christ) is the very same way that one becomes a part of Christ's church.
   1. As a penitent believer, one is:
      (a) "Baptized into Christ" (Rom. 6:3; Gal. 3:27).
      (b) "Baptized into one body" (1 Cor. 12:13; cf. Eph. 4:4+1:22-23).
      (c) Baptized into the church of Christ (Acts 2:41-47+5:11).
      (d) Baptized into the family of God (Gal. 3:26-27).
      (e) Baptized into the kingdom of God (John 3:3-5).
   2. Following these steps:
      (a) Is how one becomes a Christian—a New Testament Christian.
      (b) Is how one becomes a member of Christ and His church—the church of Christ.
      (c) Does not place one in a denomination of any kind.
   3. These are the same steps followed by individuals in New Testament times (Acts 2:36-47; 8:12-13, 26-40; 9:18; 10:47-48; 16:14-15, 30-34; 18:8; 19:4-5; 22:16).
      (a) Doing what they did makes one what they were—a New Testament Christian!
      (b) Doing what they did places one where they were—in the New Testament church.
      (c) No one in New Testament times became a part of a denomination (for no denomination existed).
      (d) Therefore, when one follows God's steps, he will not become a part of a denomination either.
   4. The steps of salvation taught by denominations and the steps to become a part of a denominational group are NOT the steps taught in the New Testament.
      (a) Following steps taught by a denominational preacher or denominational church:
         (1) Will place one in a denomination.
         (2) Will not make one a Christian or place one in Christ's saved body.
      (b) Being baptized to join a denomination is not the same as being baptized for the remission of sins in order to be added to the saved body of Christ by the Lord.
      (c) The answer to—"Are there faithful Christians in denominations?"—becomes clear.
D. When one "becomes" a "Christian" and takes on the name of "Christ," the Lord expects him to live faithfully to that name (1 Pet. 4:16).
   1. Faithful living involves and requires:
      (a) Walking in the light of God's Word (1 John 1:7).
      (b) Staying true to the truth of God (Matt. 7:21-23).
      (c) Regularly worshiping as authorized with the saints in His church (Heb. 10:24-25).

(d) Teaching God's steps of salvation (Mark 16:15-16; Matt. 28:18-20).
(e) Teaching the essentiality of baptism for the forgiveness of sins (Acts 2:38; 22:16).
(f) Standing for and defending God's truth (Jude 3; Phil. 1:16-17; Gal. 4:16).
(g) Standing against and opposing error (Eph. 5:11; Rom. 16:17; Gal. 2:5).
(h) Having no fellowship with or showing approval for false doctrine (2 John 9-11).
2. Read this list again. Recognize it is not exhaustive. Then, ask:
(a) Can one do these things while being a member of a denomination?
(b) Can one be part of a denomination and still "live faithfully" to God's will?
3. The answer is a resounding, "No."
(a) One does not become a New Testament Christian by following denominational doctrine.
(b) One cannot live as a faithful New Testament Christian while a part of a denomination.
(c) The answer to—"Are there faithful Christians in denominations?"—is clear.

E. Answering this question is not a judgment against the sincerity of someone's heart.
1. One may sincerely believe that they have become a Christian in the way God would approve, and one may sincerely believe that their denomination is approved by God.
2. But, sincerity is not what saves. Only Jesus and His truth will save us (John 14:6).
3. The apostle Paul wrote of how sincere he was when he was persecuting Christians.
(a) "I have lived in all good conscience before God until this day" (Acts 23:1).
(b) "Indeed, I myself thought I must do many things contrary to the name of Jesus of Nazareth" (Acts 26:9).
4. Nevertheless, he recognized that in his sincerity he had become the "chief" of sinners (1 Tim. 1:15).
(a) One can be sincere and devout and even a spiritual leader (like Saul of Tarsus among the Jews), and yet that same person can be living in and practicing error.
5. The purpose of this study is not to judge someone's heart, but to shed some light on the creeds and practices of denominational groups that are not according to God's will.
(a) If creeds and practices of denominational groups are not in harmony with Scripture, then:
(1) Those who teach them are not in harmony with God and
(2) Those who follow them are not in harmony with God.

F. When we go back to the Bible, we find:
1. Who is truly a Christian in the eyes of God (i.e., a penitent believer who is baptized for the express purpose of obtaining the forgiveness of sins).
2. What church God places Christians within (i.e., the church that Jesus built).
3. That those who are saved are in His church (Acts 2:47), and (correspondingly) those who are in His church are the ones who are saved (Eph. 5:23-27).
4. That it is impossible to separate (1) those who have been saved and made Christians through faith, repentance and baptism from (2) those who are in Christ's church.
5. That those who are outside of Christ's body cannot be considered to belong to Christ.
6. That there are no faithful Christians in denominations.

G. If we seek to justify a "plan of salvation from sins" that is not in accordance with the New Testament, or if we seek to justify a "church" that is not the one that Jesus established in the New Testament, we are preaching "a different gospel" (cf. Gal. 1:6-9).
1. For one to be part of a denomination, one must join a denomination, which is, in and of itself, a departure from the truth (in their teaching and practice).

2. How can a person, who is willingly part of a departure from "the faith," be considered a faithful Christian?

H. It is not Biblically possible to be taught denominational doctrine, believe denominational doctrine, obey denominational doctrine, be a member of a denominational church, participate in denominational worship, hold to denominational creeds and still be saved and considered a faithful New Testament Christian.

VI. Should Christians or Churches of Christ Extend Fellowship to Denominations?

A. Let's first define "extend fellowship."
   1. In this context, it means (or would include things like):
      (a) To collaborate with them in the planning and/or implementation of some project.
      (b) To participate with them in their worship services.
      (c) To announce and promote their events or services.
      (d) To invite their leaders to speak to our congregation.
      (e) To have preachers form and engage in "Ministerial Alliances" with denominational leaders and "ministers."
      (f) To conduct ourselves as if we approve of and recommend their doctrines and practices to others.
   2. Admittedly, this can be a sensitive matter. But, let's approach it from God's view.

B. Remember these crucial points of emphasis in the New Testament.
   1. Jesus prayed for His people to be united as one (John 17:20-21).
   2. God calls for His people to all speak the same thing and have no divisions (1 Cor. 1:10).
   3. God condemns anyone who adds to or takes away from His Word (Rev. 22:18-19).
   4. God warns us about "anyone" who "preaches any other gospel" than what is plainly taught in the New Testament (Gal. 1:6-9).

C. There is a sweet "fellowship" that those who "walk in the light" of the gospel of Christ have with God and with fellow believers (1 John 1:3-7).
   1. This fellowship is defined by God.
   2. This fellowship is offered by God.
   3. This fellowship is restricted by God.
   4. Man may not define, offer or restrict this fellowship in any way that God Himself has not!
   5. We should gladly extend fellowship to those who are in fellowship with God Himself.
   6. Still, we must not extend our approval to any who are not in fellowship with God.

D. It has been established that:
   1. Denominations are of human origin.
   2. Denominations are founded upon and perpetuate human doctrines.
   3. Denominations teach different things than the Bible.
   4. Denominations do not teach the New Testament plan of salvation.
   5. Denominations are not the "one church" that is detailed in the New Testament.

E. Thus, it should not surprise us that the Bible issues clear warnings and censures to God's people to not extend fellowship to denominations.

F. The Bible teaches that fellowship with God is conditional.
   1. "If you abide in My word, you are My disciples indeed" (John 8:31).
   2. God is in fellowship with those who "abide" in His word, and thus, He is not in fellowship with those who do not "abide" in His word.
   3. Therefore, the fellowship that we have with others should also be conditional upon them abiding in God's Word.

G. The Bible teaches that Christians are to have no fellowship with those in error.
   1. "Have no fellowship with the unfruitful works of darkness, but rather expose them" (Eph. 5:11).
   2. "Do not be unequally yoked together with unbelievers. For what fellowship has righteousness with lawlessness? And what communion has light with darkness? ...Therefore 'Come out from among them and be separate'" (2 Cor. 6:14, 17).
   3. "As we have said before, so now I say again, if anyone preaches any other gospel to you than what you have received, let him be accursed" (Gal. 1:9).
   4. "Fellowship must exist vertically before it can exist horizontally" (Alan Highers).
      (a) The basis of fellowship with others is fellowship with God.
      (b) If others are walking in darkness and error, there is no basis for extending our approval through having fellowship with them.
H. The Bible teaches that extending fellowship is joining in with them in their error.
   1. "Whoever transgresses and does not abide in the doctrine of Christ does not have God. He who abides in the doctrine of Christ has both the Father and the Son. If anyone comes to you and does not bring this doctrine, do not receive him into your house nor greet him; for he who greets him shares in his evil deeds" (2 John 9-11).
   2. Note carefully what the inspired apostle is teaching:
      (a) There would be those who do not abide in the doctrine of God.
      (b) The consequences of not abiding in the doctrine of Christ is forfeiting any relationship with God or Christ.
      (c) Christians are commanded not to show any acceptance or approval of them by extending fellowship to them.
      (d) Christians are warned that showing any approval makes us to be "participants" in their sinful ways.
   3. Consider also the instructions in 1 Corinthians 10 regarding idolatry (i.e., false religions).
      (a) Christians are commanded to "flee from idolatry" (10:14).
         (1) Do not see how close you can get!
         (2) Flee from it! Stay away from their temples (10:19-28).
      (b) Christians are reminded of the special communion they have with the Christ, and that special communion binds New Testament Christians in "one body" (10:16-21).
      (c) Christians are warned of becoming "partakers of the altars" of false religions by joining with them in their worship (10:18-20).
      (d) Christians are commanded not to have fellowship with false religions:
         (1) "I do not want you to have fellowship with demons" (10:20).
         (2) "You cannot drink the cup of the Lord and the cup of demons; you cannot partake of the Lord's table and of the table of demons" (10:21).
         (3) By extending fellowship, a Christian would be sharing in their error.
I. The Bible teaches that Christians are to avoid those who live or teach contrary to God's truth.
   1. "Now I urge you, brethren, note those who cause divisions and offenses, contrary to the doctrine which you learned, and avoid them. For those who are such do not serve our Lord Jesus Christ" (Rom. 16:17-18).
      (a) There would be those who would hold to, teach and practice doctrines that are "contrary to the doctrine" of Christ.
      (b) These diverse and divisive doctrines would clearly lead to division.
      (c) God commands His people to not only avoid the false doctrines and the division but also to avoid those who "cause" the "divisions and offenses."

2. Even within the church, Christians are commanded:
   (a) "...withdraw from every brother who walks disorderly and not according to the tradition" (2 Thess. 3:6).
   (b) "And if anyone does not obey our word in this epistle, note that person and do not keep company with him, that he may be ashamed" (2 Thess. 3:14).
J. While to some it may seem completely harmless (and could even be worthwhile) to extend fellowship to denominations, Scripture is not unclear in the Christian's responsibility to maintain definite lines between truth and error.
   1. If Christians were to extend fellowship to denominations:
      (a) It may indicate to them that we do not consider our doctrinal differences a big deal (which we should).
      (b) It may indicate to them that we do not actually believe they are in error (when the Scripture teaches that they are).
      (c) It may indicate to them that we are in full harmony with them in their teachings and practices (many of which can be shown to be contrary to Scripture).
      (d) It may indicate to them that we are in acceptance of their false teaching about how one can be saved from sin (when they do not teach what God teaches).
      (e) It may indicate to them that we consider them to be saved and to be our brethren "in Christ" (when they have not followed God's plan of salvation).
      (f) It may indicate to them that we do not believe that it really matters how one worships (when the Bible strongly teaches that it certainly does).
      (g) It may further their belief that the "Church of Christ" is just another denomination (when it most certainly is not).
K. We must see the seriousness of the matter.
   1. When we extend fellowship to denominations:
      (a) We show approval for what they are teaching and practicing (even if we think we do not).
      (b) We become a part of and guilty of their false teachings and practices (even if we think we do not).
      (c) We take ourselves out of a relationship with the Father and the Son (even if we think we do not).
      (d) We make the church of Christ appear to be a denomination and just "one of the many" (even if we think we do not).
   2. Christian fellowship is a blessing for those who are themselves in fellowship with God!
      (a) It must be defined, offered and restricted in the way that God has defined, offered and restricted it.
      (b) It must be extended to those who are in fellowship with God.
      (c) But, it cannot be extended (showing our approval) to those who are not in fellowship with God.

VII. What Is the Appropriate Response of Christians to Denominationalism?
A. The Christian's responsibility toward denominationalism as a whole and toward specific denominational groups and toward members of denominations can be summarized in the words of Ephesians 4:15 – "speaking the truth in love."
   1. We must maintain a spirit of love and compassion.
      (a) Agape love wants what is best for the one receiving the love.
      (b) We should want what is best for those who are in error—salvation of their souls.

(c) Our efforts in their direction should be saturated with "meekness and fear" (1 Pet. 3:15, NKJV) or "gentleness and respect" (ESV).
(d) This does not suggest softening or compromise at all, but it does emphasize the Christ-like attitude we must maintain toward others.
2. We must stand for, hold to and speak forth truth.
(a) The truth of God in the Bible is not relative – to fit certain conditions.
(b) The truth of God in the Bible is not subjective – to fit certain preferences.
(c) The truth of God in the Bible is not wavering – to fit certain interpretations.
(d) It is not up to us to determine truth – that's already done.
(e) It is up to us to unashamedly stand for the truth of God!
B. With a spirit of love and compassion, Christians must stand relentlessly opposed to all man-made religion, man-made churches and man-made doctrines!
1. Christians cannot afford to compromise!
2. Truth, the gospel and the Lord's church must not be divided or negotiated!
C. Christians need to realize that the Lord's church is not in competition with denominations.
1. Some denominations might be more "open and inclusive" in who they consider to be "saved," but that is no pressure on the church to compromise what the Bible says (Mark 16:15-16; Acts 2:36-38; 22:16; Rom. 6:3-4; Gal. 3:26-27).
2. Some denominations might be more "accepting and permissive" in the lifestyles that they permit and approve, but that is no pressure on the church to compromise what the Bible says (Tit. 2:11-12; 1 Pet. 2:9-12; Rom. 1:18-32; Gal. 5:19-21).
3. Some denominations might be more "entertaining and expressive" in their worship styles, but that is no pressure on the church to compromise what the Bible says (John 4:23-24; Eph. 5:19; Col. 3:16-17; Heb. 13:15; Matt. 4:10).
D. Christians must have an unreserved, unashamed and unwavering commitment to the Bible as the single authority and sole standard in religious matters today!
E. We must turn to the Word of God! We must go back, all the way back to the establishment of the church in the New Testament!

VIII. We Must Recognize the Seriousness of Denominationalism.
A. Consider these Scriptural observations about the eternal condition of denominationalism.
1. Jesus will say, "I never knew you, depart from Me" (Matt. 7:21-23).
(a) Some well-meaning but misguided religious folks might call Jesus, "Lord, Lord," but Jesus says that "not everyone who" does that "shall enter the kingdom of heaven."
(b) These well-meaning but misguided religious folks will say on the day of judgment, "Lord, have we not" done so many things "in Your name"?
(c) Well-meaning but misguided religious folks will be told by Jesus, "I never knew you; depart from Me, you who practice lawlessness!"
(d) Doing what one believes in his heart to be right does not make it right with God!
(e) Only the one "who does the will of My Father in heaven" shall enter heaven (7:21)!
(f) Doing the will of the Father has never added anyone to a human denomination.
2. Jesus said, "Every plant, which My heavenly Father has not planted, will be rooted up" (Matt. 15:13).
(a) Jesus had spoken in this context about those who:
(1) "Transgress the commandment of God" with their own teachings (15:3).
(2) Make "the commandment of God of no effect" by their own teachings (15:6).
(3) Worship in vain, "teaching as doctrines the commandments of men" (15:8-9).

- (b) Thus, Jesus addressed those who plant and cultivate human doctrines and institutions when He said that they "will be rooted up."
- (c) Jesus warned His followers about the influence of such individuals and the eternal ramifications of following them: "Let them alone. They are blind leaders of the blind. And if the blind leads the blind, both will fall into a ditch" (15:14).
- (d) Biblical authority never planted a single denomination.
                3. When Jesus returns, He will take "vengeance on those who...do not obey the gospel of Christ" (2 Thess. 1:7-9).
                    - (a) Adhering to manmade doctrines and churches is not obeying the gospel.
                    - (b) Obeying the gospel does not lead one to denominationalism but away from it.
                    - (c) Obeying the gospel makes one a New Testament Christian, with no affiliation at all with any modern-day denomination.
        B. Consider these logical observations about denominationalism.
            1. Denominations are set apart from one another by their differing doctrines and practices.
                - (a) Would not differing doctrines and practices also set them apart from the Bible and from the church of the Bible? Such would seem to be true!
            2. Denominations believe, teach and practice different things.
                - (a) If denominationalism is acceptable, then does it really matter what one believes, teaches and practices? It does not appear that it matters!
            3. The Bible is full of warnings about division and manmade doctrines.
                - (a) Why would God put these in the Bible if it does not matter what man teaches and practices in the realm of religion? It makes the Bible meaningless!
            4. "What if a preacher (we'll call him 'preacher A') preached one thing one Sunday but on the next Sunday contradicted the very thing which he preached on the previous Sunday? And what if 'preacher A' preached on another topic the next Sunday, only to contradict himself the following Sunday?
                - (a) "What do you think would happen? How long would he be employed? How long would people listen to such a man?
                - (b) "Yet, that is essentially what is happening every Sunday in denominationalism. 'Preacher A' preaches one doctrine while 'preacher B' contradicts 'preacher A.' And 'preacher C' preaches something that contradicts 'preacher D.'
                - (c) "Now, how can such be ludicrous if found in one preacher but acceptable in different preachers?" (David Sain, 43).
        C. Denominationalism cannot be defended logically.
        D. Denominationalism cannot be defended Scripturally.

IX. Let's Go Back to the Bible and Restore the Church of the New Testament!
   A. From our study of God's Word, it is apparent that denominationalism:
      1. Is contrary to Scripture and to God's plan for the church.
      2. Does not find its origin in God or find any approval from divine authority.
      3. Finds its origin in man, as men divided themselves into new "churches" over the last 500 years due to doctrinal differences or personality conflicts.
      4. Is a clear illustration of when man "goes too far and does not abide in the teaching of Christ" (2 John 9, NASB), but instead is "teaching as doctrines the commandments of men" (Matt. 15:9).
   B. From a study of the New Testament, it should be apparent to the reader that:
      1. The Lord established His church on the day of Pentecost in Acts 2.
      2. His church was neither Catholic, Protestant nor Jew.

3. The Lord's church was not a denomination—it was not Catholic, Lutheran, Presbyterian, Baptist or Methodist!
4. First-century Christians were not Catholics, Lutherans, Presbyterians, Baptists, Methodists, etc.!
5. Denominationalism was completely unknown when the church began.
    (a) There were no denominations to join.
    (b) There were no denominational creeds to follow.
    (c) There were no denominational doctrines to teach.
    (d) There were no denominational names to wear.
    (e) There were no denominational preachers to hear.
    (f) There were not different plans of salvation promoted.
    (g) There were not different forms of worship practiced.
6. No person in the New Testament was ever part of any denomination.

C. In the New Testament, when honest seekers of truth heard the pure gospel taught:
1. They believed the message about Jesus Christ (Acts 4:4; 8:12, 13; 18:8).
2. They repented of their sins and turned to God (Acts 2:38; 3:19; 11:18; 17:30; 26:20).
3. They confessed their faith in Jesus (Acts 8:36-38; Romans 10:9-10).
4. They were baptized for the forgiveness of their sins (Acts 2:38-41; 16:33; 18:8; 22:16).
5. They obeyed the gospel (Rom. 1:5; 2:8; 6:17; 16:26; Heb. 5:9; 1 Pet. 1:22).
6. They became New Testament Christians (Matt. 28:18-20; Acts 11:26; 26:28).
7. They were added to the Lord's church (Acts 2:41, 47; 1 Cor. 12:13; John 3:3-5).
    (a) Everyone became a member of the same body—the "church of Christ."
    (b) Everyone wore the same name—simply "Christian."
    (c) They did all of this without ever being a part of a denomination.
    (d) In fact, one would have to do something more or something less in order to be in a denomination.

D. Let us go back to the Bible and restore New Testament Christianity.
1. Let us go back beyond all Catholic and Protestant denominations.
2. Let us go back beyond all human divisions and human creeds.
3. Let us go back and restore the church that we read about in the New Testament.
    (a) The church that was undenominational.
    (b) The church that was pre-denominational.
4. In restoring the New Testament church today:
    (a) We can be part of the same church that the apostles were.
    (b) We can teach and obey the same truths that they taught and obeyed.
    (c) We can wear the same name that they wore.
    (d) If it was good enough for them, should it not also be good enough for us?
5. If we will:
    (a) Teach what they taught (nothing more, nothing less),
    (b) Obey what they obeyed (nothing more, nothing less), and
    (c) Practice what they practiced (nothing more, nothing less),
6. Then we will:
    (a) Become what they became (simply Christians)—nothing more, nothing less.
    (b) Be members of the same church of which they were members (the church of Christ)—nothing more, nothing less.
    (c) Have no ties whatsoever to any denomination.
    (d) Wear no other name than "Christian."

E. The plea of the New Testament church today is:
   1. Let us go back to the Bible.
   2. Let us restore first-century Christianity in the twenty-first century.
   3. Let us speak where the Bible speaks.
   4. Let us remain silent where the Bible is silent.
   5. Let us call Bible things by Bible names.
   6. Let us do Bible things in Bible ways.

Recommended Resources

Books

Jennings, Alvin. *Traditions of Men Versus the Word of God.* Fort Worth: Star Bible Publications, 1996.

Mattox, F.W. *The Eternal Kingdom.* Delight, AR: Gospel Light Publishing, 1961.

North, Stafford. *Handbook on Church Doctrines.* Nashville: 21st Century Christian, 2007.

Shepherd, J.W. *The Church, the Falling Away, and the Restoration.* Nashville: Gospel Advocate, 1948.

Tomlinson, L.G. *Churches of Today in the Light of Scripture.* Nashville: Gospel Advocate, 1957.

Winkler, Wendell. *The Church Everybody Is Asking About.* Tuscaloosa, AL: Winkler Publications, 1988.

Articles

Boren, Maxie B. "The Preciousness of Fellowship." *Everyday Christianity (Freed-Hardeman College Lectures).* Ed. Winford Claiborne. Henderson, TN: Freed-Hardeman College, 1984. 18-25.

Cotham, Perry B. "The Church." *A Plea for Fundamentals (Freed-Hardeman College Lectures).* Ed. William Woodson. Henderson, TN: Freed-Hardeman College, 1977. 252-256.

---. "Is the Church of Christ a Denomination?" *A Plea for Fundamentals (Freed-Hardeman College Lectures).* Ed. William Woodson. Henderson, TN: Freed-Hardeman College, 1977. 257-258.

---. "Should the Church of Christ Unite with the Denominations?" *A Plea for Fundamentals (Freed-Hardeman College Lectures).* Ed. William Woodson. Henderson, TN: Freed-Hardeman College, 1977. 259-260.

---. "What Should the Church Do with False Teachers?" *A Plea for Fundamentals (Freed-Hardeman College Lectures).* Ed. William Woodson. Henderson, TN: Freed-Hardeman College, 1977. 261-264.

Duncan, Bobby. "Shall We Have Fellowship with Denominations?" *The Spiritual Sword* (Apr. 1998): 14-17.

Highers, Alan. "The Undenominational Church." *The Spiritual Sword* (Oct. 2011): 38-42

Jackson, Wayne. "Denominationalism—Permissible or Reprehensible?" *ChristianCourier.com* https://www.christiancourier.com/articles/798-denominationalism-permissible-or-reprehensible

Pharr, David R. "Are There Christians in All Denominations?" *The Spiritual Sword* (Oct. 2007): 33-37.

Sain, David. "Denominational Division Is Sinful." *The Spiritual Sword* (April 1999): 41-44.

Smith, Kelby. "Can One Be a Christian Outside the Church?" *Just a Christian (Freed-Hardeman College Lectures).* Ed. Winford Claiborne. Henderson, TN: Freed-Hardeman College, 1985. 310-314.

Wallace, G.K. "Our Attitude Toward Denominationalism." *The Church Faces Liberalism (Freed-Hardeman College Lectures)*. Ed. Thomas B. Warren. Nashville: Gospel Advocate, 1971. 197-209.

Winkler, Dan. "Is the Church of Christ a Denomination?" *The Church: The Sect Everywhere Spoken Against (Spiritual Sword Lectureship)*. Ed. Jim Laws. Memphis: Getwell church of Christ, 1997. 106-123.

Winkler, Wendell. "Is the Church of Christ a Denomination?" *The Church Everybody Is Asking About*. Tuscaloosa, AL: Winkler Publications, 1988. 24-31.

Periodicals

The Spiritual Sword. October 1979. "The Church of Christ—The Body, Not a Denomination."

The Spiritual Sword. January 2001. "The Church and Denominationalism."

The Spiritual Sword. July 2009. "A Handy Guide to Denominationalism."

The Spiritual Sword. October 2011. "There Is One Body."

The Spiritual Sword. January 2016. "Denominationalism on the Decline."

Lesson 12: The Organization of the Church

I. **The Church Is Spoken of in Different Senses in the New Testament.**
   A. See Roman numeral V in Lesson 8, "The Distinct Nature of the Church" (page 88).
   B. The church is spoken of in a universal sense in the New Testament (Matt. 16:18; Acts 20:28; Eph. 1:22-23; 5:23, 25; 1 Cor. 7:17; 11:16; 14:33; 2 Cor. 11:28; 1 Tim. 3:15).
      1. The universal sense embraces all saved persons of the earth from the first century until the end of time.
      2. The universal sense does not focus on any specific congregation of the Lord's people but on all of the Lord's people in the worldwide body or kingdom of Christ.
      3. The universal sense can appear in the singular "church" (Matt. 16:18) and the plural "churches" (1 Cor. 7:17), but all still referencing the single "one body" (Eph. 4:4).
   C. The church is spoken of in a local sense in the New Testament (Acts 8:1; 13:1; 14:23; 20:17; Rom. 16:5; 1 Cor. 1:2).
      1. The local sense focuses on a congregation of the Lord's people in a specific locality, community or city.
      2. These are not different denominations (with different names, creeds and practices), but these are individual, local congregations of the one universal church.
      3. This is the sense in which the bulk of this lesson will focus.
   D. The church is spoken of in a regional/provincial sense in the New Testament (Acts 9:31; 1 Cor. 16:19; 2 Cor. 8:1; Gal. 1:2; Rev. 1:4).
      1. The regional/provincial sense embraces multiple congregations within a given area.
      2. Each of these congregations is separate from the others in the region (see IV below).
      3. Yet, each of these congregations is part of the one, global, universal church.

II. **Christ Is the Head of the Church.**
   A. This point cannot be overemphasized. In the organization of the church, Christ is head!
   B. The church is not a democracy, where the majority (as determined by human beings) rules.
   C. The church is a theocracy, with Christ ruling as King of kings and Lord of lords (Rev. 17:14).
      1. Christ is "the head of the church" (Eph. 5:23; Col. 1:18).
      2. Christ is the "only one Lawgiver and Judge, the One who is able to save and to destroy" (Jas. 4:12).
      3. His Word is the final authority in all matters (John 12:48; Col. 3:17).
   D. There is only one who has a right to rule or dictate in the church, and that is the One who has "all authority" (Matt. 28:18; Eph. 1:22-23; Acts 2:36).
      1. Jesus alone has that *"exousia"* authority in the church—"the power of one whose will and commands must be submitted to by others and obeyed" (Thayer).
      2. No man on earth has *"exousia"* authority! There is no earthly head of the church!
      3. There is no person or group who has the authority to change anything the Head says!
      4. The following find no mention, no place, and, therefore, no authority in the church: the Pope, Presiding Bishop, Right Reverend, Archdeacon, Cardinal, President, etc.
      5. There is also no mention and no authority in the church for: ecclesiastical conventions, synods, councils, presbyteries, etc.
   E. In its universal sense, the church has no earthly organization or headquarters.
      1. The New Testament has not authorized any church government beyond the local congregation (see III and IV below).
      2. Therefore, the New Testament does not authorize:
      (a) Any earthly headquarters for the church.

           (b) Any earthly organization/government of (or over) the church.
        3. The "headquarters" of the church is where the Head resides.
           (a) The church's Head (i.e., Christ) resides in heaven (1 Pet. 3:22; Eph. 1:20-21).
           (b) The church must adhere to the orders given from heaven.
        4. There is no authority in Scripture for a "leader" or "council" outside a local congregation that makes decisions for one or more congregations, requiring the compliance and adherence of those congregations.
    F. Christ alone has authority (and all authority) over the universal church.
        1. His word and His truth are universal and must be universally taught, universally required and universally followed.
        2. There is no room at the universal level, regional level or local level for any modification of divine law. This point, also, cannot be overemphasized.
    G. Christ is the head of the church—at the local level and the universal level!
III. **Each Local Church/Congregation Is to Be Overseen By Elders.**
    A. At the local level, the church is to be organized according to the New Testament pattern.
    B. God has an "order" (i.e., an organizational structure) that He intends for His church to have at the local level (note carefully the word "order" in Titus 1:5).
        1. The word "order" emphasizes the "orderliness" which God intended the organization of His church to have.
        2. The church today must follow His pattern (i.e., His "order") for the church.
    C. The divine "order" calls for His church to "appoint elders in every city" (Tit. 1:5).
        1. Paul followed this pattern when he "appointed elders in every church" (Acts 14:23).
        2. These men:
           (a) Served as the local overseers of the local congregation,
           (b) Under the rule and authority of Christ over His church.
    D. The divine "order" gives very specific qualifications that a man must meet in order to be considered for appointment as an elder.
        1. Read these qualifications in 1 Timothy 3:1-7, 11 and Titus 1:5-9.
        2. These qualifications are not optional, multiple choice or best-case scenarios.
        3. These qualifications are absolutely essential and will be investigated in the next lesson.
    E. The divine "order" for the local congregation was a plurality of elders in each church.
        1. Note the plural "elders" in Acts 14:23; 20:17; Philippians 1:1; Titus 1:5 & 1 Peter 5:1.
        2. The plural emphasizes that no one man can exercise oversight over a congregation. There must be more than one elder in each congregation.
        3. This also emphasizes that the oversight and authority within a congregation is not in "an elder" but in the "eldership." All elders in a congregation have equal authority and responsibility toward the congregation. No elder is above another elder.
        4. Therefore, there is no authority in the New Testament for a "pastor" to rule and govern over a congregation. A "preacher" is not, by definition, a "pastor." (See VI.)
    F. The divine "order" also limits an eldership's oversight to the one local congregation.
        1. Note carefully the word "among" in Acts 20:28 and 1 Peter 5:1-2.
        2. The eldership's responsibility is limited to the church "among" which the elders lead (Acts 20:28; 1 Pet. 5:1-2). They must be "among" them to exercise oversight.
        3. Just as one congregation must have a plurality of elders, those elders may only oversee the affairs of that one congregation and no other. (See IV.)
        4. There is no higher authority (besides Christ Himself) in a local congregation than the local eldership.

G. Elders are designated by three Greek words, usually translated into six English words.
   1. The Greek *presbuteros* is translated into "presbyter" (KJV, ASV, NASB) and "elder."
      (a) This word signifies an older man who has experience and wisdom.
   2. The Greek *episkopos* is translated into "overseer" and "bishop."
      (a) This word emphasizes the responsibility of oversight, superintendency and rule.
   3. The Greek *poimein* is translated into "shepherd" and "pastor."
      (a) This word emphasizes the work of caring, feeding and protecting the church.
   4. These three Greek words are used together in two key passages about elders.
      (a) Acts 20:17, 28 – "[Paul] sent to Ephesus and called for the elders *(presbuteros)* of the church. And when they had come to him, he said to them, '…Therefore take heed to yourselves and to all the flock, among which the Holy Spirit has made you overseers *(episkopos)*, to shepherd *(poimein)* the church of God which He purchased with His own blood.'"
         (1) There is no difference made between an elder, bishop/overseer or shepherd.
         (2) Each word simply views the same man from a different vantage point.
      (b) 1 Peter 5:1-2 – "The elders *(presbuteros)* who are among you I exhort…Shepherd *(poimaino)* the flock of God which is among you, serving as overseers *(episkopos)*…"
         (1) There is no difference made between an elder, bishop/overseer or shepherd.
         (2) Each word simply views the same man from a different vantage point.
   5. The six English words can be summarized with the acronym, B-E-P-O-P-S (as an elder is to be a father or "pop" of faithful children):
      (a) Bishops
      (b) Elders
      (c) Presbyters
      (d) Overseers
      (e) Pastors
      (f) Shepherds
   6. It is important to note that these six words (i.e., three Greek words) are used interchangeably in the New Testament to refer to the very same office.
      (a) They all refer to men serving at the local level and not over multiple congregations.
      (b) Bishops do not have more authority than elders. They are the same men.
      (c) The passages in Acts 20 and 1 Peter 5 show this very clearly.
H. The duty and work of elders is summarized in these various designations for them.
   1. Elders have the responsibility to see that the local congregation functions according to the will of God and does so in the very best way possible.
   2. The primary work of elders is to tend to, care for, feed and protect the church.
      (a) This is emphasized in Acts 20:28-30; 1 Peter 5:1-3; 1 Timothy 3:1-7 & Titus 1:5-9.
      (b) The utmost importance of guiding the church to heaven is stressed in Hebrews 13:17—"they watch out for your souls, as those who must give account."
   3. Also underscored in the verses above is the elders' responsibility to "take care of the church" that is "entrusted" to them through proper oversight and example.
   4. Elders do not have authority to create new "laws," rescind "laws" or modify divine laws. They only have authority to administer and require adherence to God's law.
   5. The duty and work of elders will be studied more fully in the next lesson.
I. God's design is for qualified men (called "elders") to lead His church to heaven.
   1. Members of the church need to "consider the outcome of [the elders'] way of life,"
   2. And then "imitate their faith" (Heb. 13:7, ESV).

IV. Each Local Church/Congregation Is Autonomous.
　A. "Autonomy" is a compound word, combining "auto"=self and "nomos"=law/rule. Thus, the word itself has the meaning of "self-rule" or "self-governing."
　　1. English dictionaries define autonomy as "the quality or state of being self-governing; the right of self-government; the state of existing or acting separately from others; an independent state or body."
　　2. The Bible does not use the word "autonomous," but it teaches this concept regarding the church, emphasizing the independence of the local congregation.
　B. Don't misunderstand or misapply the autonomy of the local congregation.
　　1. A local congregation's autonomy does not negate or contradict the universal rule of Christ.
　　　(a) Christ has ALL authority (Matt. 28:18; Eph. 1:22-23).
　　　(b) The governing of the church on the local level is done under the authority of Christ!
　　　(c) The authority of Christ has already decided truth; no congregation sets or legislates truth.
　　2. The rule of Christ has already decided and dictated the acceptable work and functioning for all congregations of the church. For example:
　　　(a) A local congregation has no authority to decide the qualifications of its leaders.
　　　(b) A local congregation has no authority to decide on what day to worship.
　　　(c) A local congregation has no authority to decide when to have the Lord's Supper.
　　　(d) A local congregation has no authority to decide the role of women in the church.
　　　(e) Again, Christ has already decided and dictated these things for the church.
　　3. In the New Testament, the church was made up of local congregations.
　　　(a) Letters were written to specific congregations in specific locales.
　　　(b) Yet, those individual congregations were all part of the one universal church.
　　　(c) They were not different denominations with different laws to govern them.
　　4. Therefore, every local congregation is subject to the same universal law – i.e., the New Testament, which must be taught the same (1 Cor. 4:17; 7:17) and obeyed the same (1 Cor. 1:10; Rom. 6:17) in every congregation of the Lord's church.
　　　(a) What was taught to one congregation was taught to all congregations (cf. Col. 4:16).
　　　(b) Note carefully that when letters were written to the seven churches of Asia, each separate congregation was urged to "hear what the Spirit says to the churches" (Rev. 2:7, 11, 17, 29; 3:6, 13, 22). All letters had application to all congregations.
　　　(c) The law of the New Testament is universal and to be applied universally to every congregation.
　C. The Bible does teach that each local congregation of the Lord's church is autonomous (i.e., self-governing) in that:
　　1. They are independent of and not subject to any other congregation or ecclesiastical organization/government.
　　2. There is no authority of an individual or body outside or above the local congregation.
　　3. No man or body from outside a congregation may exercise rule or authority over that congregation.
　　4. No congregation is over the affairs of another congregation, as a "mother" church.
　　　(a) This includes even in mission work. A missionary's sponsoring/overseeing congregation is not "over" the congregation in the mission field.
　　　(b) The congregation in the mission field is as autonomous as any other congregation of the Lord's church.

5. Each congregation is to independently:
   (a) Appoint its own leaders/elders.
   (b) Choose its own preachers.
   (c) Judge matters of expediency.
   (d) Manage its own affairs.
   (e) Controls its own resources.
   (f) Settle its own problems.
   (g) Handle its own discipline.
   (h) Carry out its own work.
   (i) Deal with various circumstances that arise in accordance with the revealed will of Christ recorded in His all-authoritative Word.
6. Each congregation has the right to decide and govern themselves in matters of expediency and no other congregation has a right to interfere or seek to overrule.

D. Overseers of each congregation are permitted oversight only over the single congregation of which they are "among" (Acts 20:28; 1 Pet. 5:1-2). (See III, F.)
   1. Individual overseers may not exercise authority outside their congregation, but only "over those entrusted" to them (1 Pet. 5:3).
   2. No congregation can be overseen or directed by someone not "among" them.
   3. Overseers are responsible to lead, watch for, care for and deal with those within their own congregation (Heb. 13:17).

E. Each congregation of the Lord's church is its own separate body with its own leadership to govern only within (or "among") that body.
   1. "The absence of any centralized earthly government among the churches of the New Testament and the responsibility of each local church to hold to the pattern of the apostles' teaching insist upon the autonomy of each local church. Local church autonomy is the safety valve against full-scale apostasy" (Wharton 81).
   2. "The wisdom of God is seen in such an arrangement for [H]is churches. If one became corrupted in doctrine or affected by evil practices, other churches would not be so affected. If dissension arose in one, it would not spread to the others; if one perished, the others would not be dragged down. If a window is made of one large pane, a break injures the entire pane; but if it be made of several panes, it is not so bad to break one. The independence of the churches is a protection for each one" (H. Leo Boles, *Gospel Advocate,* Feb. 15, 1940).

F. Individual local congregations are authorized in the New Testament to cooperate with each other in various efforts or endeavors.
   1. This is seen in efforts of evangelism (Acts 11:19-30; Phil. 4:15-16).
   2. This is seen in efforts of edification (Acts 15:1-29; 18:27).
   3. This is seen in efforts of benevolence (Acts 11:27-30; Rom. 15:26-27; 1 Cor. 16:1-2).
   4. However, each congregation must continue to maintain its autonomy, and no authority may be exercised by one man or congregation over another congregation.

G. The first major departure from N.T. Christianity came in the organization of the church.
   1. Men were not satisfied with (1) the plurality of elders required, (2) the limited "rule" of elders over only one congregation, or (3) the autonomy of each congregation.
   2. Men began to create a hierarchal structure which:
      (a) elevated one of the elders above the rest, calling him the "bishop";
      (b) positioned the "bishop" over multiple congregations in that region;
      (c) appointed "archbishops" over multiple regions;

(d) and finally assigned one man as the supreme bishop over all the church.
3. This deviation from God's pattern for the organization of the church led to a major departure (cf. Acts 20:28-31; 1 Tim. 4:1-3) and gave birth to Roman Catholicism.

H. The church today must go back to the original organizational pattern for the church!
1. There is no organizational structure for the church outside or above the local congregation.
2. Restoring the New Testament church requires restoring the organizational structure that God designed and intended for His church.

V. **Each Local Church/Congregation Is to Have Deacons to Serve the Church.**
A. While all Christians are servants, deacons are special servants with specified duties.
B. The Greek word for "deacon" is *diakonos* (Phil. 1:1).
  1. The Greek word means "one who executes the commands of another...a servant, attendant, minister" *(Thayer's Greek Lexicon)*.
  2. The Greek word is translated: deacon, servant, minister.
    (a) The word is used generally of all Christians (1 Cor. 3:5; Col. 1:7; Rom. 16:1; Rev. 2:19).
    (b) The word is used interestingly of Jesus Himself (Rom. 15:8; Matt. 20:28).
    (c) The word is used specifically of "deacons" in the local church (Phil. 1:1; 1 Tim. 3:8-13).
    (d) In each use, the definition of the term is essentially the same—servants who serve.
  3. Thus, we understand that deacons are specialized servants in the church.
C. Scripture gives very specific qualifications that a man must meet in order to be considered for appointment as a deacon. Read these qualifications in 1 Timothy 3:8-13:
  1. Reverent
  2. Blameless
  3. Husband of one wife
  4. Ruling his children and his own house well
  5. Holding the mystery of the faith with a pure conscience
  6. First be tested
  7. Not double-tongued
  8. Not given to much wine
  9. Not greedy for money
  10. His wife must be reverent, not a slanderer, temperate, faithful in all things.
D. Insight can be gained into the work of deacons from Acts 6:1-7.
  1. While these men are not called "deacons," they appear to be functioning as such.
  2. There was a work (or "business," v. 3) that needed to be done.
    (a) The nature of this work was to "serve tables" or "deacon tables"—a special task.
    (b) Just as in 1 Timothy 3:8-13, these men were to be qualified for the job (v. 3).
  3. The deacons were not "underlings"; they were appointed "over this business" (v. 3).
E. The work of deacons (as all works of the church) is overseen by the elders.
  1. A deacon's authority is "over" whatever "business" the elders may assign to him. (See both of these terms in Acts 6:3b).
  2. Once a task is delegated, the deacon must work diligently to perform it and complete it. "For those who have served well as deacons obtain for themselves a good standing and great boldness in the faith which is in Christ Jesus" (1 Tim. 3:13).
  3. Works of deacons will be in all areas of the work of the church—evangelism, edification and benevolence. Their work is essential to the overall health of the church.
F. In the church, there are important roles to be filled for the work of the church to thrive.
  1. In Acts 6, the apostles had work to do, and the "deacons" had assigned work to do.

2. Today, the elders have work to do, and the deacons have assigned work to do.
   (a) If elders do not allow deacons to be "over" the work that is assigned to them, by default the elders will end up doing the deacons' work.
   (b) If deacons do not do the work that is assigned to them, by default the elders will end up doing the deacons' work and neglect their work of shepherding souls.
3. By definition, the work of deacons will be "service" oriented and assigned to them.
4. When everyone fulfills their God-given roles, the church can grow (Acts 6:7; Eph. 4:16).

VI. Each Local Church/Congregation Needs to Have an Evangelist to Preach the Gospel.
A. While all Christians are to preach the gospel to the lost, the church needs evangelists.
B. The Greek words used for these men emphasize their role.
   1. Evangelists are to be "heralds"—proclaiming the message of the King (1 Tim. 2:7).
   2. Evangelists are to be "gospelizers"—spreading the good news of Jesus (2 Tim. 4:5).
   3. Evangelists have been charged with a heavenly message, which they must convey faithfully and completely, without modification. "Preach the word" (2 Tim. 4:2)!
C. In preaching, evangelists are to (2 Tim. 4:2; 1 Cor. 14:3):
   1. "Preach the word" as their first priority.
   2. "Be ready in season and out of season," being on duty whether convenient or not.
   3. "Convince" or "convict" or "reprove" to bring about conviction (and confession) of sin.
   4. "Rebuke" or "warn" with sharp censure.
   5. "Exhort" or "plead" with urging, encouraging, comforting and admonishing.
   6. Be "longsuffering" with "great patience" for the one being taught.
   7. "Teach" or "instruct" faithfully the doctrine of Christ.
   8. "Edify" or "build up" or "strengthen" hearts and minds with the Word of God.
   9. "Comfort" or "console" to help people overcome the difficulties of life through Christ.
D. An evangelist has the Scriptural responsibility to:
   1. Proclaim the pure gospel and thereby win souls to Christ (2 Tim. 4:2-5).
   2. Preach "the whole counsel of God," holding back nothing that is helpful (Acts 20:27, 20).
   3. Edify, build up and equip the local congregation (Eph. 4:11-16; 1 & 2 Tim. and Titus).
   4. Protect the church and defend the faith (1 Tim. 1:3; 4:1-6; 6:20-21; 2 Tim. 4:1-5).
   5. Appoint and maintain qualified leadership in the local congregation (Tit. 1:5; 1 Tim. 3).
   6. Prepare and train other men to be preachers and teachers (2 Tim. 2:2).
   7. Rebuke wayward elders who "persist in sin" (1 Tim. 5:20, ESV).
E. The preacher/evangelist is not the "pastor" or the "reverend."
   1. The elders (plurality) are the pastors, shepherds and overseers of the church.
   2. The preacher (just like every member, every deacon and every elder) is one of the members (sheep) of the congregation and is subject to the eldership.
   3. Scripture makes a distinction between "evangelists" and "pastors" (Eph. 4:11).
   4. The preacher is not on a level "above" anyone else or to be "revered" as such.
      (a) Of Jehovah, Scripture states, "Holy and reverend is [H]is name" (Psa. 111:9, KJV).
         (1) No man is God. No man has authority to be called "Reverend."
      (b) Jesus commanded, "Do not call anyone on earth your father; for One is your Father, He who is in heaven" (Matt. 23:9; cf. 23:5-12).
         (1) Since the only true "Father" is in heaven, no man has authority on earth to be called "Father" in a religious context.
   5. There is no Scriptural authority to refer to the preacher/evangelist in the local congregation as "Pastor" or "Reverend" or "Father."

VII. Conclusion
A. There is only ONE head of the church and that is Christ – not any man or woman.
B. The Lord's church must be organized and appoint leadership as instructed by the Lord.
C. There is no Scriptural authority for modern forms of church government among the denominations, which do not follow the plurality of elders among a single congregation.
D. Any deviation from God's pattern creates a man-made organization.
E. The New Testament church will be organized according to the pattern in the New Testament.
   1. Elders will lead, guide, oversee and rule the congregation (Acts 20:28-30; 1 Pet. 5:1-2).
   2. Deacons will work as special servants in the congregation (Acts 6:1-8; 1 Tim. 3:13).
   3. Evangelists will preach (2 Tim. 4:1-5).
   4. Members will submit to the elders and work in the congregation (Heb. 13:17; Eph. 4:16).
   5. Restoring the New Testament church requires restoring the organizational structure that God designed and intended for His church.

Recommended Resources

Books

Brownlow, Leroy. *Why I Am a Member of the Church of Christ.* Fort Worth: Brownlow Publishing, 1973.

Cox, James D. *"...With the Bishops and Deacons."* Tustin, CA: James D. Cox, 1976.

Jennings, Alvin, ed. *Introducing the Church of Christ.* Fort Worth: Star Bible, 1981.

Massey, Jim. *Scriptural Organization of the Churches of Christ.* Winona, MS: Choate Publications, 1985.

Phillips, H.E. *Scriptural Elders and Deacons.* Bowling Green, KY: Guardian of Truth, 1959.

Wharton, Edward C. *The Church of Christ.* Nashville: Gospel Advocate, 1997.

Wilson, L. R. *Congregational Development.* Nashville: Gospel Advocate, 1963.

Articles

Alexander, Wallace. "Each Local Church Is Self-Governing Under Christ." *Introducing the Church of Christ.* Ed. Alvin Jennings. Fort Worth: Star Bible, 1981. 71-75.

Brownlow, Leroy. "Because It Is Scriptural in Organization." *Why I Am a Member of the Church of Christ.* Fort Worth: Brownlow Publishing, 1973. 38-44.

Cogdill, Roy E. "Church Government." *New Testament Church.* Fairmount, IN: Truth Magazine Bookstore, 1982. 55-64.

Flatt, Ben S. "As in Bible Times, Deacons Serve the Church." *Introducing the Church of Christ.* Ed. Alvin Jennings. Fort Worth: Star Bible, 1981. 81-84.

Gardner, A. Kay. "The Role of Preachers in the Lord's Church." *Introducing the Church of Christ.* Ed. Alvin Jennings. Fort Worth: Star Bible, 1981. 85-89.

Jackson, Wayne. "Congregational Autonomy: Not a Shield for Error." *ChristianCourier.com* https://www.christiancourier.com/articles/743-congregational-autonomy-not-a-shield-for-error

Liddell, Bobby. "The Organization of the Lord's Church." *The Lord's Church: Past, Present and Future (POWER Lectures).* Ed. B.J. Clarke. Southaven, MS: Southaven church of Christ, 1999. 468-485.

McDade, Jason. "The Work and Qualifications of Deacons." *The Spiritual Sword* (Oct. 2003): 20-23.

Sanders, Phil. "Church Government." *The Spiritual Sword* (Oct. 2003): 3-7.

Wharton, Edward C. "The Organizational Structure of the Church." *The Church of Christ.* Nashville: Gospel Advocate, 1997. 63-113.

Winkler, Wendell. "Where Are the Headquarters of the Church of Christ?" *The Church Everybody Is Asking About.* Tuscaloosa, AL: Winkler Publications, 1988. 14-20.

Periodicals

The Spiritual Sword. July 1996. "Leadership in the Church."

The Spiritual Sword. October 2003. "The Model Church."

Lesson 13: Qualifications & Responsibilities of Elders

I. **The New Testament Church Was Designed By God to Have Elders.**
   A. God's design for His church was for every congregation to have elders (Tit. 1:5).
      1. Paul returned to congregations that he helped to establish and he "appointed elders in every church" (Acts 14:23).
   B. God's design for His church was for a plurality of men to serve as elders (1 Pet. 5:1).
      1. There was never divine approval for a congregation to have one elder serving alone.
      2. Every mention of elders in local congregations in the New Testament indicates that there was always more than one, and each elder was to be equal within the eldership.
   C. God's design for His church was for only men who were qualified to serve as elders.
      1. The Lord gave very specific qualifications which Christian men "must" meet before they might be considered for the eldership.
      2. These qualifications (in 1 Timothy 3 and Titus 1) will be studied in this lesson.
   D. God's design for His church was for the elders to be the leaders within the local congregation, to govern and to supervise the work and direction of the church.
      1. Elders have authority "over" their local congregation (1 Thess. 5:12; Heb. 13:17).
      2. Elders only possess authority "among" their own congregation (Acts 20:28; 1 Pet. 5:2).
      3. No elder may exercise any authority on his own within his local congregation (as the authority resides within the eldership), and no elder may exercise authority outside of his local congregation (as he is only an elder "among" his local church).
      4. The responsibilities of elders within the local congregation will be studied in this lesson.
   E. Understanding the qualifications and responsibilities of elders is crucial to a proper and full understanding of New Testament Christianity.
   F. As a reminder from Lesson 12, elders are designated by three Greek words.
      1. The Greek *presbuteros* is translated into "presbyter" and "elder."
         (a) This word signifies an older man who has experience and wisdom.
      2. The Greek *episkopos* is translated into "overseer" and "bishop."
         (a) This word emphasizes the responsibility of oversight, superintendency and rule.
      3. The Greek *poimein* is translated into "shepherd" and "pastor."
         (a) This word emphasizes the work of caring, feeding and protecting the church.
      4. These three Greek words are used together in two key passages about elders.
         (a) Acts 20:17, 28 – "[Paul] sent to Ephesus and called for the elders *(presbuteros)* of the church. And…he said to them, '…Therefore take heed to yourselves and to all the flock, among which the Holy Spirit has made you overseers *(episkopos)*, to shepherd *(poimein)* the church of God which He purchased with His own blood.'"
            (1) There is no difference made between an elder, bishop/overseer or shepherd.
            (2) Each word simply views the same man from a different vantage point.
         (b) 1 Peter 5:1-2 – "The elders *(presbuteros)* who are among you I exhort…Shepherd *(poimaino)* the flock of God which is among you, serving as overseers *(episkopos)*…"
            (1) There is no difference made between an elder, bishop/overseer or shepherd.
            (2) Each word simply views the same man from a different vantage point.
      5. These three Greek words are found in six English words in our Bible today: Bishops, Elders, Presbyters, Overseers, Pastors, Shepherds.
         (a) It is important to note that these six words (i.e., three Greek words) are used interchangeably in the New Testament to refer to the very same office.

II. **The New Testament Gives Explicit Qualifications That Elders Must Meet in Order to Serve.**
   A. Having a knowledge of the qualifications that God specified for elders to possess:
      1. Helps Bible students to understand the gravity of the work that these men do.
      2. Helps congregations to know how they are to be Scripturally organized.
      3. Gives Christian men a clear target for the kind of man God wants them to be.
   B. Every Christian man should strive to possess and grow in each of these areas.
      1. Serving as an elder should be a goal for every Christian man.
      2. Elders have an opportunity to emulate Jesus in ways that other Christians do not.
      3. Even if a man never serves as an elder, these qualities will make him a better husband, a better father, a better Christian and a better man.
   C. The qualifications for elders are not:
      1. Arbitrary – these are not a random list of various helpful traits.
      2. Optional – a man *"must"* possess them to be considered for possible appointment.
      3. Short-term – a man must *continue* to possess them to continue to serve.
      4. Multiple choice – a man must possess *all of them* to be considered for appointment.
      5. Best-case scenarios – no man can be "the next best thing" to being qualified.
      6. A group effort – each elder must possess every qualification, and not simply as a group.
      7. Automatic appointment as an elder – men must be selected, approved and then appointed to serve.
   D. God specifies His qualifications for elders in His church in 1 Timothy 3:1-7 and Titus 1:5-9.
      1. Each one is absolutely essential, thus God stated that a bishop "must be" (1 Tim. 3:2).
      2. A man must be more than just "a good man" or "the best we have" to be appointed an elder—he must meet all of the qualifications divinely set forth in Scripture.
      3. God is concerned about a man's character, his capabilities, his relationships, his experience, his Biblical proficiency and his motivation.
   E. Some qualifications for elders can be designated as **"domestic qualifications."**
      1. *"Husband of one wife"* – he is a one-woman man, neither polygamist nor bachelor.
      2. *"Rules (or manages) his own house well"* – he is the head of his house, who "stands in front of" and leads the way, but not acting as an authoritarian with an iron fist.
      3. *"Having his children in submission with all reverence"* – he has his "children under control" and they are in subjection to him "with all dignity" while under his leadership.
      4. *"Having faithful children"* or *"children who believe"* – his children are old enough to have made the decision to become Christians and live faithfully while in his house.
      5. *"Having children not accused of dissipation or insubordination (rebellion)"* – he has raised his children to be of good character, upright behavior and an orderly life.
      6. How a man "rules" his house is indicative of how he will "rule" the church (1 Tim. 3:4-5).
      (a) Scripture directs us to make this comparison in the life of a potential elder.
      7. His *wife* "must be" (not optional):
      (a) *"Reverent"* or *"dignified,"*
      (b) *"Not a slanderer"* or a *"malicious gossip,"*
      (c) *"Temperate"* or *"sober-minded,"*
      (d) *"Faithful in all things."*
      8. It should be noted that "children" in these passages, although in the plural, does not require that the man have more than one child. Having one child (who fits the specified qualifications for the children) would qualify the man. Consider these other passages where the word "children" (in the plural) quite obviously has application even to one child – Genesis 21:7; Luke 14:26; 1 Timothy 5:4.

F. Some qualifications for elders can be designated as **"positive qualifications."**
   1. *"Blameless" or "above reproach"* – he is irreproachable, not open to censure, where a charge can rightly be laid on him; he's not perfect, but he rightly handles his mistakes.
   2. *"Temperate"* – vigilant, circumspect, evenly tempered, exercising self-control.
   3. *"Sober-minded"* – prudent, self-controlled, sensible, balanced in judgment, exercising restraint.
   4. *"Of good behavior"* – respectable, orderly, well-ordered demeanor, disciplined, modest, measured, balanced.
   5. *"Hospitable"* – lit, "friendly to strangers"; generous to guests, courteous, friendly, rejoices in fellowship, pleased to share his goods, aware of the needs of others.
   6. *"Gentle"* – equitable, fair, mild, peaceful, kind, considerate.
   7. *"A lover of what is good"* – loving goodness, properly-placed priorities, loves things that are true and pure and of the highest kind of morality, finds happiness and joy in good people and good things, delights in godliness.
   8. *"Just"* – treating one's fellowmen in a fair and equitable manner, upright and honest in his dealings, recognizes and acts to protect the rights and privileges of others, refraining from partiality in the treatment of others.
   9. *"Holy"* – one who is dedicated to God, pleasing to God, properly discharges his Christian duties toward God, striving to live undefiled from sin.
   10. *"Able to teach"* – skillful in teaching, either publicly or privately, either believers or unbelievers; a good student of the Word, having a good knowledge of the Word and some skill in imparting it to others.
   11. *"Holding fast the faithful word…able, by sound doctrine, both to exhort and convict those who contradict"* – clings to sound doctrine, highly devoted to sound doctrine, takes a strong and firm stand on doctrinal truth, has courage to be uncompromising in his stand, able to recognize false doctrines and attacks on truth, defends the truth of God's Word, refutes and stops false teachers.
   12. *"A good testimony among outsiders"* – has a good reputation among non-Christians, who believe him to be honest, of high integrity and devoted to the cause of Christ.
G. Some qualifications for elders can be designated as **"negative qualifications."**
   1. *"Not given to wine"* – lit, "not near wine"; one who sits near wine, allowing himself to come under its allure and its control. He stays away from it.
   2. *"Not covetous"* – lit, "fond of silver"; loves money, greedy for filthy lucre, having an unholy desire for wealth, priorities which place more emphasis on material things.
   3. *"Not greedy for money"* – greedy for gain, inclined to an unhealthy desire for material possessions, avarice which can lead to mis-prioritization and dishonesty.
   4. *"Not violent"* – pugnacious, bruiser, striker, contentious, one who fights, a bully, resentful, possessed of a violent temper.
   5. *"Not quarrelsome"* – one who is peaceable rather than being a brawler, fighter, argumentative, belligerent, engaging in disputes of every kind.
   6. *"Not quick-tempered"* – prone to anger, quick to fly off the handle and make rash statements, vengeful, hot-headed, impetuous, easily irritated, short-fused.
   7. *"Not self-willed"* – self-pleasing, dominated by self-interest, inconsiderate of others, asserts his own will, has to have his way, arrogant, places his judgment ahead of others, stubborn, obstinate, inflexible, refuses to listen to other points of view.
   8. *"Not a novice"* or *"a recent convert"* – inexperienced, spiritually immature.

H. In summary:
   1. He must have a desire to serve, rather than be served.
   2. He must be a man of integrity.
   3. He must be a man of courage.
   4. He must be a man of the Book, with proven knowledge and ability.
   5. He must be the leader of his own home and have proven himself therein.
   6. He must be mindful of spiritual things more than material things.
   7. He must be able to work with others and lovingly lead others.
   8. He must be a people-person, love souls and want to help others go to heaven.
   9. He must be strong enough to stand for and defend truth without compromise.
   10. He must be willing and desirous to continue to grow and develop in all areas.
I. When a man has developed these character traits in his life, he is well-suited (as designated so by God Himself) to faithfully fulfill the work of a Biblical elder.
   1. Before a man can "take heed to the flock," God first expects the man to "take heed to himself" (cf. Acts 20:28).
   2. He must be a true man of God (in meeting these qualifications) before he can help other men/women of God faithfully serve God and reach their home in heaven.

III. The New Testament Gives Specific Responsibilities That Elders Must Fulfill in Their Work.
A. The Lord limits those who can serve as elders because His task for them is of critical importance to the health, growth and maturing of His church.
   1. Truly, if a man does not meet the Biblical qualifications for an elder, he will not be competent to fulfill the responsibilities that God has for him.
   2. The qualifications are not arbitrary but are necessary for the task.
B. The average church member may have very different ideas as to "what elders do."
   1. Some may see elders strictly as "the decision makers."
   2. Some may see elders as "those who sign the checks."
   3. Some may see elders as "the ones who make announcements."
   4. Some may see elders as "the ones who came to visit me in the hospital."
   5. Varying concepts exist as to the everyday duties of elders.
   6. They are so much more than any of these ideas even come close to expressing.
C. The reality is that "elders have the most solemn and serious responsibility of any group of men on earth" (Camp, "The Bible and Elders," p. 258). It must not be taken lightly.
D. Let's examine the responsibilities of elders from a Biblical perspective.
   1. There are 7 key passages that give us great insight into their work: Acts 20:28-31; 1 Thess. 5:12-13; 1 Timothy 3:1-7; 5:17-19; Titus 1:5-11; Hebrews 13:17; 1 Peter 5:1-4.
E. Elders have the responsibility to the congregation to **"take heed."**
   1. The Greek word for "take heed" in Acts 20:28 *(prosecho)* literally means "to hold to," signifying that one is to "hold his mind to" or "turn his attention to" something.
      (a) Perhaps it is better understood to "give heed."
      (b) This Greek word is often translated "beware" in the New Testament.
   2. Other translations have "be on guard for" (NASB) and "pay careful attention to" (ESV).
   3. The verb is a present imperative, commanding a continual, habitual action.
   4. The elders' responsibility in this regard is: "to yourselves" and "to all the flock."
   5. Note the word "all" which emphasizes the responsibility to hold one's attention toward each individual member and not just to the overall institution of the church.
   6. Being an elder is not an honorary position in which the men just "take it easy" and receive accolades for long tenures. It requires constant diligence and attentiveness.

F. Elders have the responsibility to the congregation to **"watch."**
   1. The Greek word for "watch" in Acts 20:31 *(gregoreo)* emphasizes a "spiritual alertness," or "staying awake spiritually."
      (a) This same Greek word:
         (1) Was used by Jesus in Matthew 25:13, regarding the second coming.
         (2) Was used by Peter in 1 Peter 5:8, regarding the devil.
      (b) Other translations have "be on the alert" (NASB) and "be alert" (ESV).
      (c) The verb is a present imperative, commanding a continual, habitual action.
      (d) Elders must stay awake and stay alert.
   2. The Greek word for "watch" in Hebrews 13:17 *(agrupneo)* emphasizes "to be without sleep" or "to be sleepless."
      (a) Vine remarks, "The word expresses not mere wakefulness, but the 'watchfulness' of those who are intent upon a thing" (667).
      (b) Paul uses this same word in Ephesians 6:18, regarding a Christian soldier's constancy in prayer.
      (c) The verb is present tense, indicating a continual action.
      (d) Note especially the object of the verb in this passage:
         (1) Elders "watch out for" (NKJV) or "watch over" (NASB) or "watch in behalf of" (ASV) "your souls."
         (2) An elder's sleeplessness is not due to material matters but spiritual matters.
      (e) Elders go without sleep in their effort to "watch out for" the souls of the church.
   3. The word "watch" inherently denotes those who were "watchmen" in ancient cities.
      (a) Often ancient cities would have "watchtowers" where "watchmen" would work.
      (b) Their responsibility was to:
         (1) keep a sharp eye out for the enemy and
         (2) warn the city of any approaching danger,
         (3) in order to keep the city safe and secure from enemy attack.
      (c) Thus, elders must protect the church by serving as "watchmen":
         (1) keeping a sharp eye out for the enemy and for danger (cf. Matt. 7:15-20),
         (2) warning the members of any approaching danger or pitfalls (cf. Acts 20:28-31),
         (3) in order to keep the Lord's church safe and secure from enemy attack.
      (d) Read carefully God's expectations of His watchmen in Ezekiel 3:16-21.
         (1) There is a grave responsibility placed upon watchmen.
         (2) Their very souls are at stake in the fulfillment of their task (cf. Heb. 13:17).
         (3) Watchmen (especially elders) must use God's Word to warn God's people!
G. Elders have the responsibility to the congregation to **"shepherd."**
   1. The Greek noun for "shepherd" *(poimen)* is used once in the New Testament to refer to the elders of the church, and most versions translate it as "pastors" (Eph. 4:11).
   2. The Greek verb for "shepherd" *(poimaino)* is used twice in the New Testament in some very instructive passages (Acts 20:28; 1 Pet. 5:2) regarding the work of elders.
      (a) Interestingly, this was a word "used of rulers" (Thayer), who would govern, manage and direct. It is often translated "rule" in the New Testament. This denotes that a shepherd was viewed as a position of authority in the church.
   3. Paul addressed elders in Acts 20:28, "Therefore take heed to yourselves and to all **the flock**, among which the Holy Spirit has made you overseers, **to shepherd the church** of God which He purchased with His own blood."
      (a) The verb "shepherd" in this verse is an infinitive of purpose.

- (b) Why are elders to "take heed" and to serve as "overseers"? What's the purpose?
- (c) The purpose that God has for elders in the church is to "shepherd" it.
4. Peter addressed elders in 1 Peter 5:2, "**Shepherd the flock of God** which is among you, serving as overseers, not by compulsion but willingly, not for dishonest gain but eagerly."
   - (a) The verb "shepherd" in this verse is an aorist imperative, commanding a specific act to be done with urgency.
   - (b) The Greek word for "flock" *(poimnion)* is found only 5 times in the New Testament, and it is always used metaphorically for Christians (Luke 12:32; Acts 20:28-29; 1 Pet. 5:2-3). Christians are sheep!
   - (c) Note how "the church" and "the flock" are used synonymously in these passages to help Bible readers understand the nature of the church.
5. Scripture has much to teach about the work of shepherding and often uses the word in a metaphorical sense to emphasize the special role God has given to elders.
   - (a) Older translations have the word "feed" in Acts 20:28.
     - (1) There is a different Greek word *(bosko)* that is most often the word used for "feed" (Luke 15:15, of feeding "swine"; John 21:15, 17, of feeding "sheep").
     - (2) Shepherding involves "feeding," but that is not the only aspect of the work.
     - (3) The Greek verb used for "shepherding" *(poimaino)* is sometimes translated "tend" (John 21:16; 1 Pet. 5:2, ASV). Elders are to "tend the flock."
     - (4) This is such a vivid word used to portray an elder's responsibility to the church.
   - (b) Like an actual shepherd, a shepherd (elder) of the Lord's church needs to:
     - (1) "Know," speak to and "call" the members by name (John 10:3, 14).
     - (2) "Lead" the members and "go before them," showing the way (John 10:4).
     - (3) Be one who "gives his life for the sheep" (John 10:11).
     - (4) "Care about the sheep" (John 10:13).
     - (5) Be "known by" the members (John 10:14).
     - (6) Be on guard against "savage wolves" (false teachers) (Acts 20:30-31).
     - (7) Care about and search diligently for "one [sheep] which is lost" (Luke 15:4).
     - (8) Be an "example to the flock" (1 Pet. 5:3).
   - (c) Consider how special a relationship there must be between a shepherd and the sheep for a shepherd to be able to fulfill these intimate responsibilities.
     - (1) A shepherd must spend time with the members outside the church building.
     - (2) A shepherd must be around the members casually and socially.
     - (3) A shepherd must know (personally) the sheep and be known (personally).
     - (4) A shepherd must never show partiality in his dealings with the members.
     - (5) A shepherd, by the nature of his work, will:
       - (i) Feed the members, teaching privately and publicly.
       - (ii) Show how to live a Christian life through his own daily walk.
       - (iii) Tend to the needs of the members.
       - (iv) Guide the flock to green pastures of rich and profitable Bible teaching.
       - (v) Protect the flock (individual members and the congregation as a whole).
       - (vi) Notice when a member has strayed and seek tirelessly to find and restore.
       - (vii) Correct wayward members, when necessary.
       - (viii) Soothe broken hearts and gently bind up broken lives.
       - (ix) Seek for opportunities to make a daily and eternal difference.

6. God takes the work of shepherding His people so seriously that He gave one of the strongest warnings in Scripture to shepherds who failed at shepherding God's people (Ezek. 34:1-10).
   (a) Some of the shepherds of Israel lost sight of their God-given purpose:
      (1) "Woe to the shepherds of Israel who feed themselves!"
      (2) "Should not the shepherds feed the flocks?"
   (b) The Lord specifies exactly where they had failed in their role as shepherds:
      (1) "You do not feed the flock.
      (2) "The weak you have not strengthened,
      (3) "nor have you healed those who were sick,
      (4) "nor bound up the broken,
      (5) "nor brought back what was driven away,
      (6) "nor sought what was lost…
      (7) "So [the sheep] were scattered because there was no shepherd…
      (8) "My sheep wandered…My flock was scattered…
      (9) "and no one was seeking or searching for them."
   (c) The Lord's displeasure with the shepherds is expressed in their punishment:
      (1) "Behold, I am against the shepherds,
      (2) "and I will require My flock at their hand."
   (d) Could the God of heaven ever say the same thing about shepherds in His church?
      (1) These things "were written for our learning" (Rom. 15:4), "as an example" and "for our admonition" (1 Cor. 10:11).
      (2) God wants His shepherds to take their shepherding seriously.
7. Like "the good shepherd" (John 10:11, 14) and "the Chief Shepherd" (1 Pet. 5:4) who shepherds the "souls" (1 Pet. 2:25) of His flock, elders in the Lord's church are "under-shepherds," who are charged with shepherding the souls of the local congregation "among" which they serve.

H. Elders have the responsibility to the congregation to be **"overseers."**
   1. The Greek verb for "oversee" *(episkopeo)* is used once in the New Testament to refer to the work of elders in the church (1 Pet. 5:2).
      (a) It is translated "serving as overseers" (NKJV), "taking the oversight" (KJV), "exercising oversight" (NASB), "exercising the oversight" (ASV).
   2. The Greek noun for "overseers" *(episkopos)* is used four times in the New Testament to refer to elders of the church (Acts 20:28; Phil. 1:1; 1 Tim. 3:1; Tit. 1:7).
      (a) It is translated as "overseers" and as "bishops."
      (b) Thus, the words "overseers" and "bishops" are synonymous terms for "elders."
   3. As "overseers," elders inherently have authority and responsibility in the local church.
      (a) The Greek word *episkopos* is a compound word meaning "to look or watch" *(skopos)* "over" *(epi)*. They have the responsibility to see that "things to be done by others are done rightly" (Thayer).
      (b) An overseer has accepted the responsibility to care for, watch over and guard the church.
      (c) Elders are responsible for the direction of a congregation.
      (d) Elders are responsible for the teaching done within a congregation.
      (e) Elders are responsible for the overall spiritual health of a congregation.
      (f) Elders are responsible for ensuring that sound doctrine is taught from the pulpit and all classes, and that the activities of the church are all Scriptural in nature.

4. An elder's primary "oversight" is of "souls" and of their eternal salvation.
   (a) The only time that *episkopos* is not used for an elder in the church is in 1 Peter 2:25 – "For you were like sheep going astray, but have now returned to the Shepherd and *Overseer* of your souls."
   (b) Jesus is called "the Overseer of souls."
   (c) Thus, "under-bishops" or "under-overseers" or "under-shepherds" must place their emphasis on being overseers of that which Jesus is an Overseer—"of souls"!
   (d) The eternal destiny of souls is of utmost and unparalleled importance!
5. An eldership's "oversight" also necessarily includes many responsibilities, including:
   (a) Appointing leaders in the local congregation, including deacons and preachers.
   (b) Organizing and assigning the various works of the church.
   (c) The operation of the church.
   (d) The finances of the church.
   (e) Discipline within the church.

I. Elders have the responsibility to the congregation to **"labor."**
   1. A Greek word commonly used for "labor" *(kopiao)* is used three times in the New Testament in reference to the work of elders (Acts 20:35; 1 Thess. 5:12; 1 Tim. 5:17).
      (a) The word signifies "growing weary," "laborious toil," "work with effort."
      (b) The term emphasizes working to the point of exhaustion and even while exhausted.
      (c) Each use of the verb is in the present tense, indicating a continual action.
   2. Some first-century elders were able to "labor in the word and doctrine" (1 Tim. 5:17).
      (a) These seem to be men who devoted themselves to full-time efforts in teaching.
      (b) All elders are to be "able to teach" (1 Tim. 3:2), and all elders are to "be able, by sound doctrine, both to exhort and convict those who contradict" (Tit. 1:9), but some, perhaps because of time or talent, can do this on an ongoing, daily basis.
      (c) Whether full-time or not, all elders need to "labor" in "teaching" the church.
   3. It is in the other two passages (Acts 20:35; 1 Thess. 5:12) where we find a fuller picture of an elder's labor.
      (a) Elders need to get into and study "the word of His grace" (Acts 20:32).
      (b) Elders need to "support the weak" (Acts 20:35).
      (c) Elders need to "admonish," "warn" and "give instruction" (1 Thess. 5:12).
      (d) Elders need to "admonish the disorderly" (1 Thess. 5:14).
         (1) Elders must "warn" those who are walking "out of step" to come back.
      (e) Elders need to "encourage the fainthearted" (1 Thess. 5:14).
         (1) Elders must "comfort" those who are discouraged and want to give up.
      (f) Elders need to "uphold the weak" (1 Thess. 5:14).
         (1) Elders must "hold firmly to" and "help" those who are weak in their faith.
      (g) Elders need to "be patient with all" (1 Thess 5:14).
         (1) Elders must be "longsuffering" and "enduring" with all members.
   4. When the Bible speaks about elders and "their work" (1 Thess. 5:13), it does not focus upon a business meeting but upon personal involvement in the lives of the members and laboring to help the souls in their care to reach heaven.

J. Elders have the responsibility to the congregation to **"steward."**
   1. The Greek word for "steward" literally means a "house manager."
      (a) A steward is himself subject to his lord, but he is "over" other people and things.
      (b) The goods under his care do not belong to him but to the master.

- (c) A steward is constantly aware of his responsibility to faithfully care for whatever or whoever has been placed in his charge.
- (d) Eventually, a steward will give an account to his master for his stewardship.
2. An elder in the Lord's church is "a steward of God" (Tit. 1:7).
   - (a) The elder is subject to the Lord, but he is "over" other people (1 Th. 5:12; Ac. 20:28).
   - (b) Those in his care do not belong to the elder himself, but to the Lord, for the church is "the flock *of God*" (1 Pet. 5:2).
   - (c) An elder must be faithful in discharging his duty as a steward (1 Cor. 4:2).
   - (d) An elder will eventually give an account for his stewardship (Heb. 13:17).
3. While an elder's primary stewardship is for the souls in his care, essentially every aspect of the work of the local congregation is under his stewardship.
   - (a) As such, an elder should remember that the church does not belong to him.
   - (b) The physical building and grounds do not belong to him.
   - (c) The money in the church's bank account does not belong to him.
   - (d) Everything about the Lord's church belongs to the Lord and should be faithfully managed and used to bring honor and glory to His name (1 Tim. 1:17).
4. An elder has the responsibility to "take care of the church of God" (1 Tim. 3:5).
   - (a) The Greek word for "take care" *(epimeleomai)* is only found here and in one other passage—the story of the Good Samaritan (Luke 10:34-35).
     - (1) The Samaritan went to the man who had been beaten and left for dead, and he "bandaged his wounds, pouring on oil and wine; and he set him on his own animal, brought him to an inn, and *took care of him*" (Luke 10:34).
     - (2) "On the next day, when he departed, he took out two denarii, gave them to the innkeeper, and said to him, *'Take care of him'*" (Luke 10:35).
   - (b) What a vivid illustration of how an elder is to "take care" of the church!
     - (1) This involves much more than making decisions—shepherds are not business managers who sit around an office.
     - (2) This necessitates seeing those who are hurting, going to them, bandaging their wounds, picking them up, carrying them along and taking care of them.
     - (3) Elders are in the "people business."
- K. Elders have the responsibility to the congregation to **"lead."**
  1. The English word "rule" is used at least four times in New Testament passages regarding elders, and it comes from two different Greek words.
  2. The Greek word for "rule" in Hebrews 13:17 *(hegeomai)* indicates being in a "supervisory capacity" as one who "leads" or "guides."
     - (a) Elders function in such a capacity, as they lead and guide the local congregation.
     - (b) The verb is present tense, indicating a continual action.
  3. Another Greek word for "rule" used for elders *(proistemi)* literally means "to stand before or in front of, to rule over, to manage."
     - (a) This word is used three times in 1 Timothy regarding elders:
       - (1) An elder must be "one who *rules* his own house well" (3:4).
       - (2) "For if a man does not know how to *rule* his own house, how will he take care of the church of God?" (3:5).
       - (3) "Let the elders who *rule* well be counted worthy of double honor" (5:17).
     - (b) While elders are not "the head of the church" (which is Christ, Eph. 5:23), they are the ones who "stand before the church" and "lead" the church. Thus, in that sense, they "rule" and must, therefore, "rule well."

(c) There is another usage of this Greek word in 1 Thessalonians 5:12 in reference to elders, but the word "rule" or "lead" is not in most translations.
   (1) "And we urge you, brethren, to recognize those who labor among you, and *are over you* in the Lord and admonish you."
   (2) As those who "stand before" the church and "rule over" the church, elders are understood as being "over you in the Lord" or those who "have charge over you in the Lord" (NASB). There is authority inherent in their work.
4. Elders are to lead, guide, direct, rule, manage and stand before the church.
   (a) An elder must be one "who leads, with diligence" (Rom. 12:8).
   (b) An elder must be one who leads "according to the integrity of his heart" (Ps. 78:72).
   (c) An elder must be one who "directs steps by the Word of God" (cf. Psa. 119:133).
   (d) An elder must be one who "leads in the paths of righteousness" (cf. Psa. 23:3).
   (e) An elder must be one who "leads by example" (cf. 1 Pet. 5:3).
   (f) An elder must be one who guides "every man" to be "perfect in Christ" (Col. 1:28).
   (g) An elder must be one who respects that he only leads "in the Lord" (1 Th. 5:12).
5. Elders are responsible for leading the church in withdrawing of fellowship from wayward brethren (cf. 1 Cor. 5:1-13; 2 Thess. 3:6-15; Matt. 18:15-18).
   (a) As the ones responsible for keeping the church pure, they will take sin seriously.
   (b) As the ones responsible for shepherding souls, they will know the sheep.
   (c) As the ones responsible for overseeing souls, they will be focused on eternity.
   (d) As the ones responsible for leading souls, they will guide the church in following the commands of Scripture and doing all that is necessary to save souls.
   (e) As the ones who are the under-shepherds, they will simply be following the lead of the Shepherd and Overseer of souls (1 Pet. 2:25), who Himself has withdrawn from those who walk disorderly (1 Cor. 5:4-5; 2 Thess. 3:6).
   (f) An entire lesson will focus on withdrawing fellowship later in this series.

L. Elders have the responsibility to the congregation to **"pray."**
1. The "Chief Shepherd" (1 Pet. 5:4), "who is "the Shepherd and Overseer of souls" (1 Pet. 2:25), prayed for those under His charge (John 17:6-26).
2. If the Chief Shepherd and Overseer saw the urgency of such a practice, then under-shepherds and under-overseers in the church must pray for those under their charge!
3. In fact, Christians are instructed, "Is anyone among you sick? Let him call for the elders of the church, and let them pray over him" (Jas. 5:14).
4. Elders should spend much time in private prayer in their own homes and in group prayers with the eldership.
   (a) Elders should pray for wisdom (Jas. 1:5).
   (b) Elders should pray for themselves.
   (c) Elders should pray for their fellow elders.
   (d) Elders should pray for the preachers and deacons.
   (e) Elders should pray for the children and young families.
   (f) Elders should pray, most importantly, for every soul within the congregation. While they need to pray for their physical well-being, more importantly, they need to pray for the spiritual well-being of every member (cf. 3 John 2).
5. Elders need to be men of prayer and should be recognized by the congregation as those who are in close communication with the Lord.
   (a) An elder may ask, "Is there anything for which you'd like me to be praying?"
   (b) An elder may share, "I want you to know that I've been praying for you."

M. In giving specific responsibilities to elders in the church, the Lord also addressed their motivation for serving (1 Pet. 5:2-3).
  1. Elders need to serve:
     (a) "Willingly" or "voluntarily" (NASB).
     (b) "Eagerly" or "zealously," with enthusiasm.
     (c) In order to be an "example to the flock" of Christian living and Christian service.
  2. Elders must not serve:
     (a) "Under compulsion," as if forced or coerced.
     (b) "For dishonest (or shameful) gain," acting out of greed for financial gain.
        (1) If an elder is compensated for his labor (1 Tim. 5:17-18), that must not be his motivation or purpose for serving as an elder.
        (2) Also, an elder must keep in mind that the treasury does not belong to him.
     (c) "As being lords (or lording it) over those entrusted to" them, with an arrogant or domineering spirit.
  3. A reading of Ezekiel 34 helps to keep a proper motivation in serving as an elder.
N. Faithful shepherds of the Lord's church are promised blessings and rewards.
  1. Those who "rule well" and "labor in word and doctrine" are "worthy of double honor" (1 Tim. 5:17). Specifically, they are to be compensated for their labor, for the Scripture teaches, "The laborer is worthy of his wages" (5:18).
  2. Even more rewarding than earthly compensation is the promise to under-shepherds that "when the Chief Shepherd appears, you will receive the crown of glory that does not fade away" (1 Pet. 5:4).

IV. The New Testament Teaches That Elders Have Authority Within the Local Congregation.
A. Some have tried to deny that elders have authority in the local congregation, but such a claim is without Biblical foundation.
B. When one surveys the qualifications that the Lord gives for elders, it is obvious that He has in mind for them to have a position of "authority" within a local congregation.
C. When one surveys the responsibilities that the Lord gives to elders (watching, shepherding, overseeing, leading, etc.), it is obvious that He has in mind for these men to have a position of "authority" within a local congregation.
D. In and of himself, one elder does not have any authority within or over a congregation.
  1. One elder does not have more authority than another elder.
  2. Authority is found within "the eldership" and not within "an elder."
  3. A single elder actually has no more authority in a congregation than any other member.
  4. Even within the eldership, one elder should not possess more authority than another.
  5. There is no place for "minority rule" within the eldership.
     (a) Each elder needs to subject himself to the other elders and to the eldership.
     (b) When an eldership makes a decision, all elders must unite behind it as "a unified decision of the eldership." There is no place for "dissenting" voices.
     (c) This is one reason that an elder must "not be self-willed" (Tit. 1:7), but humble.
     (d) A plurality of men is Scripturally required so that one or two do not dominate.
E. There is authority inherent within the eldership.
  1. They are "overseers" (Acts 20:28; Phil. 1:1).
  2. They "exercise oversight" (1 Pet. 5:2, NASB).
  3. They are "shepherds" (Acts 20:28; 1 Pet. 5:2-3).
  4. They are told to "take heed to the flock" (Acts 20:28).
  5. They are to work as "watchmen" (Heb. 13:17; Acts 20:28-32).

6. They are to "take care" of the church just as fathers rule their household (1 Tim. 3:4-5).
7. They "rule" (1 Tim. 5:17; Heb. 13:7, 17, 24).
8. They are to be "obeyed" (Heb. 13:17).
9. They "admonish" the church (1 Thess. 5:12).
10. They "stop the mouths" of false teachers (Titus 1:11).
11. They are "over you" (1 Thess. 5:12; Heb. 13:7, 17, 24).
12. They shall one day "give account" (Heb. 13:17).

F. All of this (and more) proves that the Lord Himself placed authority within the eldership.
G. The authority that an eldership has is not the same authority that Jesus has.
   1. Jesus has "all authority...in heaven and on earth" (Matt. 28:18).
      (a) That authority is *"exousia"* authority, indicating "the power of one whose will and commands must be submitted to by others and obeyed" (Thayer).
   2. While elders do not have Jesus' authority, that does not mean they have no authority.
H. An eldership has "authority" *under* the One who has "all authority."
   1. Their authority over a congregation is limited to the authority of Scripture.
   2. They have no authority to make law, change law or rescind law.
   3. They have no authority to bind anything that Christ has not bound.
   4. They do have authority to teach and expect members to obey the law of Christ.
   5. They do have authority to make decisions in the realm of judgment.
   6. They do have authority to protect the church from false teachings and teachers.
   7. They do have authority to protect the church from sin and impurities from within.
I. While possessing authority within a local congregation, elders recognize that they are not to "lord it over the flock" (1 Pet. 5:2-3).
   1. Elders should recognize and respect the limits of their authority in the congregation.
   2. Elders have no right to "lord it over" any member, including other elders.
   3. Elders should never behave like "office-seeking politicians."
   4. Elders must view their work as a God-given responsibility and not a matter of rank.
   5. Elders must be humble, like the Chief Shepherd (Phil. 2:3-8).
   6. Christ-like elders look at the word "serve" more than the word "rule" (cf. Mt. 20:28).

V. **The New Testament Gives Specific Responsibilities of the Members Toward the Elders.**
   A. There are some general responsibilities that members have toward the elders.
      1. They should have a working knowledge of the eldership as described in the N.T.
      2. They should know the Scriptural designations for these men and their significance.
         (a) The elders are "overseers."
             Therefore, the members (including each elder) are the "overseen."
         (b) The elders are "shepherds."
             Therefore, the members (including each elder) are the "sheep."
      3. They should be acquainted with the qualifications given in 1 Timothy 3 and Titus 1.
      4. They should recognize the authority inherent within the eldership.
      5. They should realize the tremendous (and grave) responsibility of being an elder.
         (a) It is not an office of "privilege" with a lot of "perks."
         (b) It is not a popularity contest.
         (c) It is not a promotion for "well-behaved deacons."
         (d) Elders are men who are willing to make daily personal sacrifices for the sake of the kingdom of God and the souls of the members.
      6. They should recognize what the flock owes the shepherds.
      7. They should trust their shepherds and follow their lead.

B. There are some specific responsibilities that members have toward the elders.
   1. Members need to "know," "respect" and "appreciate" the elders (1 Thess. 5:12)
   2. Members need to "recognize" the elders are "over" them "in the Lord" (1 Th. 5:12).
   3. Members need to "esteem them very highly in love for their work's sake" (1 Th. 5:13).
   4. Members need to "be at peace among" themselves (1 Thess. 5:13).
   5. Members need to "be submissive" to the elders (Heb. 13:17).
   6. Members need to "obey" the elders (Heb. 13:17), respecting their authority.
   7. Members need to "count" all elders worthy of "honor" (cf. 1 Tim. 5:17).
   8. Members need to "count" full-time elders "worthy of double honor" (i.e., compensation) (1 Tim. 5:17-18; cf. 1 Cor. 9:9-14).
   9. Members need to never accept "an accusation against an elder" from one person (1 Tim. 5:19).
   10. Members need to be slow and cautious with criticism (1 Tim. 5:19).
   11. Members need to follow the "example" of the elders (1 Pet. 5:3).
   12. Members need to "consider the outcome of their way of life, and imitate their faith," following their steps to heaven (Heb. 13:7).
   13. Members need to call the elders when in need (Jas. 5:14).
   14. Members need to pray for the elders (1 Tim. 2:1-2).
   15. Members need to make the work of elders a "joy" and not a "grief" (Heb. 13:17).
C. Members need to fulfill their responsibilities to the elders, just as much as the elders need to fulfill their responsibilities to the members. For, it is all "to the Lord"!

VI. There Is a Great Need in the Church Today.
A. There is a great need for men who will look at the qualifications for elders and challenge themselves to meet each of those qualifications.
   1. Even if a man never serves as an elder, he will be a better Christian (and husband, father, citizen, employee, neighbor, etc.) if he possesses and cultivates those qualities.
   2. Young men need to realize that they can make choices early in their life that could disqualify them from serving as an elder much later in their life.
   3. The qualifications are not suggestions. They are goals. They are requirements.
B. There is a great need for men who will accept the responsibility and honor of serving the church as an elder.
   1. No man is perfect. No elder is perfect. Only "The Shepherd and Overseer" is perfect!
   2. But, together, a plurality of men is able to strengthen each other and lead effectively.
   3. The church today needs more men who long to be shepherds of the flock of God.
C. There is a great need for members who will honor, submit to and obey the elders.
   1. It is not easy to be an elder, but it is easier when members fulfill their responsibilities.
   2. Members need to remember that elders "must give account" for the souls under their charge (Heb. 13:17). Therefore, members have a God-given responsibility to let the elders "watch out for [their] souls....with joy and not with grief."

Recommended Resources

Books

Brewer, G.C. *The Model Church.* Nashville: Gospel Advocate, 1957.

Brownlow, Leroy. *Why I Am a Member of the Church of Christ.* Fort Worth: Brownlow Publishing, 1973.

Camp, Franklin. *Principles and Perils of Leadership.* Birmingham, AL: Roberts & Sons, nd.

Cox, James D. *"...With the Bishops and Deacons."* Tustin, CA: James D. Cox, 1976.

Duncan, Bobby. *The Elders Which Are Among You.* Huntsville, AL: Publishing Designs, 1989.

Holland, Thomas H. *Encouraging Elders.* Brentwood, TN: Penmann Press, 1996.

Jennings, Alvin, ed. *Introducing the Church of Christ.* Fort Worth: Star Bible, 1981.

Lyles, Cleon. *Bigger Men for Better Churches.* Little Rock: Cleon Lyles, 1971.

McGarvey, J.W. *The Eldership.* Murfreesboro, TN: DeHoff Publications, 1990.

Phillips, H.E. *Scriptural Elders and Deacons.* Bowling Green, KY: Guardian of Truth, 1959.

Wharton, Edward C. *The Church of Christ.* Nashville: Gospel Advocate, 1997.

Wilson, L. R. *Congregational Development.* Nashville: Gospel Advocate, 1963.

Winkler, Wendell. *Leadership: The Crisis of Our Time.* Tuscaloosa, AL: Winkler Publications, 2003.

---. *The Mission of the Local Church.* Tuscaloosa, AL: Winkler Publications, 1971.

Articles

Camp, Franklin. "Developing Leadership." *Church Growth: A Blueprint For Stronger Churches (Freed-Hardeman College Lectureship).* Ed. William Woodson. Henderson, TN: Freed-Hardeman College, 1981. 73-83.

---. "Leadership." *Church Growth: A Blueprint For Stronger Churches (Freed-Hardeman College Lectureship).* Ed. William Woodson. Henderson, TN: Freed-Hardeman College, 1981. 43-72.

---. "The Bible and Elders." *The Bible Versus Liberalism (Freed-Hardeman College Lectureship).* Ed. W.A. Bradfield. Nashville: Gospel Advocate, 1972. 257-269.

---. "The Greatest Business in the World." *Church Growth: A Blueprint For Stronger Churches (Freed-Hardeman College Lectureship).* Ed. William Woodson. Henderson, TN: Freed-Hardeman College, 1981. 84-91.

Deaver, Mac. "Authority." *Advancing Christianity (Freed-Hardeman University Lectureship).* Ed. Winford Claiborne. Henderson, TN: Freed-Hardeman University, 1991. 86-89.

---. "A General Study of the Eldership." *Advancing Christianity (Freed-Hardeman University Lectureship)*. Ed. Winford Claiborne. Henderson, TN: Freed-Hardeman University, 1991. 77-81.

---. "Protecting the Flock." *Advancing Christianity (Freed-Hardeman University Lectureship)*. Ed. Winford Claiborne. Henderson, TN: Freed-Hardeman University, 1991. 82-85.

Gilmore, Joe. "The Authority of Elders in the Local Congregation." *The Church: The Beautiful Bride of Christ (Spiritual Sword Lectureship)*. Eds. Garland Elkins & Thomas B. Warren. Memphis: Getwell church of Christ, 1980. 60-62.

Jenkins, Jeff. "What the Church Owes Elders." *The Spiritual Sword* (Oct. 2003): 11-15.

Jenkins, Jerry. "What Elders Owe the Church." *The Spiritual Sword* (Oct. 2003): 7-11.

Nichols, Gus. "Authority of Elders." *The Church Today (Freed-Hardeman College Lectures)*. Ed. William Woodson. Henderson, TN: Freed-Hardeman College, 1975. 16-21.

Petrillo, Denny. "Why Would Any Man Want to be an Elder?" (Originally published by TheJenkinsInstitute.com)

Pharr, David R. "Qualifications of Elders." *The Spiritual Sword* (Oct. 2003): 15-19.

Stevens, Eldred. "The Eldership and Their Authority." *Freedom: Heritage, Accomplishments, and Prospects in Christ (Freed-Hardeman College Lectureship)*. Ed. William Woodson. Henderson, TN: Freed-Hardeman College, 1976. 221-231.

Wharton, Edward C. "The Pastoral Work and Qualifications of Elders." *The Church of Christ.* Nashville: Gospel Advocate, 1997. 83-94.

Periodicals

The Spiritual Sword. April 1978. "The Duty and Authority of Elders."

The Spiritual Sword. July 1996. "Leadership in the Church."

The Spiritual Sword. October 2009. "The Responsibility of Elders."

The Spiritual Sword. October 2009. "The Responsibility of Elders."

The Spiritual Sword. October 2003. "The Model Church."

The Spiritual Sword. January 2011. "Give Us Real Leaders."

Lesson 14: The Mission and Work of the Church

I. **The Church of Christ Has a Glorious Purpose!**
   A. The church is made up of those who have been saved from their sins by Christ Jesus.
   B. All the saved have been banded together in one body, with a unified purpose.
   C. The ultimate and glorious purpose of the church is to glorify God, its Creator and Savior!
      1. "…to Him be glory in the church by Christ Jesus to all generations, forever and ever. Amen" (Eph. 3:20-21; cf. Rom. 11:36; Heb. 13:21).
      2. "…now the manifold wisdom of God might be made known by the church…according to the eternal purpose which He accomplished in Christ Jesus our Lord" (Eph. 3:10-11).
      3. "…that you may proclaim the praises of Him who called you out of darkness" (1 Pet. 2:9).
   D. The church has no other and no greater purpose than giving (and being) glory to God!
      1. If a church aims for or finds itself serving some other purpose, it is not God's church!
      2. As the church "of Christ," the church seeks to be like Christ and to be able to say to the Father, as Christ did, "I have glorified You on the earth. I have finished the work which You have given Me to do" (John 17:4).

II. **The Church of Christ Has a Glorious Mission!**
   A. As the church "of Christ," the church bears the same mission as Christ did.
   B. Christ and His church are inseparably connected.
      1. Christ is the head; the church is the body (Eph. 1:22-23; 5:23).
      2. Therefore, whatever mission He had is the mission that we have!
   C. The mission of Christ on earth was stated plainly, "For the Son of Man has come to seek and to save that which was lost" (Luke 19:10).
      1. All have sinned and fallen short of the glory of God (Rom. 3:9-10, 23).
      2. All are in desperate need of salvation from their sins (Isa. 59:1-2; Rom. 1:16-17).
      3. The mission of Christ was to die that He might bring salvation to all.
      4. The mission of the church is to proclaim the message that brings salvation to all.
      5. The mission of Christ was given to His disciples to continue (cf. John 17:1-19).
   D. **The mission of the church is saving souls!**
      1. Everything, E-V-E-R-Y-T-H-I-N-G that the church does must be to save souls!
      2. Every program in which the church engages must be directed to save souls!
      3. Every decision made by the leadership must be directed to save souls!
      4. The Lord's church has only one mission—to save souls! Everything falls under that!
   E. In order to fulfill its purpose of glorifying God, the church must fulfill Christ's mission!
      1. The mission of the church is intricately linked to the mission of Christ!
      2. As His body on this earth, we stand in the place of Christ and "we implore…on Christ's behalf," pleading with men to "be reconciled to God" (2 Cor. 5:20).

III. **The Church of Christ Has a Glorious Responsibility!**
   A. In glorifying God and saving souls, the church also bears a responsibility to God's truth.
   B. Paul wrote the following to Timothy:
   "I write so that you may know how you ought to conduct yourself in the house of God, which is the church of the living God, the pillar and ground of the truth" (1 Tim. 3:15).
   C. Calling the church "the pillar and ground of the truth" is powerful:
      1. Note the definite article "the" before truth. The church is not just the pillar and ground of "a" truth, but of "<u>the</u> truth"—pure, objective, absolute, singular truth (cf. John 8:32)!

2. In reality, the truth of God is its own pillar and ground (regarding its inspiration and authenticity), but in its mission to save souls, the church must support, maintain, stabilize, represent and defend the truth of God before all men.
3. If the church does not faithfully stand as the pillar and ground of the truth among the various times and cultures of the world (cf. 1 Cor. 16:13; Eph. 6:11-14), who will?

IV. **The Church of Christ Has a Glorious Work!**
   A. The church has work to do!
      1. We are not merely saved to be saved!
      2. We are saved to work (Eph. 2:8-10)!
   B. There are several things that make the church's work a glorious work:
      1. It is the work of the Lord (1 Cor. 15:58).
      2. It is work that we can and must do together (Phil. 1:27).
      3. The Lord equips us to do His work (Heb. 13:21).
      4. The Lord works <u>with</u> us as we work for Him (1 Cor. 3:5-9).
      5. The Lord works <u>in</u> us as we work for Him (Phil. 2:12-13; Heb. 13:21).
   C. God wanted His people to be happy, so He gave them something to do for Him!
      1. The work of the Lord ought to bring us a joy and satisfaction unlike anything else on this earth!
      2. The Lord's church has been "created in Christ Jesus for good works" (Eph. 2:10).

V. **The Purpose, Mission, Responsibility and Work of the Church Is Carried Out By Local Congregations.**
   A. It is possible and practical (and Biblical) for congregations to cooperate with one another and collaborate to carry out certain works, including in:
      1. The area of evangelism (Acts 11:19-30; Phil. 4:15-16).
      2. The area of edification (Acts 15:1-29; 18:27).
      3. The area of benevolence (Acts 11:27-30; Rom. 15:26-27; 1 Cor. 16:1-2; 2 Cor. 8-9).
   B. However, the Lord holds individual congregations responsible for how they carry out His work and remain faithful to His cause (Rev. 2-3).
   C. The Lord established His church to have autonomous (i.e., independent, self-governing) local congregations. (See pages 133-134.)
      1. The responsibility for carrying out His work is squarely and equally on each congregation.
      2. This indicates that each congregation will be held accountable for how they have carried out the work of the Lord.
      3. One congregation's success or failure will not be conveyed to a sister congregation.
   D. While congregations can cooperate with each other and work together, one congregation's great ability and successes in one aspect of the Lord's work does not ease the burden on other congregations to fulfill their responsibility in that same work.
      1. Because one congregation is particularly successful in evangelism or global mission work does not mean that another congregation has less of a burden to the same works.

VI. **In Its Mission of Saving Souls, the Church of Christ Is Given the Work of Evangelism.**
   A. The Greek word for "evangelism" comes from the same root as the word "gospel."
      1. "Gospel" means "good news," and "evangelism" means "bringing good news."
      2. So, evangelism involves preaching, announcing, making known good news.
      3. There is good news about sin and about salvation in Jesus Christ!
         (a) "All have sinned and fall short of the glory of God" (Rom. 3:23).
         (b) "The wages of sin is death" (Rom. 6:23). "The soul who sins shall die" (Ezek. 18:20).

-
  -
    - (c) However, the good news or "gospel of Christ" is the "power of God unto salvation" from sin (Rom. 1:16).
    - (d) It is good news "that Christ Jesus came into the world to save sinners" (1 Tim. 1:15) and "desires all men to be saved" (1 Tim. 2:4).
  - 4. Every accountable person in the world needs the gospel of Christ (Mark 16:15)!
    - (a) Every person outside of Christ is lost (Eph. 2:12; 2 Tim. 2:10).
    - (b) No lost person on this earth can be saved without the gospel (Rom. 1:16).
    - (c) How did God intend for the lost to find and hear the gospel of Jesus?
    - (d) That is the mission of His church!
- B. The church has been commissioned by Christ Himself.
  1. "And Jesus came and spoke to them, saying, 'All authority has been given to Me in heaven and on earth. Go therefore and make disciples of all the nations, baptizing them in the name of the Father and of the Son and of the Holy Spirit, teaching them to observe all things that I have commanded you; and lo, I am with you always, even to the end of the age.' Amen" (Matt. 28:18-20).
  2. "And He said to them, 'Go into all the world and preach the gospel to every creature. He who believes and is baptized will be saved; but he who does not believe will be condemned'" (Mark 16:15-16).
- C. In evangelism, the church is to spread the good news:
  1. The good news of the manifold wisdom of God (Eph. 3:10-11).
  2. The good news about the death, burial and resurrection of Christ (1 Cor. 15:1-4).
  3. The good news of the saving power of the blood of Jesus (Matt. 26:28; Rev. 1:5).
  4. The good news of the abundant grace of God (1 Tim. 1:12-15; Tit. 2:11).
  5. The good news of forgiveness and freedom from sin (Acts 2:38; 22:16; Rom. 6:6-7).
  6. The good news of coming "out of darkness into His marvelous light" (1 Pet. 2:9).
  7. The good news of justification by faith in Christ (Rom. 3:21-26; 5:1-2; 1 Cor. 6:11).
  8. The good news of an eternal home promised in heaven (2 Cor. 5:1-8; John 14:1-3).
  9. "Go into all the world and preach the gospel (i.e., the good news)..." (Mark 16:15).
- D. In evangelism, the church is to spread the good news to everyone:
  1. To our family members (John 1:39-42; Acts 16:31-34).
  2. To our friends (John 1:43-51; Acts 10:24-33).
  3. To our neighbors (Acts 1:8; 5:42).
  4. To our enemies (Acts 8:4-13; 9:10-18; 10:28).
  5. To complete strangers (Acts 13-28).
  6. To everyone lost in sin (Matt. 18:11; Acts 17:16-34).
  7. To lost souls in our immediate area (1 Cor. 9:11-14; Acts 11:26).
  8. To lost souls around the world (Acts 1:8; 8:4; Col. 1:23).
  9. "Go into all the world and preach the gospel to every creature" (Mark 16:15).
- E. The church in the New Testament followed the commission and set an example for us.
  1. "They spoke the word of God with boldness" (Acts 4:31).
  2. "Daily in the temple, and in every house, they did not cease teaching and preaching Jesus as the Christ" (Acts 5:42).
  3. They "went everywhere preaching the word" (Acts 8:4).
  4. They "turned the world upside down" (Acts 17:6).
  5. From them "the word of the Lord has sounded forth...in every place" (1 Thess. 1:8).
  6. Only thirty years after the establishment of the church in Acts 2, Paul was able to write, "the gospel...was preached to every creature under heaven" (Col. 1:23+6).

F. The work of evangelism is a global and local operation.
  1. The church must send preachers/missionaries "into all the world" (Mark 16:15).
     (a) There are billions of souls around this planet who need to hear the gospel.
     (b) Wherever there is a lost soul, the gospel needs to be proclaimed.
     (c) Missionaries must be sent and supported to preach the gospel (Acts 13:1-3; 2 Cor. 11:8-9; Phil. 4:14-19).
  2. The church must be active in seeing lost souls in the local community and reaching out to them with the gospel (John 4:35; Rom. 1:14-16; Acts 5:42; 8:4).
     (a) "Evangelism" and "mission work" are not works reserved for missionaries (trained preachers) to fulfill in other places around the world!
     (b) "Evangelism" and "mission work" are responsibilities of every local congregation to fulfill in their own back yard!
  3. The gospel must be taken to every lost soul, regardless of who they are (Gal. 3:28).
G. The Lord's church is solely responsible for taking the gospel to the lost world! It is critical that we understand the urgency of the task and our own accountability.
  1. The Lord told Ezekiel more than 2,500 years ago:
     "So you, son of man: I have made you a watchman for the house of Israel; therefore you shall hear a word from My mouth and warn them for Me. When I say to the wicked, 'O wicked man, you shall surely die!' and you do not speak to warn the wicked from his way, that wicked man shall die in his iniquity; but his blood I will require at your hand. Nevertheless if you warn the wicked to turn from his way, and he does not turn from his way, he shall die in his iniquity; but you have delivered your soul" (Ezek. 33:7-9).
  2. H.A. Dixon (1904-1969), President of Freed-Hardeman College (1950-1969), often said: "The real reasons we have not evangelized this world are: We have never convinced ourselves that the world is lost without the gospel, and we have never convinced ourselves that we are lost if we don't take it to the world."
H. The church's work in evangelism must be focused on saving souls.

VII. **In Its Mission of Saving Souls, the Church of Christ Is Given the Work of Edification.**
A. "Edification" has to do with building up and promoting growth (spiritual growth).
  1. When the work of evangelism is fruitful and individuals become Christians, the mission of saving souls (their souls) is not complete.
  2. Once they're saved, Christians need to be "rooted and built up in Him and established in the faith" (Col. 2:7).
  3. In the Great Commission, true disciples are made not only by baptizing them but by "teaching them to observe all things" (Matt. 28:20).
B. It is essential for every Christian to grow spiritually!
  1. Every Christian must "grow in the grace and knowledge of our Lord" (2 Pet. 3:18).
  2. Christians, who were not growing properly in the first century, were reprimanded for their stagnation and lack of spiritual growth (Heb. 5:12).
     (a) When God told early Christians, "by this time you ought to be teachers," He indicated that it does not take a lifetime to get ready to teach.
     (b) Christians must grow and ready themselves to teach, and do so with rapidity rather than sluggishness or procrastination.
  3. Spiritual growth must take place with an increase in knowledge of sound doctrine and then must be exhibited with an increase in faithful Christian living (2 Pet. 1:5-7).
     (a) True spiritual growth requires "giving all diligence" (1:5+10).

4. Failing to grow properly will lead to unfruitfulness and unfaithfulness (2 Pet. 1:8-9).
5. Satan is ever-busy, seeking opportunities to prevent, stunt, divert and reverse spiritual growth in a Christian's life (Luke 8:12; Eph. 6:10-13); therefore, we must be ever vigilant and determined in our efforts (1 Pet. 5:8-9).

C. In edification, the church is responsible for helping all members to grow.
   1. The church needs to "pursue the things...by which one may edify another" (Rom. 14:19).
   2. God has organized and structured His church, in order that (Eph. 4:12-15):
      (a) The saints can be <u>equipped</u> for the work of the ministry (v. 12).
      (b) The body can be <u>edified</u> and <u>built up</u> (v. 12).
      (c) The church can reach a unified level of <u>faith and knowledge</u> of Christ (v. 13).
      (d) The brethren may <u>not be carried</u> about by false doctrines and cunning (v. 14).
      (e) The body may <u>grow up</u> in all things into the head, Christ (v. 15).
      (f) The whole body might be <u>joined and knit</u> together (v. 16).
      (g) The body can be properly fed and engage in effective exercise (individually and collectively).
   3. When a local congregation is properly edifying the body, it will result in (Eph. 4:16):
      (a) Every member effectively working to do <u>his/her share</u> (v. 16).
      (b) Continual <u>growth</u> of the body and continued <u>edification</u> of itself (v. 16).
      (c) The building up of the individual member and the entire body.
   4. We must all "strive to excel in building up the church" (1 Cor. 14:12, ESV).

D. Collectively, the church is edified and edifies one another through a variety of means:
   1. Encouraging one another edifies the church (individually and collectively).
      (a) Barnabas, the Son of Encouragement, "...was glad, and encouraged them all that with purpose of heart they should continue with the Lord" (Acts 11:23).
      (b) "Exhort one another daily, while it is called 'Today'" (Heb. 3:13).
      (c) "Therefore comfort each other and edify one another" (1 Thess. 5:11).
   2. Worshiping together edifies the church (individually and collectively).
      (a) In the context of worship, "Let all things be done for edification" (1 Cor. 14:26).
      (b) "And let us consider one another in order to stir up love and good works, not forsaking the assembling...but exhorting one another..." (Heb. 10:24-25).
      (c) "...many are weak and sick among you...Therefore, my brethren, when you come together to eat, wait for one another" (1 Cor. 11:30, 34).
   3. Studying the Bible together edifies the church (individually and collectively).
      (a) "...Desire the pure milk of the word, that you may grow thereby" (1 Pet. 2:2).
      (b) "...the word of His grace, which is able to build you up" (Acts 20:32).
   4. Engaging in fellowship together edifies the church (individually and collectively).
      (a) "I thank my God...for your fellowship in the gospel..." (Phil. 1:3-5).
      (b) "So they...entered the house...they encouraged [the brethren]" (Acts 16:40).
      (c) Christians need to be "given to hospitality" (Rom. 12:13; cf. 1 Pet. 4:9).

E. While all brethren in the church need encouragement, Scripture makes special mention of:
   1. Those who are younger (Tit. 2:1-8; 1 Tim. 4:12).
   2. Those who are older (1 Pet. 5:5; 1 Tim. 5:1-2).
   3. Those who are widows and orphans (Jas. 1:27).
   4. Those who are new converts (Acts 11:21-24; 14:21-22).
   5. Those who are weak in the faith (Rom. 15:1; 1 Thess. 5:14).
   6. Those who are discouraged (1 Thess. 5:14; Rom. 12:10-11).
   7. Those who are wayward and need to be restored (Jas. 5:19-20; Gal. 6:1).

F. The church's work in edification must be focused on saving souls.
   1. True and Biblical edification must be designed to save souls!
   2. A church must not become so engrossed in edification programs that it loses sight of evangelizing the world and reaching the lost. The church must not stop evangelizing!

VIII. In Its Mission of Saving Souls, the Church of Christ Is Given the Work of Benevolence.
   A. "Benevolence" has to do with supplying physical, material and temporal service and help to persons in need.
      1. Note that benevolence is dealing with physical and material needs (not spiritual).
      2. Note that benevolence is supplying only temporary assistance (not permanent).
      3. However, the ultimate goal of all benevolence must be on the eternal.
   B. Helping and serving those in need is a command (and an expectation) of God!
      1. "Let him who stole steal no longer, but rather let him labor, working with his hands what is good, that he may have something to give him who has need" (Eph. 4:28).
      2. "Therefore, as we have opportunity, let us do good to all, especially to those who are of the household of faith" (Gal. 6:10; cf. 1 Tim. 5:16).
      3. "Pure and undefiled religion before God and the Father is this: to visit orphans and widows in their trouble, and to keep oneself unspotted from the world" (Jas. 1:27).
      4. "And just as you want men to do to you, you also do to them likewise" (Luke 6:31).
      5. "Let us not love in word or in tongue, but in deed and in truth" (1 John 3:18).
   C. Helping and serving those in need emulates and serves Christ Himself!
      1. "...The Son of Man did not come to be served, but to serve" (Matt. 20:28).
      2. "Jesus of Nazareth...went about doing good" (Acts 10:38; cf. Luke 4:16-19).
      3. On the day of judgment, Jesus "will say to those on His right hand, 'Come, you blessed of My Father, inherit the kingdom prepared for you from the foundation of the world: for I was hungry and you gave Me food; I was thirsty and you gave Me drink; I was a stranger and you took Me in; I was naked and you clothed Me; I was sick and you visited Me; I was in prison and you came to Me.' Then the righteous will answer Him, saying, 'Lord, when did we see You hungry and feed You, or thirsty and give You drink? When did we see You a stranger and take You in, or naked and clothe You? Or when did we see You sick, or in prison, and come to You?' And the King will answer and say to them, 'Assuredly, I say to you, inasmuch as you did it to one of the least of these My brethren, you did it to Me'" (Matt. 25:34-40; cf. 41-45).
   D. Helping and serving those in need was a priority of the early church.
      1. "Now all who believed were together, and had all things in common, and sold their possessions and goods, and divided them among all, as anyone had need" (Acts 2:44-45).
      2. "Now the multitude of those who believed were of one heart and one soul; neither did anyone say that any of the things he possessed was his own, but they had all things in common" (Acts 4:32).
      3. "Nor was there anyone among them who lacked; for all who were possessors of lands or houses sold them, and brought the proceeds of the things that were sold, and laid them at the apostles' feet; and they distributed to each as anyone had need" (Acts 4:34-35).
      4. The ministering to the widows in Acts 6:1-6 is another great example.
   E. Helping and serving those in need is to be done by the church (not just individuals)!
      1. The church must be characterized by a generous spirit and a compassionate heart!

2. The church in Antioch "determined to send relief to the brethren dwelling in Judea. This they also did, and sent it…" (Acts 11:27-30).
3. The churches in Macedonia and Achaia were pleased "to make a certain contribution for the poor among the saints who are in Jerusalem" (Rom. 15:25-27).
4. Churches in the first century were cooperating with each other to help those in need (1 Cor. 16:1-2; 2 Cor. 8:1-24; 9:1-15).
5. As benevolence is a work to be done by the church ("to Him be glory in the church," Eph. 3:21), Christians should look for opportunities to help others through (and in) the church before organizations that are tied to denominational groups.

F. Helping and serving those in need includes those inside and outside the church.
1. We are to help brethren who are in need (Acts 11:27-30).
    (a) In fact, they are to be given a special portion of our attention (Gal. 6:10b).
    (b) One way in which Christians are to "[b]e kindly affectionate to one another with brotherly love" is by "distributing to the needs of the saints" (Rom. 12:10, 13).
2. "As we have opportunity," we are to "do good to all" (Gal. 6:10a).
    (a) This would include those outside the church, since the last part of the verse makes a contrast with those inside the church.
    (b) See the word "all" again in 2 Corinthians 9:12-13.
    (c) The Parable of the Good Samaritan teaches us to do good to our "neighbor," whoever he might be (Luke 10:25-37).
3. Widows and orphans in the church are to be given special care.
    (a) This responsibility again is for both the congregation and the individual members (Jas. 1:27; Acts 11:27-30; Gal. 6:10).
    (b) Children have the primary responsibility to care for their parents (1 Tim. 5:8), and if not children, then relatives have a special charge to look after widows in their family (1 Tim. 5:4, 16).
    (c) When widows need special care and families cannot provide, the church is charged to help (1 Tim. 5:1-16; Acts 6:1-8; Jas. 1:27).

G. Helping and serving those in need must focus on souls and getting them to heaven!
1. The church is not set up as a charitable organization engaged in social betterment!
2. The church is not set up to minister merely to physical and temporal needs!
3. The church IS set up to seek and save the lost with the gospel of Christ (Rom. 1:16)!

H. The church's work in benevolence must be focused on saving souls.
1. True and Biblical benevolence must be designed to save souls!
2. A church must not become so engrossed in benevolence programs that it loses sight of evangelizing the world and reaching the lost. The church must not stop evangelizing!

IX. **Conclusion**
A. The purpose and work of the church is NOT to:
1. Operate in the political arena or shape public policy.
2. Operate as a community center or social welfare organization.
3. Take the place of the home or the parents in the lives of children.
4. Furnish entertainment or be a recreation center.
5. Compete with other organizations of men.
6. Confuse worshiping every week with actually working for the Lord.
7. Make deposits in the bank and keep a large balance of funds.
8. Focus on the material or non-spiritual needs of members or non-members.

B. The purpose and work of the church IS to:
   1. Glorify God and manifest His wisdom.
   2. Fulfill Christ's mission to save souls.
   3. Stand firm as the pillar and ground of the truth.
   4. Labor for God and with God in carrying out His work on this earth through:
      (a) Evangelism, spreading the good news of Christ and salvation through Him.
      (b) Edification, building up the brethren to faithful lives of service to Him.
      (c) Benevolence, assisting those in need with material and temporary help.
   5. Focus on souls and leading them to heaven.
C. The church must have authority for all that it does in the work of the Lord.
   1. The church must "do all in the name of the Lord" (Col. 3:17).
   2. The church must see the work of the church as *the Lord's work, and not man's!*
   3. When the work is understood to be the Lord's, then the church will:
      (a) Want to do the work in the Lord's way.
      (b) Want to do the work for the Lord's reasons.
      (c) Want to do the work for the Lord's glory.
D. The mission and work of the church is great and glorious because the God we serve is Himself great and glorious!
   1. The work of the church is a much greater work than any human organization!
   2. The work of the church is of divine origin and purpose!
   3. The work of the church is focused on the spiritual and eternal needs of man!
   4. The work of the church is designed for one primary purpose: save souls!
   5. The work of the church is to work!

Recommended Resources

Books

Baxter, Batsell Barrett. *The Family of God.* Nashville: Gospel Advocate, 1980.

Winkler, Wendell. *The Mission of the Local Church.* Tuscaloosa, AL: Winkler Publications, 1971.

Articles

Bland, Billy. "Restoring the Mission of the Church." *Restoring the New Testament Church (Spiritual Sword Lectureship).* Ed. Gary McDade. Memphis: Getwell church of Christ, 2006. 325-337.

Brownlow, Leroy. "Because It Is Scriptural in Doing Missionary Work." *Why I Am a Member of the Church of Christ.* Fort Worth: Brownlow Publishing, 1973. 78-85.

Clevenger, Eugene W. "The Church of Christ—Its Mission." *The Church of Christ (Freed-Hardeman College Lectures).* Ed. Thomas B. Warren. Nashville: Gospel Advocate, 1971. 154-162.

Connally, Andrew M. "The Church—And Its World-Wide Mission." *The Church: The Beautiful Bride of Christ (Spiritual Sword Lectureship).* Eds. Garland Elkins & Thomas B. Warren. Memphis: Getwell church of Christ, 1980. 37-40.

Ferguson, Everett. "The Work of the Church." *The New Testament Church.* Abilene, TX: Biblical Research Press, 1968. 67-73.

Light, Michael. "The Mission of the Lord's Church." *The Lord's Church: Past, Present and Future (POWER Lectures).* Ed. B.J. Clarke. Southaven, MS: Southaven church of Christ, 1999. 547-558.

McGill, James R. "The Church—And Its Concern for the Poor." *The Church: The Beautiful Bride of Christ (Spiritual Sword Lectureship).* Eds. Garland Elkins & Thomas B. Warren. Memphis: Getwell church of Christ, 1980. 90-97.

Lesson 15: The Worship of the Church

I. **God Created Man with an Instinctive Need to Worship.**
   A. Created in God's image, man is innately designed to seek Him (Acts 17:26-27).
      1. As civilizations have been studied (both past and present), it is apparent that worshiping someone or something is a universal, basic human need—as if mankind was designed that way.
      2. The immortal soul longs to worship the eternal God.
   B. Sometimes, when there is no proper instruction, this instinct will lead to worshiping the wrong image (Ex. 32:8; 2 Kgs. 21:3; Dan. 3:7; Acts 10:25; 14:12-18; 17:16; Rev. 22:8).
   C. By following proper instruction, there is something intensely thrilling and satisfying about worshiping God (Psa. 26:8; 27:4-6; 42:1-2), so that the heart of every worshiper can shout, "I was glad when they said to me, 'Let us go into the house of the Lord'" (Psa. 122:1).
   D. One of the first recorded activities of man in the Bible was worship (Gen. 4:3-5).

II. **God Has Always Provided Mankind with Instruction Regarding Acceptable Worship.**
   A. The first record of worship in the Bible (in Genesis 4:3-5) shows there is such a thing as acceptable worship and such a thing as unacceptable worship.
      1. God had two very different responses to the first record of worship in the Bible:
         (a) "The Lord...respected Abel and his offering..."
         (b) "...but [the Lord] did not respect Cain and his offering" (Gen. 4:4-5).
      2. Right away Bible readers learn that not all worship is alike, nor is all worship accepted.
      3. The Bible later gives a possible explanation of what led to these differences in worship.
         (a) Hebrews 11:4 states, "By faith Abel offered to God a more excellent sacrifice than Cain, through which he obtained witness that he was righteous..."
         (b) Tie that verse of Abel's worship being offered "by faith" with Romans 10:17 – "So then faith comes by hearing, and hearing by the word of God."
         (c) Abel heard the Word of God on the matter of worship and, by faith, obeyed the Word of God on that matter.
         (d) What might be said, then, of the cause of Cain's worship?
      4. Thus, we can know that God provided Cain and Abel with instruction regarding worship.
   B. God continued to provide instruction through the Mosaic and Christian Dispensations.
      1. Exodus, Leviticus and Deuteronomy gave details for acceptable Jewish worship.
      2. The books of the New Testament give details for acceptable Christian worship.
      3. God has always explained the purpose, means and benefits of acceptable worship, and it has always been man's responsibility to learn, read and follow His instructions.
   C. It is essential that worshipers understand and offer acceptable worship to God!

III. **God Has Warned Christians About Worship That Is Not Acceptable.**
   A. Idol worship is not acceptable to God (1 Cor. 10:14).
      1. Idols can be stone/wooden objects (Acts 17:23), money (Col. 3:5) or self (Phil. 2:21).
      2. Any form that an idol takes in a person's life can become an object of worship.
      3. Obviously, this form of worship is unacceptable to God.
   B. Ignorant worship is not acceptable to God (Acts 17:23).
      1. To seek to worship God "without knowing" Him or understanding His will for worship is to worship in ignorance.
      2. If ignorant worship were acceptable to God, there would be no need to correct it or change it.
      3. Obviously, this form of worship is unacceptable to God.

C. Vain worship is not acceptable to God (Matt. 15:8-9).
   1. To seek to worship God merely externally (without the heart) or to worship based on the doctrines or commandments of men is to worship in vain.
   2. Jesus clearly affirmed that it is possible to go through the motions of worship but for a person's heart to be "far from" Him.
   3. Jesus would not tolerate those who substituted their own teachings and traditions in worship over the commandments of God. This form of worship is unacceptable to God.
D. Will-worship is not acceptable to God (Col. 2:23).
   1. To seek to worship God according to "self-imposed religion, false humility" or according to one's own feelings, rules and innovations is "will-worship" (ASV).
   2. Will-worship completely loses sight of *what* and *who* worship is all about. *Man* is neither the *what* nor the *who* of worship. GOD IS!
   3. Obviously, this form of worship is unacceptable to God.
E. Since Scripture devotes so much space to addressing worship that is not acceptable to God:
   1. Man must be diligent to investigate Scripture for what is acceptable to God.
   2. Man must be vigilant to inspect his worship and ensure it is God-approved.

IV. God Has Clearly Defined True and Acceptable Worship for Christians.
   A. The primary Greek word for "worship" is a compound word, *proskuneo*.
      1. *Pros* means "towards" and *kuneo* means "to kiss"; literally, "to kiss towards."
      2. The word is defined, "to make obeisance, do reverence to; an act of homage."
      3. In worship, the worshiper acts to show reverence to the one being worshiped.
      4. In worship of Jehovah, the worshiper is filled with a deep sense of awe for the One who alone is worthy of all praise, adoration and devotion.
   B. True and acceptable worship is a definite act that:
      1. One performs, with a start and a finish to it.
         (a) The wise men, who were in search of the child Jesus, said that they had "come to worship Him" (Matt. 2:2). A definite act, with a start to it.
         (b) "And when they had come into the house, they saw the young Child with Mary His mother, and fell down and worshiped Him…Then…they departed…" (Matt. 2:11-12). A definite act, with a start and a finish to it. (See also 1 Samuel 1:3.)
         (c) Abraham told his servants, "The lad and I will go yonder and worship, and we will come back to you" (Gen. 22:5). A definite act, with a start and a finish to it.
         (d) "And behold, a man of Ethiopia, a eunuch…who…had come to Jerusalem to worship, was returning" (Acts 8:27). A definite act, with a start and a finish to it.
      2. Requires one's full participation to accomplish it fully.
         (a) "So Abraham took the wood of the burnt offering…the fire…and a knife…And Abraham built an altar there and placed the wood in order…And Abraham stretched out his hand and took the knife" (Gen. 22:6-10). What Abraham had called "worship" required his full participation to accomplish.
         (b) Jehovah gave instructions to Israel when they came into Canaan: "You shall not worship the Lord your God with such things. But you shall seek the place where the Lord your God chooses…and there you shall go. There you shall take your burnt offerings…And there you shall eat before the Lord your God, and you shall rejoice…" (Deut. 12:4-7). Worship required their full participation to accomplish.
      3. These passages also help us to understand that "all of life" is not worship, as some have attempted to teach. All that we do as a Christian is not worship!
         (a) The Bible uses a different Greek word to describe Christian service.

            (1) The Greek verb *latreuo* means "to serve, to render religious service or homage" (Vine 686).
            (2) The Greek noun *latreia* means "service" (Vine 563).
            (3) This is the way the words are most often translated in the New Testament.
        (b) It is helpful to know that this is the word used at the end of Romans 12:1.
            (1) While some translations have "worship" in this passage, the Greek word is *latreia,* which means "service."
            (2) Based upon the rest of the Scriptural evidence (in B, 1 and B, 2 above), it should be clear that the sacrificial, Christian life is one of "service," as everything that a Christian does in his life for Christ is not worship.
        (c) There is a difference between Christian "service" and Christian "worship"!
    C. True and acceptable worship is a solemn, sacred and holy act!
        1. It requires man's utmost! Not his least!
        2. It demands man's awe! Not indifference!
        3. It calls for man to participate! Not spectate!
        4. It shows man that worship is not about what we "receive" but about what we "give."
V. **God Has Clearly Detailed the Proper Elements for True and Acceptable Worship.**
    A. "True worship" is an expression used by Jesus, not invented by man.
        1. "But the hour is coming, and now is, when the true worshipers will worship the Father in spirit and truth; for the Father is seeking such to worship Him. God is Spirit, and those who worship <u>Him</u> must worship in <u>spirit</u> and <u>truth</u>" (John 4:23-24).
        2. God is seeking "true worshipers," which implies there are "false worshipers" (see III).
        3. God is seeking "true worshipers" and has revealed how to be a "true worshiper."
        4. God has never left man to his own thoughts and devices in how to worship Him.
            (a) In fact, when man has followed his own inclinations regarding worship, the results have always been disastrous. Consider the examples of Cain (Gen. 4:3-5), Nadah and Abihu (Lev. 10:1-3), King Saul (1 Sam. 13:1-4), King Jeroboam (1 Kgs. 12:25-33), King Uzziah (2 Chron. 26:16-21), etc.
        5. The fact that God is seeking such distinctive worship means it must be identifiable.
            (a) One of the identifying marks of the unique church of the Bible is that it worships as authorized by the New Testament (see page 94).
            (b) True and acceptable worship is identifiable to God.
            (c) True and acceptable worship must be identifiable to man.
    B. True worship must be <u>directed TOWARD the proper object – GOD</u>.
        1. In John 4:24, Jesus said, "**God** is Spirit, and those who worship **Him**…"
        2. "You shall worship the Lord your God, and Him only you shall serve" (Matt. 4:10).
        3. "Worship God" (Rev. 22:9).
        4. Worship involves proper reverence and awe for God and for God alone (Heb. 12:28).
        5. True reverence for God will lead to worship from the heart according to His Word!
        6. God alone is the only worthy object of worship!
            (a) Mary, the mother of Jesus, is not an authorized focus of worship.
            (b) Departed saints are not an authorized focus of worship.
            (c) Angels are not an authorized focus of worship.
        7. God alone is the only worthy audience of worship! Man is not the audience!
        8. Rather than waiting to be entertained, true worship seeks to give God all of the glory!
        9. Therefore, true and acceptable worship is not about man and what is pleasing to man, but it is all about God and what is pleasing to God!

C. True worship must be <u>directed FROM the proper attitude – IN SPIRIT</u>.
   1. In John 4:24, Jesus said, "God is Spirit, and those who worship Him **must worship in spirit** and truth."
   2. Worship is a spiritual activity, in which Christians (spiritual beings), who are part of "a spiritual house," "offer up spiritual sacrifices acceptable to God" (1 Pet. 2:5).
   3. Worship must come from man's spirit—his heart (see "heart" in Eph. 5:19; Col. 3:16).
   4. Worship must be directed from a heart filled with faith and love (John 14:15).
   5. Worship must be directed from a heart fully devoted to the Lord (Matt. 22:37-38).
   6. Worship must be directed from a heart of joy, gladness and thanksgiving (Psa. 118:24).
   7. Worship is not merely an outward act, but true and acceptable worship must start from deep within a man's heart (Matt. 15:7-9).
      (a) If worship does not come from man's heart, it is vain hypocrisy!
   8. Worshiping in spirit requires preparing the heart in advance for worship and then keeping the heart engaged throughout the entire worship service.
      (a) When we do this, we will become less concerned about "what we get out of the worship," and more concerned about what we can "give into the worship."
      (b) True and acceptable worship requires real effort and work! But, it is worth it, for there is true satisfaction in giving God the glory of which He alone is worthy!
D. True worship must be <u>directed BY the proper standard – IN TRUTH</u>.
   1. In John 4:24, Jesus said, "God is Spirit, and those who worship Him **must worship in** spirit and **truth**."
   2. Worship done "in truth" is by the standard of God's Word (John 17:17).
      (a) There is a vast difference between worship that is according to "God's truth" and worship that is according to "the commandments of men" (Matt. 15:8-9).
      (b) When man worships according to his own traditions, commandments or standards, Jesus makes it clear that they are:
         (1) "…laying aside the commandment of God" (Mark 7:8).
         (2) "…rejecting the commandment of God" (Mark 7:9).
         (3) "…making the word of God of no effect" (Mark 7:13).
   3. God alone has the authority to tell man what to do in worship to be acceptable.
   4. All things, including worship, must be done "in the name of the Lord Jesus"—by His authority (Col. 3:17).
      (a) Our very "gathering together" is to be done "in His name" (cf. Matt. 18:20).
   5. All parts of worship must be measured by the standard of God's Word.
      (a) We are not to "think beyond" or "go beyond" "what is written" (1 Cor. 4:6).
      (b) We are not to "speak" beyond what is written (1 Pet. 4:11; 1 Cor. 1:10).
      (c) To do less in our worship than the New Testament authorizes is to "fall short of the glory of God" (Rom. 3:23).
      (d) To do more in our worship than the New Testament authorizes is to "transgress and abide not in the doctrine of Christ" (2 John 9).
      (e) Engaging in worship that is "not authorized" brings the judgment of God (Lev. 11:1-3).
   6. If something done in worship to God is not in accordance with God's Word, how can one possibly seek to justify it or explain how it must be pleasing to God?
E. True worship—to God in spirit and in truth—is a MUST.
   1. Note the word "must" in John 4:24. This is not optional. It is absolute.
   2. True worship "MUST" be BOTH from the heart and according to His Word to be true!

VI. God Has Authorized Five Avenues for Worship in the New Testament Church.
  A. When the church was established in Acts 2, Scripture records for us that "they continued steadfastly in the apostles' doctrine and fellowship, in the breaking of bread, and in prayers...praising God and having favor with all the people" (Acts 2:42, 47).
    1. They worshiped through five avenues:
       (a) Preaching ("the apostles' doctrine"),
       (b) Giving ("fellowship"), a Greek word also translated "contribution" in Romans 15:26,
       (c) The Lord's Supper ("the breaking of bread"), "the" denotes a specific event and "breaking of bread" is a common synecdoche which embraced both elements,
       (d) Praying ("prayers"), and
       (e) Singing ("praising God").
    2. Let us consider each of these five authorized avenues of worship.
  B. God has authorized <u>preaching the Word of God</u> as an avenue of worship.
    1. The church is to engage in a teaching and study of Scripture in its worship (Acts 20:7; Col. 4:16).
    2. Preaching is an avenue of worship.
       (a) While Jesus' statement in Matthew 15:9 is a rebuke, it still reveals that "worship" involves "teaching."
       (b) If vain worship involves false teaching, then true worship must involve true teaching.
       (c) Preaching is addressed in the context of worship in 1 Corinthians 14:24-31.
    3. Preachers must "preach the word" (2 Tim. 4:2), handle aright the word (2 Tim. 2:15), speak only the oracles of God (1 Pet. 4:11; Gal. 1:8-9) and teach "the whole counsel of God" (Acts 20:27).
    4. Worshipers/Listeners must desire the word (1 Pet. 2:2), demand the unadulterated truth (Gal. 1:8-9) and receive the message as the Bereans did (Acts 17:10-11).
    5. Only men are Scripturally authorized to preach in the public assembly of the church (1 Cor. 14:33-35; 1 Tim. 2:8-14). (See Lesson 18.)
  C. God has authorized <u>giving of our means</u> as an avenue of worship.
    1. Giving was done as a part of N.T. worship "every first day of the week" (1 Cor. 16:1-2).
    2. Common "orders" were given to all churches for giving (1 Cor. 16:1).
       (a) Before giving "orders" to the church at Corinth, Paul had already given "orders" to the churches of Galatia.
       (b) This emphasizes that giving was a command of God, not merely an option.
       (c) This emphasizes that the command was not just for Corinth, to address a specific matter of a limited time, but was for all churches to be practiced perpetually.
    3. Giving is to be done according as one "may prosper" (1 Cor. 16:2).
    4. Giving is to be done as one "purposes in his heart" and "not grudgingly or of necessity," remembering that "God loves a cheerful giver" (2 Cor. 9:7).
       (a) While giving is an obligation, a Christian should have "cheerful" joy in the opportunity to give back to God! Think of all that He has given to us and the joyful willingness with which He has given in abundance!
       (b) One's giving as worship is a freewill offering between a worshiper and his God.
    5. God's blessings to us are in proportion to our giving to Him.
       (a) "He who sows sparingly will also reap sparingly, and he who sows bountifully will also reap bountifully" (2 Cor. 9:6).
       (b) "Give, and it will be given to you: good measure, pressed down, shaken together, and running over will be put into your bosom" (Luke 6:38).

6. The funds are to be used for reaching the lost, teaching the saved and helping the needy.
   (a) Giving is God's only authorized method for funding the work of the church.
   (b) While some claim that the giving in the first-century church was only for benevolent purposes, the fullness of Scripture must be consulted.
      (1) The infant church in Philippi "sent aid once and again" to Paul to support him in preaching the gospel in Thessalonica (Phil. 4:16).
      (2) In fact, Paul said that the Philippian church handled the "giving and receiving" for him (Phil. 4:15).
      (3) Under inspiration of the Holy Spirit, Paul wrote to the church in Corinth that those who preach the gospel should be financially supported by the church (1 Cor. 9:1-18). This support would come from the weekly contribution.
7. While giving has purposes beyond the worship assembly, it should be remembered that the act of giving is to be done as an act of worship to God.

D. God has authorized the <u>observance of the Lord's Supper</u> as an avenue of worship.
   1. The Lord's Supper involves two elements (Mark 14:22-25):
      (a) Unleavened bread, an emblem of the Lord's body, and
      (b) Fruit of the vine, an emblem of the Lord's blood,
      (c) Of which all New Testament Christians are to partake (see "all" in Matt. 26:27).
   2. Partaking of the elements is a memorial to Christ (1 Cor. 11:24-25) and the ultimate sacrifice that He made on the cross for our sins (Matt. 26:28; 1 Cor. 15:3; Isa. 53:4-8).
   3. By partaking of the Lord's Supper, we "proclaim His death" (1 Cor. 11:26).
   4. When partaking of the Lord's Supper, we must discern the Lord's body and examine ourselves (1 Cor. 11:27-29).
   5. Partaking of the Lord's Supper is to be done every Sunday.
      (a) The New Testament church met "every first day of the week" (1 Cor. 16:2, NASB).
      (b) The purpose of the assembly was "to" (infinitive of purpose) "break bread" (Ac. 20:7).
      (c) When the New Testament church "came together" on the first day of the week, it was "to eat" the Lord's Supper (1 Cor. 11:33).
   6. Lesson 16 will study the Lord's Supper in more detail.

E. God has authorized <u>praying to God</u> as an avenue of worship.
   1. The early church "continued steadfastly in...prayers" (Acts 2:42).
   2. Prayers must be directed to deity (Matt. 6:9), in accordance with His will (1 John 5:14).
   3. Prayers in public worship must be practiced as authorized by God (1 Cor. 14:14-16).
   4. In the assembly, one leads the prayers and others say, "Amen," at the end (1 Cor. 14:16).
      (a) Prayer in worship is not designed as a period of "private" praying.
      (b) Prayer in worship is not designed for all to pray at once, leading to confusion.
   5. Prayers in public worship must be sincere and understandable (1 Cor. 14:15).
   6. As with all avenues of worship, men are to take the lead in the prayer (1 Tim. 2:8).
   7. Collective prayer in worship acknowledges a mutual love and dependence on God.

F. God has authorized <u>singing together as a congregation</u> as an avenue of worship.
   1. As with all avenues of worship, music in worship must be authorized by God.
   2. God has authorized and specified singing in worship.
      (a) "...speaking to one another in psalms and hymns and spiritual songs, singing and making melody in your heart to the Lord" (Eph. 5:19).
      (b) "Let the word of Christ dwell in you richly in all wisdom, teaching and admonishing one another in psalms and hymns and spiritual songs, singing with grace in your hearts to the Lord" (Col. 3:16).

3. From these passages, worshipers find that:
   (a) Singing in worship is intended firstly to praise God ("to the Lord"). Endeavors that seek to entertain the multitude rather than glorify the Master are vain.
   (b) Singing is also "to one another" as a form of "teaching and admonishing."
   (c) Everyone is engaged in the singing, as "one another" sing to "one another" (a reciprocal, reflexive pronoun, indicating participation by all worshipers and not just a select few, as with choirs or solos).
   (d) The heart is the melodious instrument of the true worshiper.
4. As with praying, our singing must be sincere and understandable (1 Cor. 14:15).
5. Only by singing actual words, set to music, can these requirements be fulfilled.
6. There is no authority for mechanical instruments of music in New Testament worship.
7. Lesson 17 will study music in worship in more detail.

VII. God Has NOT Authorized His Church to Worship on the Sabbath Day (Saturday).
A. There are some who contend that the church must worship on the Sabbath (Saturday).
   1. They argue that the Sabbath was part of the Ten Commandments and is still binding.
   2. They argue that the Sabbath is a perpetual (forever) ordinance to keep.
   3. They argue that Sabbath keeping goes all the way back to creation (before Judaism).
B. The teaching of the Bible regarding Sabbath observance is very clear.
   1. In Genesis 2:2-3, "the seventh day" is referenced three times, but not "the Sabbath."
      (a) "God" and "His work" are referenced three times, but man is not referenced at all.
      (b) There is nothing in this passage to teach (or suggest) that God expected anything of man regarding "the Sabbath" at the time of creation.
   2. The Sabbath is not mentioned for the first 2,500 years of Bible history (65 chapters).
      (a) There was no observance of the Sabbath during the Patriarchal Age, for God had not commanded such of them.
   3. The command to observe the Sabbath was part of the law that God made (Deut. 5:12):
      (a) With the Jews only ("Israel" + "with us" [3x], Deut. 5:1-3; cf. Ex. 34:27).
      (b) With the Jews when they came out of Egypt (Ex. 19:1-8; cf. 24:1-8).
      (c) With the Jews at Mt. Sinai (Deut. 4:13; 5:2; Ex. 19-20; Neh. 9:13-14).
      (d) But not before Mt. Sinai ("today") or "with our fathers" (Deut. 5:1-3; Neh. 9:13-14).
      (e) As a sign with Israel and no other nation(s) (Ex. 20:1-2; 31:12-17; Ezek. 20:12, 20).
      (f) To remember that they had been slaves in the land of Egypt (Deut. 5:15; Ex. 20:2).
   4. There is no command or example in the Bible of Sabbath observance by any non-Jew.
      (a) By noting its purpose, it would have been meaningless to any other people!
      (b) Since the observance of the Sabbath commemorated the deliverance of the Jews from Egypt, the day would have had no meaning to anyone before the Jews were delivered from Egypt or even to any non-Jew after the deliverance.
      (c) Observing the Sabbath was not a universal command to all mankind.
C. The covenant/law that God made at Mt. Sinai included the Ten Commandments (Ex. 34:27-28; Deut. 4:13; 9:9-11; 1 Kgs. 8:9, 21).
D. The covenant/law that God made at Mt. Sinai was abrogated by God Himself.
   1. God foretold and fulfilled the making of a "new covenant" (Jer. 31:31-34; Heb. 8:6-13).
      (a) God intentionally limited the time of the old covenant "until" "the Seed should come" (Gal. 3:19), and that Seed "is Christ" (3:16).
      (b) God designed the old covenant to be a "tutor to bring us to Christ" (Gal. 3:24), but after Christ came, "we are no longer under a tutor" (3:25).

2. The covenant/law that was abrogated included the Ten Commandments:
   (a) "The law," to which we are "dead" and from which we "have been delivered," was the one that commanded, "You shall not covet" (Rom. 7:1-7).
   (b) The law, which included "sabbaths," was "wiped out...taken out of the way...nailed to the cross" (Col. 2:14-17).
   (c) The law, which was "written and engraved on stones," has "passed away," been "taken away" and no longer "remains" (2 Cor. 3:3-18).
E. The covenant (including the Ten Commandments) was only "forever" in the sense that it was not to cease within the timeframe for which it was intended.
   1. The same word "forever" used of the Sabbath (Ex. 12:14) was used of Pentecost (Lev. 23:21) and the Feast of Tabernacles (Lev. 23:41).
   2. The same word "perpetual" used of the Sabbath (Ex. 31:16-17) was used of burning incense (Ex. 30:8), burnt offerings (Ex. 29:42) and sin offerings (Ex. 30:10).
   3. None of these things are part of God's covenant with man today, because they were only to last "perpetually" for the years that the first covenant was in force.
F. Anyone seeking to be justified by the law of Mt. Sinai (which would include adhering to that old law of "the Sabbath") is "estranged from Christ" (Gal. 5:4).
   1. In fact, the laws of the Mosaic Covenant stand or fall together.
   2. If one goes back to the Old Testament and seeks authority to bring over just one part of that law, "he is under obligation" (debtor) "to keep the whole law" (Gal. 5:3).
   3. By doing so, Scripture affirms that one becomes "severed from Christ" (NASB) and has "fallen away from grace" (ASV) (Gal. 5:4).
   4. The Christian is not under obligation to keep any part of that old law (Rom. 7:1-7)!

VIII. God Has Authorized His Church to Worship on the Lord's Day (the First Day of the Week).
A. The day of worship, as authorized by God in the New Testament, is not optional!
   1. The notion that man today may choose the day of worship (i.e., he can worship either on Saturday or on Sunday, both days being equal options) is not authorized by God!
   2. God specified and authorized one day of worship in the New Testament—"the first day of the week."
B. Under the new covenant, the Lord established a new religion, a new institution, new commandments, a new feast, and a new day to worship—"the Lord's Day" (Rev. 1:10).
   1. The first day of the week is not to be referred to as "the Christian Sabbath."
   2. The first day of the week is a unique day for Christians, distinct from any other day.
   3. The first day of the week is the day that God specified for N.T. Christians to worship.
C. The first day of the week has great significance to Christians because of what happened.
   1. It was the day that Jesus Christ was raised from the dead (Mark 16:9).
      (a) The expression, "the first day of the week," is used in every account of the resurrection of Jesus (Matt. 28:1; Mark 16:2, 9; Luke 24:1; John 20:1, 19).
   2. It was the day that Jesus was declared "to be the Son of God with power" (Rom. 1:3-4).
   3. It was the day that Jesus gathered with His disciples after His resurrection (Jn. 20:19, 26).
   4. It was the day that the Holy Spirit came upon the apostles as promised (Acts 2:1-4).
      (a) The day of Pentecost was always on the first day of the week (Lev. 23:15-16).
   5. It was the day that the gospel was preached fully for the first time (Acts 2:14-40).
   6. It was the day that the church/kingdom was established with power (Acts 2:1, 41, 47).
   7. It was the day that the church assembled in New Testament times (Acts 20:7)
   8. It was the day that the church assembled to commune with the Lord (Acts 20:7).
   9. It was the day that the church assembled every week (1 Cor. 16:1-2; 4:17; 7:17).

- D. The first day of the week has great significance to Christians because it does to the Lord!
    1. The Lord requires the "first" from us (Gen. 4:4; Prov. 3:9; Matt. 6:33).
    2. The Lord chose the "first" day of the week for Himself and His people.
        (a) The early church assembled every first day of the week (Acts 20:7; 1 Cor. 16:1-2).
        (b) The early church assembled to commune with the Lord (Acts 20:7; Mark 14:25).
        (c) Church historians record that early Christians always assembled on Sunday.
    3. Therefore, the Christian must make worship on the Lord's Day a priority (Heb. 10:25).

IX. Conclusion
- A. What a sacred privilege given to Christians that we can worship the Almighty God!
- B. Christians should eagerly desire to worship and praise the God of heaven! He is worthy!
- C. What a blessing to be given specific instructions to ensure our worship is acceptable!
- D. May our worship always be focused on God and truly glorify Him!
- E. May our worship always be offered with the proper heart of utmost reverence!
- F. May our worship always be according to God's authorized avenues specified in His Word!
- G. May our worship never focus on the performance or entertainment of the worshiper!
- H. May our worship edify (1 Cor. 14:26), without confusion (14:33), and be orderly (14:40)!
- I. May the Lord's Day have the significance to us that it has to the Lord!

Recommended Resources

Books

Baxter, Batsell Barrett. *The Family of God.* Nashville: Gospel Advocate, 1980.

Chambers, Dan. *Showtime! Worship in the Age of Show Business.* Nashville: 21st Century Christian, 1997.

Holland, Thomas H. *Man's Worship to God.* Brentwood, TN: Penmann Books, 2008.

Jividen, Jimmy. *More Than a Feeling.* Nashville: Gospel Advocate, 1999.

Articles

Cogdill, Roy E. "The Worship of the Church." *New Testament Church.* Fairmount, IN: Truth Magazine Bookstore, 1982. 87-95.

Ferguson, Everett. "The Worship of the Church." *The New Testament Church.* Abilene, TX: Biblical Research Press, 1968. 53-59.

Jackson, Wayne. "The Divine Pattern of Acceptable Worship—Part 1." *ChristianCourier.com* https://www.christiancourier.com/articles/286-the-divine-pattern-of-acceptable-worship-part-1

---. "The Divine Pattern of Acceptable Worship—Part 2." *ChristianCourier.com* https://www.christiancourier.com/articles/290-divine-pattern-of-acceptable-worship-part-2-the

Lanier, Roy H., Jr. "Rather Than on the Sabbath, She Worships on the Lord's Day." *Introducing the Church of Christ.* Ed. Alvin Jennings. Fort Worth: Star Bible, 1981. 140-143.

Miller, Max. "Why Christians Keep the First Day of the Week." *Jesus Christ, the Son of God (Freed-Hardeman College Lectureship).* Ed. William Woodson. Nashville: Gospel Advocate, 1973. 353-362.

West, W.B., Jr. "Worship (In General)." *The Church: The Beautiful Bride of Christ (Spiritual Sword Lectureship).* Eds. Garland Elkins & Thomas B. Warren. Memphis: Getwell church of Christ, 1980. 111-116.

Wharton, Edward C. "The Identity and Acceptability of Worship." *The Church of Christ.* Nashville: Gospel Advocate, 1997. 133-140.

Winkler, Wendell. "For Defeating the Error of Culturally-Based Worship." *The All-Sufficiency of the Bible (Spiritual Sword Lectureship).* Ed. Gary McDade. Memphis: Getwell church of Christ, 2000. 529-542.

---. "Worship in Spirit and in Truth." *Worship That Pleases God (South Florida Lectureship).* Ed. David Sproule. Palm Beach Gardens, FL: Palm Beach Lakes church of Christ, 2000. 275-293.

Woodson, William. "Worship in Spirit and in Truth." *The Spiritual Sword* (Apr. 2005): 29-32.

Periodicals

The Spiritual Sword. January 1993. "Worship—In Spirit and Truth."

Lesson 16: The Lord's Supper

I. **Jesus Instituted the Lord's Supper on the Night Before His Crucifixion.**
   A. The institution of the Lord's Supper is recorded in four passages:
      Matthew 26:26-29; Mark 14:22-25; Luke 22:17-20; 1 Corinthians 11:23-26.
   B. Scripture never uses the words "Eucharist" or "Sacrament."
      1. The Bible uses these terms to refer to this sacred feast:
         (a) The Lord's Supper (1 Cor. 11:20).
         (b) The communion (1 Cor. 10:16).
         (c) The Lord's table (1 Cor. 10:21).
         (d) Breaking bread (Acts 2:42; 20:7).
      2. Rather than use terms that are not found in Scripture, let us be diligent to call Bible things by Bible names.
   C. Jesus instituted the Lord's Supper after observing the Jewish Passover with His apostles.
      1. Passover commemorated God's deliverance of the Jews from Egyptian bondage.
      2. Specifically, the Passover reminded the Jews of the occasion when, because of the blood on their lintel and doorposts, the Lord did "pass over" their homes (Ex. 12:23).
      3. It was not by accident that Jesus instituted His supper at the Passover feast (cf. 1 Cor. 5:7).
      4. While the Lord's Supper is not a continuation of the Passover (for the Passover was fulfilled when the Lord's Supper was instituted, Luke 22:16) nor is it to be called "the Christian Passover," God does draw some similarities for instructional purposes.
   D. When instituting His feast, Jesus emphasized that it was "new."
      1. "I will no longer drink of the fruit of the vine until that day when I drink it <u>new</u> in the kingdom of God" (Mark 14:25). What was "new"?
      2. The Lord's Supper was a "new" feast/memorial.
         (a) The Jews had observed and celebrated many feasts/memorials under their law, commemorating a number of events in Jewish history.
         (b) This feast/memorial being instituted by Jesus was a "new" feast/memorial, commemorating a "new" deliverance made possible by the blood of Christ.
      3. The Lord's Supper was in a "new" kingdom.
         (a) Jesus foretold of His partaking of the elements "in the kingdom," which was soon to be established (Mark 9:1).
         (b) This was the kingdom which was long awaited by the Jews, who followed Old Testament prophecies. The kingdom was/is the church (Matt. 16:18-19).
      4. The Lord's Supper was of a "new" covenant.
         (a) Jesus said, "This cup is the <u>new</u> covenant in My blood" (Luke 22:20).
         (b) The blood of the old covenant was the blood of animals, but the blood of the new covenant is the blood of Jesus (Heb. 9:12-28).
         (c) The blood of Jesus would abolish the old covenant (Eph. 2:15; Col. 2:14) and usher in a new covenant (Heb. 9:15-17).
         (d) The blood of Jesus provided "remission of sins" (Matt. 26:28), in order for one to enter into the new covenant with the Lord (Heb. 9:18-10:4).
      5. The Lord's Supper was on a "new" day. (See Roman numerals VII & VIII in Lesson 15.)
         (a) On the last day of the week, Jews remembered their deliverance from bondage (Ex. 20:8-11).
         (b) On the first day of the week (the day on which Christ rose triumphant over death), Christians were to remember their deliverance from bondage.

6. The Lord's Supper was "new" – a new feast, of a new memorial, of a new deliverance, in a new kingdom, by a new covenant, on a new day, for a new people.
    (a) It should thrill our souls to study this divine feast.
    (b) Even more, it should thrill our souls to partake of this divine feast.

II. **Jesus Instituted the Lord's Supper to Be Extraordinarily Significant for the Church.**
   A. Jesus instituted the Lord's Supper as a time for communion (1 Cor. 10:15-22).
      1. "Communion" is not just what it is called; "communion" is what is happening.
      2. "The cup of blessing which we bless, is it not the communion of the blood of Christ? The bread which we break, is it not the communion of the body of Christ?" (1 Cor. 10:16).
         (a) The picture of the unity of the bread is the picture of the unity of the one body.
         (b) It truly is a "communion," in which we all (in the one body) eat the same bread.
      3. The Greek word for "communion" in this passage is *koinonia*, which is the word for "fellowship, participation, partnership, sharing."
         (a) When we partake of the Lord's Supper, we are enjoying a divine fellowship, engaging in a divine participation, entering a divine partnership and experiencing a divine sharing...with the body and blood of Christ.
         (b) This thought alone captures the extraordinary significance of this feast, and it ought to move us to greater depths of understanding and a greater desire for participation.
      4. In the Lord's Supper (emphasize "Lord's"), we commune with Christ Himself.
         (a) Jesus taught that He is in the worship assembly with His church (Heb. 2:12).
         (b) When He instituted the Lord's Supper, He promised to "drink it new with you [or us] in My Father's kingdom" (Matt. 26:29).
         (c) Imagine partaking of the Lord's Supper with Jesus partaking next to you.
         (d) This enhances the meaning and significance of this feast even more, and it ought to drive every Christian to never miss an opportunity to commune with Jesus Himself.
   B. Jesus instituted the Lord's Supper as a time for memorial (1 Cor. 11:23-25).
      1. God knew that His people needed memorials, in order to remember Him and to remember what He had done for them.
         (a) When crossing the Jordan, the Israelites selected and set up twelve stones as a memorial of what God had done (Josh. 4:1-24).
         (b) Upon delivering the Israelites from bondage in Egypt, the Lord established the Passover feast as a memorial of what He had done (Ex. 12:1-28)
         (c) Similarly, the Lord gave instructions for the Feast of Tabernacles, which commemorated Israel's wandering in the wilderness for 40 years and the Lord's provision and protection during that time (Lev. 23:33-44).
         (d) In the New Testament, God also established a feast to help His people remember Him and what He had done for them.
      2. When it came to the Lord's Supper, twice Jesus commanded, "Do this in remembrance of Me" (1 Cor. 11:24-25).
         (a) This command emphasizes that participating in this feast is not optional.
         (b) This command also emphasizes the purpose of the feast: to remember Jesus.
      3. The two elements of the Supper themselves provide the key to the memorial.
         (a) The unleavened bread was an emblem of Jesus' sinless, lifeless body: "This is My body which is given for you; do this in remembrance of Me" (Luke 22:19).
         (b) The fruit of the vine was an emblem of Jesus' precious blood: "This is My blood of the new covenant, which is shed for many" (Mark 14:24).

- (c) By specifying the two elements, there is no authority to use any other elements in the Lord's Supper.
- (d) Scripture does not teach that the elements transform into the actual body and blood of Jesus when we partake.
  - (1) "Transubstantiation" is a man-made doctrine, without any Biblical foundation.
  - (2) Notice the progression of Jesus' own words as He instituted this feast.
    - (i) "I will not drink of **the fruit of the vine** until the kingdom of God comes" (Luke 22:16).
    - (ii) "Then He took the cup, and gave thanks, and gave it to them, saying, 'Drink from it, all of you. For this is **My blood** of the new covenant, which is shed for many for the remission of sins'" (Matt. 26:27-28; Luke 22:20).
    - (iii) Then He said, "But I say to you, I will not drink of **this fruit of the vine** from now on until that day when I drink it new with you in My Father's kingdom" (Matt. 26:29).
  - (3) Even after calling it His "blood," He still said it was "fruit of the vine."
  - (4) While "the fruit of the vine" was to represent His "blood," the substance was still "**this** fruit of the vine." It had not, did not and does not change.
4. In the Lord's Supper, we are to be "discerning the Lord's body" (1 Cor. 11:29).
   - (a) Our minds are to "separate" or "discriminate" our thoughts, so that they focus on the body of Jesus hanging on the cross.
   - (b) Our hearts must remember that Christ suffered and died for us, shedding His blood, in order that we might be delivered from the slavery to sin.
   - (c) This is the whole focus of the Lord's Supper and cannot be overemphasized.
   - (d) If we fail to discern the Lord's body as we partake, then we eat and drink judgment to ourselves (1 Cor. 11:29).
C. Jesus instituted the Lord's Supper as a time for self-examination (1 Cor. 11:27-30).
   1. "But let a man examine himself, and so let him eat of the bread and drink of the cup."
   2. While reflecting upon the sacrificial death of Christ, one must reflect on his own life.
      - (a) We are not "examining others," to determine an "open" or "closed communion."
        - (1) The manmade concept of an "open communion" or "closed communion" is not found anywhere in Scripture and must not be practiced.
      - (b) Each Christian is to examine the only life he can thoroughly examine—his own.
      - (c) We must examine ourselves next to the cross of Jesus.
      - (d) We should be asking ourselves during this time of reflection:
        - (1) "How is the death of Christ affecting me?"
        - (2) "How is my life conforming to His death?"
      - (e) We are "chastened by the Lord" when we examine/judge ourselves (11:31-32).
D. Jesus instituted the Lord's Supper as a time for proclamation (1 Cor. 11:26).
   1. Paul explained that "…as you eat this bread and drink this cup, you proclaim the Lord's death till He comes."
   2. The regular observance of the Lord's Supper is a regular message to the world that Jesus died for all and shed His blood that all might be saved.
   3. The regular observance of the Lord's Supper is also a regular message to the world that Jesus is coming again and all must be prepared when He comes.
   4. If the Lord's Supper is not observed with the regularity that Christ specified, then the church is not proclaiming His death as He intended.

E. Jesus instituted the Lord's Supper to be observed in a "worthy manner" (1 Cor. 11:27, 29).
  1. This has nothing to do with the "worthiness" of the partaker to eat and drink.
     (a) The word is not an adjective to modify the partaker. No Christian is ever "worthy" to partake of the Lord's Supper! That is not the focus of this word.
     (b) The word is an adverb to modify the verb, emphasizing the manner of partaking.
  2. There are two keys in the passage for partaking in a "worthy manner."
     (a) First, one must "remember" and "discern" the body and blood of the Lord.
     (b) Second, one must "examine himself" in light of the body and blood of the Lord.
  3. To fail to do these two things leads to partaking in an "unworthy manner."
     (a) Partaking in an "unworthy manner" leads one to "be guilty of the body and blood of the Lord" (11:27), for he "eats and drinks judgment to himself" (11:29).
     (b) Therefore, it is not enough for a Christian to merely partake of the bread and the fruit of the vine. He must remember Jesus and examine himself as instructed.
  4. The Lord's Supper is a most reverent time of concentration, reflection and devotion.

III. **Jesus Instituted the Lord's Supper to Be Observed By the Church Every First Day of the Week.**
  A. Division among denominations exists over the frequency of observing the Lord's Supper.
    1. Some groups partake weekly, some monthly, some quarterly, some annually. For some, it is left up to the discretion of the leadership to determine frequency.
    2. It is obvious that God did not give different commands to each of these groups, but that they are making these choices on their own. Do they have the right to do that?
    3. Does the Bible give any direction in this matter of frequency? Or does it leave the door wide open? If God is not specific as to frequency, then observing it once during your life would be enough. Is that true? What does the Bible say?
  B. It is helpful to understand that God specified the time and frequency of all of His feasts.
    1. Reading through Leviticus 23 emphasizes this point for every Bible reader.
    2. The Sabbath was to be observed on "the seventh day" (Lev. 23:3).
       (a) The time was specified. They could not do it on another day with God's approval.
       (b) Did the Lord have to say, "*every* seventh day," or would that be understood?
    3. The Passover was to be observed on "the fourteenth day of the first month" (23:5).
       (a) The time was specified. They could not do it on another day with God's approval.
       (b) Did the Lord have to say, "*every* fourteenth day of the first month," or would that be understood?
    4. The Feast of Unleavened Bread was to be observed starting on the "fifteenth day of the same month" and continue for "seven days" (Lev. 23:6-8).
       (a) The time was specified. They could not do it on different days with God's approval.
       (b) Did the Lord have to say, "*every* fifteenth day of the first month," or would that be understood?
    5. The Feast of Weeks (or Harvest or Pentecost) was to be observed "fifty days to the day after the seventh Sabbath" (Lev. 23:15-16).
       (a) The time was specified. They could not do it on another day with God's approval.
       (b) Did the Lord have to say, "*every* fiftieth day after the seventh Sabbath," or would that be understood?
    6. The Feast of Trumpets was to be observed on "the first day" of "the seventh month" (Lev. 23:23-25).
       (a) The time was specified. They could not do it on another day with God's approval.
       (b) Did the Lord have to say, "*every* first day of the seventh month," or would that be understood?

7. The Day of Atonement was to be observed on "the tenth day of the seventh month" (Lev. 23:27).
   (a) The time was specified. They could not do it on another day with God's approval.
   (b) Did the Lord have to say, "*every* tenth day of the seventh month," or would that be understood?
8. The Feast of Tabernacles was to be observed on "the fifteenth day of the seventh month" and continue for "seven days" (Lev. 23:34).
   (a) The time was specified. They could not do it on different days with God's approval.
   (b) Did the Lord have to say, "*every* fifteenth day of the seventh month," or would that be understood?
9. The specificity of divine instruction regarding these days and frequencies leads the Bible reader to expect such specificity in the New Testament regarding the day and frequency of the Lord's Supper.
   (a) If it was to be observed annually, the Bible reader would expect to read that.
   (b) If it was to be observed monthly, the Bible reader would expect to read that.
   (c) Thus, it is not an insignificant detail that that New Testament specifies a weekly observance of the Lord's Supper on the first day of the week.
10. It is highly instructive to see that when God specifies the day and frequency of His feasts, it is not left to man to change that day and that frequency.
    (a) If the Lord specifies the first day of the week, would He have to say "*every* first day of the week," or would that be understood? Amazingly, He says both!

C. God did give very clear instructions on the regularity and frequency of partaking.
   1. By reading the books of Acts and First Corinthians, God's authority is understood.
   2. Readers are confronted with apostolic instruction and apostolic example.
   3. What the apostles taught and practiced in one church is what they taught and practiced in every church (1 Cor. 4:17; 7:17; 14:33; 16:1; cf. 2 Thess. 2:15).

D. The New Testament church continued steadfastly in the Lord's Supper.
   1. "They continued steadfastly...in the breaking of bread" (Acts 2:42).
   2. "Breaking bread" is a figurative of speech (called synecdoche) for the Lord's Supper.
      (a) It was a reference to the time when Jesus broke bread in the upper room.
      (b) Synecdoche includes both elements by the mention of one.
   3. In the Greek, there is a definite article "the" before "breaking" and before "bread."
      (a) This was a specific breaking (feast) of a specific bread (the Lord's Supper).
   4. "They continued steadfastly" is made up of two separate Greek verbs.
      (a) "They were" is in the Greek imperfect tense, indicating a habitual practice.
      (b) "Continuing steadfastly" is in the present tense, indicating continual practice.
   5. There was definitely a regularity and frequency to the Lord's Supper.
      (a) This regularity was not random or merely occasional. It must have had a pattern.
      (b) If God did not specify the exact frequency, then it might be left to man to decide.
      (c) However, we must let the Bible speak before we speak.

E. The New Testament church came together to eat the Lord's Supper (on Sunday).
   1. In Acts 20:7 is an apostolic example of the church coming together to eat the Lord's Supper every week.
      (a) "Now on the first day of the week, when the disciples came together to break bread."
      (b) The day of the week is specified. Why specify the day if it didn't matter?
         (1) Though in a hurry, Paul had waited seven days just for this occasion (20:6).
         (2) If Paul was waiting for just a "common meal," he didn't need to wait seven days.

(3) If Paul really was waiting for the Lord's Supper, how did he know it would be observed that coming Sunday and not a month or two months from then?
- (c) "When" (an adverb of time) ties the day with the gathering as an established and expected practice. The disciples were expecting to meet on that day.
- (d) "Came together" is passive, indicating it was initiated by God and not themselves.
- (e) "To break bread" is an infinitive of purpose, indicating their reason for gathering.
- (f) Acts 20:7 is an approved example for the church today to follow.
  - (1) There is apostolic approval (and teaching) for the expectation and practice.
  - (2) The Troas church was practicing what every church practiced.
  - (3) What was taught to and practiced in one church was universal (see III, C, 3).
- (g) The gathering for worship (i.e., when the church "came together") and the breaking of bread occurred at the same frequency.
  - (1) If the frequency of one could be changed, the frequency of the other could be also.
2. In 1 Corinthians 11:17-34 is direction to the church to come together for the Lord's Supper.
   - (a) There was to be a regular frequency to the Lord's Supper, as noted by the word "often" used by Paul in 1 Corinthians 11:26.
   - (b) The context emphasizes repeatedly that the focus is upon that time when the church would "come together" (11:17, 18, 20, 33, 34).
   - (c) In disapproval for their practice and to return them to the proper way, Paul said, "When you come together in one place, it is not to eat the Lord's Supper" (11:20).
     - (1) In other words, they were supposed to be gathering to eat the Lord's Supper.
     - (2) But, the supper they were gathering to eat was NOT the "Lord's" (v. 20-22).
     - (3) They had corrupted the Lord's Supper and, thus, corrupted the worship.
   - (d) The early church was supposed to be "coming together" to worship (14:23-25), to edify (14:26) and to eat the Lord's Supper (11:20, 33).
     - (1) "To eat" in verse 33 is an infinitive of purpose, indicating the reason for which they were supposed to be coming together.
     - (2) The church in Corinth was not doing what they were supposed to be doing.
     - (3) Paul was writing to bring them back to God's original design.
   - (e) The gathering for worship and the Lord's Supper was to occur at the same frequency.
     - (1) If the frequency of one could be changed, the frequency of the other could be also.
   - (f) Thus, it should not be surprising that God urges Christians, "...not forsaking the assembling of ourselves together, as is the manner of some" (Heb. 10:25).
F. The New Testament church came together every first day of the week.
   1. When God instructed Israel, "Remember the Sabbath day, to keep it holy" (Ex. 20:8), which Sabbath do you suppose they understood God to be identifying?
      - (a) The obvious answer is that they understood He meant every Sabbath, every week.
      - (b) God specified the day and the frequency, and the Jews could not change it.
   2. In 1 Corinthians 16:1-2 is instruction for Christians to gather every first day of the week.
      - (a) The orders being given were the same orders to all churches (16:1; cf. 4:17; 7:17).
        - (1) This was not something that was limited only to the church in Corinth.
        - (2) These "orders" were being given "in all the churches of the saints" (cf. 14:33).
      - (b) The NASB and ESV properly translate verse 2: "On the first day of every week."
        - (1) The Greek word *kata* (meaning "every") is in this verse.
          - (i) The same word *(kata)* is found in Acts 13:27 and 15:21 to indicate that the Law of Moses and the Prophets were read among the Jews "every Sabbath."

(ii) This weekly frequency would be expected, even if the Greek *kata* was not in the verse. But the use of the word emphasizes the point even more.
(2) Even if *kata* was not in 1 Corinthians 16:2 regarding the frequency of the gathering of the church, which weeks have first days? Every one!
(c) Churches were given instructions about their weekly gatherings on Sundays.
(1) This was their common practice, as taught to them by the apostles.
(d) Question: How often do "churches" today take up a collection?
(1) Answer: Every Sunday! Why? Because 1 Corinthians 16:1-2 teaches it.
(2) "Churches" today always take up a collection every week.
(3) But, why not partake of the Lord's Supper every week, which is what Acts 20:7 teaches is a purpose of the gathering?
G. There is no Biblical authority for partaking of the Lord's Supper on any other day other than the first day of the week.
1. By apostolic example, the church is only authorized to partake on the first day of the week, when the disciples come together (Acts 20:7).
2. By apostolic direction, the church is only authorized to partake on the first day of every week, when the church is to come together (1 Cor. 11:17, 20; 16:1-2).
3. Therefore, there is no authority in Scripture to partake of the Lord's Supper:
(a) On a day other than the first day of the week (even Paul had to wait in Acts 20).
(b) On an occasion other than the Sunday worship assembly of the church (like a wedding, a funeral, etc.).
H. Put all of the evidence together:
1. The New Testament church <u>continued steadfastly in the Lord's Supper</u>. (There was a regularity and frequency to its observation.)
2. The New Testament church <u>came together for the purpose of eating the Lord's Supper</u>. (This was the focus of their assembly.)
3. The New Testament church came together <u>every first day of the week</u>. (This was "the Lord's Day"—the day they assembled as His body.)
(a) They assembled on "the Lord's day" (Rev. 1:10) to partake of "the Lord's Supper" (1 Cor. 11:20). The "day" and the "supper" belong together and are inseparable.
(b) Interestingly, the Greek adjective for "Lord's" occurs only in these two verses.
4. Therefore, the New Testament church continued steadfastly in coming together to eat the Lord's Supper every first day of the week. The sum of God's Word is truth!
5. How can the church today do any different, any more or any less?

IV. Jesus Instituted the Lord's Supper to Be a Special Feast for His Children.
A. The Lord makes a definite distinction between the Lord's Supper and a common meal.
1. In the worship context of Acts 2:42, the definite article "the" specifies the communion.
(a) Later, in Acts 2:46, the church was "breaking bread" in a common meal.
2. In Acts 20:7, the breaking of bread was the communion of the whole church.
(a) Later, in Acts 20:11, Paul (single pronoun "he") ate a common meal.
3. In 1 Corinthians 11, the church was making the communion a common meal (20-21).
(a) Verse 33 specifies that they were to come together to eat the Lord's Supper.
(b) Verse 34 specifies that the common meals could be enjoyed at home.
4. The Lord's Supper is not to be considered a common, ordinary meal.
(a) It is a divinely appointed feast to be observed every first day of the week.
(b) It is a divinely appointed feast to commune with Jesus every week.
(c) It is a divinely appointed feast to remember what Jesus did for us on the cross.

B. The Lord identifies those for whom the Lord's Supper is intended.
 1. Jesus promised to partake in the Lord's Supper "in the kingdom of God" (Mk. 14:25).
 2. Jesus observes the communion "with" those in His "Father's kingdom" (Matt. 26:29).
 3. Therefore, the Lord's Supper is for citizens in the kingdom of God (John 3:5).
    (a) It is a special communion between Jesus and those who have been saved from their sins by the precious blood of Jesus and are in His kingdom/church.
    (b) There is a direct connection between the blood of Jesus washing one's sins away in obedience to the gospel of Christ and that same person observing the Lord's Supper as a reminder of Jesus' sacrifice and His delivering him/her from sin.
    (c) There is no authority in Scripture for the manmade doctrines and practices of "open communion" or "closed communion." This is not a time to "examine somebody else," but a time to "examine self."
 4. Jesus intended for "all" Christians to partake of the entire feast.
    (a) Every Christian is to partake of the bread as equals.
       (1) Jesus instructed, "Take, eat; this is My body which is broken for you" (1 Cor. 11:24).
    (b) Every Christian is to partake of the fruit of the vine as equals.
       (1) Jesus instructed, "Drink from it, all of you" (Matt. 26:27).
       (2) "He gave it to them, and they all drank from it" (Mark 14:23).
       (3) It is almost as if Jesus knew that a group later in history would claim that the cup was not intended for all to drink, and so He intentionally specified for all disciples to drink.
    (c) At the foot of the cross and at the Lord's table, every Christian stands on equal terms and level ground.
       (1) Every member is to partake of every element every first day of the week.

V. Conclusion
A. The Lord's Supper was instituted by Jesus to be an integral part of Christian worship.
 1. It is a communion, a memorial, a proclamation, and a time of examination.
B. The Lord's Supper was instituted by Jesus to be observed every first day of the week.
C. The Lord's Supper is "the Lord's," and He alone has authority to regulate it.
D. There is no authority in Scripture to observe the Lord's Supper:
 1. On a different day than the first day of the week.
 2. On a different frequency than every week, on the first day of every week.
 3. On a different occasion than the worship assembly of the church (like a wedding).
E. May we commune with Him every Sunday—remembering Him and examining ourselves.
F. May we make our time of communion the priority of our week and the focus of our hearts.

Recommended Resources

Books

Holland, Thomas H. *Man's Worship to God.* Brentwood, TN: Penmann Books, 2008.

Articles

Baxter, Batsell Barrett. "Worship—Supper of the Lord." *Family of God.* Nashville: Gospel Advocate, 1980. 111-117.

Brownlow, Leroy. "Because of Its Scriptural Teaching and Observance of the Lord's Supper." *Why I Am a Member of the Church of Christ.* Fort Worth: Brownlow Publishing, 1973. 168-175.

Cogdill, Roy E. "The Lord's Supper." *New Testament Church.* Fairmount, IN: Truth Magazine Bookstore, 1982. 91-92.

Ferguson, Everett. "The Lord's Supper." *The New Testament Church.* Abilene, TX: Biblical Research Press, 1968. 60-65.

Hanson, David E. "Members of the Church Commune As Christ Ordained." *Introducing the Church of Christ.* Ed. Alvin Jennings. Fort Worth: Star Bible, 1981. 55-60.

Holland, Thomas H. "Why Worship Regularly and Faithfully." *Man's Worship to God.* Brentwood, TN: Penmann Books, 2008. 25-31.

Jackson, Wayne. "The Weekly Observance of the Lord's Supper." *ChristianCourier.com* https://www.christiancourier.com/articles/240-weekly-observance-of-the-lords-supper-the

---. "What About a 'Saturday Night' Observance of the Lord's Supper?" *ChristianCourier.com* https://www.christiancourier.com/articles/725-what-about-a-saturday-night-observance-of-the-lords-supper

Merideth, J. Noel. "The Church—And the Lord's Supper." *The Church: The Beautiful Bride of Christ (Spiritual Sword Lectureship).* Eds. Garland Elkins & Thomas B. Warren. Memphis: Getwell church of Christ, 1980. 126-131.

Miller, Dave. "Sunday and the Lord's Supper." *ApologeticsPress.org* http://apologeticspress.org/APContent.aspx?category=11&article=1254&topic=81

---. "The Order of the Lord's Supper." *ApologeticsPress.org* http://www.apologeticspress.org/APContent.aspx?category=11&article=470

Nichols, Gus. "The Church of Christ—The Lord's Supper." *The Church of Christ (Freed-Hardeman College Lectures).* Ed. Thomas B. Warren. Nashville: Gospel Advocate, 1971. 286-296.

Overton, Basil. "The Lord's Supper." *The Church Faces Liberalism (Freed-Hardeman College Lectures).* Ed. Thomas B. Warren. Nashville: Gospel Advocate, 1970. 257-268.

Wharton, Edward C. "The Lord's Supper." *The Church of Christ.* Nashville: Gospel Advocate, 1997. 141-150.

Winkler, Wendell. "Why Does the Church of Christ Observe the Lord's Supper Weekly?" *The Church Everybody Is Asking About.* Tuscaloosa, AL: Winkler Publications, 1988. 64-72.

Periodicals

The Spiritual Sword. July 1982. "The Lord's Supper."

The Spiritual Sword. January 1993. "Worship—In Spirit and Truth."

Lesson 17: Music in the Worship of the Church

I. **All Worship Must Be Authorized By God to Be Acceptable to Him!**
  A. Jesus said that true worshipers worship God "in spirit and in truth" (John 4:24).
  B. To worship in truth is to worship according to His divine standard, His word (John 17:17).
  C. God is the author and object of worship, therefore, He is the only one who has the authority to determine what is acceptable and unacceptable in worship (John 4:23-24).
  D. All that we say and do (including in worship) must be by His authority (Col. 3:17).

II. **All Worship Today Must Be Authorized By the New Testament!**
  A. The church is a New Testament institution of God (Matt. 16:18; Acts 2:47; 20:28).
    1. Therefore, the church must follow the New Testament as its sole authority (Matt. 17:5; Col. 3:17).
  B. The Old Testament (with its worship) is no longer binding or an authority for man today.
    1. It was abrogated by the death of Christ (Col. 2:14-17).
    2. It was annulled by the giving of the New Testament (Jer. 31:31-34; Heb. 8:8-13; 9:15-17).
    3. We are no longer under it (Gal. 3:19-25).
    4. Therefore, we cannot use it to justify or authorize worship practices (Gal. 5:1-4).
  C. See Lesson 6 for more on the Two Covenants and the abrogation of the Old Testament.

III. **God Desires and Has Authorized Congregational Singing in Worship!**
  A. The New Testament identifies and authorizes the type of music in worship—singing.
    1. Music in worship in the New Testament was only singing.
    2. Every New Testament verse referencing music in worship is always **singing**.
      (a) "When they had **sung** a hymn, they went out to the Mount of Olives" (Mt. 26:30).
      (b) "When they had **sung** a hymn, they went out to the Mount of Olives" (Mk. 14:26).
      (c) "But at midnight Paul and Silas were praying and **singing** hymns to God..." (Ac. 16:25).
      (d) "...and that the Gentiles might glorify God for His mercy, as it is written: 'For this reason I will confess to You among the Gentiles, And **sing** to Your name'" (Rom. 15:9).
      (e) "I will **sing** with the spirit, and I will also **sing** with the understanding" (1 Cor. 14:15).
      (f) "Speaking to one another in psalms and hymns and spiritual songs, **singing** and making melody in your heart to the Lord" (Eph. 5:19).
      (g) "Let the word of Christ dwell in you richly in all wisdom, teaching and admonishing one another in psalms and hymns and spiritual songs, **singing** with grace in your hearts to the Lord" (Col. 3:16).
      (h) "...He is not ashamed to call them brethren, saying: 'I will declare Your name to My brethren; In the midst of the assembly I will **sing** praise to You'" (Heb. 2:11-12).
      (i) "Therefore by Him let us continually offer the sacrifice of praise to God, that is, the **fruit of our lips**, giving thanks to His name" (Heb. 13:15).
      (j) "Is anyone among you suffering? Let him pray. Is anyone cheerful? Let him **sing** psalms" (Jas. 5:13).
    3. In every passage that discusses music, it always specifies sing, singing, sung.
  B. The New Testament identifies and authorizes the object of singing in worship—God.
    1. By example, our singing is to be directed "to God" (Acts 16:25).
    2. By instruction, our singing is to be directed "to the Lord" (Eph. 5:19; Col. 3:16).
    3. Jesus Himself sings in the assembly "to You," the Lord (Heb. 2:12).
    4. As the object, God identifies and specifies worship that is acceptable to Him.
    5. As neither man nor his wishes are the object or focus of worship, man has no say at all in determining what is acceptable to God in worship.

C. The New Testament identifies and authorizes the two-fold purpose of singing.
  1. First and foremost, our singing is to render praise and thanksgiving to God (Rom. 15:9; Heb. 13:15; Jas. 5:13).
  2. Secondarily, our singing is to "speak to," "teach" and "admonish one another" (Eph. 5:19; Col. 3:16).
     (a) "One another" is a reflexive, reciprocal pronoun emphasizing that:
        (1) The action of the verb is a two-way action.
        (2) There is mutual action or interaction taking place.
        (3) Two people carry out an action and benefit from the consequences of that action at the same time.
     (b) God's use a reflexive, reciprocal pronoun with regard to singing demonstrates that:
        (1) God requires that the entire congregation "sing," "speak to," "teach" and "admonish" the entire congregation.
        (2) God has not authorized choirs or solos in worship, for then it is not reciprocal.
        (3) God has not authorized featuring "the best singers" in the church over others.
D. The New Testament identifies and authorizes the manner in which to sing.
  1. We are to sing "with the spirit" (1 Cor. 14:15). Our <u>hearts</u> must be engaged!
     (a) "...singing and making melody in your heart" (Eph. 5:19)
     (b) "...singing with grace in your hearts" (Col. 3:16).
  2. We are to sing "with the understanding" (1 Cor. 14:15). Our <u>minds</u> must be engaged!
E. The New Testament identifies and authorizes the instrument to be used in singing.
  1. There is an instrument authorized and demanded by God in N.T. worship.
  2. However, God does not authorize a mechanical instrument in N.T. worship.
  3. God does authorize and demand the instrument of the heart in N.T. worship.
  4. Melody is to be made "in your heart to the Lord" (Eph. 5:19).
F. God alone can and does authorize acceptable worship, and He authorizes singing.
  1. Notice that God nowhere identifies or authorizes mechanical instruments in worship.
  2. Our worship can fulfill every desire and command of God, and our worship can impart every benefit God had in mind for the worshiper, without a mechanical instrument.
  3. When churches of Christ reject the use of mechanical instruments in their worship:
     (a) It is not because they are trying to hold stubbornly to some manmade tradition.
     (b) It is not because they just want to stand out and make this "their issue."
     (c) It is because there is no Biblical authority for it!
        (1) There is no command from God to authorize its use.
        (2) There is no approved example of the early church using any.

IV. God Is Specific (Not Generic) About Singing in Worship.
A. See pages 55-59 in Lesson 5 for more on generic and specific authority in Scripture.
B. God authorizes through both generic authority and specific authority.
  1. Virtually every authorized command in the Bible has both generic & specific elements.
     (a) Specific commands set forth the specific manner in which God's ordinances are to be implemented (without addition, subtraction or substitution).
        (1) This means there is uniformity as all obey the same commands.
        (2) The specific element of the command rules out all other possible specifics.
     (b) Generic commands set forth the general manner in which God's ordinances are to be implemented, leaving the specifics to the judgment of the individual.
        (1) The generic element gives liberty, where there may be a diversity of practice.
        (2) Of course, no liberty can violate another of God's commands.

C. It is vital to understand the difference between generic authority and specific authority, and to understand how each includes inclusive and exclusive elements.
   1. A physician can give a prescription to a pharmacist that is generic or specific.
      (a) Generic Prescription: "Give the patient an antibiotic."
          (1) Inclusive: ANY antibiotic, any dosage and any frequency would be permitted.
          (2) Exclusive: ALL other kinds of drugs (antacids, laxatives, steroids, etc.).
      (b) Specific Prescription: "Give the patient 250mg of tetracycline twice a day."
          (1) Inclusive: ONLY tetracycline, but any brand would be permitted.
          (2) Exclusive: ALL other antibiotics, dosages, frequencies are prohibited.
          (3) The very thing included in the Generic Command is excluded in the Specific.
          (4) By specifying the type of antibiotic, the physician automatically (without saying another word) excludes every other type of antibiotic. A thing does not have to be specifically forbidden to be unauthorized.
   2. A mother can give instruction to a child that is generic or specific.
      (a) Generic Instruction: "Go and put on your shoes."
          (1) Inclusive: ANY shoes, any type, any color, any size would be permitted.
          (2) Exclusive: ALL other kinds of clothes (hats, earmuffs, skates, waders, etc.).
      (b) Specific Instruction: "Go and put on your black dress shoes."
          (1) Inclusive: ONLY black dress shoes, but any black dress shoes in closet.
          (2) Exclusive: ALL other color shoes and type shoes are prohibited.
          (3) The instruction is SPECIFIC (black dress shoes) and EXCLUSIVE (ALL other shoes).
          (4) The very thing included in the Generic Command is excluded in the Specific.
          (5) By specifying the type of shoe, the mother automatically (without saying another word) excludes every other type of shoe. A thing does not have to be specifically forbidden to be unauthorized.
D. God utilized Generic Authority and Specific Authority in the commands of the Bible.
   1. God told Noah, "Make yourself an ark of gopherwood..." (Gen. 6:14-16).
      (a) Inclusive: ANY tools needed to build (hammer, saw, etc.) would be permitted.
      (b) Inclusive: ONLY gopherwood, but any length/width of boards would be permitted.
      (c) Exclusive: ALL other kinds of wood are prohibited.
      (d) By specifying the type of wood, God automatically (without saying another word) excluded every other type of wood. A thing does not have to be specifically forbidden to be unauthorized.
      (e) If God had given a generic command, "Make yourself an ark of wood," then any type of wood have been acceptable. But, God specified and only gopherwood was authorized and acceptable to Him.
      (f) God's commands were to be obeyed, without addition or subtraction.
   2. God commands Christians to partake of the Lord's Supper with unleavened bread and fruit of the vine every Sunday in their "come together" assembly (Matt. 26:26-29; Acts 20:7; 1 Cor. 11:17-26; 16:1-2; Heb. 10:25).
      (a) Inclusive: ANY building, tent, home, owned, rented, etc. is permitted.
      (b) Inclusive: ONLY unleavened bread and fruit of the vine are permitted.
      (c) Exclusive: ALL other kinds of "food" (meat, apples, soda, etc.) are prohibited.
      (d) Inclusive: ANY time on Sunday (6:00 a.m., 6:00 p.m., etc.) is permitted.
      (e) Inclusive: ONLY the first day of every week (Sunday) is permitted.
      (f) Exclusive: ALL other days or frequencies.

- (g) By specifying the "food" and the day of the week, God automatically (without saying another word) excluded every other type of "food" and every other day. A thing does not have to be specifically forbidden to be unauthorized.
- (h) If God had given a generic command, "Partake of the Lord's Supper with food," then any type of food would have been acceptable. But, God specified and only unleavened bread and fruit of the vine are authorized and acceptable to Him.
- (i) God's commands are to be obeyed, without addition or subtraction.

E. Regarding music in worship, God specified singing: "…singing and making melody in your heart to the Lord" (Eph. 5:19).
  1. Inclusive: Words, tunes, pitch, 4-part harmony, 4/4 time, multiple verses, etc.
  2. Inclusive: Books, projectors, starting note/pitch, beating time, etc.
  3. Inclusive: ONLY singing as a congregation is permitted.
  4. Exclusive: ALL other kinds of music are prohibited.
     (a) There are two kinds of music: instrumental and vocal.
     (b) God could have used Generic Authority and commanded, "Make music."
        (1) If He had, then singing, playing or singing-and-playing would be permitted.
        (2) And, a diversity of those practices would be authorized and expected.
     (c) However, God chose to specify (and command) the type of music in worship.
     (d) By specifying the "music" in Christian worship, God automatically (without saying another word) excluded every other type of "music." A thing does not have to be specifically forbidden to be unauthorized.
     (e) Just like the examples above (prescriptions, wood for the ark, etc.), when the spoken words specify a particular item/action in a category, all other items/actions in that category are automatically excluded.
        (1) God did not have to say to Noah, "Do not use oak," for such was automatically excluded in the specific command to use gopherwood.
        (2) God did not have to tell the early church, "Do not use donuts and coffee in the Lord's Supper," for such was automatically excluded in the specific command to use unleavened bread and fruit of the vine.
        (3) God does not have to tell the church, "Do not use mechanical instruments of music in worship," for such is automatically excluded in the specific command to sing and make melody in our hearts.
  5. Note: It is wrong to state that the Bible does not allow music in worship.
     (a) The Bible most definitely authorizes (and demands) music in worship.
     (b) The Bible specifies the music that is authorized (and demanded): singing.
     (c) Singing is music in New Testament worship and the only authorized type.

F. We readily understand generic/specific and inclusive/exclusive in every part of life.
  1. Why do those same basic principles not readily apply to singing in worship?
  2. They must! They do!

V. God Is Silent About Instrumental Music in Worship.
A. A favorite argument in favor of instrumental music in worship is, "There isn't a verse in the Bible that says, 'Thou shalt not use instrumental music in worship.'"
  1. On the surface, one must admit that this is true. No such verse can be found.
  2. This is referred to as "the silence of the Scriptures."
B. So, how is one to properly handle the silence of the Scriptures?
  1. If a teaching or practice is not explicitly forbidden, is it permitted or prohibited?
  2. Are we to live by what the Bible does not say or by what the Bible does say?

3. If one is permitted to practice anything (yea, everything) that the Bible does not expressly forbid, what would be included in that? What would not be included?
4. Scripture still teaches that we are not to "think" (NKJV) or "go" (ASV) "beyond what is written" (1 Cor. 4:6; cf. 2 John 9-11).

C. This is not a hard issue, for we readily understand "silence" in everyday life.
 1. When a parent sends a child to the store for milk and bread, is it permissible to buy M&M's and Coke, since mom didn't say, "You may not buy M&M's and Coke"?
 2. When a boy gets in trouble for being in a Ladies' Restroom, is it permissible for him to be in there and stay in there, since the sign didn't say, "No boys or men allowed"?
 3. When a music tutor says, "Sing the National Anthem," is it permissible for her student to play it, since the tutor did not say, "Do not play the National Anthem"?
 4. When God is "silent" about instrumental music, why don't the same common-sense principles apply? They must. They do.

D. God understands the significance of silence and makes arguments based upon it.
 1. The superiority of Jesus over angels is argued from silence (Heb. 1:4-5, 13).
   (a) The Bible asks, "To which of the angels did [God] ever say, 'You are My Son...I will be to Him a Father...Sit at My right hand'?"
   (b) The Bible is silent regarding God ever saying anything like that to any angel.
   (c) However, that was said to and of Jesus (Psa. 2:7; 2 Sam. 7:14; Psa. 110:1).
   (d) God's penman made an argument, to prove the superiority of Jesus, based on something the Bible did NOT say.
 2. The superiority of Jesus as High Priest and the necessity of the change of the law is argued from silence (Heb. 7:11-15).
   (a) Jesus could not serve as a priest on earth (Heb. 8:4), because He was of the tribe of Judah and not the priestly tribe of Levi, as specified of God (Heb. 7:14).
   (b) Scripture states that Jesus "arose from Judah, of which tribe Moses spoke nothing concerning priesthood" (7:14).
     (1) When God specified Levi, He was silent regarding the other tribes.
     (2) His silence was not permissive, to allow any other tribe to be the priests.
     (3) His silence was prohibitive. Even Jesus could not be a priest from Judah.
   (c) The only way for Jesus to be High Priest was to change the law.
     (1) "For the priesthood being changed, of necessity there is also a change of the law" (7:12).
     (2) The writer of Hebrews was arguing for the change of the law, from the old covenant to the new.
     (3) The High Priesthood of Jesus demands such a change, otherwise, Jesus could not and cannot be our High Priest, which leaves us condemned in our sins.
     (4) In like manner, the only way to make God's silence permissive today (regarding any matter, including instrumental music) is to change His law, which is not acceptable in any form (Rev. 22:18-19; Gal. 1:6-9).
   (d) By arguing from the silence of the Scriptures, the author was making the strongest argument that he could make to prove the law did not support the high priesthood of Jesus according to the Levitical system. It had to change.

E. God's "silence" regarding instrumental music in worship is prohibitive, not permissive!
 1. Scripture is also "silent" about infant baptism, worshiping saints, praying to Mary, counting beads, burning incense, animal sacrifices, lighting candles for the dead, etc.
   (a) None of these practices (and many more like them) is authorized by God.

(b) "Where is the verse that says not to do these things? God doesn't say 'not to.'"
(c) Is the church permitted to add anything it likes to a perceived "silence" of God?
2. Christians must "do all in the name of the Lord Jesus" (Col. 3:17).
   (a) The music that God authorizes in N.T. worship involves "speaking," "singing," "making melody in the heart," "giving thanks," "teaching," "admonishing," "praise," "declare/tell/proclaim," etc. (Eph. 5:19-20; Col. 3:16; Heb. 2:12; 13:15).
      (1) All of these are uniquely accomplished in singing.
      (2) None of these can be fulfilled with instruments of music.
   (b) We have no right to go beyond what is written (1 Cor. 4:6; 2 John 9)!
   (c) We have no right to add to the Word of God (Rev. 22:18; Deut. 4:2; 12:32).
   (d) God's "silence" is expressly prohibitive.
F. Severe consequences await those who do not respect the silence of the Scriptures.
   1. Nadab and Abihu offered "unauthorized fire before the Lord" (Lev. 10:1-2).
   2. God specified that fire was to be obtained "from off the altar" (Lev. 16:12; Num. 16:46).
   3. Nadab and Abihu took fire from a source, "which He had not commanded them" (v.1).
   4. God was silent regarding that other fire, but His silence was prohibitive.
   5. Because they did not respect the silence of God, but treated it as permissive rather than prohibitive, "fire went out from the Lord and devoured them" (10:2).
   6. In this setting, which involved the worship of God, the Bible reader learns quite blatantly that he must respect (1) what God says and (2) what God does not say.
      (a) To worship God in a way that He has not authorized (regardless of how harmless it may seem) is completely unacceptable to God and subject to His wrath.
      (b) We must have a "thus saith the Lord" for all aspects of our worship.
G. Conclusion: To act in a realm where the Lord is silent is prohibitive and sinful!
   1. When one asks, "Where's the verse that says not to play an instrument?"...
   2. The answer is quite simple: "It's the one that specifies to sing!"
H. See pages 59-64 in Lesson 5 for more on understanding "The Silence of the Scriptures."

VI. Answering Some Common Arguments Made to Support Instrumental Music in Worship.
A. Some argue that instruments are permissible because God accepted them in the O.T.
   1. First of all, remember that we are no longer under the Old Testament (Gal. 3:19-25).
      (a) The Old Testament was fulfilled in Christ (Matt. 5:17-18; Luke 24:44; Eph. 2:14-18).
      (b) The Old Testament was nailed to the cross (Col. 2:14; Eph. 2:15-16; Heb. 9:1-10:18).
      (c) We have been "released from the law," made "free from the law," have "become dead to the law" and "have been delivered from the law" (Rom. 7:1-6).
   2. Scripture makes it very clear that attempting to bring one part of the Old Testament into the New Testament worship demands bringing it all (Gal. 5:3), including animal sacrifices, burning incense, three annual trips to Jerusalem, etc.
   3. Those who seek to justify the use of mechanical instruments based upon the law of Moses "are severed from Christ" and "are fallen away from grace" (Gal. 5:4, ASV).
B. Some argue that instruments are permissible because they are found in heaven.
   1. First of all, remember that we can only do in the church what God has authorized to be done in the church while on earth.
   2. Second, remember that Revelation is written in signs or figurative language (Rev. 1:1).
      (a) One verse says, "I heard a voice from heaven, as the voice of...harpers harping with their harps" (Rev. 14:2). Note the word "as." It is merely describing the voice.
      (b) Another verse that mentions harps also mentions "golden bowls full of incense" (5:8). Are those permitted or authorized in the church also? Are they literal?

- (c) The book also mentions that there is a "white horse" in heaven (Rev. 19:11). Shall we have one of those in worship, as well? Is it a literal horse?
    3. Is there any contextual reason to take "harps" in the book of Revelation as literal but the other items in the book as figurative? What would a spiritual being in heaven do with a material instrument (like a harp)?
    4. Something figurative in heaven is not authorization from God for His church on earth!
- C. Some argue that instruments are just an aid, like a tuning fork or pitch pipe.
    1. When we use a tuning fork, song book or projector, we've done nothing but sing.
        - (a) A song book is an "aid," which provides the words for everyone to sing together.
        - (b) A pitch pipe is an "aid," which provides the starting "tune" for the song.
        - (c) Having both words and a starting note are necessary for a group to sing together. An instrument is not necessary to fulfill God's command to sing.
    2. When an instrument is used, now there is singing *plus* playing (two kinds of music, instead of just the one that God specified and authorized).
    3. This is an unauthorized addition, because it is another kind of music (Rev. 22:18-19).
    4. Instruments cannot and do not "speak to," "teach" or "admonish," which is the purpose that God gave to music in worship (Eph. 5:19; Col. 3:16).
    5. See pages 53-54 for further discussion about expedients as aids and not additions.
- D. Some argue that the Greek word *psallo* means "to play."
    1. *Psallo* is the Greek word that is translated "sing" (Rom. 15:9; 1 Cor. 14:15), "sing psalms" (Jas. 5:13), and "making melody" (Eph. 5:19).
        - (a) No reliable Bible translation included any hint of "playing" in the translation.
        - (b) Every reliable Bible translation exclusively translated *psallo* to mean "singing."
        - (c) Some folks have not been satisfied with this translation of the word and have sought for a different meaning to the word *psallo*.
    2. *Psallo* varied in meaning over time (like "gay," "bad," "sick" and "cell" vary today).
        - (a) In some eras of the Greek language, it did mean "to strike" or "to pluck," like one might pluck a hair, a harp string, a carpenter's string or a bowstring.
        - (b) Interestingly, there was always an object upon which action was being taken.
    3. However, in N.T. times, lexical scholars and translators affirm that it meant "to sing."
        - (a) The word was not tied to any mechanical instrument of music in the New Testament.
        - (b) In his *Complete Expository Dictionary of Old & New Testament Words*, W.E. Vine defined *psallo*, "In the N.T., to sing a hymn, sing praise" (402).
        - (c) In his commentary on *First Corinthians,* Vine noted, "The word *psallo* originally meant to play a stringed instrument with the fingers, or to sing with the accompaniment of a harp. Later, however, and in the New Testament, it came to signify simply to praise without the accompaniment of an instrument" (191).
        - (d) Joseph H. Thayer defined *psallo,* "In the N.T. to sing a hymn, to celebrate the praises of God in song" (675).
        - (e) In the 1979 edition of Bauer, Arndt, Gingrich and Danker's *A Greek-English Lexicon of the New Testament, psallo* "means 'sing' exclusively…with no reference to instrumental accompaniment" (891).
    4. Consider this: Even if *psallo* did mean "to pluck" in Ephesians 5:19 (which it does not), notice where God instructs Christians to "make melody." The object is identified upon which action is to be taken (see VI, D, 2, (b) above).
        - (a) The word *psallo* itself does not include a particular instrument or object.
        - (b) God specified the instrument or object for Christians to *psallo* – the heart!

(c) By specifying the instrument/object (i.e., the heart), God excluded all others.
(d) Therefore, *psallo* did not and could not mean anything other than to "sing and make melody in the heart"!
5. If *psallo* means "to play an instrument," then it is a command. As a command of God:
   (a) It is not optional. Playing would be required EVERY time singing took place.
      (1) However, those who advocate the use of instrumental music do not believe that it must be used in every song of praise to God.
      (2) They do not believe that those who sing without instrumental accompaniment are doing anything wrong. Yet, God's commands are not optional.
   (b) Everyone in the assembly must play, for the command is to every individual.
      (1) Someone else could not fulfill that command for another worshiper by proxy.
      (2) Every worshiper would be required to personally *psallo* a mechanical instrument for himself.
   (c) It would be a sin not to play.
      (1) Is there anyone willing to make such a claim?
   (d) One might also note that if *psallo* in Ephesians 5:19 is going to be pressed to include a mechanical instrument (which it cannot), then it must be an instrument that can be "plucked" (like harps, guitars, etc.) and not one that cannot be "plucked" (like drums, horns, organs, pianos, etc.).
E. Some argue that they have a "God-given talent" for playing, so it must be acceptable.
   1. Will all talents be permitted, like dancing, twerking, juggling, yodeling, chugging, cooking, belching, etc.?
   2. Is worship intended as a talent show for God, without any boundaries?
   3. If man is permitted to use any talent he possesses to praise God in the assembly, then why did God give parameters for acceptable worship? Any such parameters would amount to nonsense, if man is permitted to do as he pleases.
   4. God is the object of worship, not us! God is the director of worship, not us!

VII. Many Do Not Realize That Instrumental Music in Worship Is a Relatively New Addition.
A. Mechanical instruments were not used in the first-century church.
   1. This has been shown already to be Biblically true.
   2. It can be shown to be historically true.
      (a) The following quotation was at one time attributed to Justin Martyr (100-165 A.D.), but it may have come from Theodoret of Cyrrhus (393-458). In either case, it provides early testimony to the practice of the early church: "Simply singing is not agreeable to children, but singing with lifeless instruments and with dancing and clapping; on which account the use of this kind of instruments and of others agreeable to children is removed from the songs in the churches, and there is left remaining simply singing."
      (b) James W. McKinnon, a musical historian (of a Catholic background), wrote in his Ph.D. dissertation, "The Church Fathers and Musical Instruments," at Columbia University in 1965:
         (1) "...early Christian music was vocal" (2).
         (2) "...the strongest possible evidence" shows "that [musical instruments] were not used in the early Church" (264).
         (3) "In respect to musical instruments, the Middle Ages inherited from the patristic era not only a practice which was free from them but a doctrine of bitter opposition to them" (267).

- (4) "More important than explicit opposition to instruments is the simple fact that they were not used in the patristic period" (268).
  - (c) *The Catholic Encyclopedia* records, "Although Josephus tells of the wonderful effects produced in the Temple by the use of instruments of music, the first Christians were of too spiritual a fiber to substitute lifeless instruments for or to use them to accompany the human voice" (1913, Vol. X, p. 651).
  - (d) The *Wycliffe Bible Dictionary* states, "There is no record in the NT of the use of instruments in the musical worship of the Christian church" (1163).
- B. Mechanical instruments began to be introduced into worship by the Roman Catholic and Latin churches, but not until several centuries after the establishment of the church.
  1. McClintock and Strong's *Cyclopedia of Biblical, Theological, and Ecclesiastical Literature* affirms,
     - (a) "The general introduction of instrumental music can certainly not be assigned to a date earlier than the 5th or 6th centuries" (Vol. VI, p. 759).
     - (b) Music "in the Eastern Church has never been any other than vocal, instrumental music being unknown in that Church, as it was in the primitive Church. Sir John Hawkins, following the Romish writers in his erudite work on the *History of Music*, makes Pope Vitalian, in A.D. 660, the first who introduced organs into churches. But students of ecclesiastical archaeology are generally agreed that instrumental music was not used in churches till a much later date" (Vol. VIII, p. 739).
  2. M.C. Kurfees quoted from *The American Encyclopedia* (Vol. 12, page 688), "Pope Vitalian is related to have first introduced organs into some of the churches of western Europe, about 670; but the earliest trustworthy account is that of the one sent as a present by the Greek emperor Constantine Copronymus to Pepin, King of the Francs, in 755" (Kurfees 152).
  3. Kurfees also quoted from *The Schaff-Herzog Encyclopedia* (Vol. 2, page 1072), "In the Greek church, the organ never came into use. But after the eighth century, it became more and more common in the Latin church; not, however, without opposition from the side of the monks. Its misuse, however, raised so great an opposition to it, that, but for the Emperor Ferdinand, it would probably have been abolished by the Council of Trent. The Reformed church discarded it; and though the Church of Basel very early re-introduced it, it was in other places admitted only sparingly, and after long hesitation" (Kurfees 152).
  4. James W. McKinnon concluded a later date, in his research, finding that the organ was the first instrument used in worship services and that it was introduced around 950 A.D. "It appeared with some frequency during the period from 1000 to 1300" (269).
- C. Mechanical instruments were not part of worship in protestant denominations when they first began (which is a surprise for many to hear).
  1. M.C. Kurfees quotes from John Spencer Curwen's work, *Studies in Worship Music* (p. 179). (Curwen was a member of "The Royal Academy of Music" and President of the Tonic Sol-Fa College in London in 1880.) "Men still living can remember the time when organs were very seldom found out of the Church of England. The Methodist, Independents, and Baptists rarely had them, and by the Presbyterians they were stoutly opposed" (qtd. in Kurfees 146).
  2. In fact, many of the early founders and leaders of protestant denominations were adamantly opposed to mechanical instruments in their worship.

(a) Martin Luther (the founder of the Lutheran Church) called the organ "an ensign of Baal" (*McClintock & Strong Cyclopedia,* "Music," Vol. VI, p. 762).

(b) John Calvin (the founder of the Presbyterian Church, along with John Knox) said, "Musical instruments in celebrating the praises of God would be no more suitable than the burning of incense, the lighting of lamps and the restoration of the other shadows of the law. The papists, therefore, have foolishly borrowed this, as well as many other things, from the Jews" (*John Calvin's Commentary* on the 23rd Psalm).

(c) John Wesley (the founder of the Methodist church) said, "I have no objection to instruments of music in our chapels, provided they are neither HEARD nor SEEN" (quoted by Adam Clarke in his comments on Amos 6:5).

(d) Adam Clarke (well-known and highly-respected Bible commentator; a Methodist)

   (1) Comments on 2 Chronicles 29:25 – "But were it even evident, which it is not, either from this or any other place in the sacred writings, that instruments of music were prescribed by Divine authority under the law, could this be adduced with any semblance of reason, that they ought to be used in Christian worship? No: the whole spirit, soul, and genius of the Christian religion are against this: and those who know the Church of God best, and what constitutes its genuine spiritual state, know that these things have been introduced as a substitute for the life and power of religion; and that where they prevail most, there is least of the power of Christianity. Away with such portentous baubles from the worship of that infinite Spirit who requires his followers to worship him in spirit and in truth, for to no such worship are those instruments friendly."

   (2) Comments on Amos 6:5 – "...I farther believe that the use of such instruments of music, in the Christian Church, is without the sanction and against the will of God; that they are subversive of the spirit of true devotion, and that they are sinful...I am an old man, and an old minister; and I here declare that I never knew them productive of any good in the worship of God; and have had reason to believe that they were productive of much evil. Music, as a science, I esteem and admire: but instruments of music in the house of God I abominate and abhor. This is the abuse of music; and here I register my protest against all such corruptions in the worship of the Author of Christianity. The late venerable and most eminent divine, the Rev. John Wesley, who was a lover of music, and an elegant poet, when asked his opinion of instruments of music being introduced into the chapels of the Methodists said, in his terse and powerful manner, 'I have no objection to instruments of music in our chapels, provided they are neither HEARD nor SEEN.' I say the same, though I think the expense of purchase had better be spared."

(e) Charles Spurgeon (the greatest Baptist preacher of the 1800's) said, "David appears to have had a peculiarly tender remembrance of *the singing* of the pilgrims, and assuredly it is the most delightful part of worship and that which comes nearest to the adoration of heaven. What a degradation to supplant the intelligent song of the whole congregation by the theatrical prettiness of a quartet, the refined niceties of a choir, or the blowing off of wind from inanimate bellows and pipes! We might as well pray by machinery as praise by it" *(The Treasury of David,* Psalm 42:4).

      3. These quotations are not given as the authoritative rule on this matter.
         (a) God's Word alone is the authoritative rule on this matter (and all others).
         (b) These quotations are given to show that:
            (1) Denominations have not always used instrumental music in their worship.
            (2) Denominational leaders were not just indifferent to the use of instrumental music in worship, but they were adamantly opposed.
            (3) Religious leaders once agreed with and practiced the music (i.e., singing) authorized by the New Testament and practiced by the church of Christ.
      4. What if we just went back to the singing that was authorized and practiced in the N.T.?

VIII. Conclusion
    A. In the New Testament, God specifies, authorizes and commands singing in worship.
      1. Christians are to "sing and melody" in their hearts to the Lord (Eph. 5:19).
    B. The New Testament does not authorize the use of mechanical instruments in worship.
      1. While many failed attempts have been made to justify the use of mechanical instruments in worship, none of them has been able to stand against the light of the truth of God's Word!
      2. We must have authority for all that we do, including in our worship (Col. 3:17).
      3. Mechanical instruments are not authorized in worship because:
         (a) By specifying "singing" in worship, God automatically excludes "playing."
         (b) There is no generic command to make music which could include instruments.
         (c) The silence of the Scriptures regarding instruments is prohibitive not permissive.
      4. To use mechanical instruments in worship is to add to God's Word (Rev. 22:18).
      5. Therefore, the use of mechanical instruments in worship is unauthorized and sinful.
    C. God is the object of our worship (John 4:24).
      1. God alone has the right to authorize what happens in worship.
      2. And man must submit humbly to God's revealed and specified will.
      3. To do otherwise makes man the object (and authority) of worship and subjugates God to a role of submission.
    D. True worship is TO God as authorized BY God!
    E. May we obey His will, in order to please Him!

Recommended Resources

<u>Books</u>

Bales, James D. *Instrumental Music and New Testament Worship.* Search, AR: Resource Publications, 1973.

Ferguson, Everett. *A Capella Worship.* Abilene: Biblical Research Press, 1972.

---. *Early Christians Speak.* Abilene: ACU Press, 1999.

Ferguson, Everett, Jack P. Lewis & Earl West. *The Instrumental Music Issue.* Nashville: Gospel Advocate, 1987.

Kurfees, M.C. *Instrumental Music in the Worship.* Nashville: Gospel Advocate, 1975.

Miller, Dave. *Richland Hills & Instrumental Music.* Montgomery, AL: Apologetics Press, 2007.

<u>Articles</u>

Brownlow, Leroy. "Because It Has Scriptural Music in the Worship." *Why I Am a Member of the Church of Christ.* Fort Worth: Brownlow Publishing, 1973. 176-185.

Cogdill, Roy E. "Instrumental Music." *New Testament Church.* Fairmount, IN: Truth Magazine Bookstore, 1982. 96-99.

Jackson, Wayne. "Psallo and the Instrumental Music Controversy." *ChristianCourier.com*
https://www.christiancourier.com/articles/829-psallo-and-the-instrumental-music-controversy

---. "The Authorized Elements of Church Music." *ChristianCourier.com*
https://www.christiancourier.com/articles/1518-authorized-elements-of-church-music-the

---. "What About Musical Instruments of Music in Christian Worship?" *ChristianCourier.com*
https://www.christiancourier.com/articles/615-what-about-mechanical-instruments-of-music-in-christian-worship

Kurfees, M.C. "Walking By Faith." *The Spiritual Sword* (July 2004): 41-48.

Miller, Dave. "Church Music." *Piloting the Strait.* Pulaski, TN: Sain Publications, 1996. 204-223.

Miller, Dave. "Instrumental Music and the Principle of Authority." *ApologeticsPress.org*
https://apologeticspress.org/APContent.aspx?category=11&article=1215&topic=288

Nichols, Flavil H. "Is Congregational Singing Authorized?" *Glory to God: Through Christian Living and Through Preaching (Freed-Hardeman College Lectureship).* Ed. Winford Claiborne. Henderson, TN: Freed-Hardeman College, 1989. 252-258.

---. "Why We Do Not Use Instrumental Music in Worship." *The Church of Tomorrow: Horizons and Destiny (Freed-Hardeman College Lectureship).* Ed. Winford Claiborne. Henderson, TN: Freed-Hardeman College, 1983. 266-273.

Nichols, Gus. "The Church of Christ—Its Singing." *The Church of Christ (Freed-Hardeman College Lectures)*. Ed. Thomas B. Warren. Nashville: Gospel Advocate, 1971. 273-285.

Tolle, James M. "Like the Early Christians, She Worships in Song." *Introducing the Church of Christ*. Ed. Alvin Jennings. Fort Worth: Star Bible, 1981. 46-49.

Wallace, Foy E., Jr. "Instrumental Music in Christian Worship." *The Spiritual Sword* (July 2004): 25-40.

Wallace, G.K. "Instrumental Music and Fellowship." *The Church and Fellowship (Freed-Hardeman College Lectures)*. Ed. William Woodson. Henderson, TN: Freed-Hardeman College, 1974. 63-68.

Warren, Thomas B. "Liberalism and the Use of Instrumental Music in the Worship of God." *The Church Faces Liberalism (Freed-Hardeman College Lectures)*. Ed. Thomas B. Warren. Nashville: Gospel Advocate, 1970. 243-255.

Wharton, Edward C. "Church Music." *The Church of Christ*. Nashville: Gospel Advocate, 1997. 151-157.

Winkler, Wendell. "Why Does the Church of Christ Not Have Mechanical Instruments of Music in Their Worship?" *The Church Everybody Is Asking About*. Tuscaloosa, AL: Winkler Publications, 1988. 73-78.

Woodson, William. "History of Instrumental Music." *The Spiritual Sword (Jan. 1993): 17-20.*

---. "Music in the Early Church." *The Spiritual Sword (July 1990): 7-10.*

Periodicals

The Spiritual Sword. October 1978. "Instrumental Music in Worship Is Sinful."

The Spiritual Sword. July 1990. "The Music Question."

The Spiritual Sword. January 2004. "Why Churches of Christ Do Not Use Instrumental Music."

The Spiritual Sword. July 2015. "A Handy Guide to the Instrumental Music Question."

Lesson 18: The Role of Women in the Church

I. **The Role of Women in the Church Is an Important, But Sensitive Subject.**
   A. Some individuals may not even know why this subject needs to be studied and taught.
   B. Some individuals may be offended that this subject is being studied and taught.
   C. The reality is that "the role of women in the church" is a Bible subject, therefore, it must be studied and taught. But, we must limit ourselves to what the Bible says about it.
   D. Some churches of Christ are struggling with this subject.
      1. This subject has created turmoil in some congregations and even led to division.
         (a) Many outside influences have made their way into the church.
         (b) Some brethren have been strongly influenced by modern society, political correctness, denominationalism and various movements.
      2. Some congregations are trying to expand the role that women have in worship and leadership positions within the church. They are asking questions like:
         (a) "Can women serve in the same leadership roles in the worship as the men?"
         (b) "Can women serve in the same leadership roles within the church as the men?"
         (c) "Why should women be considered in a different light than the men?"
         (d) "If women have been 'liberated' in our culture, why not in the church?"
   E. These are questions that some churches are trying to answer.
      1. The key to all of this is, "What does God's Word say?" That's all that matters.
      2. The church belongs to Him. The Bible is His "manual" for the church.
      3. When it comes to this issue (and all issues), whatever God's Word teaches about this matter cannot be modified. It is not left up to us but to God Himself!
      4. Rather than look to tradition or culture or current trends, we must look to His Word!

II. **God Has Designed Both Similarities and Differences in Men and Women.**
   A. God made men and women to be different.
      1. The source for each was different—"dust" (Gen. 2:7) and a "rib" (Gen. 2:21-22).
      2. The sexuality for each was different—a "man" (Gen. 2:8) and a "woman" (Gen. 2:22).
      3. The scope of each was different—"tend" (Gen. 2:15) and "helper" (Gen. 2:18).
      4. These differences in NO WAY imply a difference in worth, value or ability.
      5. It should not surprise us, then, if God gave different roles to each in the church.
         (a) God viewed men and women differently in the Old Testament (cf. Deut. 22:5).
         (b) God views men and women differently in the New Testament (1 Cor. 11:13-15).
         (c) God views men and women differently in the home (Eph. 5:21-33).
         (d) It should not surprise us that God views men and women differently in the church (1 Tim. 2:1-15; 3:1-13; Tit. 1:5-9; etc.).
         (e) Even though "times" and "cultures" change their views of men and women, that does not mean that God changes His views (and plans for) men and women.
   B. God made men and women to be equal.
      1. This may seem like a contradiction with the first point, but it is not.
      2. Men and women are equal in regard to God's love (1 John 4:7-19).
      3. Men and women are equal in regard to God's salvation (Gal. 3:28; Acts 5:14; 8:12).
         (a) Everyone who is "in Christ" has the same status before God. They are all equally "children" and equally "in Christ" (Gal. 3:26-28).
         (b) Everyone who is "in Christ" has the same privileges from God. They are all equally saved, all have access to Him through prayer, all are one (Eph. 2:1-22).

(c) But, the same status and the same privileges do not imply the same function. Galatians 3:28 may not be rightly used to address anyone's role in the church.
    4. Men and women are equal in regard to God's promise of heaven (1 Pet. 3:7).
        (a) They can be "heirs together of the grace of life."
        (b) No man or woman has more right to eternal life based upon their gender.
        (c) But, this does not imply that they are to have equal roles in the church.
C. God gave men and women different roles in the church.
    1. Before we examine those roles, we need to understand the nature of different roles.
    2. Having different roles does NOT suggest that one is superior and one is inferior.
        (a) God has always held women in high regard, never seeing an inferior (see Prov. 31).
        (b) Women were an integral part of His scheme of redemption (Gal. 4:4; Gen. 3:15).
        (c) Five women are mentioned in the genealogy of Jesus in Matthew 1 (1:3, 5, 6, 16).
        (d) Some of the greatest people in Bible history were women: Sarah, Rachel, Deborah, Hannah, Ruth, Esther, Mary, Elizabeth, Mary-and-Martha, Lois, Eunice, Priscilla, etc.
        (e) Jesus gave great attention, favor and commendation to women: the Samaritan woman, Mary-and-Martha, Mary Magdalene, widow of Nain, His own mother, etc.
        (f) In a school, the teacher is not inferior to the principal or the school board. They all have different roles, but it is not a superior-inferior relationship.
        (g) The same is true in the organization of the church.
    3. Having different roles does NOT mean any preferential treatment is being shown.
        (a) God makes a distinction between elders and deacons (1 Tim. 3:1-13).
        (b) God makes a distinction between elders and members (1 Pet. 5:1-3; Heb. 13:17).
        (c) God makes a distinction between elders and single men (1 Tim. 3:2; Tit. 1:6).
        (d) God makes a distinction between widows to support and not support (1 Ti. 5:3-16).
        (e) God is not unjustly discriminating in any of these examples, nor is He unjustly discriminating by giving men and women different roles in the church.
        (f) Having different roles does NOT mean that:
            (1) God is showing favoritism to any of these groups over the others.
            (2) God is holding women back from fulfilling their greatest potential.
            (3) There are no meaningful roles or opportunities for women in the church.
    4. God's roles within the church make for orderliness by His standards and for our good.
    5. For a man to teach what the Bible says about different roles for men and women in the church is not chauvinism or discrimination, as long as he is faithfully teaching God's truth (and doing so with a Christ-like attitude). This is God's Word, not man's.

III. God Has Specified Roles in the Church for Men and Women.
A. The book of First Timothy was written to give instructions on proper "conduct" in the "house of God, which is the church of the living God" (1 Tim. 3:15).
B. God specified the roles of leadership for the men in the church.
    1. God specified men to be leaders in the church as elders (1 Tim. 3:2).
    2. God specified men to be leaders in the church as deacons (1 Tim. 3:11-12).
    3. God specified men to be leaders in the worship of the church (1 Tim. 2:8).
        (a) The Greek word for "men" in 1 Timothy 2:8 *(aner)* is exclusively male.
            (1) This is not the Greek word for "mankind" *(anthropos),* which would include both males and females. The Greek *aner* never means men *and* women.
            (2) *Anthropos* was used in verses 1-7 to refer to all mankind: pray for "all men," God "desires all men to be saved," "one Mediator between God and men," "the Man Christ Jesus."

                (3) But, the Holy Spirit chose a specific and exclusive word for "man" in verse 8.
            (b) The men (*aner,* males only) are to lead in the acts of worship, including praying.
            (c) The men are to lead "in every place" the church assembles to worship (cf. 1 Cor. 1:2).
        4. When God specifies roles, we must pay attention and follow His instructions.
    C. God specified the role of submission for the women in the church.
        1. The Greek word for "women" used in 1 Timothy 2 *(gune)* is exclusively female.
        2. Women are called to "learn in silence with all submission" (1 Tim. 2:11).
            (a) There is a contrast made in 1 Timothy 2 between the leadership (speaking/teaching) role of the men and the submissive (learning) role of the women.
            (b) In the same assembly in which women are to remain silent the men are to lead.
            (c) In the context of worship in 1 Corinthians 14 (with repeated emphasis on "when you come together," 11:17, 18, 20, 33; 14:23-26), women are to "be submissive" (14:34).
        3. The "silence/quietness" in 1 Timothy 2:11 is not total silence (cf. Acts 21:40-22:2).
            (a) The "silence" is a quiet spirit, an attitude of attentiveness and receptiveness.
            (b) It would be difficult for them to participate in worship if they could not speak at all.
            (c) All Christians (men and women alike) are to "sing" in worship (Eph. 5:19; Col. 3:16).
        4. The "submission" is a subjecting or subordinating of herself, recognizing her role.
            (a) The word denotes a voluntary choice to place oneself under the authority of another.
                (1) The same Greek word is used of Christians being "subject to the governing authorities" (Rom. 13:1; cf. 1 Pet. 2:13), and of "younger" Christians being "subject to" older Christians (or "elders") (1 Pet. 5:5).
                (2) Christians are also to "be submissive" to the elders (Heb. 13:17).
                (3) None of these uses indicates that one is more valuable or more important than another, or even that one is superior to another who is inferior.
            (b) The word involves a recognition of a God-given position and a humble spirit that graciously assumes such with honor and dignity.
            (c) This has nothing to do with one's value or worth, or of being controlled by another.
            (d) Compare this again to the submission of a teacher to a principal. The emphasis is on roles and responsibilities, not on value, superiority or discrimination.
            (e) The context (1 Tim. 2; 1 Cor. 14) is within the church and in its assemblies, and the exercise of spiritual authority in that context.
            (f) Consider that these instructions were not being written to a Jewish culture, but they were written to a Greek culture (in Ephesus and Corinth), where women had more prominence than in the Jewish world (cf. Acts 13:50; 16:13-14; 17:4, 12).
        5. Women are not permitted "to teach or to exercise authority over a man" (1 Tim. 2:12).
            (a) Note first what this does not mean:
                (1) This does not prohibit women from all teaching (see Titus 2:3-5).
                (2) This does not prohibit women from ever teaching a man (see Acts 18:26).
                (3) This does not prohibit women from all teaching in the assembly (see Col. 3:16).
                    (i) All Christians (women and men) are commanded to be involved in "teaching and admonishing one another" while "singing" together in worship.
                (4) The word "usurp," as used in the KJV, is not a good English rendering of the Greek term, and as such, it has given rise to misapplications.
                    (i) Some have misunderstood the word "usurp" to mean that a woman forces or presses to have a role that has not been assigned to her. However, these same individuals surmise that if a position of authority or leadership is given to her by the elders, then she would not be usurping to take it.

                (ii) In other words, if the elders ask a woman to teach an adult class with men in it, or ask a woman to lead singing or public prayer, or ask a woman to serve as a deacon, then it would be permissible for her to fill those roles of leadership, for she would not be "usurping" authority over the man, since he willingly gave it to her.
                (iii) It is critical to understand that such a definition and understanding of that word is incorrect, and thus any such applications (i.e., assigning leadership roles to women so that she doesn't "usurp") are in error.
                (iv) The word means "to exercise authority" (Vine) or "to exercise dominion over" (Thayer), which is reflected in the NASB, ASV and ESV translations.
                (v) The word involves having authority over man in spiritual matters.
            (b) The dual prepositional phrase has "man" as the object of both phrases:
                (1) A woman is not permitted to teach "over a man."
                (2) A woman is not permitted to exercise authority "over a man."
            (c) This is addressing the position of authority inherent in teaching and leading.
                (1) Public leading and teaching, in general, subordinates hearers to the speaker.
                (2) The position of the teacher or preacher is a position of authority over hearers.
                (3) For a woman to "teach over" a man in the church is to violate this passage.
                    (i) Teaching or preaching in a church assembly is a position of authority.
                    (ii) Women are not permitted by God to teach or preach "over" a man.
                (4) For a woman to "exercise authority" or have dominion over a man in the church violates this passage.
                    (i) Praying or taking a lead in public worship is a position of authority.
                    (ii) Serving as an elder or deacon is a position of authority. (See III, D below.)
                    (iii) Women are not permitted by God to exercise authority "over" a man in the church.
            (d) In 1 Corinthians 14:34-35, Paul affirms that:
                (1) Women "are not permitted to speak" in the assembly of the churches.
                (2) "It is shameful for women to speak" in the assembly of the churches.
                (3) Publicly speaking to the assembly of the church (which would include preaching, leading prayers, etc.) is not permissible for women in God's design.
                (4) These instructions applied to "all the churches" (14:33).
                (5) These were not Paul's ideas but are "the commandments of the Lord" (14:37).
        6. The role of women in the church follows the role designated for them in marriage.
            (a) While husbands and wives submit to each other (Eph. 5:21), the Lord has charged wives to submit to their "own husbands" (Eph. 5:22; Col. 3:18; Tit. 2:5; 1 Pet. 3:1).
            (b) Contrary to our modern culture and the pervasive practice of our day, "It is in the role of wife and mother that women reach their zenith" (Jerry Jenkins).
        7. It is critical that we respect the roles that God has (and has not) designated for us.
    D. God did not authorize women to serve as elders or deacons.
        1. God plainly disclosed His qualifications for one to be appointed as an elder or deacon.
            (a) He must be "married" (1 Tim. 3:2, 12), therefore, a bachelor cannot serve.
            (b) He must have "children" (1 Tim. 3:4, 12), therefore, a childless man cannot serve.
            (c) He must be "the husband of one wife" (1 Tim. 3:2, 12; Tit. 1:6), therefore, a woman cannot serve as an elder or deacon.
            (d) God was not unjustly discriminating against anyone in these qualifications, including women. God has the authority to determine His qualifications.

2. God used the exclusive terms again in these passages.
   (a) The elder is to be an *aner* – the Greek word exclusively for male, in contrast to female (1 Tim. 3:2; Tit. 1:6).
   (b) The deacon is to be an *aner* (1 Tim. 3:12).
   (c) The spouses of these men are to be *gune* – the Greek word exclusively for female, in contrast to male (1 Tim. 3:2, 11, 12; Tit. 1:6).
3. The clarity of these passages proves that Phoebe was not a "deaconess of the church," as some have so wrongly concluded from Romans 16:1-2.
   (a) The Greek word *diakonos* is used in two senses in the New Testament:
       (1) A technical/specific sense (one serving as a "deacon" in the church), and
       (2) A non-technical/general sense (one who is a "servant/minister" of the Lord).
   (b) In its general sense, all Christians are servants or ministers. This is how the term is used most extensively in the Greek New Testament.
   (c) In its specific sense, only those men who qualify and are appointed are "deacons."
   (d) The context of a passage (the immediate, remote and Biblical context) must be studied to determine how the term is being used.
       (1) *Diakonos* is used of civil leaders in Romans 13:4. Not a "deacon" in the church.
       (2) *Diakonos* is used of Jesus in Romans 15:8. Not a "deacon" in the church.
       (3) *Diakonos* is used of Paul and Timothy (1 Cor. 3:5; 1 Tim. 4:6). Not "deacons."
       (4) *Diakonos* is used of Satan's "ministers" (2 Cor. 11:15). Not "deacons."
       (5) *Diakonos* is used of Phoebe (Rom. 16:1-2). Not a "deacon" in the church.
       (6) The context only demands "deacons" in 1 Timothy 3:8-13 and Philippians 1:1.
4. God has a Divine order, which man (or woman) has no right to change.
E. It is not insignificant to note that when making leadership selections:
   1. Jesus chose twelve men to be His apostles (Matt. 10:1-4).
   2. Jesus chose seventy (or seventy-two) men for a limited commission (Luke 10:1-20).
   3. Seven men were appointed "over" the "business" of serving widows (Acts 6:1-6).
   4. Every travel companion of the apostle Paul who did any public teaching or preaching was always a man (Barnabas, Silas, Timothy, Luke, Titus, etc.).
F. God has specified the roles for men and the roles for women to have in His church.
   1. We must respect where God has designated for each one to serve.

IV. God Has Provided Clear Explanation for the Different Roles of Men and Women.
A. First of all, we must recognize that God does not have to provide man with an explanation.
   1. When God gives instructions, man just needs to obey them.
   2. When God gives specifications, man just needs to accept them.
   3. Man's acceptance and obedience are not contingent on an explanation from God.
   4. He is the Father. We are the children. He is not obligated to give us a reason.
B. However, in the matter of the role of women in the church, He gives clear reasoning.
   1. What we will see is that God's rationale has nothing to do with any given culture.
   2. What we will see is that God's rationale has nothing to do with male chauvinism.
   3. God's rationale transcends all culture, all civilizations and all locales for all time.
C. God provides at least four reasons for His specified role for women in the church.
D. Reason #1: The Divine order of headship/authority (1 Cor. 11:3).
   1. "But I want you to know that the head of every man is Christ, the head of woman is man, and the head of Christ is God."
   2. God has an order of authority.

(a) God likens the relationship between Christ and the Father with the relationship between woman and man.
(b) Scripture is not teaching that women are inferior to men any more than it is teaching that Christ is inferior to the Father.
(c) Where there is subjection does not mean there is inequality (cf. Phil. 2:5-8).
3. The word "head" (1 Cor. 11:3) is not about source but authority (the Divine order).
4. A woman is "under the authority" of men (i.e., to be subordinate). That is God's order of authority.
5. This Divine order was to find universal practice for all time.
(a) "As <u>in all the churches</u> of the saints, the women should keep silent" (1 Cor. 14:33-34, ESV).
(b) "I desire therefore that the men pray <u>everywhere</u>" (1 Tim. 2:8).

E. Reason #2: The natural order derived from creation (1 Tim. 2:13; 1 Cor. 11:3, 7-12).
1. The Divine order of headship is tied to the order of creation, which is not cultural.
(a) The first word in 1 Timothy 2:13 ("For") will show the Divine reason for verses 8-12.
(b) Many argue today against the Bible's "restrictions" on women, stating that Paul was just dealing with the culture of the day and that our culture is different today.
(c) Perhaps (but not successfully) such an argument could be made if verses 13-14 were not in First Timothy. But, those verses forever eliminate the cultural argument.
(d) Paul ties the role of women in his day (and every day) all the way back to creation.
(e) God's Divine order goes back to "the beginning of the creation" (Mark 10:6).
2. God created the male first (giving him chronological priority in the creation) (1 Ti. 2:13).
(a) God did this to emphasize man's functional purpose and responsibility as head/leader in the home and church. (Priority does not mean superiority.)
3. God created the woman second (1 Tim. 2:13).
(a) Woman was specifically designed and created (from the beginning) for the purpose of being a subordinate, companion-helper, suited for man (not inferior).
4. God's creation order has intentional purpose (1 Cor. 11:8-9).
(a) God could have created the woman first or both simultaneously, but He did not.
(b) God's order was intended to convey His will regarding gender roles.
(c) God gave spiritual teaching to Adam before Eve was created (Gen. 2:15-17).
(d) God created the female as "an help meet for him" (Gen. 2:18, 20).
(e) The Bible does not teach that man was created for the woman, but woman was created "for" the man (1 Cor. 11:9), and she was "brought to" him (Gen. 2:22).
(f) In His creation, we find God's authority and His divine arrangement for leadership and submission within His creation (1 Cor. 11:8).

F. Reason #3: The introduction of sin into the world (1 Tim. 2:14).
1. The events of Genesis 3 illustrate what happens when men and women tamper with God's design and His intentions for men and women.
(a) When Eve took the spiritual leadership over her husband, sin was introduced.
(b) When Adam failed to exercise proper spiritual leadership and authority over his wife, sin was introduced.
2. Eve led humanity into sin (when she took the spiritual initiative over the man).
(a) The nature of Eve's sin is that she was "deceived," but Adam "was not deceived."
(b) Eve believed Satan's lie that she might become as God—she was "beguiled."
3. Even though Eve sinned first and introduced sin into the world, God spoke first to the head of the home—the man (Gen. 3:9). He failed to exercise proper leadership.

4. In the punishment for her sin, God reaffirmed to the woman her role of submission to her husband (Gen. 3:16). Her subjection was increased because of her sin.
G. Reason #4: The relation of Christ and the church (Eph. 5:23-33).
1. God likens the husband-wife relationship to the Christ-church relationship.
2. The husband is the "head" of the wife, as Christ is the "head" of the church (5:23).
3. The wife is to "submit" to her husband as "the church submits to Christ" (5:22, 24).
4. No more should a wife think of exercising authority over her husband than the church should think of exercising authority over Christ. The parallel is key to this passage.

V. God Has Given Wonderful Roles for Women to Fulfill in the Home and in the Church.
A. Christian women are wonderfully talented servants in the church with enormous capabilities.
B. There are many meaningful roles that godly women can and do fulfill in service to Christ.
1. In the home, God calls for women to (this is not an exhaustive list by any means):
   (a) "...bear children" and "bring up children" (1 Tim. 5:14, 10).
   (b) "...manage [rule, ASV] the house, give no opportunity to the adversary" (1 Tim. 5:14).
   (c) "...love their husbands [and] children" (Tit. 2:4).
   (d) "...be sensible, pure, workers at home" (Tit. 2:5).
   (e) The work of a godly woman in and around her home cannot be underestimated.
2. In the church, God calls for women to (this is not an exhaustive list by any means):
   (a) "be...teachers of good things" (Tit. 2:3).
   (b) Teach other women (Tit. 2:3-5).
   (c) Teach and mentor children (2 Tim. 3:14-15).
   (d) Teach alongside men (Acts 18:26; Phil. 4:3).
   (e) Help to administer church programs (Rom. 16:1-2).
   (f) Do good works for others (Acts 9:36; 1 Tim. 5:10).
   (g) Show hospitality (Acts 12:12; 16:14; 1 Tim. 5:10).
   (h) Serve those in need and assist those in distress (1 Tim. 5:10).
   (i) Continue in prayer for the church and all its members (Acts 1:14).
   (j) There is much that Christian women can do in the church with God's approval.
C. Christian women have a powerful influence—in the home, the church and the community.
1. The influence of a righteous, God-fearing, faithful-to-the-book Christian woman can have a tremendous impact on:
   (a) Her husband (1 Pet. 3:1-2).
   (b) Her children (2 Tim. 1:5; 3:14-15).
   (c) Her church (Rom. 16:1-2).
   (d) Older women (Acts 9:36-41).
   (e) Younger women (Tit. 2:3-5).
   (f) Her community (Acts 17:4, 12).
   (g) Generations to follow (Matt. 26:13).
2. Christian women should be grateful for the influence that they have and should exert that influence for good and for the glory of God.

VI. Conclusion
A. There are God-given differences between males and females.
B. God has designed specific roles for each one to have in His order, and each one is pleasing to God when he/she fulfills his/her God-given roles.
C. A Christian (man or woman) should not insist upon exercising his/her "rights."
1. The only "rights" a Christian has are the ones given by God.
2. If we insist upon our "rights" to do what we want to do, we lost sight of our place.

D. God has commanded all Christians to be in subjection to Him.
E. A woman must obey all the commands of God, as surely as any man must.
F. Submission has nothing to do with quality or worth, but it is based upon God's order.
G. The role of women in the church is not cultural, but it is universal, being tied to creation.
H. For a woman to exercise authority over men in the church violates the principle of subjection.
   1. For anyone to exercise authority that God has not granted to them is sinful (cf. 1 Sam. 13:8-14; 2 Chron. 26:16-21).
   2. No man, elder or eldership has the right to give authority or positions of authority to the woman, which God Himself has not given.
I. God's design for the role of women in the church has nothing to do with oppressing them or trying to overpower them or control them.
   1. Men and women alike are given specific roles to fulfill in the church.
   2. These distinct roles require subordination of all men and women alike to the will of God (Eph. 5:21; Jas. 4:7), and specifically to the roles that God has assigned to each.
J. God's design (and distinction) regarding the roles for men and roles for women in the church is to ensure the proper function of His church (cf. 1 Tim. 3:15).
   1. Are we willing to submit ourselves to God's design?
   2. The acceptable function of His church (and our acceptance in His sight) depends on it.
K. Let us remember that God's evaluation of greatness is found in those who serve (Matt. 20:26-38; 23:11-12), regardless of any special "role" or "office" they may have.

Recommended Resources

Books

Laws, Jim, ed. *Women: To the Glory of God.* Spiritual Sword Lectureship. Memphis: Getwell church of Christ, 1994.

McWhorter, Don. *God's Woman: Feminine or Feminist?* Huntsville, AL: Publishing Designs, 1992.

Articles

Baird, James O. "God Assigned a Special Role for Women in the Church." *Introducing the Church of Christ.* Ed. Alvin Jennings. Fort Worth: Star Bible, 1981. 121-125.

Colley, Glenn. "For Establishing Women's Role in the Church Today." *The All-Sufficiency of the Bible (Spiritual Sword Lectureship).* Ed. Gary McDade. Memphis: Getwell church of Christ, 2000. 197-210.

Deaver, Roy. "The Role of Women in the Church." *The Future of the Church (Freed-Hardeman College Lectureship).* Ed. William Woodson. Henderson, TN: Freed-Hardeman College, 1978. 96-110.

Jackson, Wayne. "In Christ—Neither Male Nor Female." *ChristianCourier.com*
https://www.christiancourier.com/articles/1397-in-christ-neither-male-nor-female

---. "Woman's Role in the Church." *ChristianCourier.com*
https://www.christiancourier.com/articles/169-womans-role-in-the-church

Jenkins, Jerry. "His Pattern for Her Role." *Respect for God's Word (South Florida Lectureship).* Ed. David Sproule. Palm Beach Gardens, FL: Palm Beach Lakes church of Christ, 2005. 99-111.

Miller, Dave. "Male and Female Roles: Gender in the Bible." *ApologeticsPress.org*
http://apologeticspress.org/APContent.aspx?category=11&article=5007&topic=389

Sanders, Phil. "Are Women Limited As Leaders?" *Gospel Advocate* (March 2015): 34-37.

Periodicals

The Spiritual Sword. July 1975. "Woman—In the View of God."

The Spiritual Sword. January 1991. "Role of Women in the Church."

The Spiritual Sword. January 1996. "A Review of Feminist Theology."

The Spiritual Sword. July 2003. "The Worthy Woman."

The Spiritual Sword. April 2015. "God's Plan for Women."

Lesson 19: The Doctrine of Salvation

I. **The Greatest Need That Man Has on This Earth Is the Salvation of His Soul.**
   A. There is no Bible doctrine more important than salvation:
      1. For this concerns the spiritual condition of one's soul.
      2. For this concerns the state of one's relationship with God.
      3. For this concerns the eternal destiny of one's soul.
   B. God created man with free will – the freedom to choose what to do with his life and how to respond to the will of God.
      1. Numerous passages in the Bible call for man to make a choice.
         (a) "…choose for yourselves this day whom you will serve…" (Josh 24:15).
         (b) "…fear the Lord, serve Him in sincerity and in truth…" (Josh. 24:14).
         (c) "I have set before you life and death, blessing and cursing; therefore choose life, that both you and your descendants may live" (Deut. 30:19).
         (d) "How long will you falter between two opinions? If the Lord is God, follow Him; but if Baal, follow him" (1 Kgs. 18:21).
         (e) "Test all things; hold fast what is good. Abstain from every form of evil" (1 Th. 5:21-22).
         (f) "Abhor what is evil. Cling to what is good" (Rom. 12:9).
         (g) "No one can serve two masters; for either he will hate the one and love the other, or else he will be loyal to the one and despise the other" (Matt. 6:24).
      2. God created mankind with free will, "so that they should seek the Lord, in the hope that they might grope for Him and find Him" (Acts 17:24-28).
         (a) The Bible teaches that God wants all men to come to Him (1 Tim. 2:4; John 3:16; Tit. 2:11; 2 Pet. 3:9; Matt. 11:28).
         (b) However, the Bible also clearly teaches that not all men will come to God (Matt. 7:13-14, 21-23; 25:31-46; 2 Thess. 1:7-9; Rev. 21:8).
         (c) There is an obvious difference in Scripture between: (1) what God wants/wills and (2) what man might choose to do. This is clear evidence of man's free will.
   C. While God longs for man to come to Him and enter into a relationship with Him (Acts 17:24-28; 1 Tim. 2:4; John 3:16), the majority of accountable persons are not interested in the will of God and they make choices that violate God's will—this is called "sin."
      1. Sin is the result of violating the will of God.
         (a) From the beginning, God has made known His will to His creation.
            (1) God told man not to eat of the tree of knowledge of good and evil (Gen. 2:17).
            (2) Then, with his free will, man chose to violate the will of God and ate (Gen. 3:6).
            (3) The Bible calls this very first act of violating God's will, "sin" (1 Tim. 2:14).
         (b) *Vine's Expository Dictionary* defines "sin" as "a missing of the mark."
            (1) The "mark" is God's will, which He has revealed to man.
            (2) "Sin" occurs and is the result of man "missing the mark" of God's will.
         (c) Scripture defines "sin" as:
            (1) Committing "lawlessness," for "sin is lawlessness" (1 John 3:4).
               (i) Remember that one can be religious and think he's doing right and still be "lawless" in God's eyes (Matt. 7:22-23).
            (2) "All unrighteousness" (1 John 5:17).
            (3) Not "doing" what God wills (Jas. 4:17).
      2. Sin is a personal choice.
         (a) As free moral agents, Adam and Eve made a choice and they sinned against God.

(b) Sin occurs when a person "commits lawlessness" (1 Jn. 3:4). "Commit" is a choice.
(c) The Bible speaks of "the soul [i.e., person] who sins" (Ezek. 18:20). "Sin" is a choice.
(d) When Satan tempts man to sin "by his own desires," a man's response to that temptation is a choice. Making the choice to yield to the temptation is "sin" (Jas. 1:13-15; cf. Rom. 1:18-32).
   (1) Note: While Jesus was tempted (Matt. 4:1-11), He chose not to sin (Heb. 4:15).

3. Sin is not inherited.
  (a) As sin is a choice to "transgress" God's law (1 John 3:4) or to refuse to "do" God's law (Jas. 4:17), it is obvious that this is not something that is or can be inherited.
    (1) The abundance of evidence in Scripture showing that sin is a personal choice is very instructive. Sin is never depicted as inherited in Scripture.
  (b) Scripture teaches that man is "created" "perfect" until he sins (Ezek. 28:15).
  (c) Scripture teaches that sin is the personal choice of each individual (Ezek. 18:20a).
  (d) Scripture teaches that "[t]he son shall not bear the guilt of the father, nor the father bear the guilt of the son" (Ezek. 18:20).
    (1) "The righteousness of the righteous shall be upon himself" (18:20)—righteousness cannot be inherited or passed down to one's offspring.
    (2) "...and the wickedness of the wicked shall be upon himself" (18:20)—wickedness cannot be inherited or passed down to one's offspring.
  (e) Scripture teaches that one must be "converted and become as little children," in order to "enter the kingdom of heaven" (Matt. 18:3).
    (1) It is obvious that "little children" do not have any sins.
    (2) God must view children as "righteous," otherwise they could not enter the kingdom (1 Cor. 6:9).
    (3) They have not inherited any sins from their parents or from Adam and Eve.
    (4) They have not yet committed any sins, until their understanding matures to know and respond to the law of God (Rom. 7:8-9).
  (f) Scripture teaches that for man to be right with God he must deal with his personal sins (not sins that he fictitiously inherited).
    (1) "Let the wicked forsake *his* way, And the unrighteous man *his* thoughts; Let him return to the Lord... for He will abundantly pardon" *his* sin (Isa. 55:7).
    (2) Sin is personal! It is not inherited!

4. Sin results in separation from God.
  (a) By one's personal choice to sin, one is personally responsible for the consequences.
  (b) God warned of sin's consequences in the beginning—"you shall surely die" (Gen. 2:17).
  (c) When man sinned, he was driven from the presence of God (Gen. 3:24).
  (d) As physical death is a separation of the spirit from the body (Jas. 2:26), spiritual death is a separation of the spirit from God—man separating himself from God.
  (e) "The wages of sin is death" (Rom. 6:23; cf. Jas. 1:13-15). "Death" is separation.
  (f) "Your iniquities have separated you from your God; and your sins have hidden His face from you, so that He will not hear" (Isa. 59:1-2).
  (g) Separation from God due to one's sins is a condition that will plague man in this life while on earth (Rom. 6:23; Isa. 59:1-2).
  (h) But even more dreadful, separation from God due to one's sins is a condition that will doom man to "everlasting destruction away from the presence of the Lord and from the glory of His power" (2 Thess. 1:8-9).

D. It is essential to understand the true nature and gravity of sin, so that man can understand his desperate need for salvation from his sin.
   1. When man chooses to violate the law of God, he sins against God and is then separated from God.
   2. His greatest need is to be saved from his sins and return to a right relationship with God.

II. It Is Essential to Understand What "Being Saved" Means.
A. While it is critical to understand "how" one can be "saved" (which will be studied in this lesson), it is equally critical to understand "what" it even means "to be saved."
   1. Religious individuals frequently use the word "saved":
      (a) "Are you saved?" "I remember when I was saved." "You need to get saved."
   2. However, being "saved" is not an expression to be used lightly or casually.
   3. For eternal reasons, it is vital to use and understand the word by its Biblical standard.
B. "Being saved" involves what one is being saved "from."
   1. Sin is a personal choice that separates man from God in this life (Isa. 59:2).
      (a) "Being saved" removes that separation and puts man back in a right relationship with God. This is not a matter to be taken lightly or casually.
   2. Sin brings the wrath of God upon oneself (Rom. 1:18; Col. 3:6).
      (a) "Being saved" reverses the wrath of God and puts man back in a right relationship with God. This is not a matter to be taken lightly or causally.
   3. Sin will result in an eternity in hell (2 Thess. 1:8-9; Rev. 21:8).
      (a) "Being saved" pulls one "out of the fire" (Jude 23) and puts man back in a right relationship with God. This is not a matter to be taken lightly or causally.
C. "Being saved" involves what one is being saved "by."
   1. Sins are "washed" away by the "blood" of Jesus (Rev. 1:5; Eph. 1:7).
   2. The blood of Jesus is not a matter to be taken lightly or casually.
   3. Salvation through His blood will be considered more fully later in this lesson.
D. "Being saved" involves what one is being saved "to."
   1. When one is saved, he becomes "right" with God (Rom. 1:16-17; 2 Cor. 5:20).
   2. When one is saved, he becomes a "child" of God (Gal. 3:26; Rom. 8:16).
   3. When one is saved, he becomes a "servant" of God (Rom. 6:13-23; Heb. 9:14).
   4. When one is saved, he becomes an "heir" of God (Rom. 8:17).
   5. When one is saved, he becomes a "citizen" of heaven (Phil. 3:20-21).
   6. A new and proper relationship with God is not a matter to be taken lightly or casually.
E. "Being saved" involves what one is being saved "for."
   1. One is saved in order to do "good works" (Eph. 2:10).
   2. One is saved in order to be an "instrument of righteousness" (Rom. 6:13).
   3. One is saved in order to "serve the living God" (Heb. 9:14).
   4. One is saved in order to "teach others also" (2 Tim. 2:2).
   5. One is saved in order to "present every man perfect in Christ Jesus" (Col. 1:28).
   6. One is saved in order to "always abound in the work of the Lord" (1 Cor. 15:58).
   7. One is saved in order to "glorify God" (1 Cor. 6:20).
   8. The purpose of God's gift of salvation is not a matter to be taken lightly or casually.
F. Just as the Bible uses various terms for "sin" (i.e., iniquity, transgression, trespass, lawless deed, lawlessness, unrighteousness, ungodliness, wickedness, disobedience, etc.), the Bible uses various terms for "salvation." Each one helps us to understand the meaning that God intends for us to have about the salvation He offers. The following are Scriptural synonyms for salvation:

1. "Saved" or "salvation" (Mark 16:16; Acts 4:12; 16:30-31; Rom. 10:9-10; Heb. 5:9).
2. "Forgiveness" (Eph. 1:7; Col. 1:14; 2:13; 1 John 1:9; 2:12; Acts 8:22).
3. "Remission" (Acts 2:38; Matt. 26:28; Mark 1:4; Luke 24:47; Heb. 9:22).
4. "Redeemed" (Eph. 1:7; Col. 1:14; 1 Pet. 1:18-19; Tit. 2:14; Rev. 5:9; Rom. 3:24).
5. "Washed" (Acts 22:16; 1 Cor. 6:11; Eph. 5:26; Tit. 3:5; Rev. 1:5; Psa. 51:2, 7).
6. "Cleansed" (1 Cor. 6:11; Eph. 5:26; Heb. 9:14; 1 John 1:7, 9; 2 Pet. 1:9).
7. "Sanctified" (1 Cor. 1:2; 6:11; Eph. 5:26; 1 Thess. 4:3; 5:23; Heb. 2:12; 10:10; 13:12).
8. "Justified" (Rom. 3:24-28; 5:1, 9; 1 Cor. 6:11; Gal. 3:24; Jas. 2:21-25).
9. "Delivered" (Rom. 7:6; 2 Cor. 1:10; Col. 1:13; 1 Thess. 1:10).
10. "Set free" or "made free" (John 8:32-36; Rom. 6:7, 18, 22; Rom. 8:2; Gal. 5:1).
11. "Reconciled" (Rom. 5:10-11; 2 Cor. 5:18-21; Eph. 2:16; Col. 1:20-21).
12. "Born again" (John 3:3-7; 1 Pet. 1:23).
13. "Conversion" (Acts 15:3).
14. "Life" (John 3:16; 5:24, 40; Acts 11:18; Eph. 2:5; Col. 2:13; 1 John 2:25; Rom. 6:23).
15. "Newness of life" (Rom. 6:4; 2 Cor. 5:17).
16. "Blotted out" (Acts 3:19; Psa. 51:1, 9).
17. Being "in Christ" or "in the one body" (Eph. 1:3-7; 2:10, 13-16; Gal. 3:27; Rom. 6:3).

G. "Being saved" is not an expression to be used without appreciating the weight of its Biblical meaning—including what one is being saved "from," "by," "to" and "for."

H. Using Bible terms to talk about a Bible subject demands using those words in Bible ways and using the Bible as one's only authority.

III. Salvation from Sin, According to the Bible, Is Intended for and Offered to All.

A. There are many in the denominational world who do not believe that all people have the God-given opportunity to be saved.
1. These individuals have been led to believe that God pre-selected those who would be saved and those who would be lost.
2. They believe that the number of the saved is fixed and cannot be altered.
3. They believe that, as a result, Jesus only died for the elect, limiting the availability of the atonement of His blood only to those who were predetermined to be saved.
4. Consequently, they do not teach that salvation is open, intended and offered to all.
5. This false doctrine is the heart of Calvinism, which is accepted and taught widely in the denominational world. But, what does the Bible say about it?

B. The Bible teaches that ALL are lost!
1. "ALL are under sin" (Rom. 3:9).
2. "ALL have turned aside" (Rom. 3:12).
3. "ALL have sinned" (Rom. 3:23).
4. "We ALL stumble in many things" (Jas. 3:2).
5. Does the Bible teach that ALL are lost but ALL cannot be saved?

C. The Bible teaches that ALL will be judged!
1. "ALL the nations will be gathered before Him" (Matt. 25:32, 31-46).
2. "We must ALL appear before the judgment seat of Christ" (2 Cor. 5:10).
3. "We shall ALL stand before the judgment seat of Christ" (Rom. 14:10).
4. "EVERY knee shall bow to Me" (Rom. 14:11).
5. "EVERY tongue shall confess to God" (Rom. 14:11).
6. "I am coming quickly, and My reward is with Me, to give to EVERY one according to his work" (Rev. 22:12).

7. "EVERY soul who will not hear that Prophet shall be utterly destroyed from among the people" (Acts 3:23).
8. Does the Bible teach that ALL will be judged but ALL cannot be prepared for judgment?

D. The Bible teaches that God wants ALL to be saved!
1. God "desires ALL men to be saved" (1 Tim. 2:4).
2. "The Lord is…not willing that any should perish but that ALL should come to repentance" (2 Pet. 3:9).
3. "To you first, God…sent Him to bless you, in turning away EVERY one of you from your iniquities" (Acts 3:26).
4. "In your seed ALL the families of the earth shall be blessed" (Acts 3:25).
5. "At the name of Jesus EVERY knee should bow" (Phil. 2:10).
6. "And that EVERY tongue should confess that Jesus Christ is Lord" (Phil. 2:11).
7. If God wants ALL to be saved, then ALL must have the opportunity to be saved!

E. The Bible teaches that Jesus died for ALL!
1. "That by the grace of God He might taste death for EVERYONE" (Heb. 2:9).
2. "He died for ALL" (2 Cor. 5:14-15).
3. "Christ Jesus…gave Himself a ransom for ALL" (1 Tim. 2:6).
4. "I, if I am lifted up from the earth, will draw ALL peoples to Myself" (John 12:32).
5. "He…delivered Him up for us ALL" (Rom. 8:32).
6. "He became the author of eternal salvation to ALL" (Heb. 5:9).
7. "You were slain and have redeemed us to God by Your blood out of EVERY tribe and tongue and people and nation" (Rev. 5:9).
8. "He Himself is the propitiation for our sins, and not for ours only but also for the WHOLE world" (1 John 2:2).
9. While some teach a "limited atonement" available from the death of Christ, Scripture plainly affirms that the blood of Jesus was shed for ALL people.

F. The Bible teaches that Jesus has commissioned His disciples to go to ALL people.
1. "Go therefore and make disciples of ALL the nations" (Matt. 28:19).
2. "Go into ALL the world and preach the gospel to EVERY creature" (Mark 16:15).
3. "…Repentance and remission of sins should be preached in His name to ALL nations" (Luke 24:47).
4. "…Preach, warning EVERY man and teaching EVERY man in all wisdom, that we may present EVERY man perfect in Christ Jesus" (Col. 1:28).
5. "…the everlasting gospel to preach to those who dwell on the earth—to EVERY nation, tribe, tongue, and people" (Rev. 14:6).
6. Why would God send His disciples to teach ALL people if ALL could not be saved?

G. The Bible teaches that the invitation to come to Christ and be saved is extended to ALL.
1. "Come to Me, ALL you who labor and are heavy laden, and I will give you rest" (Matt. 11:28).
2. "The grace of God that brings salvation has appeared to ALL men" (Tit. 2:11).
3. "The gospel of Christ…is the power of God to salvation for EVERYONE" (Rom. 1:16).
4. "If ANYONE wants to do His will, he shall know concerning the doctrine…" (John 7:17).
5. "If ANYONE desires to come after Me, let him deny himself, and take up his cross, and follow Me" (Matt. 16:24).
6. "Therefore, if ANYONE is in Christ, he is a new creation" (2 Cor. 5:17).
7. "Behold, I stand at the door and knock. If ANYONE hears My voice and opens the door, I will come in to him and dine with him, and he with Me" (Rev. 3:20).

8. "WHOEVER desires, let him take the water of life freely" (Rev. 22:17).
9. "WHOEVER believes in Him should not perish" (John 3:15-16).
10. "You are ALL sons of God through faith in Christ Jesus" (Gal. 3:26).
11. "WHOEVER believes that Jesus is the Christ is born of God" (1 John 5:1).
12. "WHOEVER calls on the name of the Lord shall be saved" (Rom. 10:13).
13. "God…now commands ALL men EVERYWHERE to repent" (Acts 17:30).
14. "Unless you repent you will ALL likewise perish" (Luke 13:3).
15. "The Lord is…not willing that ANY should perish but that ALL should come to repentance" (2 Pet. 3:9).
16. "WHOEVER confesses Me before men, him I will also confess before My Father who is in heaven" (Matt. 10:32).
17. "WHOEVER confesses that Jesus is the Son of God, God abides in him, and he in God" (1 John 4:15).
18. "Let EVERY one of you be baptized in the name of Jesus Christ for the remission of sins" (Acts 2:38).
19. "He became the author of eternal salvation to ALL who obey Him" (Heb. 5:9).
20. "EVERYONE who practices righteousness is born of Him" (1 John 2:29).
21. Salvation truly is offered and available to EVERYONE!

H. The Bible teaches that God is no respecter of persons when it comes to salvation.
1. "God shows NO partiality. But in EVERY nation WHOEVER fears Him and works righteousness is accepted by Him" (Acts 10:34-35).
2. "God…will render…glory, honor, and peace to EVERYONE who works what is good, to the Jew first and also to the Greek. For there is NO partiality with God" (Rom. 2:5-11).
3. "The righteousness of God…is revealed…to ALL and on ALL who believe. For there is NO difference" (Rom. 3:21-22).
4. "For there is NO distinction between Jew and Greek, for the same Lord over ALL is rich to ALL who call upon Him" (Rom. 10:12).
5. "There is neither Jew nor Greek, there is neither slave nor free, there is neither male nor female; for you are ALL one in Christ Jesus" (Gal. 3:28).
6. "'As I live,' says the Lord God, 'I have no pleasure in the death of the wicked, but that the wicked turn from his way and live'" (Ezek. 33:11).

I. From a careful study of God's Word, it is readily apparent that:
1. The Bible does not teach the denominational doctrine of predestination.
2. The Bible does not teach the denominational doctrine of unconditional election.
3. The Bible does not teach the denominational doctrine of limited atonement.
4. The Bible does teach that God wants ALL men to be saved and that He has offered His salvation to ALL mankind to accept. What a glorious blessing for all mankind!

IV. Salvation from Sin, According to the Bible, Is By the Grace of God.
A. The grace of God is wonderfully beautiful and so desperately needed!
1. Thayer's *Greek-English Lexicon* defines the Greek word for grace *(charis)* as: "good-will, loving-kindness, favor… used of the kindness of a master toward his inferiors or servants, and so especially of God toward men… kindness which bestows upon one what he has not deserved…that kindness by which God bestows favors even upon the ill-deserving, and grants to sinners the pardon of their offences, and bids them accept of eternal salvation through Christ" (p. 665-666).
2. Trench's *Synonyms of the New Testament* defines the Greek word for grace *(charis)* as: "signifying the favor, grace, and goodness of God to man…the grace of the

worthy to the unworthy, of the holy to the sinful...the absolute freeness of the lovingkindness of God to men" (p. 157-158).
3. Dan Winkler finds "grace" defined in Scripture as the perfect combination of God's "mercy," "love" and "kindness" (see those words in Ephesians 2:4+7 and Titus 3:4-7).
4. Grace has often been defined simply as the "unmerited favor" of God, or man receiving from God what he doesn't deserve.

B. Scripture affirms the only way that man can be saved from sin is by the grace of God.
1. God's grace is what saves us.
    (a) "By grace you have been saved" (Eph. 2:5, 8).
    (b) We can be "justified freely by His grace through the redemption that is in Christ Jesus" (Rom. 3:24).
2. God's grace saves us through the death of Christ.
    (a) "Redemption" is "through His blood...according to the riches of His grace" (Eph. 1:7).
    (b) "And the grace of our Lord was exceedingly abundant, with faith and love which are in Christ Jesus," who "came into the world to save sinners" (1 Tim. 1:14-15).
3. God's grace is available to all.
    (a) "For the grace of God that brings salvation has appeared to all men" (Tit. 2:11).
    (b) God's grace is not intended only for the "elect," as Calvinism claims.

C. However, Scripture does not teach that salvation is by grace alone.
1. There are some denominations who teach that salvation is by grace alone.
2. However, the Bible teaches there are conditions for accessing the grace of God.
3. Salvation by grace is accessed "through faith" (Eph. 2:8).
4. Salvation by grace is accessed by obeying its "teaching" (Tit. 2:12).
5. Salvation by grace is accessed "through the washing of regeneration" (Tit. 3:5-7).
6. If salvation was actually by grace alone, then all would be saved (Tit. 2:11).

D. It is impossible for man to earn or merit his salvation.
1. Salvation is a "gift *(doron)* of God" (Eph. 2:8).
    (a) *Doron* signifies a gift which involves a sacrifice and involves a "cost" to the giver.
    (b) God sacrificed His Son as a "gift" for our salvation.
2. Salvation is a "gift *(charisma)* of God" (Rom. 6:23).
    (a) *Charisma* comes from the Greek *charis*, which means "grace."
    (b) God's salvation is a "gracious gift" or sometimes translated "free gift," which cannot be earned or deserved.
3. God does not extend His grace to man because of any merit on man's part.

E. Man is saved by grace (Eph. 2:5, 8), but we can only find "access...into this grace" (Rom. 5:1-2) by a proper response to the revealed will of the gracious God!

V. Salvation from Sin, According to the Bible, Is By the Blood of Jesus Christ.
A. The grace of God, which was fueled by "the love of God":
1. "...Sent His only begotten Son into the world" (1 John 4:9),
2. To offer "the sacrifice of Himself" (Heb. 9:26),
3. "...To give His life a ransom for many" (Matt. 20:28),
4. In order to "shed [His blood] for many for the remission of sins" (Matt. 26:28).

B. Why was it essential for Jesus to shed His blood?
1. There is a direct correlation in Scripture between blood and one's relationship with God.
2. It would not have been sufficient for Jesus to merely die and willingly give His life.
3. It was essential in His death that He give His blood.
4. God has always placed the power of atonement in a sacrifice of blood.

5. Only "by His blood" (Rom. 3:25) could Jesus "make propitiation for the sins of the people" (Heb. 2:17; 1 John 2:2; 4:10).
C. In the Patriarchal Age, the sacrifice of blood was essential.
 1. The first acceptable sacrifice of man was one of blood (Gen. 4:3-5).
 2. Noah offered sacrifices involving blood (Gen. 8:20).
 3. Abraham offered sacrifices involving blood (Gen. 12:7-8).
 4. The Passover was instituted with offered sacrifices involving blood (Ex. 12:1-13).
D. In the Mosaic Age, the sacrifice of blood was essential.
 1. The old covenant was sealed with blood (Heb. 9:18-20; Ex. 24:6-8).
 2. The tabernacle and all the vessels of the ministry were sanctified by blood (Heb. 9:21-22).
 3. The Law of Moses required multiple animal sacrifices daily (Lev. 1-7; Heb. 10:11).
 4. However, the blood of those animal sacrifices could never take away sin (Heb. 10:1-4).
    (a) Every year the sins of Israel were remembered (Heb. 10:3; Lev. 16).
    (b) Every year atonement was secured by the blood of an animal (Heb. 9:7, 25).
    (c) The priests were "offering repeatedly the same sacrifices, which can never take away sins" (Heb. 10:11).
 5. Yet, "without shedding of blood there is no remission" (Heb. 9:22).
E. The shedding of Jesus' blood was absolutely essential for our salvation from sin.
 1. Old Testament prophets foretold of the Savior's sacrifice (Isa. 53:5-6; Zech. 13:1).
 2. Wendell Winkler notes nine essential benefits of the blood of Christ (p. 39-41):
    (a) The blood of Christ redeems (Eph. 1:7; Heb. 9:12; Rev. 5:9; 1 Pet. 1:18-19).
    (b) The blood of Christ washes away sins (Rev. 1:5; 7:14; Zech. 13:1).
    (c) The blood of Christ justifies (Rom. 5:9).
    (d) The blood of Christ sanctifies (Heb. 10:29; 13:12).
    (e) The blood of Christ reconciles (Eph. 2:13; Col. 1:20).
    (f) The blood of Christ cleanses (1 John 1:7).
    (g) The blood of Christ remits (Matt. 26:28; Heb. 9:22).
    (h) The blood of Christ purges the conscience (Heb. 9:13-14).
    (i) The blood of Christ purchased the church (Acts 20:28; Eph. 5:25-27).
 3. Our salvation is only possible because of the precious blood of Jesus Christ!
F. Man is saved by Christ's blood (Eph. 1:7), but we can only be "washed...in the blood of the Lamb" (Rev. 7:14) by a proper response to the revealed will of the loving Savior!

VI. Salvation from Sin, According to the Bible, Is By the Word of the Holy Spirit.
A. The entire Godhead is involved in our salvation from sin.
 1. We are saved by the grace of God.
 2. We are saved by the blood of Jesus Christ.
 3. We are saved by the Word of the Holy Spirit.
B. Every word in our Bible is a product of the Holy Spirit.
 1. "...Prophecy never came by the will of man, but holy men of God spoke as they were moved by the Holy Spirit" (2 Pet. 1:20-21).
 2. "Now we have received, not the spirit of the world, but the Spirit who is from God, so that we may know the things freely given to us by God, which things we also speak, not in words taught by human wisdom, but in those taught by the Spirit, combining spiritual thoughts with spiritual words" (1 Cor. 2:11-13, NASB).
 3. "However, when He, the Spirit of truth, has come, He will guide you into all truth; for He will not speak on His own authority, but whatever He hears He will speak; and He will tell you things to come" (John 16:13).

C. Scripture teaches that the Spirit-given Word in our Bible is essential to salvation from sin.
   1. The Word "is the power of God to salvation" (Rom. 1:16).
   2. The Word "is able to save your souls" (Jas. 1:21).
   3. The Word has the "words by which you…will be saved" (Acts 11:14).
   4. One absolutely cannot be saved without the Bible!
D. Scripture teaches that the Spirit-given Word leads one to the point of salvation from sin.
   1. The Word "teaches" about sin, Jesus and righteousness (1 Cor. 2:13; 2 Tim. 3:16).
   2. The Word "convicts" of sin and error (2 Tim. 3:16; John 16:8; Tit. 1:9).
   3. The Word "corrects" from sin and error (2 Tim. 3:16; Acts 18:26-28; Matt. 13:15).
   4. The Word "instructs" in righteous living (2 Tim. 3:16; Col. 3:17).
   5. The Word "gives light" to lead one's feet in the right path (Psa. 119:105; Prov. 6:23).
   6. The Word "gives understanding" to know the will of God (Psa. 119:130; Eph. 3:3-4).
   7. The Word "generates faith" in God and the deity of Jesus (Rom. 10:17; John 20:30-31).
   8. One absolutely cannot be saved without the Bible!
E. Scripture teaches that the Spirit-given Word is involved in the actual salvation from sin.
   1. The Word "converts" the soul when it is obeyed (Psa. 19:7).
   2. The Word "cleanses" from sin when it is obeyed (Eph. 5:26; Psa. 119:9).
   3. The Word "purifies" the soul when it is obeyed (1 Pet. 1:22).
   4. The Word "makes free" from sin when it is obeyed (John 8:32).
   5. The Word "liberates" from sin when it is obeyed (Jas. 1:25).
   6. The Word "sanctifies" from sin and unto God when it is obeyed (Eph. 5:26; Jn. 17:17).
   7. The Word "gives life" when it is obeyed (Psa. 119:50).
   8. The Word "births" one into God's family when it is obeyed (John 3:5; 1 Pet. 1:23).
   9. The Word "reconciles" one back to God when it is obeyed (2 Cor. 5:19-20).
   10. One absolutely cannot be saved without the Bible!
F. The Word of God will be that which judges all mankind at the end of time (John 12:48).
   1. We must hear it, in order to "believe" that we must be saved (Rom. 10:17; Heb. 11:6).
   2. We must study it, in order to "know" how to be saved (John 8:32; 2 Tim. 3:16).
   3. We must obey it, in order to "be" saved (Acts 2:40; Heb. 5:9).
G. Man is saved by the Word of the Holy Spirit (1 Cor. 15:1-4), but we can only be made "alive" (Rom. 6:11-17) by a proper response to the revealed will in that Word!

VII. Salvation from Sin, According to the Bible, Is By Faith (on Man's Part).
A. Man's salvation is truly, clearly and only possible by the grace of God (Eph. 2:5).
   1. There is nothing that man can do to "earn" his salvation (Eph. 2:9).
   2. There is nothing that man can do to "deserve" his salvation (Rom. 3:23).
B. However, the Bible does teach that man has a part in his salvation.
   1. The foundation of man's proper response to God is faith.
   2. The Bible was written in order to create faith in man (Rom. 10:17; John 20:30-31).
   3. It is critical to understand and to speak of faith in the way the Bible uses that term.
C. It is helpful to have an accurate definition of faith, from Scripture and from lexicons.
   1. The Bible does not necessarily "define" faith, like a dictionary would. But, the Bible gives a very clear description of what Biblical faith is.
      (a) "Faith is the substance of things hoped for…" (Heb. 11:1).
         (1) The English word "substance" is from the Greek *hupostasis*, which means "a setting or placing under; thing put under, substructure, foundation" (Thayer).
         (2) The word is translated "assurance" in the NASB, ESV and ASV.

             (3) The idea is that "faith" is the guarantee, the basis for, the very foundation of "things hoped for" that are promised by God.
          (b) "Faith is…the evidence of things not seen" (Heb. 11:1).
             (1) The English word "evidence" is from the Greek *elegchos,* which means "a proof, that by which a thing is proved or tested" (Thayer).
             (2) The word is translated "conviction" in the NASB, ESV and ASV.
             (3) The idea is that "faith" is NOT a leap in the dark, but it is the proof or confidence that Biblical things which we have not seen or do not see are indeed real.
          (c) Faith is "being fully convinced that what [God] had promised He was also able to perform" (Rom. 4:21).
       2. After providing an inspired description of faith, the Bible goes on (in Hebrews 11) to illustrate what Biblical faith is.
          (a) Knowing that man often learns best by example, the Lord provided numerous (and familiar) examples from the Old Testament to show what true faith is.
          (b) There were many things that the Old Testament faithful had "not yet seen" (11:7), and they had not yet "received the promises" (11:13, 39), yet through faith, they "looked to the reward" (11:26), having "seen [it] afar off" (11:13). That is the very definition of "faith."
          (c) Then, with one favorite character after another, the Holy Spirit marches His readers into the field of faith to see that true, Biblical faith is one that "moves with godly fear" (11:7) and "obeys" (11:8) the will of the Lord.
          (d) The Old Testament faithful lived "by faith." The prepositional phrase "by faith" (at the beginning of so many verses in Hebrews 11) points to the leading verb of each sentence to show that faith was the motivating factor and underlying foundation of their active obedience.
          (e) God's illustration clearly teaches that faith and obedience go hand-in-hand.
       3. This description of "faith" in the Bible corresponds precisely with the definition that scholars have given of the word.
          (a) In his definition of "faith," W.E. Vine notes, "The main elements in 'faith'…are:
             (1) "a firm conviction, producing a full acknowledgement of God's revelation or truth,
             (2) "a personal surrender to Him,
             (3) "a conduct inspired by such surrender."
          (b) In his definition of the Greek word for "believe" *(pisteuo),* J.H. Thayer notes that this faith is "a conviction, full of joyful trust, that Jesus is the Messiah—the divinely appointed author of eternal salvation in the kingdom of God, conjoined with obedience to Christ."
          (c) Note carefully the three common components of "faith" in these definitions, which correspond perfectly with the Biblical description of "faith":
             (1) Conviction
             (2) Trust/Surrender
             (3) Obedience/Conduct
       4. Biblical faith involves (1) firm conviction, (2) trustful surrender and (3) obedience.
   D. It is essential to know that Scripture teaches that faith saves man from sin.
       1. Faith is produced in man's heart by hearing and studying God's Word (Rom. 10:17; John 20:30-31; Luke 8:12; Acts 15:7; Rom. 10:13-17).
       2. That faith is requisite in order to acquire true salvation.
       3. Faith is essential in order to "please" God (Heb. 11:6).

4. Faith is essential in order to be "justified" (Rom. 5:1).
5. Faith is essential in order to be "saved" (Acts 16:31; Mark 16:16; Eph. 2:8).
6. Faith is essential in order to "receive remission of sins" (Acts 10:43).
7. Faith is essential in order to have "everlasting life" (John 3:16, 36).
8. Faith is essential in order to "become children of God" (John 1:12; Gal. 3:26).
9. Faith is essential in order to avoid "the lake [of] fire and brimstone" (Rev. 21:8).
10. So, if we have been "saved through faith" (Eph. 2:8), are we saved by faith alone?
E. It is critical to understand that Scripture does not teach that faith alone saves.
 1. Man has created quite a controversy over the connection between faith and salvation. Notice that the issue has been created by "man," not God.
    (a) The discussion centers around the question, "Does faith alone save?"
    (b) Much of the controversy is due to improper and differing definitions of "faith."
        (1) Some have defined "faith" as a mental assent—i.e., merely accepting and believing the teachings of the Bible to be true and even life-changing.
        (2) Some have taken "faith" a little further to include not only accepting Bible teachings to be true but also being compelled in their hearts to put their trust in the Lord, surrender their lives to Him and ask Him into their hearts.
        (3) The problem with these definitions or understandings of faith is that they do not coincide at all with the Biblical and lexical definitions. (See VII, C above.)
    (c) Biblical faith has three equally essential components: (1) firm conviction, (2) trustful surrender and (3) obedience.
        (1) "Faith alone" advocates defy the very definition of faith.
        (2) They will not accept this definition because it includes "obedience."
        (3) Therefore, they have sought to redefine "faith" to fit their theology.
 2. Some denominations have stated their case quite clearly in their church manuals.
    (a) In paragraph 69 of the "The Constitution of the Methodist Church" section of the *Discipline of the Methodist Church* (1948), the claim is made: "Wherefore, that we are justified by faith only is a most wholesome doctrine, and very full of comfort" (p. 27).
    (b) In the "Christian Doctrine" section of Edward T. Hiscox's *The Standard Manual for Baptist Churches,* the claim is made: "We believe the Scriptures teach that the great gospel blessing which Christ secures to such as believe in him is justification; that justification includes the pardon of sin, and the gift of eternal life on principles of righteousness; that it is bestowed, not in consideration of any works of righteousness which we have done, but solely through faith in Christ" (p. 62).
    (c) In his German translation of the New Testament (in 1522), Martin Luther added the word "alone" to the text in Romans 3:28, so that it read, "…man is justified by faith alone."
    (d) But, do these statements agree with what the Scriptures teach?
 3. Scripture teaches that "a man is justified…not by faith only" (Jas. 2:24).
 4. Scripture teaches that "faith by itself…is dead" (Jas. 2:17).
 5. Scripture teaches that "faith alone" does not save, otherwise "the demons," who "believe and tremble," would be saved (Jas. 2:19).
 6. Scripture teaches that if one can be saved by faith alone, then he can be saved:
    (a) Before and without repenting of his sins (Luke 13:3; Acts 2:38; 17:30; 2 Pet. 3:9).
    (b) Before and without confessing his faith in Jesus (Matt. 10:32-33; Rom. 10:9-10).

- (c) Before and without being baptized (Mark 16:16; Acts 2:38; 8:12-12; Gal. 3:26-27).
- (d) Before and without calling on the name of the Lord (Acts 2:21; Rom. 10:13-17).
- (e) Before and without confessing Christ (John 12:42-43).
- (f) Before and without becoming a child of God (John 1:11-12).
- (g) Before and without coming to God (Heb. 11:6).
  7. Scripture teaches one who "believes" is synonymous with one who "obeys" (John 3:36, NASB).
     - (a) The jailor, in Acts 16, "rejoiced, having believed in God" (16:34).
     - (b) He repented and was baptized in verse 33. That is summarized as "having believed" in verse 34.
     - (c) Biblical faith that saves is not "faith alone." Biblical faith "obeys."
  8. Scripture presents numerous examples of individuals who believed but were not saved.
     - (a) There were "many" Jews who "believed in" Jesus in John 8. But to those Jews:
       - (1) Jesus said, "If God were your Father..." (8:42), for God was not their Father.
       - (2) Jesus said, "You are of your father the devil" (8:44).
       - (3) Here were believers in Jesus who were not saved.
     - (b) "Among the [Jewish] rulers" in John 12, "many believed in Him" (12:42).
       - (1) "But because of the Pharisees they did not confess Him" (12:42).
       - (2) "For they loved the praise of men more than the praise of God" (12:43).
       - (3) Here were believers in Jesus who were not saved.
- F. Salvation requires faith, and true faith will save.
  1. But true faith is not merely a mental assent.
  2. But true faith is not merely a trusting in Jesus and inviting him into one's heart.
  3. True faith is an active faith that is convicted, surrenders and obeys.
  4. Study the next two major points (on works and obedience) carefully.
  5. Man is saved by faith, but not by faith alone.

VIII. Salvation from Sin, According to the Bible, Is By Works (on Man's Part).
- A. Saying that man is saved by works makes some people very uncomfortable.
  1. Scripture teaches that man is saved by faith, but not by faith alone.
  2. Likewise, Scripture teaches that man is saved by works, but not by works alone.
  3. To say that man is saved by works is NOT affirming:
     - (a) That one can earn his salvation by doing enough "works."
     - (b) That faith is not necessary.
     - (c) That the totality of salvation is in man's hands to achieve.
- B. Like with grace and with faith, it is important to define terms.
  1. "Works" is from the Greek *ergon*, which simply means "a work, deed or act" (Vine).
  2. There are numerous kinds of "works" mentioned in Scripture:
     - (a) Works of God (John 6:28-29; Acts 2:11; Heb. 1:10).
     - (b) Works of Christ (Matt. 11:2; John 5:36; 15:24).
     - (c) Works of the Spirit (1 Cor. 12:11).
     - (d) Works of darkness (Rom. 13:12; Eph. 5:11).
     - (e) Works of the devil (1 John 3:8; John 8:41).
     - (f) Works of those who say and do not do (Matt. 23:3).
     - (g) Works to be seen by men (Matt. 23:5).
     - (h) Works of men's own hands (Acts 7:41).
     - (i) Works of which one may boast (Rom. 3:27; Eph. 2:9).
     - (j) Works of the flesh (Gal. 5:19-21).

(k) Works of the law (Rom. 9:32; Gal. 2:16; 3:2, 5, 10).
(l) Works befitting repentance (Acts 26:20).
(m) Works that perfect faith (Jas. 2:22; 1 Thess. 1:3).
(n) Work that justify (Jas. 2:21, 24, 25).
(o) Good works (Matt. 5:16; Acts 9:36; Eph. 2:10; 1 Tim. 5:10; Tit. 2:7, 14; 3:8, 14).
(p) Evil works (John 7:7).
(q) Wicked works (Col. 1:21).
(r) Dead works (Heb. 6:1; 9:14).
(s) Our own works (2 Tim. 1:9; Tit. 3:5).
3. Thus, it becomes evident that it would be highly inappropriate in a study of Scripture to lump all works together into one category and treat them all alike.
   (a) For those who claim that "works" have nothing to do with salvation, is it not obvious that they must be able to distinguish of which works they speak?
   (b) Likewise, for those who claim that salvation is by "works alone," is it not obvious that they must be able to distinguish of which works they speak?
   (c) The word "works" is used variously in Scripture. It is not possible to lump all "works" into one category and then affirm or deny that they are necessary for salvation.
4. The Bible teaches that (1) one is not saved by works and (2) one is saved by works.
   (a) This is not contradictory.
   (b) One must determine which kind of "works" is under discussion in each passage.
C. Scripture teaches that salvation is "not of works."
   1. Some "works" are unnecessary (and even counterproductive) to salvation.
   2. "Works" "of the law" of Moses will not save.
      (a) Romans 3:28 teaches, "...a man is justified by faith apart from works of the law."
      (b) Galatians 2:16 teaches, "knowing that a man is not justified by the works of the law but by faith in Jesus Christ, even we have believed in Christ Jesus, that we might be justified by faith in Christ and not by the works of the law; for by the works of the law no flesh shall be justified."
      (c) While Scripture teaches that one is not (and cannot be) saved by the works of the law of Moses, that does not mean that one is not saved by works.
   3. "Works" of which one may "boast" will not save.
      (a) Works of human merit, by which one might earn salvation, do not, will not and cannot save.
      (b) Ephesians 2:8-9 teaches, "For by grace you have been saved through faith, and that **not of yourselves**; it is the gift of God, **not** of works, lest anyone should **boast**."
         (1) This passage is often used (improperly) to "prove" that "works" are not necessary for salvation. But notice the "kind" of "works" under discussion.
         (2) The works excluded from salvation in this passage are meritorious works—works that are "of yourselves" and works of which one can "boast."
         (3) The emphasis in this passage is that salvation is by the grace of God (which is composed of His mercy, love and kindness) (2:4-8).
         (4) There is no salvation for man apart from what God's gracious mercy, love and kindness have done for us in Jesus Christ. That's the point!
         (5) However, in this passage, Paul is not excluding all works from salvation, else he would contradict the rest of the New Testament.
      (c) While Scripture teaches that one is not (and cannot be) saved by works of merit, that does not mean that one is not saved by works.

D. Scripture teaches that salvation is "by works."
   1. It is not a contradiction to say on one hand, "Salvation is not of works," and to say on the other hand, "Salvation is by works":
      (a) If one is defining "works" in the way that the Bible defines works, and
      (b) If one is differentiating between "works" in the way the Bible differentiates.
   2. In James 2, the inspired writer asks this question, "What does it profit…if someone says he has faith but does not have works? Can faith (without works) save him?"
   3. James provides the inspired answer:
      (a) "Faith by itself, if it does not have works, is dead" (Jas. 2:17).
      (b) If salvation is by faith alone, then "even the demons [who] believe—and tremble" would be saved (2:19).
      (c) "Faith without work is dead" (2:20).
      (d) "Faith was working together with his works, and by works faith was made perfect" (2:22).
      (e) "A man is justified by works, and not by faith only" (2:24).
      (f) "Faith without works is dead" (2:26).
      (g) It is obvious in this passage that James is dealing with a different kind of works than Paul was addressing in Ephesians 2.
      (h) James makes it very clear that without faith-perfecting works, one cannot be saved. Faith without works is dead!
   4. There is a vast difference between meritorious works and works that perfect faith.
      (a) Paul was excluding meritorious works from salvation in Ephesians 2:8-9.
      (b) James was including works that perfect faith in James 2:14-26.
      (c) Incidentally, Paul goes on in Ephesians 2:10 to avow that we are "created in Christ Jesus for good works." He excludes one type of works but includes another.
E. Scripture teaches that some "works" are absolutely essential to one's salvation.
   1. While some try to exclude "works" as essential for salvation, Scripture teaches otherwise.
   2. Jesus said that one must "labor for…everlasting life" (John 6:27), and that to **believe in Him** is a "work" appointed by God (6:29). Jesus called faith a "work."
   3. The act of "**repentance**" requires "works befitting repentance" in order to truly "turn to God" (Acts 26:20; cf. Matt. 12:41+Jon. 3:10).
   4. It is often the case that, when it comes to those who argue that salvation is by "faith only" and that "works" are not necessary for salvation, these individuals frequently are trying to discount or eliminate the place of baptism in one's salvation. Consider some interesting points regarding this unsustainable position.
      (a) "Belief" and "repentance" are both identified with the word "work" in Scripture (John 6:29; Acts 26:20). Baptism never is.
         (1) That is not to say that baptism is not a work.
         (2) But the word "work" is never used for baptism.
         (3) To be honest, one must identify faith and repentance as works.
      (b) There are "active" verbs and "passive" verbs in the Greek New Testament.
         (1) Believing in Jesus is an active response to the gospel of Christ (Acts 16:31).
         (2) Repenting of sin is an active response to the gospel of Christ (Acts 17:30).
         (3) Being baptized is a passive verb (Ac. 2:38), where the subject of baptism is actually passive, as the one administering the baptism is the active one (Matt. 28:19).
         (4) One is active in the decision to be baptized but is passive in the actual administration of it.

5. There is one verse that speaks of baptism as a work. Note it carefully.
   (a) Colossians 2:12 depicts baptism as being "buried with" Christ and "raised with Him."
   (b) But that process is not identified in this passage as a work of man.
   (c) Rather salvation in baptism is accomplished "through faith in the **working of God**."
   (d) In baptism, the subject is passive. In baptism, God is active (working).
   (e) God is the one "doing the saving" in baptism. It is not a work of merit but of God!
6. Are "works" necessary in order to be right with God? Consider Acts 10:35.
   (a) "In every nation whoever fears Him and works righteousness is accepted by Him" (Acts 10:35).
   (b) To be "accepted" by God, certain works (that He identifies) are essential!

F. Not only are the works identified by God essential for salvation, but a Christian must continue to maintain faith-saving works to remain in a right relationship with God.
   1. A Christian is "created in Christ Jesus for good works" (Eph. 2:10).
   2. A Christian must have a "faith working through love" to "avail anything" "in Christ Jesus" (Gal. 5:6). "Faith" must be "working" in order to bring about a positive result.
   3. A Christian must "work out [his] own salvation with fear and trembling" (Phil. 2:12).
   4. A Christian must "abound in every good work" (2 Cor. 9:8, ESV).
   5. A Christian must be "fruitful in every good work" (Col. 1:10).
   6. A Christian must be "rich in good works" (1 Tim. 6:18).
   7. A Christian must be "a pattern of good works" (Tit. 2:7).
   8. A Christian must be "zealous for good works" (Tit. 2:14).
   9. A Christian must "learn" and "be careful to maintain good works" (Tit. 3:8, 14).
   10. A Christian must be "always abounding in the work of the Lord" (1 Cor. 15:58).
   11. A Christian will be judged "according to his works" (Rom. 2:6; Matt. 16:27; 1 Pet. 1:17).
   12. A Christian will "receive the things done in the body, according to what he has done, whether good or bad" (2 Cor. 5:10).
   13. Even after death, Christians' "works follow them" (Rev. 14:13).

G. Man is saved by works.
   1. That is not to say that man is saved by "works alone."
   2. But Scripture clearly ties man's "faith" with his "works" in the saving/justification process (Jas. 2:14-26). Faith without works cannot save!
   3. Like Jesus, man "must work the works" that God identifies as necessary (John 9:4).

IX. Salvation from Sin, According to the Bible, Is By Obedience (on Man's Part).

A. There are two primary Greek words used in the New Testament for "obey."
   1. *Hupakouo* means "to listen, attend" (Vine); "to hearken to a command" (Thayer). It literally means "to hear" (*akouo*) "under" (*hupo*). It involves a submission to authority.
   2. *Peitho* means "to be persuaded, yield to, comply with" (Thayer). It is an obedience that results from persuasion.
   3. Both terms are used of the obedience necessary for one's salvation in Christ.

B. Very practically speaking, "Obedience is doing *what* the Lord prescribed, in the *manner* authorized, and for the *purpose* specified" (Wayne Jackson, *Bible Words and Theological Terms Made Easy,* p. 129).

C. While the doctrine of "faith only" is widely believed today as the means for salvation, Scripture does not support such a doctrine.

D. The Scripture plainly teaches that one cannot be saved without obeying the will of the Lord revealed in the New Testament!

E. In fact, when Scripture is consulted, one finds that the New Testament uses the terms and concepts of true/saving faith synonymously and interchangeably with that of obedience.
  1. Note carefully the contrast made between one who "believes" and one who "disobeys."
     (a) John 3:36 states:
        "He who **believes** on the Son has eternal life;
        "but he who does **not obey** the Son will not see life..." (NASB).
     (b) Hebrews 3:18-19 states:
        "...they would not enter His rest...those who were **disobedient**...
        "...they were not able to enter because of **unbelief**" (NASB).
     (c) Acts 14:1-2 states:
        "A great multitude both of the Jews and of the Greeks **believed**.
        "But the Jews that were **disobedient** stirred up the souls..." (ASV).
     (d) Romans 10:16 states:
        "But they have not all **obeyed** the gospel.
        For Isaiah says, 'Lord, who has **believed** our report?'"
     (e) We find in these passages that the Bible teaches:
        (1) To "believe" the Lord is to "obey what He says."
        (2) And "a refusal to obey" is "disbelief."
  2. Note carefully how those who obeyed were said to have "believed."
     (a) In Acts 2, there were individuals who believed the message (2:37), repented (2:38) and were baptized (2:41) for the remission of their sins (2:38).
        (1) As a summary term for their obedience, Luke states, "Now all who **believed** were together" (2:44).
        (2) Those who "believed" were those who had repented and been baptized.
     (b) In Acts 16, the jailor and his household heard the Word (16:32), believed the Word (16:31), repented (16:33a) and were baptized (16:33b).
        (1) As a summary term for their obedience, Luke states, "He rejoiced, having **believed** in God with all his household" (16:34).
        (2) Those who "believed" were those who had repented and been baptized.
     (c) In Acts 19, Paul met some men who had been previously baptized (19:3-4).
        (1) As a summary term for their perceived obedience, Paul asked, "Did you receive the Holy Spirit when you believed?" (19:2).
        (2) Paul used the term "believed" to refer to those who had been baptized.
  3. The terms that involve true faith and obedience are used interchangeably.
F. Every example of one who was saved by faith in the Bible was saved by an obedient faith.
  1. The great "Faith Chapter" (Hebrews 11) affirms this truth over and over.
     (a) Verse after verse begins, "By faith," to describe the Old Testament faithful.
     (b) But they were only blessed when their faith obeyed. Note the action verbs.
     (c) "By faith Abel offered..." (11:4).
     (d) "By faith Enoch...pleased God" (11:5).
     (e) "By faith Noah...prepared an ark..." (11:7).
     (f) "By faith Abraham obeyed...went out...dwelt in the land...waited" (11:8-10).
     (g) "By faith Abraham offered..." (11:17).
     (h) "By faith Moses...refused to be called...for he looked to the reward" (11:24-26).
     (i) "By faith they passed through the Red sea as by dry land..." (11:29).
     (j) "By faith the walls of Jericho fell down..." (11:30).
     (k) True, Biblical, God-approving faith is an obedient faith.

2. In Jerusalem, "a great many of the priests were obedient to the faith" (Acts 6:7).
3. In Rome, individuals were "set free from sin" (Rom. 6:18) and "justified freely by His grace" (3:24) when:
   (a) They "obeyed from the heart that form of doctrine to which [they] were delivered" (Rom. 6:17-18).
   (b) They responded with "obedience to the faith" (1:5; 16:26).
4. True faith which saves is an obedient faith!

G. Scripture teaches that obedience is required by God.
   1. "If you love Me, keep My commandments" (John 14:15).
   2. "But be doers of the word, and not hearers only, deceiving yourselves" (Jas. 1:22).
   3. "But why do you call Me 'Lord, Lord,' and do not do the things which I say?" (Luke 6:46).

H. Scripture teaches that obedience will be rewarded by God.
   1. "You have purified your souls in obeying the truth" (1 Pet. 1:22).
   2. "Not everyone who says to Me, 'Lord, Lord,' shall enter the kingdom of heaven, but he who does the will of My Father in heaven" (Matt. 7:21).
   3. "He became the author of eternal salvation to all who obey Him" (Heb. 5:9).

I. Scripture teaches that those who do not obey will be punished by God.
   1. "Because of these things the wrath of God is coming upon the sons of disobedience" (Col. 3:6).
   2. "…when the Lord Jesus is revealed from heaven with His mighty angels, in flaming fire taking vengeance on those who do not know God, and on those who do not obey the gospel of our Lord Jesus Christ. These shall be punished with everlasting destruction from the presence of the Lord and from the glory of His power" (2 Thess. 1:7-9).

J. When one properly understands the Scriptural teaching necessitating man's obedience to God's plan of salvation, he comes to understand that manmade doctrines have no place in the divine scheme of redemption, including the doctrines of:
   1. "Unconditional Election"
      (a) One of the tenets of Calvinism affirms that God, in His sovereignty, elects individual persons to salvation irrespective of any conditions on their part. In other words, there is nothing that a person must do (or can do) to receive salvation.
      (b) However, God has enumerated certain conditions that are essential to salvation:
         (1) Faith (John 3:16; 5:24; 8:24; Rom. 5:1; 10:9-10; Acts 16:31).
         (2) Repentance (Luke 13:3, 5; 24:47; Acts 2:38; 3:19; 17:30; 2 Pet. 3:9).
         (3) Confession of faith (Matt. 10:32-33; Rom. 10:9-10).
         (4) Immersion into Christ (Mark 16:16; Acts 2:38; 22:16; Rom. 6:3-4; Gal. 3:27).
         (5) Obedience (Matt. 7:21; Luke 6:46; Heb. 5:9; Jas. 1:22-25; 2:14-26).
         (6) Continued growth and faithfulness (2 Pet. 1:5-11; 1 Cor. 15:58; Rev. 2:10).
      (c) Salvation is not unconditional! Man must meet the conditions specified by God!
   2. "A Good Moral Life"
      (a) Some have the idea that if you just live a good moral life that heaven is assured.
      (b) It is sometimes said about one who is deceased, "He was a good person. He's probably in heaven."
      (c) But, being a "good person" (by man's evaluation) does not determine one's eternal destiny.
      (d) Cornelius was "a devout man and one who feared God with all his household, who gave alms generously to the people, and prayed to God always" (Acts 10:2). But Cornelius was not "saved" (Acts 11:14, 18; 10:43).

(e) Someone who claims to live a "good moral life," which should therefore, in their estimation, be "acceptable to God," is using their "works" in precisely the way that:
   (1) Paul speaks of "works" in Ephesians 2:8, when he talks about "works" by which one may "boast" in order to saved.
   (2) Paul speaks of "works" in Titus 3:5, when he talks about "works of righteousness which we have done," as if we are good enough to save ourselves.
(f) "Eternal salvation" is only for those who "obey" Christ and "do the will" of the Father in heaven (Heb. 5:9; Matt. 7:21). That is what makes us "good" in His eyes.
3. "The Sinner's Prayer"
   (a) It is commonly believed, taught and practiced in denominational groups today that all one must do in order to be saved from sins is to say, "The Sinner's Prayer."
   (b) The prayer is something like this: "Dear Lord Jesus, I know that I am a sinner, and I ask for Your forgiveness. I believe You died for my sins and rose from the dead. I turn from my sins and invite You to come into my heart and life. I want to trust and follow You as my Lord and Savior. In Your Name. Amen."
   (c) Saying "The Sinner's Prayer" is not a Scriptural path to salvation, for:
      (1) Jesus said that it is not enough to say unto Him, "Lord, Lord," and to not do what He has commanded (Matt. 7:21; Luke 6:46).
      (2) "If I regard iniquity in my heart, the Lord will not hear" me (Psa. 66:18).
      (3) Jesus identified prayer as an avenue of communication for those who were already children of God and can rightfully call God their "Father" (Matt. 6:9).
      (4) We have the example of Saul of Tarsus praying (and fasting) for three days after Jesus appeared to him (Acts 9:9-11), but he still had his sins (which needed to be "washed away") when Ananias came to him (Acts 22:16). His praying had not removed one single sin.
      (5) There is not one single verse in the New Testament that teaches (by precept or example) that an alien sinner can say a prayer to be saved.
      (6) The concept is completely foreign to the word of God! One has to look to the teachings and traditions of man to find it, rather than to the teachings of God.
   (d) Some have tried to justify it by equating it to "calling on the name of the Lord."
      (1) However, Scripture teaches that "calling on the name of the Lord":
         (i) Is a step required of God after one believes in Jesus (Rom. 10:13-17).
         (ii) Is equivalent to repenting and being baptized (compare Acts 2:21 + 2:38).
         (iii) Is achieved in the process of being baptized to wash away sins (Acts 22:16). (See pages 236-237 for more on this subject.)
      (2) Nowhere does Scripture identify "calling on the name of the Lord" as something that is accomplished by an alien sinner reciting a prayer.
4. God has laid out His conditions for our salvation.
   (a) Let us not make modifications or add our own conditions (Rev. 22:18-19; Gal. 1:6-9).
   (b) Let us have the heart that says, "All that the Lord has said we will do, and be obedient" (Ex. 24:7).
   (c) Let us comply with His conditions in order to secure His blessings!

X. Conclusion
A. The most important question that can ever be asked is, "What Must I Do to Be Saved?"
   1. There is nothing more important than being right with God.
   2. Man's greatest problem is that his sins separate him from God (Isa. 59:1-2).
   3. Man's greatest need is to have his sins removed and taken out of the way.

B. In Biblical salvation:
   1. There is God's part in it (God's grace, Jesus' blood, the Spirit's Word), and
   2. There is man's part in it (faith, works, obedience).
   3. Salvation is God's gift, but a gift must be appropriated by a proper response on man's part, in order to receive it as God intended.
C. The salvation that we so desperately need and that God offers is summarized in John 3:16.
   1. Salvation is by grace – "God so loved."
   2. Salvation is universally designed—"the world...whoever."
   3. Salvation is by blood—"He gave His only begotten Son."
   4. Salvation is through Christ—"in Him."
   5. Salvation is conditional—"believes."
   6. Salvation is dependent upon faithful obedience—"should not perish."
   7. Salvation is eternal in scope—"have everlasting life."
D. There is only one plan of salvation.
   1. The one plan places man in God's one church.
   2. The one plan makes Christians only and only Christians.
   3. The one plan prepares man to live eternally with God.

Recommended Resources

Books

Brents, T.W. *The Gospel Plan of Salvation.* Nashville: Gospel Advocate, 1957.

Winkler, Wendell. *Things That Accompany Salvation.* Tuscaloosa, AL: Winkler Publications, 1972.

Articles

Brownlow, Leroy. "Because It Gives Scriptural Answers to the Question—What Must I Do to Be Saved?" *Why I Am a Member of the Church of Christ.* Fort Worth: Brownlow Publishing, 1973. 94-100.

---. "Because It Teaches That Man Is Saved By Faith But Not By Faith Only." *Why I Am a Member of the Church of Christ.* Fort Worth: Brownlow Publishing, 1973. 101-108.

---. "Because It Teaches That Man Is Saved By the Blood of Christ." *Why I Am a Member of the Church of Christ.* Fort Worth: Brownlow Publishing, 1973. 109-115.

---. "Because It Teaches That a Change of Heart Is Indispensable to Man's Salvation." *Why I Am a Member of the Church of Christ.* Fort Worth: Brownlow Publishing, 1973. 116-123.

---. "Because It Teaches That Infants Are Born Pure and Innocent Rather Than Depraved." *Why I Am a Member of the Church of Christ.* Fort Worth: Brownlow Publishing, 1973. 154-158.

Camp, Franklin. "Grace and Works." *The Church of Tomorrow: Horizons and Destiny (Freed-Hardeman College Lectureship).* Ed. Winford Claiborne. Henderson, TN: Freed-Hardeman College, 1983. 55-70.

DeLoach, Clarence, Jr. "She Proclaims Salvation to Whosoever Will Accept." *Introducing the Church of Christ.* Ed. Alvin Jennings. Fort Worth: Star Bible, 1981. 173-176.

Jackson, Wayne. "Acts 2:21 – Calling on the Lord's Name." *ChristianCourier.com*
https://www.christiancourier.com/articles/934-acts-2-21-calling-on-the-lords-name

---. "Justification: By Faith or Works?" *ChristianCourier.com*
https://www.christiancourier.com/articles/294-justification-by-faith-or-works

---. "Logic and the Plan of Salvation." *ChristianCourier.com*
https://www.christiancourier.com/articles/1520-logic-and-the-plan-of-salvation

---. "The Role of 'Works' in God's Plan of Redemption." *ChristianCourier.com*
https://www.christiancourier.com/articles/729-role-of-works-in-gods-plan-of-redemption-the

---. "The Sinner's Prayer—Is It Biblical?" *ChristianCourier.com*
https://www.christiancourier.com/articles/368-sinners-prayer-is-it-biblical-the

Sain, David. "What Must I Do To Be Saved?" *The Spiritual Sword* (Oct. 2007): 17-20.

Wallace, G.K. "The Plan of Salvation—Man's Part: Obedience." *A Plea for Fundamentals (Freed-Hardeman College Lectures)*. Ed. William Woodson. Henderson, TN: Freed-Hardeman College, 1977. 65-67.

---. "The New Birth." *A Plea for Fundamentals (Freed-Hardeman College Lectures)*. Ed. William Woodson. Henderson, TN: Freed-Hardeman College, 1977. 68-70.

---. "What Must I Do to Be Saved?" *A Plea for Fundamentals (Freed-Hardeman College Lectures)*. Ed. William Woodson. Henderson, TN: Freed-Hardeman College, 1977. 71-73.

---. "Not By Faith Only." *A Plea for Fundamentals (Freed-Hardeman College Lectures)*. Ed. William Woodson. Henderson, TN: Freed-Hardeman College, 1977. 74-76.

Winkler, Wendell. "How Does One Enter the Church of Christ?" *The Church Everybody Is Asking About*. Tuscaloosa, AL: Winkler Publications, 1988. 103-109.

---. Winkler, Wendell. "Willing That None Should Perish." *The Spiritual Sword* (Apr. 2005): 45-48.

Woodson, William. "Grace, Faith, Works and Obedience." *Grace Abounding (Freed-Hardeman College Lectureship)*. Ed. Winford Claiborne. Henderson, TN: Freed-Hardeman College, 1987. 390-402.

Periodicals

The Spiritual Sword. January 1976. "Grace, Law and Love."

The Spiritual Sword. April 1976. "What Must I Do to Be Saved?"

The Spiritual Sword. July 1986. "The Amazing Grace of God."

The Spiritual Sword. January 1998. "What Must I Do to Be Saved?"

Lesson 20: The Person, Process & Purpose of Baptism

I. **The Subject of Baptism Is Vitally Important and Yet Highly Controversial.**
   A. The subject of baptism is mentioned more than 100 times in the New Testament.
      1. The words "baptism," "Baptist," "baptize," "baptized" and "baptizing" are found in about 115 verses in the New Testament.
      2. Additionally, there are numerous passages that speak of the subject of baptism without using a "bapt-" root word.
   B. The subject of baptism is vitally important for us, for it comes to us from God Himself.
      1. The subject of baptism did not originate with man but with God.
      2. If it were not for the N.T., man would know nothing of the topic or practice.
      3. Man finds all that he can and needs to know about this subject within his N.T.
      4. Thus, a careful study of the N.T. is required to understand this subject as God intended.
   C. Unfortunately, man has made the subject of baptism quite controversial.
      1. Different people have developed different ideas about "who" should be baptized.
      2. Different people have developed different ideas about "what" baptism is.
      3. Different people have developed different ideas about "why" one is to be baptized.
      4. With these different ideas has come confusion and frustration over this subject.
      5. The confusion and frustration has led many to believe that anything goes on the matter—i.e., that any teaching or practice on baptism should be equally accepted.
      6. However, the confusion and frustration is not because of any ambiguity on God's part in the New Testament, for God's teaching are very clear on this subject.
   D. Let us allow the Bible to speak on this vitally important subject, since:
      1. The very concept of baptism comes from heaven and not from man (Matt. 21:25).
      2. The authority of Christ (not man) commanded baptism (Matt. 28:18-20).
      3. The Word of Christ (not man) will judge us in the end (John 12:48).
   E. At the conclusion of this study regarding what the Scripture teaches about baptism:
      1. If you have never been baptized, you will need to answer the question that Ananias asked, "And now why are you waiting?" (Acts 22:16).
      2. If you have been baptized in the past, you will need to ask yourself, "Was I baptized in the way that the Bible teaches and for the reason that the Bible teaches?"
      3. If your baptism was not in the way that the Bible teaches and for the reason that the Bible teaches, what would stand in your way of being baptized as taught in the Bible?
      (a) Scripture shows (especially in passages like Acts 19:1-5):
         (1) The importance of the "who," the "how and the "why" of baptism.
         (2) It is not wrong to be baptized a second time if the first time was not in accordance with the teaching of Scripture.
      (b) Baptism is certainly a "right thing" to do, for it comes from heaven (Matt. 21:25).
         (1) But a "right thing" must be done in the "right way" and for the "right reason" to be "right" in the eyes of God. (Compare the teaching about the Lord's Supper in 1 Corinthians 11:17-34, where a "right thing" was not being done in the "right way" and for the "right reason," and Paul was trying to correct it.)
         (2) There is one way to find out if your baptism was "right" as defined by Scripture.
            (i) Let's study together and allow God's Word to teach us.
            (ii) Then, let's make sure we are "right" in God's eyes.

II. **The Bible Specifies That There Is One Baptism.**
   A. The New Testament mentions several baptisms in the gospel accounts and the book of Acts.
   B. But, when the book of Ephesians was written, there was then only "one baptism" (4:5).
   C. This is not a contradiction, but it affirms that there is only one baptism which is now valid and in effect for Christians to teach and practice.
   D. Which baptism, mentioned in the New Testament, is the "one baptism"?
      1. It is not "the baptism of John," for that baptism was to prepare for the coming of Christ (John 3:26-30) and was not "in the name of the Lord Jesus" (Acts 19:3-5).
         (a) When Apollos "knew only the baptism of John" and was teaching that baptism to individuals in Acts 18, Aquila and Priscilla "took him aside and explained to him the way of God more accurately" (Acts 18:24-28).
         (b) When Paul found twelve men in Ephesus, who had been baptized "into John's baptism," he taught them and "they were baptized in the name of the Lord Jesus" (Acts 19:1-7).
      2. It is not "the baptism of the Holy Spirit," for that baptism:
         (a) Was administered only by the Lord Himself, not man (Matt. 3:11; John 1:33).
         (b) Involved receiving a promise rather than obeying a command (Luke 24:49; Acts 1:4-8; 2:1-4).
         (c) Occurred on only two occasions in Scripture—when the first Jews were converted to Christ (Acts 2) and when the first Gentiles were converted to Christ (Acts 10).
      3. It is not "the baptism of sufferings," for that was fulfilled in Christ's death and the persecution of the saints that followed (Matt. 22:22-23; Mark 10:38-39; Luke 12:50).
      4. It is not "the baptism of fire," for that is the eternal fires of hell yet to come (Matt. 3:11; Luke 3:16).
   E. Therefore, the "ONE baptism" is water baptism of Christ's Great Commission.
      1. It is the universal baptism for all mankind (Matt. 28:19; Mark 16:15).
      2. It is the baptism that is commanded to be obeyed (Matt. 28:19; Acts 10:48).
      3. It is the baptism administered by man (Matt. 28:19; Acts 8:38).
      4. It is the baptism administered in water (Acts 8:36-39; 10:47; 1 Pet. 3:20-31).
      5. It is the baptism done "in the name of the Lord Jesus" (Acts 2:38; 10:48; 19:5).
      6. It is the baptism to be taught and practiced until the end of time (Matt. 28:19-20).
   F. This one baptism of Christ must be studied, understood and obeyed.
III. **The Bible Specifies the Person Who Is the Biblical Candidate for Baptism.**
   A. Who can be baptized? Who should we baptize?
      1. Much controversy exists over the persons who are proper candidates for baptism.
         (a) May (or should) newborns be baptized?
         (b) May (or should) infants be baptized?
         (c) May (or should) only those who are older and more mature be baptized?
         (d) Does it really matter, as long as one is baptized?
      2. The Bible speaks clearly about the proper subjects for Scriptural baptism.
   B. The person who is baptized must meet certain Biblical conditions before baptism:
      1. One must be taught the gospel (Matt. 28:19-20; Mark 16:15-16).
      2. One must gladly receive the gospel (Acts 2:41).
      3. One must believe the gospel (Mark 16:16; Acts 8:12-13, 36-37; 16:31-33).
      4. One must be convicted of sins (Acts 2:37).
      5. One must repent of sins (Acts 2:38).
      6. One must knowingly acknowledge (confess) his faith (Acts 8:36-38).

7. One must arise of his own free will and not that of others (Acts 22:16).
8. One must be capable of obeying from his own heart (Rom. 6:17-18, 3-7).
9. One must be in search of a clean conscience from the guilt of sin (1 Pet. 3:21).
10. One must desire (and need) to fulfill the purpose of baptism in his/her own life (see Roman numeral V below).
11. One must be prepared for the commitment that baptism requires (Rom. 6:4; Gal. 3:27; 2 Cor. 5:17; 1 Cor. 15:58).

C. Only those who meet these conditions can be Scripturally (and properly) baptized.
   1. If a person does not (or cannot) meet all of these conditions, he is not a candidate.
   2. Baptism is ineffectual to fulfill its purpose until a person fulfills each condition.
D. Therefore, it is readily apparent that infants are not Scriptural candidates for baptism.
   1. Infants do not and cannot meet the conditions for baptism listed above.
   2. Since the conditions listed above must *precede* one's baptism, it is entirely improper to baptize an infant, who cannot meet these conditions until years *after* his baptism.
   3. The fact is that infants have no need to be baptized, for they are:
      (a) Sinless, pure, holy and safe in the eyes of God (Matt. 18:3; 19:14; 2 Sam. 12:23).
      (b) Not born with any inherited sins from their parents or from Adam (Ezek. 18:20).
      (c) Just like baby Jesus, who was born innocent and pure, without any sin.
   4. Nowhere in the New Testament does it speak of or approve the baptism of infants.
      (a) To teach or practice infant baptism is a departure from Scripture.

IV. The Bible Specifies the Process That Is the Biblical Method for Baptism.
A. What is the proper mode of baptism? How is baptism to be administered?
   1. English dictionaries define the word "baptize" as it is commonly and currently used today: "to immerse in water or sprinkle or pour water on."
   2. Is it true that one can be properly "baptized" in any of these ways?
   3. As long as one is "baptized," does it really matter "how" he is "baptized"?
   4. Is it wrong to teach that one can be "baptized" only by sprinkling or pouring water?
   5. Is it wrong to teach that one can be "baptized" only by immersion into water?
   6. We must allow the Bible (not English dictionaries) to be our authority and to explain what is the acceptable mode of baptism in the eyes of God!
B. The Bible very plainly describes what is involved in Bible baptism:
   1. "Much water" is required to be baptized with Bible baptism (John 3:23).
   2. The person being baptized must come "to" the water (Matt. 3:11; Acts 8:36).
   3. The person being baptized and the baptizer must go "down into the water" (Ac. 8:36).
   4. The person being baptized must be "buried...in baptism" (Col. 2:12; Rom. 6:4).
   5. The person being baptized must be "raised" from the water (Rom. 6:4; Col. 2:12).
   6. The person being baptized and the baptizer must come "up out of the water" (Ac. 8:39).
   7. The Bible makes it very clear that baptism is immersion of the body into water. Read these six requirements of Bible baptism again and ask, "Does sprinkling or pouring require what Bible baptism requires?"
C. By simply substituting the words "sprinkling, pouring, immersing" for the word "baptism" or "baptize," the Bible reader can easily understand what baptism is. Which word "fits" and "makes sense" in the following verses?
   1. All the people "were sprinkled/poured/immersed by [John] in the Jordan" (Mt. 3:6).
   2. "After being sprinkled/poured/immersed, Jesus came up from the water" (Mt. 3:16).
   3. "John also was sprinkling/pouring/immersing in Aenon near Salim, because there was much water there" (John 3:23).

4. "They went down into the water, and he sprinkled/poured/immersed him" (Acts 8:38).
5. "We were buried with Him through sprinkling/pouring/immersing into death" (Ro. 6:4).
6. "Make disciples of all the nations, sprinkling/pouring/immersing them into the name of the Father and of the Son and of the Holy Spirit" (Matt. 28:19, ASV).
7. When substituted for "baptism," immersion makes perfect sense. The others do not.
D. The original Greek makes it clear that the verb "baptize" means "to immerse."
 1. Confusion over the mode of baptism exists in large part due to a transliteration of the original Greek word rather than an actual translation of the word.
  (a) When English Bible translators (500 years ago) came to the Greek word *baptizo*, they merely transposed the letters of the Greek word into an English word, leaving a word in the Bible ("baptize") that was (and still is) imprecise in its meaning.
  (b) The word "baptize" is used indiscriminately today of sprinkling water on someone, pouring water over someone or immersing someone into water.
  (c) However, the original word (chosen by God) is not so imprecise.
 2. The Greek verb *baptizo* is defined throughout Greek lexicons to mean, "to dip, immerse, submerge, plunge, overwhelm."
  (a) The original word itself specifically means "to immerse."
  (b) The original word itself will not allow for "sprinkling" or "pouring" as an option.
  (c) One must use a different Greek word altogether to speak of sprinkling or pouring.
 3. Even in the Old Testament, there was a distinction made between the actions of "dipping," "sprinkling" and "pouring."
  (a) "And the priest shall take some of the log of oil, and <u>pour</u> it into the palm of his own left hand. Then the priest shall <u>dip</u> his right finger in the oil that is in his left hand, and shall <u>sprinkle</u> some of the oil with his finger seven times before the Lord" (Lev. 14:15-16).
  (b) These are three distinct words for three distinct actions.
  (c) These three distinct acts were not equivalents or interchangeable.
  (d) Thus, when the New Testament uses the word "immersion," it is distinct from the actions of sprinkling and pouring, and it is not interchangeable with them.
 4. If we will define words the way that the Bible defines words and then use words in the way that the Bible uses words, then we will speak of baptism only as immersion.
E. When one is baptized, he obeys the "form of doctrine" laid out by Jesus (Rom. 6:17).
 1. The "form" that Jesus left to be followed was a death, burial and resurrection (6:3-4).
 2. In baptism, one "dies to sin" (6:3, 11), is "buried" and is "raised" to a new life (6:4).
 3. Scripture teaches plainly that baptism is a "burial" (Rom. 6:3-4; Col. 2:12), followed by a "raising up" (resurrection) out of the water (Col. 3:1; Rom. 6:5; Eph. 2:6).
F. Bible baptism is clearly an immersion into water, which all Biblical evidence demands.

V. The Bible Specifies the Purpose That God Assigns to Baptism.
A. Suppose that you wrote on a piece of paper, "What is the purpose of baptism?"
 1. Then, suppose you mailed that question to ten different "churches" around town.
 2. Do you suppose that you'd receive the exact same answer from all ten "churches"?
 3. Or, do you suppose that you would receive different and even conflicting answers?
 4. You likely know, without even attempting such an experiment, that with a wide variety of "churches" comes a wide variety of ideas about baptism's purpose.
 5. Thus, this is a controversial issue, which requires our utmost attention.
 6. Let us put aside our own opinions for a moment, and let us take that same question to the Bible and let the Bible answer—"What is the purpose of baptism?"

B. According to the Bible, a purpose of baptism is <u>to obey the command of Christ</u>.
1. Jesus commanded His disciples to go and "make disciples" by "baptizing" (Mt. 28:19).
2. Peter "commanded them to be baptized in the name of the Lord" (Acts 10:47-48).
3. Jesus commanded Saul of Tarsus to "go into the city," and there he would be "told what [he] must do" (Acts 9:6). The "must" included, "Arise and be baptized" (22:16).
4. When one disregards the command to be baptized, one has "rejected the will of God" (Luke 7:29-30).
5. It is important to note that while one may be baptized in an effort to obey the command of God, if he is not baptized for the right reason, it is not Bible baptism.
C. According to the Bible, a purpose of baptism is <u>to be saved from past sins</u>.
1. Our sins separate us from God and a relationship with Him (Isa. 59:1-2; Hab. 1:13).
   (a) Sin brings the judgment and wrath of God upon us (Rom. 1:18; 2:8; 5:15-18).
   (b) Sin enslaves us to sin and its enticements (John 8:34; Rom. 6:12-21; 2 Pet. 2:19).
   (c) Man's desperate is need to be "saved" from sin and its horrible consequences!
2. Jesus taught, "He who believes and is baptized will be saved" (Mark 16:16).
   (a) The conjunction "and" joins two items of equal grammatical importance.
      (1) "And" means that "believing" is equally as important as being "baptized."
      (2) The end result ("saved") is not possible without both elements being present.
   (b) Jesus places being "saved" AFTER being "baptized." That is Jesus' order.
      (1) One cannot be saved and then be baptized. That is not Jesus' order.
      (2) One cannot be baptized and then believe. That is not Jesus' order.
      (3) Jesus' order can be summarized as: Believes + Baptized = Saved.
      (4) To alter Jesus' formula one iota will nullify the results completely.
3. Peter emphatically stated, "Baptism now saves you" (1 Pet. 3:21, NASB).
   (a) As sure as Noah and his family "were saved through water" (1 Pet. 3:20), penitent believers are "saved" through the waters of baptism today (3:21).
   (b) Those Biblical truths stand or fall together.
   (c) Notice again that God places the result (i.e., "saves") AFTER "baptism."
D. According to the Bible, a purpose of baptism is <u>to obtain the remission of sins</u>.
1. The word "remission" in Acts 2:38 is also translated "forgiveness" in the NASB and ESV.
2. In seeking forgiveness of their sins, the Jews in Acts 2:37 asked, "What shall we do?"
   (a) Whatever Peter answered was inspired by God and, therefore, essential.
3. Peter commanded, "Repent, and let every one of you be baptized in the name of Jesus Christ for the remission of sins" (Acts 2:38).
   (a) There are numerous key elements to note in this response.
4. The coordinating conjunction "and" joins two items of equal grammatical importance.
   (a) "And" means that "repent" is equally as important as "be baptized."
   (b) The end result ("remission") is not possible without both elements being present.
5. Peter places "remission of sins" AFTER being "baptized." That is heaven's order.
   (a) One cannot secure remission and then be baptized. That is not heaven's order.
   (b) One cannot be baptized and then repent. That is not heaven's order.
6. Being baptized is "for" the remission of sins. What does "for" mean in this verse?
   (a) The Greek word for "for" *(eis)* means "to obtain, in order to" and "denotes purpose." The word is always prospective (looking forward and never backward).
   (b) "For" means the same thing for "repent" as it does for "be baptized."
   (c) One does not "repent" or "be baptized" because he has already been forgiven (looking backward) but in order to obtain remission (looking forward).

                (d) The same expression is used in Matthew 26:28, where Jesus said, "For this is My blood of the new covenant, which is shed for many for the remission of sins."
                    (1) Jesus shed His blood in order that many might obtain remission (purpose).
                    (2) Man must be baptized in order to obtain remission of sins (purpose).
            7. Baptism is to be done by the authority of ("in the name of") Jesus Christ.
                (a) This is not man's idea but that of Christ (Matt. 28:18-20; Mark 16:16; Luke 24:47).
                (b) Submitting to the authority of Jesus Christ requires baptism.
    E. According to the Bible, a purpose of baptism is <u>to have sins washed away</u>.
        1. Ananias urged Saul, "Arise and be baptized, and wash away your sins" (Acts 22:16).
        2. Being baptized was part of the "must" that Saul was told to do in the city (Acts 9:6).
        3. There was an urgency, requiring an immediate response, as evident from the question Ananias asked, "Why are you waiting?"
        4. The washing away of sins is inseparably tied (by the word "and") to baptism. It would have been impossible for Saul to "wash away" his sins without being baptized.
        5. By telling him to wash away his sins, Ananias affirmed that Saul still had his sins.
            (a) Saul realized in his heart (i.e., believed) on the road to Damascus that Jesus had been raised from the dead (Acts 9:1-8), but he still had his sins in Acts 22:16.
            (b) Saul spent three days in the city praying fervently (while blind and fasting) (Acts 9:9, 11), but he still had his sins in Acts 22:16.
            (c) The only way that Saul could have his sins washed away was by being baptized.
        6. In baptism, one is washed and cleansed (Eph. 5:26; 1 Cor. 6:11), but not before.
    F. According to the Bible, a purpose of baptism is <u>to be sanctified, cleansed and justified</u>.
        1. In baptism, one has his sins washed away (Acts 22:16). See V, E above.
        2. The N.T. uses the concept of "washing" repeatedly to refer to baptism and its blessings.
        3. In baptism, one is "sanctified" and "cleansed" "with the washing of water" (Eph. 5:26).
        4. At the same time one is "washed," he is also "sanctified" and "justified" (1 Cor. 6:11).
        5. It is through "the washing of regeneration" that God's mercy has "saved us" (Tit. 3:5).
        6. Putting it all together, one finds that upon baptism (and not before):
            (a) One is sanctified by God, set apart from sin and unto Him for His service.
            (b) One is justified and made right in the eyes of God.
            (c) One is cleansed from his past sins to be presented pure unto Christ.
    G. According to the Bible, a purpose of baptism is <u>to be made free from sin</u>.
        1. Romans 6 teaches that when one is buried with Christ and raised with Christ in baptism:
            (a) "The body of sin [is] done away with" (6:6).
            (b) He is "no longer" counted among "slaves of sin" (6:6, 17).
            (c) He has "been freed from sin" (6:7).
            (d) He has "been set free from sin" (6:18).
        2. Colossians 2 teaches that when one is buried with and raised with Christ in baptism:
            (a) He puts "off the body of the sins of the flesh" (2:11).
            (b) God has "forgiven [him] all trespasses" (2:13).
        3. Freedom from sin cannot be secured apart from Bible baptism!
    H. According to the Bible, a purpose of baptism is <u>to contact the saving blood of Christ</u>.
        1. Jesus shed His saving blood in His death (John 19:34; Heb. 9:12; 13:12).
            (a) We contact that blood when we are baptized into His death (Rom. 6:3).
        2. Jesus shed His blood "for the remission of sins" (Matt. 26:28).
            (a) We contact that blood when we are baptized "for the remission of sins" (Ac. 2:38).
        3. Jesus shed His blood to "wash us from our sins" (Rev. 1:5).

(a) We contact that blood when we are baptized to "wash away [our] sins" (Ac. 22:16).
4. From Scripture, it is obvious that the blood of Christ saves us when we are baptized.

I. According to the Bible, a purpose of baptism is <u>to enter a new relationship with God</u>.
   1. One is baptized "into the name of the Father…Son and…Holy Spirit" (Mt. 28:19, ASV).
   2. The word "into" emphasizes a change of relationship from "outside" a relationship with the Godhead to "inside" a relationship with the Godhead.
   3. Vine states, "The phrase in Matt. 28:19, 'baptizing them into the Name'…would indicate that the baptized person was closely bound to, or became the property of, the one into whose Name he was baptized."
   4. Until the moment that we are "baptized into the name of" the Godhead:
      (a) We do not belong to the Godhead.
      (b) We cannot take on the name of the Godhead.
      (c) We cannot call upon God as our "Father."
   5. Baptism is the point at which one goes from outside fellowship with God to inside.

J. According to the Bible, a purpose of baptism is <u>to be born again</u>.
   1. Jesus taught that one "must" be "born of water and the Spirit" (John 3:3, 5, 7).
   2. By (1) "the Spirit" and (2) "water," one can (3) "enter the kingdom of God."
   3. By (1) "the Word" and (2) "washing of water," one is (3) "cleanse[d]" (Eph. 5:26).
   4. By (1) "the Holy Spirit" and (2) "the washing of regeneration," one is (3) "saved" (Tit. 3:5).
   5. Note the parallel in each of these passages, emphasizing the essentiality of baptism.

John 3:5	The Spirit	Water	Enter the kingdom of God
1 Cor. 12:13	One Spirit	Baptized	Into one body
Eph. 5:26	The Word	Washing of water	Cleansed
Titus 3:5	Holy Spirit	Washing of regeneration	Saved

   6. One is not born again until he follows "the Word" and is baptized in "water."
   7. "Water" (baptism) and "the Spirit" (the Word) are two elements of the one birth.

K. According to the Bible, a purpose of baptism is <u>to enter the kingdom of God</u>.
   1. The kingdom of God is the church (Matt. 16:18-19), wherein are the saved (Ac. 2:47).
   2. Only the kingdom/church is saved by Christ (Eph. 5:23).
   3. Only those in the kingdom will be delivered to the Father in the end (1 Cor. 15:24).
   4. Jesus taught, "Unless one is born again, he cannot see the kingdom of God" (Jn. 3:3).
   5. "Unless one is born of water and the Spirit, he cannot enter the kingdom of God" (3:5).
   6. One must be baptized to enter the kingdom of God and be promised eternity in heaven.

L. According to the Bible, a purpose of baptism is <u>to enter the one body of Christ</u>.
   1. The Bible teaches that there is only "one body" (Eph. 4:4), and the body is the church (Eph. 1:22-23).
   2. Only those in the body/church are saved by Christ (Eph. 5:23).
   3. Only those in the body/church have been reconciled to God (Eph. 2:16).
   4. Only those in the body/church have access to God (Eph. 2:18).
   5. On Pentecost, about 3,000 were baptized and "added to the church" (Acts 2:41, 47).
   6. In baptism, "we were all baptized into one body" (i.e., the church) (1 Cor. 12:13).
   7. Only through baptism can one enter the blessed body of Christ.

M. According to the Bible, a purpose of baptism is <u>to become a child of God</u>.
   1. Those who believe in Christ are given "the right to become children of God" (Jn. 1:12).
      (a) In other words, simply believing in Christ does not make one a child of God.

(b) A believer is given authority to become something he is not—God's child.
2. "Sons of God" are those who "through faith" have been "baptized" (Gal. 3:26-27).
   (a) Faith is the avenue by which it is made possible, but baptism is the final step.
   (b) The word "for" at the beginning of verse 27 explains how one became a child of God in verse 26. The conjunction "for" marks the cause.
3. Becoming a child of God is the new relationship (cf. Matt. 28:19) that is obtained when is "born again" (John 3:3-7). He is born into the family of God as His child!

N. According to the Bible, a purpose of baptism is <u>to put on Christ</u>.
   1. In baptism, one is able to then "put on Christ" (Gal. 3:27).
   2. Before baptism, one does not have Christ!
   3. In baptism, one is literally clothed with Christ (like putting on a garment).
      (a) The "old man" is crucified (Rom. 6:6).
      (b) The "new man" is put on, who is Christ (Gal. 2:20).

O. According to the Bible, a purpose of baptism is <u>to enter into Christ, wherein is salvation</u>.
   1. The Bible emphatically teaches that "all spiritual blessings are IN CHRIST" (Eph. 1:3).
      (a) In Christ is where one is "chosen" and "accepted" (Eph. 1:4, 6).
      (b) In Christ is "redemption" (Col. 1:13-14; Eph. 1:7).
      (c) In Christ is "the forgiveness of sins" (Eph. 1:7).
      (d) In Christ is "an inheritance" (Eph. 1:11).
      (e) In Christ is "no condemnation" (Rom. 8:1).
      (f) In Christ is "sanctification" (1 Cor. 1:2).
      (g) In Christ is "hope" (1 Cor. 15:19).
      (h) In Christ are "all the promises of God" (2 Cor. 1:20).
      (i) In Christ is "a new creation" (2 Cor. 5:17).
      (j) In Christ is "consolation" (Phil. 2:1).
      (k) In Christ is "grace" (2 Tim. 2:1).
      (l) In Christ is "eternal life" (1 John 5:11).
      (m) In Christ is "salvation" (2 Tim. 2:10).
      (n) If one is NOT in Christ, then he has NONE of these spiritual blessings, for they are "all...in Christ"!
   2. There are only two New Testament verses which teach how one can get "into Christ."
      (a) "Or do you not know that as many of us as were **baptized into Christ Jesus** were baptized into His death?" (Rom. 6:3).
      (b) "For as many of you as were **baptized into Christ** have put on Christ" (Gal. 3:27).
   3. Those two verses emphatically teach that baptism is the only one way INTO CHRIST.
   4. Before baptism, one is outside of Christ and deficient of EVERY spiritual blessing.
   5. Only when a penitent believer is baptized does he move from being outside of Christ to now being "in Christ," wherein are all spiritual blessings, including salvation.

P. According to the Bible, a purpose of baptism is <u>to become a New Testament Christian</u>.
   1. Jesus taught that "disciples" are made by being "baptized" (Matt. 28:19).
      (a) The present participle ("baptizing") points back to the main verb in the sentence ("make disciples") and declares the manner in which one is made a disciple.
      (b) According to Jesus, one is not made one of His disciples until he is baptized.
   2. "The disciples were first called Christians in Antioch" (Acts 11:26).
      (a) The terms "disciples" and "Christians" were used synonymously in this passage and throughout the rest of the New Testament.

- (b) Therefore, the very way that one is made a "disciple" is the precise and only way that one is made a "Christian."
- (c) One becomes a Christian (i.e., a disciple) by being baptized as instructed by Jesus.
- (d) If one does not follow the prescribed plan of Jesus in the Great Commission (i.e., to "believe," Mark 16:16 + "repent," Luke 24:47 + "be baptized," Matt. 28:19; Mark 16:16), then he cannot be called a Christian as defined in the New Testament.
3. There was division within the church at Corinth and different ones were claiming, "'I am of Paul,' or 'I am of Apollos,' or 'I am of Cephas,' or 'I am of Christ'" (1 Cor. 1:12).
    - (a) Paul taught that to wear his name (in a religious sense) required two things:
        - (1) Paul would have had to be "crucified for you," and
        - (2) You would have to be "baptized in the name of Paul" (1 Cor. 1:13).
        - (3) Then and only then could one wear the name of Paul.
        - (4) Paul argued rhetorically that since neither of those conditions were true, then no one had a right to say, "I am of Paul."
        - (5) He therefore implies the same about wearing the name of Apollos or Cephas.
    - (b) Emphatically affirmed is that the same is true in order to wear the name of Christ.
        - (1) Paul's argumentation equally requires two conditions to say, "I am of Christ":
            - (i) Christ would have had to be "crucified for you," and
            - (ii) You would have to be "baptized in the name of Christ."
        - (2) The power of the truthfulness of his argumentation is overwhelming!
            - (i) Baptism is absolutely essential in order to wear the name of Christ.
            - (ii) One cannot be called a "Christ-ian" unless he has been "baptized in the name of Christ" "for the remission of sins" (Acts 2:38).

Q. According to the Bible, a purpose of baptism is <u>to walk in newness of life</u>.
1. Paul summarizes the act of baptism in Romans 6:4 – "Therefore we were buried with Him through baptism into death, that just as Christ was raised from the dead by the glory of the Father, even so we also should walk in newness of life."
2. The word "that" (Greek, *hina*) denotes purpose or result.
3. In this passage, the purpose/result of being buried and raised with Christ (in baptism) is to be able to "walk in newness of life."
    - (a) Before baptism, one is walking in the old life of sin.
    - (b) Upon baptism, one does not continue in the same life as before baptism.
    - (c) Upon baptism, one begins a new life, which entails freedom from sin (6:2, 7).
    - (d) The new life in Christ is not available or even possible until one is baptized.
4. Upon baptism, one is "raised" to "walk in newness of life" (Rom. 6:3-4).
5. As baptism is in the only way "into Christ" (see V, O above), it is only after baptism that one becomes "a new creation" with an all-new life (2 Cor. 5:17).

R. According to the Bible, a purpose of baptism is <u>to call on the name of the Lord</u>.
1. The Bible plainly teaches, "Whoever calls on the name of the Lord shall be saved" (Acts 2:21; Rom. 10:13; Joel 2:32).
2. Peter quoted this verse in his sermon on the Day of Pentecost in Acts 2.
    - (a) The hearers were told they could be "saved" by calling on the name of the Lord.
        - (1) Remember what the word "saved" emphasizes—it is speaking of being saved, delivered, rescued from the horrible guilt and consequences of sin.
        - (2) In order to be saved from one's sins, he must call on the name of the Lord.
        - (3) What did that mean? Peter would explain later in his sermon.

(b) The hearers were told they could obtain "the remission of sins" by repenting and being baptized (2:38).
   (1) Being "saved" in Acts 2:21 is parallel to "remission of sins" in Acts 2:38.
   (2) Therefore, everything mentioned in verse 21 and in verse 38 were required conditions for securing salvation and forgiveness of sins.
      (i) It cannot be properly assumed that the "call" and being "baptized" are mutually exclusive.
      (ii) In fact, the Bible is going to teach that "calling on the name of the Lord" takes place when one repents and is baptized.
3. In Romans 10:13, Paul writes, "Whoever calls on the name of the Lord shall be saved."
   (a) In order to "call on Him," one must have "believed" (10:14a).
   (b) In order to "believe in Him," one must have "heard" (10:14b).
   (c) In order to "hear," a "preacher" must have been "sent" (10:14c, 15a).
   (d) Notice the order specified by the inspired penman:
      (1) A preacher is "sent."
      (2) The preacher "preaches."
      (3) People "hear" the preacher.
      (4) Hearers "believe" in Jesus.
      (5) Believers "call on Him."
   (e) Note carefully that "calling on the name of the Lord" is a step that one takes after believing in Jesus.
      (1) One is not saved when he believes (as is often taught), for he has not yet "called on the name of the Lord."
      (2) What step could there be after believing in Jesus that would lead one to be saved? What does it mean to "call on the name of the Lord"? How does he do that? When does he do that?
4. When Ananias preached to Saul of Tarsus, he commanded him, "Arise and be baptized, and wash away your sins" (Acts 22:16).
   (a) Ananias went on to use a Greek aorist participle, which pointed back to the main verbs ("be baptized" and "wash away") to indicate that there was something happening either simultaneously or immediately preceding it.
   (b) "Arise and be baptized, and wash away your sins, *calling on the name of the Lord.*"
   (c) The "calling" takes place in the process of being baptized and washing away sins. The grammar of the text demands that conclusion.
5. "Calling on the name of the Lord" cannot be merely a verbal plea, for Jesus condemned appeals that stopped at a verbal plea (Matt. 7:21; Luke 6:46).
   (a) Interestingly, the same Greek word for "calling" is used in Acts 25 but is translated "appeal" (25:10-11).
   (b) One could substitute the word "appealing" in Acts 22:16 for the word "calling."
   (c) "Calling on the name of the Lord" is not merely a prayer, asking Jesus to come into one's heart and forgive. (See the section on "The Sinner's Prayer" on page 224.)
   (d) In baptism, one is making an "appeal" to God. The "calling" is happening in the baptism.
6. Consider the "sum" of Scriptural teaching on this matter:

Rom. 10:13-17	Sent	Preacher	Heard	Believed	Call	Saved
Acts 2:21					Call	Saved
Acts 2:37-38	Peter was sent	Peter said	Heard	Believed	Repent & baptized	Remission of sins
Mark 16:15-16	Go	Preach	(Hear)	Believes	Baptized	Saved
Acts 22:12-16	Ananias came	Ananias said	Heard	(Believed)	Baptized (calling)	Wash away sins
1 Peter 3:21					Baptism (appeal)	Saves

      7. Repentance and baptism are the means by which a sinner calls upon (appeals to) the Lord for salvation from sin.

S. According to the Bible, a purpose of baptism is <u>to appeal to God for a good conscience</u>.
   1. Peter affirms very plainly that "baptism now saves you" (1 Pet. 3:21, NASB).
   2. Peter proceeds to state that baptism is "an appeal to God for a good conscience" (NASB).
      (a) The Greek word *(eperotema)* is a "demand or appeal" (Vine), "an inquiry, a question, a demand, desire" (Thayer).
      (b) The translation of the word as "appeal" in 1 Peter 3:21 is supported by the lexicons and the context.
   3. In baptism, an appeal is made "to God." An appeal is either made "for" a good conscience (NASB) or "of" (from) a good conscience (ASV).
   4. In other words, by the very act of baptism, one is calling upon God and appealing to Him to do, in that moment, what He has promised to do.
      (a) This "appeal to God" parallels Acts 22:16 – "…be baptized, and wash away your sins, calling on the name of the Lord" (cf. Rom. 10:13).
      (b) In baptism, one is "buried [and]…raised with Him through faith in the working of God" (Col. 2:12).
      (c) God is the One who saves! God is the One who does the work!
      (d) In baptism, one "appeals to God" (or calls upon God) to do "the working" (i.e., the saving) that He promised to do.
   5. The true securing of "a good conscience" does not take place until one is baptized.
T. According to the Bible, a purpose of baptism is <u>to be able to truly rejoice</u>.
   1. After the Ethiopian eunuch was baptized, "he went on his way rejoicing" (Acts 8:39).
   2. After the Philippian jailer was baptized, "he rejoiced" (Acts 16:34).
   3. It is significant that they did not rejoice until AFTER they were baptized.
   4. There was something that transpired during the act of baptism (and NOT before) which gave them reason to rejoice. What better reason to rejoice than to have been saved from all of their sins and to enter into the body of Christ.
U. The conversions in the book of Acts demonstrate that baptism is essential to salvation.
   1. The book of Acts has sometimes been called "The Book of Conversions."
   2. In the Great Commission, Jesus gave instructions for how one can be saved.
      (a) One must believe   in order to   be saved (Mark 16:16).
      (b) One must repent   in order to   have remission of sins (Luke 24:47).
      (c) One must be baptized   in order to   be made a disciple (Mt. 28:19; Mk. 16:16).

3. In the Book of Acts, Jesus shows us example after example of people being saved.
   (a) In the book of Acts, we have vivid illustrations of individuals being saved in exactly the same manner that Jesus required in the Great Commission.
       (1) People believed   in order to   be saved (Acts 16:31).
       (2) People repented   in order to   have remission of sins (Acts 2:38).
       (3) People were baptized   in order to   be made a disciple (22:16; 11:26).
   (b) The purpose of the book of Acts is to present multiple cases of conversion in order to answer the question, "What must I do to be saved?"
   (c) Clear and precise instructions (in the Great Commission) combined with clear, precise and copious examples in the book of Acts (that correspond unambiguously with the instructions) makes God's plan to save man crystal clear.
4. Study these accounts of conversion carefully and note what the Scripture specifically states that these individuals did in order to be converted to Christ.

Those Who Were Taught	Believed Heb. 11:6	Repented Luke 13:3	Confessed Rom. 10:10	Baptized Gal. 3:27	Saved 2 Tim. 2:10
Jews Acts 2:1-47	Cut to heart (37)	Repent (38)		Baptized (38, 41)	Remission (38) Added (47)
Samaritans Acts 8:5-12	Believed (12)			Baptized (12)	
Simon Acts 8:13	Believed (13)			Baptized (13)	
Eunuch Acts 8:26-40	Believed (36-37)		Confessed (37)	Baptized (36-38)	Rejoiced (39)
Saul Acts 9:1-18				Baptized (9:18; 22:16)	Sins washed away (22:16)
Cornelius Acts 10:25-58	Believed (43)	Repentance (11:18)		Baptized (47-48)	Remission of sins (43)
Lydia Acts 16:11-15				Baptized (15)	
The Jailer Acts 16:25-34	Believed (31, 34)	Washed their stripes (33)		Baptized (33)	Saved (30) Rejoiced (34)
Corinthians Acts 18:4-11	Believed (8)			Baptized (8)	
Ephesians Acts 19:1-7	Believed (2, 4)			Baptized (5)	

5. In these ten accounts of conversion, something of great significance is observed.
   (a) The record does not specifically mention that each convert had believed, although we are confident that each one must have believed to be converted.
   (b) The record does not specifically mention that each convert had repented and confessed their faith in Jesus, although we are confident that each one must have repented and confessed their faith, for such is essential to salvation.
   (c) But, each one of the accounts specifically records that each person was baptized.
   (d) If baptism is not essential to salvation, why did God include it in every account?
   (e) The very act that so many readily dismiss today as being nonessential for salvation (i.e., baptism) is explicitly and purposefully mentioned in every conversion account.
   (f) When one compiles all accounts of conversion in God's "Book of Conversions," he will have a full and complete picture of God's conversion plan, for "the sum" of God's "word is truth" (Psa. 119:160). Add them up and baptism is essential!

6. Those who were converted in the New Testament did:
   (a) Exactly what they were told to do.
   (b) Immediately what they were told to do.
   (c) Uniformly (in every case) what they were told to do.
   (d) Graciously receive the same blessing of salvation upon their obedience.

V. The Bible clearly specifies the purpose that God assigns to baptism, and it is quite overwhelming how very plain He makes it. One absolutely must be baptized in order to:
   1. Obey the command of Christ.
   2. Be saved from past sins.
   3. Obtain the remission of sins.
   4. Have sins washed away.
   5. Be sanctified, cleansed and justified.
   6. Be made free from sin.
   7. Contact the saving blood of Christ.
   8. Enter a new relationship with God.
   9. Be born again.
   10. Enter the kingdom of God.
   11. Enter the one body of Christ.
   12. Become a child of God.
   13. Put on Christ.
   14. Enter into Christ, wherein is salvation.
   15. Become a New Testament Christian.
   16. Walk in newness of life.
   17. Call on the name of the Lord.
   18. Appeal to God for a good conscience.
   19. Be able to truly rejoice.
   20. Be converted in the same way as everyone else in the New Testament.

VI. While the Bible Is Very Plain and Offers Abundant Teaching, Some Still Offer Objections.
   A. Some steadfastly assert that one is already saved before he is baptized.
      1. However, read all of the verses about baptism which include any mention of being saved or a blessing associated with baptism.
      2. In every single one of these passages (without exception), God precisely orders the words to place baptism BEFORE salvation the blessing. Note the order in just a few:
         (a) "He who believes and is baptized will be saved" (Mark 16:16). Baptism is before.
         (b) "Repent, and…be baptized…for the remission of sins" (Acts 2:38). Baptism is before.
         (c) "Arise and be baptized, and wash away your sins" (Acts 22:16). Baptism is before.
         (d) "Baptism now saves you" (1 Pet. 3:21, NASB). Baptism is before.
         (e) "As many of you as were baptized into Christ have put on Christ" (Gal. 3:27). Baptism is before.
      3. There is not one single verse in the Bible that speaks about baptism coming after one is saved. Not one! God places it as an essential step in the salvation process.
   B. Some appeal to the thief on the cross, stating that he was saved but was never baptized.
      1. However, it cannot be proven that the thief had not been baptized.
         (a) John was baptizing throughout Judea and "all went out to him" (Matt. 3:5-6).
         (b) It is possible that the thief had been baptized by John at some point.
         (c) The burden of proof is upon those who claim that he was never baptized.
      2. The thief knew about Jesus and His kingdom (Luke 23:41-42).

(a) He knew that Jesus had done nothing wrong. How did he know that?
(b) He knew that Jesus had the power to bless him. How did he know that?
(c) He knew something about Jesus' kingdom. How did he know that?
(d) He appears to have some prior knowledge, perhaps due to the preaching of John.
3. The New Testament was not in force when Jesus saved the thief on the cross.
   (a) Consider Hebrews 9:15-17 carefully: "And for this reason He is the Mediator of the new covenant, by means of death, for the redemption of the transgressions under the first covenant, that those who are called may receive the promise of the eternal inheritance. For where there is a testament, there must also of necessity be the death of the testator. For a testament is in force after men are dead, since it has no power at all while the testator lives."
   (b) The thief lived under the Law of Moses—a covenant that did not require baptism.
   (c) It was only after the death of Jesus that His law was put into effect.
   (d) The thief lived under a different covenant than we do.
   (e) We live under the new covenant, which demands baptism to be saved.
   (f) It is irresponsible to tie one's self to a case of salvation before the cross and ignore the thousands of cases of conversion after the cross (in the book of Acts).
4. Ultimately, the Son of God had the power to forgive sin while on earth.
   (a) When Jesus was living on this earth and before His will went into effect, He had "power on earth to forgive sins" of whomever He desired (Matt. 9:6), independent of any conditions on their part, including baptism.
   (b) Just as Jesus forgave the thief on the cross (because He had that authority):
       (1) He also forgave the paralytic in Mark 2:5.
       (2) He also forgave the sinful woman in Luke 7:48.
       (3) He also forgave the adulteress in John 8:11.
       (4) He also forgave Zacchaeus in Luke 19:9.
   (c) Upon His death, Jesus' last will and testament (i.e., His new covenant) became effective, requiring that one believe and be baptized to be saved (Mark 16:16).
   (d) That is the law under which we live, which we must obey and which we have no right to alter one iota.
   (e) Before that law became operative, Jesus could (and did) forgive sin as He willed.
5. The thief is not our example for conversion today! The book of Acts is!
6. Rather than place our hope in the thief on the cross, let us obey the Savior on the cross!

C. Some point to verses that teach one is saved by faith and claim baptism is not included.
   1. There is not a single verse in the Bible that teaches one is saved by faith alone.
   2. In fact, Scripture plainly teaches that justification is "not by faith only" (Jas. 2:24).
   3. If it is a proper hermeneutic to pick a verse that teaches that faith saves us and then claim that anything not mentioned in that verse (like baptism) is not essential:
      (a) Then one could likewise use Luke 13:3 to teach repentance only saves.
      (b) Then one could likewise use Matthew 10:32 to teach confession only saves.
      (c) Then one could likewise use 1 Peter 3:21 to teach baptism only saves.
   4. The truth of God's Word is found in the "sum" of God's Word, not just in a part.
   5. See pages 215-218 in Lesson 19 for more on salvation by faith.

D. Some suggest that baptism is a work and that salvation is not of works.
   1. The works in Ephesians 2:8-9 are works of human merit, which will never save.
   2. However, works of obedience are essential to salvation (Jas. 2:14-26).
   3. Scripture teaches that "faith without works is dead" (Jas. 2:26).

    4. While the Bible never uses the word "work" to describe baptism, Jesus does call belief in Him a "work" (John 6:28-29). Does that mean it is not essential?
    5. The New Testament makes a clear distinction between works of human merit and works of faithful obedience. One will never save! One is essential to save!
    6. Baptism is an act of faithful obedience to the revealed will of God.
    7. See pages 218-221 in Lesson 19 for more on salvation by works.
  E. While some offer objections to the essentiality of baptism for salvation, the Bible still teaches very plainly that baptism saves from sin.
    1. In fact, the verses that teach baptism's inseparable connection to one's salvation are some of the simplest verses in the New Testament (in structure and content).
    2. One cannot reject clear Bible teaching and still secure God's salvation (cf. Luke 7:29-30).

VII. Conclusion
  A. Baptism is such a wonderful and exciting topic to study!
  B. Without the Word of God, we would know nothing about its meaning or its necessity!
  C. It is not up to man to decide the place of baptism in God's plan—that's up to God!
  D. It is up to man to study, accept and teach the person, process and purpose of Bible baptism!
  E. Scripture teaches that the proper (and only) subjects for Bible baptism are those who have been taught, have believed in Jesus, have repented of their sins and are willing to confess their faith in Jesus. Infants do not need to be baptized.
  F. Scripture teaches that baptism is a burial (an immersion) in water.
  G. Scripture teaches that baptism is essential for one's salvation from sins.
  H. Scripture teaches that it is through the blood of Jesus that one is saved in Bible baptism.
  I. Scripture gives abundant and explicit teaching regarding the essentiality of baptism, and Scripture gives abundant and specific examples of those who were baptized to be saved.
  J. The very last words of Jesus before His ascension called upon man to be baptized in order to be "saved" (Mark 16:16) and to become one of His "disciples" (Matt. 28:19).
  K. Rather than reject plain Bible teaching:
    1. Let us conform ourselves to the teaching of Jesus.
    2. Let us follow the example of every conversion to Christ in the New Testament.
    3. Let us embrace God's truth.
    4. Let us love God's truth.
    5. Let us teach God's truth.
    6. Let us obey God's truth.

VIII. Have You Ever Been Baptized? If So, Was It According to Scripture?
  A. If you have never been baptized, there's no need to delay.
    1. Ananias asked Saul, "And now why are you waiting?" (Acts 22:16).
    2. Having studied what the Bible teaches about baptism and its essential role in your salvation, "Behold, now is the accepted time; behold, now is the day of salvation" (2 Cor. 6:2).
    3. As Ananias urged Saul, "Arise and be baptized."
  B. If you have been baptized in the past:
    1. Was your baptism by immersion, in the way that the Bible teaches?
    2. Was your baptism in order to obtain the forgiveness of sins, as the Bible teaches?
      (a) One way to figure this out to ask yourself, "Did I believe that I was already saved before I was baptized?"
      (b) Another way to figure this out is to look at what you were taught before you were baptized and what that particular religious group teaches about baptism.

- (1) If they teach that salvation comes at the point of faith before one is baptized, then you were not baptized for the purpose defined in the Bible.
- (2) If they teach that baptism is something one needs to do after they are saved, then you were not baptized for the purpose defined in the Bible.
- (3) If it is not their practice to teach and administer baptism immediately upon one's faith in Jesus and desire to follow Him, then you were not baptized for the purpose defined in the Bible.

C. If your baptism was not in the way that the Bible teaches and for the reason that the Bible teaches, is there any reason that you should not be baptized as the Bible teaches right now?
   1. Scripture shows (esp. in passages like Acts 19:1-5) that it is not wrong to be baptized a second time if the first time was not in accordance with the teaching of Scripture.
   2. Baptism is certainly a "right thing" to do, for it comes from heaven (Matt. 21:25), but a "right thing" must be done in the "right way" and for the "right reason" to be "right" in the eyes of God.
   3. If you were not baptized in the right way (by immersion) and for the right reason (for the express purpose of having your sins taken away at that moment by the blood of Jesus), then "why are you waiting?" Be baptized, in accordance with the teaching of the Bible, today!

Recommended Resources

<u>Books</u>

Chambers, Dan. *Is Baptism Really Necessary?* Nashville: Gospel Advocate, 2002.

Chesser, Frank. *Voyage of Faith.* Huntsville, AL: Publishing Designs, 2010.

Choate, J.C. *New Testament Conversions.* Winona, MS: Choate Publications, 2002.

Overton, Basil. *Conversions in Acts.* Winona, MS: Choate Publications, 1981.

Winkler, Wendell. *Things That Accompany Salvation.* Tuscaloosa, AL: Winkler Publications, 1972.

<u>Articles</u>

Brownlow, Leroy. "Because It Teaches and Administers Scriptural Baptism." *Why I Am a Member of the Church of Christ.* Fort Worth: Brownlow Publishing, 1973. 132-142.

Duncan, Bobby. "As in Bible Times Adults Are the Subjects of Baptism." *Introducing the Church of Christ.* Ed. Alvin Jennings. Fort Worth: Star Bible, 1981. 115-119.

Edwards, Earl D. "What Is Scriptural Baptism?" *The Spiritual Sword* (Oct. 2007): 21-25.

Hamilton, W.T. "Born of Water and of the Spirit." *"What Do You Know About the Holy Spirit?" (Fort Worth Lectures).* Ed. Wendell Winkler. Montgomery, AL: Winkler Publication, 1980. 328-336.

Jackson, Wayne. "Conversions in Acts." *ChristianCourier.com*
https://www.christiancourier.com/articles/1277-conversions-in-acts

---. "Does Ephesians 2:8-9 Exclude Baptism?" *ChristianCourier.com*
https://www.christiancourier.com/articles/1483-does-ephesians-2-8-9-exclude-baptism

---. "What Does It Mean To Be a Born Again Christian?" *ChristianCourier.com*
https://www.christiancourier.com/articles/115-what-does-it-mean-to-be-a-born-again-christian

McClish, Dub. "The Apostles' Pattern Is Followed in the Practice of Baptism." *Introducing the Church of Christ.* Ed. Alvin Jennings. Fort Worth: Star Bible, 1981. 109-114.

Sain, David. "Baptism Is a Requirement." *The Spiritual Sword* (Apr. 2005): 25-28.

Winkler, Wendell. "Bible Baptism." *Things That Accompany Salvation.* Tuscaloosa, AL: Winkler Publications, 1972. 112-119.

---. "Do Members of the Church of Christ Believe in Water Salvation?" *The Church Everybody Is Asking About.* Tuscaloosa, AL: Winkler Publications, 1988. 112-118.

---. "Ye Must Be Born Again." *Things That Accompany Salvation.* Tuscaloosa, AL: Winkler Publications, 1972. 63-68.

Periodicals

The Spiritual Sword. January 1979. "Baptism Is Unto the Remission of Sins."

The Spiritual Sword. January 1994. "Baptism in the New Testament."

The Spiritual Sword. April 2004. "Baptism in the Plan of God."

Lesson 21: The Danger and Reality of Apostasy

I. **God Makes Wonderfully Reassuring Promises to Those Who Are Saved.**
   A. God's greatest desire for man is that he might be saved (John 3:16; 1 Tim. 2:4; 2 Pet. 3:9).
   B. When one is saved from his sins, he enters into a new and special relationship with God, which God longs might persist until the end of time (John 14:1-6; Rev. 21-22).
   C. To those who have been saved, God makes numerous precious promises.
      1. God's children have great assurance that no external power "shall be able to separate us from the love of God which is in Christ Jesus our Lord" (Rom. 8:35-39).
      2. God's children have tremendous hope, knowing that God's intent for them is that they "should not perish but have eternal life" (John 3:14-16).
      3. God's children have been given "eternal life, and they shall never perish; neither shall anyone snatch them out" of Jesus' hand or the Father's hand (John 10:27-29).
      4. God's children have comfort, for God "is able to keep you from stumbling, and to present you faultless before the presence of His glory with exceeding joy" (Jude 24).
   D. There is nothing that God wants more than for His children to spend eternity with Him.
   E. But, are these promises that God gives to His children conditional?
      1. "Conditional" means "subject to one or more conditions or requirements being met."
      2. Conditions are stipulations, premises, prerequisites which are essential for the fulfillment of an agreement.
      3. The question must be answered: When God makes promises, are there any conditions or requirements necessary to the fulfillment of those promises, or are God's promises completely unconditional, requiring no response from man at all?
      4. Once man is saved by God:
         (a) Is there anything that man *must do* to remain in that relationship?
         (b) Is there anything that man *can do* to fall out of that relationship?
      5. As with all Bible questions, we must go to the Bible and allow the Bible to answer!

II. **A Person Is Saved Only By the Grace of God, But God's Grace Is Conditional.**
   A. The Bible clearly teaches that man is saved from his sins by the grace of God (Eph. 2:1-9; Rom. 3:23-24; 5:15; Tit. 2:11; 3:4-5). (See pages 212-213.)
      1. Grace is God's "unmerited favor," which is a gift that is not earned or deserved.
      2. While it is God's grace that saves man, the Bible clearly teaches there are conditions that man must meet in order to be saved (Mark 16:16; Acts 2:38; Eph. 2:8).
         (a) God's saving grace requires faith (Heb. 11:6). (See pages 215-218.)
         (b) God's saving grace requires works (Jas. 2:14-16). (See pages 218-221.)
         (c) God's saving grace requires obedience (Heb. 5:8-9). (See pages 221-224.)
      3. Salvation by God's grace is conditional!
   B. The Bible clearly teaches that man, once saved, continues to be saved by the grace of God.
      1. By God's grace, we continue to have "redemption through His blood" (Eph. 1:7).
      2. By God's grace, we continue to have cleansing from our sins (1 John 1:6-10).
      3. By God's grace, we continue to have "the propitiation for our sins" (1 John 2:1-2).
      4. By God's grace, we continue to have Jesus making "intercession" for us (Heb. 7:25).
      5. While God's grace continues to save, the Bible clearly teaches there are conditions that man must meet to continue to be saved (John 8:31-32; 1 John 1:7-9; Rev. 2:10).
         (a) That is the thrust of this lesson.
         (b) Is the securing of eternal salvation conditional?
         (c) Or, once a man is saved, is he always saved, regardless of any conditions?

C. Consider this: If an alien sinner fails to meet God's conditions for salvation, he cannot be saved from his sins.
   1. "**...if you do not believe** that I am He, you will die in your sins" (John 8:24).
   2. "I tell you, no; but **unless you repent** you will all likewise perish" (Luke 13:3).
   3. "But **whoever denies Me** before men, him I will also deny..." (Matt. 10:33).
   4. "...**Unless one is born of water and the Spirit**, he cannot enter the kingdom of God" (John 3:3-5).
   5. God made His salvation conditional and said it could not be secured otherwise!
D. Likewise: Would it not make sense that if a Christian, once saved, fails to continue to meet God's conditions for continued salvation, such a Christian cannot continue to be saved from his sins? That is the question to be considered and answered in this lesson.
   1. The Bible teaches that for one who has been saved by the grace of God to continue in the grace of God:
      (a) He must continue to "abide in" Jesus (John 15:4-7; 1 John 2:28).
      (b) He must continue to "abide in" Jesus' "word" (John 8:31-32).
      (c) He must continue to have Jesus' "words abide in" him (John 15:7; 1 John 2:24-25).
      (d) He must continue to "keep" Jesus' "commandments" (John 15:10).
   2. The very fact that God enumerated conditions indicates unequivocally that if those conditions are not met that the promise is negated.
      (a) If one fails to continue to meet the conditions of God's grace, then one consequently falls out of the favor of God's grace.
      (b) Such is the nature of conditional promises.
E. Many Protestant denominations have been influenced by Calvinism and teach the doctrine of "Perseverance of the Saints."
   1. This doctrine has also been called:
      (a) "Once Saved, Always Saved."
      (b) "The Eternal Security of the Believer."
      (c) "The Impossibility of Apostasy."
   2. The doctrine asserts that once a person enters into a saved state with God there is nothing that saved person (i.e., Christian) can do to fall from that state of grace.
      (a) Stated another way, Calvinism teaches that no child of God can so sin as to be lost in hell eternally—no sin could ever endanger his soul.
      (b) Many adamantly believe and teach that once a person is saved that he is always saved—how he lives has nothing to do with the salvation of his soul.
   3. Is the doctrine of "Once Saved, Always Saved" supported by Scripture?
      (a) If is it impossible for one to fall away from God, then such a doctrine removes free will and the consequences thereof.
      (b) If once a person is saved that person is always saved, then he is not free to determine his own destiny and could not go to hell, even if he tried.
F. The Scriptural evidence concludes quite clearly: Apostasy is possible!
   1. Apostasy means "falling away, turning away from or abandoning faith."
   2. Scripture teaches and warns that such is absolutely possible.
   3. A Christian can so sin that he can fall away from God, be separated from God and be lost in sin (again).
   4. The Bible does not teach the man-made doctrine of "once saved, always saved."
   5. In fact, the Bible denies and crushes the false doctrine again and again.
   6. Let us consider the abundance of evidence provided in God's Word.

III. The Bible Emphatically Teaches That One Can Fall Away from God and Lose His Salvation!
   A. Perhaps the most vivid passage on falling away is in 2 Peter 2.
      1. This chapter alerts Christians to the dangers of false teachers among them and the consequences of following their "destructive ways."
         (a) One has to wonder—if the doctrine of "once saved, always saved" is supported by Scripture, what difference would it make if there were false teachers?
         (b) Would it really matter if a false teacher led a Christian (who could never be lost) to believe or practice something that was contrary to God's will? (See Rev. 2:20-23.)
      2. Christians were taught in this chapter that these false teachers were "among you" (2:1).
         (a) These teachers were not "outside" the church but were "inside."
         (b) While they had once followed "the way of truth" (2:2), they themselves now "have forsaken the right way" (2:15).
      3. These individuals, in 2 Peter 2, were unquestionably saved at some time in the past.
         (a) They had "escaped the corruption that is in the world" (1:4).
         (b) They had "escaped from those who live in error" (2:18).
         (c) They had "escaped the pollutions of the world" (2:20).
         (d) Those who have "escaped" the world and its lusts are ones who have been saved.
      4. But, these individuals, who were once saved, were now "overcome" and "enslaved."
         (a) Verse 19 teaches, "by what a man is overcome, by this he is enslaved" (NASB).
         (b) Any man can be overcome by something (including sin) and become enslaved.
         (c) Verse 20 teaches that they were "again entangled...and overcome."
         (d) Note these two words in verse 20: "after" and "again."
            (1) "*After* they have escaped" – something happens after they are saved.
            (2) "They are *again* entangled" in the world – like they were before being saved.
            (3) This obviously points to a Christian falling back into sin and separated from God.
      5. This passage clearly depicts individuals who:
         (a) Knew "the way of righteousness" (2:21),
         (b) Once walked "the right way" (2:15),
         (c) Had obeyed "the way of truth" (2:1-2),
         (d) But then they "turn from the holy commandment delivered to them" (2:21).
      6. They had been saved, but now they had "turned" and reverted back to the ways and the entanglements of sinful living. That turning from truth and from a saved state:
         (a) Is likened to a "dog" who "returns to his own vomit" (2:22).
         (b) Is likened to "a sow, having washed," who returns "to her wallowing in the mire."
      7. "The latter end is worse for them than the beginning" (2:20).
         (a) Peter states that "it would have been better for them not to have known the way of righteousness, than having known it, to turn from" it (2:21).
         (b) Does this sound like they're still saved and going to heaven? Certainly not!
      8. Christians can become entangled in the world again, fall away and be lost! A vivid truth!
   B. The book of Galatians, as a whole, teaches that one can fall away, especially 5:1-4.
      1. Galatians was written to Christians, who were "turning away" from the gospel and the truth of Christ (1:6-7; 3:1; 4:9; 5:7), in order to urge them to remain steadfast (5:1).
         (a) These Christians enjoyed "the liberty by which Christ has made us free" (5:1).
         (b) They are charged to "keep standing firm" in that liberty (NASB).
      2. Paul urged these freed Christians not to be "entangled again with a yoke of bondage."
         (a) Having been freed from the bondage, this plea of Paul proves they could fall back into bondage and abandon the freedom they had in Christ.

- (b) Why would Paul make this plea if apostasy was not possible and if their souls were not in jeopardy of being lost? Why would they need to be charged to "stand firm" and why would they need to be warned of being "entangled again"?
  3. Verse 4 makes it very plain.
     - (a) Paul emphatically affirmed that, by "seeking to be justified by law," these Christians had "been severed from Christ" and had "fallen from grace" (5:4).
     - (b) The verb tenses do not merely indicate a possibility of something in the future, but they are past tense, indicating that apostasy had actually happened.
     - (c) Those who had been saved by the grace of God had now "fallen from grace."
  4. Christians, once saved, can be lost and severed from Christ! A very clear passage!
C. The book of Hebrews, as a whole, teaches that one can fall away, especially 6:4-6.
  1. Hebrews was written to Christians who were on the verge of "drifting away" (2:1-4), for their hearts were being "hardened" (3:7-19) and they were "dull of hearing" God's word and growing therein (5:11-14).
  2. In chapter 6, the writer describes, in vivid terms, individuals who had become Christians:
     - (a) They "were once enlightened" (6:4).
     - (b) They had "tasted the heavenly gift" (6:4).
     - (c) They had "become partakers of the Holy Spirit" (6:4).
     - (d) They had "tasted the good word of God" (6:5).
     - (e) They had "tasted...the powers of the age to come" (6:5).
     - (f) No more beautiful depiction of salvation could be penned. This is an obvious description of ones who had become Christians by the grace of God.
  3. Then, in the next verse, the writer continues with a sudden turn of events—"...and then have fallen away" (6:6, NASB).
     - (a) It is not merely "if they fall away," but the verb tense indicates an actuality.
     - (b) They clearly had been saved, and then they clearly had "fallen away" from that state.
     - (c) Apostasy was more than just a possibility. It was a reality.
  4. Such persons, who were once saved and in the grace of God, now "crucify again for themselves the Son of God, and put Him to an open shame" (6:6). They have fallen!
  5. Christians can fall away! If they cannot, then this passage is pointless!
D. The book of James, a very practical book about Christian living, ends with a very clear teaching about the possibility of apostasy in 5:19-20.
  1. These verses are addressed to "Brethren," therefore, Christians are in view.
  2. These verses announce the real possibility that a brother can "wander from the truth."
  3. These verses emphasize that "any" brother can wander away and be lost.
  4. These verses show that the lost brother needs "someone" to "turn him back."
  5. These verses refer to the brother who has wandered away as "a sinner."
  6. These verses demonstrate that the lost brother is in "error."
  7. These verses contrast the action of a brother who wanders "FROM the truth" with the need of that brother to turn "FROM the error."
  8. These verses highlight that the brother's sinful condition is "of his way"—i.e., it was his personal choice to turn from truth and it will be his personal choice to turn back.
  9. These verses emphasize that the brother who has fallen away is truly lost, for he needs someone who will "save" him. He is not presently in a "saved" condition.
  10. These verses teach that, unless someone helps the lost brother to turn back, his "soul" will suffer the consequences of his "sins"—namely, spiritual "death."

11. The emphasis of these verses is on saving a "soul from death."
    (a) The brother will die physically whether he turns back or not.
    (b) The salvation he (i.e., a brother in Christ) needs in this passage is of his soul.
    (c) This brother is separated from God and will remain so in eternity if he does not turn.
    (d) It is obvious that this is a brother in Christ who is not in a saved condition.
12. Christians can wander from God and be lost! If not, this passage is meaningless!

E. Jesus' Parable of the Soils teaches that those who are saved can be lost (Luke 8:4-15).
   1. The parable is of "a sower" who "went out to sow his seed" (8:5).
      (a) The "seed" in the parable represents "the word of God" (8:11).
      (b) The "soils" in the parable represent various "hearts" (8:12, 15).
   2. There are four different soils, representing four different responses to the gospel.
      (a) The wayside heart hears the word but is not "saved" (8:12).
      (b) The rocky/stony heart accepts the word and becomes a Christian—it "sprang up...with joy" (8:6, 13).
         (1) These Christians "believe for a while and in time of temptation fall away" (13).
         (2) This one "endures only for a while. For when tribulation or persecution arises because of the word, immediately he stumbles" (Matt. 13:21).
         (3) Look at those words: "fall away," "endures only for a while" and "stumbles."
      (c) The thorny heart also becomes a Christian—it "sprang up" (8:7)
         (1) However, his faith is "choked with cares, riches and pleasures of life" (8:14).
         (2) And, he "becomes unfruitful" (Matt. 13:22) and brings "no fruit to maturity" (Luke 8:14).
      (d) The good heart "hears the word" and becomes a Christian—it "sprang up" (8:8).
         (1) These Christians "hold [the word] fast, and bear fruit with perseverance" (8:15, NASB).
         (2) There is an obvious faithful endurance on the part of these Christians.
   3. This parable of Jesus draws a vivid contrast of the hearts of those who hear the Word.
      (a) "Many" (cf. Matt. 7:13) will hear the word and not become a Christian.
      (b) "Few" (cf. Matt. 7:14) will hear the word and become a narrow-walking Christian.
      (c) "Some" (Luke 8:6-7) will hear the word and become a Christian, but will "fall away," "stumble" and not "persevere."
      (d) Of the four hearts that Jesus described, half of them prove the possibility of apostasy.
   4. It is possible for one who is saved to fall away and be lost!

F. Jesus' teaching about the vine and the branches shows the saved can be lost (Jn. 15:1-8).
   1. Jesus taught that He is "the true vine" and the "Father is the vinedresser" (15:1).
   2. Jesus taught that each individual follower ("branch") of Christ is "in Me" (15:2).
      (a) Jesus used the expression "in Me" six times in six verses (15:2-7).
      (b) Jesus was not merely describing individuals who were "close" to Him or "attached" to Him. Jesus says that Christians (i.e., those who are saved) are "in" Him.
   3. But, Jesus taught in John 15 that even one who is "in Me" can so live that:
      (a) God, the vinedresser, "takes away" that person from being "in" Jesus (15:2).
      (b) "He is cast out," thrown "into the fire" and "burned" (15:6).
   4. Jesus clearly taught that in order to enjoy the blessings of being "in Christ":
      (a) One must continually "abide in" Him (15:4).
      (b) One must continually "bear much fruit" (15:5).
      (c) One must continually "abide in" His words (15:7).

(d) Read and circle the words "if" and "unless" in this passage. These are words that demand conditions be met (and continue to be met) before blessings and promises are granted. (See II, D.)
  5. It is possible for one who is saved "in Christ" to fall away and be lost eternally!
 G. If a Christian cannot fall away and lose his salvation, then these passages have no meaning.

IV. The Bible Repeatedly Warns That One Can Fall Away from God and Lose His Salvation!
 A. It is obvious from the preceding point that the teachings of the Bible about apostasy (in passages like 2 Pet. 2, Gal. 5, Heb. 6, Jas. 5, Luke 8, John 15) are warnings in themselves.
   1. However, there are additional passages that state warnings very clearly.
   2. One must ask: If the Bible spends any time warning a Christian about falling away and being lost, is there any rational way to argue that apostasy is not possible?
 B. Paul warns, "Therefore let him who thinks he stands take heed lest he fall" (1 Cor. 10:12).
   1. This verse was written to Christians in Corinth. They were saved.
   2. The verb "take heed" is in the present tense, indicating continuous action.
   3. What if the Christian does not "take heed"? He will "fall"!
   4. If a Christian cannot fall away, why was this warning given to Christians?
   5. The warning is given because the possibility of apostasy is real and severe.
 C. Hebrews warns, "Beware, brethren, lest there be in any of you an evil heart of unbelief in departing from the living God" (Heb. 3:12).
   1. This verse was written to first-century Christians ("brethren"). They were saved.
   2. The word "beware" indicates the most solemn of warnings—watch out!
   3. The word "lest" underscores that the danger is very real and must be prevented.
   4. The word "any" emphasizes this perilous possibility for ANY Christian (see 3:13; 4:1, 11).
   5. The words "an evil heart of unbelief" emphasize the depth to which a believer in Christ could fall—to the point of no longer believing in Him (cf. 2 Pet. 2:1).
   6. The words "in departing from the living God" leave no doubt about apostasy.
     (a) The ASV translates it, "…in falling away from the living God."
   7. This is one of the strongest warnings against apostasy in Scripture.
   8. If a Christian cannot stop believing and depart from God, why was this warning given?
 D. Peter warns, "Therefore, brethren, be even more diligent to make your call and election sure, for if you do these things you will never stumble" (2 Pet. 1:10).
   1. This passage was written to Christians to motivate them to spiritual growth.
     (a) The readers had been saved (cf. 1:9b) and now needed to grow in their faith.
     (b) Verses 5-7 list areas of growth in which these Christians needed to concentrate.
   2. Peter warns that the Christian who fails to grow in these areas "has forgotten that he was cleansed from his old sins" (1:9).
   3. In order to keep from falling, Peter warns these Christians to:
     (a) "Be even more diligent…" (NKJV) or "be all the more diligent" (NASB),
     (b) "To make certain" (NASB), "to confirm" (ESV), "to make…sure" (NKJV),
     (c) "Your calling and election."
     (d) "Every effort" (NIV) and "diligence" is required to keep oneself saved.
     (e) "Once saved, always saved" does not fit in this passage in any way, shape or form!
   4. Circle the word "if" in verses 8 and 10.
     (a) The word "if" is a conditional term.
       (1) God's promises are only secured by meeting His conditions.
       (2) "For if these things are yours and abound…" (1:8).
       (3) "…for if you do these things…" (1:10).

- (b) "If" a Christian grows in these areas, he will not be "useless or unfruitful" (NASB).
  - (1) But, "if" a Christian does not grow in these areas, he will be useless and unfruitful.
- (c) "If" a Christian grows in these areas, he will "never stumble" or "fall" (ESV).
  - (1) But, "if" a Christian does not grow in these areas, he will stumble and fall.
- (d) "If" a Christian grows in these areas, "an entrance will be supplied...abundantly into the everlasting kingdom of our Lord and Savior Jesus Christ" (1:11).
  - (1) But, "if" a Christian does not grow in these areas, an entrance into the everlasting kingdom of our Lord and Savior Jesus Christ will not be supplied.
- (e) God's conditions must be met in order to enjoy God's promises! (See II, D.)
5. If a Christian cannot stumble and fall away, why was this warning given to Christians?

E. Warning after warning is issued to God's people to alert them to the danger of apostasy!
  1. A loving God would not so severely warn about something that was not possible!

V. The Bible Gives Numerous Examples of Those Who Did Fall Away and Lose Their Salvation!

A. Those things written in Scripture are for "our learning" (Rom. 15:4).
  1. God shared examples in His Word as an "admonition" or "warning" (1 Cor. 10:11).
  2. Christians must take heed to these examples and learn from them.

B. The example of apostasy used repeatedly in the Bible is that of the Israelite nation itself.
  1. Before Paul gave the warning in 1 Corinthians 10:12—"Take heed lest he fall"—he used the Israelites as "examples" (10:6, 11) from which we need to learn.
    - (a) The children of Israel were "all" blessed tremendously by the Lord (10:1-4).
    - (b) "But with most of them God was not well pleased" (10:5), and as a result:
      - (1) "Their bodies were scattered in the wilderness" (10:5).
      - (2) "In one day twenty-three thousand fell" (10:8).
      - (3) "Some...were destroyed by serpents" (10:9).
      - (4) "Some...were destroyed by the destroyer" (10:10).
    - (c) God's own people disobeyed Him and were lost—a clear example of apostasy!
    - (d) That's why Paul said, "Let him who thinks he stands take heed lest he fall."
  2. As the Hebrew writer was delivering the strong warning in Hebrews 3:12—"Lest there be in any of you an evil heart of unbelief in departing from the living God"—he used the Israelites as a vivid example of how such could happen among God's people.
    - (a) "All who came out of Egypt" "rebelled" against God (3:16).
    - (b) Because they "sinned" against the Lord, He was "angry" with them (3:17, 10).
    - (c) As a result, their "corpses fell in the wilderness" (3:17).
    - (d) Because God's own people did not "obey" the Lord, He "swore" that they "would not enter His rest" (3:18, 11).
    - (e) The first "generation" (3:10) of Jews who came out of Egypt "could not enter" the Promised Land "because of unbelief" (3:18) —a clear example of apostasy!
    - (f) That's why the writer said, "Beware, brethren, lest there be in any of you an evil heart of unbelief in departing from the living God." If it could happen to the Israelites (after all they saw God do), it can happen to you!

C. Judas, one of the apostles, "fell away" (Acts 1:25, ASV) and he was "lost" (John 17:12).

D. A Christian in Corinth had fallen into sin, and the church needed to take disciplinary action against him so that he might "be saved in the day of the Lord" (1 Cor. 5:5).
  1. If he did not change from his evil ways, he would not be saved when Christ came.
  2. Here was a brother in Christ whose soul was in jeopardy of eternity in hell.

E. Hymenaeus and Alexander had been "delivered to Satan," because they "rejected" the faith and "suffered shipwreck in regard to their faith" (1 Tim. 1:18-20).

F. Hymenaeus and Philetus "strayed concerning the truth" (2 Tim. 2:17-18).
G. Ananias and Sapphira willfully sinned against the Lord and fell (Acts 5:1-11).
H. Simon the sorcerer, after becoming a Christian, behaved in such a way that his "heart [was] not right in the sight of God," he needed to "repent" and be forgiven (Acts 8:9-24).
I. The congregation in Ephesus had "left [its] first love" and "fallen," and Christ was going to "remove" them and their right to "the tree of life," if they did not "repent" (Rev. 2:1-7; 1:20).
J. The congregation in Pergamos was commanded to "repent" or the Lord would "fight against them" (Rev. 2:16).
K. The congregation in Sardis was commanded to "repent" or the Lord would "come upon you as a thief" (Rev. 3:3).
L. The congregation in Laodicea was commanded to "repent" or the Lord would "vomit you out of My mouth" (Rev. 3:19, 16).
M. The apostle Paul himself recognized that even he could fall away and be lost, so he stated, "I discipline my body and bring it into subjection, lest, when I have preached to others, I myself should become disqualified" (1 Cor. 9:27).
N. If a Christian cannot fall away and lose his salvation, then these examples are deceptive and absolutely meaningless.

VI. The Bible Vividly Predicted That Some Would Fall Away and Lose Their Salvation!
A. God not only said that one could fall away, He expressly said that some would fall away.
B. In writing about the assurance of the return of Christ, the inspired apostle affirmed that Christ's return would not happen "unless the falling away comes first" (2 Thess. 2:3).
   1. "Falling away" is from the Greek *apostasia*, from which we get our word "apostasy."
   2. The NASB translates it, "unless the apostasy comes first."
   3. The definite article "the" identifies a definite and expected digression from the faith.
   4. God foresaw and foretold specifically that there would be a falling away!
   5. One cannot "fall away" from something of which he was never a part.
C. When speaking with the elders from Ephesus, Paul warned them that, after his departure, "...savage wolves will come in among you, not sparing the flock" (Acts 20:29).
   1. He then predicted, "Also from among yourselves men will rise up, speaking perverse things, to draw away the disciples after themselves" (20:30).
   2. The Greek word for "draw away" (*apospao*) is elsewhere translated "withdrawn" (Luke 22:41) and "departed" or "parted" (Acts 21:1).
   3. Scripture not only states that one can be drawn away from and depart from the faith, but, in this passage, it explicitly teaches that some would!
   4. One cannot be drawn away from something of which he was never a part.
D. In Paul's letters to his fellow evangelist, Timothy, he foretold of future apostasy.
   1. "Now the Spirit expressly says that in latter times some will depart from the faith, giving heed to deceiving spirits and doctrines of demons..." (1 Tim. 4:1-3).
   2. "For the time will come when they will not endure sound doctrine...and they will turn their ears away from the truth, and be turned aside to fables" (2 Tim. 4:3-4).
   3. Scripture not only states that one can depart from the faith and turn away from the truth, but, in this passage, it explicitly teaches that some would!
   4. One cannot depart from something of which he was never a part.
E. If a Christian cannot fall away and lose his salvation, then these passages are senseless.
   1. The very fact that God predicted apostasy proves that such is possible!

VII. The Bible Offers Various Causes of Christians Falling Away and Losing Their Salvation!
   A. The devil is ever busy, looking for ways and opportunities to turn Christians away from their faith and back to a life of sinful, worldly living.
      1. He finds success in various places and causes Christians to fall for various reasons.
      2. Side note: If a Christian could never fall away and be lost (i.e., if once a Christian was saved, he was always saved and could never depart from God and back into the devil's hands), then why does the devil even bother tempting Christians to sin and to turn away from God?
   B. Some Christians fall away because of a lack of faith (Heb. 3:12; Luke 8:13).
   C. Some Christians fall away because of the deceitfulness of sin (Heb. 3:13).
   D. Some Christians fall away because of lusts and pride (1 John 2:15-17).
   E. Some Christians fall away because of persecution (Matt. 13:20-21; 2 Tim. 3:12).
   F. Some Christians fall away because of the cares, riches and pleasures of life (Luke 8:14).
   G. Some Christians fall away because of the love of money (1 Tim. 6:10; Luke 12:15-21).
   H. Some Christians fall away because of the hardships of life (Job; 1 Thess. 3:7; 2 Cor. 8:2).
   I. Some Christians fall away because of the deceitfulness of riches (1 Tim. 6:9-10; Mk. 4:19).
   J. Some Christians fall away because of false teachers/teaching (Ac. 20:29-30; 2 Tim. 4:3-4).
   K. Some Christians fall away because they fail to love the truth (2 Tim. 4:3-4; 2 Th. 2:9-12).
   L. Some Christians fall away because they fail to grow as they should (Heb. 2:3; 5:11-14).
   M. Some Christians fall away because they are mistreated by their brethren (3 John 9-11).
   N. Some Christians fall away because they do not develop relationships in the church (1 Cor. 12:12-27).
   O. Some Christians fall away because they do not count the cost (Luke 14:28-30).
   P. Some Christians fall away because they do not prioritize the assembly (Heb. 10:24-27).
   Q. Some Christians fall away because they underestimate the devil (1 Pet. 5:8-9).
   R. Some Christians fall away because they conform themselves to the world (Rom. 12:1-2).
   S. Some Christians fall away because they love the praise of men (3 Jn. 9-11; Jn. 12:42-43).
   T. Some Christians fall away because they revert back to their old ways (Acts 8:9-24).
   U. Some Christians fall away because they revert back to an old religion (Gal. 5:4).
   V. Some Christians fall away because they revert back to old friends (1 Cor. 15:33).
   W. The list of reasons that Christians fall away is truly endless.
      1. Knowing that apostasy is real and that it is possible for anyone, let us do all we can to "make [our] call and election sure" (2 Pet. 1:10).
      2. Knowing that there are countless methods used by the devil to cause a Christian to fall away and be lost, let us "be sober" and "vigilant" (1 Pet. 5:8).
      3. Let us look back over this list of causes, identify certain ones that could be our point of weakness, and work diligently, with the Lord's help, to overcome them.

VIII. The Bible Clearly Depicts the Condition and Future of Those Who Have Fallen Away!
   A. The Bible portrays the condition of one who has fallen away in a very dreadful way.
      1. The one who has fallen away:
         (a) Is in "worse" condition than he was before he was converted (2 Pet. 2:20).
         (b) Has wandered "from the truth" to "the error of his way" (Jas. 5:19-20).
         (c) Has turned from God's "holy commandment" (2 Pet. 2:21).
         (d) Has "trampled the Son of God underfoot, counted the blood of the covenant...a common thing, and insulted the Spirit of grace" (Heb. 10:29).
         (e) Is likened to "a dog" that "returns to his own vomit" (2 Pet. 2:22).
         (f) Is likened to a "washed" sow returning "to wallowing in the mire" (2 Pet. 2:22).

                (g) Crucifies "the Son of God afresh" and puts Him "to an open shame" (Heb. 6:6).
                (h) Would have been "better" off not knowing the truth than "to turn from it" (2:21).
            2. What a dreadfully sad and pitifully desperate condition in which to put one's self!
            3. Who would ever want to knowingly remain in this condition?
            4. Falling away is done by one's personal choice!
                Likewise, returning to the Lord is done by one's personal choice!
        B. The Bible portrays the future of one who has fallen away in a very dreadful way.
            1. The one who has fallen away:
                (a) Is in danger of ultimate "death" (Jas. 5:19-20).
                (b) Has "a certain fearful expectation of judgment" (Heb. 10:27).
                (c) Is subject to a "much worse punishment" than those who "rejected Moses' law" and died "without mercy" (Heb. 10:28-29).
                (d) Is subject to the "vengeance" of God (Heb. 10:30-31).
                (e) Has drawn himself "back to destruction" (Heb. 10:39).
                (f) Is on the road to "perish" in his own destruction (Acts 8:20).
                (g) Will be "cast…into outer darkness" (Matt. 25:14, 26, 30).
                (h) Will be cast "into the furnace of fire," where "there will be wailing and gnashing of teeth" (Matt. 13:40-42).
            2. What a dreadfully fearful and dire future to have secured for one's self!
            3. Who would ever want to knowingly remain on course for that future?
            4. Falling away is done by one's personal choice!
                Likewise, returning to the Lord is done by one's personal choice!
        C. Why would God describe the condition and future of an apostate in such detail and with such reiteration?
            1. God loves everyone, even those who have strayed away (Luke 15:1-32).
            2. God wants all of those who have strayed to repent and return (2 Pet. 3:9).
            3. God wants to rattle the lost out of their indifference and complacency, and into godly sorrow, repentance and salvation (Heb. 10:26-39; 2 Cor. 7:8-10).
IX. **The Bible Lovingly Details How One Who Has Fallen Away Can Return and Be Saved!**
    A. One who has fallen away has wandered from God, rejected God's ways, turned to his own way and is subject to the eternal punishment of God's justice.
        1. God has every right to leave such a person in his self-inflicted, woeful condition.
        2. God could just let His justice run its course and not offer any chance of pardon.
    B. Yet, God's love still longs for His wayward child to return to Him and be saved. What an amazing love!
        1. Even when God's people refuse to obey, harden their necks and rebel against Him, He is still "ready to pardon, gracious and merciful, slow to anger" (Neh. 9:17).
        2. Like the father of the prodigal, God is eager:
            (a) For His lost child to come home (15:20).
            (b) To run to receive His lost child back (15:20).
            (c) To embrace His lost child in His loving arms (15:20).
            (d) To forgive His lost child of all sins and wrongdoings (15:21-24).
            (e) To restore His lost child completely to a right relationship with Him – from "dead" to "alive again," from "lost" to "found" (15:21-24, 32).
        3. What a wonderful and breath-taking portrait of a wonderful, amazing God!

C. As God has conditions (a law of pardon) for alien sinner's to be saved, God has conditions (a second law of pardon) for those who have fallen away to be saved. God wants to pardon His lost children, but there are conditions they must meet (Acts 8:22)!
   1. First, a wayward Christian must REPENT!
      (a) Simon the sorcerer was told, "Repent…of this your wickedness" (Acts 8:22).
      (b) The church in Ephesus was told, "Remember therefore from where you have fallen; repent and do the first works" (Rev. 2:5).
      (c) The churches in Pergamos, Sardis and Laodicea were also told to repent (Rev. 2:16; 3:3, 19).
      (d) Even God's wayward children in the Old Testament were commanded to repent (Ezek. 14:6; 18:30).
      (e) To truly repent:
         (1) One must rekindle his faith that has faded into "unbelief" (Heb. 3:12).
         (2) One must be "pricked" in his heart that he is doing wrong (Acts 2:37-38).
         (3) One must "humble" himself before God (2 Chron. 7:14).
         (4) One must have "a broken and a contrite heart" (Psa. 51:17).
         (5) One must have true "godly sorrow" for his sin (2 Cor. 7:9-10; Rom. 2:4).
         (6) One must renounce his sinfulness and return to God (Luke 15:18-21).
         (7) One must reform his ways and practice righteousness (Rev. 2:5; 2 Cor. 5:11).
         (8) One must "bear fruits worthy of repentance" (Matt. 3:8).
   2. Second, a wayward Christian must PRAY!
      (a) Simon the sorcerer was told, "Repent…and pray God if perhaps the thought of your heart may be forgiven you" (Acts 8:22).
      (b) When one has humbled himself, God calls upon him to "pray and seek My face, and turn from their wicked ways, then I will hear from heaven" (2 Chron. 7:14).
      (c) After David sinned against God with Bathsheba, he cried out to God.
         (1) "Have mercy upon me…Blot out my transgressions. Wash me thoroughly from my iniquity, and cleanse me from my sin…Purge me…Wash me…Make me hear joy and gladness…Hide Your face from my sins…Blot out all my iniquities…Create in me a clean heart…Do not cast me away from Your presence…Restore to me the joy of Your salvation…" (Psa. 51:1-12).
         (2) What an example! What a heart!
      (d) The prodigal son could not be forgiven and restored to his father unless he first:
         (1) "Came to himself" (Luke 15:17).
         (2) Remembered his "father's house" (15:17).
         (3) Went "to" his father (15:18).
         (4) And spoke directly to his father, one-on-one (15:18).
      (e) While prayer cannot save an alien sinner in God's first law of pardon (because the alien sinner is not God's child), prayer will (and does) save in God's second law of pardon for His lost child!
      (f) When we pray, our intercessor and advocate, Jesus, pleads our case to the Father.
         (1) Jesus is our "merciful and faithful High Priest," who longs to "aid" God's children who need their "sins" forgiven (Heb. 2:17-18).
         (2) Jesus is our "great" and "sympathetic" High Priest, who gives God's children access to "the throne of grace, that we may obtain mercy" (Heb. 4:14-16).
         (3) Jesus is our "intercessor," who is "able to save to the uttermost" children of God when they sin (Heb. 7:24-25).

(4) Jesus is our "Advocate with the Father," who is "Himself the propitiation for our sins" (1 John 2:1-2).
3. Third, a wayward Christian must CONFESS!
    (a) The Greek word for "confession" *(homologeo)* is a compound word which means "to speak" *(lego)* the "same" *(homos)*.
        (1) The word literally carries an understanding of "agreement."
        (2) When one confesses sin, he is acknowledging, agreeing and "speaking the same thing" as God. God says it is "sin," therefore, I say it is "sin"!
    (b) First, a wayward Christian must confess his sinfulness to God.
        (1) Simon the sorcerer was told to pray that "the thought of your heart may be forgiven" (Acts 8:22).
        (2) Jesus told us to pray, "Forgive us our sins" (Luke 11:4; Matt. 6:12).
        (3) "If we confess our sins, He is faithful and just to forgive us our sins and to cleanse us from all unrighteousness" (1 John 1:9).
        (4) The prodigal returned to his father and acknowledged, "I have sinned against heaven and in your sight" (Luke 15:21).
        (5) David confessed, "I acknowledge my transgressions…Against You, You only, have I sinned, and done this evil in Your sight" (Psa. 51:3-4).
        (6) Our sins are ultimately against God Himself, therefore, we must acknowledge them before Him and beg His forgiveness! What could be more important than ensuring that one is right with God?
        (7) For sins that are of a personal nature only and not known to others, confession to God is necessary, but it need not be broadcast any further.
    (c) Second, a wayward Christian must confess his sinfulness to his brethren.
        (1) The Bible instructs Christians, "Confess your trespasses to one another, and pray for one another" (Jas. 5:16).
        (2) A sin against others should be confessed to whatever degree the sin is known.
            (i) If it is a private matter, then it should be handled in private, "between you and [that person] alone" (Matt. 18:15; cf. 5:23-24).
            (ii) If a sin is known more widely, then a public confession should be made before the church, "in the sight of all" (cf. Acts 19:18-19)
            (iii) If reproach has been brought against the church by one's actions, then such should be confessed and forgiveness sought.
            (iv) We should remember that sins are not only acts of commission but acts of omission, as well.
        (3) One should make a confession as public as the sin itself.
        (4) It is not necessary for a Christian to confess his private sins to another man. Private sins are between a man and God.
        (5) When one has confessed sin to his brethren:
            (i) The brethren need to pray together (Jas. 5:16; Acts 8:24; 1 John 5:16).
            (ii) The brethren need to forgive the returning brother (2 Cor. 2:6-8; Matt. 6:14-15; Luke 17:3-4; Eph. 4:32; Col. 3:13).
   D. If a Christian cannot fall away and lose his salvation, why provide him a law of pardon?
X. **The Bible Unmistakably Portrays Falling Away As a Danger for Every Christian to Avoid!**
   A. God wants us to make sure that we "take heed lest [we] fall" (1 Cor. 10:12).
      1. It is possible for any Christian to fall away, if he does not take heed to God's Word!
      2. This is a danger for which we must be watchful and to avoid at all costs!

B. God wants us to "be even more diligent to make [our] call and election sure" (2 Pet. 1:10).
   1. We make our call and election sure by:
      (a) Adding the Christian graces to our faith (1:5-7).
      (b) Abounding in the Christian graces (1:8).
      (c) Giving "all" and "more" diligence in our growth unto God (1:5, 10).
   2. When we make our call and election sure, we "will never stumble" (1:10-11).
   3. If we do not grow as instructed by the Lord, we will assuredly stumble and fall!
   4. This is a danger for which we must be watchful and to avoid at all costs!
C. God wants us to make sure our names are in the Book of Life (Luke 10:20).
   1. Why is "the Book of Life" of unparalleled importance?
      (a) The Book of Life will be opened on the day of judgment (Rev. 20:12).
      (b) Only those with their names written in the Book of Life will enter heaven (Rev. 21:27).
      (c) "Anyone not found written in the Book of Life" will be cast into hell (Rev. 20:15).
   2. Who has their names in the Book of Life?
      (a) Those who are saved and in the Lord's church "are registered in heaven" (Heb. 12:23).
      (b) Faithful workers in the Lord's kingdom are "in the Book of Life" (Phil. 4:3).
   3. But, once a name is written by God in the Book of Life, does that mean it is forever there and could never be removed? (Once one is saved, is he always saved?)
      (a) It is possible, once a name is written in the Book of Life, for one to have his name blotted out of the Book (Ex. 32:33; Rev. 3:5). And if a name is no longer in the Book, then he will be "cast into the lake of fire" (Rev. 20:15).
      (b) It is possible for any Christian to be blotted out, if he fails to live by God's laws.
      (c) This is a danger for which we must be watchful and to avoid at all costs!

XI. Conclusion

A. God makes numerous precious promises to His children, such as:
   1. Nothing "shall be able to separate us from the love of God" (Rom. 8:35-39).
   2. They "should not perish but have eternal life" (John 3:14-16).
   3. No one "shall...snatch them out" of Jesus' hand or the Father's hand (John 10:27-29).
B. Christians have been given great assurance by God. Apostasy is not necessary or inevitable.
   1. We have the "hope of eternal life" (Tit. 1:2) given to us by God.
   2. We do not possess it yet (Rom. 8:24-25), but we have God's promise of it (1 John 2:25).
C. But, Scripture plainly teaches that God's promises are conditional.
   1. While it is true that no other person or force may be able to separate God's children from Him or snatch them from His hand...
   2. It is equally true (Scripturally) that a child of God has the God-given ability (and right) to separate Himself from God and to be eternally lost, by his own personal choices.
D. God's Word repeatedly teaches and warns that a child of God can fall away and be lost.
E. Scripture makes it very clear that there are eternal consequences for Christians who turn from the truth and are again entangled in the affairs of the world.
F. If a saved person could not fall away, then thousands of verses would be meaningless.
G. Although a Christian may wander from the truth, God longs for him to return to Him and provides a path of pardon for His lost child to come home.
H. God's Word provides clear instructions for remaining faithful and avoiding apostasy.
I. Only those who are faithful workers in the Lord's kingdom until their death have their names written in the Book of Life (Phil. 4:3; Luke 10:20) and will enter heaven (Rev. 2:10; 21:27)! Those who fall away will not!
J. Let us be diligent to keep the faith and make our call and election sure!

Recommended Resources

Books

Jackson, Wayne. *Eternal Security.* Stockton, CA: Courier Publications, 1993.

Articles

Brownlow, Leroy. "Because It Teaches that a Child of God Can So Sin As to Be Eternally Lost." *Why I Am a Member of the Church of Christ.* Fort Worth: Brownlow Publishing, 1973. 143-153.

DeHoff, George W. "Man Can Forfeit Their Salvation By Turning Away from Christ." *Introducing the Church of Christ.* Ed. Alvin Jennings. Fort Worth: Star Bible, 1981. 158-161.

Duncan, Bobby. "A Child of God Can Fall." *The Spiritual Sword* (Apr. 1999): 18-21.

Fulford, Hugh. "A Child of God Can Fall." *The Spiritual Sword* (Apr. 2005): 22-25.

Gulledge, Dennis. "A Christian Can Fall From Grace." *God's Amazing Grace (Spiritual Sword Lectureship).* Ed. Jim Laws. Memphis, TN: Getwell church of Christ, 1995. 222-240.

Jackson, Wayne. "Apostasy—A Clear and Ever-Present Danger." *ChristianCourier.com*
https://www.christiancourier.com/articles/1505-apostasy-a-clear-and-ever-present-danger

---. "Can a Christian Ever Be Lost?" *ChristianCourier.com*
https://www.christiancourier.com/articles/1131-can-a-christian-ever-be-lost

---. "God's Plan of Salvation for His Lost Children." *ChristianCourier.com*
https://www.christiancourier.com/articles/832-gods-plan-of-salvation-for-his-lost-children

---. "Take Heed Lest You Fall." *ChristianCourier.com*
https://www.christiancourier.com/articles/845-take-heed-lest-you-fall

Merideth, J. Noel. "God's Word and Apostasy." *God's Word—The All-Sufficient Guide (Garfield Heights Lectureship).* Ed. Kenneth, McClain. Indianapolis, IN: Garfield Heights church of Christ, 1988. 108-114.

Wharton, Edward C. "Keeping Saved: Danger of Apostasy." *The Church of Christ.* Nashville: Gospel Advocate, 1997. 181-183.

Periodicals

The Spiritual Sword. April 1977. "A Child of God Can Be Lost Eternally."

Lesson 22: Withdraw of Fellowship

I. **One of the Great Blessings of Being in Christ Is the Fellowship Enjoyed.**
  A. The word "fellowship" comes from the Greek word *koinonia,* which means "partnership, association, joint participation, sharing" (see Thayer 352).
    1. *Koinonia* is translated "fellowship" (Acts 2:42; 1 Cor. 1:9; Gal. 2:9; 1 John 1:3, 6-7); "communion" (1 Cor. 10:16; 2 Cor. 6:14; 13:14); "sharing" (NASB in 1 Cor. 10:16; Heb. 13:16); "participation" (NASB in 2 Cor. 8:4; Phile. 1:5); "distribution" (2 Cor. 9:13); "contribution" (Rom. 15:26).
    2. At its core, the word means "common" or to have "in common."
    3. The same root word is used repeatedly of "partners" (Lk. 5:10; Phil. 1:17; 2 Cor. 8:23).
  B. When one is "baptized into Christ" (Gal. 3:27), he enters into a wonderful fellowship with the Godhead—a vertical fellowship.
    1. Those in Christ enjoy fellowship "with the Father..." (1 John 1:3).
    2. Those in Christ enjoy fellowship with "His Son, Jesus Christ our Lord" (1 Cor. 1:9).
    3. Those in Christ enjoy fellowship with "the Holy Spirit" (2 Cor. 13:14).
    4. The Greek construction in Matthew 28:19 indicates a complete change in relationship and entry into that fellowship with the Godhead when one is "baptized <u>into</u> the name of the Father and of the Son and of the Holy Spirit" (ASV, emp. added).
    5. This fellowship is described in passages that teach:
      (a) Faithful Christians become "partakers of the divine nature" (2 Pet. 1:4).
      (b) Faithful Christians have their "life...hidden with Christ in God" (Col. 3:3).
      (c) Faithful Christians have "Christ" living "in" them (Gal. 2:20).
      (d) Faithful Christians are "children" of God and "joint heirs with Christ" (Rom. 8:16-17).
    6. This vertical fellowship involves a communion, joint participation and sharing with the God of heaven. What a tremendous blessing!
  C. When one is "baptized into one body" (1 Cor. 12:13), he enters into a wonderful fellowship with fellow Christians in the body of Christ—a horizontal fellowship.
    1. The fellowship that one has with Christ upon his baptism into Christ (Gal. 3:27) is a communion that one then shares with fellow Christians who are also in "the one body."
    2. There is an intrinsic unity intended in this "one body."
      (a) Jesus prayed that all believers "might be one" (John 17:20-21).
      (b) The Lord commanded that there "be no divisions" (1 Cor. 1:10).
      (c) In the Lord's church, we "are all one in Christ Jesus" (Gal. 3:28).
      (d) Inherent within God's intended unity is a partnership, fellowship, sharing, etc.
    3. There is a special fellowship intended in this "one body."
      (a) Fellow Christians share a common "fellowship" with each other (1 John 1:3).
      (b) The early church "continued steadfastly in...fellowship" (Acts 2:42).
        (1) The close fellowship of the early church is seen in that:
          (i) They "had all things in common *(koinos)*" (Acts 2:44).
          (ii) They "were of one heart and one soul" (Acts 4:32).
        (2) That same fellowship is to continue in the church today.
      (c) The closeness of this fellowship is emphasized when Christians are described as being "members of one another" (Rom. 12:5), wherein "each member belongs to all the others" (NIV).
        (1) As "members of one another," we need each other (1 Cor. 12:12-27).

                (i) We are mutually dependent on each other, for no member of the Lord's body can exist independently.
                (ii) Each member is responsible for helping the others get to heaven.
            (2) As "members of one another," we are to "love one another" (John 13:34-35).
                (i) This love is to be exhibited in our attitudes toward one another (1 Pet. 3:8; Rom. 12:10; Eph. 4:2) and in our actions toward one another (1 Thess. 5:11; Gal. 5:13; Heb. 3:13; 10:24-25; Jas. 5:16).
                (ii) Agape love in "the body" places the needs of our brethren above our own.
        (d) The camaraderie of this fellowship is emphasized with the prefix "fellow."
            (1) Christians are "fellow workers" (Rom. 16:3; 1 Cor. 3:9; 2 Cor. 1:24; Col. 4:11).
            (2) Christians are "fellow laborers" (1 Thess. 3:2; Phile. 1:1, 24).
            (3) Christians are "fellow servants" (Col. 1:7; 4:7).
            (4) Christians are "fellow soldiers" (Phil. 2:25; Phile. 1:2).
            (5) Christians are "fellow citizens" (Eph. 2:19).
            (6) Christians are "fellow heirs" (Eph. 3:6).
    4. This horizontal fellowship in "the one body" involves a communion, joint participation and sharing with one another. What a tremendous blessing!
        (a) We need each other in order to effectively serve the Lord.
        (b) We need each other in order to make it to heaven.
        (c) We are responsible for helping each other remain faithful and enter eternal life.
  D. This wonderful fellowship is conditional.
    1. First John 1:7 begins with the word "if" – a conditional statement.
        (a) In order to be in fellowship with God (1:3, 6), one must "walk in the light as He is in the light" (1 John 1:7).
        (b) Likewise, in order to "have fellowship with one another," one must "walk in the light."
    2. "If" that condition of walking in the light ceases, then the fellowship also ceases.
        (a) Christians only enjoy fellowship with Christ if they are walking in the light.
        (b) Christian are only to extend and enjoy fellowship with fellow Christians who likewise walk in the light.
    3. One cannot be in fellowship horizontally with those who are not in fellowship with God vertically.
    4. This point is critically important to understand in the study of withdrawing fellowship.

II. There Are Times When a Christian Must Withdraw His Fellowship from Some.
  A. Because fellowship is such a special gift bestowed by God, it must also be limited by the standards that He imposes.
  B. The fellowship of a Christian is not to be extended to the sinful ways of the world.
    1. Christians are to "have no fellowship with the unfruitful works of darkness" (Eph. 5:11).
    2. Christians are reminded that "righteousness" is to have no "fellowship...with lawlessness" and "light" is to have no "communion...with darkness" (2 Cor. 6:14).
    3. Christians readily understand that our fellowship is limited when it comes to the world, but could our fellowship also be limited when it comes to our brethren?
  C. The fellowship of a Christian is not to be extended to brethren living in sin.
    1. The fellowship that Christians enjoy with each other is precious indeed.
    2. But, that fellowship with our brethren can be severed by sin.
        (a) Sin is divisive.
        (b) Sin separates man from God (Isa. 59:1-2).
        (c) Sin also separates brethren from brethren.

3. Scripture specifically teaches, "Do not...share *(koinoneo)* in other people's sins" (1 Tim. 5:22). This would include our own brethren.
4. If a brother's sinful actions take him outside "the light" (1 John 1:7), God does not permit us to follow him outside "the light" and continue to fellowship with him in darkness (2 Cor. 6:14).
    (a) By his own actions, this wayward Christian has put his fellow Christians in a position to sever ties with him. Such is the demand of God's fellowship.
    (b) In fact, if a faithful Christian, who is still walking "in the light," shows approval for and extends fellowship to a wayward brother who is no longer walking " in the light," Scripture teaches that he "shares *(koinoneo)* in his evil deeds" (2 John 10-11).
    (c) That kind of fellowship is contrary to and runs completely against the precious fellowship that is to be enjoyed with and extended to those in the body of Christ.

D. Therefore, it must be noted that God commands Christians to withdraw from brethren who choose to walk outside "the light." This is not optional.
    1. Note these imperatives (commands of God, which will be studied in more detail):
        (a) "Avoid" or "turn away from" (Rom. 16:17, suggesting continuous action).
        (b) "Put away" or "remove" (1 Cor. 5:13, with a sense of urgency).
        (c) "Purge" or "clean out" or "get rid of" (1 Cor. 5:7, with a sense of urgency).
        (d) "Note" or "take special note" (2 Thess. 3:14, suggesting continuous action).
        (e) "Reject" or "have nothing more to do with" (Tit. 3:10, suggesting continuous action).
        (f) "Let him be to you..." (Matt. 18:17, suggesting continuous action).
        (g) "Admonish" or "warn" (2 Thess. 3:15, suggesting continuous action).
    2. There are other words used that are not imperatives (which will be studied in this lesson), but these verbs are noted here to emphasize that withdraw of fellowship is not a suggestion of God but rather a command.
        (a) These verb tenses were specifically chosen by God to command action.
        (b) In fact, the word "command" is found four times in Paul's discussion of withdraw of fellowship 2 Thessalonians 3.

E. The subject of withdrawing fellowship is certainly a difficult subject to study.
    1. Some people misunderstand the nature of the action that is to be taken.
    2. Some people misunderstand the purpose of the action that is to be taken.
    3. Some people view the action as heartless, judgmental and old-fashioned.
    4. Some people have mistakenly likened withdraw of fellowship to the Catholic practice of "excommunication," which it is not.
    5. Some people cannot believe or accept that God calls upon His people to withdraw from their own brethren.
    6. Some congregations of the Lord's church have never (or very rarely) practiced this method of church discipline, and the methodology has certainly varied within the small number of congregations that do practice it.
    7. Some Christians have never heard any Biblical teaching on this subject and have never seen it put into practice.
    8. This is a very sensitive matter, as it deals with the lifestyle choices of fellow Christians and the church's response to such.
    9. Therefore, any study of this subject must be handled carefully and yet Scripturally.

F. It is important to understand at this point in the study that withdrawing fellowship is not a subject that originated in the mind or heart of any man.
    1. Withdrawing fellowship is a command of God.

2. Therefore, while it may not be easy or popular, it must be studied and followed as the church would any other authorized command of God in the New Testament.

III. The New Testament Teaches Us "What" Withdraw of Fellowship Is.
A. Fellowship with Christ and with His church is a precious blessing for Christians to enjoy.
 1. However, when one chooses to step outside of that precious fellowship, Christians are instructed to discontinue extending and having fellowship with him.
 2. But, what does that mean? What is involved in that action?
 3. Specifically "who" is to be withdrawn from, and "why" and "how" withdraw is to be practiced will be studied in subsequent points. But, first, what exactly does it mean?
B. Christians are instructed to "withdraw from" (2 Thess. 3:6).
 1. The Greek word *stello* is found only here and in 2 Corinthians 8:20.
    (a) The word means "to remove oneself" and more specifically, "to abstain from familiar contact with one" (Thayer 587).
    (b) Vine indicates that it signifies "to shrink from a person or thing" (680).
 2. The word is translated "keep away from" in the NASB and ESV.
 3. The word is translated "avoiding" (NKJV) in 2 Corinthians 8:20.
 4. There are certain brethren that God instructs Christians to steadfastly withdraw from, abstain from and avoid.
C. Christians are instructed to "put away from" or have "taken away from" (1 Cor. 5:2, 13).
 1. The Greek word *airo* means "to bear away; carry off; to remove" (Thayer 16).
 2. In 1 Corinthians 5, the word is combined with the preposition *ek*, "out of."
 3. The word is translated "removed from" in the NASB and ESV in 5:2.
 4. The word is translated "remove" (NASB) and "purge" (ESV) in 5:13.
 5. There are certain brethren that God instructs Christians (with a sense of urgency) to put away from ("out of") themselves and remove from ("out of") themselves.
D. Christians are instructed to "avoid" (Rom. 16:17).
 1. The Greek word *ekklino* means "to turn away from, keep aloof from; to shun" (Thayer 196).
    (a) The Greek word is a compound word combining *klino* ("to incline, bow") and *ek* ("from, away, out").
    (b) Literally, the word means, "incline oneself away from" or "to bend out of."
 2. The word is translated "turn away from" in the NASB (also in 1 Peter 3:11).
 3. The word is translated "turn aside" in Romans 3:12.
 4. There are certain brethren from which God instructs Christians to steadfastly incline oneself away from, turn away and avoid.
E. Christians are instructed to "reject" (Tit. 3:10-11).
 1. The Greek word *paraiteomai* means "to avert; to shun, avoid; to refuse, reject" (Thayer 482). *Robertson's Word Pictures* includes, "to beg off from."
 2. The word is translated "refuse" (ASV) and "have nothing more to do with" (ESV).
 3. The word is translated "have nothing to do with" (NASB, ESV) in 1 Timothy 4:7.
 4. There are certain brethren with whom God instructs Christians to steadfastly have nothing to do, to avoid and refuse fellowship.
F. Christians are instructed to "purge out the old leaven" (1 Cor. 5:7).
 1. The Greek word *ekkathairo* means "to cleanse out, clean thoroughly, purge out," emphasizing that "something is made clean" by its "removal" (Thayer 195).
 2. The word is translated "cleanses" in 2 Timothy 2:21 (its only other use in the N.T.).
 3. The word is translated "clean out" (NASB) and "cleanse out" (ESV) in 1 Cor. 5:7.

4. Note that with the prefix *ek*, the word means more than just "cleanse" or "purge," but it means to "cleanse *out from*" and to "purge *out from*."
5. This action is likened to the Jewish practice in which they would remove all leaven from their house in the celebration of Passover (Ex. 12:8-19).
6. There are certain brethren that God instructs Christians (with a sense of urgency) to purge out, cleanse out and remove from their midst that they might be clean.

G. Christians are instructed "not to keep company with" (1 Cor. 5:11).
   1. The Greek word *sunanamignumi* means "to mix up together, to keep company with" (Thayer 601), to have association with, "to mingle" (Vine 116).
      (a) The Greek word is a compound word combining *mignumi* ("mingle, mix") and *ana* ("up," used for intensity) and *sun* ("with, together").
      (b) Literally, the word means, "mingle up together with."
   2. The word is translated "not to associate with" in the NASB and ESV.
   3. The word is translated "have nothing to do with him" (ESV) in 2 Thessalonians 3:14.
   4. There are certain brethren with whom God instructs Christians to steadfastly have no association or familiar company. God even specifies, "Not even to eat with such a person" (5:11). Social contact of a familiar nature is forbidden.

H. Christians are instructed to "note that person" (2 Thess. 3:14).
   1. The Greek word *semeioo* means "to mark, note, distinguish by marking" (Thayer 574). *Robertson's Word Pictures* says, "Put a tag on that man."
   2. The word is translated "take note of" (ESV) and "take special note of" (NASB).
   3. This instruction is not merely to Christians individually but to the church collectively. There was some action that was to be taken by the church to denote such a one.
   4. There are certain brethren that God instructs Christians (with a sense of urgency) to distinguish from themselves by taking special note of them in the church.

I. Christians are instructed to "keep an eye on" (Rom. 16:17).
   1. The Greek word *skopeo* means "to look at, behold, watch, contemplate" (Vine 394).
      (a) *Robertson's Word Pictures* notes, "Keep an eye on so as to avoid."
      (b) The word is translated "note" (NKJV), "mark" (ASV), "keep your eye on" (NASB) and "watch out for" (ESV).
   2. There are certain brethren of which God wants the church to be observant and to be carefully mindful of their negative influence upon the Lord's church.

J. Christians are instructed to "deliver such a one to Satan" (1 Cor. 5:5).
   1. The Greek word *paradidomi* means "to give over; to give over into one's power or use; to deliver to one to keep" (Thayer 481).
   2. The word is translated "gave them up" or "gave them over" in Romans 1:24, 26, 28.
      (a) In this context, there were individuals who were determined to live outside the will of God, so God gave them over to it. He delivered them over to the lifestyle that they were so determined to have.
      (b) God did not arbitrarily choose individuals to give over to "impurity," "vile passions" and "a depraved mind." They were already there in their hearts.
      (c) The word is used in the same way in 1 Corinthians 5:5.
   3. The same expression is found in 1 Timothy 1:20—"Hymenaeus and Alexander, whom I delivered to Satan that they may learn not to blaspheme."
   4. There are certain brethren that God instructs Christians to give over to the desires of their heart (i.e., give them over to do the will of Satan, for that is where their heart is).
      (a) This may sound so foreign and harsh to the Christian walk, but the context explains.

                (b) In the context, Christians are admonished to not keep company with such a one.
                (c) In the context, the purpose of such an action is explained. (See V, B-C).
                (d) The church is simply delivering the erring brother over to the lifestyle (albeit one of sin and of the devil) that the brother has chosen for himself.
        K. Christians are instructed to "let him be to you like a heathen and a tax collector" (Mt. 18:17).
            1. There are at least two concepts involved in this action:
                (a) These individuals are to be viewed as outsiders. Heathens and tax collectors were not welcome "inside" the close fellowship of the Jews.
                (b) These individuals are to be removed and cut off from social interaction. The Jews had nothing to do with the heathen and tax collectors.
            2. There are certain brethren that God instructs Christians to steadfastly put outside their number and avoid familiar social interaction.
                (a) The wording of this instruction may sound overly harsh for a Christian.
                (b) But, understand it in the larger context of the Bible's instructions regarding withdrawing fellowship.
                (c) And, understand it in the context of the overall purpose of the action intended by a loving God. (See V, B-C).
        L. Review closely for a moment the specificity and the abundance on this subject.
            1. With a variety of words (which all point to the same action), God gives specific instructions to His people regarding certain Christians.
                (a) They are to withdraw from, keep away from, avoid, put away from themselves, purge out, remove, turn aside from, reject, shun, have nothing to do with, keep no company with, note, distinguish from the rest, give over to Satan and treat like an outsider.
                (b) These are strong words, and yet they are clearly understandable and specific.
            2. In addition to the specificity, consider the abundance of Biblical testimony.
                (a) God gives commands to His children on this matter over and over again.
                (b) This is not a matter than can be overlooked or missed in any way.
                (c) The church cannot claim to not have sufficient evidence or instruction.
            3. From the specificity and the abundance of Biblical instruction, it is evident that:
                (a) Withdrawing of fellowship is not a manmade ordinance.
                (b) Withdrawing of fellowship is not an optional policy for elders to consider.
                (c) Withdrawing of fellowship is a command and clear expectation from God Himself.
IV. **The New Testament Teaches Us "From Whom" Fellowship Is to Be Withdrawn.**
    A. The subject of withdraw of fellowship can be a very difficult and sensitive matter, in addition to being very personal.
    B. Rather than being left to our own devices, Scripture identifies the sort of person from whom fellowship is to be withdrawn.
    C. First of all, it must be noted that the action of withdraw is taken against a Christian.
        1. Withdraw of fellowship is not exercised against a non-Christian, for they are not "in fellowship" with Christ (Gal. 3:26-27) or His body (1 Cor. 12:13). (See pages 260-261.)
        2. Paul specified, "I certainly did not mean...people of this world...since then you would need to go out of the world. But now I have written to you not to keep company with anyone named a brother..." (1 Cor. 5:9-11).
        3. Twice in 2 Thessalonian 3, Paul specifies that withdraw of fellowship is to be practiced against one who is a "brother" (3:6, 15).

4. Fellowship cannot be withdrawn from someone with whom a spiritual union and partnership has never been formed.
D. The church is to withdraw fellowship from brethren who "walk disorderly" (2 Thess. 3:6).
  1. Paul wrote, "But we command you, brethren, in the name of our Lord Jesus Christ, that you withdraw from every brother who walks disorderly and not according to the tradition which he received from us" (3:6; cf. 3:11).
  2. Note the all-inclusiveness of those for whom we must be concerned: "every brother" (3:6) and "anyone" (3:14).
  3. The Greek word for "disorderly" *(ataktos)* was a military term that denoted a soldier who was "not keeping rank, insubordinate" (Vine 174) or "out of step" because he was "deviating from the prescribed order or rule" (Thayer 83).
    (a) Vine notes that the same Greek word "is used in 1 Thess. 5:14, describing certain church members who manifested an insubordinate spirit, whether by excitability or officiousness or idleness" (174).
  4. The "prescribed order or rule" from which these Christians have deviated is specified in this verse—"the tradition which he received from us."
    (a) This was not a man-made tradition from which they had deviated.
    (b) This is the inspired and authoritative tradition, instruction and doctrine which they "were taught" according to 2 Thessalonians 2:15.
    (c) When a Christian deliberately chooses to habitually walk (present tense) contrary to the teachings of Scripture, he is not to be kept in fellowship with the church.
  5. This is further emphasized in 3:14, "If anyone does not obey our word in this epistle."
    (a) When a Christian deliberately chooses to habitually disobey (present tense) the word of God delivered in Scripture, he is not to be kept in fellowship with the church.
  6. To "walk disorderly" is a broad term that is used to encompass "every" (3:6) and "any" (3:14) brother who does not keep rank with the prescribed order of God's Word, but instead marches down a path that is contrary to Biblical truth.
E. The church is to withdraw fellowship from brethren who become impenitently enslaved to a life of habitual sin (1 Cor. 5:9-11).
  1. "But now I have written to you not to keep company with anyone named a brother, who is sexually immoral, or covetous, or an idolater, or a reviler, or a drunkard, or an extortioner—not even to eat with such a person" (5:11).
    (a) This passage is not addressing a one-time mistake made by a Christian.
    (b) Rather, this passage is addressing habitual sin practiced by a brother in Christ.
  2. "Sexually immoral" is a general term that comes from the Greek word *porneia*, which means "illicit sexual intercourse."
    (a) This has application to both the married and the unmarried.
    (b) Sexual immorality *(porneia)* includes fornication, adultery, homosexuality, etc.
  3. "Covetous" is from the Greek word *pleonektes*, which means "one eager to have more, especially what belongs to others" (Thayer 516).
    (a) This person is greedy for money, and especially of having more and more.
    (b) Vine notes that this Greek word is "always in a bad sense" (136).
  4. "Idolater" is from the Greek word *eidololatres*, meaning "a worshipper of false gods."
    (a) Of course, this is not limited to idols of stone, wood or metal.
    (b) Even desire for money and material possessions can become a god (Col. 3:5).
  5. "Reviler" is from the Greek word *loidoros*, which involves "abusive" language.

(a) It is sometimes translated by the word "railing," denoting one who reviles or scolds with harsh, insulting, abusive language.
(b) While some sins are merely personal, this involves the treatment of others.
6. "Drunkard" is from the Greek word *methusos*, indicating one who has "become intoxicated."
   (a) Christians will "abstain from fleshly lusts which war against the soul" (1 Pet. 2:11), which includes alcoholic beverages.
   (b) Christians are commanded, "Do not get drunk" (Eph. 5:18)—"an inceptive verb, marking the process or the state" of becoming intoxicated (Vine 186).
7. "Extortioner" is from the Greek word *harpax*, which is defined as "rapacious, ravenous" in an adjective form and "a robber" in substantive form (Thayer 75).
   (a) The word is translated "swindler" in the NASB and ESV.
   (b) It denotes one who is excessively grasping or covetous, and selfishly takes the goods of another by force or by fraud.
8. Of course, this list of habitual sins is not an exhaustive list of those from whom the church is to withdraw fellowship (as is seen in IV, D and IV, F, G, H, I).
   (a) It is apparent that the Lord was not attempting to list every possible immorality against which the church must take action. This list does not mention thieves or murderers, but certainly those would be included.
   (b) Nevertheless, God wants His church to know how seriously affected His church can be by one who becomes impenitently enslaved to a life of sin.
   (c) That habitual sin must not be permitted to settle itself down in the church, like a piece of leaven would settle itself down into the lump of dough (1 Cor. 5:6-7).
   (d) The Lord's church is too precious and too pure to allow an enslavement to sin to permeate and ravage it.

F. The church is to withdraw fellowship from an impenitent brother, who has sinned against a fellow brother in Christ and refuses to repent (Matt. 18:15-17).
   1. Jesus is the one who introduced and taught about withdrawing fellowship, even during His earthly ministry.
   2. Jesus addressed the matter of when a "brother sins against" another brother (18:15).
   3. If private rebuke does not resolve the matter and bring about repentance, then the matter is to be taken to the church.
   4. If the church as a whole cannot bring about repentance, the brother is to be regarded "like a heathen and a tax collector" (18:17).
   5. The church (consisting of those striving to faithfully follow the Lord) is not to keep company with (i.e., is to withdraw itself from) brethren who are impenitent and have no intention of faithfully following the Lord.

G. The church is to withdraw fellowship from one who is factious or divisive (Rom. 16:17-18; Tit. 3:10-11).
   1. In Romans 16, the church is instructed to "note those who cause divisions and offenses, contrary to the doctrine."
   2. In Titus 3, the church is instructed to "reject a divisive man after the first and second admonition."
   3. Scripture is very clear that we are to keep an eye on and avoid those brethren who:
      (a) Create divisions or possess a divisive spirit.
      (b) Cause brethren to stumble.
      (c) Teach contrary to sound doctrine.

4. Such individuals are not serving the good of the church but their own desires (Rom. 16:18; cf. Phil. 3:18-19).
5. Among the seven things listed in Proverbs 6 that are an abomination to Lord is "one who sows discord among brethren" (6:16-19).
6. These individuals stand "self-condemned" (Tit. 3:11) and cannot be accepted in the Lord's church.

H. The church is to withdraw fellowship from those who teach false doctrine.
1. The New Testament places a strong emphasis on remaining true to the doctrine of Christ and watching for those who teach against or oppose sound doctrine.
2. In Acts 20:28-30, elders of the Lord's church were warned, "Also from among yourselves men will rise up, speaking perverse things, to draw away the disciples after themselves."
   (a) What should the church do with brethren who lead other brethren astray?
3. In Romans 16:17, the church is to "avoid" those who "cause divisions and create obstacles contrary to the doctrine" (ESV).
4. The book of First Timothy begins and ends with a strict call for doctrinal purity.
   (a) Timothy was to "charge some that they teach no other doctrine" (1 Tim. 1:3).
   (b) And, "If anyone teaches otherwise and does not consent to wholesome words, even the words of our Lord Jesus Christ, and to the doctrine which accords with godliness," the instruction was clear, "From such withdraw yourself" (6:3-5).
   (c) Thus, in this context, Paul identifies certain ones who had taught false doctrines, caused trouble in the church, and against whom the church had taken action.
      (1) Hymenaeus and Alexander had "suffered shipwreck" concerning "the faith," and they were "delivered to Satan that they may learn not to blaspheme" (1 Tim. 1:19-20).
      (2) Hymenaeus and Philetus "strayed concerning the truth, saying that the resurrection is already past; and they overthrow the faith of some" (2 Tim. 2:16-18).
   (d) Such false teaching could not be tolerated in the body of Christ—then or now.
5. The apostle John makes it very clear that Christians are to give no encouragement or show any level of approval to those who teach false doctrine.
   (a) Christians are alerted that anyone who "goes too far" (NASB) and "does not abide in the doctrine of Christ does not have God" (2 John 9). That is quite a statement!
   (b) Christians are warned, "If anyone comes to you and does not bring this doctrine, do not receive him into your house nor greet him" (2 John 10).
      (1) We are not to show any acceptance or approval (by our words, our actions or even our presence) for that which is contrary to sound doctrine.
   (c) Christians are cautioned that if any child of God shows acceptance or approval to one who is advocating false doctrine, then he "shares in" (NKJV), "participates in" (NASB), "takes part in" (ESV) "his evil deeds" (2 John 11).
6. It is dangerous to the church and to the individual Christian to have any fellowship with or indicate any endorsement for teachings that are contrary to sound doctrine.

I. The church is to withdraw fellowship from those who willfully forsake the assembly.
1. This particular point may seem overly specific, but it must be addressed.
2. Is there any Scriptural authority or precedent for withdrawing from a fellow Christian who habitually and willfully absents himself from the assemblies of the church?

3. Scripture clearly instructs Christians that they are responsible for "not forsaking the assembling of ourselves together, as is the manner of some, but exhorting one another, and so much the more as you see the Day approaching" (Heb. 10:25).
4. For a child of God who "knows" that God has called upon him to do "the right thing" (which would include assembling with the church) and he "does not do it" (present tense, habitually), Scripture plainly says, "it is" (present tense, ongoing) "sin" (Jas. 4:17).
5. To habitually and willfully sin by forsaking the assembly of the church is to walk "disorderly and not according to the tradition" delivered by the Lord (2 Thess. 3:6).
6. Those who walk disorderly and out of step with the Divine tradition are to have fellowship withdrawn from them (2 Thess. 3:6), and such would include those who "manifest an insubordinate attitude toward the Lord, toward [H]is word, and toward the shepherds who watch for their souls (Heb. 13:17)" (W. Winkler 84).
7. Forsaking the assembly of the church is not some "minor issue" or "little sin" that can be overlooked. It is one of the most public sins that a Christian can commit.

J. Scripture is specific and clear regarding those from whom fellowship is to be withdrawn.
1. While Scripture does not give an exhaustive list of every sin and every situation in which church discipline is to be exercised, it does give ample guidance in this matter.
2. While some have tried to limit withdraw only to those engaged in gross immorality or those deliberately not working, Scripture makes application to multiple categories of the unfaithful:
(a) Those brethren who walk disorderly.
(b) Those brethren who are impenitently enslaved to habitual sin.
(c) Those brethren who are impenitent in their sin against a fellow Christian.
(d) Those brethren who are factious or divisive.
(e) Those brethren who teach or advocate false doctrine.
3. When any brother impenitently walks out of step with God's instructions and in defiance to His Word, God commands that he must be put away from the church.

V. The New Testament Teaches Us "Why" Fellowship Is to Be Withdrawn.
A. This point is critically important!
1. A study of withdrawing fellowship without understanding the Scriptural purpose behind it is incomplete and subject to total misunderstanding and misapplication.
2. Because many have not properly understood the Scriptural purpose of withdraw, many have mischaracterized the practice as:
(a) Being "harsh," "unloving," "cruel and unusual," "hateful," etc.
(b) "Kicking someone out of the church" to "get rid of them" with an attitude of "good riddance!"
(c) Equivalent to the Catholic tradition of "excommunication" (which it is not).
3. If withdraw of fellowship is not properly practiced, perhaps it could be viewed in that way, but such is not the Scriptural view of this important matter.
4. We must see withdraw of fellowship through the eyes of God!
Why would God ever command us to put someone away from the church?

B. The New Testament commands withdraw because God wants the wayward to be saved!
1. God's design for withdraw of fellowship is to "save" a wayward brother.
(a) "...Deliver such a one to Satan...that his spirit may be saved in the day of the Lord Jesus" (1 Cor. 5:5).
(b) This is an obvious indication from God that such a person (yes, even a brother) is not in a saved condition.

(1) He is living like the world (1 Cor. 5:1), following after Satan (5:5), walking disorderly (2 Thess. 3:6) and not obeying the Word of God (2 Thess. 3:14).
(2) The purpose of withdrawing fellowship from him is to "save" him.
- (c) Consider the result of turning an erring brother back, as stated in James 5:19-20, "Brethren, if anyone among you wanders from the truth, and someone turns him back, let him know that he who turns a sinner from the error of his way will <u>save</u> a soul from death and cover a multitude of sins."
- (d) "Church discipline is redemptive in design, not retaliatory or vindictive" (Winkler 81).
2. God's design for withdraw of fellowship is "the destruction of the flesh" of the wayward brother.
    - (a) "...Deliver such a one to Satan for the destruction of the flesh" (1 Cor. 5:5).
    - (b) The New Testament addresses emphatically the dangers of "the flesh" (cf. Gal. 5:19-21) and the Christian's responsibility to:
        (1) "Not walk according to the flesh" (Rom. 8:1, 4).
        (2) "[Put] off the body of the sins of the flesh" (Col. 2:11).
        (3) "Make no provision for the flesh, to fulfill its lusts" (Rom. 13:14).
        (4) "[Crucify] the flesh with its passions and desires" (Gal. 5:24).
        (5) "Abstain from fleshly lusts which war against the soul" (1 Pet. 2:11).
    - (c) Christians are warned, "If you live according to the flesh you will die" (Rom. 8:13).
    - (d) Thus, the purpose of withdrawing fellowship from the wayward brother is to prompt him to "the destruction of the flesh" by making changes in his life.
        (1) He must see the destructive path of walking in the flesh.
        (2) He must make the choice to "destroy" that influence and direction in his life.
3. God's design for withdraw of fellowship is to "gain" a wayward brother.
    - (a) "If your brother sins against you, go and tell him his fault between you and him alone. If he hears you, you have gained your brother" (Matt. 18:15).
    - (b) The goal of the first step in church discipline, as outlined by Jesus, is the goal of the entire process—to gain a brother back!
    - (c) Church discipline is not designed to "get rid of" a brother!
    - (d) Church discipline is designed to "win" a brother back!
4. God's design for withdraw of fellowship is to produce "shame" in a wayward brother.
    - (a) "And if anyone does not obey our word in this epistle, note that person and do not keep company with him, that he may be ashamed" (2 Thess. 3:14).
    - (b) The Greek word for "ashamed" *(entrepo)* literally means "to turn in."
    - (c) Vine notes that it means "to turn one upon himself and so produce a feeling of 'shame,' a wholesome 'shame' which involves a change of conduct" (39).
    - (d) Before one will turn from his sinful ways and be restored, he must feel ashamed for where he is spiritually. That is the purpose behind withdrawing fellowship.
5. God's design for withdraw of fellowship is to produce "sorrow" in a wayward brother.
    - (a) The church in Corinth was instructed to withdraw fellowship from a man who had taken "his father's wife" (1 Cor. 5:1).
    - (b) When the church took this action against this brother, it created "sorrow," for the church was instructed to "forgive and comfort" the man, "lest perhaps such a one be swallowed up with too much sorrow" (2 Cor. 2:7).
    - (c) Later in the same epistle, Paul wrote that "godly sorrow produces repentance leading to salvation" (2 Cor. 7:10).

(d) Before one will turn from his sinful ways and be restored, he must feel sorrow for where he is spiritually. That is the purpose behind withdrawing fellowship.
6. Put all of this together and the conclusion is evident: God commands His church to withdraw fellowship because He wants the wayward to be saved! This is critical!
C. The New Testament commands withdraw because God wants the church to be saved.
1. God is equally interested in the salvation of the souls of each of His children.
    (a) He wants the soul of His wayward child to be saved. (V, B)
    (b) He also wants the souls of His faithful children to remain saved and kept safe.
    (c) Withdraw of fellowship aims to accomplish both purposes of God.
2. The church is the beautiful bride of Christ and must be protected from sin.
    (a) Withdraw of fellowship is designed by God to protect and preserve His church.
3. God's design for withdraw of fellowship is to protect His church from the influence of sin.
    (a) The church in Corinth allowed unrepentant sin to remain in its midst (1 Cor. 5:1-2).
        (1) This sin was "among" them (5:1).
        (2) The one committing this sin was not "taken away from among" them (5:2).
    (b) The presence and acceptance of unrepentant sin "among" the church will adversely impact the members of that congregation.
    (c) Paul said, "Do you not know that a little leaven leavens the whole lump?" (5:6).
        (1) Even if leaven did not intend to exert its influence on the rest of the lump, it would. And, even if the rest of the lump did not want the influence of the leaven, it would still be influenced. Why? That's the nature of leaven!
        (2) Even if an unrepentant sinner did not intend to exert his influence on the rest of the congregation, he would. And, even if the rest of the congregation did not want to be influenced by the unrepentant brother, it would still be influenced. Why? That's the nature of sin.
        (3) It only takes a little tolerance of sin to leaven its way through the whole church, which is likely why God used the word "little." His focus was on any unrepentant sin (big or "little") that could adversely affect His church.
    (d) The church of our Lord is likened to a "body" (Col. 1:18).
        (1) When an illness like cancer is left unchecked within a human body, it begins to spread and take over a body until death ensues. That's the nature of cancer.
            (i) That is why the presence of cancer must be removed from a body.
            (ii) The cancer is removed to save the body.
        (2) When sin is left unchecked within the church body, it begins to spread and become more accepted and prevalent within the body until spiritual death ensues (cf. Rev. 2:5, 16; 3:3, 15-19). That's the nature of sin.
            (i) That is why the presence of sin must be removed from the body of Christ.
            (ii) The unrepentant sinner is removed to save the body.
    (e) One member of a church turning from Christ could lead to the whole congregation turning from Christ, if the church does not remove that influence.
        (1) To argue against that is to argue against God and the principle of the leaven.
        (2) A congregation that tolerates sin will not escape (cf. Rev. 2:14-15, 20).
4. God's design for withdraw of fellowship is to keep His church pure.
    (a) Like a bride, the church is to remain clean and pure in the eyes of Christ.
    (b) Christ "loved the church and gave Himself for her, that He might sanctify and cleanse her with the washing of water by the word" (Eph. 5:25-26).
        (1) In baptism, one is sanctified and cleansed by Christ (see also 1 Cor. 6:11).

- (2) Christ purifies His church in order that she might remain pure. Paul goes on to explain His purpose: "...that He might present her to Himself a glorious church, not having spot or wrinkle or any such thing, but that she should be holy and without blemish" (Eph. 5:27).
- (c) Thus, Paul instructed the church in Corinth, "Purge out the old leaven, that you may be a new lump, since you truly are unleavened" (1 Cor. 5:7).
  - (1) While withdraw of fellowship is a painful process (like going through surgery), it is necessary in order to keep the church herself pure.
  - (2) Perhaps this was also in Paul's mind when he penned these words in his second letter, "In everything ye approved yourselves to be pure in the matter" (2 Cor. 7:11, ASV). She could have become impure herself.
- (d) One can become impure due to sin and due to false teaching.
  - (1) Thus, Paul warned of those "who cause divisions and offenses, contrary to the doctrine which you learned," for "by smooth words and flattering speech [they] deceive the hearts of the simple" (Rom. 16:17-18).
  - (2) Again, Paul warned that the "message" of false teachers "will spread like cancer" (or "gangrene," NASB) and "overthrow the faith of some" (2 Tim. 2:17-18).
  - (3) Thus, they must be "delivered to Satan that they may learn not to blaspheme" (1 Tim. 1:19-20). This is done with the intent (1) to save the false teachers (see V, B) and (2) to save the church!
5. God's design for withdraw of fellowship is to urge Christians to remain faithful.
   - (a) When a faithful Christian observes the influence of sin in the church and a faithful congregation's response to that sin (through withdraw of fellowship):
     - (1) It should prompt that Christian to examine himself (cf. 2 Cor. 13:5).
     - (2) It should prompt that Christian to avoid sin in his own life (cf. 1 John 2:1).
     - (3) It should prompt that Christian to strive for faithfulness himself (cf. Rev. 2:10).
   - (b) When a congregation properly addresses sin, "the rest also may fear" (1 Tim. 5:20).
6. Put all of this together and the conclusion is evident: God commands His church to withdraw fellowship because He wants His church to be saved! This is critical!

D. The New Testament commands withdraw because God wants the world to be saved.
1. In all that the church does, the Lord must be exalted and magnified!
   - (a) As "the light of the world," we are to help outsiders "glorify" God (Matt. 5:14-16).
   - (b) As "a holy nation," we are to help outsiders "glorify God" (1 Pet. 2:9-12).
   - (c) The church must never allow sin to so infiltrate and influence it that it fails to glorify God itself and fails to lead outsiders to do the same.
2. The image of the Lord's church to outsiders is critical in the conversion effort.
   - (a) The gospel of Christ demands repentance and transformation of life (Acts 17:30).
   - (b) However, if those "in the church" are living just like those "out of the church" (cf. 1 Cor. 5:1), then how will a non-Christian be convicted of sin and turn from it?
3. God's design for withdraw of fellowship is to preserve the image of the church in the eyes of the world.
   - (a) Harboring sin in a congregation makes the church look like the world (cf. Rom. 12:2).
   - (b) There is no proper incentive or appeal for one to leave the world in order to enter the Lord's church, if the church is no different than the world (cf. 2 Cor. 6:14-7:1).
   - (c) If withdraw of fellowship is properly exercised:
     - (1) It shows the world that sin is a serious matter.
     - (2) It shows the world that the church is serious about dealing with sin.

                (3) It shows the world that the church believes and practices the Bible.
                (4) It shows the world that the church is a people of integrity, who practice what they preach.
                (5) It shows the world that there is a God-given path for making it to heaven.
            (d) When the sin of Ananias and Sapphira was dealt with in the early church and discipline was enacted (by God Himself):
                (1) It did not cause the church to lose its influence and die (as many claim today).
                (2) It actually caused "great fear [to come] upon all the church and upon all who heard these things" (Acts 5:11).
                (3) And in the days that immediately followed, "believers were increasingly added to the Lord, multitudes of both men and women" (Acts 5:14).
        4. Put all of this together and the conclusion is evident: God commands His church to withdraw fellowship because He wants the world to be saved! This is critical!
    E. Many have misunderstood withdraw of fellowship and its purpose.
        1. Its purpose is not vindictive or malicious.
        2. Its purpose is not arrogant or conceited.
        3. Its purpose is based upon a love for souls!
        4. Its purpose, when Scripturally practiced, is designed to save:
            (a) To save the wayward Christian!
            (b) To save the church!
            (c) To save the world!

VI. The New Testament Teaches Us "How" Fellowship Is to Be Withdrawn.
   A. Scripture teaches that withdrawing is to be done by the authority of Christ.
      1. The practice of withdrawing fellowship is not based on any man-made authority.
         (a) It was not the Corinthian church's idea to deliver their brother unto Satan.
             (1) Paul wrote, "It is actually reported that there is sexual immorality among you...And you are puffed up, and [you] have not rather mourned, that he who has done this deed might be taken away from among you...Your glorying is not good" (1 Cor. 5:1-2, 6).
             (2) If the church in Corinth had it their way, they would not done nothing, because they were already doing nothing!
         (b) Withdrawing fellowship is not something man devised!
      2. The practice of withdrawing fellowship is based on authority directly from heaven!
         (a) Many times people wonder, "Who gave the church the right to do this?"
         (b) God clearly tells us where the authority for withdraw originates:
             (1) "In the name of our Lord Jesus Christ, when you are gathered together, along with my spirit, with the power of our Lord Jesus Christ..." (1 Cor. 5:4).
             (2) "But we command you, brethren, in the name of our Lord Jesus Christ, that you withdraw from every brother who walks disorderly and not according to the tradition which he received from us" (2 Thess. 3:6).
         (c) The authority for withdraw is the authority of Jesus Christ Himself!
             (1) The same authority ("in the name of the Lord Jesus Christ") by which the church is to withdraw fellowship is the same authority that demands:
                 (i) Preaching repentance and remission of sins to all nations (Luke 24:46-47).
                 (ii) Repenting of sin (Acts 2:38).
                 (iii) Being baptized for the remission of sins (Acts 2:38; 10:48).
                 (iv) Measuring all we do and say by His authority (Col. 3:17).

                (2) These are all done "in the name of Christ," as is withdrawing fellowship!
            (d) Notice the word "command" associated with withdrawing fellowship.
                (1) This practice is not optional. It must be obeyed.
                (2) In fact, Paul wrote in 2 Corinthians 2, "For to this end I also wrote, that I might put you to the test, whether you are <u>obedient</u> in all things" (2:9).
                (3) As with all commands of God, the command of withdrawing must be obeyed!
            (e) A church has no right to decide IF it will teach on or practice withdraw!
                (1) A faithful church will teach and practice the essentiality of faith in Jesus, repentance of sins and baptism for the remission of sins. It does so because of the authority of Christ (Acts 2:38; 10:48; 17:30; Luke 24:46-47).
                (2) How, then, could a church refuse to teach and practice withdraw of fellowship, when the same authority of Christ demands it?
        3. The practice of withdrawing fellowship is following the lead of Jesus Himself!
            (a) We know that the Godhead practices withdraw of fellowship, for Romans 1 states:
                (1) "God also gave them up to uncleanness" (1:24).
                (2) "God gave them up to vile passions" (1:26).
                (3) "God gave them over to a debased mind" (1:28).
                (4) This same word (for "gave them up") is used when the church is commanded to "deliver such a one to Satan" (1 Cor. 5:5).
            (b) Paul stated that his actions in the matter of withdraw had been done "in the presence of Christ" (2 Cor. 2:10).
                (1) This indicates the authority of Christ.
                (2) This indicates the approval and validation of Christ.
                (3) This also indicates that Paul was following in the steps of Christ.
            (c) In the context of dealing with an unrepentant brother, Jesus stated: "But if he refuses even to hear the church, let him be to you like a heathen and a tax collector...For where two or three are <u>gathered together in My name</u>, <u>I am there</u> in the midst of them" (Matt. 18:17, 20).
                (1) The presence of Jesus indicates the authority of Jesus.
                (2) The presence of Jesus indicates the approval and validation of Jesus.
                (3) The presence of Jesus also indicates that the church is following in His steps.
            (d) When Jesus' church withdraws fellowship, Jesus Himself has withdrawn fellowship!
                (1) What does that say about the seriousness of withdraw of fellowship?
                (2) What does that say about the members who refuse to withdraw fellowship?
    B. Scripture teaches that withdrawing is to be done by the church, in a public assembly.
        1. Withdraw of fellowship is an action to be done when the church is "gathered together."
            (a) Paul wrote, "In the name of our Lord Jesus Christ, when you are gathered together...deliver such a one to Satan" (1 Cor. 5:4-5).
            (b) Jesus stated, in the context of dealing with an unrepentant brother, that the actions of the church were done when they were "gathered together in My name" (Matt. 18:20).
        2. Withdraw of fellowship is an action to be done by the whole church, and not just the eldership.
            (a) The elders of the congregation would certainly take the lead in withdrawing fellowship, as they do in all matters of the local congregation (cf. Heb. 13:7, 17).
                (1) The elders would initiate the process, carry it through each step and then lead the church in its final effort to restore the erring by withdrawing from him.

- (b) However, withdrawing fellowship is to be exercised by the whole congregation.
  - (1) The instructions are given for when the church is "gathered together" (5:4).
  - (2) The instructions are given to "brethren" (2 Thess. 3:6), not just elders.
  - (3) The instructions were followed by the church in Corinth, albeit the "majority" of the membership (2 Cor. 2:6).
- 3. Withdraw of fellowship is not done in secret or only by the church leadership.
- 4. Withdraw of fellowship is to be implemented and practiced by the entire congregation.
  - (a) When dealing with an unrepentant brother, Jesus said that eventually (if the brother refuses all other efforts to restore him) it would be necessary to "tell it to the church" (Matt. 18:17).
  - (b) In the matter of an unrepentant elder, Timothy was instructed, "Those who are sinning rebuke in the presence of all, that the rest also may fear" (1 Tim. 5:20).
  - (c) Paul's praise of the "majority" (2 Cor. 2:6) was, by implication, a censure of the minority who had apparently refused to honor and participate in the withdraw.
  - (d) For the whole congregation to practice something together requires notification and explanation to be made in a public assembly (when "gathered together").
  - (e) Remember that the purpose of withdraw is not to publicly celebrate the expulsion of a member but to collectively endeavor to save a soul!
- C. Scripture teaches that withdrawing is to be done with urgency.
  - 1. "Urgency" does not mean sloppy or careless or without proper thought and care.
    - (a) But, "urgency" emphasizes that this matter is important and cannot be delayed.
    - (b) "Urgency" emphasizes that this matter needs close and immediate attention.
  - 2. Withdraw requires urgency because of the Greek verbs involved.
    - (a) There are two aorist imperative verbs used in 1 Corinthians 5: "purge out" (5:7) and "put away" (5:13).
    - (b) While present imperative verbs command habitual action, aorist imperative verbs (as used in these verses) often involve a sense of urgency.
  - 3. Withdraw requires urgency because of the lost soul involved.
    - (a) If a brother is "walking disorderly" (2 Thess. 3:6), then his soul is in jeopardy.
    - (b) If a brother is impenitently enslaved to habitual sin (1 Cor. 5), he is lost (v. 5).
    - (c) If you yourself had fallen away from Christ and were lost, how long would you want the church to wait before doing everything it could to save you?
    - (d) Withdrawing of fellowship is included in "everything a church can do" to save a wayward brother. Salvation from sin is urgent and cannot be delayed.
- D. Scripture teaches that withdrawing is to be done in a methodical and prayer-filled procedure.
  - 1. There are obviously multiple steps involved in the process of withdrawing fellowship.
    - (a) There are steps that are taken leading up to the withdraw of fellowship.
    - (b) There are steps that are taken in the process of withdrawing fellowship.
    - (c) There are steps that are taken when fellowship has been withdrawn.
    - (d) The following steps are not outlined specifically in this order in Scripture (although each is required), but they are suggested as a starting point.
    - (e) While Scripture commands withdraw and gives some specifications, much of the actual procedure is a matter of expediency for each congregation (and eldership) to choose the most effective way to implement it in their congregation.
  - 2. Step #1: Be mindful of all brethren and their spiritual condition.
    - (a) Elders have responsibility to know the sheep (John 10:1-14).
    - (b) Elders have responsibility to "watch out" for the "souls" in their care (Heb. 13:17).

- (c) Christians have responsibility to "consider one another" (Heb. 10:24).
- (d) Christians are to "look out...for the interests of others" (Phil. 2:4). Would that include their spiritual needs, interests and condition?
3. Step #2: Warn the wayward brother.
    - (a) Fellow Christians are to "warn those who are unruly" (1 Thess. 5:14).
        - (1) "Unruly" is from the same Greek word as "disorderly" in 2 Thessalonians 3:6.
        - (2) This is a military term of one who is walking "out of step."
        - (3) We warn him in order to get him back into step with God.
    - (b) Fellow Christians are to "warn" their wayward brother more than once (Tit. 3:10).
        - (1) "Reject a factious man after a first and second warning" (Tit. 3:10, NASB).
        - (2) "As for a person who stirs up division, after warning him once and then twice, have nothing more to do with him" (Tit. 3:10, ESV).
    - (c) Make every effort to let him know of "the error of his way" (Jas. 5:20).
4. Step #3: Make every effort to restore the brother.
    - (a) Paul gave instructions to every Christian in Galatians 6:1, "Brethren, if a man is overtaken in any trespass, you who are spiritual restore such a one in a spirit of gentleness, considering yourself lest you also be tempted."
        - (1) The word "restore" is a present imperative verb, indicating continual action.
        - (2) Restoring (in this verse) is not just a one-time attempt.
        - (3) Restoring is a continuous, repeated, on-going effort.
    - (b) James encouraged every Christian to take action in James 5:19-20, "Brethren, if anyone among you wanders from the truth, and someone turns him back, let him know that he who turns a sinner from the error of his way will save a soul from death and cover a multitude of sins."
        - (1) Again, as in Galatians 6:1, this passage is addressed to all "brethren."
        - (2) The word "turn" means "to cause to return, to bring back" (Thayer 243).
        - (3) "Knowing" the blessed result of our efforts to bring an erring brother back (i.e., save his soul and cover sins), these efforts ought to be constant.
    - (c) The church ought to expend every effort possible to restore the erring brother before it withdraws fellowship from him. Nevertheless, withdraw should not be avoided or delayed.
5. Step #4: Withdraw fellowship from the erring brother.
    - (a) When all previous efforts have not been successful in turning the erring brother back to the narrow way, the church must withdraw fellowship from the brother.
        - (1) This is to be commenced in a public assembly, so that all the members can know and can be involved in this soul-saving action. (See VI, B.)
    - (b) This involves:
        - (1) Putting him away from the church (1 Cor. 5:2, 13; 2 Thess. 3:6).
        - (2) Not keeping company with him (1 Cor. 5:11).
        - (3) Having nothing to do with him (2 Thess. 3:14).
        - (4) Letting him be as a heathen and tax collector to the church (Matt. 18:17).
    - (c) It is vital that the entire congregation engage in this exercise, for the sake of the soul of the erring brother, that he might be saved.
        - (1) While the elders take the lead, this is not an action taken only by them.
        - (2) God's commands regarding withdraw are all directed to the church as a whole.
6. EACH of these steps must be saturated with PRAYER.
    - (a) The church should pray for the wayward brother.

- (b) The church should pray for themselves, as they endeavor to restore this brother.
- (c) The church should pray for God's love, guidance and blessings in their efforts.
- E. Scripture teaches that withdrawing is to be done as an ongoing endeavor to restore.
    1. Withdraw is not a one-time act.
    2. Withdraw is not the announcement.
    3. Withdraw is a continual effort of the church until the wayward brother returns.
    4. Scripture uses several present tense verbs regarding the action of the church against the erring brother, to indicate that the action is continual and ongoing.
        - (a) The church is "not to keep company with" or "not to associate with" (present tense) the erring brother (1 Cor. 5:9-11).
        - (b) The church is to "have nothing more to do with" (present tense) the erring brother (Tit. 3:10).
        - (c) The church is "not even to eat with" (present tense) the erring brother (5:11).
        - (d) The church is to "admonish/warn" (present tense) the erring brother (2 Thess. 3:15).
        - (e) Of course, the church in these statements refers to each member of the church.
- F. Scripture teaches that withdrawing is to be done as an act of love.
    1. Withdraw of fellowship, as instructed in Scripture and properly obeyed by the church is to be (1) motivated by love, (2) practiced in love and (3) continued in love.
    2. Discipline, when properly motivated and properly practiced, is always out of love.
        - (a) While discipline may be painful and hard, that does not mean that love is absent.
        - (b) When a parent disciplines his child, it may hurt, but it is an act of love.
        - (c) Church discipline is painful for all involved, but it is always to be done out of love.
        - (d) Hebrews 12 teaches this very principle – discipline is painful but an act of love.
            - (1) "All discipline for the moment seems not to be joyful, but sorrowful; yet to those who have been trained by it, afterwards it yields the peaceful fruit of righteousness" (12:11, NASB).
            - (2) "For those whom the Lord loves He disciplines" (12:6, NASB).
        - (e) Jesus stated in Revelation 3:19, "As many as I love *(phileo)*, I rebuke and chasten."
        - (f) The church withdraws fellowship from an erring brother out of love for him!
    3. Because of the church's love for the wayward brother, it continues to warn him.
        - (a) After instructing the church to "withdraw from every brother who walks disorderly," Paul commanded the church, "Yet do not count him as an enemy, but admonish him as a brother" (2 Thess. 3:15).
        - (b) Both verbs in this verse are in the present tense, indicating continual action.
        - (c) The church is not to continually treat the withdrawn-from brother "as an enemy."
            - (1) He is not an enemy. He is not hated. He is not ever to be treated as such.
        - (d) The church is to continually "warn" (ESV) the withdrawn-from brother.
            - (1) The Greek *noutheteo* literally means, "to put in mind," involving a gentle rebuke.
            - (2) The church is to continually put in the mind of the withdrawn-from brother the seriousness of his spiritual condition and the eternal destiny awaiting.
    4. The point about "warning" the brother is intentionally placed under the point of withdrawing fellowship being an "act of love."
        - (a) We warn our wayward brother, not to be mean or harsh or vindictive.
        - (b) We warn our wayward brother, because we love him and want him to be saved.
        - (c) Our brother must know of our concern for the direction of his life and he must know that we can have no part in it. But, he must know this from a heart of love.

VII. The New Testament Teaches Us That Withdrawing Fellowship Is Effective in Its Purpose.
  A. Every person on this earth—Christian and non-Christian—possesses freedom of will, which they may exercise to their heart's content, regardless of our wishes or efforts.
     1. However, a person's freedom of will should never stop us from trying to save them.
     2. We should do all we can to reach out to the alien sinner and bring him to Christ.
     3. We should do all we can to reach out to the erring brother and restore him to Christ.
     4. If we follow God's prescribed plan of withdrawing fellowship, His Word shows us that such an effort can work in restoring the erring brother.
     5. While some people might claim that withdraw of fellowship doesn't work and therefore the church shouldn't do it, both Scripture and practical experience would teach just the opposite.
        (a) Does it work every time it is practiced? No.
        (b) Does it work some of the time it is practiced? Yes.
        (c) Should we comply with the commands of God even if it "doesn't work"? Yes.
  B. Scripture teaches us that withdrawing fellowship can cause an erring brother to return.
     1. The church in Corinth was commanded to withdraw fellowship from the man who had taken his father's wife (1 Cor. 5:1-2).
     2. The church in Corinth was "obedient" (2 Cor. 2:9) and withdrew from this brother.
        (a) Actually, "the majority" of the church followed the apostle's instructions (2:6).
        (b) Paul called the withdraw a "punishment" (2 Cor. 2:6).
     3. The withdraw of fellowship succeeded in its purpose, and the brother came back.
        (a) Paul said that the withdraw was "sufficient for such a man" (2:6).
     4. How refreshing it is that Scripture shows a brother being restored after the church withdrew fellowship from him!
     5. Hebrews 12 speaks of the blessed result of discipline when an open heart is "trained by it"—"it yields the peaceable fruit of righteousness" (Heb. 12:11).
  C. Scripture teaches us how the church must respond when an erring brother returns.
     1. Scripture does not teach to "keep the man at arm's length" until "he proves himself."
     2. Scripture does not teach to treat him with suspicion, as the apostles initially did with Saul of Tarsus.
     3. Scripture does not teach to respond like the elder brother in Luke 15:25-32.
     4. Rather, Scripture is very clear that the church must "stand ready to receive such a one back into complete fellowship when he repents" (Meadows 217).
     5. The brethren must respond positively and quickly to the brother when he returns.
        (a) First, "forgive" (2 Cor. 2:7).
           (1) "If your brother sins against you, rebuke him; and if he repents, forgive him" (Luke 17:3; cf. Eph. 4:32).
        (b) Second, "comfort" (2 Cor. 2:7).
           (1) The Greek *parakaleo* literally means, "to call to one's side."
           (2) The design is to console, encourage and strengthen.
        (c) Third, "reaffirm your love" (2 Cor. 2:8).
           (1) The act of withdraw itself was done out of love (cf. Heb. 12:6).
           (2) When the erring brother returns, the church's love for him must be confirmed.
           (3) This is to be done individually (1 Thess. 3:12-13; 4:9-10).
           (4) Especially, in this word "reaffirm," it is to be done publicly.
              (i) The Greek *kuroo* means "to make valid; to confirm publicly or solemnly, to ratify" (Thayer 366).

                (ii) As the withdraw was done publicly (VI, B), so is the reaffirmation of love.
                (iii) As the withdraw was done in the presence of Christ (V, A, 2-3), so is the forgiveness and restoration (2 Cor. 2:10).
        6. All of this must be done, and done promptly, in order to:
            (a) End the "punishment" (2 Cor. 2:6-7a).
            (b) Prevent the brother from being "swallowed up with too much sorrow" (2:7b).
            (c) Prove ourselves "obedient in all things" (2:9).
            (d) Guard against Satan, lest he "should take advantage of us" (2:11).

VIII. Conclusion
   A. The topic of withdraw of fellowship is a very serious and difficult subject.
      1. Enjoying fellowship with God and with the church is a tremendous blessing.
      2. Therefore, there is nothing more detrimental than having that fellowship severed.
   B. It is possible for a child of God to so sin that he refuses to repent and falls away from a faithful and acceptable relationship with God (Gal. 5:4; Heb. 6:4-6). (See Lesson 21.)
      1. In such cases, the Bible teaches that God withdraws His fellowship from that man.
      2. Additionally, the Bible teaches that God instructs the church to withdraw from him.
      3. Whether a church chooses to withdraw fellowship is a test of its obedience to the commands of the Lord (2 Cor. 2:9).
         (a) It is not popular in the twenty-first century church to withdraw fellowship.
         (b) Many congregations have neglected to heed the clear commands of God.
         (c) But, is sin any less prevalent, any less pervasive and any less "destructive" today than it was in the first century?
         (d) Is there any compelling reason not to obey the commands of God today?
   C. When a church withdraws fellowship from an erring brother, it is designed to:
      1. Lovingly put him away, have no association with him and not even to eat with him.
      2. Continually warn him, with the hope that he will return before it is too late.
      3. Prayerfully create shame, sorrow and a desire to return in the brother's heart.
   D. Some have the idea that the church is condemning a person to hell when they withdraw fellowship from them, but such is certainly not the case.
      1. The way one lives his life will determine his eternal destination (2 Cor. 5:10).
      2. Scripture teaches that one who chooses to stray from the truth and walks in a disorderly fashion is "self-condemned" (Tit. 3:11).
         (a) His own choices have and are condemning him—not the choices of others.
      3. Withdrawing fellowship actually has as its purpose to "save" the lost brother, not condemn him!
   E. Members of the Lord's church enjoy a special relationship with each other.
      1. All that Christians do as a part of the body of Christ is to be motivated and implemented by *agape* love, including the withdrawing of fellowship from brethren who walk disorderly.
      2. We need each other in order that we might help one another go to heaven together. Again, that is the purpose of withdrawing fellowship.
   F. May God help us to obey all of His commands without being selective, in order that we might:
      1. Save the lost!
      2. Save our wayward brethren!
      3. Save the church!
      4. Save ourselves!

Recommended Resources

<u>Books</u>

Butt, Kyle. *That Their Souls Might Be Saved.* Montgomery, AL: Peaceful House Publishing, 2008.

Holland, Thomas H. *Entreating the Erring.* Brentwood, TN: Penmann Books, 2006.

Meadows, James. *A Study of Church Discipline.* Nashville: 21st Century Christian, 1970.

Smithson, Ed. *The Forgotten Commandment.* Oklahoma City: Ed Smithson, 1976.

Usrey, Robert S. *Church Discipline for Caring Christians.* Searcy, AR: Resource Publications, 1983.

<u>Articles</u>

Baxter, Batsell Barrett. "Fellowship." *Family of God.* Nashville: Gospel Advocate, 1980. 141-146.

Brewer, G.C. "Dealing with the Disorderly." *The Model Church.* Nashville: Gospel Advocate, 1957. 107-122.

Carr, B.C. "The Scriptures Are Her Discipline." *Introducing the Church of Christ.* Ed. Alvin Jennings. Fort Worth: Star Bible, 1981. 136-139.

Edwards, Earl D. "Is Withdrawing Fellowship Too Harsh?" *Respect for God's Word (South Florida Lectureship).* Ed. David Sproule. Palm Beach Gardens, FL: Palm Beach Lakes church of Christ, 2005. 41-60.

Ferguson, Everett. "Fellowship of the Church." *The New Testament Church.* Abilene, TX: Biblical Research Press, 1968. 46-52.

Highers, Alan E. "Restoring the New Testament Church in Church Discipline." *Restoring the New Testament (Fort Worth Christian College Lectures).* Ed. Foy Kirkpatrick. Fort Worth: Fort Worth Christian College, 1966. 97-103.

Jackson, Wayne. "Church Discipline—A Tragic Neglect." *ChristianCourier.com* https://www.christiancourier.com/articles/207-church-discipline-a-tragic-neglect

---. "Should 'Weak' Christians Be Disfellowshipped?" *ChristianCourier.com* https://www.christiancourier.com/articles/239-should-weak-christians-be-disfellowshipped

---. "When Christ Withdraws His Fellowship." *ChristianCourier.com* https://www.christiancourier.com/articles/355-when-christ-withdraws-his-fellowship

McDade, Gary. "Church Discipline." *The Spiritual Sword (Oct. 2003): 27-32.*

Meadows, James. "Withdrawing Fellowship." *The Church and Fellowship (Freed-Hardeman College Lectures).* Ed. William Woodson. Henderson, TN: Freed-Hardeman College, 1974. 208-218.

Winkler, Dan. "Maintain the Purity of Christian Fellowship with Proper Church Discipline." *Harmony Among the Heirs of God.* Huntingdon, TN: Practical Publications, 1986.

Winkler, Wendell. "The Church—And Self-Discipline (Disfellowship—Negative)." *The Church: The Beautiful Bride of Christ (Spiritual Sword Lectureship).* Eds. Garland Elkins & Thomas B. Warren. Memphis: Getwell church of Christ, 1980. 75-89.

Periodicals

The Spiritual Sword. January 1974. "Christian Fellowship."

Lesson 23: The Second Coming of Christ

I. **The Second Coming of Jesus Christ Is a Thrilling Doctrine of the New Testament.**
   A. The second coming of Christ is referenced a few times in the Old Testament (Job 19:25-27; Dan. 12:2-3; Psa. 110:1; Isa. 45:23).
      1. The Old Testament is focused primarily on the first coming of Jesus.
      2. Once Jesus came, the New Testament then focuses on the second coming of Jesus.
   B. The second coming of Christ is a major subject of the New Testament.
      1. The Bible can be summarized in three sentences:
         (a) "Someone is coming" – the Old Testament.
         (b) "Someone is here" – Matthew, Mark, Luke and John.
         (c) "Someone is coming again" – Acts through Revelation.
      2. From the end of Jesus' life to the end of the N.T., the second coming is central theme.
      3. The second coming is mentioned or alluded to in over 300 verses in the New Testament. (That is about 1 out of every 25 N.T. verses that deals with this subject in some way.)
   C. There are various terms used in the New Testament to identify this day.
      1. It is called "the coming of our Lord Jesus Christ" (2 Thess. 2:1; 1 Thess. 2:19; 3:13; 4:15; 5:23; 1 Cor. 15:23; Jas. 5:7; 2 Pet. 1:16; 3:4, 12; 1 John 2:28).
         (a) The Greek word is *parousia,* which literally means "a presence" or "a being with," and thus "denotes both an 'arrival' and a consequent 'presence with'" (Vine 111).
         (b) Thayer notes, "In the N.T. especially of the advent, i.e. the future, visible, return from heaven of Jesus, the Messiah" (490).
         (c) *Parousia* "became the official term for a visit of a person of high rank, especially of kings and emperors visiting a province" (BDAG [2000], p. 781).
      2. It is called "the appearing of our Lord Jesus Christ" (1 Tim. 6:14; 2 Tim. 4:1, 8; Tit. 2:13).
         (a) The Greek word is *epiphaneia*, "used of the 'appearance' of a god to men" (Vine 32).
         (b) Jesus will shine forth in His return, as the one true God appears to all men.
      3. It is called "the revelation of our Lord Jesus Christ" (1 Cor. 1:7; 2 Th. 1:7; 1 Pet. 1:7, 13).
         (a) The Greek word is *apokalupsis*, which literally means "an uncovering or unveiling."
         (b) Jesus will be manifested, revealed when He returns, for the first time since 33 A.D.
         (c) Robertson makes this note in his comments on 2 Thessalonians 2:1, "*Parousia* lays emphasis on the **presence** of the Lord with his people, *epiphaneia* on his **manifestation** of the power and love of God, *apokalupsis* on the **revelation** of God's purpose and plan in the Second Coming of the Lord Jesus."
      4. It is called "the day of our Lord Jesus Christ" (1 Cor. 1:8).
         (a) The Greek word for "day" *(hemera)* is often used to refer to "the last day of the present age…the day in which Christ will return from heaven, raise the dead, hold the final judgment, and perfect his kingdom" (Thayer 278).
         (b) The word is used in various ways about the second coming of Christ, including:
            (1) "The day of the Lord" (1 Thess. 5:2; 2 Pet. 3:10; cf. 2 Thess. 2:2).
            (2) "The day of the Lord Jesus" (1 Cor. 5:5; cf. 1 Cor. 1:8; Phil. 1:6, 10).
            (3) "The day of God" (2 Pet. 3:12).
            (4) "That day" (Matt. 7:22; 24:36; 2 Thess. 1:10; 2 Tim. 1:12, 18; 4:8).
            (5) "The last day" (John 6:39, 40, 44, 54; 11:24; 12:48).
            (6) "The great day" (Jude 6).
            (7) "The day of judgment" (Matt. 10:15; 11:22, 24; 12:36; 2 Pet. 2:9; 3:7).
            (8) "The day of wrath" (Rom. 2:5).

                (9) "The day of redemption" (Eph. 4:30).
    D. The New Testament speaks of various "comings" of Christ, both figurative and literal.
        1. This is an important point to understand.
        2. The "second" coming of Christ is spoken of throughout Scripture in literal, personal terms, which is the focus of this study.
        3. However, there are some "comings" of Christ spoken of in Scripture other than His second coming, and these are always seen as imminent, and yet figurative "comings" of Christ in a representative form, rather than a literal form.
        4. It is critical for a Bible student to be able to differentiate between these "comings."
        5. Christ was spoken of as "coming" in:
            (a) The establishment of the kingdom on Pentecost (Matt. 16:28; cf. Mark 9:1).
            (b) The giving of the Holy Spirit to the apostles (John 14:18).
            (c) The destruction of Jerusalem in 70 A.D. (Matt. 24:30, 34).
            (d) However, none of these were literal appearances.
                (1) All were figurative or representative in nature.
                (2) All of these "comings" have already taken place (occurring in the first century).
        6. Then, after all of these nonliteral "comings," He "will appear a second time" (Heb. 9:28).
            (a) The word "second" points to His "first" and literal coming.
            (b) The word "second" emphasizes a coming that will be like the first (i.e., literal).
            (c) Thus, the word "second" emphasizes the nonliteral nature of the other comings.
            (d) Jesus has not yet returned a second time (regardless of what some claim). The earth and its inhabitants are still awaiting that thrilling event!
    E. This lesson will examine what the Scriptures teach about Christ's second coming.
II. **The Future Event of the Second Coming of Jesus Christ Is Certain!**
    A. The second coming of Christ is an absolutely certain event.
        1. Jesus Himself promised it (John 14:1-3).
        2. The angels testified of it at Jesus' ascension (Acts 1:9-11).
        3. The apostles and inspired penmen of the New Testament focused on it throughout their ministries and writings (1 Cor. 15:50-58; 2 Cor. 5:1-11; Phil. 3:20-21; 1 Thess. 4:13-5:11; 2 Thess. 1:7-9; Heb. 9:28; 2 Pet. 3:3-13; 1 John 3:1-2; Rev. 1:7).
        4. The resurrection of Christ guarantees His return (Acts 17:30-31).
    B. The second coming of Christ must take place as the culmination of God's eternal plan.
        1. God's whole scheme has been designed to unite His people with Him for eternity.
        2. Christ was sent the first time to save man, as part of God's eternal plan (1 Pet. 1:18-21).
        3. Christ will come the second time to usher in His eternal salvation (Heb. 5:9; 9:27-28).
        4. Christ is coming "to be glorified in His saints" and "admired" by believers (2 Th. 1:10).
    C. The Bible foretells the thrilling event of Jesus Christ's second coming and guarantees it!
III. **The Exact Time of the Second Coming of Christ Is Unknown!**
    A. Over the centuries, many have tried to predict the timing of Christ's coming.
        1. Some have done this because they misunderstood the "signs" in Matthew 24.
            (a) Some have thought that Matthew 24:1-34 is speaking of the second coming.
            (b) However, the context and language of the passage will not allow such a meaning.
                (1) Mark's account indicates that Jesus was in a "private" conversation with "Peter, James, John and Andrew" (Mark 13:3). He was speaking specifically to them.
                    (i) In that context, Jesus used the second person pronoun "you" or "your" repeatedly. (Matthew records 17 uses; Mark 21 uses; Luke 26 uses.)

- (ii) These were signs that would be seen by "you"—Peter, James, John and Andrew. If these events are yet future to us, then the context is senseless.
- (2) Jesus showed "the buildings of the temple" to His disciples and told them that "not one stone shall be left here upon another" (24:2).
- (3) The disciples asked Jesus when "these things" would happen and what "sign" would precede "the end" (24:3). To a Jew, the destruction of the temple would have likely seemed like the end of the world.
- (4) Jesus spoke to them specifically of "the end of the age," which was the end of the Jewish age (24:3, 6, 14). See 1 Corinthians 10:11 and Hebrews 9:26.
- (5) Jesus used figurative language (even of "the sun being darkened" and "the stars will fall from heaven") that was commonly used of the destruction and fall of a nation. Read Isaiah 13; Ezekiel 32:1-16; Amos 8:1-10.
- (6) Jesus plainly taught, regarding the "signs" in that passage, "This generation will by no means pass away till all these things take place" (Matt. 24:34).
- (c) All "signs" before verse 34 were pointing toward the destruction of Jerusalem and the fall of the Jewish nation in 70 A.D., which occurred in the lifetime of "this generation" to whom Jesus spoke. This is a highly significant verse!
  - (1) To attempt to make any verse before verse 34 apply to some current or yet future event of modern man is to ignore what Jesus plainly taught in verse 34.
  - (2) People living in that "generation" would see the fulfillment of the "signs." Not us.
2. It is altogether without Scriptural basis to use Matthew 24:1-34 to look for "signs" of Christ's second coming today and to predict His imminent return.
   - (a) It is clear that Jesus spoke of two separate events in Matthew 24.
   - (b) He first spoke of the destruction of Jerusalem (24:1-34).
     - (1) Jesus said that there were "signs" that would precede or forewarn of this event.
     - (2) Jesus Himself knew when this would happen.
   - (c) He then spoke of His second coming and the destruction of the world (24:35-25:46).
     - (1) Jesus said that there were no signs that would precede or forewarn of this event.
     - (2) Jesus Himself, while on earth, did not know when this would happen (Mk. 13:32).
   - (d) Since there are signs for one event in Matthew 24 but not the other, and since Jesus knew when one event would occur but not the other, it follows quite clearly that the two events of Matthew 24 are not the same event, nor will they occur at the same time. Verse 34 draws a line of demarcation between them.
   - (e) Jesus has not already returned the "second" and final time, as some claim!
   - (f) The destruction of Jerusalem in 70 A.D. was not the second coming of Christ!
   - (g) There is not a dual fulfillment of these signs in Matthew 24:1-34, as some suppose, referring to both the destruction of Jerusalem in 70 A.D. and to the end of time.
     - (1) Nowhere in this context or any context does the Lord suggest such. Thus, it would be pure speculation for man to try to force a dual meaning.
     - (2) Jesus said that "all these things" would take place (four times in Matthew 24).
       - (i) He did not say "some of these things" or say "representative things."
       - (ii) He emphasized that ALL things of which He spoke would take place in the destruction of Jerusalem.
     - (3) Jesus said that the worst tribulation ever would occur—"such as has not been since the beginning of the world until this time, no, nor ever shall be" (Matt. 24:21). It is impossible for the "worst ever" to happen twice. There can only be one worst tribulation ever.

3. Many predictions of years and exact dates have been made, and every one failed.
   (a) William Miller, founder of the Seventh Day Adventists, predicted that Christ would come in 1843. When that didn't happen, he changed his prediction to 1844.
   (b) Joseph Smith, founder of the Mormons, predicted that Christ would come by 1891.
   (c) Charles T. Russell, founder of the Jehovah's Witnesses, predicted that Christ would come in 1914.
   (d) Hal Lindsey, who influenced tremendously the premillennial movement of the twentieth century, predicted that Christ would come in 1988.
   (e) Without exception, every time man has ever predicted the time of the return of Christ, he has found himself in error. There is a very clear reason for that!
B. The Bible clearly teaches that the timing of Jesus' return is unknown by man.
   1. Jesus taught that "no one knows" the day and hour, "but My Father only" (Mt. 24:36).
   2. Jesus taught that during His earthly ministry, He Himself did not know (Mark 13:32).
   3. Jesus taught that He would return "at an hour you do not expect" (Luke 12:40).
   4. Jesus taught that the day would be as unexpected as a thief in the night (Mt. 24:42-44).
      (a) Paul echoed that the day would come "as a thief in the night" (1 Thess. 5:2).
      (b) Peter echoed that the day would come "as a thief in the night" (2 Pet. 3:10).
   5. Jesus taught that it is not for man "to know times or seasons" of the Father (Ac. 1:7).
   6. Jesus taught that man must "watch" because he does not know the time (Mt. 25:13).
   7. Jesus marked a sharp difference between the "signs" that would lead up to and signal the coming destruction of Jerusalem (Matt. 24:1-34) and the complete absence of any signs whatsoever that would lead up to and signal His second coming and the end of the world (Matt. 24:35-44). It is critical to note that difference!
C. It is irresponsible and unscriptural to speculate as to a certain timing. We do not know!
   1. If Christ didn't know and taught that man doesn't know, how arrogant to claim to know!

IV. The Manner of the Second Coming of Christ Is Going to Be Glorious!
A. Jesus will come suddenly, without warning (1 Thess. 5:2; 2 Pet. 3:10; Matt. 24:36-44).
B. Jesus will come personally and literally Himself.
   1. It will not be a figurative or representative coming (see I, D).
   2. The angels announced, "This same Jesus...will so come..." (Acts 1:11).
   3. Paul announced, "The Lord Himself will descend from heaven" (1 Thess. 4:16).
C. Jesus will come "in like manner" as He ascended (Acts 1:11).
   1. Jesus will be "revealed from heaven" (2 Thess. 1:7).
   2. As Jesus "was taken up," "a cloud received Him" (Acts 1:9).
   3. Thus, Jesus will return "in the clouds" (1 Thess. 4:17) and "with clouds" (Rev. 1:7).
D. Jesus will come in such a way that "every eye will see Him" (Rev. 1:7).
   1. There will not be anything invisible or secretive about Jesus' return.
   2. As Jesus' return will be "in like manner" as His ascension (Acts 1:11), note that:
      (a) They "watched" Jesus ascend, therefore, we will "watch" Him return (Acts 1:9).
      (b) Jesus ascended from their "sight," therefore, He will return to our "sight" (Acts 1:9).
   3. He will be "revealed" *(apokalupsis)*, signifying an unveiling for all to see (2 Thess. 1:7).
   4. He will "appear" *(phaneroo)*, signifying a visible manifestation to all (1 John 2:28).
   5. He will "appear" *(optanomai)*, signifying the eye (optical) will see (Heb. 9:28).
   6. There will be no second coming of Jesus that is not witnessed by "every eye"!
E. Jesus will come "in His glory" and "in the glory of His Father" (Matt. 25:31; Mark 8:38).
   1. His deity will be evident to all, as "we shall see Him as He is" (1 John 3:2).
   2. Everything about His return will show forth His glory, including His throne (Mt. 25:31b).

F. Jesus will come with "all the holy [and mighty, 2 Th. 1:7] angels with Him" (Matt. 25:31).
G. Jesus will come "from heaven with a shout" (1 Thess. 4:16).
H. Jesus will come "with the voice of an archangel and with the trumpet of God" (1 Th. 4:16).
I. Jesus will come "with all His saints" who "have fallen asleep" (1 Thess. 3:13; 4:13, 17).
J. Jesus will come "to be glorified in His saints" (2 Thess. 1:10).
K. There is no possible way that Jesus has already come, as some attempt to suggest.
L. What a glorious event awaits us all in the second coming of our Lord Jesus!

V. **The Events of the Second Coming of Christ Will Be Overwhelmingly Spectacular!**
   A. When Jesus returns, every dead person will be raised at the same time. (See VI.)
   B. When Jesus returns, those who are still alive will be lifted up from the earth and transformed into the likeness of Christ.
      1. "The dead in Christ will rise first" (1 Thess. 4:16b).
         (a) This passage does not teach that the dead outside of Christ will be raised "second" or sometime later, as is often erroneously taught. (See VI, H.)
         (b) This passage is only focused on those who are "in Christ." Those who are outside of Christ are not in view (or in discussion) in this passage.
      2. "Then [after the "first"] we who are alive and remain will be caught up together with them [i.e., the dead in Christ who have already been raised]" (1 Thess. 4:17a).
         (a) There is a definite order expressed in this passage.
         (b) The living "in Christ" will not "precede" the dead "in Christ" (1 Thess. 4:15).
         (c) Once the dead "in Christ" have been raised, "then" the living "in Christ" will rise.
      3. At that moment:
         (a) "We shall see [Jesus] as He is" (1 John 3:2).
         (b) "We shall all be changed" (1 Cor. 15:51).
         (c) He "will transform our lowly body that it may be conformed to His glorious body" (Phil. 3:21).
         (d) "We shall be like Him" (1 John 3:2).
   C. When Jesus returns, He will deliver the kingdom to His Father (1 Cor. 15:24).
      1. Many wrongly teach that Jesus is going to "set up" His kingdom when He returns.
      2. But the Bible plainly teaches that He is going to "deliver up" His kingdom.
         (a) This emphasizes that the kingdom (i.e., church, Matt. 16:18-19) is already in existence now (i.e., the saved are in the kingdom now; cf. Col. 1:13; Rev. 1:9; Acts 2:47), and is not going to then be established at His coming.
         (b) This emphasizes that only those who are in His kingdom/church will go to heaven and be delivered to the Father when Jesus returns.
         (c) Jesus will deliver and present His "glorious church, not having spot or wrinkle or any such thing, but that she should be holy and without blemish" (Eph. 5:27).
      3. Scripture emphasizes that this will occur at "the end," when He "puts an end to all rule and all authority and power" (1 Cor. 15:24).
         (a) Every power in existence that exalts itself against Christ will be brought to an end (15:24-25).
         (b) His "reign" as mediator (Rev. 1:6; 3:21) will no longer continue or be necessary (1 Cor. 15:25).
            (1) His first coming was to deal with sin and "bear the sins of many" (Heb. 9:28).
               (i) With "His own blood" He has "obtained eternal redemption" (Heb. 9:12).
            (2) When He ascended into heaven, His purpose was "now to appear in the presence of God for us" (Heb. 9:24).

                (i) "He always lives to make intercession" for God's children (Heb. 7:25).
                (ii) He is still dealing with sin, as our "Advocate with the Father," pleading our case when we sin (1 John 2:1-2).
            (3) But, His "second" coming will "not [be] to deal with sin but to save those who are eagerly waiting for Him" (Heb. 9:28, ESV).
            (4) This will all happen at "the end."
        (c) "The last enemy that will be destroyed [at the end] is death" (1 Cor. 15:26).
            (1) If "death" is still present on the earth, then "the end" has not yet come!
            (2) If the dead have not all been raised yet, then "the end" has not yet come!
    4. Those in His kingdom/church upon His return will enter into "the everlasting kingdom" of heaven itself (2 Pet. 1:11).
    5. When Christ returns, His reign will "end" and He will deliver the kingdom to His Father.
        (a) Therefore, we know with certainty that Jesus is reigning now over His kingdom.
        (b) Therefore, we know that His kingdom is in existence now.
        (c) Therefore, we know that He will not be establishing His kingdom upon His return.
        (d) There is no room in Scripture for the theory of premillennialism.
  D. When Jesus returns, the earth and everything in it will be destroyed. (See VII.)
  E. When Jesus returns, every person who has ever lived will be judged. (See VIII.)
  F. When Jesus returns, eternal destinies will be rewarded to all. (See IX.)
  G. Let us turn our attention to the four major events that will occur when Christ returns.

VI. At the Second Coming of Christ, Every Dead Person Will Be Raised at the Same Time!
  A. It is important to know that when the Bible speaks of the resurrection of the dead, it is clearly the body that is being raised from the grave and not the soul or spirit.
    1. Death is a separation, when the spirit leaves the body.
        (a) The soul or spirit of a man is that eternal part of man that is made in the image of God (Matt. 10:28; Gen. 1:26-27), which resides in a human body (2 Cor. 5:6).
        (b) Death involves the "soul...departing" from the body (Gen. 35:18; cf. 25:8).
        (c) "...The body without the spirit is dead..." (Jas. 2:26).
        (d) "Then the dust will return to the earth as it was, And the spirit will return to God who gave it" (Ecc. 12:7).
    2. Therefore, it is a person's body that dies and not the soul or spirit.
        (a) The soul or spirit of a man does not die. Thus, it cannot be raised!
        (b) While the body is buried, the soul or spirit continues to exist in a conscious existence in Hades, the intermediate realm of the dead (Luke 16:22-25).
        (c) While in death one is "absent from the body" (2 Cor. 5:8), he is still very much alive in the spirit (Luke 16:19-31; Rev. 6:9-11).
    3. In the resurrection, the spirits will be brought forth from Hades (Rev. 1:18; 20:13; 1 Thess. 3:13) and reunited with the dead bodies that come forth from the graves (1 Cor. 15:52-54).
  B. Some today are like the Sadducees of Bible times—they do not believe in the resurrection of the dead (Matt. 22:23; Acts 23:6-8).
    1. However, the resurrection of the dead is a foundational and guaranteed element of God's eternal plan. While some men might deny it, God guarantees it!
    2. The "resurrection of the dead" is an "elementary principle of Christ" (Heb. 6:1-2).
  C. The doctrine of the resurrection from the dead was known, believed and taught in the Old Testament.
    1. The doctrine of the resurrection is not a new idea introduced in the New Testament.

2. During the Patriarchal Age, God's people believed in the resurrection of the dead.
   (a) Job asked God, "If a man dies, shall he live again?" (Job 14:14).
   (b) Job already knew the answer, "For I know that my Redeemer lives, And He shall stand at last on the earth; And after my skin is destroyed, this I know, That in my flesh I shall see God, Whom I shall see for myself, And my eyes shall behold, and not another. How my heart yearns within me!" (Job 19:25-27).
   (c) Abraham had faith "that God was able to raise [Isaac] up, even from the dead" (Heb. 11:17-19).
3. During the Mosaic Age, God's people believed in the resurrection of the dead.
   (a) God taught Moses about the resurrection of the dead in Exodus 3:6.
      (1) God said, "I am the God of your father—the God of Abraham, the God of Isaac, and the God of Jacob."
      (2) Jesus affirmed that God was speaking of "the resurrection of the dead" (Matt. 22:31-32).
   (b) Daniel quite clearly spoke of the resurrection in Daniel 12:2.
      (1) "And many of those who sleep in the dust of the earth shall awake, Some to everlasting life, Some to shame and everlasting contempt."
      (2) He even recognized that all would be raised at the same "time" (v. 1), "some" to eternal life and "some" to condemnation (cf. John 5:28-29).
4. There are other Old Testament passages that anticipate the resurrection of the dead (Psa. 16:8-11; 17:15; 49:15; 73:24; Isa. 25:8; 26:19; Hos. 13:14).

D. The doctrine of the resurrection of the dead was taught by Jesus Himself.
   1. Jesus often disputed with the Sadducees, who did not believe in the resurrection.
      (a) Jesus told them that by holding to their false doctrine, "You are mistaken, not knowing the Scripture not the power of God" (Matt. 22:23-29).
      (b) Jesus told them that their own Scriptures (i.e., the Old Testament) clearly taught the resurrection of the dead (Matt. 22:31-32; cf. Ex. 3:6).
      (c) While they denied the actual bodily resurrection (as some still do today), Jesus said that they did not know the power of God or the Scripture! Thus both the power of God and the Scripture demand an actual bodily resurrection!
   2. When the Jews sought "to kill" Jesus because He made "Himself equal with God" (John 5:18), Jesus impressed upon them that:
      (a) "As the Father raises the dead and gives life to them, even so the Son gives life to whom He will" (5:21)
      (b) "The hour is coming, and now is, when the dead will hear the voice of the Son of God; and those who hear will live" (5:25).
      (c) "All who are in the graves will hear His voice and come forth" (5:28-29).
   3. When the Jews continued to question the deity of Jesus, He repeated over and over, "I will raise him up at the last day" (John 6:39, 40, 44, 54).

E. The doctrine of the resurrection was central to the apostles' preaching.
   1. The first gospel sermon focused primarily on the resurrection of Jesus (Acts 2:24-36).
   2. The apostles were arrested because "they preached in Jesus the resurrection from the dead" (Acts 4:1-2).
   3. At the center of Paul's preaching was the resurrection.
      (a) "I have hope in God...that there will be a resurrection of the dead" (Acts 24:15).
      (b) Paul was arrested and put on trial because of what he preached "concerning the resurrection of the dead" (Acts 23:6; 24:21).

    4. The summary of their teaching was this: "God both raised up the Lord and will also raise us up by His power" (1 Cor. 6:14).
F. The doctrine of the resurrection of the dead is taught emphatically in 1 Corinthians 15.
    1. The resurrection of Christ is an essential part of the gospel (15:1-4).
    2. The resurrection of Christ was confirmed by eyewitness testimony (15:5-11).
    3. There are serious consequences if Christ was not raised from the dead (15:12-19).
    4. The resurrection of Christ guarantees the resurrection of all dead (15:20-28).
        (a) As the "firstfruits," Christ's resurrection is a pledge that the remainder of the Lord's harvest (i.e., the future resurrection of the dead) is forthcoming (15:20).
        (b) As certain as "all" die because of Adam, "all" will be raised from the dead because of Christ (15:21-22).
        (c) "All" of the dead will be raised at "the end" (15:24), when Jesus returns and when all enemies (including death) are subdued once and for all (15:25-26).
        (d) "The last enemy that will be destroyed is death" (1 Cor. 15:26).
    5. There are serious consequences for denying the resurrection of the dead (15:29-34).
    6. Some questions/objections are answered about the resurrection (15:35-49).
    7. The bodies of the living will be changed into a spiritual body at Jesus' return (15:50-53).
    8. The resurrection of the dead is the final conquering of death and ultimate victory of the purpose of God (15:54-57).
    9. Christians are exhorted to steadfastness in view of our ultimate victory (15:58).
G. The apostle John described the resurrection in the closing pages of the Bible.
    1. In a vision, John "saw the dead" (Rev. 20:12), indicating that he saw all of them.
    2. He saw all of them "before God" because, "The sea gave up the dead who were in it, and Death and Hades delivered up the dead who were in them" (Rev. 20:13).
    3. Every receptacle of death delivered up its dead. Every last one of them was raised.
H. Here is a key point: The resurrection of the dead involves all of the dead, the righteous and the unrighteous, at the same time.
    1. At the return of Christ, there will be "a shout," "the voice of an archangel," and "the trumpet of God" (1 Thess. 4:16).
    2. "The trumpet of God" that will sound will be "the last trumpet" (1 Cor. 15:52).
    3. "The last trumpet" will sound on "the last day" (John 6:40, 44, 54).
        (a) If this is the last trumpet, how many trumpets will sound after this one? None!
        (b) If this is the last day, how many days will there be after this one? Not a single one!
        (c) It will be "the last day" for the righteous and the wicked (John 12:48; cf. 11:24)!
        (d) There will not be another day, or another year, or another millennium! It is the last!
    4. Upon the sounding of the last trumpet, "the dead will be raised" (1 Cor. 15:52).
        (a) When the trumpet sounds, "the dead in Christ will rise first" (1 Thess. 4:16).
        (b) While some have attempted to make this mean that the dead out of Christ would rise second (and even 1,000 years later), that is not what the passage teaches.
        (c) The only persons in view in 1 Thessalonians 4 are Christians—dead ones and living ones. Those "outside of Christ" are not anywhere in this context.
        (d) Those who have died "in Christ" would rise first.
        (e) "Then (i.e., second) we [in Christ] who are alive and remain shall be caught up together with them" (1 Thess. 4:17).
        (f) The fullness of Scripture teaches that the dead (in Christ and out of Christ) will be raised at the same time.

5. Notice closely and carefully what Jesus taught about the resurrection of the dead.
   (a) Simultaneously, "all who are in the graves will hear His voice" (John 5:28).
   (b) Simultaneously, "all who are in the graves will...come forth" (John 5:28-29).
   (c) There is not a long span of time between any of the resurrections.
   (d) All of the dead are raised all in the same "hour"! This includes the righteous and the wicked (i.e., "they that have done good" and "they that have done evil")!
   (e) And, remember, all of this will happen on "the last day" (John 6:40, 44, 54).
      (1) There will not be even one more day (or even one more hour) on this earth after the one, only and final resurrection.
      (2) If there is not one day more, then there is certainly not 1,000 years!
6. Paul preached that "there will be a resurrection of the dead" (Acts 24:15).
   (a) Interestingly, the word "resurrection" is singular. There will be only one.
   (b) This one simultaneous resurrection will be "both of the just and the unjust" (24:15).
   (c) The conjunction "and" ties these two resurrections together inseparably!
7. There is no Bible verse that explicitly or implicitly teaches the premillennial doctrine of the righteous being raised first and then the unrighteous raised 1,000 years later.
8. The Bible explicitly and repeatedly teaches that all will be raised at the same time.

I. While all will be raised at the same time, the righteous and unrighteous will experience two very different resurrections.
   1. The righteous will "come forth...to the resurrection of life" (John 5:28-29).
      (a) Those who are "in Christ...shall be made alive" (1 Cor. 15:22).
      (b) Daniel prophesied that the righteous would "awake...to everlasting life" (12:2).
      (c) He whose "life is hidden with Christ...will appear with Him in glory" (Col. 3:3-4).
      (d) When raised, the righteous will receive incorruptible bodies (1 Cor. 15:41-45).
      (e) "When He is revealed, we shall be like Him, for we shall see Him as He is" (1 Jn. 3:2).
      (f) Christ "will transform our lowly body that it may be conformed to His glorious body" (Phil. 3:20-21).
      (g) Those still alive will be caught up with them to meet the Lord in the air (1 Th. 4:17).
   2. The unrighteous will "come forth...to the resurrection of condemnation" (Jn. 5:29).
      (a) The unrighteous "shall awake...to shame and everlasting contempt" (Dan. 12:2).
      (b) Their resurrected bodies will be susceptible to pain and suffering (Mark 9:42-48).

J. When Jesus returns, all of the dead will be raised out of the graves at the same time!
   1. What a sight that will be!
   2. All of those bodies will be changed into bodies that will exist forever!
   3. All of those still alive will be removed from the earth to join the dead for eternity!

VII. At the Second Coming of Christ, the Earth and Everything in It Will Be Destroyed.
A. When all of the people (living and dead) are removed from the earth, the Bible plainly teaches that this material planet, and everything in it, will be destroyed by fire.
B. The Bible teaches that this will happen on the very day that Christ returns.
C. However, some are teaching that the earth will not be destroyed when Christ returns.
   1. Those who espouse the doctrine of premillennialism claim that Jesus will establish an earthly kingdom and reign on the earth for 1,000 years.
      (a) However, on the "day" Jesus returns, the earth will be destroyed. The earth will not be in existence for any earthly kingdom or reign.
      (b) The Bible nowhere speaks of Jesus ever stepping one foot back on the earth. In fact, it specifically teaches that He will return "in the air" (1 Thess. 4:15-17).
      (c) There is no room in any Bible verse for a 1,000-year reign of Christ on earth.

2. There are others who are teaching that the earth is going to be purified by fire and then it will become "heaven" for God's people for all of eternity.
   (a) Groups like the Seventh Day Adventists and the Jehovah's Witnesses hold that followers of God will reside on earth for eternity. Heaven will be on earth.
   (b) Premillennialists believe that there will be a literal new heavens and new earth on a purified earth.
   (c) This doctrine has made its way into the church and has convinced some Christians that their eternal reward will be a renovated and purified earth.
   (d) Scripture must be examined carefully. It clearly teaches that the earth will be destroyed and that it will cease to exist when Jesus returns.
D. The Bible makes a clear distinction between heaven and earth.
   1. Jesus frequently sharply contrasted heaven and earth—they could never be the same!
      (a) "Heaven...is God's throne" and "earth...is His footstool" (Matt. 5:34-35).
      (b) We should pray that God's "will be done on earth as it is in heaven" (Matt. 6:10).
      (c) We are "not" to "lay up...treasures on earth," but instead we are to "lay up...treasures in heaven" (Matt. 6:19-20). They are NOT the same place!
      (d) Jesus told His disciples about His "Father's house," and then said:
         (1) "I go to prepare a place for you" (John 14:2). He was going to heaven, where His Father is (cf. Jn. 13:33, 36; 16:16, 28; 20:17). He was not going to prepare earth!
         (2) "I will come again and receive you to Myself; that where I am, there you may be also" (John 14:3). Wherever Jesus was going to prepare a place was not the same place where His disciples already were (i.e., on earth). Otherwise, Jesus' words are nonsensical in this passage.
         (3) Jesus was going to heaven. When He returned, He would take His followers to heaven (i.e., His Father's house) with Him. This is NOT on earth!
         (4) While some teach that the Father and the Son are going to come down and reside on earth with their people, Jesus taught just the opposite!
   2. The apostles frequently sharply contrasted heaven and earth—not the same place!
      (a) Paul reassured Christians that their true citizenship is not of "earthly things" but "is in heaven," and Christians "eagerly wait for the Savior" to come for them "from" heaven (Phil. 3:19-21). Heaven and earth are not the same!
      (b) Paul urged Christians to "seek those things which are above, where Christ is, sitting at the right hand of God." He then contrasted, "Set your mind on things above, not on things on the earth" (Col. 3:1-2). Heaven is NOT on earth!
         (1) Earlier in the same book, Paul reassured these Christians that their "hope" was "laid up for [them] in heaven" (Col. 1:5). NOT on earth!
      (c) Peter wrote of the Christian's "living hope" that is "reserved in heaven" (1 Pet. 1:3-4). Why didn't he say "reserved on earth," if heaven is going to be here?
   3. Heaven and earth are NOT the same and never will be! The Bible makes that clear!
      (a) Heaven, the dwelling place of God, existed eternally before earth was ever created.
      (b) Heaven, the dwelling place of God, will exist eternally after earth is destroyed!
      (c) To limit man's eternal dwelling place to earth is to limit the eternal God!
E. When Jesus returns, the earth and everything in it will be destroyed.
   1. The New Testament repeatedly teaches that the earth and the heavens (i.e., the skies, atmosphere, planets and universe [Gen. 1:1, 14, 20; 22:17; Ezek. 31:6]) will "pass away."
      (a) Jesus said, "Heaven and earth will pass away" (Matt. 24:35).
      (b) Peter said, "...the heavens will pass away with a great noise" (2 Pet. 3:10).

(c) John said, "...the first heaven and the first earth had passed away" (Rev. 21:1).
(d) The Greek word in these verses for "pass away" *(parerchomai)* means "to come to an end and so no longer be there, *pass away, disappear*" (BDAG [2000], p. 776). Vine says that it will "perish" (461).
(e) When Jesus comes back, the earth will "perish" and "no longer be there."
2. The apostle John saw a vision of the return of Christ and stated that "the earth and the heaven fled away" "from [Jesus'] face" (Rev. 20:11).
   (a) The Greek word for "fled away" *(pheugo)* means "to cease being visible, *vanish, disappear*" (BDAG [2000], p. 1052).
   (b) John goes on to state, "And there was found no place for them."
   (c) When Jesus comes back, the earth will not remain. It will vanish from His presence.
3. In the context of "the day of the Lord," when Christ returns at the end of time and the material creation perishes and passes away, Peter describes it in great detail.
   (a) "The heavens will pass away with a great noise" (2 Pet. 3:10).
      (1) The great noise is a "whizzing sound of rapid motion" *(Robertson's Word Pictures)* or "noise made by something passing with great force and rapidity" (BDAG [2000], p. 907).
      (2) It will be obvious. It will be catastrophic.
   (b) "The elements will melt with fervent heat" (2 Pet. 3:10).
      (1) Note how descriptive and detailed God is (down to the very elements) in the total destruction of His creation.
      (2) The "elements" (Greek *stoicheion*) refer to "basic components of something... of substances underlying the natural world, the basic elements from which everything in the world is made and of which it is composed" (BDAG [2000], 946).
      (3) The word "melt" is also translated "destroyed" (NASB), "dissolved" (ASV).
      (4) The Greek word for "melt" *(luo)* is found three times in 2 Peter 3:10-12 – "melt" in verse 10 and "dissolved" in verses 11-12. Verse 11 states that "all these things will be dissolved."
      (5) The Greek word *luo* means "to reduce something by violence into its components, *destroy*...Of the parts of the universe, as it is broken up and destroyed in the final conflagration" (BDAG [2000], p. 607).
      (6) The word "melt" in verse 12 is a different Greek word *(teko)*, which means "to cause something to become liquid, *melt*" (BDAG [2000], p. 1001).
      (7) The elements will be made liquid and destroyed by a "fervent heat" (Greek *kausoo)*, a word which means to "be consumed by heat, burn up...destroyed by burning" (BDAG [2000], p. 536).
      (8) The very fundamental components that make up the earth, everything in it and everything surrounding it will be completely consumed. There will be nothing left, and for sure no place for man to abide for 1,000 years or for all eternity!
   (c) "The earth and the works that are in it will be burned up" (2 Pet. 3:10).
      (1) "Burned up" is from the Greek *katakaio,* which means "burn down, burn up, consume by fire" (BDAG [2000], p. 517). (Verse 12 also mentions "fire.")
      (2) Some translations instead read "laid bare," "exposed," "found," "discovered."
         (i) These words come from a different Greek word that is found in some Greek manuscripts.
         (ii) However, the idea of the earth being "found" or "discovered" at Jesus' return does not match the context of this passage at all (or the context of

the New Testament as a whole). Every single thought and word in this text is about the heavens and the earth being completely destroyed by fire. There will be nothing left to be found or exposed. That's the point of the context.
- (iii) If the word in 2 Peter 3:10 really meant that the earth would be "found" (Greek *heurisko),* Thayer notes that it "shall be found namely for destruction, i.e., will be unable to hide themselves from the doom decreed them by God" (261).
- (d) A consuming heat will completely burn up, dissolve and melt the earth into nothing!
4. Peter and John both spoke of a "new heavens and a new earth" when Jesus returns.
   - (a) Peter said, "We, according to His promise, look for new heavens and a new earth in which righteousness dwells" (2 Pet. 3:13).
   - (b) John said, "Now I saw a new heaven and a new earth, for the first heaven and the first earth had passed away. Also there was no more sea" (Rev. 21:1).
   - (c) What is "a new heaven(s) and a new earth"?
     - (1) The phrase is found two other times in Scripture, both in the book of Isaiah (65:17; 66:22), where it is used figuratively of Israel's future (i.e., "new") in the Messianic age, when they return from Babylonian captivity.
     - (2) If the phrase is used figuratively in these passages, would it not also be expected to be figurative (i.e., not a literal heavens and earth) in other uses?
   - (d) Put the phrase into the context of the passages in 2 Peter 3 and Revelation 21.
     - (1) The events being described are at the end of time when Christ returns.
     - (2) The present material heavens and earth will have passed away and been destroyed. It will be "no more."
     - (3) Physical bodies will have been changed to new incorruptible bodies, because the physical body is not suited for the new world to come (1 Cor. 15:51-58).
     - (4) The new heavens and new earth could not be a renovated earth, for Scripture emphatically teaches that it will be consumed and no longer be there.
   - (e) The Greek New Testament has two words that are translated "new."
     - (1) The word "new" in these verses is from the Greek word *kainos*, which is not "new" in time but "new" in quality (Vine 430-431; Trench 220).
     - (2) Kittel's *Theological Dictionary of the New Testament* holds that it means "new in nature" and something that is "not yet used" (III, 447-448).
     - (3) Vine also indicates that it is "unused" (430).
     - (4) Thayer includes "unused, unworn" in his definition (317).
     - (5) Trench's *New Testament Synonyms* emphasizes that *kainos* denotes "the new, as set over against that which has seen service, the outworn, the effete or marred through age" (220).
     - (6) It is apparent that the "new" heaven and "new" earth has nothing to do with the present material earth, which is used, outworn and ultimately dissolved. There is no true hope laid up in this earth...at all!
   - (f) So what is the "new heavens and new earth"?
     - (1) There is an obvious comparison and contrast drawn between "the first heaven and the first earth" and the "new heaven and new earth."
     - (2) "The first" is where we dwell now.
     - (3) "The new" is where we will dwell later.
       - (i) Scripture affirms that "heaven" is where faithful Christians will dwell later.
       - (ii) "Heaven" is the place to which Jesus ascended (Mark 16:19; Acts 1:11).

                1. As our "forerunner (Heb. 6:19-20), He has "consecrated for us" "a new and living way" (Heb. 10:20) into the same place He entered.
                2. Jesus did not ascend or enter into a renovated earth but into the presence of the eternal dwelling of God! So will faithful Christians!
            (iii) "Heaven" is the place from which Jesus will descend (1 Thess. 4:16).
            (iv) "Heaven" is the dwelling place of God (Matt. 6:9).
            (v) "Heaven" is the place of reward for the people of God (Matt. 5:12).
            (vi) "Heaven" is where God's faithful will ultimately dwell (Phil. 3:20).
            (vii) Jesus went to "prepare a place" for us (John 14:2). It will be a new world for us! It will be a new dwelling place where we have never been before.
        (4) It is thus apparent that "the new heaven and new earth" must be a figurative way of describing where God's people will dwell eternally with Him in "heaven." Heaven is truly where "righteousness dwells" (2 Pet. 3:13).
        (5) Wayne Jackson concluded, "The 'new heavens and new earth' becomes a *figure of speech* signifying a new environment. Just as we now live in an environment in which we breathe the air of 'heaven,' and take sustenance of the bounties of the 'earth,' even so, we look forward to a future realm, not material in nature, but a 'new heavens and new earth' of *spiritual* composition" (*Bible Words and Theological Terms Made Easy,* p. 80).
    F. By understanding the Bible's clear teaching about the raising of all the dead and the utter destruction of the earth upon Christ's return at "the end," it is quite obvious that:
        1. The end has not yet come (as some so advocate).
        2. There will be no 1,000-year reign of Jesus on the earth (as some so advocate).
        3. Heaven will not be on earth (as some so advocate).
        4. Let us stay true to what the Scriptures teach and rejoice in them!

VIII. At the Second Coming of Christ, Every Person Who Has Ever Lived Will Be Judged!
   A. The Bible has much to say about the day of judgment.
        1. The day of judgment is a major theme of both the Old and New Testaments.
        2. The doctrine of "eternal judgment" is an "elementary principle of Christ" (Heb. 6:1-2).
        3. While justice may not always be apparent or even present for wrongs and crimes that people do on this earth, the Bible teaches that there is a final judgment coming.
        (a) The New Testament calls it:
            (1) "The judgment" (Matt. 5:21, 22; 12:41, 42; Luke 10:14; 11:31, 32; Heb. 9:27).
            (2) "The day of judgment" (Mt. 10:15; 11:22, 24; 12:36; 2 Pet. 2:9; 3:7; 1 Jn. 4:17).
            (3) "The judgment of the great day" (Jude 6)
            (4) "The judgment to come" (Acts 24:25).
            (5) "The day of wrath and revelation of the righteous judgment of God" (Rom. 2:5).
            (6) "Eternal judgment" (Heb. 6:2).
        (b) Although one may "get away with sin" on this earth, there is a judgment coming!
            (1) "Beloved, do not avenge yourselves, but rather give place to wrath; for it is written, 'Vengeance is Mine, I will repay,' says the Lord" (Rom. 12:19).
            (2) "...When the Lord Jesus is revealed from heaven," He will return in flaming fire taking vengeance on those who do not know God, and on those who do not obey the gospel of our Lord Jesus Christ" (2 Thess. 1:7-8).
            (3) "For if we sin willfully after we have received the knowledge of the truth, there no longer remains a sacrifice for sins, but a certain fearful expectation of judgment" (Heb. 10:26-27).

                (4) "God is not mocked; for whatever a man sows, that he will also reap" (Gal. 6:7).
        4. Above all other days, this is the day for which every person must be prepared!
    B. The Bible teaches that Jesus Christ will be the Judge.
        1. God is "the Judge of all the earth" (Gen. 18:25).
            (a) He is the one who has determined the who, the how, the when and the why of judgment.
            (b) He is the one who has determined Who will sit on the throne of judgment.
        2. Jesus said that "the Father...has committed all judgment to the Son...and has given Him authority to execute judgment" (John 5:22, 27).
            (a) Jesus is God and therefore omniscient, knowing perfectly the will of God and knowing perfectly the judgment that must be rendered.
            (b) God has given Jesus authority to judge.
        3. Paul told the Athenians that "God...will judge the world in righteousness by the Man whom He has ordained" (Acts 17:31; cf. 10:42).
            (a) It is not just the divine side of Jesus that will judge mankind (John 5:22, 27), but the man/human side of Jesus will also judge. Jesus, as the Judge, retains identity with man and is able to sympathize with our weaknesses (Heb. 2:17-18; 4:15).
            (b) God has "ordained" or "appointed" (NASB) Jesus, "the Man," to judge.
            (c) He will judge as both the Son of God (John 5:22) and the Son of Man (Acts 17:31).
        4. All judgment will take place "before the judgment seat of Christ" (2 Cor. 5:10).
            (a) He is "the righteous judge" (2 Tim. 4:8). It is His throne. It is His judgment seat.
            (b) Paul told Timothy that "the Lord Jesus Christ...will judge" (2 Tim. 4:1).
            (c) Peter told his readers that Christ "is ready to judge" (1 Pet. 4:5).
    C. The Bible teaches about the timing of the day of judgment.
        1. Jesus taught that the day of judgment would occur "when the Son of Man comes in His glory, and all the holy angels with Him" (Matt. 25:31-32).
        2. Paul taught that the day of judgment would occur "at His appearing" (2 Tim. 4:1), "when the Lord Jesus is revealed from heaven with His mighty angels" (2 Th. 1:7-9).
        3. Peter taught that "the day of judgment" (2 Pet. 3:7) would occur at "His coming" (3:4), when "the day of the Lord will come as a thief in the night" (3:10).
        4. John taught that the day of judgment would occur (and the Judge would sit on His "great white throne") after "the earth and the heaven fled away" (Rev. 20:11-12).
        5. Therefore, the day of judgment will occur upon the return of Jesus Christ, and after all of the dead are raised and after the heavens and the earth are destroyed.
    D. The Bible teaches about the certainty of the day of judgment.
        1. Paul "reasoned" with Felix about "the judgment to come" (Acts 24:25). It is coming!
        2. The Bible says that the time of "the judgment" is "appointed" (Heb. 9:27).
            (a) "Appointed" is from the Greek word *apokeimai,* which literally means "laid up."
            (b) "It is unavoidable in view of inevitable circumstance, *it is certain, one is destined*" (BDAG [2000], p. 113).
            (c) Vine says that it means, "reserved." Judgment is a "must" (2 Cor. 5:10).
            (d) Judgment is as certain, as reserved, as unavoidable as physical death (Heb. 9:27).
        3. The Bible says that God "has appointed a day on which He will judge" (Acts 17:30-31).
            (a) "Appointed" in this text is from the Greek word *histemi*, which means to "set/fix a time" (BDAG [2000], p. 482). It denotes that something is "made to stand."
            (b) God has set the day on which the world will be judged. It is a fixed day!

- (c) And He has guaranteed it as such "by raising [Jesus] from the dead" (17:31). As historically certain as the resurrection of Jesus Christ is, so is the judgment!
- (d) No wonder, in this context, Paul cites this as a motive for all men to repent!

E. The Bible teaches about the persons who will be judged on the day of judgment.
1. When Jesus returns, "All the nations will be gathered before Him" (Matt. 25:32).
2. Jesus will "judge the world," which includes "all men everywhere" (Acts 17:30-31).
3. Jesus "will judge the living and the dead at His appearing" (2 Tim. 4:1; cf. Acts 10:42).
4. Jesus will judge the "small and great" (Rev. 20:11-12).
5. Jesus will judge the "righteous" and the "unrighteous" (Matt. 25:31-46).
6. "We must all appear before the judgment seat of Christ" (2 Cor. 5:10).
7. "We shall all stand before the judgment seat of Christ" (Rom. 14:10).
8. Every person who has ever lived is amenable to God and will be judged by Jesus on the day of judgment (Acts 17:30-31).
9. "God is no respecter of persons" (Acts 10:34; cf. 1 Pet. 1:17). No one will miss this day!

F. The Bible teaches about the standard that will be used on the day of judgment.
1. Man will not be judged by:
   (a) Anyone's opinions or feelings or personal beliefs.
   (b) Anyone's subjective standard of right and wrong.
   (c) What a church taught, what a parent believed or what a preacher said.
2. The all-authoritative Word of God will be the standard of judgment.
   (a) Jesus made this very clear when He said, "He who rejects Me, and does not receive My words, has that which judges him—the word that I have spoken will judge him in the last day" (John 12:48).
3. Every person will be judged according to the law of God under which each one lived.
   (a) Those who lived in the Patriarchal Age will be judged by the law revealed to them, which includes the Gentiles throughout the Old Testament (Rom. 2:12-15).
   (b) Those who lived and died in the Mosaic Age (specifically, the Jews) will be judged by the law of Moses (Rom. 2:12; Luke 16:29-31).
   (c) Those who lived in the Christian Age will be judged by the gospel, the new covenant of Christ (Rom. 2:16; John 12:48).
   (d) Each person was, is and will be amenable to the law of God under which he/she lived and will be held accountable (Acts 17:30-31).
4. The apostle John was shown a vision of the great and awesome day of judgment.
   (a) On the day of judgment, "books" (plural) will be "opened" (Rev. 20:12).
   (b) There can be no doubt that the Word of God will be opened on that day (Jn. 12:48).
   (c) Another book that will be opened is "the Book of Life" (Rev. 20:12).
      (1) Only those whose names are in the Book of Life will enter heaven (Rev. 21:27).
   (d) Every person will be judged "by the things...written in the books" (Rev. 20:12).
5. The standard of judgment will be the absolute truth of God's Word—nothing else!

G. The Bible teaches about the conduct that will be judged on the day of judgment.
1. The judgment made on that final day will not be arbitrary or unfair.
   (a) The "righteous judge" (2 Tim. 4:8) will judge "in righteousness" (Acts 17:31), for "true and righteous are [His] judgments" (Rev. 16:7).
   (b) The judgment will be done fairly, justly and properly (1 Pet. 1:17).
2. Here's a key to remember: One's obedience (or disobedience) to the will of God determines (and will determine) his standing before God on that day (Matt. 7:21-23).
3. On that day, "each of us shall give account of himself to God" (Rom. 14:12).

4. On that day, each one will "receive the things done in the body, according to what he has done, whether good or bad" (2 Cor. 5:10).
   (a) Each person will be judged (and receive) "according to":
      (1) His "works" (Rev. 20:13; 22:12; 1 Pet. 1:17; Rom. 2:6; Ecc. 12:14; 11:9).
      (2) His "words" (Matt. 12:36-37; Jas. 3:1-12; 1:26; Rev. 21:8; Eph. 4:29).
      (3) His "thoughts" (1 Cor. 4:5; 2 Cor. 10:4-5; Mark 7:21-23; Heb. 4:12; Gen. 6:5).
      (4) His "secrets" (Rom. 2:16; Ecc. 12:14; 1 Cor. 4:5; Heb. 4:13).
      (5) His sins of commission (1 John 3:4; John 8:34; Ezek. 18:20; Rom. 1:18-32).
      (6) His sins of omission (Jas. 4:17; Luke 6:46; Luke 12:47).
      (7) His response to the gospel (hearing, repenting, obeying) (Matt. 10:14-15; 11:20-25; 12:38-42; Rom. 2:3-11; 1 Pet. 4:17-18; 2 Thess. 1:7-10).
   (b) Thankfully, no forgiven sin will be remembered against us (Heb. 8:12).
5. The way one has lived (righteously or unrighteously) will determine his judgment.

H. The Bible teaches about the separation and the sentencing of the day of judgment.
   1. When Jesus, the Righteous Judge and the Son of Man, returns:
      (a) "He will sit on the throne of His glory" (Matt. 25:31).
      (b) "He will separate them one from another" (Matt. 25:32).
      (c) "He will set the sheep on His right hand, but the goats on the left" (Matt. 25:33).
      (d) There will be a great separation that takes place, and it will be based upon what one has "done in the body, whether good or bad" (2 Cor. 5:10).
      (e) Jesus will separate the righteous from the unrighteous.
   2. The Judge will weigh a man's life against the absolute standard of judgment.
      (a) The purpose of the day of judgment will not be to determine one's eternal destiny.
         (1) Upon one's death, his final destiny is already known, and it is fixed and unalterable (Luke 16:22-26; 2 Pet. 2:9).
         (2) One's final destiny is based upon what he has "done in the body…whether good or bad" (2 Cor. 5:10) and how that compares to God's Word (John 12:48).
      (b) Rather, the purpose of the day of judgment will be to reveal "the righteous judgment of God" (Rom. 2:5).
   3. The Judge will pronounce final sentences. That is the ultimate purpose of the day!
      (a) There are only two possible sentences that the Judge will issue on that day:
         (1) To the righteous, eternal life (Matt. 25:23, 34, 46):
            (i) "Well done, good and faithful servant… Enter into the joy of your lord."
            (ii) "Come, you blessed of My Father, inherit the kingdom prepared for you from the foundation of the world."
            (iii) "…The righteous [will go away] into eternal life."
         (2) To the unrighteous, eternal punishment (Matt. 7:23; 25:41, 46):
            (i) "I never knew you; depart from Me, you who practice lawlessness!"
            (ii) "Depart from Me, you cursed, into the everlasting fire prepared for the devil and his angels."
            (iii) "These will go away into everlasting punishment."
      (b) The judgment and the sentence of Christ on that day will be irreversible!
         (1) There will not be a "last chance" given or a "stay of execution."
         (2) There will not be an opportunity to "appeal the ruling."
         (3) His sentence is final (Luke 16:22-26). His sentence is forever (Matt. 25:46).

I. Regardless of the sentence on that day, "Every knee shall bow to [the Lord], and every tongue shall confess to God" (Rom. 14:11).

1. On that day, every person who has ever lived will be gathered before Christ.
2. On that day, every person who has ever lived will give account of himself to God.
3. On that day, every person who has ever lived will bow to and confess the Lord.
4. On that day, every person who has ever lived will believe Jesus is God's Son.
5. How much better would it be to bow the knee and confess with the tongue NOW, rather than let the day of judgment be the first time!

IX. At the Second Coming of Christ, Eternal Destinies Will Be Rewarded to All!
  A. The second coming of Christ will be "the end" of many things (1 Cor. 15:24).
     1. It will be the end of this earth and all life and things on this earth (2 Pet. 3:10-13).
     2. It will be the end of opportunities to be saved from sin (2 Cor. 6:2; Heb. 3:12-15).
     3. It will be the end of opportunities to make preparations (Matt. 25:1-13, 14-30).
     4. It will be the end of all second chances and access to His grace (Luke 17:26-30).
     5. It will be the end of the reign of Christ over His kingdom (1 Cor. 15:20-28).
  B. At the same time, the second coming will be the "beginning" of eternity for all people.
     1. Jesus said, The unrighteous "will go away into eternal punishment" (Matt. 25:46).
     2. Jesus said, "The righteous" will go "into eternal life" (Matt. 25:46).
     3. The same word "eternal" (Greek *aionios*) is used for both heaven and hell.
        (a) The Greek word *aionios* "pertains to a period of unending duration, *without end*" (BDAG [2000], p. 33), *"never to cease, everlasting"* (Thayer 20).
        (b) *Aionios* is set in contrast with the "temporary" (Greek *proskairos*, "for a season") in 2 Corinthians 4:18 (Vine 207). "For the things which are seen are temporary, but the things which are not seen are eternal."
        (c) The same word *(aionios)* that is used for God (Rom. 16:26), for He is the eternal/everlasting God, is used of the duration of the final destinies of all mankind.
        (d) There will be eternal, everlasting, without-end, never-to-cease "life" for those who obey God and His will (John 3:16; Heb. 5:9; Tit. 1:2).
        (e) There will be eternal, everlasting, without-end, never-to-cease "punishment" for those who do not obey God and His will (2 Thess. 1:8-9; Matt. 25:41; Jude 7).
        (f) Just as one will last forever and ever, so equally will the other.
  C. The righteous shall be rewarded with eternity in heaven.
     1. Heaven is a real, literal (but not material) place (Matt. 25:31-46; John 14:1-6).
     2. Heaven is the eternal dwelling place of the Godhead and of His angels.
        (a) It is the abode of God (Matt. 5:16; 6:9; 12:50; Heb. 9:24; Rev. 21:2-3).
        (b) It is the abode:
           (1) From which Jesus descended (John 3:13, 31; 6:38).
           (2) To which Jesus ascended (Acts 1:9-11; Heb. 4:14; 6:20; 9:24; John 14:1-3).
           (3) Where Jesus is now, at the right hand of God (Heb. 8:1; Eph. 1:20; Col. 3:1; Heb. 1:3; 10:12; 12:2; 1 Pet. 3:22).
           (4) From which Jesus will descend at His return (1 Thess. 4:16; Phil. 3:20-21).
        (c) It is the abode of the Holy Spirit (Acts 2:1-4, 33; 1 Pet. 1:12; Luke 3:22; 1 John 5:7).
        (d) It is the abode of angels (Matt. 18:10; 22:30; 24:36).
     3. Heaven will be the eternal dwelling place of:
        (a) The faithful saints of days gone by (Matt. 8:11; Gen. 25:8; 35:29; 1 Thess. 2:19-20).
        (b) Young children who died in childhood or in the womb (2 Sam. 12:23).
        (c) Those who are obedient to Jesus Christ and His will (Heb. 5:8-9).
        (d) Those who are in the Lord's church and part of His bride (Heb. 12:23; Rev. 21:1-3).
        (e) Those who have their citizenship in heaven (Phil. 3:20-21).

(f) Those whose names are written in the Book of Life (Rev. 20:15; 21:27; Heb. 12:23).
(g) The "few" who walk the "narrow way which leads to life" (Matt. 7:13-14).
4. As the eternal dwelling place of God's faithful, heaven is described in God's Word as:
   (a) The "place" that Jesus went to "prepare," which has "many rooms" (John 14:1-3).
   (b) The place where "God will dwell with…His people" forever and ever (Rev. 21:3).
   (c) The place where God's people get "to be at home with the Lord" (2 Cor. 5:8).
   (d) The place where God's people "shall see His face" (Rev. 22:4).
   (e) "The eternal inheritance" (Heb. 9:15; cf. Eph. 1:11; Rom. 8:17; Col. 3:24; Tit. 3:7).
   (f) "An inheritance incorruptible, undefiled and that does not fade away" (1 Pet. 1:4).
   (g) "Paradise" (2 Cor. 12:4; Rev. 2:7).
   (h) An "eternal home" (2 Cor. 5:1; Ecc. 12:5).
   (i) An eternal "rest" from one's labors (Heb. 4:9-11; Rev. 14:13; 2 Thess. 1:7).
   (j) A "reward" (Matt. 5:12; Col. 3:24; Heb. 11:26).
   (k) A "gain" that is "very much better" than being on earth (Phil. 1:21-23).
   (l) "The joy of your Lord" (Matt. 25:21, 23).
   (m) A place where no sin or abomination will ever invade (Rev. 21:8, 27; 22:3, 15).
   (n) A place of "no more death, nor sorrow, nor crying…no more pain" (Rev. 21:4).
   (o) A place where there is "no night" and no need for the "sun" (Rev. 21:25; 22:5).
   (p) A place where "His servants shall serve Him" (Rev. 22:3).
   (q) A "new heavens and a new earth in which righteousness dwells" (2 Pet. 3:13).
   (r) "The everlasting kingdom of our Lord" (2 Pet. 1:11; cf. Matt. 25:34).
   (s) The place where "we shall always be with the Lord" (1 Thess. 4:17; cf. 2 Cor. 5:8).
   (t) The place of "eternal life" (John 3:15-16; Mark 10:30; Rom. 2:7; 1 John 5:11).
   (u) "The great city…having the glory of God," and adorned with beauty that is more than our minds can imagine in earthly terms (Rev. 21:10-11; cf. 21:12-22:5).
5. Knowing what God tells us about heaven ought to motivate every person to go there!

D. The unrighteous shall be rewarded with eternity in hell.
1. There are some Greek and Hebrew words that need to be properly defined and accurately used to understand what the Bible teaches about hell.
   (a) The King James Version translates three different Greek words as "hell," but only one of them is actually the word for the eternal place called hell.
   (b) The Greek word *hades* is translated "hell" in the KJV (Matt. 11:23; 16:18; Luke 10:15; 16:23; Acts 2:27, 31; Rev. 1:18; 6:8; 20:13-14), but it is not the eternal place.
      (1) *Hades*, rather, is "the nether world, as place of the dead" (BDAG [2000], p. 19), "the common receptacle of disembodies spirits" (Thayer 11).
      (2) *Hades* is the intermediate state of the dead, where the departed spirits/souls are awaiting the return of Jesus. They are very much alive and conscious (Luke 16:19-31).
      (3) The story in Luke 16 of the rich man and Lazarus demonstrates that there are two sides or compartments in the Hadean realm.
         (i) The side of the righteous is called "Abraham's bosom" (Luke 16:22) or "Paradise" (Luke 23:43).
         (ii) The side of the wicked is called "torments" (Luke 16:23) or "tartarus" (from the Greek word in 2 Peter 2:4 for "cast down to hell").
      (4) Upon the return of Jesus, Hades will deliver "up the dead who were in" it (i.e., all of the dead will be raised) and Hades will then be "cast into the lake

of fire" (Rev. 20:13-14). The realm of Hades will have fulfilled its purpose, as those spirits, who once abode therein, will then enter an eternal realm.
- (c) The Greek word *hades* corresponds with the Hebrew word *sheol,* which is sometimes translated "grave," but is also the realm of the dead who are awaiting Christ's return. (Compare Psalm 16:10 with Acts 2:27.)
- (d) The Greek word for "hell" (as the eternal place of fire and punishment of the wicked) is *gehenna.*
    - (1) *Gehenna* is found 12 times in the Greek New Testament, and Jesus Himself spoke eleven of those twelve (Matt. 5:22, 29, 30; 10:28; 18:9; 23:15, 33; Mark 9:43, 45, 47; Luke 12:5; Jas. 3:6).
    - (2) The word originally referred to the Valley of Hinnom, which was outside the south walls of the city of Jerusalem.
        - (i) In the dark days of Israel, children were sacrificed there to the pagan god Molech, by being thrown into the fiery arms of the idol (2 Kgs. 23:10).
        - (ii) After this practice ceased, the Jews disposed of all the refuse and rubbish from the city into this valley and also dead bodies of animals and unburied criminals. Fires were continually burning at Hinnom to consume the piles of trash and bodies (see Thayer 111).
        - (iii) *Gehenna* is the word that Jesus used more than anyone else to vividly depict the horrors of a place where fires of torment burn for eternity.
        - (iv) This is the word that "was adopted as a symbol for the eternal, conscious punishment of the wicked, both in body and soul (Mt. 10:28), following the judgment" (Jackson, *Bible Words and Theological Terms*, p. 82).
2. Just as heaven is a real, literal place, so hell is a real, literal place (Matt. 25:31-46).
3. Hell will be the eternal dwelling place of:
    - (a) "The devil and his angels" (Matt. 25:41; Rev. 20:10).
    - (b) "The ungodly and the sinner" (1 Pet. 4:17-18).
    - (c) Those characterized by "disobedience" (Col. 3:6; Eph. 5:6; Heb. 2:2).
    - (d) "Those who do not obey the gospel" (2 Thess. 1:8; 1 Pet. 4:17).
    - (e) "The cowardly, unbelieving, abominable, murderers, sexually immoral, sorcerers, idolaters, and all liars" (Rev. 21:8; cf. 22:15).
    - (f) Those who "practice" "adultery, fornication, uncleanness, lewdness, idolatry, sorcery, hatred, contentions, jealousies, outbursts of wrath, selfish ambitions, dissensions, heresies, envy, murders, drunkenness, revelries, and the like" (Gal. 5:19-21; cf. Rom. 1:18-32).
    - (g) Those who are "fornicators...idolaters...adulterers...homosexuals...sodomites... thieves...covetous...drunkards...revilers...extortioners" (1 Cor. 6:9-10).
    - (h) Those who do not serve the needs of "one of the least of these" (Matt. 25:41-46).
    - (i) Christians who are "lukewarm" (Rev. 3:15-16).
    - (j) Christians who have turned from the way of truth (2 Pet. 2:20-22; Jas. 5:19-20).
    - (k) Some religious people who do not actually "do the will of the Father" (Mt. 7:21-23).
    - (l) Those who "add to" and "take away from" the Word of God (Rev. 22:18-19).
    - (m) "Anyone not found written in the Book of Life" (Rev. 20:15).
    - (n) The "many" who walk the "broad way that leads to destruction" (Matt. 7:13).
4. As the eternal dwelling place of those who are lost, hell is described in God's Word as:
    - (a) A place that will be "everlasting" (2 Thess. 1:9).
    - (b) A place that will last "forever and ever" (Rev. 14:11).

- (c) A place of "eternal punishment" (Matt. 25:46).
- (d) A place where "both soul and body" will suffer eternal misery (Matt. 10:28).
- (e) A place of "indignation and wrath, tribulation and anguish" (Rom. 2:8-9).
- (f) A place where "they will be tormented day and night forever and ever" (Rev. 20:10).
- (g) A place where "the smoke of their torment ascends forever and ever" (Rev. 14:11).
- (h) A place where "they have no rest day or night" (Rev. 14:11).
- (i) A place of "outer darkness" and "blackness of darkness" (Matt. 25:30; Jude 13).
- (j) A place of "fire" that is described as:
  - (1) "everlasting fire" (Matt. 25:41).
  - (2) "the furnace of fire" (Matt. 13:42, 50).
  - (3) "the lake of fire" (Rev. 20:14-15).
  - (4) "the lake which burns with fire and brimstone" (Rev. 21:8; 20:10).
  - (5) "the fire is not quenched...the fire that shall never be quenched" (Mk. 9:44-48).
- (k) A place where "their worm does not die" (Mark 9:44, 46, 48).
- (l) A place where "there will be wailing and gnashing of teeth" (Matt. 13:42, 50).
- (m) A place where there is no relief and no hope (Matt. 25:41, 46; cf. Luke 16:26).
- (n) A "worse punishment" than death "without mercy" (Heb. 10:28-31).
- (o) A place of "everlasting punishment away from the presence of the Lord and from the glory of His power" (2 Thess. 1:9; cf. 1 John 1:5).

5. There is no Biblical evidence to support the false doctrine that those who are sentenced to hell will be annihilated (i.e., cease to exist) and not endure the fires of hell of all eternity!
   - (a) Some try to use the word "destroy" in Matthew 10:28 to teach that the lost in hell will simply go out of existence after a short period of time.
   - (b) However, the same Greek word for "destroy" *(apollumi)* is used elsewhere in the New Testament of "wineskins" that "break" (Matt. 9:17), "sheep" that are "lost" (Matt. 10:6), the "lost" people Jesus came to save (Matt. 18:11), a "coin" that was "lost" (Luke 15:8-9), a "son" who was "lost" (Luke 15:24), etc.
     - (1) None of these things could be said to be annihilated or going out of existence. Obviously, that is not what this word means.
   - (c) Regarding the Greek word *apollumi,* "The idea is not extinction but ruin, loss, not of being, but of well-being" (Vine 164).
     - (1) "'Destroy' here is not annihilation, but eternal punishment in Gehenna" (*Robertson's Word Pictures*).
     - (2) "Metaphorically, to devote or give over to eternal misery" (Thayer 64).
   - (d) One needs only to read the Biblical descriptions of hell to understand that it is both an (1) eternal and (2) conscious torment. (Read over the list under IX, D, 4 again.)
     - (1) Inhabitants will suffer tribulation and anguish forever and ever!
     - (2) Inhabitants will have no rest day or night forever and ever!
     - (3) Inhabitants will wail and gnash their teeth forever and ever!
     - (4) Inhabitants will suffer with worms that do not die forever and ever!
     - (5) Inhabitants will be tormented day and night forever and ever!
     - (6) Inhabitants will have smoke from their torment ascending forever and ever!
6. Knowing what God tells us about hell ought to motivate every person not to go there!

E. There are eternal rewards awaiting every person who has ever lived:
  1. The eternal bliss of heaven, in the presence of God, for His obedient children.
  2. The eternal damnation of hell, away from God's presence, for those who do not obey.

X. Every Person Needs to Be Prepared for the Second Coming of Christ!
A. God does not want any person to be lost (2 Pet. 3:9; 1 Tim. 2:4).
B. God wants every person to spend eternity in heaven with Him (John 3:16; Rom. 5:8).
C. Christ came the first time to save man from sins (Isa. 53:3-6; Mt. 1:21; Gal. 1:3-4; Jn. 3:17).
D. Christ will come the second time to gather His saved to home in heaven (1 Thess. 4:17).
E. At that moment, every person must be prepared to meet Him (Matt. 24:44) by:
   1. Bowing the knee before Him now and confessing Him as Lord now (Phil. 2:10-11).
   2. Working out his salvation with fear and trembling according to God's will (Phil. 2:12-13).
   3. Doing the will of the Father and obeying His commands (Matt. 7:21-23; Heb. 5:9).
   4. Enduring the trials and temptations of life and resisting sin in our lives (Jas. 1:2-21).
   5. Remaining faithful to the Lord and walking with Him every day (Rev. 2:10; 1 Jn. 1:7).
F. If we neglect opportunities to obey, it will increase our guilt on that day (Matt. 11:20-24).
G. Through the prophet Amos, God told His people, "Prepare to meet your God!" (4:12).
H. Through the New Testament, God tells His people today, "Prepare to meet your God!"

XI. Conclusion
A. So many false doctrines have been invented by man regarding the topic of the Lord's second coming, all of which have risen from attempts to make a text say something it does not.
   1. We must be ever vigilant to speak where the Bible speaks and remain silent where the Bible is silent.
   2. Jesus has not already returned the second time, as some claim He did in 70 A.D.
   3. There will not be any signs or warnings that precede His second coming, as some claim.
   4. Jesus will not come and reign on the earth for 1,000 years, as some claim.
   5. There will not be two separate resurrections (of the just and unjust), as some claim.
   6. Heaven will not be on a purified and renovated earth, as some claim.
   7. Those who go to hell will not be annihilated and go out of existence, as some claim.
   8. We must let the Bible speak, and not add to or take away from its teachings!
B. Jesus Christ is coming again the second time, but the day and hour are unknown!
C. The second coming of Christ will be a great and glorious day of victory!
D. The day of Christ's coming will be the last day on earth and the beginning of eternity!
E. The second coming of Christ is going to be a thrilling event!
   1. Hearing the heavenly shout and the trumpet of God will be thrilling!
   2. Spotting Jesus Himself descending from heaven with the clouds will be thrilling!
   3. Watching all of the graves open and all the dead coming forth will be thrilling!
   4. Seeing the living saints begin to ascend into the air will be thrilling!
   5. Witnessing bodies being transformed into new, celestial bodies will be thrilling!
   6. Beholding this temporary, physical dwelling of earth disappearing will be thrilling!
   7. Standing before our Friend and Savior as our Judge will be thrilling!
   8. Hearing His voice as He sentences our final destinies will be thrilling!
   9. BUT, there will be NOTHING more thrilling than entering into eternity with Him!
   10. Of course, all of this assumes that you are ready and longing for His return!
F. The eternal destinies of heaven and hell will be rewarded, based on one's life in Christ!
   1. Those who obeyed the Lord will enter into the joys of heaven with Him (Matt. 25:34).
   2. Those who have not obeyed the Lord will depart from Him into eternal fire (Mt. 25:41).
G. There is no reason or excuse for us to be "caught off guard" at His coming (1 Thess. 5:4)!
H. Christians should long for it and anticipate it with joyous expectation (Phil. 3:20; Tit. 2:13)!
I. Now is the time to make the necessary decisions and preparations for that day (Mt. 24:44)!
J. Let us be diligent to always be prepared for our Savior's return!

Recommended Resources

Books

Brown, David. *Christ's Second Coming: Will It Be Premillennial?* Rosemead, CA: Old Paths Book Club, 1953.

Cox, William E. *Biblical Studies in Final Things.* Phillipsburg, NJ: Presbyterian and Reformed, 1966.

Harper, E.R. *Prophecy Foretold Prophecy Fulfilled.* Abilene: E.R. Harper, n.d.

Jackson, Wayne. *The A.D. 70 Theory.* Stockton, CA: Courier Publications, 1990.

Laws, Jims, ed. *Then Cometh the End (Spiritual Sword Lectureship).* Memphis, TN: Getwell church of Christ, 1999.

Lipe, David L., ed. *At His Coming (Freed-Hardeman University Lectureship).* Henderson, TN: Freed-Hardeman University, 1998.

Lyon, Mack. *Did You Miss the Rapture?* Huntsville, AL: Publishing Designs, 1993.

Manor, J. Curtis. *Workbook on Denominational Doctrines (Vol. 2): Premillennialism or the Thousand-Year Reign of Christ on Earth.* Dallas: Gospel Teachers, 1984.

Meadows, James L. *Matthew 24.* Nashville: 21st Century Christian, 1996.

Pharr, David R. *Thy Kingdom Come: The Truth About the Rapture.* Huntsville, AL: Publishing Designs, 2003.

Taylor, Robert R., Jr. *The Bible Doctrine of Final Things.* Ripley, TN: Taylor Publications, 1993.

Thomas, Leslie G. *Truth, the Millennium, and the Battle of Armageddon.* Nashville: Gospel Advocate, 1979.

Wallace, Foy E., Jr. *God's Prophetic Word.* Fort Worth: Foy E. Wallace, Jr., 1960.

Willis, Mike. *"Then Cometh the End..."* Bowling Green, KY: Guardian of Truth, 1999.

Winkler, Dan. *Heaven: My Father's House.* Tuscaloosa, AL: Winkler Publications, 2003.

Winkler, Wendell, ed. *Premillennialism: True or False?* Montgomery, AL: Winkler Publications, 1978.

Articles

Brownlow, Leroy. "Because It Teaches the Kingdom Has Been Established and Christ Is Now Reigning." *Why I Am a Member of the Church of Christ.* Fort Worth: Brownlow Publishing, 1973. 86-93.

Butt, Kyle. "What Will Happen When Jesus Comes Again?" *ApologeticsPress.org* http://www.apologeticspress.org/APContent.aspx?category=11&article=1261&topic=83

Caskey, Guy V. "The Church Anxiously Awaits the Return of Jesus." *Introducing the Church of Christ.* Ed. Alvin Jennings. Fort Worth: Star Bible, 1981. 242-247.

Connally, Andrew M. "Is the Lord's Coming Imminent?" *Premillennialism: True or False?* Ed. Wendell Winkler. Montgomery, AL: Winkler Publications, 1978. 34-39.

Deaver, Roy. "Matthew 24." *Premillennialism: True or False?* Ed. Wendell Winkler. Montgomery, AL: Winkler Publications, 1978. 105-114.

Duncan, Bobby. "Premillennialism." *The Spiritual Sword* (Apr. 1997): 38-41.

Elkins, Garland. "The Last Days." *Premillennialism: True or False?* Ed. Wendell Winkler. Montgomery, AL: Winkler Publications, 1978. 68-73.

Gardner, Albert. "She Teaches the Future Punishment of the Wicked." *Introducing the Church of Christ.* Ed. Alvin Jennings. Fort Worth: Star Bible, 1981. 187-191.

Harper, E.R. "The Church of Christ—The Kingdom of the King of Kings." *The Church of Christ (Freed-Hardeman College Lectures).* Ed. Thomas B. Warren. Nashville: Gospel Advocate, 1971. 107-133.

Highers, Alan E. "Hell Is Eternal." *The Spiritual Sword* (Apr. 2005): 41-44.

Jackson, Wayne. "A New Heavens and a New Earth." *Revelation: Jesus Christ's Last Message of Hope.* Stockton, CA: Courier Publications, 2004. 109-115.

---. "Are There 'Signs' of the Second Coming of Christ?" *ChristianCourier.com*
https://www.christiancourier.com/articles/551-are-there-signs-of-the-second-coming-of-christ

---. "Facts About the Second Coming of Christ." *ChristianCourier.com*
https://www.christiancourier.com/articles/1559-facts-about-the-second-coming-of-christ

---. "Was Christ Mistaken About His Second Coming?" *ChristianCourier.com*
https://www.christiancourier.com/articles/1567-was-christ-mistaken-about-his-second-coming

---. "Will Heaven Be on Earth?" *ChristianCourier.com*
https://www.christiancourier.com/articles/1353-will-heaven-be-on-earth

Lanier, Roy H., Sr. "Revelation 20—Analysis and Exegesis." *Premillennialism: True or False?* Ed. Wendell Winkler. Montgomery, AL: Winkler Publications, 1978. 229-240.

McDade, Gary. "The Biblical Doctrine of Hell." *The Spiritual Sword* (Apr. 2003): 32-35.

Miller, Dave. "Is the Kingdom Yet to Be Established?" *ApologeticsPress.org*
https://apologeticspress.org/APContent.aspx?category=11&article=1088&topic=83

Nichols, Gus. "Christ and His Second Coming." *Jesus Christ, the Son of God (Freed-Hardeman College Lectures).* Ed. William Woodson. Nashville: Gospel Advocate, 1973. 9-18.

---. "Christ and the General Resurrection." *Jesus Christ, the Son of God (Freed-Hardeman College Lectures).* Ed. William Woodson. Nashville: Gospel Advocate, 1973. 19-30.

---. "Christ and the Judgment." *Jesus Christ, the Son of God (Freed-Hardeman College Lectures)*. Ed. William Woodson. Nashville: Gospel Advocate, 1973. 31-39.

---. "Christ and His Teaching on Heaven and Hell." *Jesus Christ, the Son of God (Freed-Hardeman College Lectures)*. Ed. William Woodson. Nashville: Gospel Advocate, 1973. 40-51.

Powell, David. "Heaven Is Real." *The Spiritual Sword* (Apr. 2005): 37-40.

Sain, David. "What Does the Bible Say About the Judgment?" *The Spiritual Sword* (Apr. 2003): 16-19.

Sanders, Phil. "Conscious Torment or Annihilation?" *The Spiritual Sword* (Jan. 2005): 38-42.

Taylor, Robert R., Jr. "Prophecy and Premillennialism." *Freedom: Heritage, Accomplishments, and Prospects in Christ (Freed-Hardeman College Lectures)*. Ed. William Woodson. Henderson, TN: Freed-Hardeman College, 1976. 206-220.

---. "Will There Be a Rapture?" *The Church of Tomorrow: Horizons and Destiny (Freed-Hardeman College Lectures)*. Ed. Winford Claiborne. Henderson, TN: Freed-Hardeman College, 1983. 326-331.

---. "Will There Be an Armageddon?" *The Church of Tomorrow: Horizons and Destiny (Freed-Hardeman College Lectures)*. Ed. Winford Claiborne. Henderson, TN: Freed-Hardeman College, 1983. 332-335.

---. "Will There Be a Thousand Year Reign of Christ on Earth?" *The Church of Tomorrow: Horizons and Destiny (Freed-Hardeman College Lectures)*. Ed. Winford Claiborne. Henderson, TN: Freed-Hardeman College, 1983. 336-340.

---. "Will There Be a Conversion to Christ of the Jewish Nation?" *The Church of Tomorrow: Horizons and Destiny (Freed-Hardeman College Lectures)*. Ed. Winford Claiborne. Henderson, TN: Freed-Hardeman College, 1983. 341-345.

Warren, David H. "Will Heaven Be on Earth?" *The Spiritual Sword* (July 2016): 26-30.

Winkler, Dan. "How Long Is Everlasting?" *The Spiritual Sword* (Jan. 2005): 16-20.

Winters, Clayton. "She Teaches the Bodily Resurrection of the Just and Unjust." *Introducing the Church of Christ*. Ed. Alvin Jennings. Fort Worth: Star Bible, 1981. 248-252.

Woodson, Williams. "Premillennialism." *The Future of the Church (Freed-Hardeman College Lectures)*. Ed. William Woodson. Henderson, TN: Freed-Hardeman College, 1978. 297-303.

Workman, Gary. "Is There an Eternal Hell?" *The Spiritual Sword* (Apr. 1992): 30-34.

---. "The Premillennial Theory." *Then Cometh the End (Spiritual Sword Lectureship)*. Ed. Jim Laws. Memphis, TN: Getwell church of Christ, 1999. 343-374.

---. "The Second of Christ: Will It Be Premillennial?" *Christ in You, the Hope of Glory (Freed-Hardeman College Lectures)*. Ed. Winford Claiborne. Henderson, TN: Freed-Hardeman University, 1993. 341-351.

---. "The Second of Christ: Will the Earth Be Destroyed and the Saved All Be in Heaven?" *Christ in You, the Hope of Glory (Freed-Hardeman College Lectures).* Ed. Winford Claiborne. Henderson, TN: Freed-Hardeman University, 1993. 352-360.

---. "The Second of Christ: Will the Wicked Be Eternally Punished or Annihilated?" *Christ in You, the Hope of Glory (Freed-Hardeman College Lectures).* Ed. Winford Claiborne. Henderson, TN: Freed-Hardeman University, 1993. 361-367.

<u>Periodicals</u>

The Spiritual Sword. January 1977. "Eternity—Heaven or Hell?"

The Spiritual Sword. October 1977. "Premillenialism—Part 1"

The Spiritual Sword. January 1978. "Premillenialism—Part 2"

The Spiritual Sword. April 1992. "The Final Things."

The Spiritual Sword. January 1999. "A Study of Premillenialism"

The Spiritual Sword. April 2003. "Life After Death."

The Spiritual Sword. January 2005. "Eternal Punishment."

The Spiritual Sword. July 2016. "A Handy Guide to Final Things."

Lesson 24: The Purpose and Duration of Miracles

I. **Understanding the Nature of Bible Miracles Is Fascinating and Essential.**
   A. The Bible is a book that is full of miracles, which intensifies the intrigue of its study.
      1. The Bible begins with the miracle of Creation (Gen. 1:1-31).
      2. Miracles surrounded the exodus from Egypt and the conquest of Canaan.
      3. Miracles were performed by Elijah and Elisha during the days of the divided kingdom.
      4. Miracles were even present during the period of the Babylonian Captivity.
      5. Most exciting of all are the miracles of Jesus and the apostles in the New Testament.
   B. While miracles permeate the Bible, they were not always prevalent throughout history.
      1. How many miracles did the great Noah, the preacher of righteousness, do?
      2. How many miracles did the great Abraham, the father of the Jewish nation, do?
      3. How many miracles did the great David, the man after God's own heart, do?
      4. This fact alone indicates that there must have been a purpose to the miracles—both to the deeds themselves and to the timing of them being done.
   C. Defining terms is essential and critical in any Biblical study, including a study of miracles.
      1. Miracles are referred to by various terms in the New Testament.
      2. Three times there are three terms used together—"miracles, wonders and signs" (Acts 2:22; 2 Cor. 12:12; 2 Thess. 2:9).
      3. "Miracles" is from the Greek word *dunamis* and denotes, "'power, inherent ability,' is used of works of a supernatural origin and character, such as could not be produced by natural agents and means" (Vine 412).
         (a) It is "a deed that exhibits ability to function powerfully, *deed of power*" (BDAG [2000], p. 263).
         (b) In the New Testament, *dunamis* is translated "miracles," "power" and "mighty works." It is the basis for our English words, "dynamite," "dynamic" and "dynamo."
         (c) The emphasis of the word "miracles" is on the *power* of their divine source.
      4. "Wonders" is from the Greek word *teras* and denotes, "something that astounds" (BDAG [2000], p. 999), "causing the beholder to marvel" (Vine 682).
         (a) A "wonder" is that which grabs the attention of the observer.
         (b) The emphasis of the word "wonder" is on the *effect* that it creates in the eyes and minds of the beholder, and thus the "power" of God is a "wonder" to behold.
      5. "Signs" is from the Greek word *semeion*, which served as a "mark, indication, token...of divine authority and power" (Vine 575).
         (a) *Semeion* denotes "an event that is an indication or confirmation of intervention by transcendent powers" (BDAG [2000], p. 920).
         (b) A "sign" points to something beyond itself, showing the significance of the miracles as being of divine power, and thus the one performing the miracle was sent by God, with His power and with His message.
         (c) Regarding *semeion,* Thayer notes, "of miracles and wonders by which God authenticates the men sent by him, or by which men prove that the cause they are pleading is God's" (573).
         (d) The emphasis of the word "sign" is on the *proof* that is demonstrated of divine authority, divine authenticity and divine purpose. The people looked for a "sign."
      6. Regarding these three terms, Vine notes, "A sign is intended to appeal to the understanding, a 'wonder' appeals to the imagination, a power (*dunamis*) indicates its source as supernatural" (Vine 682).

7. All three of these can be seen in each miracle recorded in the Bible. For example, consider the work that Philip did in Samaria.
   (a) Philip was doing "miracles" (Acts 8:6, 13), including casting out demons and healing many who were paralyzed and lame (8:7).
   (b) Philip was doing wonders, for Simon "was amazed" ("wondered," KJV) when he saw the deeds that Philip did (8:13).
   (c) Philip was doing "signs" (8:13), which obviously pointed to someone or something outside him and greater than him, which led "multitudes" to "heed the things spoken by Philip" (8:6) and to be "baptized" (8:12-13).
8. Thus, a miracle is a work of:
   (a) "supernatural origin and character, such as could not be produced by natural agents and means" (Vine 412)
   (b) "divine operation that transcends what is normally perceived as natural law; it cannot be explained upon any natural basis" (W. Jackson, "What Does...?").

D. Dividing the miracles recorded in the Bible into general categories can help the Bible student to grasp the breadth of the power of God as demonstrated in His Word. In his article, "What Does the Bible Say About Miracles?" Wayne Jackson classifies miracles in these seven general categories.
   1. Supernatural acts of creation
      (a) All things were created by the word of God (Heb. 11:3; Psa. 33:9) in only six days (Ex. 20:11) and were finished at the end of that week (Gen. 2:1-2).
      (b) God has power over all things.
   2. Suspension of natural laws (temporarily and locally)
      (a) Examples: Jesus calming the storm (Matt. 8:23-27), Jesus walking on water (Matt. 14:22-33).
      (b) God has power over His creation.
   3. Subjection of the physical body
      (a) Examples: The blind could see (John 9:1-7) and the lame could walk (Acts 3:1-11).
      (b) On other occasions, bodily punishments were inflicted (1 Kgs. 13:4; Acts 13:11).
      (c) God has power over disease and the human body.
   4. Power over death
      (a) Examples: The resurrection of Lazarus after four days (John 11:1-44) and the resurrection of Christ Himself (1 Cor. 15:16-19).
      (b) God has power over man's greatest fear – death.
   5. Casting out demons
      (a) Examples: The demon cast out of a boy that was suffering convulsions (Luke 9:37-42), the demons (named "Legion") cast out into a herd of swine (Luke 8:26-39).
      (b) God has power over man's greatest enemy – Satan.
   6. Manipulation of material things
      (a) Examples: Turning water into wine (John 2:1-11), multiplying five loaves and two fish to feed 5,000 men, plus women and children (John 6:1-14).
      (b) God has power over the elements.
   7. Authority over plant and animal kingdoms
      (a) Examples: Balaam's donkey speaking (Num. 22:28-30), Jesus destroying a fig tree (Matt. 21:18-20).
      (b) God has power over life and every living thing.

E. The study of Bible miracles is fascinating!
   1. There is and can be no doubt that God worked incredible miracles in Bible times, especially during the ministry of Jesus Christ and the labors of His apostles.
   2. "God" was absolutely "bearing witness both with signs and wonders, with various miracles, and gifts of the Holy Spirit, according to His own will" (Heb. 2:4).
F. But the critical question that must be answered is: "Are Bible-type miracles still happening today?" What does the Bible have to say?
   1. There are many folks who claim that miracles are still happening today.
      (a) Some claim that miraculous powers, like the ones in the Bible, are still in effect today.
      (b) Some claim that the baptism of the Holy Spirit is still available today.
      (c) Some claim that the miraculous spiritual gifts are still being bestowed today.
      (d) Some claim that the miraculous gift of speaking in tongues is still practiced today.
      (e) Some claim that the revelation of inspired messages are still being given today.
      (f) Some claim that continual confirmation of a confirmed message is needed today.
      (g) Some claim that they have witnessed a modern-day miracle.
   2. The only way to know if these claims are true is not to consult man but to consult God!
      (a) What does the Bible teach about the purpose of miracles?
      (b) What does the Bible teach about the persons who could perform miracles?
      (c) What does the Bible teach about the perpetuity of miracles?
      (d) Our greatest concern must be—what does the Bible teach?
   3. The focus of this study will be upon the miracles and the teaching of the New Testament.
      (a) Here is a point to consider: If the Bible teaches that miracles were to continue to the present day (and beyond), then it could not also teach that they were to have ceased.
      (b) If the Bible teaches that miracles were to have ceased already, then it could not also teach that miracles are still happening today.
      (c) The Bible does not contradict itself. It cannot teach both of these doctrines, so it must teach one to the exclusion of the other.
G. The conclusion that will be inescapable by the end of this study is that the day of Bible miracles has ceased and that no true miracles are being done by man today.

II. **The Bible Teaches That There Was a Defined Purpose for Miracles.**
A. Here's a question to consider:
   1. If the Bible defines the divine purpose for Bible miracles,
   2. And if the Bible demonstrates that the defined purpose for miracles has been fulfilled,
   3. Then, does it not necessarily follow that miracles (having fulfilled their purpose) are no longer happening today, in accordance with God's will? Let's study this together.
B. Miracles were essential in order to reveal the truth of God.
   1. Without miraculous revelation to man of God's inspired message, man could have never known the will of God on his own.
      (a) Paul stated this very plainly in 1 Corinthians 2: "But God has revealed them to us through His Spirit. For the Spirit searches all things, yes, the deep things of God. For what man knows the things of a man except the spirit of the man which is in him? Even so no one knows the things of God except the Spirit of God. Now we have received, not the spirit of the world, but the Spirit who is from God, that we might know the things that have been freely given to us by God" (2:10-12).
      (b) Those first-century preachers could not have preached the truth of God without the miracles necessary to give that message to them.

2. It was essential that the Holy Spirit be given to the apostles and inspired writers:
   (a) In order to "teach [them] all things" (John 14:26).
   (b) In order to "bring to [their] remembrance all things" Jesus said to them (14:26).
   (c) In order to receive the testimony of Jesus (John 15:26).
   (d) In order to "guide [them] into all truth" (John 16:13).
   (e) In order to know and be able to speak about "things to come" (John 16:13).
   (f) In order for truth, the whole truth and nothing but the truth to be made known.
3. Through the miraculous intervention of the Holy Spirit upon the apostles and inspired messengers in the first century, the truth of God was revealed.
   (a) The Holy Spirit either taught them "all things" as Jesus said, or He did not.
   (b) The Holy Spirit either reminded them of "all things" as Jesus said, or He did not.
   (c) The Holy Spirit either guided them into "all truth" as Jesus said, or He did not.
   (d) We know, because the Bible teaches us, that the Holy Spirit:
      (1) "Revealed" God's truth, so that those men could "speak" it (1 Cor. 2:10, 13).
      (2) "Made known" the mystery of God to His "apostles and prophets" (Eph. 3:3-5).
      (3) "Made known" "the gospel" that was "preached" (Gal. 1:11-12).
      (4) "Moved" men of God to "speak" and "prophesy" God's Word (2 Pet. 1:20-21).
      (5) Gave "all things that pertain to life and godliness" (2 Pet. 1:3).
      (6) Gave "all Scripture," "that the man of God may be complete, thoroughly equipped for every good work" (2 Tim. 3:16-17).
      (7) "Delivered" God's truth (i.e., "the faith") "once for all...to the saints" (Jude 3).
4. Put this together and draw the only rational conclusion:
   (a) If the Bible is true and the fullness of God's truth has already been revealed, then miraculous powers are no longer needed today and no longer present today.
   (b) If miraculous powers are needed today and are present today, then the Bible is not true and the fullness of God's truth has not actually been revealed to man.
   (c) See IV, B-C below for further Scriptural development of the connection between the full revelation of the complete truth of God and the cessation of miracles.
5. Those who claim that miracles, and even inspired revelations, are still happening today:
   (a) Reject that the Bible is the revealed truth of God.
   (b) Reject that the Bible is the full and complete revelation of God.
   (c) Lead to the confusion and discouragement of others who are seeking the truth.
   (d) Contribute to the religious division that exists today (cf. John 17:20-21).

C. Miracles were essential in order to confirm the truth of God that was being preached.
   1. In the first century, how could individuals know if a message being preached was truth?
      (a) In those days, there was a man named Jesus who claimed to be the Son of God.
         (1) How could people know if His claims were true?
         (2) If all He had was the verbal message, how could He authenticate His message and prove it was actually from God?
      (b) In those days, the apostles and other messengers went into various cities and preached about the Christ and His will for mankind.
         (1) How could people know if what they said was true?
         (2) If all they had was the verbal message, how could they authenticate the message and prove it was actually from God?
      (c) Was there something that could be used alongside the message as proof?
   2. Jesus performed miracles to confirm that His message was from God.
      (a) To prove that the message was of God, the power of God was laid down beside it.

(b) The miracles that Jesus did confirmed that He was the Son of God, as He claimed.
   (1) Nicodemus said, "Rabbi, we know that You are a teacher come from God; for no one can do these signs that You do unless God is with him" (John 3:2).
   (2) When John the Baptist asked, "Are You the Coming One, or do we look for another?" Jesus pointed to His miracles as confirmation (Matt. 11:2-5).
   (3) It should have been obvious that "the [miraculous] works" of Jesus truly did "bear witness of [Him], that the Father" sent Him (John 5:36; 10:25).
(c) The recording of the miracles that Jesus did confirm that He is the Son of God.
   (1) While no one today ever personally witnessed a miracle of Jesus, the recording of them in the New Testament is designed to produce the same result as having seen the miracles in person.
   (2) John said, "And truly Jesus did many other signs in the presence of His disciples, which are not written in this book; but these are written that you may believe that Jesus is the Christ, the Son of God" (John 20:30-31).
   (3) There were other signs done, but they were not recorded. Why? Because the ones recorded were sufficient for the designated task—namely, to confirm for every reader for all time that Jesus is who He claimed to be.
(d) Jesus does not need to return to earth today and perform miracles in order to prove the truth of His deity. The inspired recording of His miracles in the New Testament does that, as was its design.

3. The apostles and other men in the first century performed miracles to confirm the message that they were preaching was from God.
   (a) To prove that the message was of God, the power of God was laid down beside it.
   (b) Mark 16:17-20 is a key passage in understanding that the purpose of miracles was to confirm the message being preached.
      (1) Jesus sent His apostles "into all world" to "preach the gospel" in Mark 16:15.
      (2) Two verses later, He stated, "And these signs will follow those who believe: In My name they will cast out demons; they will speak with new tongues; they will take up serpents; and if they drink anything deadly, it will by no means hurt them; they will lay hands on the sick, and they will recover" (16:17-18).
      (3) There was a direct connection between the apostles "preaching the gospel" and the "signs" that would "accompany" (NASB) their preaching.
         (i) What was that connection?
         (ii) What was the purpose of the apostles being able to do miracles?
         (iii) Two verses later, after the Lord ascended into heaven, Scripture tells us.
      (4) "And they went out and preached everywhere, the Lord working with them and confirming the word through the accompanying signs" (16:20).
         (i) "The Lord" ascended "into heaven" in verse 19.
         (ii) Now "the Lord" was "working with them" in verse 20.
         (iii) "The Lord" working the miracles through them was for the purpose of "confirming the word" that they were speaking.
   (c) Hebrews 2:3-4 is a key passage in understanding that the purpose of miracles was to confirm the message being preached.
      (1) The message that was being preached concerned "salvation" (2:3).
      (2) The Hebrews writer states, "After it was at the first spoken through the Lord, it was confirmed to us by those who heard [Him], God also testifying with

them, both by signs and wonders and by various miracles and by gifts of the Holy Spirit according to His own will" (2:3-4, NASB).
- (3) Notice what happened:
  - (i) The apostles and inspired messengers began to preach the word of salvation, which the Lord had given to them.
  - (ii) Along with the message came signs, wonders and miracles.
  - (iii) What was the connection between the preaching and the miracles?
  - (iv) What was the purpose of these men being able to do these signs?
- (4) The text states that the message was "confirmed" by the signs.
  - (i) The men were preaching and it was God who was "testifying with them."
  - (ii) God was "testifying," through the miracles, that the message was His!
  - (iii) The purpose of the signs was to confirm the authenticity of the message.
- (d) The Greek word for "confirm" in Mark 16:20 and Hebrews 2:4 is *bebaioo*, which means "to make firm, establish, confirm, make sure" (Thayer 99), "to put something beyond doubt" (BDAG [2000], p. 173).
  - (1) Miracles accompanied those who were preaching the gospel in the days of the early church to "establish" the heavenly origin of the message and "to prove its truth and divinity" (Thayer 99).
  - (2) Without the accompanying signs, the message could not be authenticated!
  - (3) But with the accompanying signs, the message was authenticated as divine!
  - (4) That was the purpose of miracles, as stated in the Bible itself!
4. The conclusion that follows is incontrovertible:
   (a) The purpose of miracles in the New Testament was to confirm the message.
   (b) The message has been confirmed today through the recorded miracles.
   (c) Therefore, having fulfilled their purpose, miracles are no longer necessary today.
5. The following point will solidify this conclusion.

D. Miracles were designed by God to produce faith.
1. In the Bible, miracles were not designed by God to merely benefit the recipient(s).
   (a) Paul had a "thorn in the flesh" (2 Cor. 12:7)—whatever that was—but he was not permitted to use his miraculously endowed power to remove it.
   (b) On one of his last journeys, Paul left his friend, Trophimus, "in Miletus sick" (2 Tim. 4:20). If he could work miracles, why would he not heal his friend?
   (c) While in prison in Rome, a companion of Paul, Epaphroditus, "was sick almost unto death" (Phil. 2:27), and he recovered, but Scripture does not indicate that it was by any miracle performed by Paul.
2. The purpose of miracles in the early church was to confirm the message (see II, C), but why did the message being preached in the first century need to be confirmed?
   (a) It was not merely to prove that the message was from God.
   (b) It was designed to produce faith in the heart of the hearers that the message was from God and that the hearer needed to respond to it.
3. The miracles recorded in the Bible were designed by God to produce faith:
   (a) First, in the hearts of the individuals upon whom the miracles were done (John 2:23; 6:2; 10:42; 11:45; 20:8; Mark 11:20-22; Luke 17:15; 18:43; Acts 2:5-37; 8:6-8, 12-13; 13:11-12; 19:11-18).
   (b) Second (and equally so), in the hearts of individuals in the centuries that would follow, who read of these miraculous deeds in the pages of the New Testament.

4. There is divine record, in John 20:30-31, of the purpose of miracles being recorded in written form in the Bible. Why are the miracles documented in Scripture?
   (a) "And truly Jesus did many other signs in the presence of His disciples, which are not written in this book; but these are written that you may believe that Jesus is the Christ, the Son of God, and that believing you may have life in His name."
   (b) The Lord recorded the miracles in Scripture that readers "may believe that Jesus is the Christ, the Son of God."
5. Today, the written Word does produce faith.
   (a) "So then faith comes by hearing, and hearing by the word of God" (Rom. 10:17).
   (b) If the written Word was designed to produce faith (John 20:30-31),
       and if the written Word does in fact produce faith (Rom. 10:17),
       what then would be the purpose of any miracles being performed today?
6. The conclusion is inescapable that God recorded miracles in the Bible for the purpose of producing faith, and, therefore, no miracles are needed today to produce faith.
   (a) If there are miracles being done today, what is their purpose?
   (b) If there are miracles being done today, then God's word is inept in its purpose.
   (c) Either God's Word is sufficient for the task designed by God or it is not.

E. In summary, miracles were designed by God to confirm the Word.
   1. First, they accomplished their purpose when the message was actually being spoken.
      (a) The power of God witnessed in the miracles established that the message was from God.
      (b) When God's New Testament (emphasis on "new") was being revealed (since it had never been revealed before), it required confirmation of its divine origin.
      (c) But, once a message is confirmed, it is confirmed forever and does not need perpetual acts of confirmation.
   2. Second, the recording of the miracles fulfills their purpose in hearts of readers today.
      (a) There is not any new revelation being given, therefore, no miraculous acts of confirmation are necessary today.
      (b) The Bible is the completed revelation of God for man today, for it is :
         (1) Inspired by God (2 Tim. 3:16).
         (2) All-sufficient (2 Pet. 1:3; 2 Tim. 3:17).
         (3) Fully delivered (Jude 3).
      (c) In its completed and written form (which is available around the world today), the Bible does what the miracles and signs did in the first century:
         (1) It proves that the message is from God.
         (2) It produces faith in the hearts of its readers.
      (d) Therefore, since the Bible fulfills the purpose of miracles today, there is no need for any miraculous signs today.
   3. Wendell Winkler uses the illustration of scaffolding. "Just as there is a need for scaffolding when a house is under construction, but when the house is completed the scaffolding is removed, so in the beginning of Christianity there was a need for miracles; but, when the New Testament was completed, there ceased to be a need for such" (83).

F. The miraculous powers of the apostolic age were confined by God to that age!
   1. Once the purpose of confirmation was fulfilled, the miraculous power ceased.
   2. There are no miracles happening today, and further, there is no need for miracles today.

III. The Bible Teaches That There Was a Defined Reception of the Power to Perform Miracles.
   A. Here's a question to consider:
      1. If the Bible defines the means of receiving the power to perform miracles,
      2. And if the Bible demonstrates that the defined means of reception no longer exists,
      3. Then, does it not necessarily follow that miracles (without any means by which man can obtain the power to do them) are no longer happening today, in accordance with God's will? Let's study this together.
   B. In New Testament times, there were only two means of receiving miraculous powers:
      1. The baptism of the Holy Spirit.
      2. The laying on of the apostles' hands.
   C. The power to perform miracles came first through the baptism of the Holy Spirit.
      1. The New Testament records only two instances of the baptism of the Holy Spirit:
         (a) First, upon the apostles (Jews) in Acts 2.
         (b) Second, upon Cornelius and his household (Gentiles) in Acts 10.
         (c) There are no other records of Holy Spirit baptism taking place at any other time.
      2. The "baptism" of the Holy Spirit indicated "to overwhelm" with "an outpouring" (Thayer 94) of the Spirit's power.
         (a) Such was clearly evident in both instances in the New Testament, but the baptism of the Holy Spirit was limited to the early days of the church, as will be studied.
         (b) It will also be evident that the purpose and the result of these two instances in the New Testament were not the same.
      3. The purpose of the baptism of the Holy Spirit upon the apostles was to reveal all truth to them and to confirm all truth through them.
         (a) Holy Spirit baptism was prophesied through Joel (Joel 2:28-32).
         (b) Holy Spirit baptism was promised by John the Baptist (Matt. 3:11; Mark 1:8).
         (c) Holy Spirit baptism was administered by Christ Himself (Matt. 3:11; John 1:33; 15:26; Acts 2:32-33).
         (d) Holy Spirit baptism was promised to the apostles by Jesus Himself (Acts 1:4, 5, 8).
            (1) The Holy Spirit would "abide" "with" and "in" the apostles (John 14:16-17).
            (2) The Holy Spirit would "teach" the apostles "all things" (John 14:26).
            (3) The Holy Spirit would "bring" to the apostles' "remembrance all things" that Jesus taught them (John 14:26).
            (4) The Holy Spirit would "testify" of Jesus to and through the apostles (John 15:26).
            (5) The Holy Spirit would "guide" the apostles "into all truth" (John 16:13).
            (6) The Holy Spirit would "tell" the apostles "things to come" (John 16:13).
            (7) The Holy Spirit would "give" the apostles "what to speak" (Mark 13:11).
            (8) The Holy Spirit would "clothe" the apostles "with power from on high" (Mark 9:1, NASB), when He would "come upon" them (Acts 1:8).
               (i) This is the power by which they would speak God's Word.
               (ii) This is the power by which they would confirm God's Word through miracles.
            (9) Stop for a moment and consider:
               (i) If the Holy Spirit did come upon the apostles as Jesus promised,
                  and if the Holy Spirit did reveal all truth to the apostles,
                  and if, by the Spirit's power, the apostles miraculously spoke and confirmed the Word as truly being from God,
                  then, there is no place for miracles today.

            (ii) If there are still miracles taking place today,
                 then the promise of Jesus did not come true,
                 and all of the truth of God was not revealed,
                 and nothing that the Bible says can be trusted.
        (e) Holy Spirit baptism overwhelmed the apostles in Acts 2.
            (1) Just as was prophesied by Joel and promised by John the Baptist and Jesus:
                (i) The Spirit miraculously empowered them to speak "with other tongues" (2:4).
                (ii) The "Spirit gave them" the words to speak (2:4).
                (iii) "...Many wonders and signs were done by the apostles" (2:43).
            (2) As a fulfillment of the purpose of Holy Spirit baptism and the miracles:
                (i) The people "were all amazed and marveled" (2:7, 12).
                (ii) "When they heard" the message, "they were cut to the heart" (2:37).
                (iii) They "gladly received [the] word" as being authentically from God (2:41).
            (3) Holy Spirit baptism revealed the truth of God and confirmed the truth of God!
    4. The purpose and results of the baptism of the Holy Spirit upon the Gentiles was not the same as it was in Acts 2.
        (a) The Jews were very hesitant to take the gospel to the Gentiles (Acts 10:15, 28).
        (b) Thus, when Peter and his Jewish companions saw the Holy Spirit overwhelm Cornelius and his household, "as upon [the Jews] at the beginning" (Acts 11:15):
            (1) They knew that the Gentiles were equal recipients of the gospel as the Jews (Acts 11:16-18). All doubts should have been removed.
            (2) They knew that God "made no distinction between" Jews and Gentiles any longer (Acts 15:7-9). "God gave them *the same gift* as He gave us" (11:17).
        (c) Peter recognized what happened at Cornelius' home had not transpired since "the beginning" of the gospel on Pentecost (11:15).
            (1) A common element in the two occurrences of Holy Spirit baptism was that the recipients spoke in tongues—real, known languages of that day (2:4, 6, 8, 11; 10:46).
            (2) No doubt, when Peter "heard [Cornelius and his household] speak with tongues" (Acts 10:46), that pointed him back to that occasion on Pentecost.
        (d) After these two occurrences, it would never happen again!
            (1) Holy Spirit baptism occurred to bring salvation to the Jews (Acts 2).
            (2) Holy Spirit baptism occurred to bring salvation to the Gentiles (Acts 10).
            (3) Having fulfilled its divine purpose, the Lord never again administered this baptism.
        (e) The baptism of the Holy Spirit upon Cornelius and his household did not save them.
            (1) The Spirit came upon them "as [Peter] began to speak" (Acts 11:15).
            (2) But, they needed to be told "words" by which they would be saved (11:14).
            (3) Once they heard the gospel, Peter commanded them to be baptized (10:47-48).
            (4) At that point (and not before), Cornelius and his household received the remission of sins, just like those on the day of Pentecost who were also "baptized in the name of the Lord" (10:48; cf. 2:38).
    5. In Ephesians 4:5 (written about 62 A.D.), the Bible affirms that there is "one baptism."
        (a) This is not Holy Spirit baptism, but it is water baptism of the Great Commission.
        (b) Water baptism of the Great Commission was to continue "to the end of the age," as long as disciples were being made through teaching and baptism (Matt. 28:19-20), but the Bible does not make the same affirmation regarding Holy Spirit baptism.

- (c) Water baptism of the Great Commission was to be administered by man "to the end of the age" (Matt. 28:19-20; Acts 8:38), but Holy Spirit baptism was administered by Christ only twice (in Acts 2 and Acts 10; cf. Matt. 3:11; John 1:33; Acts 2:32-33).
- (d) Water baptism of the Great Commission was an age-lasting command to be obeyed (Matt. 28:18-20; Acts 2:38; 10:47-48), while Holy Spirit baptism was a promise to be bestowed (Matt. 3:11; Luke 24:49; Acts 1:4-5, 8).
- (e) Water baptism of the Great Commission was done "in the name of Jesus Christ" (Acts 2:38; 10:47-48), while Holy Spirit baptism was not.
- (f) When Paul stated, "There is…one baptism" (Eph. 4:4-5), he was unequivocally affirming that Holy Spirit baptism had fulfilled its course and that only water baptism of the Great Commission was in practice (in 62 A.D.) and was to continue.
   6. Therefore, the Biblical evidence is clear that miraculous powers are no longer being endowed today through the baptism of the Holy Spirit.
      - (a) Holy Spirit baptism upon the apostles was essential for them to be able to proclaim the gospel "with infallible and unerring certainty" (Brownlow 162).
      - (b) Having fulfilled that Scriptural purpose, Holy Spirit baptism became obsolete.
      - (c) The two instances in the New Testament were the extent of God's administration of this overwhelming measure of the Spirit.
   7. There was only one other means of receiving the power to do miracles in the first century.
- D. The power to perform miracles came through the laying on of the apostles' hands.
   1. In the beginning of the church (in the early chapters of Acts), the apostles were the only ones recorded as having the power to perform miracles (cf. 2:43; 3:1-11; 4:10, 14, 16, 22, 30; 5:12, 15-16).
   2. When the apostles "laid hands" (specifically stated in 6:6) on the seven men in Acts 6, then there were other men who did "miracles" (8:6), "wonders and signs" (6:8).
      - (a) Therein lies the key to understanding who could do miracles in the first century and how that power was conferred from person to person.
      - (b) Notice how that is purposefully detailed for Bible readers in Acts 8.
   3. Philip (one of the seven men upon whom the apostles laid their hands in Acts 6), went to Samaria in Acts 8 and "preached Christ" (8:5).
      - (a) The multitudes "heeded the things spoken by Philip, hearing and seeing the miracles which he did" (8:6).
      - (b) His miracles included casting out demons and healing the paralyzed and lame (8:7).
      - (c) Thus, many were baptized (8:12), including a sorcerer named Simon (8:13).
   4. The apostles sent Peter and John (two of the apostles) to Samaria, and "they laid hands on [the new converts to Christ], and they received the Holy Spirit" (8:17).
      - (a) No one had received this miraculous measure of the Spirit prior to the arrival of the apostles, according to Acts 8:16.
      - (b) It was evident that only "through the laying on of the apostles' hands the Holy Spirit was given" (8:18).
         - (1) Simon wanted to purchase "this power" to impart the Holy Spirit (8:19).
         - (2) But, he had "neither part nor portion in this matter" (8:21), for he had not the power to administer the miraculous gifts of the Spirit through his hands.
   5. Notice very closely that Philip was in Samaria and had the power to do great miracles (8:6-7), but his power was limited.
      - (a) If Philip could impart the miraculous endowment of the Spirit, why were two apostles, Peter and John, dispatched to Samaria?

(b) Philip, while able to perform miracles, could not pass that power on to others.
(c) It is obvious from the text that:
  (1) The apostles alone had the power to confer the Holy Spirit.
  (2) It was only through the laying on of the apostles' hands that the miraculous power of the Spirit was imparted.
  (3) The miraculous gifts of the Spirit could not be bestowed in any other way.
(d) If it was only through the laying on of the apostles' hands that the miraculous power of the Spirit could be given, what does that tell us about the availability and bestowment of miraculous powers today?

6. There are other New Testament examples that further emphasize that only the apostles could confer the Holy Spirit upon others.
  (a) In Acts 19:6, "when Paul had laid hands on [the twelve men converted in Ephesus], the Holy Spirit came upon them, and they spoke with tongues and prophesied." It took an apostle's hands to do that.
  (b) In Romans 1:11, Paul longed to see the brethren in Rome that he "may impart to [them] some spiritual gift, so that [they] may be established." He had to be physically present with them in order to impart this gift.
  (c) In 2 Timothy 1:6, Paul urged Timothy to "stir up the gift of God which is in you *through* the laying on of my hands." Note the word "through."
    (1) The Greek word *dia* denotes "the Means or Instrument by which anything is effected; because what is done by means of a person or thing seems to pass as it were *through* the same" (Thayer 133).
    (2) Paul was the "agency" (BDAG [2000], p. 225) through which "God" acted to give the power of the Holy Spirit (Thayer 133).
    (3) It may have been on this same occasion when the "the eldership" also laid their hands on Timothy (1 Tim. 4:14).
      (i) But Paul specifies in that text that the gift was given to Timothy "*with* the laying on of the hands of the eldership" (4:14)
      (ii) The Greek word for "with" *(meta)* denotes a "marker of attendant circumstances of something that takes place" (BDAG [2000], p. 637).
      (iii) While the elders were present and also laid their hands on Timothy (perhaps as a gesture of love, prayer and support in his coming mission, similar to that of the Antioch church in Acts 13:1-3), it was only "through" Paul's hands that the miraculous power of the Spirit was given.

E. It is quite clear that miracles cannot possibly be performed by any persons today, for no person is able to receive the power to perform them.
  1. The power to perform miracles cannot be conferred today because:
    (a) There is no baptism of the Holy Spirit today.
    (b) There are no apostles to lay their hands and impart the miraculous gift.
      (1) Each of the apostles was "a witness" of the resurrected Jesus (Acts 1:22), and each of them died at some time during the first century.
      (2) In fact, Paul called himself the "last" apostle of all (1 Cor. 15:8).
      (3) After the apostles died, no one else could bestow the Spirit's miraculous power.
    (c) With the means of reception (which required the presence and involvement of an apostle) no longer available today, miracles are no longer happening today.
  2. Since all of those upon whom the apostles laid their hands have all died, it is can also be affirmed that there are no miracles being performed today.

IV. The Bible Teaches That There Was a Defined Duration of Miracles.
  A. Here's a question to consider:
     1. If the Bible defines the appointed duration for Bible miracles,
     2. And if the Bible demonstrates that the defined duration for miracles has passed,
     3. Then, does it not necessarily follow that miracles (which were only for a specified duration) are no longer happening today, in accordance with God's will? Let's study this together.
  B. The Bible teaches that miracles were to last "until" "the unity of the faith" came (Eph. 4:8-13).
     1. Ephesians 4:8-13 is a key passage in understanding the duration of Bible miracles.
     2. The occasion of these gifts is specified – the miraculous "gifts" were given when Jesus "ascended on high" (4:8; see Mark 16:17-20).
     3. The nature of these gifts is specified – the miraculous "gifts" involved bestowal of miraculous functions to the church leadership (i.e., apostles, prophets, evangelists, pastors, teachers) (4:11).
     4. The purpose of these gifts is specified:
        (a) The miraculous "gifts" were designed "for the equipping of the saints for the work of the ministry, for the edifying of the body of Christ" (4:12).
        (b) The miraculous "gifts" were designed so that Christians "should no longer be children, tossed to and fro and carried about with every wind of doctrine, by the trickery of men, in the cunning craftiness of deceitful plotting" (4:14).
     5. Now, the duration of these gifts is specified – the miraculous "gifts" were to last "till we all come to the unity of the faith and of the knowledge of the Son of God, to a perfect man, to the measure of the stature of the fullness of Christ" (4:13).
        (a) The word "till" is from the Greek *mechri,* which is a "marker of continuance in time up to a point" (BDAG [2000], p. 644), noted by Thayer as "a particle indicating the terminus ad quem: *as far as, unto, until*" (408).
           (1) "Terminus ad quem" is a Latin phrase meaning, "the point at which something ends or finishes."
           (2) God's use of this adverb indicates that there was a point at which He planned for miracles to terminate. If they were not to cease, the use of this word is meaningless.
        (b) Miracles (including the miraculous spiritual gifts mentioned in the New Testament) would terminate when "the unity of the faith" came.
           (1) This does not say when "a unity of faith" came, as if talking about all men believing and teaching alike. The use of the definite articles ("the") proves that.
           (2) At its core, "unity" (Greek, *henotes*) is a "state of oneness" (BDAG [2000], p. 338), finding its root in the Greek word for "one" (Greek, *heis*), which emphasizes that which is "in contrast to the parts, of which a whole is made up" (BDAG [2000], p. 291).
        (c) That which is to come to a state of unity or oneness (in contrast to being in parts), at which time miracles would cease, is "the faith."
           (1) Paul defines what "the faith" is when he parallels it with "the gospel" (Gal. 1:11+1:23). "The unity of the faith" is talking about the gospel being complete.
           (2) Jude assures Bible readers that "the faith" had been "once for all delivered to the saints" (Jude 3).
           (3) This accords with the rest of Ephesians 4:13, which speaks of "the unity...of the knowledge of the Son of God," when the state of "a mature man" was reached.

(d) The conclusion that miracles (including spiritual gifts) would cease in the first century is unavoidable in this passage, for:
    (1) The oneness of the faith (i.e., the full revelation of the gospel, rather than being in parts) was completed by the end of the first century.
    (2) Once that state of maturity was reached, in which the unity of the knowledge of Christ was contained in one place (i.e., the completed New Testament), Scripture teaches us that miracles would cease.
    (3) Every word in Ephesians 4:13 demands that conclusion.
C. The Bible teaches that miracles were to last until "that which is perfect" came (1 Cor. 13:8-13).
    1. 1 Corinthians 13:8-13 is a key passage in understanding the duration of Bible miracles.
    2. The thirteenth chapter of First Corinthians is in the middle of an inspired, comprehensive, three-chapter dissertation on miraculous gifts of the Holy Spirit.
        (a) Chapter 12 emphasizes the presence or existence of the miraculous, spiritual gifts.
            (1) They are introduced and listed, with an emphasis on their origin and unity.
        (b) Chapter 13 emphasizes the passing or expiration of the miraculous, spiritual gifts.
            (1) They are contrasted with *agape* love, which is permanent and enduring.
        (c) Chapter 14 emphasizes the practice or exercise of the miraculous, spiritual gifts.
            (1) They are regulated in their use, with an emphasis on decency and order.
    3. The nature of these gifts is specified – the miraculous "gifts" involved a diverse range of powers that were bestowed upon early Christians.
        (a) Nine miraculous abilities are listed: the word of wisdom, the word of knowledge, faith, gifts of healings, the working of miracles, prophecy, discerning of spirits, different kinds of tongues, the interpretation of tongues (12:8-10).
    4. The origin of these gifts is specified – the miraculous "gifts" were all given "by the same Spirit...as He wills" (12:4-11).
    5. The purpose of these gifts is specified – the miraculous "gifts" were designed to promote the unity of the believers in one body (12:12-28).
    6. The limitations of these gifts is specified – the miraculous "gifts" were not all possessed by all of the early Christians (12:29-30).
    7. The inferiority of these gifts is specified – the miraculous "gifts," while exciting to have, were inferior to the "greatest" of God's enduring gifts – *agape* love.
        (a) At the end of chapter 12, Paul set forth to "show you a more excellent way" (12:31).
        (b) By the end of chapter 13, Paul had presented the "greatest" gift of all – love (13:13).
    8. Now, the duration of these gifts is specified (13:8-13).
        (a) Paul sets forth a great contrast, which demands that a change is forthcoming.
            (1) There is something that "never fails" and something that "will fail" (13:8).
            (2) There is something "in part" and something "which is perfect" (13:9).
            (3) There is the time of being "a child" and the time of being "a man" (13:11).
            (4) There is seeing in a "mirror dimly" and seeing "face to face" (13:12).
            (5) There is something that will "fail...cease...vanish away...be done away...[be] put away" and there is something that will "abide" (13:8-13).
            (6) The strong emphasis on the contrast shows that these gifts will not last.
        (b) Paul sets forth clearly "that which is in part" and its temporary nature.
            (1) The subject matter under discussion is the miraculous, spiritual gifts.
                (i) As representative of the nine gifts from chapter 12, Paul lists three of them in chapter 13: prophecies, tongues and knowledge.
                (ii) The gifts pertained especially to the revelation of the will of God.

(iii) But these gifts were not intended to last.
- (2) The miraculous, spiritual gifts are said to be "in part" things (13:9, 10, 12).
  - (i) The use of the words "in part" emphasizes that which is incomplete.
  - (ii) The use of the words "in part" points toward the goal of being "complete."
  - (iii) The use of the words "in part" shows that they were not intended to last.
- (3) These "parts" (i.e., these miraculous gifts, including tongues, prophecies, healing, etc.) would "fail…cease…vanish away…be done away…[be] put away."
- (c) Paul sets forth the time "when" these gifts would pass away.
  - (1) It is evident that these gifts were not intended to last for all time.
  - (2) Paul states, "But when that which is perfect has come, then that which is in part will be done away" (13:10).
  - (3) Note the words "when" and "then." These are key words and markers of time.
    - (i) "When" something happens, "then" the spiritual gifts "will be done away."
    - (ii) What is "that which is perfect"?
  - (4) The word "perfect" is from the Greek *teleion*.
    - (i) When speaking of people, the word means "fully grown, mature."
    - (ii) When speaking of things, the words means "complete" (Vine 466).
  - (5) "That which is perfect" is the completion of "that which is in part."
    - (i) The "in part" things pertained to the revelation of God's will.
    - (ii) Therefore, the "perfect/complete" thing pertains to the revelation of God's will in its completed form (no longer "in part").
    - (iii) Vine admits that the word "perfect" is "referring to the complete revelation of God's will and ways" (466).
    - (iv) Once the "complete" revelation had "come," the "parts" were no longer necessary.
  - (6) It is critical to note, in our modern age, that Paul specified tongues as one of the miraculous gifts that would "cease" and "be done away."
    - (i) "Tongues," in the New Testament, were real, actual, known, spoken, intelligible languages of people in that day (Acts 2:4, 6, 8, 11), but in the context of miracles, they were spoken by those who did not personally know the language but were miraculously endowed to speak them.
      1. Tongues were "easy to understand" by those who knew that real language (1 Cor. 14:9-11). They were not unintelligible sounds.
      2. Tongues were not to be spoken unless people could "understand" (1 Cor. 14:12, 14, 16, 17, 19). For what would be the purpose?
      3. Tongues were regulated to only two or three speakers taking turns, and that was only if an interpreter was present (1 Cor. 14:28).
      4. Tongue speakers were to "keep silent" if no interpreter was present, which shows that such an ability was within the speaker's control (1 Cor. 14:28, 32).
      5. In the context of these miraculous gifts in the assembly, the Bible says that "God is not the author of confusion" (1 Cor. 14:33).
    - (ii) Along with all of the other miraculous, spiritual gifts, the power to speak in tongues ceased at the completion of the New Testament.
      1. If speaking in tongues is still in existence today, then all of the other spiritual gifts must be also. They either stand or cease together.

2. If tongues are still present, then that indicates the Bible is not the complete and final revelation of God, which it claims to be.
3. If tongues still exist today, then you cannot trust the Bible!
              (d) Put all of the evidence together:
                  (1) For a time, God's will was being revealed "part" by "part" through miraculous powers of the Spirit upon early Christians (including tongues and prophecies).
                  (2) But, "when" the whole, complete, full, perfect revelation of God's will would "come," "then" the part-by-part revelation (miraculous gifts) would cease.
                  (3) God's revelation was complete upon the writing of the book of Revelation.
                  (4) At that point, revelation ceased; therefore, at that point, miraculous gifts ceased.
                      (i) This coincides perfectly with their purpose—to confirm the message.
                      (ii) This coincides perfectly with their reception—through the apostles.
              (e) Miraculous, spiritual gifts no longer exist today:
                  (1) For the days of childhood have given way to the maturity of a man (13:11).
                  (2) For that which was seen dimly has given way to seeing face-to-face (13:12).
                  (3) For partial knowledge has given way to a full knowledge of God's will (13:12).
                  (4) All of these metaphors point to the completion of God's revelation in the Bible.
              (f) The revelation of God has been "once for all delivered" (Jude 3; cf. John 16:13).
                  (1) There is no further revelation to be given.
                  (2) Therefore, there is no further presence of miraculous gifts.
                  (3) The revealing of God's will and the presence of miracles went hand-in-hand.
                  (4) To claim the presence of miraculous powers today is to claim that God's Word is not complete, which it definitively claims and proves to be.
              (g) Some claim "that which is perfect" is the coming of Christ at the end of time.
                  (1) However, "perfect," in this context, means "complete, whole" and not "sinless."
                  (2) "Perfect," in this context, has reference to the completion of "parts" in that day.
                  (3) Verse 13 specifies that faith and hope were to "abide" (i.e., continue/remain) after the gifts ceased, but faith and hope will not "abide" (i.e., continue/remain) when Jesus comes, for they will be fulfilled and not continue in heaven.
    D. The Bible clearly defines the duration of miracles in the church was to last until "the faith" (i.e., the gospel) was no longer "in part" but was "complete"!
        1. Spend time comparing Ephesians 4:8-13 and 1 Corinthians 13:8-13—the two passages complement one another perfectly regarding the duration of miracles.
        2. The revelation of the New Testament was completed in the first century.
        3. All of the apostles died by the end of the first century.
        4. Therefore, the miraculous powers that were endowed upon early Christians by the Holy Spirit, through the laying on of the apostles' hands, ceased by the end of the first century.
        5. There are no miracles taking place today! Their Biblically-defined duration has been completed!

V. **The Genuine, Supernatural Miracles of the Bible Are No Longer Occurring Today!**
    A. There are those who claim that miracles are still happening today.
        1. In addition to the Biblical evidence already examined (which proves incontrovertibly that the age of miracles has passed), let us compare the genuine miracles of the Bible with so-called, modern-day miracles.
        2. Actually, by definition, it is a sharp "contrast" and not a "comparison."

B. The types of miracles that were done in the Bible are not being done anywhere today.
   1. Think about the types of miracles that people claim are done today and then consider the types of genuine miracles that were actually done in the New Testament.
   2. Some miracles of the early Christians were done directly upon various persons.
      (a) People were raised from the dead (Acts 9:36-42; 20:10-12).
      (b) People were struck blind (Acts 13:11).
      (c) Demons were cast out (Acts 5:16; 8:7; 16:16-18; 19:10-11; Mark 16:17).
      (d) The sick were healed (Acts 5:15-16; 19:11-12; 28:8-9; Mark 16:18).
      (e) The blind were given sight (Acts 9:12, 17-18).
      (f) The lame or cripple were able to walk for the first time (Acts 3:1-11; 8:7; 14:8-10).
      (g) The paralyzed were healed to be able to walk again (Acts 9:33-34; 8:7).
      (h) "Unusual miracles" were done where "even handkerchiefs or aprons were brought from [Paul's] body to the sick, and the diseases left them and the evil spirits went out of them" (Acts 19:10-11).
   3. Some miracles of the early Christians were done within one's self but for the benefit of those who witnessed the deed, such as:
      (a) Speaking in "new tongues" (languages) they did not personally know (Mark 16:17).
      (b) Taking up "serpents" (Mark 16:18) or suffering "no harm" from a viper (Acts 28:3-5).
      (c) Drinking "anything deadly" (Mark 16:18) or "deadly poison" (ESV).
   4. Read over this list again. How many of these things are actually being done today? That's not, "How many are claimed to be done?" But, "How many actually are?"
      (a) "Is it not logical that if some miraculous gifts are still with us, it should follow that all of them would be? Yet those who claim certain gifts usually ignore others. Those who claim the gifts often cite Mark 16:17-18 as authority for tongues and healing, but except for a few fanatics, they want no part of the snakes and poison" (Pharr, "Miraculous Gifts Have Ceased," 40).
   5. ALL of these miracles COULD be done and WERE done in the first century!
      (a) Therefore, it follows, that when one ceased they ALL ceased!
      (b) There are no genuine Bible miracles done today!
      (c) ALL miraculous powers among men have ceased!
C. The characteristics of miracles that were done in the Bible are not found anywhere today.
   1. Think about "how" people claim miracles are done today and then compare that with "how" the genuine miracles of the Bible were actually done.
   2. The miracles of the early Christians:
      (a) Were done publicly (Acts 2:6-12, 22; 3:1-11, 16; 26:26).
      (b) Were affirmed even by enemies (Acts 4:16, 21).
      (c) Were instantaneously effective, without a single failure (Acts 3:6-7; 9:18; 13:11).
      (d) Made people complete and whole, with no record of relapses (Acts 3:16; 4:10).
      (e) Left no doubt in the minds of the witnesses that a true miracle had been done!
   3. What should strike modern-day readers is that the miracles of the early Christians:
      (a) Were never done to bring attention, honor or glory to the miracle worker.
      (b) Were never done with great pomp, ceremony and sensationalism.
      (c) Were never done to financially benefit the miracle worker.
      (d) Were never followed by taking up a collection.
      (e) Were never done in an incomplete or secretive fashion.
      (f) Never took more than a split second to be fully, 100% effective.
      (g) Did not always require faith or a positive response from the one healed.

(h) Could not be explained by any natural causes but were, without doubt, miracles.
4. No genuine miracles, with these Biblical characteristics, are being done today!
   (a) If there are any miracles being done today, they would have all of these Biblical characteristics.
   (b) No so-called miracles today have any of these Biblical characteristics; therefore, there are no Bible-type miracles happening today!

D. Even with all of the Biblical evidence, some still object to the cessation of miracles.
   1. Some argue, "God does not change. He is the same God. Therefore, miracles must still happen."
      (a) It is true that the nature of God does not change (Mal. 3:6; Heb. 13:8).
      (b) But God's activity on this earth has been shown to change.
         (1) God is no longer creating our material world out of nothing, as He did in Genesis 1. He is the same God, but His activity on earth changed.
         (2) While God once flooded the entire earth (Gen. 6-9), He promised that He would not do that again. He's the same God but working differently.
         (3) God once fed His people with quails in the evening and manna in the morning (Ex. 16:11-31). He's still the same God but His activity is different.
      (c) While His activity on earth may change, that does not mean that God changes.
      (d) It is God's Word (which must not be changed, Gal. 1:6-9; Rev. 22:18-19) which teaches us plainly about the existence and then the expiration of miracles. We must trust God and trust His Word. We must focus on His will for our lives today.
   2. Some argue, "God is still all-powerful. He can do anything today that He did in the past."
      (a) It is true that God is all-powerful (Gen. 18:14; Psa. 89:8; Mt. 19:26; Eph. 3:20-21).
      (b) But, again, it is not a question of what God can do or what God has done (see V, D, 1 above), but the focus must be on what He is doing and what He expects of us.
      (c) Hebrews 1:1-2 is one example in Scripture showing that God used His power in different ways at different times to accomplish different purposes.
      (d) The issue has to do with what Scripture teaches us about the exercise of God's power today, and Scripture plainly teaches us that God planned to (and did) cease miraculous interventions on this earth when the Bible was completed.
   3. Some argue, "Scripture promises in the book of James that prayer will save the sick."
      (a) James 5:14-15 says, "Is anyone among you sick? Let him call for the elders of the church, and let them pray over him, anointing him with oil in the name of the Lord. And the prayer of faith will save the sick, and the Lord will raise him up. And if he has committed sins, he will be forgiven."
      (b) The specificity of James 5:15 is pointing to a miraculous healing that was practiced in (but confined to) the days of the early church.
      (c) James specifies "the prayer of faith" not "a prayer of a heart of faith."
         (1) One of the spiritual gifts was a miraculous level of "faith" (1 Cor. 12:9).
         (2) One of the spiritual gifts was "healings" (1 Cor. 12:9).
         (3) This is what is in view in James 5:15.
      (d) James guaranteed a healing in that day.
         (1) It is not "may" or "might" or "could" be healed.
         (2) It is that the prayer of faith "will" save, and the Lord "will" raise him up.
         (3) These are absolute promises/guarantees of healing by miraculous means.
         (4) There are no natural or medicinal means in view in this passage.

(e) The specific application of this passage was to a time in history when miraculous healings were taking place every time "the prayer of faith" was offered.
    (1) That is not happening today.
    (2) Even modern-day healers would admit "it doesn't work every time."
    (3) It is not happening today because the Bible teaches that miracles have ceased.
4. Some argue that they have seen a miracle done today.
    (a) There is no doubt that some sincere individuals believe they have witnessed a modern-day miracle.
    (b) But, if God's Word is true, then there would, of necessity, be a natural explanation to the supposed supernatural act.
    (c) Interestingly, Paul warned that there would be deceptive "signs and lying wonders" that people would see and believe (2 Thess. 2:8-10).
        (1) These are not real signs and wonders, but to some, they appear that way.
        (2) Appearances can be deceiving, and God warns us about that.
    (d) Even the Samaritans were fooled by the "sorceries" of Simon and believed he was "the great power of God" (Acts 8:10-11).
        (1) "They heeded him because he had astonished them" (8:11).
        (2) But when they saw real, genuine miracles performed by Philip and powered by God, the Samaritans realized they had been following a hoax and they turned to follow God's true pattern (8:5-13).
    (e) Read again the characteristics of Bible-type miracles (V, C above), and realize that those characteristics are not representative of so-called modern miracles. There is a very good, Bible-based reason for that—miracles really have ceased.
5. We must be ever so careful in raising objections that we do not place ourselves in the place of God and our wills in the place of God's will.
    (a) Whatever the Bible teaches is what the Bible teaches. We must not change that.
    (b) Whatever the Bible teaches is what we must believe and teach ourselves.

E. Those who claim that Bible-type miracles are happening today are contributing to the religious division that exists in the modern world.
1. To claim that miracles are happening today is to claim that the Biblical purpose of miracles is still valid and not yet complete.
2. Since the Biblical purpose of miracles was to reveal and to confirm the Word of God, modern-day miracle workers must affirm that the Bible is not complete and that modern-day revelations from God are still occurring.
    (a) If that is the case:
        (1) Is God revealing and confirming all of the contradictory doctrines of modern-day miracles workers (for they do not all teach and practice the same thing)?
        (2) The Bible cannot be trusted, for it claims to be complete (2 Tim. 3:16-17; Jude 3).
    (b) But when the Bible teaches that is the final, complete, once-for-all-delivered revelation of God, we must believe that and reject all claims for modern-day miracles.
    (c) Today, God is not authenticating contradictory teachings of these various groups by endowing them with supposed miraculous powers! Miracles have ceased!
3. Miracle workers in the first century all taught the same thing; they were all part of the same church; they all worshiped the same way.
    (a) There were no differences in their doctrines or practices.
    (b) In the context of miraculous gifts, the Bible says that "God is the not the author of confusion" (1 Cor. 14:33). Any confusion or division is a result of man, not God.

VI. Conclusion
- A. The study of miracles in the Bible is one of the most fascinating and rewarding endeavors that one can have into God's Word!
    1. One truly stands in awe of the majesty and power of God when he explores these inspired treasures of magnificent wonder!
    2. Our God truly is an awesome God!
- B. Unfortunately, some claim that miracles are still happening today, when the Bible quite clearly teaches that they have ceased.
    1. Some use the term "miracle" lightly to describe various events.
        (a) Some refer to the birth of a child as "a miracle."
        (b) Some refer to the near-miss of a serious auto accident as "a miracle."
        (c) But that is not the way the Bible uses or describes the term "miracle."
        (d) A miracle, as that term is properly used in the Bible, is a work of "supernatural origin and character, such as could not be produced by natural agents and means" (Vine 412).
        (e) That which occurs naturally or coincidentally is not a miracle.
    2. Some claim that the miraculous, spiritual gifts of the New Testament are still present and being practiced by various ones today.
        (a) However, these miraculous gifts were inherently connected to the apostles.
            (1) They were endowed upon the apostles through the baptism of the Holy Spirit.
            (2) They were endowed by the apostles through the laying on of their hands.
            (3) Since there are no apostles alive today, and since there are no men alive today upon whom the apostles had laid their hands, there are no miraculous gifts still present or being practiced in our modern day.
        (b) These miraculous gifts were inherently connected to the confirmation of the Word.
            (1) The purpose of miracles was to reveal and confirm all truth.
            (2) Since the Bible states that all truth has been revealed and confirmed by God, there is no place for miraculous gifts to still be present and practiced today.
            (3) Without any new revelations to confirm, there are no miracles needed today.
            (4) When the age of miracles ended, all miraculous gifts ended with it, including all miraculous healing, speaking in tongues, direct revelations, etc.
- C. When the revelation of God was completed (and available in a written, enduring form), all miraculous, spiritual gifts ended, for their purpose for existence had ended.
- D. How blessed we are to have the full, complete revelation of God!
    1. Unlike the first-century church, we have all of God's revelation at our fingertips.
    2. Unlike the first-century church, we can read every word of God's revelation.
    3. Unlike the first-century church, we do not need any miracles today, for we have the permanent source of all truth in our Bibles!
    4. How blessed we are!
- E. While miracles have ceased, we have enduring "the power of God" in written form today!
    1. His Word "is living and powerful, and sharper than any two-edged sword" (Heb. 4:12).
    2. His Word "is the power of God to salvation for everyone who believes" (Rom. 1:16).
    3. His Word, unlike miracles, "lives and abide" and "endures forever" (1 Pet. 1:23, 25).
    4. His Word supplies us with "all things that pertain to life and godliness" (2 Pet. 1:3).
    5. His Word "thoroughly [equips us] for every good work" (2 Tim. 3:17).
    6. Who needs miracles when we have the powerful, living, edifying Word of God!

F. While God no longer works through miraculous means today, that does not mean that God is not working in this world and in the lives of His people today!
  1. God is always with His children today (Heb. 13:5-6; Matt. 28:20).
  2. God takes care of His children today (Psa. 37:23-25; 33:20; Matt. 6:19-34).
  3. God supplies the needs of His children today (Phil. 4:19; 2 Cor. 9:8; Mt. 6:11; 7:7-11).
  4. God protects His children today (Psa. 34:7, 15-17; 21:11; Rom. 8:18, 28, 31-35).
  5. God bears the burdens and needs of His children today (Ps. 55:22; 1 Pet. 5:6-7; Mt. 6:8).
  6. God blesses His children with an abundant life on earth (John 10:10; Mt. 6:4, 6, 18).
  7. God guides and delivers His children safely through temptations today (2 Pet. 2:7-9; Matt. 6:13; 1 Cor. 10:13; Prov. 3:5-6).
  8. God does not do any of this through supernatural means, but He does all of it through His superintendency of the natural world that He created—through His providence!
  9. We do not need the miraculous today, for we serve the almighty God who is **able**!
     (a) God "is **able** to aid those who are tempted" (Heb. 2:18).
     (b) "God is **able** to make all grace abound toward you" (2 Cor. 9:8).
     (c) God "is **able** to keep what I have committed to Him until that Day" (2 Tim. 1:12).
     (d) God "is **able** to keep you from stumbling" (Jude 24).
     (e) "Now to Him who is **able** to do exceedingly abundantly above all that we ask or think, according to the power that works in us, to Him be glory in the church by Christ Jesus to all generations, forever and ever. Amen" (Eph. 3:20-21).
G. Let us trust and serve the God of heaven!
H. Let us honor and submit to His eternal and divine will!

Recommended Resources

Books

Bales, James D. *Miracles or Mirages?* Austin: Firm Foundation, 1956.

Jividen, Jimmy. *Glossolalia: From God or Man?* Fort Worth: Star Bible, 1971.

---. *Miracles: From God or Man?* Abilene: ACU Press, 1987.

Miller, Waymon D. *Faith Healing: Faith or Fiction?* Tulsa, OK: Plaza Press, 1990.

---. *Modern Divine Healing.* Rosemead, CA: Old Paths Book Club, 1956.

Articles

Brownlow, Leroy. "Because It Teaches That the Miraculous Manifestations of the Spirit Have Ceased." *Why I Am a Member of the Church of Christ.* Fort Worth: Brownlow Publishing, 1973. 159-167.

Fulford, Hugh. "The Holy Spirit and Laying on of Hands." *"What Do You Know About the Holy Spirit?" (Fort Worth Lectures).* Ed. Wendell Winkler. Montgomery, AL: Winkler Publication, 1980. 250-255.

Guild, Claude A. "She Believes the Miracles of Bible Times Are No Longer Available." *Introducing the Church of Christ.* Ed. Alvin Jennings. Fort Worth: Star Bible, 1981. 168-172.

Jackson, Bill. "Does God Manifest Himself Miraculously, Or in Special Form, Today?" *Questions Men Ask About God (Fort Worth Lectures.)* Ed. Eddie Whitten. Bedford, TX: Christian Supply Center, 1987. 174-182.

Jackson, Wayne. "What Does the Bible Say About Miracles?" *ChristianCourier.com* https://www.christiancourier.com/articles/5-what-does-the-bible-say-about-miracles

Jividen, Jimmy. "Can Men Speak in Tongues Today?" *"What Do You Know About the Holy Spirit?" (Fort Worth Lectures).* Ed. Wendell Winkler. Montgomery, AL: Winkler Publication, 1980. 291-300.

Lipe, David L. "Miracles in the Church." *Applying Acts in the 21st Century (South Florida Lectureship).* Ed. David Sproule. Palm Beach Gardens, FL: Palm Beach Lakes church of Christ, 2002. 129-139.

Miller, Dave. "Modern-Day Miracles, Tongue-Speaking, and Holy Spirit Baptism: A Refutation." *ApologeticsPress.org* http://apologeticspress.org/APContent.aspx?category=11&article=1399&topic=293

Nichols, Flavil H. "Meeting the Argument of the 'Faith Healers.'" *"What Do You Know About the Holy Spirit?" (Fort Worth Lectures).* Ed. Wendell Winkler. Montgomery, AL: Winkler Publication, 1980. 135-143.

Nichols, Gus. "Tongue-Speaking." *The Church Faces Liberalism (Freed-Hardeman College Lectures).* Ed. Thomas B. Warren. Nashville: Gospel Advocate, 1970. 297-305.

Pharr, David. "Miraculous and Temporary or Non-Miraculous and Continuing." *The Spiritual Sword (July 2000):* 17-20.

---. "Miraculous Gifts Have Ceased." *The Spiritual Sword (April 1999):* 36-40.

Pryor, Neale. "The Nine Spiritual Gifts of the Holy Spirit." *"What Do You Know About the Holy Spirit?" (Fort Worth Lectures).* Ed. Wendell Winkler. Montgomery, AL: Winkler Publication, 1980. 65-73.

Robinson, Garland M. "God's Word and Speaking in Tongues." *God's Word—The All-Sufficient Guide (Garfield Heights Lectureship).* Ed. Kenneth McClain. Indianapolis: Garfield Heights church of Christ, 1988. 62-77.

Smith, Foy L. "Are Miracles Still Being Performed Today?" *"What Do You Know About the Holy Spirit?" (Fort Worth Lectures).* Ed. Wendell Winkler. Montgomery, AL: Winkler Publication, 1980. 211-225.

Taylor, Robert R., Jr. "An Exegetical Study of Ephesians 4:7-16." *"What Do You Know About the Holy Spirit?" (Fort Worth Lectures).* Ed. Wendell Winkler. Montgomery, AL: Winkler Publication, 1980. 301-310.

Winkler, Wendell. "Do Members of the Church of Christ Believe Miracles and Speaking in Tongues Can Still Be Performed Today?" *The Church Everybody Is Asking About.* Tuscaloosa, AL: Winkler Publications, 1988. 82-89.

Periodicals

The Spiritual Sword. April 1974. "Pentecostalism."

The Spiritual Sword. July 1994. "The Charismatic Movement."

Lesson 25: Marriage, Divorce and Remarriage

I. **Having a Biblical Understanding of This Subject (MDR) Is of Critical Importance!**
   A. First of all, it is a matter of eternal significance!
      1. The earthly relationship of marriage directly affects our relationship with God!
      2. And, our relationship with God determines whether we go to heaven or not!
   B. This matter has a national significance!
      1. Marriage and the family are the foundation of a nation's health (ours is crumbling).
      2. The marriage relationship, as defined by God, has been on a steep decline in the U.S.
         (a) Our nation has left the laws and morality of God for their own subjective morality.
         (b) The rise of the divorce rate, the prevalence of multiple marriages, the rejection of marriage in general and the promotion of homosexuality have destroyed marriage.
   C. This matter has a church significance!
      1. The church and its members have not been immune to this issue.
      2. Even Christians are divorcing and remarrying at alarming rates (for various reasons).
      3. Some Christians have left the laws and morality of God for their own subjective morality.
      4. Evangelistic efforts are impacted by the previous marriages of prospects.
      5. Brethren often disagree on this issue, leading to controversy within the church.
      6. Some Christians "preacher-shop" for one who will validate their marriage.
      7. Shepherds are placed in difficult positions, requiring tough (unpopular) decisions.
   D. This matter has a Biblical significance!
      1. Marriage and the home are the first and oldest institution known to man (Gen. 2).
      2. Biblical precepts outline God's will for the marriage relationship and must be obeyed.
   E. This is not an insignificant subject! We need to know and follow God's truth on it!

II. **Studying Marriage, Divorce and Remarriage Must Be Entered with the Proper Attitude!**
   A. Studying and teaching this subject is a very sensitive matter!
      1. This subject touches everyone – personally, emotionally, with family, etc.
      2. Self-justification and justification of loved ones, at any cost, often takes precedence.
      3. When there are children involved, the matter is often complicated exponentially.
      4. The highly controversial nature of this subject has divided congregations and families.
      5. Discerning and abiding by God's law is often set aside for one's personal preferences.
      6. The sensitivity of the subject must be kept in mind and handled with care, but the delicacy of the matter must not prevent a full analysis of and true compliance with God's truth.
   B. Proper study must include a proper attitude toward marriage itself!
      1. Marriage is not unnecessary, a tradition of the past or a product of culture.
      2. Marriage was the first institution created by God, and it must be respected as such.
      3. See Roman numeral IV, beginning on page 331, for more on God's view of marriage.
   C. Proper study must include a proper attitude toward God Himself (J. Laws, pp. 13-16)!
      1. Our love for God must exceed our love for anyone else, and nothing should be permitted to impede that love (Luke 10:27; 14:26).
      2. Our submission to God must override our submission to anyone else (John 6:38-40; 8:29; Col. 1:10; 2 Tim. 2:4; 3:4; Heb. 10:7; Luke 22:42).
      3. Our attitude of love and submission should lead us to true repentance from sin (Matt. 3:8; 2 Cor. 7:9-10; Acts 26:20; Rom. 2:4).
      4. Our respect for God will not allow us to improperly invoke His love and mercy as justification for sinful actions (Rom. 6:1, 15; 3:8; Psa. 25:10; 69:13; 85:10).

- D. Proper study must include a proper attitude toward God's Word (J. Laws, pp. 17-22)!
    1. A proper attitude respects the perfection of God's revelation, knowing it is complete (2 Tim. 3:16-17; 2 Pet. 1:21; Jas. 1:25; 2 Pet. 1:3; Jude 3).
    2. A proper attitude objectively seeks the truth without preconceived ideas (Prov. 14:12; Phil. 3:7; John 7:17; Matt. 5:6; 2 Thess. 2:10).
    3. A proper attitude recognizes that the Bible is knowable and understandable (John 8:32; 17:17; Eph. 3:4; 5:17; Matt. 22:23-29; 2 Tim. 2:15; 1 John 2:21).
    4. A proper attitude desires to obey God's truth regardless of cost or where it leads (Rom. 12:1; John 6:67-68; Matt. 8:19-22; Luke 9:23-26; 2 Tim. 3:12; Rom. 6:7-19).
    5. A proper attitude accepts that some consequences to sin are unalterable (Gal. 6:7).
- E. Proper study must include a proper attitude toward one another (J. Laws, pp. 22-25)!
    1. A proper attitude possesses and demonstrates *agape* love for all (Col. 3:12-14; Matt. 5:43-48; John 13:34-35; 1 Cor. 16:14; Rom. 12:10; 1 Cor. 13:4-7).
    2. A proper attitude is gracious and forgiving but not compromising (Jas. 4:4; Eph. 4:32; John 17:17; Gal. 2:5; 4:16).

III. Studying Marriage, Divorce and Remarriage Must Be Entered with the Proper Authority!
- A. When it comes to the subject of MDR, which standard shall we use? (See D. Rader, pp. 2-3)
- B. Proper Authority Option #1: Fickle Emotions
    1. Our emotions sometimes prevail when something doesn't seem fair or right (examples: Ezra 10:10-11; Josh. 7:24-26; Matt. 19:16-22).
        (a) But, if God commands something, that makes it inherently fair and right!
    2. Our emotions sometimes prevail when something doesn't make sense (examples: 2 Kgs. 5:10-14; Num. 21:14-19; Josh. 6:1-7; John 9:6-7).
        (a) But, if God commands something, that is the only sense it needs to make!
    3. Our emotions are not qualified to be the authority (Jer. 10:23; Isa. 55:8-9; Prov. 16:25; 3:5-6; Rom. 11:34)!
        (a) We are not qualified to question or doubt God or His standard.
        (b) We are qualified, as His creation, to believe Him and do what He says.
    4. Our emotions do not determine or change Biblical teaching!
- C. Proper Authority Option #2: Family Situations
    1. It is extremely unsettling when a family member chooses a path away from God's path.
        (a) Sometimes a Christian will be tempted to justify their family member's choice.
        (b) Sometimes, to avoid condemning the sinful choice, a "new standard" is created.
    2. However, the Bible "says what it means" and "means what it says"! It is the standard!
    3. If one family situation can be used to prove God's approval, then any family situation could be used to prove God's approval, which means no situation would ever be wrong.
    4. Our families and their marriages do not determine or change Biblical teaching!
- D. Proper Authority Option #3: Fellow Brethren
    1. Some try to find a preacher who agrees with them and approves of their marriage.
    2. Some may argue that more brethren agree with them and their marriage than do not.
    3. How could fellow human beings ever be considered as a proper authority (Ex. 23:2; Matt. 7:13-14; John 12:42-43; 2 Cor. 5:9; 10:12; Prov. 14:12; 1 John 4:1)?
    4. Our brethren do not determine or change Biblical teaching!
- E. Proper Authority Option #4: Flawless Word of God (which is actually the only "option"!)
    1. The Word of God is the only standard that is objective, divine and pleasing to God.
    2. The Word of God is the sole authority for all religious matters (Mt. 28:18; Col. 3:17).
    3. The Word of God is the final authority that will judge us (John 12:48; 2 Cor. 5:10).

F. When God's authority is rejected, then anything and everything becomes acceptable. Here are a few of the varying positions on marriage, divorce and remarriage that exist today:
1. Marriage is merely a cultural development which has evolved over the years.
2. Living together, without and/or before being married, is acceptable and advisable.
3. Having an open marriage (agreeing to have sex outside of marriage) is healthy.
4. Homosexual marriages are equally as legitimate as heterosexual marriages.
5. The practice of polygamy (having multiple spouses) is authorized and approved by God.
6. God's marriage laws are not amenable to non-Christians.
7. Matthew 19:9 is not part of the New Testament and is not applicable to Christians.
8. Matthew 19:9 applies only to Christians, as a "covenant passage."
9. Divorce and remarriage is permitted for any cause.
10. Divorce and remarriage is not permitted for any cause.
11. Whatever marriage or divorce the civil law permits is acceptable to God.
12. Everyone has a right to be married.
13. Death is the only cause for remarriage.
14. Baptism washes away all divorces/remarriages and absolves all adulterous relationships.
15. A person may abide in whatever marital relationship he finds himself when he's baptized, as Christianity has sanctified that relationship.
16. Repentance only requires one to be sorry and to promise to never do it again.
17. Adultery means only "covenant breaking" (not actually any sexual activity), after which one can pray, ask forgiveness and remarry.
18. A Christian may remarry if his/her non-Christian spouse departs and leaves him/her.
19. Divorce and remarriage is permitted for viewing pornography.
20. A spouse who is guilty of fornication (and put away for it) may remarry.
21. Divorce and remarriage is only permitted for the innocent spouse who puts away his/her mate for fornication.
22. Now, which of these (if any) are acceptable to God? God's Word (i.e., His absolute standard of authority) must be studied, respected, taught and obeyed (cf. Mt. 7:21)!

IV. It Is Critical to Understand Marriage in the Eyes of God (the Only View That Matters)!
A. God gave the plan for marriage (the only plan that matters)!
1. Consider this: Most conflict over marriage, divorce and remarriage could be prevented and resolved if God's people would learn and accept God's plan.
   (a) God's plan today is the same plan He had at the beginning (Mark 10:6-9).
   (b) God is the one who created and established the divine and sacred relationship of marriage, thus He alone has the right to regulate it (Gen. 2:24; Matt. 19:6).
   (c) The Bible's teaching about MDR is not complicated, cloaked or contradictory.
   (d) The Bible's teaching about MDR is straightforward, simple and systematic.
2. Marriage was created by God, as detailed in Genesis 2.
   (a) God created the man (2:7) and woman (2:21-22), creating them for each other.
   (b) God created marriage in the beginning, when "He brought her to the man" (2:22).
   (c) Thus, God alone, not man, has the right to govern all things marriage-related.
3. Marriage is regulated by God in His Word.
   (a) Scripture gives "us all things that pertain to life and godliness" (2 Pet. 1:3).
   (b) Marriage, by God's creation, incorporates both "life" and "godliness."
   (c) As soon as God created marriage, He gave the principles to govern it – "Therefore a man shall leave his father and mother and be joined to his wife, and they shall become one flesh" (Gen. 2:24).

        (d) Jesus used the same words, showing the timeless nature of God's regulation (Mt. 19:5).
        (e) The Holy Spirit had Paul to quote the same principles again in Ephesians 5:22-33.
        (f) Marriage has existed "from the beginning" (Mark 10:6), and so have God's laws.
    4. Marriage is defined by God in His Word.
        (a) God's Word defines marriage as (adapted from Flavil Nichols):
            (1) The lifelong
            (2) Covenant (contract or commitment)
            (3) According to the law of God
            (4) And the laws of the land
            (5) Between two eligible persons
            (6) Of opposite sex (one male and one female)
            (7) Who become one with each other
            (8) With the privilege of sexual cohabitation
            (9) And the obligation to *agape* love one another
            (10) Until separated (disjoined) by death.
        (b) Where would the world be today, or even where would the church be today, if everyone defined marriage in the way that God defines marriage?
  B. God gave the participants for marriage.
    1. "From the beginning of the creation, God 'made them male and female'" (Mk. 10:6).
        (a) "Male and female He created them" (Gen. 1:27).
        (b) When God made a mate for the man, He created woman. That's God's plan!
    2. Monogamy (one male and one female) is authorized, not polygamy.
        (a) "[T]he two shall become…" (Mt. 19:5). There are only two—one man, one woman.
        (b) Spouses are always referred to as singular (1 Cor. 7:2; 9:5; Eph. 5:23-33).
    3. Heterosexuality (a male with a female) is authorized, not homosexuality.
        (a) Marriage, in God's eyes, is always between a man and a woman.
            (1) God joins a "man" to "his wife." He does not approve any other "union."
        (b) Every reference to homosexuality in Scripture always condemns it (Gen. 1:27; 18:16-19:29; Matt. 19:4; Lev. 18:22; 20:13; Rom. 1:26-32; 1 Cor. 6:9; Jude 7).
    4. God, who alone can regulate marriage, restricts those who can enter marriage to:
        (a) A person who has never been married (1 Cor. 7:28; 9:5)
        (b) A person who was married but whose spouse is now dead (Rom. 7:2-3; 1 Cor. 7:39).
        (c) A person once married but who put away his/her spouse for fornication (Matt. 19:9).
    5. Of course, both parties in a marriage must be eligible in God's sight to marry.
  C. God gave the priority for marriage.
    1. The husband-wife bond is to take precedence over all other earthly relationships.
    2. This requires decisiveness – "a man shall leave his father and mother" (Gen. 2:24).
        (a) What was once a man's closest relationship must now yield to his marriage.
        (b) Loyalty to one's spouse must take precedence over loyalty to father or mother.
    3. This requires commitment – "and shall cleave unto his wife" (Gen. 2:24)
        (a) The Hebrew word for "cleave" (*dabaq*) means "to cling, cleave, keep close…to stick to, adhere to…glue" (Unger 37).
        (b) The Greek word for "cleave" (*kollao*) means "to join fast together, to glue, cement" (Vine 104).
        (c) Husband and wife must stick together no matter what!
        (d) This is an exclusive and continuing commitment.

4. This requires unity – "and they shall become one flesh" (Gen. 2:24).
   (a) "One flesh" emphasizes a special kind of union between husband and wife:
      (1) The totalities of two lives are joined together into one life with one goal.
      (2) They become one physically, spiritually, emotionally, socially, psychologically, etc.
      (3) Adam said, "This is now bone of my bones and flesh of my flesh" (Gen. 2:23).
   (b) For two to become one, each must surrender part of themselves.
      (1) The unity of a husband and wife is seen in the change of pronouns they use: "I"→"We" + "Me"→"Us" + "My"→"Our" + "Mine"→"Ours"
   (c) Marriages weaken when one of the "two" begins to take priority over the "one."
5. This requires exclusivity – "They were both naked, the man and his wife" (Gen. 2:25).
   (a) Husbands and wives must demonstrate absolute fidelity to each other.
   (b) The priority of marriage is seen in that no other person may enter into this relationship between a "man and his wife."
6. This requires a higher loyalty – "out of reverence for Christ" (Eph. 5:21, ESV).
   (a) The marriage relationship must share a mutual allegiance first to Jesus Christ!
   (b) Not only does Jesus give priority to every marriage, but Jesus must become the priority of every marriage.

D. God gave the provisos for marriage.
   1. There must be intention to live together as husband and wife (Matt. 19:5-6).
      (a) Leaving parents and cleaving to one's mate denotes an agreement to be married.
   2. There must be a commitment to each other (Gen. 2:24).
      (a) There must be a vow of devotion to each other, with each one understanding and accepting that vow.
   3. There must be compliance with the laws of the land or the society in which one lives.
      (a) Christians must obey the laws of the land (Rom. 13:1-7).
      (b) Whatever the laws of the land require for marriage, Christians must comply (unless they violate the revealed will of God, which must come first—Acts 5:29).
   4. There must be love for and submission to one another (Eph. 5:22-25, 28; 1 Pet. 3:1).
      (a) *Agape* love must dominate the marriage and permeate all aspects of it (1 Cor. 13:4-7).
   5. Cohabitation does not equate to marriage (Heb. 13:4; John 4:18; Matt. 1:25).
      (a) One must adhere to the conditions set out by God in order to be "married."

E. God gave purpose to marriage.
   1. As the Creator of marriage, God designed this exclusive union to fulfill the following purposes (Nichols 243):
   2. To provide self-completion and wonderful companionship (Gen. 2:18).
      (a) God said, "It is not good that man should be alone."
      (b) God said that the man needed one who was "comparable to him."
      (c) In God's eyes, a husband and wife are incomplete without the other.
   3. To enjoy sexual intimacy and fulfillment (Gen. 2:25; 1 Cor. 7:1-5; Heb. 13:4).
      (a) Marriage is the only divinely authorized situation for a man and woman to have sex.
      (b) Husbands and wives are "husband and wife" at the end of the marriage ceremony.
      (c) Each spouse has the exclusive right to the body of his/her mate, to be "one flesh."
   4. To propagate the human race (Gen. 1:27-28).
      (a) Multiply a godly offspring (Mal. 2:15) and teach them diligently (Deut. 6:7).
   5. To prevent or avoid fornication, sexual immorality (1 Cor. 7:2-4)
   6. To help each other get to heaven (1 Cor. 7:14, 16; 1 Pet. 3:1, 7).
   7. To promote better understanding of Christ's relationship to the church (Eph. 5:22-33).

F. God gave permanence to marriage.
1. This point is absolutely critical: God's general law of marriage is that it is FOR LIFE (Mark 10:9-12; Rom. 7:2-3; 1 Cor. 7:10-11).
2. From the beginning, marriage was to be a permanent bond.
   (a) "Leave father and mother" does not ever have returning in view. It's permanent!
   (b) "Cleave unto his wife" does not ever have "un-cleaving" in view. It's permanent!
   (c) "Shall become one flesh" does not ever have "two flesh" in view. It's permanent!
3. Jesus emphatically affirmed the permanency of marriage.
   (a) Jesus contrasted the popular view of His day (i.e., to end marriage for any reason).
   (b) Jesus taught "leaving," "cleaving" and two becoming "one flesh" (Matt. 19:5).
   (c) Jesus taught, "They are no longer two but one flesh" (Matt. 19:6).
   (d) Jesus taught, "God has joined together" AND "Let not man separate" (19:6).
      (1) The Greek word for "joined together" (*suzeugnumi*) means "to fasten to one yoke, yoke together" (Thayer 594), "to make a pair" (BDAG [2000], p. 954).
      (2) When God "fastens" a husband and his wife "to one yoke," His design is for them to stay together (as a pair) in that yoke and "not separate."
      (3) God alone can "pair," "yoke" and "fasten," therefore, God alone can "un-pair," "un-yoke" and "un-fasten" (if such is to be done).
4. God intended (and still intends) for marriage to last until death separates them.
   (a) God planned for marriage to be FOR LIFE!
   (b) "The woman who has a husband is bound by the law to her husband as long as he lives. But if the husband dies, she is released from the law of her husband" (Ro. 7:2).
   (c) "A wife is bound by law as long as her husband lives" (1 Cor. 7:39).
   (d) Leaving, cleaving and weaving two lives together, in God's eyes, is irrevocable!
5. In the study of MDR, this foundational truth cannot be overemphasized!
   (a) It helps us to see how seriously God views this relationship and its perpetuity!
   (b) It helps us to see how very limited any exceptions would be to this permanency (if any would be given), and how seriously we must weigh those exceptions!

V. **It Is Critical to Understand Divorce in the Eyes of God (the Only View That Matters)!**
   A. Understanding how seriously God views marriage (Roman numeral IV) lays the groundwork for how seriously one can expect God to view the matter of divorce.
   B. Man's view of divorce is very different from God's view of divorce.
      1. Divorce is very common today. Is that in line with God's plan?
      2. Divorce is done for almost any reason today. Is that in line with God's plan?
      3. Divorce is considered merely a legal transaction today. Is that in line with God's plan?
      4. Divorce is just no big deal today. Is that in line with God's plan?
      5. Man must strive to understand divorce from God's viewpoint and abide therein.
   C. The New Testament Greek word for divorce is *apoluo*. This is an important word.
      1. *Apoluo* literally means "to loose from."
      2. *Apoluo* means "to set free; to let go, dismiss; to bid depart, send away" (Thayer 66).
         (a) It was used in "releasing" prisoners (Matt. 27:15-26; John 18:39; Acts 4:21-23).
         (b) It was used in "sending away" the multitudes (Matt. 14:15-23; 15:32-39).
         (c) It was used in "loosing" infirmities (Luke 13:12).
      3. In the context of divorce, the KJV and ASV often translate this term as "put away."
      4. To "put away" someone in the New Testament involved a mental consideration, an intentional decision/action and following any legal requirements of the land.
         (a) While it involves the civil courts, divorce is more than a civil action.

(b) And, even though one goes through the process of divorce, it does not necessarily mean that one has found approval in the eyes of God.
5. The modern concept of divorce merely being the legal act of signing a document and the court of law processing that document is not the limited meaning of *apoluo*.
6. *Apoluo* involves the decision, the communication and the act of "putting away."
D. Marriage involves a contract/covenant between three parties: man, woman, God.
1. Regardless of whether one is a Christian or not, marriage involves more than just a man and a woman.
2. Marriage is a sacred institution created by God, thus God's laws apply to every marriage.
3. In discussing the marriage relationship (as designed by God), Jesus taught that "God joins" a man and a woman together. Thus, three parties are involved in a marriage.
   (a) If marriage involves more than just the two human parties (which it does), then divorce also must involve more than just the two human parties.
   (b) If the only marriages "acceptable" to God are ones He joins together, then, it would seem to follow that, the only divorces "acceptable" to God are ones He "disjoins."
4. If three parties are involved in proper marriages, One cannot be omitted during divorce.
   (a) Only God can "join" two people together.
   (b) Therefore, only God can "disjoin" two people from each other.
   (c) Why does that matter? See V, F below.
5. Therefore, God's view of divorce must be studied, understood and accepted.
E. God's plan for marriage (from the beginning) never included or intended divorce at all.
1. This point is absolutely critical, and it goes hand-in-hand with the foundational premise (in IV, F above) that God gave permanence to marriage.
2. From the beginning, God's design for marriage was for one man and one woman to become one flesh and remain together for one lifetime.
3. While there was a temporary "concession" ("permitting" and "suffering" divorce for a time), such was not commanded, required or desired by God. Hence, when Jesus came and taught on the matter, He restored God's original plan from the beginning.
4. God's view of divorce is simple, yet strong – "He hates divorce" (Mal. 2:16)!
   (a) God said, "A wife is bound by law as long as her husband lives" (1 Cor. 7:39).
   (b) God said, "A wife is not to depart from her husband" (1 Cor. 7:10).
   (c) God said, "A husband is not to divorce his wife" (1 Cor. 7:11).
   (d) That is God's view of divorce, emphasizing God's desire for marriage!
5. The Biblical testimony is clear and conclusive: Divorce is a sin in the eyes of God!
   (a) Divorce is a sin because it puts asunder what God joined together (Matt. 19:6).
   (b) Divorce is a sin because it contributes to fornication (Matt. 5:32; 1 Cor. 7:2).
   (c) Divorce is a sin because it violates the direct command of God (1 Cor. 7:10b, 11b).
   (d) Divorce is a sin because it commits an act that God expressly hates (Mal. 2:16).
6. For a spiritual view of God's view of violating marital fidelity, read Ezekiel 16.
F. God's marriage laws are not bound, loosed or altered by what man approves or legislates.
1. God's divine law is not subservient to civil law! Ever!
   (a) We are to "submit...for the Lord's sake to every human institution" (1 Pet. 2:13).
   (b) But, when human law is not in harmony with divine law, God's law trumps (Ac. 5:29).
   (c) Human/Civil law only has authority that God has provided it (Ro. 13:4; Jn. 19:11).
   (d) Human law has no power to *sanction a wrong* or *forbid something that's right*.
   (e) While civil law differs from culture-to-culture and will change even within a single culture, God's law remains constant and consistent.

2. If civil law joins two people together, that does not mean that God has joined them.
   (a) Just because a marriage is "legal" (to man) does not mean it is Scriptural (to God).
   (b) Just because two people marry does not mean they had a right to marry.
   (c) Herod "married" Herodias (legally), but it wasn't lawful in God's eyes (Mk. 6:17-18).
3. If civil law disjoins two people, that does not mean that God has disjoined them.
   (a) Just because a divorce is "legal" (to man) does not mean it is Scriptural (to God).
   (b) Just because a divorced person remarries does not mean they had a right to do it.

G. Divorce is, therefore, not some flippant word to use or some casual conversation to have.
   1. Before one ever gets a divorce, he/she should look at it through God's eyes.
   2. God hates it! God limits it! God regulates it!
   3. A good Bible student will dig in to God's Word to study it, understand it and accept it.

VI. It Is Critical to Understand Remarriage in the Eyes of God (and Key Terms Associated with It).

A. Having an understanding of how seriously God views marriage and how severely God views divorce should assist a Bible student in understanding how God views remarriage.
   1. The topic of remarriage is a basis for many jokes today, in laughing about how many husbands or how many wives a person has had.
   2. But marriage, divorce and remarriage is not a laughing matter to God!
   3. If God limits marriage and limits divorce, one should expect He limits remarriage.

B. God's general rule regarding marriage, divorce and remarriage is vital to understand.
   1. Remember the permanence that God gives to marriage (Gen. 2:24; Matt. 19:6).
   2. Remember that God's plan for marriage never intended for divorce (Gen. 2:24; Mal. 2:16).
   3. So, in general, if one marries, divorces and then remarries, how does God see that?
      (a) Jesus taught very plainly, "Whoever divorces and marries another commits adultery" (Mark 10:11-12).
      (b) Paul affirmed that if one "marries another" while his/her spouse still "lives," he/she "will be called an adulteress" or adulterer (Rom. 7:3).
      (c) Scripture teaches that if a spouse "does depart" (even if the husband or wife did not want that to happen), there are two options: "remain unmarried or be reconciled" (1 Cor. 7:11). Notice that remarrying was not one of God's options.
      (d) While this may not be easy to accept, it is certainly not difficult to understand.
   4. Scripture does teach that a widow or widower may remarry (1 Cor. 7:39; Rom. 7:2).
   5. God's original plan for marriage was a lifelong commitment (Gen; 2:24; Mal. 2:16)!
   6. Therefore, God's general rule is that, without a clear Scriptural justification (including the death of a spouse), a second marriage is not acceptable to God, but it is sinful!
   7. If there was no divine exception given to that divine rule, then there could be NO divorce and remarriage at all without adultery.
   8. God does give ONLY ONE divine exception, but it must be understood in God's eyes.

C. Besides the death of a spouse (1 Cor. 7:39; Rom. 7:2-3), God allows only one exception to His general rule for marriage, divorce and remarriage (Matt. 19:9; 5:31-32).
   1. If divorce was acceptable to God for any/every cause, then His laws are meaningless.
   2. In marriage, neither spouse has a God-given right to break their union to each other.
   3. The ONE exception that God permits to His general rule of "marriage for life, no divorce," is the intrusion of a third party that strikes at the heart this God-ordained "one-flesh union" – i.e., when a spouse takes that "one flesh" outside the marriage.
      (a) Jesus said, "And I say to you, whoever divorces his wife, except for sexual immorality, and marries another, commits adultery; and whoever marries her who is divorced commits adultery" (Matt. 19:9).

(b) Jesus said, "But I say to you that whoever divorces his wife for any reason except sexual immorality causes her to commit adultery; and whoever marries a woman who is divorced commits adultery" (Matt. 5:32).
4. If one's spouse is guilty of fornication, the innocent spouse has a God-given right to break the union, "put away" his/her spouse and marry another without committing adultery.
(a) This is the one and only one exception to God's divine law for marriage!
(b) See Roman numeral VII on page 340 for a deeper study of the one exception.
D. In a study of MDR, it is crucial to understand the term "fornication" as God uses it.
1. "Fornication" is rendered in some translations as "sexual immorality."
2. In the categorizing of sexual sins, fornication (sexual immorality) is a broad term.
3. The Greek word *porneia* denotes "illicit sexual intercourse in general" (Thayer 532) and "various kinds of 'unsanctioned sexual intercourse'; unlawful sexual intercourse" (BDAG [2000], p. 854).
4. This broad, inclusive term *(porneia)* includes:
(a) Sexual intercourse between unmarried people (1 Cor. 7:2).
(b) Sexual intercourse between individuals who may be married but not to each other (Matt. 19:9).
(c) Homosexuality (Jude 7; 1 Cor. 6:9-10).
(d) Pedophilia, bestiality, prostitution, rape, etc.
5. "For the cause of fornication" (i.e., sexual intercourse of any kind with anyone else) is the only exception that God gives to His law of married for life.
(a) The innocent spouse is not required to divorce because of fornication.
(b) But, the innocent spouse is permitted by God, at the time of the infidelity, to divorce for the cause of fornication, and if he/she so chooses at some future time, marry another without committing adultery.
6. Fornication is, by definition, a sexual sin that involves intercourse.
(a) Fornication is more than just a sin of the mind.
(1) Many have wondered if pornography (in any form, along with the acts associated with it) is "fornication" in the eyes of God.
(2) But, fornication (by definition) involves intercourse, and pornography does not.
(3) Pornography is sinful (cf. Matt. 5:28; 1 Pet. 2:11; 1 John 2:15-16), but it does not qualify as the one "exception" given by Jesus for divorce and remarriage.
(b) Fornication is more than lasciviousness.
(1) The Greek word *aselgeia* means, "unbridled lust, wantonness, shamelessness....wanton (acts or) manners, as filthy words, indecent bodily movements, unchaste handling of males and females, etc." (Thayer 79).
(i) It means to "follow the inclination to sensuality" (BDAG [1979], p. 114).
(2) The English word "lasciviousness" means "tending to excite lustful desires."
(i) "Lewdness" means "showing, or intended to excite, lust or sexual desire."
(3) Fornication is not lasciviousness, for fornication involves intercourse.
(4) Lasciviousness is sinful (cf. Gal. 5:19; 1 Pet. 4:3; Rom. 13:13), but it is not the same as fornication.
7. God includes "fornication" as a sin for which one "will not inherit the kingdom of God" (Gal. 5:19-21), but of which one may repent, discontinue and be forgiven (1 Cor. 6:9-11).
E. In a study of MDR, it is crucial to understand the term "adultery" as God uses it.
1. From beginning to end, the Bible speaks of "adultery" very disparagingly.
(a) In the Old Testament, "adultery" was a seriously vile and contemptible act.

(1) It was an act one might "commit," which was condemned by God (Ex. 20:14).
(2) It was an act "committed" with another person, which was punishable by "death" (Lev. 20:10).
(3) It was an act that one "commits" to the peril of "his own soul" (Prov. 6:32).
(4) "Adultery" is often equated with "harlotry/prostitution" (Isa. 57:3; Jer. 5:7; 13:27; Ezek. 6:9; 23:43; Hos. 2:2; 4:13-14). It was a sexual act.
  (b) In the New Testament, the Lord is just as clear and just as disapproving.
   (1) However, in an attempt to escape the force of the word, some try redefining it.
   (2) They think that redefining (i.e., softening) the word will ease their responsibility.
2. God's definition of "adultery" is unambiguous and has been unchanged.
  (a) The Hebrew term *na'aph* means, "The violation of the marriage relationship whereby either husband or wife has an illicit sexual relationship with a third party" (Renn 15).
  (b) The Greek word *moicheia* denotes one "who has unlawful intercourse with the spouse of another" (Vine 14).
  (c) Even today, the English word still carries that meaning: "sex between a married person and someone who is not that person's wife or husband" (Merriam-Webster).
  (d) "Adultery" involves a married person having sexual intercourse with a third party.
3. Yet, some have tried to make "adultery" mean something less than the sexual act.
  (a) It is falsely taught by some (in the church) that adultery is only "covenant-breaking."
   (1) They claim adultery is not sex but the act of leaving and divorcing one's mate.
   (2) They view adultery as breaking one's marriage covenant at the time of divorce.
   (3) They claim that adultery does not continue into a second marriage.
     (i) As long as one apologizes to God and promises not to break a covenant again, he can remain in the second marriage with God's blessing.
     (ii) All sexual activity after that point is pure and acceptable to God.
   (4) It is obvious, by this theory, that they are trying to justify unscriptural marriages.
  (b) A few questions will show the fallacious and irresponsible nature of this position:
   (1) When the word "adultery" is used of the Israelites' unfaithfulness to God:
     (i) Could they have simply said, "I'm sorry," and then continue in idolatry?
     (ii) If that forgave their sin, wouldn't God have approved of their idolatry?
   (2) What about a man who "looks at a woman to lust for her" (Matt. 5:28)?
     (i) What does "already committed adultery with her in his heart" mean?
     (ii) Was he passionately visualizing breaking a covenant with her?
   (3) What about the woman "caught in adultery, in the very act" (John 8:3-4)?
     (i) Did the Pharisees catch her "covenant-breaking"?
     (ii) If the woman was sorry, could she go back to the man?
   (4) Why does Hebrews 13:4 tie the "marriage bed" to "adulterers"?
     (i) How does an adulterer ("a covenant breaker") defile the marriage bed?
     (ii) God tells us that defiling the bed has to do with sex (Gen. 49:4; 35:22).
     (iii) Even when used figuratively, adultery is committed on a bed (Rev. 2:22).
   (5) If "adultery" is actually "covenant breaking" and does not involve a sexual act, how did all of the lexicons (without a single exception) get this definition wrong?
4. The true definition of adultery sheds tremendous light on God's view of marriage.
  (a) Jesus teaches that whoever divorces and remarries commits "adultery" (Mk. 10:11).
   (1) But, from man's view, that first marriage is dissolved and over.
   (2) Why would Jesus use a word (i.e., adultery) that means one of the parties is married to someone else? He specifically chose that word to prove that point!

             (3) Jesus did not accidentally use the wrong word or change the word's definition!
         (b) Jesus teaches that whoever marries a divorced person commits adultery (Mt. 5:32).
             (1) "A divorced woman" (5:32), one word in Greek, is a perfect passive participle.
             (2) The perfect tense denotes that results of a past action still exist in the present.
             (3) The force of the perfect tense shows she is still a having-been-put-away woman.
             (4) Therefore, the "third party" enters into an adulterous relationship/marriage.
         (c) The second marriage is adulterous in God's eyes:
             (1) Because that person is still obligated by law to the first marriage (Rom. 7:2-3).
             (2) Because God still sees that spouse bound to His law of marriage by which He joined.
             (3) Because the "third party" has no right to marry one who is still bound by law.
         (d) The definition of adultery demands these conclusions.
      5. It is critical to understand the force of Jesus using the present tense, "commits adultery."
         (a) "Commits adultery" is one word in the Greek New Testament *(moichao).*
         (b) "Commits adultery" is in the Greek present tense, which denotes continuous action.
             (1) The adultery is not a one-time act (like breaking a covenant) and then it's over.
             (2) One who divorces and marries "keeps on committing adultery."
             (3) The second marriage is continuous adultery every time they are intimate.
             (4) Thus, one can "live in adultery," separated from God (1 Cor. 6:9-11; Col. 3:5-7).
         (c) If the adultery was just an act of covenant-breaking that a person committed when
             he divorced his wife, why would Jesus say he was continually committing adultery?
             (1) Knowing that Jesus used the present tense answers all sorts of false arguments.
      6. God includes "adultery" as a sin for which one "will not inherit the kingdom of God"
         (Gal. 5:19-21), but of which one may repent, discontinue and be forgiven (1 Cor. 6:9-11).
   F. In a study of MDR, it is crucial to understand the term "repentance" as God uses it.
      1. If one is guilty of the sexual sin of fornication (including adultery), what is involved in
         and required in the matter of repentance?
         (a) Some have suggested that expressing sorrow and asking for forgiveness is all
             that is involved in repentance.
         (b) Thus, according to this view, a person could stay in an unlawful relationship just
             by saying, "I'm sorry. I won't do it again."
         (c) But, is that the extent of Biblical repentance?
      2. The Greek word for "repentance" (*metanoia*) is primarily "a change of mind" that
         involves a "turning about, conversion," as one "turns away" from their sinful
         behavior (BDAG [2000], p. 640).
         (a) Thayer notes that "it embraces both a recognition of sin and sorrow for it and
             hearty amendment, the tokens and effects of which are good deeds" (406).
         (b) Therefore, the "change of mind" in repentance leads to a "change of conduct."
      3. Repentance is more than just sorrow for one's actions.
         (a) The Jews in Acts 2 where "cut to the heart," but they still had to "repent" (2:37-38).
         (b) Paul taught that "godly sorrow produces repentance" (2 Cor. 7:10).
      4. Repentance demands the "fruit in keeping with repentance" (Matt. 3:8, NASB).
         (a) While repentance is a change of mind, God equally requires a resulting change of
             life, behavior and relationship, as evidence of genuine repentance.
         (b) To be sorrowful for a sinful relationship and even express sorrow for that sinful
             relationship, but then to remain in that sinful relationship, is not Bible repentance!
      5. True repentance involves:
         (a) Sorrow for sin (2 Cor. 7:10).

(b) Change of mind (Matt. 21:29).
(c) Change of conduct, including discontinuing sinful living (Matt. 3:8; 12:41).
(d) Discontinuing a sinful relationship, which is viewed by God as adultery.
6. See VIII, F, 5 on page 365 for further defining of Biblical repentance.
G. In a study of MDR, it is crucial to understand and accept God's view and God's laws.
1. In a day of disposable marriages and divorce "for every cause":
(a) God's divine rule regarding MDR likely seems harsh to many folks (or most).
(b) To hold to God's restrictive view of marriage can be unpopular and "unloving."
2. The reaction of Jesus' disciples shows that God's view is intentionally narrow (Mt. 19:10).
3. There is a monumental difference between "married" acceptably in man's sight and "married" acceptably in God's sight—one is carnal, and the other is eternal!
(a) In marriage that is acceptable to God, He joins them together (Matt. 19:6).
(b) But, not all marriages that are legal in man's sight are joined together by God.
4. Rejection of God's marriage laws, leading one to engage in unscriptural divorces and remarriages, will cost that one (and any new "spouses") a home in heaven.
(a) "Fornicators and adulterers God will judge" (Heb. 13:4).
(b) "Neither fornicators...nor adulterers...will inherit the kingdom of God" (1 Cor. 6:9-10).
5. Our greatest desire should be to see things God's way and to obey His will.
(a) But, even if one "cannot see it," that does not change the responsibility to obey it!
(b) If man would follow God's laws of marriage, so many problems would disappear!

VII. It Is Critical to Understand the One Exception in the Eyes of God (the Only View That Matters)!
A. In the beginning, God created man, God created woman and God created marriage.
1. In the beginning of the New Testament, God came to earth and taught about marriage.
2. It would follow that the teaching of Jesus on this subject would be a pivotal place to start and an essential foundation to have in order to understand God's will on MDR.
3. Matthew 19:3-9 is the key passage to examine to find God's original plan for marriage.
B. Consider the parallel passages of Matthew 19:9 and their unique emphases.
1. God's overall rule on MDR is stated in **Mark 10:11 and verse 12**.
(a) "Whoever divorces his wife and marries another commits adultery against her."
(b) "If a woman divorces her husband and marries another, she commits adultery."
(c) The law applies equally to the man or woman who divorces his/her mate.
(d) The consequences for violating God's marriage law are equal for all – adultery.
2. God's overall rule on MDR is stated in **Luke 16:18** and includes the put-away spouse.
(a) "Whoever divorces his wife and marries another commits adultery..."
(b) "...and whoever marries her who is divorced from her husband commits adultery."
(c) Again, the consequences for violating God's marriage law apply equally to all.
(1) The spouse, who puts away and then marries another, commits adultery.
(2) The spouse, who is put away and then marries another, commits adultery.
(3) The third party, who marries one who has been put away, commits adultery.
3. God's overall rule on MDR is stated in **Matthew 5:32** and stresses the gravity of putting away.
(a) "Whoever divorces his wife for any reason except sexual immorality causes her to commit adultery; and whoever marries a woman who is divorced commits adultery."
(b) By putting away his spouse, a husband puts his wife in a tough position:
(1) Either remain unmarried for the rest of her life, OR
(2) Marry another man and thus become an adulterer, along with her new husband.

4. God's overall rule on MDR is stated in **Matthew 19:9** and answers the question of "divorce for every cause."
   (a) "Whoever divorces his wife, except for sexual immorality, and marries another, commits adultery; and whoever marries her who is divorced commits adultery."
   (b) The Pharisees had asked about putting away a spouse "for every cause."
   (c) Jesus authoritatively answered there is only one cause for divorce and remarriage.
5. Let's study this key text (Matthew 19:9 and the verses leading up to it) more closely.

C. The Pharisees' question gives insight into the teaching and practice of that day (19:3).
   1. The Greek indicates that the Pharisees were repeatedly testing Jesus and repeatedly asking Him, "Is it lawful for a man to divorce his wife for just any reason?"
   2. Their interest in "lawful" had to do with the Law of Moses and not the Law of God.
      (a) They wanted to know what Jesus would teach (parallel or contrary) about the law.
      (b) Of course, "lawful" in the Pharisees' mind also had more to do with their doctrines.
   3. The real emphasis of the question is at the end, "...for just any reason?"
      (a) It is also translated: "...for every cause?" (ASV); "...for any reason at all?" (NASB); "...for any cause?" (ESV).
      (b) They were not asking if divorce was lawful but asking what reasons were lawful.
      (c) Divorce was common and accepted among the Jews, even for trifle reasons.
   4. There were two major (and heatedly contested) schools of thought regarding "cause."
      (a) Their divide was based upon differing interpretations of Deuteronomy 24:1-4.
         (1) Specifically, the divide was over the meaning of "uncleanness/indecency" (24:1).
         (2) Whatever this was, in their minds, provided acceptable grounds for divorce.
         (3) The Hebrew term, somewhat vague, means, "nakedness of a thing."
         (4) It likely involved some indecent or lewd act, but its exact meaning is not known.
      (b) The two major schools of thought followed the positions held by two Rabbis.
         (1) The school of Shammai taught divorce was only lawful for lewdness or worse.
            (i) They emphasized the "nakedness" part of the meaning.
            (ii) Some may have limited it to adultery, and others to a lewd/indecent act.
         (2) The school of Hillel taught that divorce was lawful for every cause.
            (i) They emphasized the more "generic" part of the meaning – "some thing."
            (ii) Thus, divorce was allowed (by the Jews) for the smallest of reasons.
            (iii) This was the more popular view and widely "practiced" among the Jews.
      (c) As we will see below, Deuteronomy 24 was not God's law approving divorce.
         (1) It was God's law restricting divorce, to gain control over their practice of it.
         (2) It was intended to provide protection for the Jewish wives.

D. Jesus' response to the Pharisees was a restoration of the original plan of God (19:4-6).
   1. The Pharisees wanted to see if Jesus would side with Shammai or Hillel.
      (a) But the Lord of all man was not obligated to side with any manmade doctrine!
      (b) Rather, the Lord of all man emphasized HIS doctrine regarding divorce.
   2. Jesus charged the Pharisees for their ignorance of God's original intent for marriage.
      (a) To Pharisees who took pride in their "knowledge," Jesus said, "Have you not read?"
   3. While the Pharisees argued over Deuteronomy 24, Jesus went back beyond it (19:4-5).
      (a) He went back before Moses, before their traditions and before their rabbis.
      (b) Jesus went all the way back to God's design for marriage "at the very beginning."
         (1) He could do that, for He was God...He was there...and He knew God's design!
         (2) Jesus created all things (John 1:3; Col. 1:16), including man and woman.
         (3) Therefore, Jesus created marriage and knew the Creator's original design.

- (4) Jesus taught there was marriage "from the beginning of the creation" (Mk. 10:6).
- (c) Jesus quoted Scripture to answer, "Is it lawful to divorce for any reason?"
  - (1) A Bible question was asked and Jesus gave a Bible answer (Gen. 1:27; 2:24).
  - (2) Divorce was not part of God's original plan, for He only created one man for one woman (or one woman for one man). There were no other possible mates!
  - (3) Divorce was not part of God's original plan, for they were to "cleave" to each other, with "glue, cement" that made a permanent union.
4. Jesus emphasized the "one flesh" nature of marriage (19:6).
   - (a) The word "So" draws a conclusion regarding the bond that had resulted.
   - (b) "So then, they are no longer two but one flesh."
     - (1) In marriage, God takes two and makes one. One person cannot be divided.
     - (2) Divorce was not part of God's original plan, for it violates the will of God, as it severs the unity that He created in marriage.
5. Jesus summarized and underscored the respect man must have for God's marriage (19:6).
   - (a) In a Scriptural marriage, God joins together (or yokes together) husband and wife.
   - (b) Who is man to undo what God has done? To disjoin what God has joined?
   - (c) Jesus demands proper respect for marriage: "What God has joined together, let not man separate."
     - (1) "Let not man separate" is a present tense imperative verb (preceded by "not").
     - (2) The actual command (in Greek) is for man to "*stop* doing what he is doing."
       - (i) Even the "most religious" of that day were disregarding God's original plan.
       - (ii) Jesus commanded them to "stop it!" *Stop disjoining what God joins!*
       - (iii) Regardless of civil law, religious tradition or human desires, follow God's will!
E. The Pharisees mistakenly thought they had Jesus cornered and in conflict with Moses (19:7-8).
  1. In verse 7, they asked (not seeking truth or understanding, but continuing to test Him):
     - (a) "Why then did Moses command to give a certificate of divorce, and to put her away?"
       - (1) They presumed Jesus was wrong, because what He said contradicted Moses.
       - (2) However, they had perverted Moses to wrongly justify any cause for divorce.
     - (b) The Jews had erroneously concluded that Moses "commanded" divorce.
       - (1) They had taken Deuteronomy 24 as God-given right and support of divorce.
       - (2) Such perversion of Deuteronomy 24 had led to rampant divorce among Jews.
     - (c) Deuteronomy 24:1-4 was simply addressing possible conditions that could occur and what to do when/if they did occur. God was not saying, "It's ok. Go and do it."
       - (1) This is a clear case of "casuistic law," which uses "if…then" clauses.
         - (i) Casuistic law is not commands or showing approval for things that happen.
         - (ii) Casuistic law is what must be done when certain things (the "ifs") happen.
         - (iii) The "if" clause is called the protasis; the "then" (main) clause is the apodosis.
         - (iv) In Deuteronomy 24, verses 1-3 are the protases and verse 4 is the apodosis.
       - (2) Consider some examples of casuistic law in everyday life (to understand it):
         - (i) Sign in store: "If you break it, you buy it." (This is not a command or permission to break anything.)
         - (ii) Parent to child: "If you make a mess, you will clean it up." (This is not a command or permission to make a mess.)
       - (3) Consider some examples of casuistic law in other Scriptures:
         - (i) "If he takes another wife, he shall not diminish her food…" (Ex. 21:10).
         - (ii) "If you buy a Hebrew servant, he shall serve six years…" (Ex. 21:2).
         - (iii) "If a man steals an ox…he shall restore…" (Ex. 22:1).

- (iv) "When a man goes to the woods...and the head slips from the handle and strikes his neighbor so that he dies, he shall flee..." (Deut. 19:5).
- (4) Deuteronomy 24:1-3 are the conditions (not approved) that could occur (the "ifs").
  - (i) A man gives wife certificate of divorce for "uncleanness" and sends her away.
  - (ii) The woman goes and becomes another man's wife.
  - (iii) The second husband also divorces the woman or he dies.
- (5) Deuteronomy 24:4 is what must be done if the (unacceptable) conditions occur.
  - (i) The first husband "is not allowed to take her again to be his wife."
  - (ii) God did not approve of the first divorce or of the second marriage, for:
    1. "She has been defiled" (see also Jer. 3:1; Lev. 18:20; Num. 5:13).
    2. "That is an abomination before the Lord" (see also Lev. 18:24-30; 19:29; Num. 35:33-34).
- (6) In Deuteronomy 24, God wanted the rampant practice of divorce under control.
  - (i) He wanted to dissuade the Jews from divorcing for any and every cause.
  - (ii) He wanted to make men think hard about divorce, as no reconciliation allowed.
  - (iii) He wanted to protect the wife, who was often handled harshly and severely.
  - (iv) He was not encouraging, commanding or approving divorce. How could He?
  - (v) Compare also Leviticus 21:7, 14; 22:13; Numbers 30:9.
- (d) The "uncleanness/indecency" in Deuteronomy 24:1 is rather difficult to define.
  - (1) Hillel wanted it to include "any cause at all," but it is more substantial than that.
  - (2) Shammai may have wanted it to be adultery, but it was "less" than that.
  - (3) It could not have been adultery, for that led to the death penalty (Deut. 22:22).
  - (4) It was likely some immoral indecency that was short of intercourse.
2. In verse 8, Jesus corrected their obvious (and even willful) distortion of Moses' words.
  - (a) First of all, Moses did not "command" divorce, as they suggested and taught. Rather, Moses "permitted you to divorce your wives."
    - (1) The Law only "permitted" (NKJV), "allowed" (ESV), "suffered" (ASV) this action.
    - (2) The Law did not command it, and God, for sure, did not want it.
    - (3) "Suffered/Permitted" does not denote approval but rather toleration for a time.
  - (b) God permitted it "because of the hardness of your hearts." Divorce was not His will!
    - (1) This was not a part of God's original plan; He allowed a temporary relaxation.
    - (2) The reason: their hearts were hardened and rebellious toward God's law.
    - (3) For a time, God tolerated other practices (ex: polygamy) which He didn't approve.
    - (4) It is interesting (and not happenstance) that God did not (and could not) close the Old Testament without a reminder of His will (cf. Mal. 2:16).
  - (c) Again, Jesus returned to the original plan: "but from the beginning it was not so."
    - (1) Jesus wanted these Jews to know that God's "concession" was only temporary.
    - (2) He wanted them to know that God's original intent for marriage did not change.
    - (3) Jesus was about to tell them that the temporary accommodation was over.
    - (4) "But" contrasts what had been taught and permitted with what He was about to say. (Notice that verse 9 begins, "And I say to you...")
    - (5) "From the beginning" takes it all the way back beyond Moses (cf. Mark 10:6).
    - (6) "It was not so" is a perfect tense verb, which is very significant.
      - (i) Greek perfect tense indicates a past action with abiding results in the present.
      - (ii) The emphasis is this: "it was not so" in the past and "it is still not so" today.
      - (iii) God's will and God's law about marriage is permanent and never changed.
  - (d) Therefore, the Lord was restoring the marriage relationship back to His original intent.

(1) As Jesus leads into Matthew 19:9, He was reestablishing God's marriage laws.
(2) Regardless of what Moses taught or permitted, God's law on MDR is God's law!
(3) To divorce and remarry for any/every cause results in adultery.
(4) God allows an innocent spouse to divorce a fornicating spouse, and that's it.

F. Jesus gave one and only one exception to God's original plan for a lifelong marriage (19:9).
1. God's overall rule on MDR is, "Whoever divorces and remarries commits adultery."
2. If no exception was given, there could be NO divorce and remarriage without adultery.
3. In Matthew 19:9 and 5:32, Jesus gives the only reason one may divorce and remarry.
   (a) While many folks divorce and remarry for many causes, they stand guilty before God.
   (b) Jesus gave one reason a person could be innocent through a divorce and remarriage.
4. In Matthew 19:9 and 5:32, Jesus used two different Greek words for "except."
   (a) In Matthew 19:9, "except for" is from a two-word Greek expression, *me epi*.
      (1) *Me* is a Greek negative particle that serves as a "marker of negation" and means "not" (BDAG [2000], p. 644).
         (i) Thayer notes that it is conditional and means "unless, if not" (408).
      (2) *Epi* is a Greek preposition that serves as a "marker of basis for a state of being, action or result" and can mean, in this passage, "on" or "on the basis of" (BDAG [2000], p. 364).
         (i) Thayer defines it as "upon the ground of...for, on account of" (232-233).
      (3) In Matthew 19:9, "except for" means that "unless" the divorce is "on the basis of" ("if not...upon the ground of") fornication, any marriage that follows is adultery.
      (4) The word "except" would allow no other conditions for divorce and remarriage.
   (b) In Matthew 5:32, "for any reason except" is from the Greek *parektos logos*.
      (1) *Parektos* is a Greek preposition that "pertains to something left out of other considerations" and means "apart from, except for" (BDAG [2000], p. 774).
         (i) Vine includes the meaning "saving" (as in "saving for") (Vine 215).
      (2) *Logos* in this context means the "reason," "cause," "ground" or "motive" for one's actions (BDAG [2000], p. 601).
      (3) In Matthew 5:32, "apart from" or "saving for" the "reason, cause, ground or motive" of divorce being fornication, any marriage that follows is adultery.
5. By using the expression "except for" and "for any reason except," Jesus was saying:
   (a) "If and only if" fornication is present may the innocent spouse divorce and remarry.
   (b) This is the "one and only one" exception for God's overall rule on MDR.
   (c) There is no other reason, cause or motive that will be accepted! This is it!
   (d) "Fornication" is the only basis/reason for divorce and must be that basis/reason.
6. Jesus specified and restricted "fornication" as the only grounds for an innocent party to divorce and remarry.
   (a) "Fornication" (from the Greek *porneia*) is a "generic" term that:
      (1) Means "every kind of unlawful sexual intercourse" (BDAG [1979], p. 693).
      (2) Includes all sexual activity that is not between a husband and wife joined by God.
   (b) "Fornication," also translated "sexual immorality," must be taken very seriously!
      (1) In God's overall rule for marriage, only death can sever a marriage (Rom. 7:2-3).
      (2) And, He only gave ONE exception to that rule: fornication.
      (3) He viewed becoming one flesh with a third party as the only cause for divorce.
7. In order for an innocent party to have God's approval to divorce and remarry:
   (a) He/She must be an innocent party, not having committed fornication himself/herself.
   (b) Fornication must be the actual reason/cause for taking the action of divorce.

- (c) Fornication is not a reason/cause that can be applied later after a divorce.
    - (1) Sometimes after a divorce for "any other cause," a spouse will commit fornication.
    - (2) This is not grounds for the other spouse to retroactively apply that to the divorce.
    - (3) Fornication as a result of divorce is not the same as fornication as the cause.
- 8. Understanding and applying Jesus' one exception is critical to a proper understanding of God's view of remarriage.

G. Matthew 19:9 stands as a central text in God's authority on the subject of MDR.
  1. Authority on this subject was being established in Matthew 19.
     - (a) The Pharisees did not see Jesus as an authority—they were "testing Him" (19:3).
     - (b) To the Jews, Moses was looked to as their authority (19:7).
     - (c) In Matthew 19, Jesus was establishing Himself as THE authority on MDR.
  2. Jesus took His opponents back to "the beginning" twice to emphasize original authority (4, 8).
     - (a) The context of Matthew 19:1-12 is rich in contrasts:
       - (1) Contrast between Jesus and the Pharisees.
       - (2) Contrast between the school of Hillel and the school of Shammai.
       - (3) Contrast between divorce for any cause and divorce for only one cause.
       - (4) Contrast between the law of man (civil) and the law of God (divine/superior).
       - (5) Contrast between "put away" and "certificate of divorce."
       - (6) Contrast between God's will "at the beginning" and man's will "at present."
       - (7) Contrast between two becoming one and one becoming two (again).
       - (8) Contrast between God joining together and man putting asunder.
       - (9) Contrast between Moses commanding and Moses permitting.
       - (10) Contrast between hardness of hearts and making oneself a eunuch for Christ.
       - (11) Contrast between what Moses/Pharisees/Rabbis said and what "I say to you."
  3. The authority in Matthew 19:9 is Jesus Himself!
     - (a) After they tested Jesus and twisted the Scripture, Jesus finally said, "I say to you."
     - (b) Notice that His authority is divine and reaches back to the beginning:
       - (1) "**He who** made them at the beginning" (19:4; cf. Col. 1:16).
       - (2) "What **God** has joined together" (19:6; cf. John 1:3).
       - (3) "From **the beginning**" (19:8; cf. John 1:1).
     - (c) Jesus contrasted man's authority and Moses' authority with His/Divine authority!
       - (1) "**And I say to you**" (19:9; cf. 5:32).
       - (2) Moses was the lawgiver (Jn. 1:17); now Christ is the lawgiver (1 Co. 9:21; Ga. 6:2).
  4. Matthew 19:9 is God's law on marriage, divorce and remarriage.

VIII. **Many False Doctrines on MDR Have Arisen, Which Must Be Answered from the Bible.**
  A. While divine law on MDR is fairly simple (i.e., *one* man and *one* woman becoming *one* flesh for *one* lifetime with only *one* exception), various teachings contrary to divine law have been advocated over the years. (See page 331 for a list of some of them.)
    1. False doctrines regarding MDR cannot be tolerated, for multiple souls are at risk!
       - (a) Scripture strongly affirms, "Fornicators and adulterers God will judge" (Heb. 13:4).
       - (b) "Neither fornicators...nor adulterers...will inherit the kingdom of God" (1 Cor. 6:9-10).
       - (c) This is not a matter on which one can afford to be wrong.
    2. A few of the more common doctrines need to be answered from the Bible.
  B. **False Doctrine: Matthew 19:9 is not amenable to Christians today.**
    1. Advocates argue that the N.T. took effect on Pentecost in Acts 2, and therefore, anything stated in the Bible before Acts 2 (incl. Mathew 19:9) is not part of the N.T.

(a) They claim Matthew, Mark, Luke, John and Acts 1 are not part of the new covenant.
   (1) They say that as the "last O.T. prophet," Jesus lived under the old law (not the New), and what He taught was part of the old law (and not the New), for He had to keep the Old perfectly and could not alter it with any "new" teaching.
   (2) Jesus' teachings were merely explanatory of the Law of Moses.
   (3) Therefore, since the law was nailed to the cross, Jesus' teachings were as well.
(b) They claim the law for the church (Christians) was not given until Pentecost and after.
   (1) If anything Jesus taught was part of the N.T., it must be stated again after Acts 2.
   (2) Therefore, they will not accept as law anything in the Bible before Acts 2.
(c) In their minds, the "exception clause" in Matthew 19:9 is not N.T. doctrine.
   (1) They require the exception to be repeated after Acts 2 to be amenable today.
   (2) Therefore, they argue that the exception clause is not law for us today.
(d) This doctrine (Matthew 19:9 is not amenable to Christians) is blatantly false!
2. Answering this false doctrine with the truth is necessary and fairly simple.
   (a) Truth: To reject one verse/doctrine (i.e., Matthew 19:9) as part of the N.T.:
      (1) Necessitates the rejection of the entire chapter (19) and book (Matthew).
      (2) Necessitates the rejection of all four gospel accounts as part of N.T.
   (b) Truth: Jesus came to both fulfill the Old and to establish the New. He did both!
      (1) "I did not come to destroy [the Law or the Prophets] but to fulfill" (Mt. 5:17).
      (2) "...the word that I have spoken will judge him in the last day" (John 12:48).
   (c) Truth: While Jesus did explain parts of the Law of Moses, He also taught the New.
      (1) Are verses like these part of the Old (i.e., Jesus explaining it) or part of the New?
         (i) "Unless one is born again, he cannot see the kingdom of God" (John 3:3, 5).
         (ii) "No one comes to the Father but by [Jesus]" (John 14:6).
         (iii) "Make disciples of all the nations" (Matt. 28:18-20).
         (iv) "Preach the gospel to every creature" (Mark 16:15-16).
      (2) Jesus taught many things that were not part of the Law of Moses.
         (i) Many of Jesus' teachings were not found in the Old or bound by the Old.
         (ii) He could not be merely explaining old laws if they were not laws of the Old.
         (iii) To keep the Old perfectly, even Jesus couldn't "add" to it (Dt. 12:32; Pr. 30:6).
         (iv) Therefore, if Jesus' words were bound on anyone, it is on us (after Acts 2).
      (3) Jesus taught many things (binding on us today) not repeated after Acts 2.
         (i) "...to lust for her has already committed adultery in his heart" (Matt. 5:28).
         (ii) "Do not call anyone on earth your father; for One is your Father" (Mt. 23:9).
         (iii) Neither of these verses (and many like them) are ever repeated after Acts 2.
         (iv) Therefore, Jesus' teachings before Acts 2 are part of N.T. and amenable to us.
   (d) Truth: Jesus often contrasted the teaching of the Old with His teaching.
      (1) He could not be merely clarifying/explaining the Old if He was differentiating.
         (i) This is seen repeatedly in Matthew 5 (vv. 21-22, 28, 31-32, 33-34, 38-39, 43-44).
         (ii) This is seen even in Matthew 19: "Moses permitted...And I say to you..."
         (iii) While Jesus did provide explanation and interpretation of the Law of Moses on occasion, He also contrasted definitively His law from the Old.
      (2) If Matthew 19:9 merely explained the Law of Moses, then Jesus contradicted it.
         (i) The Law of Moses permitted divorce for "uncleanness" (Deut. 24:1-4).
         (ii) "Uncleanness" could not be adultery, for that meant death (Lev. 20:10).
         (iii) Jesus could not have been explaining the Old, else He was contradicting it.
         (iv) Therefore, Jesus' teachings were different from the Old and thus New.

(3) Even the Pharisees recognized He was contrasting His teaching with Moses (19:7).
- (e) Truth: Law can be spoken and taught before it takes effect as law.
    (1) Illustration: Legislatures do this all the time—making laws and explaining laws before those laws take effect.
    (2) Before Acts 2, Jesus taught things that (by His authority) would go into effect later:
        (i) The Great Commission: preach the gospel to save the world (Mark 16:15).
        (ii) The plan of salvation: "He who believes and is baptized will be saved" (16:16).
        (iii) The Lord's Supper: "this is my body…this is my blood" (Matt. 26:26-29).
        (iv) Extensive teaching on "the kingdom of God," not established until Acts 2.
        (v) His church and the practice of church discipline (Matt. 16:16-18; 18:15-18).
        (vi) The work of the apostles and growth of the church in Acts 1:8.
    (3) Before Acts 2, Jesus taught "new" things not authorized in the Law of Moses:
        (i) "All meats clean": something not authorized for the Jews (Mark 7:19).
        (ii) Worship not limited to the mountain, Jerusalem, etc. (John 4:21).
        (iii) Bringing Gentiles into covenant without becoming Jews (Jn. 10:16; 11:47-53).
    (4) Before Acts 2, Jesus taught for men to keep His commandments (Jn. 14:15; 15:14).
        (i) His new law, under His authority, would require a change in the law.
        (ii) Once the old law was removed, His new law took effect.
        (iii) This transition took place at the cross (cf. Col. 2:14; Heb. 7:12; 9:15-17).
    (5) How can Matthew 28, Mark 16, Luke 24 and John 21 not be law today?
        (i) Those who advocate this false position have a hard time being consistent.
        (ii) They don't want Matthew 19:9 to be amenable to them; therefore, they must also eliminate everything else in the New Testament before Acts 2.
- (f) Truth: Matthew, Mark, Luke and John were ALL WRITTEN AFTER Pentecost.
    (1) If Jesus' teachings (in the gospel accounts) do not apply to us, then to whom?
    (2) If Matthew 19:9 is not amenable to us today, it was never amenable to anyone.
        (i) It was not amenable to the Jews, for fornicators were put to death (Dt. 22:22).
        (ii) It will not be amenable in heaven, for there will be no marriage (Mt. 22:30).
        (iii) Therefore, it is either amenable to us today or it is a meaningless text.
    (3) These books were written by the authority of Christ!
        (i) Would the authority of Christ add to the Law of Moses after it was dead?
        (ii) Or write a book to the Greeks (i.e., Luke) that had nothing to do with them?
3. Matthew 19:9 is most certainly amenable to Christians today!

C. **False Doctrine: Matthew 19:9 is amenable ONLY to Christians.**
1. Advocates argue that this is a "covenant passage" that is amenable only to husbands and wives who are both Christians (i.e., members of the church of Christ).
    - (a) In an effort to justify and accept adulterous relationships among non-Christians (and to not condemn them or teach that they must sever unscriptural relationships), some teach that Matthew 19:9 only applies to those already in the church and already in a "covenant" relationship with God (i.e., a "covenant passage").
    - (b) They teach that this text does not apply to two non-Christians married to each other or to a Christian married to a non-Christian.
    - (c) And, since these individuals are not amenable to it, they cannot commit adultery.
2. Answering this false doctrine with the truth is necessary and fairly simple.
    - (a) Truth: It is obvious that Jesus was returning to God's original marriage laws, not based upon culture or tradition or concession, but upon eternal divine principles.
        (1) These marriage laws embraced the whole of humanity, not just Christians.

           (2) Wayne Jackson noted, "There was no church of Christ in the Garden of Eden" (*The Teaching of Jesus,* 6).
           (3) Therefore, the laws are not limited to "covenant people" but extend to all people.
       (b) Truth: There was not a single Christian present when Jesus was speaking.
           (1) There were great multitudes (19:2-3), Pharisees (19:3) and disciples (19:10).
           (2) If this verse is only amenable to Christians, why was Jesus wasting His breath?
           (3) If His words were not addressed to His Jewish inquirers, He dodged the question.
       (c) Truth: Since those outside the church can commit the sins of fornication and adultery, then the marriage laws of God must apply to them.
           (1) The Christians in Corinth were reminded of their lifestyle before Christ.
               (i) "Neither fornicators...nor adulterers...will inherit the kingdom of God."
               (ii) "And such were some of you" (1 Cor. 6:9-11), before becoming Christians.
               (iii) God says that they were adulterers, but based upon whose law (if they were not subject to the law of God on marriage, divorce and remarriage)?
               (iv) By definition, to be called "adulterers," these non-Christians must have been amenable to God's marriage law before they became Christians!
           (2) God created marriage as His authorized "bed" for sex (Heb. 13:4; 1 Cor. 7:2).
               (i) If non-Christians are not amenable to God's marriage laws, then are they permitted to fulfill their sexual desires in any way or place they want?
               (ii) What verse would teach otherwise?
       (d) Truth: Jesus universally applied His teaching with unlimited application to "whoever."
           (1) "Whoever" is not a word limited by Jesus to Christians in a "covenant."
               (i) "Whoever murders will be in danger of the judgment" (Matt. 5:21).
               (ii) "Whoever is angry with his brother without a cause..." (Matt. 5:22).
               (iii) "Whoever looks at a woman to lust for her..." (Matt. 5:28).
               (iv) "Whoever desires to save his life will lose it..." (Matt. 16:25).
               (v) "Whoever divorces his wife for any reason except..." (Matt. 5:32).
               (vi) "Whoever divorces his wife, except for sexual immorality..." (Matt. 19:9).
               (vii) Do Jesus' warnings about murder, anger and lust apply to both Christians and non-Christians? Obviously, they do, as do His words in 5:32 and 19:9.
           (2) "Whoever" is used interchangeably by Jesus with "everyone."
               (i) "*Everyone* who is angry with his brother...*whoever* says to his brother" (5:22).
               (ii) "*Whoever* sends his wife away...*everyone* who divorces his wife" (5:31-32).
           (3) Jesus' universal use of "whoever" matches the rest of the New Testament.
               (i) "Whoever calls on the name of the Lord shall be saved" (Rom. 10:13).
               (ii) "Whoever desires, let him take the water of life freely" (Rev. 22:17).
       (e) Consider this logical argumentation from Wayne Jackson (*The Teaching of Jesus...*):
           (1) "Christ's teaching on marriage was a restoration of Heaven's original plan.
           (2) "But God's original plan encompassed mankind as a whole.
           (3) "Thus, Christ's teaching on marriage encompasses mankind as a whole" (6).
   3. Matthew 19:9 is amenable to all men and all women in all marriages today.
D. **False Doctrine: A spouse who commits fornication may be put away and marry again.**
   1. The claim is made that the guilty party has equal right to remarry as the innocent party.
       (a) Some claim that if the bond of marriage is dissolved so that the innocent party can remarry, the marriage bond must also be dissolved for the guilty party to remarry.
       (b) Some claim that "except for fornication" clause must also apply to the guilty party.

(1) They suggest that the exception in the first part of Matthew 19:9 carries over to and is implied in the second part of the verse to mean, "Whoever marries her who is divorced (except it was for fornication) commits adultery."
(2) They suggest that the exception applies to both the innocent and the guilty, so that it is not adultery to marry a guilty party or for the guilty party to remarry.
2. Truth: The put away-fornicator may not remarry: Biblical authority will not allow it!
   (a) There is NO Scriptural authority for a put-away fornicator to remarry.
      (1) Everything we do must be done by (and with) the authority of Christ (Col. 3:17).
      (2) The New Testament clearly authorizes three categories of persons to marry:
         (i) One who has never been married (1 Cor. 7:28; 9:5).
         (ii) One who has been married but whose spouse is dead (Ro. 7:2-3; 1 Co. 7:39).
         (iii) One who was married but put away his/her spouse for fornication (Mt. 19:9).
      (3) By what or whose authority can a guilty party be authorized to marry?
         (i) There is no passage in the New Testament that authorizes the put-away fornicator to remarry (or the put-away non-fornicator)!
         (ii) To suggest that the put-away fornicator has the same right to remarry as the innocent party is to go beyond what Scripture explicitly or implicitly teaches.
   (b) There is a difference between "the marriage" and "the bond."
      (1) It is possible for one to be "married" to another person (in human terms) but still be "bound" elsewhere and not permitted to be "remarried" (in God's terms).
         (i) "For the woman who has a husband is **bound by the law to her husband** as long as he lives. But if the husband dies, she is released from **the law of her husband**. So then if, while her husband lives, she marries another man, she will be called an adulteress; but if her husband dies, she is **free from that law**, so that she is no adulteress, though she has married another man" (Rom. 7:2-3).
            1. A divorced person is "bound" BY and TO the LAW of his/her spouse.
               a. God calls it, "The law of the" spouse (ASV); "The law concerning the" spouse (NASB); "The law of marriage" (ESV).
               b. This is the law to which a person promises to be faithful "until death do us part."
               c. This is the law that governs when each spouse surrenders the right to marry anyone else as long as the other lives.
            2. A divorced person is bound BY and TO the LAW of God:
               a. In regard to God's divine plan for marriage.
               b. For it is to God that a person promises to live faithfully in marriage.
            3. A parallel passage in 1 Corinthians 7:39 states:
               a. "A wife is bound by law as long as her husband lives" (NKJV).
               b. "A wife is bound as long as her husband lives" (NASB).
               c. "A wife is bound to her husband as long as he lives" (ESV).
               d. "A wife is bound for so long time as her husband liveth" (ASV).
            4. Thus, if an innocent party chooses to put away a fornicating spouse:
               a. God releases the innocent party from that law (for that is the will of God toward the one who did nothing wrong),
               b. But He does not release the guilty party from that law (for that is the will of God toward the one who violated that law).

- (ii) John the Baptist kept telling Herod, "**It is not lawful** (present tense) **for you to have** your brother's wife'" (Mark 6:18).
  1. There was a law that Herod had violated.
  2. To put it another way, there was **a law still binding** that made their relationship adulterous.
- (2) Civil law might call it a "marriage" but God calls it adultery.
  - (i) God does not "loose" the guilty party from "the law of marriage."
  - (ii) A guilty party remains bound to all obligations to which he had yielded.
- (3) Since God is the One who does the joining (Matt. 19:6):
  - (i) God is the One who can keep one "bound" to His law, and
  - (ii) God is the One who can "loose" and keep one "loosed" from His law.
- (4) It is possible, since God is in charge and with God all things are possible:
  - (i) For one spouse to be bound to the law of God and the other spouse not, and
  - (ii) For one spouse to be released from the law of God and the other spouse not.
- (c) The Bible outright forbids the guilty party to remarry.
  - (1) When a put-away person remarries, God calls it "adultery" every time.
  - (2) "...whoever marries her who is divorced...commits adultery" (Luke 16:18).
  - (3) "...whoever marries a woman who is divorced commits adultery" (Mt. 5:32).
  - (4) "...whoever marries her who is divorced commits adultery" (Matt. 19:9).
  - (5) The guilty party, along with every other put-away person, is included in this.
3. Truth: The put away-fornicator may not remarry: Matthew 19:9 will not allow it!
   (a) Jesus' words in Matthew 19:9 literally read:
     (1) "And I am saying to you, that every man who shall send (put) away his wife and shall marry another woman, except it be for the one and only cause (reason) of her sexual unfaithfulness, keeps on committing adultery; and the one who has married a having-been-put-away woman keeps on committing adultery."
   (b) There are three persons in this passage who keep on committing adultery:
     (1) The person who divorces his wife and marries another (except for fornication).
     (2) The person who has married a woman who has been put away by her husband.
     (3) The having-been-put-away woman who is married by another man.
   (c) There are two divorced persons (implied) in this passage who do not commit adultery:
     (1) The person who divorces his wife and marries another (on grounds of fornication).
     (2) The person who has been put away and remains unmarried.
     (3) Note: A remarried fornicator does not fit in either of these categories.
   (d) Simply stated, all who divorce (not for fornication) and remarry are adulterers!
     (1) A guilty party cannot divorce for fornication. Jesus said he/she is an adulterer!
     (2) A spouse who has sex outside of marriage has forfeited the right to remarry.
   (e) The Lord's one exception restricts the guilty party from the right to remarry.
     (1) The word "except" (meaning "if and only if") provides the one and ONLY grounds for divorce and remarriage in God's plan.
       (i) "Apart from" or "saving for" the cause of fornication, one who divorces his/her spouse and marries again commits adultery.
       (ii) No person has a right to divorce and remarry, except the one sinned against.
     (2) If the guilty party is also "excepted" in Matthew 19:9 and can also remarry:
       (i) Then Jesus did not mean "except."
       (ii) Then all are "excepted," leaving no exceptions.
       (iii) Then "except" does not mean "except" in Matthew 19:9 or in John 3:5.

(3) If both the innocent and guilty parties have a right to remarry, then:
   (i) "Except" is meaningless in the teaching of Jesus.
   (ii) There would be more than one exception, denying the definition of "except."
   (iii) How would anyone ever be guilty of "committing" (present tense, continuous action) adultery? Once a person is involved in adultery, that person would become a "guilty party," who would then be free to remarry at will.
   (iv) Why was Jesus protecting the rights of the innocent in the first part of 19:9?
   (v) Why did Jesus even discuss this at all? It is nonsensical and superfluous.
(f) Unless Jesus contradicts Himself inside one verse, a guilty party has no right to remarry.
   (1) Some people miss the force and simplicity of Mark 16:16.
      (i) They argue baptism is not in the second part of the verse, so it isn't necessary.
      (ii) However, Jesus plainly states at the beginning those who shall be saved.
      (iii) The only persons who shall be saved are those who believe and are baptized.
      (iv) Jesus did not say something in the second part that contradicted the first.
      (v) The same is true with Jesus' teaching in Matthew 19:9.
   (2) There are two forceful and simple conclusions to be drawn from Matthew 19:9.
      (i) The ONLY person who has a right in God's eyes to divorce one spouse and marry another is the person whose spouse is guilty of sexual unfaithfulness.
      (ii) EVERYONE who marries any having-been-put-away person commits adultery.
      (iii) Based on these simple conclusions, the guilty party has NO right to remarry:
         1. The guilty party is not the person who had divorced his spouse and married another for the reason that his spouse was guilty of fornication.
         2. And, the guilty party IS a having-been-put-away person.
   (3) To argue that the guilty party does have a right to remarry in God's eyes:
      (i) Makes Jesus completely contradict Himself just inside one verse!
      (ii) Makes Jesus say something in the second part that contradicts the first.
      (iii) Makes Jesus' teaching on marriage, divorce and remarriage useless!
      (iv) Makes it nearly impossible for any marriage to not be labeled "Scriptural"!
(g) The exception in Matthew 19:9 cannot apply to the first and second clauses.
   (1) Practically speaking, the exception cannot be applied to both clauses in the verse.
      (i) In the first part, Jesus' exception permits only the offended party to divorce and remarry.
      (ii) If applied in the second part, it would permit the offending party to remarry.
      (iii) Obviously, that would make Jesus contradict Himself (which He did not do!).
      (iv) Is it true that whoever marries a put-away, marriage-destroying fornicator does not commit adultery but is perfectly ok and accepted in God's eyes?
   (2) Grammatically speaking, the exception cannot be applied to both clauses.
      (i) "Except for fornication" is an adverbial clause that modifies the verbs, "divorces and remarries," in the first part of the verse.
      (ii) The exception clause is NOT repeated in the second part of the verse, and it cannot be proven to be implied.
         1. If it was implied, what word would it modify?
         2. Grammatically, an adverbial modifier cannot just be changed into an adjectival modifier to modify the woman who has been put away.
   (3) Jesus never gave an exception for the put-away fornicator to remarry.
      (i) Every put-away person (fornicator or non-fornicator) must remain unmarried.
      (ii) To teach otherwise makes Jesus contradict Himself or speak utter nonsense.

- (h) The fact that Jesus omits the definite article in the second part of the verse forbids the guilty party to remarry.
    - (1) Every word in the Bible is inspired of God, down to the smallest words, like "the."
        - (i) Since God chose every word to put in, He also chose the words to leave out.
    - (2) If Jesus used the definite article in the second clause it would have read:
        - (i) "…whoever marries THE/THAT woman who is divorced commits adultery."
        - (ii) The definite article would point to the woman put away for trivial reasons.
        - (iii) This, potentially, might have helped the guilty-party-may-remarry position, by specifying the put-away non-fornicator and leaving the fornicator unmarked.
        - (iv) But, Jesus, by omitting the article, was not specifying any particular woman.
    - (3) Instead, the identity of the "having-been-put-woman" is indefinite.
        - (i) Meaning, Jesus taught that marrying any put-away woman results in adultery.
        - (ii) And, there is no exception to that! It includes one put away for fornication!
        - (iii) Hugo McCord, a Greek scholar wrote: "If the Greek article…were present to point back to the put-away woman of the first clause, then the exceptive phrase could be inferred in the second clause. But, as written, the second clause asserts that no put-away woman is eligible for remarriage" (*The Guilty Party,* 438).
4. Truth: The put away-fornicator may not remarry: Sound rationale will not allow it!
    - (a) If the guilty party can remarry, then the just and the holy nature of God are impugned.
        - (1) Is there a heavier obligation put on a put-away non-fornicator than fornicator?
        - (2) The guilty-party-can-remarry doctrine is affirming the following:
            - (i) The spouse put away for anything other than fornication cannot remarry.
            - (ii) And, the spouse who is put away for committing fornication can remarry.
            - (iii) How does that align with the justice and holiness of God?
        - (3) The guilty-party-can-remarry doctrine is also affirming the following:
            - (i) If a man divorces his wife because she becomes ugly, fat, boring or a Christian…She CANNOT remarry!
            - (ii) If a woman divorces her husband because he is a drunk, addict, violent or bum…She CANNOT remarry!
            - (iii) HOWEVER, if SHE had only had sex with another man (or a woman or an animal)…She COULD remarry!
            - (iv) How does that align with the justice and holiness of God?
        - (4) Does God's holiness allow a fornicator put away by his spouse to remarry?
    - (b) If the guilty party can remarry, then there is a premium and profit placed on sin.
        - (1) The wife and mother of young children (who is physically, verbally and emotionally abused by her non-Christian husband) has no right to divorce and remarry a nice Christian man.
            - (i) If she decides to leave her husband, she must remain unmarried.
            - (ii) She knows that is not what God wants, and she could not support herself.
        - (2) However, suppose this same woman learned from a preacher that she would be free from her husband and eligible to remarry if she had sex with another man.
            - (i) Hearing that a guilty party has God's blessing to divorce and remarry, this abused woman takes matters into her own hands to protect her children.
            - (ii) She has sex with another man, makes sure her husband finds out and now she is able to secure the God-approved freedom that she had been wanting.
        - (3) Advocates of this doctrine would not endorse this scenario, but it is valid.

(4) Does the God of the Bible place a premium on sin?
   (i) Are there some loopholes (or even permissions) whereby one may find profit or reward through sinning and reap benefits from his own wrong?
   (ii) Are those who are guilty of sexual unfaithfulness provided greater advantages in God's sight than those who remain sexually faithful?
   (iii) God condemns doing "evil that good may come" (Rom. 3:8).
   (iv) God affirms that "whatever a man sows, that he will also reap" (Gal. 6:7).
   (v) "Of course the guilty party could not, for no one is allowed by law to reap the benefits of his own wrong" (J.W. McGarvey, *The Fourfold Gospel*, p. 242).
(5) How many marriages have been held together by Jesus' strict teaching on MDR?
   (i) How many couples have worked to solve problems due to God's severe law?
   (ii) If the guilty party can remarry, wouldn't that discourage solving problems?
   (iii) If the guilty party can remarry, wouldn't that encourage more fornication?
   (iv) If the guilty party can remarry, wouldn't that tempt unhappy spouses to sin?
   (v) If there is perceived to be lesser penalty (and no penalty) for a greater sin and a greater penalty for a lesser sin, wouldn't that support more fornication?
(c) If the guilty party can remarry, then it empowers the fornicator to illogical absurdity.
   (1) In 19:9, "whoever...marries another" is the one who can initiate the divorce.
      (i) The coordinating conjunction "and" joins "divorces" and "marries."
      (ii) Thus, whoever has a right to marry another has the right to initiate divorce.
   (2) Hence, an unhappy spouse wishing to be freed, in order to marry another:
      (i) May, by following this theory, go out and commit fornication.
      (ii) Then, based on his own fornication, initiate ("file for") the divorce.
      (iii) And, be free to marry again (all with God's approval).
   (3) That may seem absurd and unreasonable, but it follows the same line of reason.
      (i) This reasoning empowers the fornicator to circumvent God's plan!
      (ii) And, simultaneously, it destroys the sanctity of God's creation—marriage.
(d) If the guilty party can remarry, then spouse-swapping and synchronized unfaithfulness would be acceptable.
   (1) If a husband and wife become unhappy in their marriage, they could:
      (i) Plan and agree for both of them to have sex outside of marriage.
      (ii) Then, plan and agree for both of them to put the other away for fornication.
      (iii) Then, be free from each other and free to remarry at will with God's blessing.
      (iv) Then, having found a "way out" of God's original plan, live happily ever after.
   (2) If a husband and wife meet another couple that attracts them, they could:
      (i) Plan and agree among the four of them to swap spouses.
      (ii) Make two new happy marriages out of two old unhappy marriages.
      (iii) And, do all of this with Jesus' permission.
   (3) Both of these scenarios could be repeated at will without limit and without fault!
(e) If the guilty party can remarry, then extremely heinous sex acts would free one to remarry.
   (1) "Fornication" (Greek *porneia*) means "every kind of unlawful sexual intercourse."
   (2) The word includes more than just "having an affair" (as we might define it).
   (3) Therefore, while a faithful Christian who was abused and abandoned by a spouse cannot remarry, according to the guilty-party-can-remarry doctrine:
      (i) Someone who has had sex with a person of the same gender, or with an animal, or with a relative, or with a child is FREED (by God) to remarry.

(ii) Regardless of civil or criminal laws, if a put-away fornicator has a God-given right to remarry, then God's law (superseding man's law) would allow it.
- (f) It is not suggested that advocates of this doctrine (that a put-away fornicator can remarry) would ever teach or allow such conclusions.
  - (1) But, their doctrine does teach and allow it!
  - (2) This is not an attempt to be unfair to those who believe and teach this doctrine.
  - (3) But, it is an exercise to expose a very serious and dangerous false doctrine.
5. Souls are at risk when they believe and act upon this false doctrine!
    - (a) God wanted man to understand how serious fornication and its consequences are!
      - (1) Taking the gift of sexual relations outside of marriage is a sin against God, one's own body, one's spouse, one's children, the church and even mankind!
      - (2) God gave ONLY ONE cause for a spouse to put away his/her mate—fornication!
      - (3) It is the ONLY action so intolerable to a marriage that God permitted divorce!
      - (4) It is the ONE act that can make a spouse "one flesh" with a third party (1 Co. 6:16).
      - (5) Therefore, it is no wonder that God removes a fornicator's right to be married again, if his/her innocent spouse chooses to put him/her away.
    - (b) If a put-away fornicator could really remarry with God's 100% hearty approval:
      - (1) Then shouldn't we stop preaching on the sanctity of marriage?
      - (2) Where is the sacredness of marriage if one can take sex outside of it and have no accountability?
      - (3) If nothing else, it creates a lower standard for today's families to live by.
    - (c) Too many guilty parties weigh their options and still choose to "take the risk."
      - (1) Some believe that they have approval from God.
      - (2) Some hope that God will understand and just be merciful.
      - (3) Yet, few ever consider that they're not only condemning their own souls, but also the souls of the ones with whom they enter these adulterous relationships.
    - (d) Roy Lanier, Jr. posed these two questions (in "Discussion Forum, No. VIII"):
      - (1) "What will be the fate of those who may not commit these sins, but by their teaching encourage men to commit them?"
      - (2) "What will be the fate of encouragers of fornication and adultery?" (477).
    - (e) God's Word does not permit fornicators to remarry.
      - (1) Fornication is fornication!
      - (2) Jesus did NOT open the door for ANY put-away fornicator to remarry!
      - (3) In fact, He kept that door completely shut!
      - (4) Marrying any having-been-put-away fornicator is adultery every time!
- **E. False Doctrine: The desertion of an unbelieving spouse allows for remarriage.**
  1. The claim is made (based on a faulty view of 1 Corinthians 7:15) that if a non-Christian spouse leaves a Christian spouse, then the Christian is free to divorce and remarry.
      - (a) Some argue that 1 Corinthians 7:15 provides cause for divorce in addition to Jesus' exception in Matthew 19:9. (Thus, "except" doesn't mean "except.")
      - (b) Some argue that Matthew 19:9 is a covenant passage that only applies to Christians (i.e., a Christian married to a Christian), and that 1 Corinthians 7:12-16 is God's marriage laws for a Christian married to a non-Christian (since Matthew 19:9 doesn't apply to them). (Thus, 1 Corinthians 7 contradicts Matthew 19.)
      - (c) Some argue that "desertion" is another cause for divorce and remarriage.
        - (1) They hold that a believer deserted by an unbeliever can remarry without adultery.
        - (2) This is in addition to the one exception that Jesus gave (i.e., for fornication).

(3) They suggest that it is not a contradiction of Jesus but simply addressing a situation He did not address.
(4) This cause for divorce is often referred to as "The Pauline Privilege," denoting that the Apostle Paul was the one who stated this cause and not Jesus.
  (d) Some argue that "not under bondage" (in 1 Cor. 7:15) releases the Christian.
(1) They argue a Christian is no longer bound to the marriage but the bond is broken.
(2) Thus, if they are no longer bound to the marriage, then they are free to remarry.
2. Preliminary #1: A brief examination of 1 Corinthians 7:10-16 is necessary.
  (a) In 1 Corinthians 7, Paul addressed about seven questions regarding marriage.
(1) The Christians in Corinth had written to Paul to ask him some questions (7:1).
(2) As with all Biblical writings, Paul's words in response were inspired of God.
(3) While Jesus may not have specifically addressed these in His earthly ministry:
  (i) All of their questions can and must be answered in light of Jesus' teaching on the subject of marriage (particularly in Matthew 5:32; 19:9).
  (ii) His teachings have universal application to every marriage and divorce.
  (b) Instructions are given to all husbands and wives (1 Cor. 7:10-11).
(1) First of all, as Jesus taught while on earth, they are to remain married (7:10).
  (i) Marriage is for life, "till death parts" (Rom. 7:2-3; 1 Cor. 7:39).
  (ii) There is only one exception, given by Jesus in Matthew 19:9.
  (iii) Paul is addressing the general rule and universal principles of marriage; the context of 1 Corinthians 7 is not about remarriage or the exception.
(2) If a separation does occur, however:
  (i) They are to remain unmarried or be reconciled (7:11).
  (ii) They are still considered to be married to each other—he is "her husband."
(3) Jesus, and therefore the entirety of Scripture, gives only one exception, allowing a married but sinned-against spouse to divorce and remarry (Matt. 19:9; 5:32).
  (c) Instructions are given to Christians who are married to unbelievers (7:12-16).
(1) This is the context in which the verse (v. 15) under controversy is found.
(2) "The rest" likely refers to the additional questions asked by the brethren (7:12).
(3) Being married to a non-Christian is not justification for divorce (7:12-13).
(4) It is still a marriage joined by God and holy in His sight (7:14).
(5) Verse 15 is a parentheses amidst verses 12-16, which provides an "exception" to the overall aim of the passage that the Christian should remain married to the unbeliever.
(6) A Christian, whose first allegiance is to Christ, is not so obligated/bound to keep the marriage together as to violate or surrender that first allegiance (7:15).
(7) The Christian mate must do what is right in order to lead both to salvation (7:16).
3. Preliminary #2: Every part of 1 Corinthians 7 is equally inspired and authorized by God.
  (a) Some try to make something out of Paul's statements, "I say" and "not I but the Lord"—trying to make a distinction between God's commands and Paul's opinions.
  (b) In this specific passage, the inspired apostle was distinguishing between:
(1) What the Lord taught and authorized while on earth (Matt. 5:32; 19:9), and
(2) What He taught and authorized through the Holy Spirit after He left (Eph. 3:1-5).
  (c) The overriding truth is that every word in 1 Corinthians 7 (and the rest of the Bible, for that matter) was chosen, inspired and authorized by God, and not Paul!
(1) The things Paul wrote were not his own opinions (cf. 2 Pet. 1:20-21).
(2) The things Paul wrote were not the teachings of other men (Gal. 1:11-12).

(3) The things Paul wrote were fully inspired (1 Cor. 2:9-13; 2 Tim. 3:16).
(4) The things Paul wrote were "the commandments of the Lord" (1 Cor. 14:37).
(5) The things Paul wrote were equally the words/authority of the Lord as those spoken by Jesus during His earthly ministry (John 16:13-15).

4. Truth: Desertion by a non-Christian spouse is not an authorized cause for divorce and remarriage!
   (a) To make this argument is to force something onto the text that is just not there!
   (b) It is important to understand the verb "depart" (Greek, *chorizo*).
      (1) *Chorizo* means "to separate, divide, part, put asunder" (Thayer 674).
      (2) In the phrase, "if the unbeliever departs," it is a present middle indicative, noting that the unbeliever himself is attempting to or desiring to depart.
      (3) In the phrase, "let him depart," it is a present middle imperative, indicating the Christian may permit the separation (but it is not sanctioning it at all).
   (c) As seen clearly in VII, F (on page 344), Jesus' use of the word "except":
      (1) Is a word that means "if and only if," and there's one and only one exception.
      (2) Teaches there is one and only one way to enter the kingdom (John 3:3-5).
      (3) Teaches there is one and only one cause for divorce and remarriage (Mt. 19:9).
      (4) Must be the law under which every other passage is studied and explained.
   (d) The specific context of 1 Corinthians 7:15 must be studied out and respected.
      (1) The Corinthians evidently asked Paul some questions about the status of a marriage when one spouse becomes a Christian and the other does not.
      (2) This would likely create conflict in the marriage, including demands from the unbeliever upon the Christian to make compromises to "save" their marriage.
         (i) The unbeliever may force the Christian to make a choice: "Christ or me!"
         (ii) Is it really even an option for the Christian to renounce his faith in Christ?
         (iii) A Christian choosing the unbelieving mate over Christ would be slavery!
         (iv) The Christian is permitted to "let him depart" and not compromise loyalty to Christ.
      (3) Separation is only allowed if the non-Christian forces the Christian to choose.
         (i) And, even then, divorce and remarriage are not even discussed or permitted.
   (e) Note carefully: "Divorce" is not being discussed in the context of 1 Corinthians 7:15.
      (1) The context of Matthew 19 is divorce, but the context of 1 Corinthians 7 is not!
      (2) The word used for divorce in the Greek New Testament is *apoluo*.
      (3) The word *apoluo* is noticeably absent in 1 Corinthians 7:10-15.
         (i) If this section is about "divorce," why would the common word be absent?
      (4) The word *chorizo* (the word used in 1 Cor. 7) means to "divide" or "separate."
         (i) It is a generic term (used 12 times in the N.T.), including in Matthew 19:6.
         (ii) It is also in Acts 1:4; 18:1-2; Romans 8:35, 29; Philemon 15; Hebrews 7:26.
         (iii) There is no indication that it means "divorce" in 1 Corinthians 7:10, 11, 15.
         (iv) The generic and typical meaning of "separate" is intended (and so translated).
         (v) "Departs" *(chorizo)* in 1 Corinthians 7:15 literally means "separates himself."
      (5) Jesus spoke clearly and conclusively regarding divorce (Matt. 5:32 + 19:9).
         (i) If 1 Corinthians 7 even appears to contradict Jesus' clear and conclusive teaching, then 1 Corinthians 7 cannot be addressing the subject of divorce.
   (f) Note carefully: "Remarriage" is not being discussed in the context of 1 Cor. 7:15.
      (1) While some want *chorizo* ("departs, let him depart") to imply a broken marriage bond and a right to remarry, neither the word nor the context will allow it.

  (2) The same word *(chorizo)* is used in verse 11.
    (i) It is obvious that the departure in verse 11 did not permit remarriage.
    (ii) Thus, there is no justification for remarriage after a departure in verse 15.
    (iii) The departure *(chorizo)* was not a termination of the marriage bond.
    (iv) While "divorce" has a specific meaning to us, *chorizo* is used in the New Testament with a general meaning ("separate, divide, depart").
  (3) In 1 Corinthians 7, there is NO mention of remarriage until verse 39.
    (i) And, in verse 39, it is a widow whose right to remarry is under discussion.
    (ii) There is no discussion of remarriage anywhere else in the context.
 (g) There is no divorce or second marriage in view in this passage, for:
  (1) It is still calling them "husband" and "wife."
  (2) There is still the possibility of a reunion.
  (3) Divorce is not even mentioned and no other cause is anywhere given.
 (h) If Paul had permitted divorce and remarriage in 7:15, he would have contradicted his own teaching just four verses earlier, when he taught that celibacy or reconciliation were the only two options for a spouse whose mate had departed.

5. Truth: The word "bondage" in 1 Corinthians 7:15 must be understood Biblically!
 (a) "Bondage" is from the Greek verb *douloo*, akin to the noun form *doulos*.
  (1) The verb *douloo* means "to make one subservient to one's interests, *cause to be like a slave*" (BDAG [2000], p. 260), "to make a slave of" (Vine 73).
 (b) It is significant in this study to know that the verb "bondage" *(douloo)* is never used in the New Testament to refer to the marriage bond.
  (1) It is frequently translated "enslaved" in the NASB (Acts 7:6, Tit. 2:3; 2 Pet. 2:19).
  (2) It is used of being enslaved to God and to righteousness (Rom. 6:18, 22).
  (3) But, marriage is never viewed in the Bible as "slavery."
  (4) In passages where Paul was writing of the marriage bond (and even here in 1 Corinthians 7), he used a different word—*deo* (1 Cor. 7:27, 39; Rom. 7:2).
  (5) By using a different word, readers would know this was not the marriage bond.
  (6) In 1 Corinthians 7:15, "not under bondage" is not the marriage relationship/bond.
 (c) If a non-Christian spouse "departs," the Lord assures the Christian that:
  (1) One's first allegiance is to God (Acts 5:29).
  (2) One is not expected to or enslaved to compromise his relationship with God in order to maintain a relationship with his spouse.
  (3) The Christian is not under bondage (or a slave) to relinquish his Christianity and to prevent departure or pursue (or force) reconciliation with the departed spouse.
  (4) If Christians were obligated to "desert" the Lord to maintain a marriage with a "deserted" (or threatening to "desert") spouse, that would be an enslavement.
  (5) Still, even if a non-Christian spouse departs, and if the Christian "lets her depart" to maintain his allegiance to God, the Christian is not permitted to remarry.
 (d) In 1 Corinthians 7:15, the word for "bondage" *(douloo)* is in the Greek perfect tense.
  (1) The perfect tense denotes a completed action (past) but with a present result.
    (i) Something has taken place in the past but the results are still abiding.
  (2) The perfect tense of "bondage" in 1 Corinthians 7:15 literally translates to:
    (i) "He was not bound and still is not bound."
    (ii) "He was not enslaved (before his spouse departed and was still with him) and is not now enslaved (after the departure has happened)."
    (iii) The Christian has never been in the bondage under consideration here.

                (3) The word "bondage" (in the perfect tense) cannot at all refer to the marriage.
                    (i) Since the Christian was married to his spouse (and still is), the bondage cannot be marriage.
                    (ii) If "bondage" is "marriage," then substitute the word into the sentence:
                        1. "The believer was not married and still is not married."
                        2. Substitution does not fit because it is not the marriage.
                (4) A Christian was not required to compromise his faith (when his spouse was still with him), and he is not enslaved to compromise his faith for his spouse now.
            (e) The Christian's bond to Christ is stronger than the bond to his unbelieving spouse.
                (1) The Christian's bond to Christ is to take precedence over every other bond!
                (2) If a Christian favors any other bond (ex: with parent, spouse, etc.) over his bond to Christ, then he is not worthy to be considered a disciple of Christ (Luke 14:26).
        6. Truth: Matthew 19:9 and 1 Corinthians 7:15 must stand in complete harmony!
            (a) Jesus' teaching in Matthew 19:9 applies comprehensively to ALL men ("whosoever").
            (b) Jesus' teaching in Matthew 19:9 was intended for the duration of the Christian age.
            (c) Jesus' teaching in Matthew 19:9 is based on God's original plan in Genesis 2:24.
                (1) God's original plan for marriage was intended for all of humanity.
                (2) Jesus' appeal to that original plan for marriage was intended for all of humanity.
            (d) Jesus' teaching in Matthew 19:9 must apply equally and fairly to all marriages.
                (1) If a man divorces his wife for trivial reasons, neither can remarry (Matt. 19:9).
                (2) If two Christians separate, both must remain unmarried (1 Cor. 7:10-11).
                (3) However, can a Christian deserted by a non-Christian divorce and remarry?
                (4) Wouldn't that make God a respecter of persons?
            (e) Therefore, Paul's teaching in 1 Corinthians 7 must:
                (1) Also apply to all of humanity.
                (2) Harmonize with all Biblical teaching on MDR (incl. Genesis 2 and Matthew 19).
                (3) Complement and support Jesus' teaching regarding marriage, divorce, remarriage and the one divine exception, and not contradict it!
F. **False Doctrine: Upon baptism, one may remain in their current marriage, regardless of any past marriages and divorces.**
    1. Some believe that non-Christians who have divorced and remarried without any limits in the past (for unscriptural reasons but within civil sanction) may remain with the one to whom they are married when they're baptized (and with God's full approval).
        (a) Some insist that non-Christians are not amenable to Christ's law but to civil law only.
            (1) They claim that, if a non-Christian violates God's marriage laws, there is no sin.
            (2) They claim that only those in the church are accountable to God's marriage laws.
            (3) They are only amenable to God's marriage laws after they have been baptized.
            (4) See VIII, F, 2 (on page 360) for a Scriptural response to this erroneous belief.
        (b) Some teach that Paul authorized any married non-Christian, regardless of their marital state, to "remain in the same calling in which he was called" (1 Cor. 7:20).
            (1) They teach that if someone was living in adultery when converted to Christ, they can (and must) stay married to their present spouse (without further sin).
            (2) Would this not, of necessity, also include polygamists, homosexuals, etc.? How could they be exempt from this law and God's promise of salvation?
            (3) See VIII, F, 3 (on page 362) for a Scriptural response to this erroneous belief.
        (c) Some assert that Christianity is not about abolishing relationships but sanctifying them, for "the unbelieving husband is sanctified by the wife..." (1 Cor. 7:14).

(1) However, this puts Jesus in the position of sanctifying activity which He condemned, without any change (or cessation) of the activity.
(2) It wrests a meaning which contradicts the passage and the entire Bible.
(3) Is a person set apart and made holy (acceptable) to Him merely for being married to a Christian? If so, what purpose does His plan of salvation have?
(4) 1 Corinthians 7:14 is not dealing with a sinful or adulterous marriage, but a Christian who is rightfully (lawfully in God's eyes) married to a non-Christian.
   (i) The verse has to do with the continued holy nature of marriage (cf. Mt. 19:6).
   (ii) The verse has to do with the purifying influence of the Word and the Christian life upon the non-Christian in the marriage and the children (cf. 1 Pet. 3:1).
(d) Some argue that baptism washes away adulterous relationships.
   (1) They actually believe that non-Christians are amenable to the law of Christ.
      (i) Thus, they believe that non-Christians can and do commit adultery by not following God's design for marriage and by violating Matthew 19:9.
      (ii) However, once baptized, a couple (once adulterous) can stay together.
   (2) They reason like this: when one is baptized, all past sins are forgiven.
      (i) Included in the forgiveness is the sinful act of the adulterous marriage.
      (ii) Consequently, after being baptized, one may continue in the marriage, for it is no longer adultery (which has been forgiven).
   (3) They claim that the act of baptism takes a sinful/unscriptural relationship and makes it fully acceptable/Scriptural in the eyes of God.
   (4) See VIII, F, 4 (on page 363) for a Scriptural response to this erroneous belief.
(e) Some allege adultery is among those sins that cannot be undone, and therefore, no change to a couples' relationship (even though adulterous) is necessary.
   (1) They argue that a murderer cannot bring back someone he has murdered (it is "undoable") and cannot change his relationship to the one murdered; likewise it is not essential that an adulterer force a change of relationship.
   (2) Just as the murderer can "repent" and "promise to never do it again," it is argued that an adulterer can do the same.
   (3) "Repentance" is redefined: Say, "I'm sorry," but keep living the way you are.
   (4) Could not polygamists, homosexuals, pedophiles and prostitutes do the same?
   (5) See VIII, F, 5 (on page 365) for a Scriptural response to this erroneous belief.
(f) Some believe that the early church accepted into the church (almost out of necessity) those living in adultery, without consideration of their present marital status or even thinking of requiring any change.
   (1) It is claimed that the practice and lifestyle of adultery was so prevalent that the church would have had no choice but to accept them.
   (2) Of course, one must ask how the prevalence of any sin makes it justifiable.
      (i) Does the Lord become soft on sin when "everyone is doing it"?
      (ii) Will/Can the same be applied to polygamy, homosexuality, pedophilia, etc.?
   (3) See VIII, F, 4, (c) (on page 363) for a Scriptural response to this erroneous belief.
(g) Some cannot accept that any marriage must be dissolved when children are present.
   (1) When heartstrings are tugged, marriage laws must become pliable and yield.
   (2) However, would that not also be true of all of God's other laws?
   (3) Would this not apply equally to marriages in the church and outside the church?
   (4) See VIII, F, 5, (g) (on page 366) and IX, E (on page 368) for a Scriptural response.
(h) As we consider what Scripture teaches about this matter, we must remember:

                (1) Personal beliefs and feelings have no place in determining what God authorizes.
                (2) One passage of God's Word will never contradict another passage of God's Word.
                (3) If our interpretation of one passage contradicts another passage:
                    (i) Our interpretation is wrong (not God's Word),
                    (ii) And our interpretation must be changed (not God's Word)!
    2. Truth: All mankind is amenable/answerable to the law of God, including non-Christians!
        (a) The prevalence of divorce and remarriage today has been difficult on the church:
            (1) In evangelism, should we teach prospects the whole truth about MDR?
            (2) In evangelism, should we teach the corrective action that repentance requires?
            (3) Or, in evangelism, should we relax God's MDR standards to fit our society?
            (4) Additionally, when members of the church move in from other places:
                (i) Should shepherds be concerned if sheep are living in adultery?
                (ii) Or, should shepherds just mind their own business and not create waves?
        (b) Unfortunately, many brethren have sought to ease God's plan for non-Christians.
            (1) They have tried to affirm that God's marriage law doesn't apply to non-Christians.
            (2) Thus, before becoming a Christian, unbelievers can divorce and remarry freely.
                (i) It does not matter for what reasons they had divorced prior to conversion.
                (ii) None of their previous divorces and remarriages will "count against them."
                (iii) Upon conversion, it will be as if their current marriage was their first marriage.
        (c) The truth is that all mankind is answerable to God's law on marriage!
            (1) In Matthew 19, Jesus restored marriage to God's original, "beginning" plan.
                (i) God's original plan was applicable to all mankind.
                (ii) There were no Jews or Gentiles in the beginning.
                (iii) There were no Christians or non-Christians in the beginning.
                (iv) It applied to all at the beginning; Jesus restored its universal application.
                (v) Thus, God's marriage laws apply to the entire human race, as He intended.
            (2) Jesus directed His marital teaching to "whoever" (Mt. 19:9) and "everyone" (5:32).
                (i) The Lord intentionally chose words that emphasize universal application.
                (ii) The church was not yet established, but He was giving laws for life within it.
                (iii) Would Jesus deliver His marriage law to Jews if it did not apply to them also?
                (iv) In the first century, Jesus' marriage laws applied to those people **before** they became Christians (Matt. 19) and **after** they had become Christians (1 Cor. 7.).
                (v) How could anyone believe that it would be any different today?
                (vi) The Lord's marriage laws apply to ALL "whoevers" and "everyones"!
        (d) All mankind can violate God's law on marriage, therefore, all are answerable!
            (1) In all three dispensations (Patriarchal, Mosaic and Christian):
                (i) God has had marriage laws.
                (ii) It has been possible for individuals to violate those laws.
                (iii) Violating the marriage vow was "adultery" (Job 24:15; Ex. 20:14; Mt. 19:9).
            (2) By definition, the sin of adultery is a sexual act:
                (i) That involves a married person having sexual intercourse with a third party.
                (ii) From the Greek *moicheia*, "unlawful intercourse with the spouse of another."
                (iii) Thus, the word itself necessitates that one is violating his/her marriage vow.
                (iv) There can be no "adultery" where there is no "marriage" that is violated!
            (3) If one is not amenable to a law, then it is not possible for him to violate that law.
                (i) If a non-Christian is not bound by God's marriage laws, then he cannot break them (i.e., a non-Christian could not possibly commit adultery).

- (ii) However, Scripture clearly shows non-Christians were guilty of adultery.
- (iii) In 1 Corinthians 6:9-10, Paul listed numerous sins, including adulterers.
- (iv) Then Paul says, "And such were some of you" (6:11).
- (v) How could these Christians possibly be adulterers before they were sanctified by God, if God's laws of marriage did not apply to them?
- (vi) The clear answer is that these unbelievers were answerable to God's marriage laws before they became Christians!

(e) If God's marriage laws do not apply to non-Christian marriages, and if they can divorce and remarry as often as they like before becoming Christians (for God does not recognize their pre-conversion-to-Christ marriages as falling under His law):
  (1) Wouldn't the couple need to be married "again" to each other the same day they get baptized, so that God will recognize their conversion and their marriage?
  (2) What happens if one of them is baptized and the other is not? Could the non-Christian still divorce and remarry at will, without committing sin? Would the Christian be stuck and not able to divorce/remarry like his non-Christian spouse?
  (3) How could the Bible possibly state that "God judges those outside" (1 Cor. 5:13), including "the sexually immoral of this world" (5:10), if God doesn't recognize, judge or even condemn their marriages?
  (4) This would confuse the issue when a put-away Christian marries a non-Christian.
    (i) Jesus said, "Whoever marries her who is divorced commits adultery" (19:9).
    (ii) But, what if a Christian spouse, who is put away for a non-fornication reason, marries a non-Christian?
      1. Is a non-Christian amenable to marrying a "having-been-put-away" person?
      2. In this scenario, does the non-Christian commit adultery or not?
      3. Does the Christian (put away for non-fornication) commit adultery?
      4. Can one marriage partner be committing adultery and the other not?

(f) The reality is that non-Christians are (and must be) amenable to the law of Christ, otherwise they would never sin and would never need the gospel!
  (1) "All have sinned and fall short of the glory of God" (Rom. 3:23). "All" = "All"!
    (i) "…Sin is lawlessness" (1 John 3:4).
    (ii) Therefore, since all people sin, and since sin is lawlessness, all people must be amenable to the law of God; otherwise, they would never become a sinner (in need of the gospel) in the first place!
  (2) In the Great Commission, Jesus (who has "all authority") sent Christians to all non-Christians (every creature) to preach the entirety of the gospel, a message to which they're amenable and must obey (Matt. 28:18-20; Mark 16:15-16).
  (3) Jesus plainly announced that all would be judged by His Words (John 12:48).
    (i) Can one be judged by a law to which he was not amenable?
  (4) Jesus is not merely "the Lord of Christians," but "He is Lord of all" (Acts 10:36).
  (5) If a non-Christian is not amenable to God's marriage laws, then he would not be amenable to any of God's laws (cf. Jas. 2:10; Gal. 5:3).
    (i) If he is not amenable to God's laws:
      1. Then it would not be sinful for him to reject those laws.
      2. Then he actually could not obey God's laws, for one cannot obey a law to which he is not amenable.
      3. Then his standard has become civil law and anything that civil law allows.

- (ii) If a person is accountable to the "plan of salvation" part of the law, then he is also accountable to the rest of the law!
- (iii) Essentially, in this theory, they let civil law trump divine law.
  - (6) God's marriage laws apply to all persons in all places, including every Christian and every non-Christian.
3. Truth: God does not permit a sinner to abide in a sinful relationship/activity upon conversion!
    - (a) Think about the ramifications of this position for a moment:
        - (1) They believe God accepts adulterers as adulterers who can stay in their marriage.
        - (2) Can a non-Christian "abide/remain in whatever state" he is when he is called?
        - (3) If he can, what is the purpose in becoming a Christian?
        - (4) Why does he need to become a Christian?
        - (5) If he doesn't need to change, what's wrong with what he's doing?
    - (b) Advocates of this position base their belief on words from 1 Corinthians 7:17-24.
        - (1) "…as the Lord has called each one, so let him walk…{20} Let each one remain in the same calling in which he was called…{24} Brethren, let each one remain with God in that state in which he was called."
        - (2) Their position nullifies any need to repent (see VIII, F, 5 on page 365).
    - (c) As with all Scripture, the verses of 1 Corinthians 7 must be kept in their context!
        - (1) In the overall context of Scripture, how could anyone believe that remaining in a sinful state (but "still converted") would ever be permissible to God?
        - (2) In the remote context of this chapter, there was a "present distress" (a period of hardship and persecution) that was influencing Paul's words (7:26).
            - (i) "Because of the present distress, it is good for a man to remain as he is."
            - (ii) This is talking about, in the context, whether one is married, single, etc. It is not dealing with any matter (or relationship) that is sinful!
        - (3) Look at the immediate context of these verses:
            - (i) Paul stated a general principle for Christians to remain (unchanged) in one's life situation when converted (as long as that situation was not sinful) and to walk in a manner worthy of and pleasing to the Lord (7:17).
            - (ii) To illustrate this for marriage, Paul referred to two cultural arrangements/ relationships that were not inherently sinful and need not be interrupted:
                1. A racial one: circumcision (whether circumcised or not when called).
                2. A social one: slavery (whether a slave or not when called).
            - (iii) When one became a Christian, it did not matter (to salvation purposes) if he was circumcised or not! Either way, just remain the way you were when called (7:18-20).
            - (iv) When one became a Christian, it did not matter (to salvation purposes) if he was a slave or free! Either way, just peacefully abide in the state in which you were called (7:21-24).
            - (v) Due to the big picture and the "present distress," there was no need to alter their lawful statuses, assuming such were not sinful in God's eyes!
            - (vi) Therefore, when one became a Christian, it did not matter (to salvation) if he was married or single, married to a Christian or to a non-Christian! In any case, it was better to remain in the state in which called. (This had nothing to do with any sinful/unlawful relationships or marriages. Keep it in context.)

(vii) All of these matters were moral/honorable; none of these relationships/ conditions were sinful before baptism. For the "abide-in-your-adulterous-marriage-when-called" doctrine to be valid, then all of these would equally need to be immoral (like adultery). *The context will not allow it!*
        (4) In ALL circumstances, it was not the racial or social status that mattered. What mattered was (and is) "keeping the commandments of God" (7:19)!
    (d) Follow this "abide-as-you-were-called" position out to its logical absurdity!
        (1) If an adulterer who is converted can remain (with God's approval) married:
            (i) What about a homosexual who is married to a homosexual partner?
            (ii) What about the polygamist who has multiple marriage partners?
            (iii) What about the pimp, the drug dealer, the human trafficker, etc.?
            (iv) Couldn't any or all of them remain in the state in which they were called?
        (2) Obviously, God was not permitting sinful relationships to remain after conversion!
4. Truth: God does not sanctify an adulterous relationship upon one's baptism!
    (a) The Bible teaches that baptism washes away sins (Acts 22:16; 2:38).
    (b) The Bible teaches that baptism will wash away the sin of adultery (1 Cor. 6:9-11).
        (1) Some of the Christians in Corinth had previously been adulterers (6:9-11).
        (2) "But you were washed, but you were sanctified, but you were justified in the name of the Lord Jesus and by the Spirit of our God" (6:11).
        (3) Upon baptism into Christ, the guilt of adultery was remitted by Jesus' blood.
    (c) However, there is NO PLACE in Scripture that teaches the adulterous relationship has been made pure, holy and acceptable in the eyes of God (and could be maintained)!
        (1) Advocates of this doctrine want others to believe that Christianity takes an adulterous marriage and sanctifies it to be a perfectly acceptable marriage.
        (2) However, baptism will not, does not and cannot change:
            (i) A sinful or unlawful practice into a righteous or lawful one, or
            (ii) A sinful relationship into a righteous one.
            (iii) Baptism is not some kind of magic potion that resolves and resets adulterous marriages into non-adulterous marriages.
        (3) If a once-adulterer, washed in baptism, is permitted to continue the same marriage, could not others continue their practices after baptism?
            (i) Would a once-idolater be permitted to continue worshipping idols?
            (ii) Would a once-homosexual be permitted to continue homosexuality?
            (iii) Would a once-thief be permitted to continue his life of stealing?
            (iv) Would a once-drunkard be permitted to continue getting drunk?
            (v) Obviously, those in 1 Corinthians 6:9-11 stopped their sinful practices! Baptism cleansed them from the guilt of their sin, but only after they stopped practicing it! If they continued in it, they would be sinning!
    (d) The nature of "adultery" must be understood, as it is used in Scripture.
        (1) Jesus clearly taught about adultery in Matthew 19:9.
            (i) "Whoever divorces his wife...and marries another, commits adultery..."
            (ii) "Whoever marries her who is divorced commits adultery."
        (2) "Commits adultery" is in the Greek present tense, denoting continuous action.
            (i) Adultery is not a "one-time" act (at the wedding ceremony) and that's it.
            (ii) One who divorces and marries "keeps on committing adultery."
            (iii) The second marriage is continuous adultery every time they are intimate, because one (or both) of them is still married to another (in God's eyes).

- (iv) Jesus affirmed, by using the present tense, the permanent nature of marriage.
- (3) Affirming marriage's permanent nature affirmed the ongoing nature of adultery.
  - (i) To avoid adultery there are only two options: celibacy or reconciliation (1 Cor. 7:10-11).
  - (ii) It is possible for one to sinfully "live in adultery" for the rest of one's life.
  - (iii) "Such **were** some of you" in 1 Corinthians 6:11 is a Greek imperfect tense.
    1. The imperfect tense emphasizes a continuous lifestyle in the past.
    2. It was not a single act they had committed in the past.
    3. Adulterers were involved in an ongoing sinful lifestyle/relationship.
  - (iv) "You **lived** in them" in Colossians 3:7 is a Greek imperfect tense.
    1. "Them" in verse 7 points back to the carnal behaviors in verse 5.
    2. They had "lived in…fornication," which is all illicit sex, including adultery.
    3. This was a continuous sin, for God viewed the first marriage as binding.
  - (v) God defines adultery as an ongoing act that continually violates His will.
- (4) Those who commit adultery are doing so because God has/had not joined them.
  - (i) Proper marriages of two eligible persons are joined by God.
  - (ii) Even non-Christians are joined by God in marriage (a divine institution).
  - (iii) The Bible does NOT teach that God joins two adulterers when baptized.

(e) Sex that is unlawful before baptism is still unlawful sex after baptism.
  - (1) Premarital sex before baptism is sinful, and it remains sinful after baptism.
  - (2) Homosexual sex before baptism is sinful, and it remains sinful after baptism.
  - (3) Polygamous sex before baptism is sinful, and it remains sinful after baptism.
  - (4) Pedophilia sex before baptism is sinful, and it remains sinful after baptism.
  - (5) Bestiality sex before baptism is sinful, and it remains sinful after baptism.
  - (6) Prostitution sex before baptism is sinful, and it remains sinful after baptism.
  - (7) Likewise, adultery sex before baptism is sinful, and it remains sinful after baptism.
  - (8) Baptism does not sanctify any of these unauthorized sexual lifestyles!

(f) Can baptism make an adulterous marriage only "half adulterous"?
  - (1) If only one spouse in an adulterous marriage is baptized, what does that mean?
    - (i) Is one half of that marriage now living "out of adultery" and no longer sinning,
    - (ii) While the other half is still living "in adultery" and still in a sinful relationship?
  - (2) If one half of an adulterous marriage is baptized and is no longer an adulterer (though still living with and having sex with one to whom God did not join),
    - (i) Couldn't the same reasoning be used to justify one half of a homosexual, polygamous, pedophilic marriage being sin-free in the eyes of God?
    - (ii) If not, why not? It is exactly the same from a Scriptural standpoint!
  - (3) Baptism does not sanctify one half or one whole of any sinful sexual lifestyle!
  - (4) What would happen if a put-away Christian marries a non-Christian?
    - (i) Jesus taught that "whoever marries her who is divorced commits adultery."
    - (ii) If the put-away Christian spouse remarries, he will be committing adultery.
    - (iii) But what if he remarries a non-Christian? Is there adultery? For who?
    - (iv) What if the non-Christian is later baptized? Is the non-Christian forgiven of all adulterous activity by virtue of his baptism? What about the Christian? Is the Christian still committing adultery, but the newly baptized Christian is not?

(g) Too bad John the Immerser didn't know "baptism sanctifies adulterous relationships."
  - (1) John spent his last days repeatedly telling Herod that he was sinning.
    - (i) "John had been saying [imperfect tense, continuous past action] to Herod…"

(ii) "'It is not lawful...'" [present tense, "it is and keeps on being unlawful"].
(iii) "'...For you to have...'" [present tense, "to have and to keep on having her"].
(2) John's repeated message regarding God's universal law cost him his life.
(3) If only John would have told Herod and Herodias:
(i) "While your marriage is not lawful right now, because it is adultery..."
(ii) "Just be baptized and it will be sanctified by God and you can stay together."
(iii) Shouldn't the forerunner of Jesus have known that Jesus would allow this?
(4) John did not offer that as a possibility because such a teaching is not from God!
(h) Baptism washes away sins, but it doesn't wash away previous husbands or wives!
5. Truth: God requires genuine repentance before one is saved from sins!
(a) Repentance of sin is an absolute requirement in order to be forgiven of sin!
(1) It is a requirement of non-Christians outside of Christ (Acts 2:38; 17:30-31).
(2) It is a continued requirement of Christians who are in Christ (Ac. 8:22; Rev. 2:5).
(b) Baptism is ineffective and invalid unless preceded by genuine repentance!
(1) Sinners were told, "Repent and...be baptized...for the remission..." (Acts 2:38).
(2) John preached "a baptism of repentance for the remission of sins" (Mark 1:4).
(c) "Repentance" must be defined accurately and not popularly or socially! (See VI, F.)
(1) Repentance is often paralleled (in the mind of men) with regret or sorrow.
(i) Some equate saying, "I'm sorry," with repentance.
(ii) Some have limited repentance to purely a mental act and nothing more.
(iii) However, regret or sorrow or just changing one's mind is not repentance!
(2) The noun "repentance" (Greek *metanoia)* and the verb "repent" (Greek *metanoeo)* always carry the emphasis of:
(i) A change of mind,
(ii) That involves a change of conduct,
(iii) Ultimately fulfilled in the ceasing of the past sin.
(3) It involves a "change of mind" to the point of "turning about, conversion," as one "turns away" from their sinful behavior (BDAG [2000], p. 640).
(i) It refers "exclusively to 'turning from one's sin'" (Renn 810)
(ii) It "involves both a turning from sin and a turning to God" (Vine 525).
(4) "Both noun and verb denote a radical, moral turn of the whole person from sin and to God" (Mounce 580).
(i) It is "used almost exclusively for the attitude of unbelievers and sinners returning to God...urging 'conversion' to Christianity. There is no longer any question of distinguishing between change of thoughts, of heart, of actions. The change is that of the soul, of the whole person (the new creature)" (Spicq Vol. 2, 475).
(ii) "Not just any regret or repudiation but affliction, 'remorse' that inspires a desire to make reparation, even expiation" (Spicq Vol. 2, 476).
(d) "Repentance" must be defined Biblically and not popularly or socially!
(1) Repentance involves more than being pricked in the heart (Acts 2:37-38).
(2) Repentance involves more than having godly sorrow (2 Cor. 7:10).
(3) Repentance involves more than acknowledging wrongdoing (Psa. 51:1-19).
(4) Repentance involves a change of mind and change of action (Matt. 21:28-29).
(5) Repentance involves a turning from evil ways (Matt. 12:41; Jonah 3:10).
(6) Repentance involves a "burning" of sinful practices and devices (Acts 19:19).
(7) Repentance involves a reformed lifestyle (Luke 3:8).

- (8) Repentance involves fruit that is "in keeping with repentance" (Matt. 3:8).
- (9) Therefore, defined Biblically, repentance is BETWEEN the emotional conviction of godly sorrow and the ultimate changed life resulting from repentance.
    - (i) Repentance is only possible when one loves the Lord so much that he wants to do His will rather than his own.
    - (ii) Godly sorrow leads to and produces repentance.
    - (iii) Repentance leads to and produces an amended life.
    - (iv) If one stays in an adulterous relationship, where is the amended life?
- (e) Repentance requires change, separation and cessation!
    - (1) When one genuinely repents of sin, he will cease that sinful activity in his life.
    - (2) When one does not genuinely repent, he will continue that sinful activity in life.
    - (3) The key to repentance is the cessation of sinful activity!
    - (4) Repenting of an adulterous marriage is more than just regretting a past decision and determining (and promising) to never do it again.
    - (5) Repenting of an adulterous marriage requires a cessation of that which is sinful—i.e., a cessation of the adulterous marriage.
    - (6) Repentance has not occurred if one continues to live in adultery after baptism.
    - (7) Repentance is a cessation of sinful activity that will "sin no more" (John 8:11).
    - (8) Baptism has no power to wash away sins until (or before) those sins are stopped!
- (f) Repentance demands the severing of all relationships that violate God's will.
    - (1) A prostitute, a polygamist, a homosexual, a pedophile must sever all relationships that are in violation of God's will.
    - (2) Therefore, an adulterer must sever his adulterous relationship.
    - (3) This is what John called upon Herod to do – "It is not lawful to have her!"
        - (i) In other words, you need to stop living according to your standards.
        - (ii) You need to start living according to God's standards.
        - (iii) As a result, you must sever every relationship that defies God's laws!
    - (4) Wendell Winkler illustrated it this way: "If a man stole a car from your driveway, a suit from your closet, a watch from your jewelry box and ran off with your wife, what would he have to do if he genuinely repented? Would he have to return all the stolen merchandise; but, be able to keep your wife?" (41).
- (g) Many will argue that it is not fair to teach that a married couple must sever their relationship, especially when children are involved.
    - (1) To make an appeal to human rational (what is "fair") or to an emotional element (like "the children") is to concede that there is no Biblical foundation or Scriptural support for their position, and so they must go "outside" Scripture for help.
    - (2) Even so, God did not leave us without instruction in this matter.
    - (3) The work of Ezra was restoration—to get God's people back to following God's law.
        - (i) In Ezra's day, God's people had forsaken His commandments (9:1-15).
            1. They had married persons whom God had forbidden them to marry.
            2. Thus, they had sinned against God and were subject to His punishment.
        - (ii) To make things right with God, remove sin and be restored back to God:
            1. They first recognized the seriousness of their sin (9:6-7, 14; 10:9).
            2. They were commanded by God to put away their unlawful wives (10:3, 11).
            3. They immediately followed procedure to "put away their wives" (10:12).
            4. Their names are even listed to note the seriousness (10:18-44).

(iii) In the midst of this restoration of righteousness and repentance from sin:
1. There were children "who had been born to them" (10:3).
2. The children were also "put away" (10:3) and made "separate" (10:11).
3. The last 3 words of the book emphasize, "they had children" (10:44).
(4) Human rationale and emotions should not prevent us from doing what is right!
(i) Children must be cared for, and parents must fulfill their God-given roles.
(ii) However, children do not change what God says about marriage and divorce.
(5) Shouldn't Christians want their children to see obedience to Christ as a priority?
(6) It is possible to exercise genuine repentance, sever an adulterous marriage and still provide a home and family for children! With effort, love and prayer, we "can do all things through Christ who strengthens" (Phil. 4:13).
(i) Would it be required of a polygamous marriage? Obviously it would!
(ii) And, if multiple marriages can be severed and the children still cared for and provided a home/family, then it can be done in just one marriage.
(h) When it comes to genuine and proper repentance, why would anyone want to play it close, cut corners or argue with God's expectations for true repentance?
(1) Jesus laid it out plainly in Luke 13:3 and again in Luke 13:5 –
(i) "I tell you, no; but unless you repent you will all likewise perish."
(2) God's Word clearly defines and demands genuine repentance. No human rationale can change that, soften that or eliminate that!
G. False doctrines regarding MDR cannot be tolerated, for multiple souls are at risk!
1. Scripture strongly affirms, "Fornicators and adulterers God will judge" (Heb. 13:4).
2. "Neither fornicators...nor adulterers...will inherit the kingdom of God" (1 Cor. 6:9-10).
3. This is not a matter on which one can afford to be wrong.
4. We must teach God's truth without addition, subtraction, modification or mitigation!

IX. Conclusion
A. Marriage is a sacred institution created by God.
1. It is designed by God for *one* man and *one* woman to live together for *one* lifetime.
2. As a creation of God Himself, marriage is not merely a human institution which can be regulated by human wishes and human laws.
3. As the Creator of marriage, God alone has the authority to regulate it.
B. Divorce was never a part of the original, eternal will of God for marriage.
1. God gave permanency to marriage, stating that "they shall become one" (Gen. 2:24).
2. Jesus said, "What God has joined together, let not man separate" (Matt. 19:6).
3. In fact, God bluntly reveals the sinfulness of divorce by stating "He hates" it (Mal. 2:16).
C. Remarriage is severely limited by God.
1. Since His original plan was for *one* man to be with *one* woman for *one* lifetime, it would be well outside that design for one to have a second or third spouse.
2. Such an exception to God's original design would require Him to give an "exception."
3. Besides the death of a spouse (1 Cor. 7:39; Rom. 7:2-3), Jesus permitted only one class of people to divorce and remarry—i.e., an innocent spouse whose mate committed sexual immorality. No other person has a right to divorce and remarry.
4. Divorce and remarriage for any other cause is viewed by God as ongoing adultery.
D. Marriage, divorce and remarriage is not some "side issue" that doesn't really matter.
1. There are souls involved in marriage, in the home, in the family, in the church and in the community that are affected by the relationship between a husband and a wife.
2. This matter must be treated with the utmost importance and care!

3. God's Word must the sole authority and respected guide in this crucial matter!
E. God's marriage laws are admittedly strict and rightfully so!
   1. The disciples in Matthew 19 immediately recognized the serious and restrictive nature of God's marriage laws as He designed them and as Jesus required them to be kept.
      (a) Their immediate conclusion of a life of celibacy (Matt. 19:10) shows that they understood the real binding nature (on all men) of Jesus' words regarding marriage.
   2. Jesus did not soften His teaching due to their response, but He clarified that celibacy was not God's desire and that not all men could abide by such a law (Matt. 19:11).
      (a) Jesus identified only three classes of people who could live a celibate life (19:12):
         (1) Those born eunuchs (physically impotent, incapable of sexual relations).
         (2) Those made eunuchs by men (by cruelty of men).
         (3) Those who have made themselves eunuchs for the kingdom of heaven's sake.
            (i) These are not eunuchs because of a physical condition.
            (ii) These are eunuchs by personal choice and for a spiritual reason.
            (iii) These are able to devote more time and effort to the Lord and His church.
            (iv) These may be some who do not have a right to remarry.
         (4) There are many things that are more important than physical relationships!
            (i) It may be hard, but Jesus said "strait is the way" (cf. Mt. 7:13-14; Lk. 13:24)!
            (ii) With God's help, one can follow His divine will in all things (Phil. 4:13).
   3. The strictness of a law does not make it unfair or impossible to obey.
      (a) God had a very specific plan for marriage!
      (b) God does not demand something that is impossible!
      (c) God has given us the responsibility and the ability to respect His will and obey it!
F. Understanding the divine basis for marriage can help us understand God's strictness. Consider these closing points from Wayne Jackson (*The Teaching of Jesus*, p. 24):
   1. "First of all, marriage is the most intimate of all human relationships.
      (a) "Because of this, an atmosphere is created which accommodates human vulnerability.
      (b) "When martial unions are treated casually, the victims of psychological trauma become numerous.
   2. "Second, children have the right to grow up in a stable family relationship.
      (a) "Children do not need to be shuttled from one environment to another. That is not healthy.
      (b) "A strict marriage code is doubtless designed to protect our little ones.
   3. "Third, the family relationship is the cement that contributes to the cohesiveness of society.
      (a) "In this connection, it helps to create the kind of tranquil atmosphere which facilitates the propagation of the gospel of Christ.
      (b) "A firm marriage law is a significant contributor to Heaven's redemptive plan!
   4. "When one reflects upon matters of this nature:
      (a) "It is not so difficult to understand why the Lord gave marriage regulations which appear strict,
      (b) "But which, upon closer consideration, really make sense."
G. Marriage, as designed by God, is a sacred institution and a divine blessing to enjoy!
H. Let us respect God's design for it, study God's design for it, follow God's design for it and teach God's design for it!

Recommended Resources

Books

Baird, James O. *And I Say Unto You.* Oklahoma City: B&B Bookhouse, 1981.

Jackson, Wayne. *Divorce & Remarriage (A Study Discussion).* Stockton, CA: Courier Publications, 1983.

---. *The Teaching of Jesus Christ on Divorce & Remarriage.* Stockton, CA: Courier Publications, 2002.

Laws, Jim, ed. *Marriage, Divorce, and Remarriage (Spiritual Sword Lectureship).* Memphis: Getwell church of Christ, 1992.

Miller, Dave. *To Be or "Knot" To Be.* Pulaski, TN: Sain Publications, 1986.

Music, Goebel. *Divorce.* Colleyville, TX: Music, 1987.

---. *Separation Is Sin.* Colleyville, TX: Music, 1985.

Rader, Donnie V. *Marriage, Divorce and Remarriage.* Bowling Green, KY: Guardian of Truth, 2003.

Thomas, J.D. *Divorce and Remarriage.* Abilene, TX: Biblical Research Press, 1977.

Warren, Thomas B. *Charts You Can Use in Preaching, Teaching and Studying on Divorce and Remarriage.* Jonesboro, AR: National Christian Press, 1978.

---. *Keeping the Lock in Wedlock.* Moore, OK; National Christian Press, 1980.

---. *Under Bondage to the Law of Christ—The Only Real Freedom.* Moore, OK: National Christian Press, 1989.

Warren, Thomas B., ed. *Your Marriage Can Be Great.* Jonesboro, AR: National Christian Press, 1978.

Articles

Colley, Gary. "Analysis of Romans 7:1-4." *The Spiritual Sword* (Jan. 1975): 26-28.

Connally, Andrew M. "A General Look at Some Contemporary Views of Divorce and Remarriage." *Your Marriage Can Be Great.* Ed. Thomas B. Warren. Jonesboro, AR: National Christian Press, 1978. 504-509.

Deaver, Mac. "The Biblical Definition of 'Fornication' and 'Adultery.'" *Marriage, Divorce, and Remarriage (Spiritual Sword Lectureship).* Ed. Jim Laws. Memphis, TN: Getwell, 1992. 268-280.

Deaver, Roy. "Analysis of Matthew 19:3-12 and a Review of 'Except for Fornication.'" *The Spiritual Sword* (Jan. 1975): 14-26.

---. "Is the Non-Christian Amenable to Christ's Law of Marriage, Divorce, and Remarriage?" *Marriage, Divorce, and Remarriage (Spiritual Sword Lectureship).* Ed. Jim Laws. Memphis, TN: Getwell, 1992. 487-507.

---. "Marriage, Divorce and Remarriage Discussion Forum, No. II: 1 Corinthians 7:15: 'Not Under Bondage.'" *Studies in 1 Corinthians (Denton Lectures).* Ed. Dub McClish. Denton, TX: Pearl Street, 1982. 375-390.

---. "Matthew 19:9 and 1 Corinthians 7." *The Spiritual Sword* (Oct. 1987): 6-12.

---. "Matthew 19:9 Is a Part of the New Testament." *Your Marriage Can Be Great.* Ed. Thomas B. Warren. Jonesboro, AR: National Christian Press, 1978. 76-78.

---. "Some Errors on 1 Corinthians 7 Set Forth and Refuted." *Your Marriage Can Be Great.* Ed. Thomas B. Warren. Jonesboro, AR: National Christian Press, 1978. 437-453.

---. "The 'Guilty Party' Is Not Free (In God's Sight) to Marry Again." *Your Marriage Can Be Great.* Ed. Thomas B. Warren. Jonesboro, AR: National Christian Press, 1978. 369-383.

---. "The Physical Relationship Is Not What Constitutes Marriage." *Your Marriage Can Be Great.* Ed. Thomas B. Warren. Jonesboro, AR: National Christian Press, 1978. 92-93.

Deffenbaugh, Don. "Does Baptism into Christ for the Remission of Sins Wash Away Adulterous Marriage?" *Marriage, Divorce, and Remarriage (Spiritual Sword Lectureship).* Ed. Jim Laws. Memphis, TN: Getwell, 1992. 508-519.

Dobbs, H.A. (Buster). "Is a Christian Who Has Been Divorced By an Unbelieving Spouse Free to Remarry?" *Marriage, Divorce, and Remarriage (Spiritual Sword Lectureship).* Ed. Jim Laws. Memphis, TN: Getwell, 1992. 476-486.

Duncan, Bobby. "Does Baptism Sanctify an Unscriptural Relationship?" *The Spiritual Sword* (July 1997): 40-43.

---. "Key Scriptures: Romans 7:1-4." *Marriage, Divorce, and Remarriage (Spiritual Sword Lectureship).* Ed. Jim Laws. Memphis, TN: Getwell, 1992. 364-374.

Edwards, Earl. "Exegesis of Matthew 19:3-12." *Building Stronger Christian Families (Freed-Hardeman University Lectureship).* Ed. Winford Claiborne. Henderson, TN: Freed-Hardeman University, 1992. 50-60.

---. "Exegesis of Matthew 19:3-9." *The Spiritual Sword* (July 1997): 3-8.

---. "Key Scriptures: Matthew 19:3-12." *Marriage, Divorce, and Remarriage (Spiritual Sword Lectureship).* Ed. Jim Laws. Memphis, TN: Getwell, 1992. 338-363.

---. "What About Matthew 19:9?" *The Spiritual Sword* (Apr. 2010): 26-29.

Elkins, Garland. "Is It the Case That Repentance Demands Only Saying, 'I'm Sorry'?" *The Spiritual Sword* (Oct. 1987): 20-22.

---. "Jesus' Teaching on Marriage, Divorce, and Remarriage." *Studies in Matthew (Denton Lectures).* Ed. Dub McClish. Denton, TX: Valid Publications, 1995. 385-410.

Floyd, Harvey. "More in Review of the So-Called 'Pauline Privilege.'" *The Spiritual Sword* (Jan. 1975): 37-39.

---. "The Doctrine of the So-Called 'Pauline Privilege' Is Seen to Be False By the Greek Text of 1 Corinthians 7:15." *Your Marriage Can Be Great.* Ed. Thomas B. Warren. Jonesboro, AR: National Christian Press, 1978. 498-503.

Highers, Alan E. "What the Scriptures Teach Regarding Marriage, Divorce and Remarriage." *Marriage, Divorce, and Remarriage (Spiritual Sword Lectureship).* Ed. Jim Laws. Memphis, TN: Getwell, 1992. 27-38.

Jackson, Wayne. "Divorce and Civil Law." *ChristianCourier.com* https://www.christiancourier.com/articles/581-divorce-and-civil-law

---. "Divorce and the Guilty Party." *ChristianCourier.com* https://www.christiancourier.com/articles/359-divorce-and-the-guilty-party

---. "False Ideas About Marriage." *Building Stronger Christian Families (Freed-Hardeman University Lectureship).* Ed. Winford Claiborne. Henderson, TN: Freed-Hardeman University, 1992. 137-153.

---. "She Honors and Upholds God's Teaching on Marriage and Divorce." *Introducing the Church of Christ.* Ed. Alvin Jennings. Fort Worth: Star Bible, 1981. 131-135.

---. "What Is Adultery?" *The Spiritual Sword* (July 1997): 21-26.

---. "What Is the Meaning of 'Not Under Bondage" (1 Cor. 7:15)?" *ChristianCourier.com* www.christiancourier.com/articles/683-what-is-the-meaning-of-not-under-bondage-1-cor-7-15

Jobe, Glenn A. "Is Covenant-Breaking Adultery?" *Marriage, Divorce, and Remarriage (Spiritual Sword Lectureship).* Ed. Jim Laws. Memphis, TN: Getwell, 1992. 520-541.

Jones, Edwin S. "The Biblical Definition of Divorce." *Marriage, Divorce, and Remarriage (Spiritual Sword Lectureship).* Ed. Jim Laws. Memphis, TN: Getwell, 1992. 254-267.

Kizer, Andy. "Key Scriptures: Matthew 5:31-32." *Marriage, Divorce, and Remarriage (Spiritual Sword Lectureship).* Ed. Jim Laws. Memphis, TN: Getwell, 1992. 319-337.

Lanier, Roy H., Jr. "A Look at 1 Corinthians 7:15." *The Spiritual Sword* (July 1997): 12-16.

---. "Marriage, Divorce and Remarriage Discussion Forum, No. IV: 1 Corinthians 7:17-14: 'Abide in That Calling.'" *Studies in 1 Corinthians (Denton Lectures).* Ed. Dub McClish. Denton, TX: Pearl Street, 1982. 402-414.

---. "Marriage, Divorce and Remarriage Discussion Forum, No. VIII: Matthew 19:9: 'The Rights of the Guilty Party.'" *Studies in 1 Corinthians (Denton Lectures).* Ed. Dub McClish. Denton, TX: Pearl Street, 1982. 469-478

Lanier, Roy H., Sr. "Divorce and Remarriage." *20 Years of the Problem Page (Vol. 1).* Abilene, TX: Quality Publications, 1984. 138-155.

---. "Review of the So-Called 'Pauline Privilege.'" *The Spiritual Sword* (Jan. 1975): 33-37.

---. "The So-Called 'Pauline Privilege' Is of Human Origin." *Your Marriage Can Be Great.* Ed. Thomas B. Warren. Jonesboro, AR: National Christian Press, 1978. 486-497.

---. "What Is Marriage?" *Your Marriage Can Be Great.* Ed. Thomas B. Warren. Jonesboro, AR: National Christian Press, 1978. 89-91.

Laws, Jim. "Attitudes We Should Possess Toward God, His Word, and One Another." *Marriage, Divorce, and Remarriage (Spiritual Sword Lectureship).* Ed. Jim Laws. Memphis, TN: Getwell, 1992. 11-26.

Lewis, Jack P. "From the Beginning It Was Not So." *Your Marriage Can Be Great.* Ed. Thomas B. Warren. Jonesboro, AR: National Christian Press, 1978. 410-419.

Lipe, David L. "Answering Marriage Questions." *Perfecting God's People (Freed-Hardeman University Lectureship).* Ed. David L. Lipe. Henderson, TN: Freed-Hardeman University, 2010. 74-94.

---. "1 Corinthians 7 Does <u>Not</u> Provide Another Ground for Divorce and Remarriage." *Your Marriage Can Be Great.* Ed. Thomas B. Warren. Jonesboro, AR: National Christian Press, 1978. 454-459.

---. "Exegesis of 1 Corinthians 7." *Building Stronger Christian Families (Freed-Hardeman University Lectureship)*. Ed. Winford Claiborne. Henderson, TN: Freed-Hardeman University, 1992. 192-211.

McClish, Dub. "Is Matthew 19:9 A Part of the Law of Christ?" *The Spiritual Sword* (July 1997): 32-37.

---. "Is It the Case That the Guilty Party (in Cases of Marital Unfaithfulness) Is As Free to Marry Again As the Innocent Party?" *The Spiritual Sword* (Oct. 1987): 17-20.

McCord, Hugo. "Divorce and Remarriage." *Fifty Years of Lectures.* 222-226.

---. "The Guilty Party Is Not Free to Remarry. *Volume Two: Fifty Years of Lectures.* 433-438.

McGee, Pat. "A Refutation of the View That It Is Impossible to 'Live in Adultery.'" *Your Marriage Can Be Great.* Ed. Thomas B. Warren. Jonesboro, AR: National Christian Press, 1978. 510-514.

Miller, Dave. "A Look at 1 Corinthians 7:15." *The Spiritual Sword* (Oct. 1987): 44-47.

---. "The Biblical Doctrine of 'Repentance.'" *Marriage, Divorce, and Remarriage (Spiritual Sword Lectureship).* Ed. Jim Laws. Memphis, TN: Getwell, 1992. 281-294.

Moffitt, Jerry. "Are All Men Amenable to Christ's Law?" *The Spiritual Sword* (July 1997): 37-40.

Music, Goebel. "Is It the Case That Paul (in 1 Cor. 7) Contradicted What Jesus Taught in Matthew 19:9?" *The Spiritual Sword* (Oct. 1987):15-17.

Nichols, Flavil H. "The Biblical Definition of Marriage." *Marriage, Divorce, and Remarriage (Spiritual Sword Lectureship).* Ed. Jim Laws. Memphis, TN: Getwell, 1992. 241-253.

Pharr, David. "May the Guilty Party Remarry?" *Marriage, Divorce, and Remarriage (Spiritual Sword Lectureship).* Ed. Jim Laws. Memphis, TN: Getwell, 1992. 450-461.

---. "Shall the Guilty Go Free?" *The Spiritual Sword* (July 1997): 17-21.

Powell, Ivie. "Key Scriptures: Deuteronomy 24:1-4." *Marriage, Divorce, and Remarriage (Spiritual Sword Lectureship).* Ed. Jim Laws. Memphis, TN: Getwell, 1992. 310-318.

Pryor, Neale. "Divorce—Its Meaning." *Your Marriage Can Be Great.* Ed. Thomas B. Warren. Jonesboro, AR: National Christian Press, 1978. 98-104.

Ramsey, Johnny. "Why People in Unscriptural Marriages Must Separate." *Your Marriage Can Be Great.* Ed. Thomas B. Warren. Jonesboro, AR: National Christian Press, 1978. 557-562.

Sanders, Phil. "What Is Adultery?" *The Spiritual Sword* (Apr. 2010): 30-34.

Sztanyo, Dick. "A Passage 'Requiring Them to Separate.'" *Your Marriage Can Be Great.* Ed. Thomas B. Warren. Jonesboro, AR: National Christian Press, 1978. 570-582.

Taylor, Robert R., Jr. "Crucial Questions Asked About Marriage." *Marriage, Divorce, and Remarriage (Spiritual Sword Lectureship).* Ed. Jim Laws. Memphis, TN: Getwell, 1992. 54-73.

Warren, Thomas B. "A General Look at Divorce & Remarriage." *The Spiritual Sword* (Jan. 1975): 1-9.

---. "All Men—Including Non-Christians—Are Amenable to Christ's Law on Divorce and Remarriage." *Your Marriage Can Be Great.* Ed. Thomas B. Warren. Jonesboro, AR: National Christian Press, 1978. 361-368.

---. "Only Three Classes of People Are Free (In the Sight of God) to Marry." *Your Marriage Can Be Great.* Ed. Thomas B. Warren. Jonesboro, AR: National Christian Press, 1978. 353-355.

---. "Some Crucial Questions on "The-Guilty-Party-Can-Remarry" Theory." *Your Marriage Can Be Great.* Ed. Thomas B. Warren. Jonesboro, AR: National Christian Press, 1978. 384-386.

---. "Some Questions on 'The Guilty Party Is Free' Theory." *The Spiritual Sword* (Jan. 1975): 41-43.

---. "Some More Crucial Questions Which Show the Distinction Between Truth and Error on Divorce and Remarriage." *Your Marriage Can Be Great.* Ed. Thomas B. Warren. Jonesboro, AR: National Christian Press, 1978. 387-402.

---. "There Is <u>One</u>—and <u>Only</u> One—Ground for Divorce and Remarriage." *Your Marriage Can Be Great.* Ed. Thomas B. Warren. Jonesboro, AR: National Christian Press, 1978. 356-360.

Winkler, Wendell. *Solving Problems God's Way.* Tuscaloosa, AL: Winkler Publications, 2004.

Woodson, William. "A Study of Matthew 5:31-32." *The Spiritual Sword* (Apr. 2010): 22-25

---. "Analysis of Matthew 5:31-32." *The Spiritual Sword* (July 1997): 8-12.

---. "Whoever Shall Marry Her When She Is Put Away Committeth Adultery." *Your Marriage Can Be Great.* Ed. Thomas B. Warren. Jonesboro, AR: National Christian Press, 1978. 403-409.

Workman, Gary. "Key Scriptures: 1 Corinthians 7:1-40." *Marriage, Divorce, and Remarriage (Spiritual Sword Lectureship).* Ed. Jim Laws. Memphis, TN: Getwell, 1992. 375-416.

<u>Periodicals</u>

The Spiritual Sword. January 1972. "The Christian Man and Woman in Marriage."

The Spiritual Sword. April 1972. "Problem Areas in Marriage."

The Spiritual Sword. January 1975. "Marriage, Divorce and Remarriage."

The Spiritual Sword. October 1987. "Another Look at Marriage, Divorce and Remarriage."

The Spiritual Sword. July 1997. "What Do Scriptures Say About Divorce and Remarriage?"

The Spiritual Sword. April 2010. "Marriage for Life."

Lesson 26: The Christian Life

I. **What a Glorious Blessing It Is to Be a Christian!**
   A. In a study of "Fortifying Your Faith," it is critical to know and remember that:
      1. True Christianity is not just about making sure the "externals" are right.
      2. True Christianity is not just about emphasizing pure, unadulterated doctrine.
      3. True Christianity is not just about the work and worship of the universal church.
      4. True Christianity is a heart religion, impacting a person's life from deep inside his soul.
      5. True Christianity involves a person's:
         (a) Soul – their spirit, inner-man and eternal (made-in-the-image-of-God) essence.
         (b) Heart – their emotions, feelings and inner passions and desires.
         (c) Mind – their thoughts, intellect and reasoning skills.
         (d) Body – their activity, energy, abilities and diligent effort.
      6. True Christianity is a blessed gift from God!
   B. A "Christ-ian" is one who is "of or belongs to" Christ.
      1. The blood of Christ has cleansed him from all sin (Rev. 1:5; Eph. 1:7).
      2. The blood of Christ has appeased the justice and wrath of God for him (1 John 2:1-2).
      3. The blood of Christ has redeemed him from sin and lawlessness (Col. 1:14; Heb. 9:12).
      4. The blood of Christ has purchased him as a special possession (1 Cor. 6:19-20).
      5. The "Christ-ian" is "of" Christ and he "belongs to" Christ! There is no greater blessing!
   C. When one becomes a Christian (upon obedience to the will of God), he/she becomes:
      1. A new creature in Christ (2 Cor. 5:17; Rom. 6:4; Gal. 6:15; Col. 3:10).
      2. A child of God in the household (or family) of God (Rom. 8:16-17; Eph. 3:15; John 3:3).
      3. An heir of the eternal grace and kingdom of God (Rom. 8:17; Eph. 3:6; Tit. 3:7; 1 Pet. 3:7).
      4. A member of the body (or church) of Christ (Acts 2:47; 1 Cor. 12:13-27; Eph. 1:22-23).
      5. A citizen in the kingdom of God (Col. 1:13-14; Phil. 3:20; Eph. 2:19; John 3:5).
      6. A sheep in the fold of God (Heb. 13:20; John 10:1-29; Acts 20:28-29; 1 Pet. 5:2-3).
      7. A soldier in the army of God (Eph. 6:10-20; 2 Tim. 2:3-4; 4:6-8; 1 Tim. 6:12; Phil. 2:25).
      8. A servant or laborer in the vineyard of God (1 Cor. 3:8; 15:58; Matt. 20:1-16; Phile. 1).
      9. A priest or worshiper in the temple of God (1 Pet. 2:5-9; Rev. 1:5-6; Heb. 13:15).
      10. A living stone in the building of God (1 Pet. 2:5; 1 Cor. 3:9; Eph. 2:21-22).
      11. A branch in the vine of God (John 15:1-8, 16; Matt. 15:13; Col. 1:10; Phil. 1:11).
      12. A saint separated by Christ unto God (Acts 26:10; Rom. 1:7; 1 Cor. 14:33; Eph. 2:19).
   D. When one becomes a Christian, he/she begins a "new" life in relationship to God.
      1. When one is baptized, he is "born again" (John 3:3-5) or "born anew" (ASV).
         (a) All sins have been forgiven and forgotten (Acts 2:38; Heb. 8:12).
         (b) Upon baptism, "our old man was crucified with Him" (Rom. 6:6).
         (c) As God's new creation, a Christian gets to "start over" and do it God's way.
      2. The Christian life is consecrated by "a new and living way" (Heb. 10:20).
         (a) Upon conversion to Christ, a Christian is to "walk in newness of life" (Rom. 6:4).
         (b) "Therefore, if anyone is in Christ, he is a new creation" (2 Cor. 5:7).
         (c) A Christian has "put on the new man," being made in the image of Christ (Col. 3:10).
      3. Everything about the Christian life is new—"All things have become new" (2 Cor. 5:17).
         (a) A Christian has a new dependency—he trusts God in all things (2 Cor. 1:9-11).
         (b) A Christian has a new demeanor—what he says and does is new (Col. 3:1-17).
         (c) A Christian has a new desire—to glorify God and do His will (1 Cor. 10:31; Heb. 5:9).
         (d) A Christian has a new direction—walking with Christ daily (Col. 1:9-11; 1 John 1:7).

(e) A Christian has a new destiny—a promised home in heaven (John 14:1-3).
   4. Being "a new creation" is not a drudgery to bemoan but a blessing to enjoy!
 E. When one becomes a Christian, he/she is called to a blessed life of "faithfulness" to God.
   1. The Christian life is sometimes described in the New Testament as a "run" (Heb. 12:2; 1 Cor. 9:24-27), and sometimes it is described as a "walk" (Eph. 4:1; 5:2, 8, 15; 1 John 1:7).
   2. Christians are exhorted to (continually, Greek present tense) "be steadfast, immovable, always abounding in the work of the Lord" (1 Cor. 15:58).
   3. Faithfulness involves:
      (a) "Continuing with the Lord" and "in the faith" (Acts 11:23; 14:22), and not stopping.
      (b) "Finishing the race" and "finishing the work" (2 Tim. 4:7; John 4:34), and not quitting.
      (c) "Enduring all things" (2 Tim. 2:3, 10, 12; Heb. 10:36; 12:1), and not giving up.
      (d) "Looking forward" and "reaching forward" (2 Pet. 3:14; Phil. 3:13), and not backwards.
   4. Jesus used words like "strait," "narrow" and "difficult" to describe the Christian life (Matt. 7:14; Luke 13:24). He told us that there would be trials and troubles.
      (a) Therefore, we must be "diligent" (Heb. 4:11; 11:6; 2 Pet. 1:5, 10).
      (b) Therefore, we must exercise "perseverance" (Rom. 5:3-4; Jas. 5:11; 2 Pet. 1:6).
   5. Faithfulness is required until "the finish line" – "until death" (Rev. 2:10).
 F. There is no other life on this earth like the Christian life!
   1. Christians are the most blessed people alive today!
   2. As we study what God's Word teaches about living the Christian life:
      (a) Let us examine ourselves—comparing ourselves to the divine standard.
      (b) Let us challenge ourselves—urging ourselves to conform even more to His will.
      (c) Let us improve ourselves—finding those areas that need our attention the most.
      (d) Let us commit ourselves—determining to fix our eyes on Jesus and never look back.
      (e) Let us enjoy ourselves—knowing that we are experiencing the abundant life.

II. **According to Scripture, the Christian Life Is to Be Characterized By Holy Living.**
 A. The word "holy" comes from the Greek word *hagios*.
   1. *Hagios* "fundamentally signifies 'separated'" (Vine 307).
   2. The term is used of God, whose very nature is "holy" (Rev. 4:8; Isa. 6:3).
   3. The term is used of men:
      (a) "in so far as they are devoted to God" (Vine 308),
      (b) having been "reserved for God and God's service" (BDAG [2000], p. 10),
      (c) "on account of some connection with God" (Thayer 6).
   4. When it comes to Christians, they have been:
      (a) "Separated *from* sin" or the world (Vine 307, emp. added),
      (b) "And therefore consecrated *to* God" (Vine 307, emp. added).
      (c) Essentially, upon obedience to Christ, "set apart *from* the world and *unto* Christ."
   5. In its noun form, this word is also translated:
      (a) "Sanctification," to denote "the resultant state" of "separation to God" (Vine 306).
      (b) "Saints," to designate those who have been sanctified or made holy.
   6. In its verb form, the word denotes "to set apart to God" (Vine 307).
   7. The emphasis of "holiness" is equally two parts:
      (a) Set apart FROM the world,
      (b) AND, set apart TO God.
      (c) It is more than just being different from the world. It is being like God.
   8. A Christian is to "pursue...holiness" (Heb. 12:14), "earnestly endeavor[ing] to acquire" it (Thayer 153), and giving "a chase as if in a hunt" (Robertson's *Word Pictures*).

B. As faithful Christians pursuing holiness, we must be like our God.
   1. Our God is holy, and He has called upon His people to be holy.
   2. In the Old Testament, God appealed to the Jews who had just been freed from Egypt:
      (a) "For I am the Lord your God. You shall therefore consecrate yourselves, and you shall be holy; for I am holy...For I am the Lord who brings you up out of the land of Egypt, to be your God. You shall therefore be holy, for I am holy" (Lev. 11:44-45).
      (b) "And you shall be holy to Me, for I the Lord am holy, and have separated you from the peoples, that you should be Mine" (Lev. 20:26; cf. 19:2).
   3. In the New Testament, God appeals to Christians who have been freed from sin:
      (a) "...As obedient children, not conforming yourselves to the former lusts, as in your ignorance; but as He who called you is holy, you also be holy in all your conduct, because it is written, 'Be holy, for I am holy'" (1 Pet. 1:14-16).
      (b) The same God (who is "holy") calls upon and expects His people to be "holy."
      (c) As Christians, we are to "be imitators of God as dear children" (Eph. 5:1).
   4. New Testament Christians have been "added" by God to His "church" (Acts 2:41, 47).
      (a) The word "church" is from the Greek word *ekklesia.*
         (1) *Ekklesia* is a compound word from *ek,* "out of," and *kaleo,* "to call" (Vine 42).
         (2) Thus, the church, by definition, is "the called out ones."
      (b) This is exactly how the New Testament identifies the church.
         (1) God calls the church "a holy nation" (1 Pet. 2:9).
         (2) The church has been "called...out of darkness into His marvelous light" (2:9).
         (3) A Christian has been "delivered...from the power of darkness and conveyed... into the kingdom of the Son of His love" [i.e., the church] (Col. 1:13).
      (c) Thus, individually a Christian is designated as "holy" (set apart unto God).
      (d) And, collectively the church is designated as "holy" (set apart unto God).
   5. Christians are not to "be conformed to this world" (Rom. 12:2).
      (a) The "world" is that from which a Christian has been called (1 Pet. 2:9) and has been delivered (Col. 1:13).
      (b) Scripture explains what "the world" is and why it is essential for a child of God to separate himself from it in 1 John 2:15-17.
         (1) "Do not love the world or the things in the world.
            "If anyone loves the world, the love of the Father is not in him.
            "For all that is in the world—the lust of the flesh, the lust of the eyes, and the pride of life—is not of the Father but is of the world.
            "And the world is passing away, and the lust of it;
            "but he who does the will of God abides forever."
      (c) Therefore, we must not allow ourselves to be poured into the mold of this world.
      (d) Rather, we must "come out from among them and be separate" (2 Cor. 6:17).
      (e) We must perfect "holiness in the fear of God" (2 Cor. 7:1).
      (f) We must "pursue...holiness, without which no one will see the Lord" (Heb. 12:14).
   6. Rather than look like the world and act like the world, Christians have been called out and set apart to look like Christ and act like Christ (Eph. 5:1; 4:32; 1 Cor. 11:1; Phil. 2:5).
      (a) Christ is our perfect example of holiness (cf. Heb. 7:26):
         (1) In what He did...and what He did not do!
         (2) In what He said...and what He did not say!
      (b) Christ left "us an example, that [we] should follow His steps" (1 Pet. 2:21).

- (c) When we faithfully behold "the glory of the Lord" (our perfect standard of holiness), we "are being transformed into the same image from glory to glory" (2 Cor. 3:18).
- (d) The more we become like Christ, the more we fulfill God's call to "be holy"!

C. As faithful Christians pursuing holiness, we must deny and avoid ungodliness.
  1. The Bible warns Christians about the constant dangers of the world.
     (a) One is "sanctified" when he is baptized for forgiveness of sins (Eph. 5:26; 1 Cor. 6:11).
     (b) But, "sanctification" requires diligent and constant effort (1 Thess. 4:3-4).
  2. There are changes that must take place in our lives when we become Christians.
     (a) When a Christian has "put on the new man which was created according to God, in true righteousness and holiness," he must "put off the old man" (Eph. 4:20-24).
     (b) When a Christian has been "called out of darkness," he must "cast off the works of darkness" (Rom. 13:12).
     (c) When a Christian has "put on the Lord Jesus Christ," he must "make no provision for the flesh, to fulfill its lusts" (Rom. 13:14).
     (d) When one becomes a Christian, he is no longer to "be conformed to this world" (Rom. 12:2), but "conformed to the image" of Christ (Rom. 8:29; Col. 3:10).
     (e) When one becomes a Christian, he has been "born again" (John 3:3-5), and as a "new creature" (2 Cor. 5:17), he will not be the same person that he was before.
  3. There are changes that must take place in our associations when we become Christians.
     (a) When a Christian is striving to "walk in the light as He in the light" (1 John 1:7), he must "have no fellowship with the unfruitful works of darkness" (Eph. 5:11).
     (b) When a Christian is seeking to be a "friend of God" (Jas. 2:23; cf. John 15:14-15), he cannot, at the same time, "be a friend of the world" (Jas. 4:4; cf. Matt. 6:24).
     (c) When a Christian is working on "perfecting" holy habits and morals in his life (2 Cor. 7:1), he must not "be deceived" into associating with "bad company" which "corrupts good habits" (1 Cor. 15:33) and "good morals" (NASB).
  4. While sin and unrighteousness are ever-present dangers in this life, a Christian must seek to live a life of "denying ungodliness and worldly lusts" (Tit. 2:11-12).
  5. To emphasize how strongly God views this matter, He chose some very direct verbs in His instructions to His people regarding ungodliness and worldliness:
     (a) "Avoid" (1 Tim. 6:20; 2 Tim. 2:23; Tit. 3:9).
     (b) "Abstain from" (1 Thess. 4:3; 5:22; 1 Pet. 2:11).
     (c) "Keep from" (Jas. 1:27; 1 John 5:21).
     (d) "Put off" (Eph. 4:22; Col. 3:8, 9).
     (e) "Put to death" (Rom. 8:13; Col. 3:5).
     (f) "Shun" (2 Tim. 1:16).
     (g) "Deny" (Luke 9:23; Tit. 2:12).
     (h) "Crucify" (Gal. 2:20; 5:24; 6:14; Rom. 6:6).
     (i) "Cast off" (Rom. 13:12).
     (j) "Refrain" (1 Pet. 3:10).
     (k) "Turn away" (2 Tim. 3:5; 1 Pet. 3:11).
     (l) "Flee" (1 Cor. 6:18; 10:14; 1 Tim. 6:11; 2 Tim. 2:22).
  6. Christians are instructed to "test all things" (1 Thess. 5:21).
     (a) "Examine everything carefully" (NASB) to determine good and evil.
     (b) Then, "Hold fast to that which is good. Abstain from every form of evil" (5:21-22).
     (c) Do not accept the world's evaluation or man's opinion!
     (d) Test all things in light of God's Word! Hold everything up to His light!

7. The "forms of evil" and the "fleshly lusts" from which we are to abstain are countless, but God does specify a number of them to avoid, to give us clear direction in life. Consider these examples from Scripture and all the ungodliness that they represent:

Revelry (Rom. 13:13)	Adultery (Gal. 5:19)	Deceit (Rom. 1:29)
Drunkenness (Rom. 13:13)	Fornication (Gal. 5:19)	Evil-mindedness (Rom. 1:29)
Lewdness (Rom. 13:13)	Uncleanness (Gal. 5:19)	Gossip (Rom. 1:29)
Lust (Rom. 13:13)	Idolatry (Gal. 5:20)	Backbiting (Rom. 1:30)
Strife (Rom. 13:13)	Sorcery (Gal. 5:20)	Violence (Rom. 1:30)
Envy (Rom. 13:13)	Hatred (Gal. 5:20)	Pride (Rom. 1:30)
Greediness (Eph. 4:19)	Contentions (Gal. 5:20)	Boasting (Rom. 1:30)
Lying (Eph. 4:25)	Jealousies (Gal. 5:20)	Inventing evil (Rom. 1:30)
Corrupt speech (Eph. 4:29)	Outbursts of wrath (5:20)	Disobey parents (Rom. 1:30)
Bitterness (Eph. 4:31)	Selfish ambitions (5:20)	Sexual immorality (Col. 3:5)
Wrath (Eph. 4:31)	Dissensions (Gal. 5:20)	Impurity (Col. 3:5)
Anger (Eph. 4:31)	Heresies (Gal. 5:20)	Evil desire (Col. 3:5)
Clamor (Eph. 4:31)	Murders (Gal. 5:20)	Covetousness (Col. 3:5)
Evil speaking (Eph. 4:31)	Filthiness (Eph. 5:4)	Blasphemy (Col. 3:8)
Malice (Eph. 4:31)	Foolish talking (Eph. 5:4)	Filthy language (Col. 3:8)
Homosexuality (1 Cor. 6:9)	Coarse jesting (Eph. 5:4)	Partiality (Jas. 2:9)
Stealing (1 Cor. 6:10)	Kidnapping (1 Tim. 1:10)	Lust of the flesh (1 Jn. 2:16)
Reviling (1 Cor. 6:10)	Perjury (1 Tim. 1:10)	Lust of the eyes (1 Jn. 2:16)
Extortion (1 Cor. 6:10)	Evil suspicions (1 Tim. 6:4)	Pride of life (1 Jn. 2:16)

   (a) God did not attempt to provide an exhaustive list of every sin.
   (b) In some cases, He used general terms like, "forms of evil" and "fleshly lusts."
   (c) After listing several sins, He then added, "and things like these" (Gal. 5:21).
8. As Christians who are pursuing holy lives, we must work diligently:
   (a) To "not let sin reign" (or even have a foothold) in our lives (Rom. 6:11-13), and
   (b) To "make no provision for the flesh, to gratify its desires" (Rom. 13:14).
D. As faithful Christians pursuing holiness, we must possess Christ-like attitudes.
   1. Christians are urged, "Let this mind be in you which was also in Christ Jesus" (Phil. 2:5).
      (a) One's mind (or heart or pattern-of-thought) needs to reflect that of Christ.
      (b) One's mind (or heart or pattern-of-thought) is often exhibited in one's attitudes.
      (c) "Attitude" is defined as "the way you think or feel about someone or something."
   2. Controlling our attitudes begins with controlling our thoughts.
      (a) Our inner thoughts often make us and define us (Prov. 4:23; 23:7).
      (b) Our inner thoughts will be reflected in our outer life (Matt. 5:21-28; 15:18-20).
      (c) Thus, we must learn to capture and control our thoughts (2 Cor. 10:5; 1 Pet. 1:13).
   3. When a Christian puts on Christ-like attitudes, he will certainly possess and exhibit:

Love (Gal. 5:22)	Honesty (Eph. 4:25)	Mercy (Matt. 5:7)
Joy (Gal. 5:22)	Tenderheartedness (Ep. 4:32)	Purity (Matt. 5:8)
Peace (Gal. 5:22)	Forgiveness (Eph. 4:32)	Peaceableness (Jas. 3:17)
Longsuffering (Gal. 5:22)	Compassion (Col. 3:12)	Willingness to yield (Jas. 3:17)
Kindness (Gal. 5:22)	Humility (Col. 3:12)	Impartiality (Jas. 3:17)
Goodness (Gal. 5:22)	Meekness (Col. 3:12)	Honor (Phil. 4:8)
Faithfulness (Gal. 5:22)	Patience (Col. 3:13)	Justice (Phil. 4:8)
Gentleness (Gal. 5:22)	Thankfulness (Col. 3:15)	Harmony (1 Pet. 3:8)
Self-Control (Gal. 5:22)	Contentment (1 Tim. 6:6)	Sympathy (1 Pet. 3:8)

   4. The Bible says, "For as [a man] thinks in his heart, so is he" (Prov. 23:7)
      (a) The inward spirit of a man is seen only by God (1 Sam. 16:7; John 2:24-25).

(b) But, the inward spirit is manifested in the outward attitudes (Prov. 4:23).

(c) Let us, as Christians, work to ensure that our attitudes emulate our Savior (Phil. 2:5).

5. If we truly "set [our] minds on things above" (Col. 3:2), the rest of who we are will follow.

E. As faithful Christians pursuing holiness, we must behave with Christ-like actions.

1. Christians are given clear instructions regarding their actions:

   (a) "Present your bodies a living sacrifice, holy, acceptable to God" (Rom. 12:1).

   (b) "If you love Me, keep My commandments" (John 14:15).

   (c) "Be doers of the word, and not hearers only, deceiving yourselves" (Jas. 1:22).

   (d) "Whatever you do in word or deed, do all in the name of the Lord Jesus" (Col. 3:17).

   (e) "Why do you call Me 'Lord, Lord,' and do not do the things which I say?" (Luke 6:46).

   (f) "To him who knows to do good and does not do it, to him it is sin" (Jas. 4:17).

   (g) "...Each of you should know how to possess his own vessel in sanctification and honor" (1 Thess. 4:4).

   (h) "...Be a vessel for honor, sanctified and useful for the Master, prepared for every good work" (2 Tim. 2:21).

   (i) There is a definite standard of holiness to which the Lord expects His people to cling.

2. The New Testament has much to say about Christians engaging in Christ-like living.

   (a) The first four books of the New Testament teach about Jesus and His life.

   (b) The fifth book of the New Testament teaches about how to give your life to Jesus.

   (c) The last twenty-one books of the New Testament teach how to live your life for Jesus.

3. While it is impossible to list all that a Christian is "to do," there are two insightful and detailed passages to consider. (Obviously, there are many more.)

   (a) The Sermon on the Mount (in Matthew 5-7) is intentionally positioned at the beginning of the New Testament to immediately teach a Bible reader what Jesus expects of His followers.

      (1) Fourteen times in these chapters, Jesus declares, "I say to you" or "I tell you."

      (2) Those who first heard this sermon were struck by the "authority" of the one who preached these words (Matt. 7:28-29), and we should be, too.

   (b) Romans 12 is one of the most practical chapters in the New Testament for Christian living.

      (1) Nestled in the heart of a masterful treatise on obedient faith (Rom. 1:5; 16:26) is a text that challenges the reader in every phrase.

      (2) The holiness of the Christian life is beautifully pictured in this chapter.

4. Consider carefully and implement intently some instructions for life from Matthew 5-7:

   (a) "Let your light so shine before men..." (Matt. 5:16).

   (b) "First be reconciled to your brother, and then come and offer your gift" (5:24).

   (c) "Whoever slaps you on your right cheek, turn the other to him also" (5:39).

   (d) "Whoever compels you to go one mile, go with him two" (5:41).

   (e) "Love your enemies, bless those who curse you, do good to those who hate you, and pray for those who spitefully use you and persecute you" (5:44).

   (f) "Do not do your charitable deeds before men, to be seen by them" (6:1).

   (g) "In this manner, therefore, pray: Our Father in heaven..." (6:6-13).

   (h) "If you do not forgive men their trespasses, neither will your Father forgive..." (6:15).

   (i) "Lay up for yourselves treasures in heaven" (6:20).

   (j) "You cannot serve God and wealth [money, ESV]" (6:24, NASB).

   (k) "Do not worry about your life" (6:25).

   (l) "Seek first the kingdom of God and His righteousness" (6:33).

- (m) "Do not worry about tomorrow" (6:34).
- (n) "Ask, and it will be given to you; seek, and you will find; knock, and it will be..." (7:7).
- (o) "Whatever you want men to do to you, do also to them" (7:12).
- (p) "Enter by the narrow gate" (7:13-14).
- (q) "Beware of false prophets, who come to you in sheep's clothing..." (7:15).
- (r) "Not everyone who says to Me, 'Lord, Lord,' shall enter the kingdom of heaven, but he who does the will of My Father in heaven" (7:21).
- (s) "Whoever hears these sayings of Mine, and does them, I will liken him to a wise man" (7:24).

5. Consider carefully and implement intently some instructions for life from Romans 12:
   - (a) "Let love be [genuine, ESV] without hypocrisy" (12:9).
   - (b) "Abhor what is evil. Cling to what is good" (12:9).
   - (c) "Be kindly affectionate to one another with brotherly love" (12:10).
   - (d) "In honor giving preference to one another" (12:10).
   - (e) "Outdo one another in showing honor" (12:10, ESV).
   - (f) "Do not be slothful in zeal [diligence, NKJV]" (12:11, ESV).
   - (g) "Be fervent in spirit" (12:11).
   - (h) "Serve the Lord" (12:11).
   - (i) "Rejoice in hope" (12:12).
   - (j) "Be patient in tribulation" (12:12).
   - (k) "Be constant in prayer" (12:12).
   - (l) "Contribute to the needs of the saints" (12:13).
   - (m) "Practice hospitality" (12:13).
   - (n) "Bless those who persecute you; bless and do not curse" (12:14).
   - (o) "Rejoice with those who rejoice" (12:15).
   - (p) "Weep with those who weep" (12:15).
   - (q) "Be of the same mind toward one another [Live in harmony, ESV]" (12:16).
   - (r) "Do not set your mind on high things [haughty in mind, NASB]" (12:16).
   - (s) "Associate with the humble [lowly, NASB]" (12:16).
   - (t) "Do not be wise in your own opinion" (12:16).
   - (u) "Repay no one evil for evil" (12:17).
   - (v) "Give thought to do what is honorable [right, NASB] in the sight of all" (12:17, ESV).
   - (w) "If it is possible, as much as depends on you, live peaceably with all men" (12:18).
   - (x) "Beloved, do not avenge yourselves" (12:19).
   - (y) "But rather give place to [the wrath of God, NASB]" (12:19).
   - (z) "If your enemy is hungry, feed him; if he is thirsty, give him a drink" (12:20).
   - (aa) "Do not be overcome by evil, but overcome evil with good" (12:21).

6. There are certainly more things that a Christian "must do" than can be listed here.
   - (a) In addition to the above, a Christian must teach the gospel to the lost, edify the saints, restore the wayward, worship God, grow spiritually, study His Word, etc., etc.
   - (b) These matters of the Christian life will be investigated in the pages that follow.

F. Living the life that is characterized by holiness is the best life that one can have on earth!
  1. Jesus describes it as the "more abundantly" life (John 10:10).
  2. Every Christian is blessed to wear the name of Christ (Acts 11:26; cf. Isa. 62:2).
  3. Every Christian, who wears the name of Christ, must bring it glory (1 Pet. 4:16).
  4. God is faithful and God is holy (1 Cor. 1:9; Rev. 4:8), and He has called His people to be faithful and holy (Rev. 2:10; 1 Pet. 1:15-16).

5. God abounds in His efforts toward us (2 Cor. 9:8), and we must long to abound in our efforts toward Him (1 Cor. 15:58).
6. True holiness will redirect our attention and our affection toward heaven (Col. 3:1-2).
7. Let us draw closer to God every day and grow in the likeness of Christ:
    (a) So that we love what He loves (John 13:34; 15:12; Eph. 5:2).
    (b) So that we hate what He hates (Rev. 2:6; Psa. 97:10; 119:104).
    (c) So that we think the way Jesus would have us think (Phil. 2:5; 4:8).
    (d) So that we act the way Jesus would have us to act (Col. 3:1-17; John 13:15).

III. According to Scripture, the Christian Life Is to Be Characterized By Continual Growth.
   A. God expects and commands Christians to grow and develop spiritually!
      1. It is imperative that every Christian grow spiritually.
         (a) God uses a present tense imperative verb in 2 Peter 3:18 to emphasize: "Grow! Grow now! And, keep on growing!"
         (b) As we grow in our relationship with God, we "become partakers of the divine nature" (2 Pet. 1:4), becoming more and more like Him.
      2. God requires great effort on our part to grow fully in our Christian lives.
         (a) God's expectations for our spiritual growth requires "giving all diligence" (2 Pet. 1:5), or "applying all diligence" (NASB), or "mak[ing] every effort" (ESV).
         (b) Having given all diligence to grow, then God calls upon us to "be even more diligent" (2 Pet. 1:10), or "be all the more diligent" (NASB) to grow!
         (c) Therefore, growing as a Christian is not something that is just automatic, nor does it come with minimal effort. Christian growth requires real work!
      3. God specifies the process and the virtues in which we are to diligently grow and "abound" (2 Pet. 1:5-8).
         (a) We are to give all the more diligence to grow in:
             (1) Faith – our firm trust in God, Jesus and His word, manifested in our obedience.
             (2) Virtue – moral courage to know what is right, to do it and to stand for it.
             (3) Knowledge – a working understanding of God's truth and how to apply it.
             (4) Self-control – a strong discipline to hold in one's desires and temper.
             (5) Perseverance – endurance that remains focused regardless of circumstances.
             (6) Godliness – a humble reverence and deep piety toward God, emulating Jesus.
             (7) Brotherly kindness – being gentle, gracious and kind toward fellow believers.
             (8) Love – unconditionally and unselfishly wanting the best for all others.
         (b) The word "abound" (v. 8) should prevent us from looking for the minimum we have to do to "get by." We should want to be and to do more and more for the Lord!
         (c) By giving ourselves to these things and abounding in these things:
             (1) We will become "fruitful" in our service to God (2 Pet. 1:8).
             (2) We will make our "call and election sure" (1:10).
             (3) We "will never stumble" (1:10).
             (4) We "will be supplied" "an entrance…into the everlasting kingdom" (1:11).
      4. God expects us to be "mature" and to "go on to maturity" (Heb. 5:14; 6:1).
         (a) We do this by having our spiritual "senses trained to discern good and evil" (5:14).
         (b) We do this by "growing up" into Christ to "no longer be children" (Eph. 4:14-15).
      5. Stagnation in Christian growth is not acceptable to God (Heb. 5:11-14).
         (a) Some Christians grow "dull of hearing" and do not grow as they should (5:11-12).
         (b) Some Christians remain "a babe" in their Christian development (5:13).
         (c) Christians who do not grow are reprimanded in this passage. We should take note!

B. Strong Christian growth comes from studying God's Word regularly!
   1. One of the greatest joys and privileges of being a Christian, and an essential part of Christian growth, is letting God speak to us through His Word!
   2. A vital link exists between growing as a Christian and growing in knowledge.
      (a) "Desire the pure milk of the word, that you may grow thereby" (1 Pet. 2:2).
      (b) "So then faith comes by hearing, and hearing by the word of God" (Rom. 10:17).
      (c) "...Those who hunger and thirst for righteousness...shall be filled" (Matt. 5:6).
   3. Genuine Christian growth requires reading God's Word.
      (a) Isaiah prompted the Jews to "search from the book of the Lord, and read" (34:16).
      (b) The gospel accounts record Jesus asking ten times, "Have you not read?"
      (c) God pronounced a blessing upon those who read and hear His Word (Rev. 1:3).
      (d) God promised that, "when you read, you can understand" (Eph. 3:3-4).
      (e) Paul urged congregations to read the epistles (Col. 4:16; 1 Thess. 5:27).
      (f) First-century Bible students "searched the Scriptures daily" (Acts 17:11).
      (g) At the foundation of Christian growth is the practice of reading God's Word!
   4. Genuine Christian growth requires meditating upon God's Word.
      (a) In addition to reading, we must contemplate and reflect on God's precious words.
         (1) The blessed man finds "his delight is in the law of the Lord, and in His law he meditates day and night" (Psa. 1:2).
         (2) He who loves the law of the Lord will make it his "meditation all the day," and even "awake through the night" to "meditate on [His] word" (Psa. 119:97, 148).
         (3) Meditating on God's Word is both (1) motivated by love for it and (2) increases love for it (Psa. 119:48, 97).
         (4) Deeper "understanding" of the "testimonies" of God is acquired through meditation upon them (Psa. 119:99).
      (b) Meditation takes time, planning and effort, but the rewards are immense.
   5. Genuine Christian growth requires studying God's Word.
      (a) We must give ourselves to a diligent and regular study of God's Word.
         (1) "Be diligent (Study, KJV) to present yourself approved to God as a workman who does not need to be ashamed, accurately handling the word of truth" (2 Tim. 2:15, NASB).
         (2) The phrase "accurately handling" is from one Greek word, *orthotomeo*.
            (i) *Orthotomeo* is a compound word that literally means, "to cut straight."
            (ii) "The metaphor could be that of plowing a straight furrow, or of a road foreman making his road straight, or of a mason squaring and cutting a stone to fit in its proper place" (Rogers & Rogers, *Linguistic and Exegetical Key to the New Testament,* p. 503).
            (iii) "The stress is on *orthos;* the Word of God is to be 'handled' strictly along the lines of its teaching" (Vine 289).
         (3) "Handling aright the word of truth" (ASV) requires proper and regular study.
      (b) We must have the proper approach to our Bible Study.
         (1) Our study of God's Word must be eager (1 Pet. 2:2; Matt. 5:6; Prov. 2:1-6, 10).
         (2) Our study of God's Word must be a priority (Matt. 6:33; Acts 17:11).
         (3) Our study of God's Word must be diligent and regular (2 Pet. 1:5-6; Matt. 7:7).
         (4) Our study of God's Word must be full of love (Prov. 12:1; 2 Thess. 2:10-11).
         (5) Our study of God's Word must be reverent (2 Tim. 3:16; Neh. 8:5).
         (6) Our study of God's Word must be humble (Jer. 10:23; Matt. 7:7; Jas. 4:10).

(7) Our study of God's Word must be thorough and honest (Ac. 17:11; Ps. 119:160).
(8) Our study of God's Word must be objective and impartial (Jn. 12:48; Gal. 1:6-9).
(9) Our study of God's Word must be with understanding (Eph. 3:3-4; 5:17).
(10) Our study of God's Word must be self-examining (2 Cor. 13:5; Acts 2:37).
(11) Our study of God's Word must be patient (2 Pet. 1:5-11).
- (c) We must expand our personal library of tools for Bible study.
    - (1) This should include multiple translations for comparison, a concordance, dictionaries, an expository dictionary, Bible encyclopedias, an atlas, sound commentaries, brotherhood periodicals, books on various Bible topics, etc.
    - (2) This should include computer software, websites and audio/video recordings.
- (d) We can use various methods in our Bible study.
    - (1) We can study the Bible conventionally, by reading it from cover to cover.
    - (2) We can study the Bible chronologically, by reading it in the order of actual events.
    - (3) We can study the Bible topically, by investigating all that it teaches on a topic.
    - (4) We can study the Bible devotionally, by using it for comfort, strength, hope, etc.
    - (5) We can study the Bible systematically, by using a trustworthy study guide.
    - (6) The method used is not nearly as important as the actual study itself.
- (e) Whenever we study the Bible, we need to remember to read it slowly.
    - (1) We often try to study the Bible too quickly or too methodically.
    - (2) Slow down, read each word and digest all that God has given to us.

6. Genuine Christian growth requires memorizing God's Word.
    - (a) Don't let "memorizing" scare you. Your mind (a creation of God) has great power.
    - (b) Memorizing God's Word (or writing it on your heart) will benefit you:
        - (1) When you are faced with temptations (Matt. 4:1-11; Psa. 119:11).
        - (2) When you are sad, lonely or anxious (Psa. 100:1-5; 46:1-10).
        - (3) When you are in need of direction and guidance (Psa. 119:105).
        - (4) When you are called upon to give a defense for your faith (1 Pet. 3:15).
    - (c) Memorizing has various levels, all of which are useful:
        - (1) You can memorize a verse word-for-word, along with its location.
        - (2) You can memorize the "gist" of the verse, along with its location.
        - (3) You can memorize the location of a verse that teaches/says a certain thing.
    - (d) Memorizing Scripture follows in the footsteps of Jesus.
        - (1) Jesus quoted Scripture often (Matt. 4:1-11; 13:14-15; Luke 20:41-44; 22:37).
        - (2) Jesus quoted Scripture to answer questions (Matt. 19:3-5, 16-19; 22:35-40).
        - (3) Jesus sometimes cited where the passage was found (Lk. 20:37, 42; Mt. 15:7-9).
        - (4) Jesus knew how to find a passage to share it with others (Luke 4:16-21).
        - (5) Jesus used the expression, "It is written," 21 times in the gospel accounts.
        - (6) Much could be said about Jesus quoting Scripture, but the point is that even Jesus had to spend time reading, meditating upon, studying and memorizing Scripture, in order to be able to quote it and share it with others.
    - (e) Memorizing is not a test of your knowledge or intellect.
    Memorizing is a blessing to your faith and to your daily life as a Christian.
    - (f) When you really get into God's Word, God's Word will really get into you!

7. Set goals for your Bible study and identify specific steps to reach those goals.
    - (a) Set a goal to read the Bible for ___ (10?) minutes every day.
    - (b) Set a goal to meditate on the Bible for ___ (20?) minutes every week.
    - (c) Set a goal to study the Bible for ___ (45?) minutes every week.

(d) Set a goal to memorize ___ (1-2?) verse(s) every week or month.
(e) Set a place in your home as "the place where I read, meditate and study God's Word."
(f) If you won't miss a meal or won't forget your medicine, don't miss or forget your time with God and His Word. Do not let anything get in the way!
(g) The health and well-being of your soul is tied directly to the time you spend with God's Word. Your physical body needs daily nourishment, and so does your soul!

C. Strong Christian growth comes from praying to God regularly!
1. One of the greatest joys and privileges of being a Christian, and an essential part of Christian growth, is speaking to God through prayer!
   (a) Reading Scripture allows God to talk to us. Praying allows us to talk to God.
   (b) Praying allows us to draw closer to God (Jas. 4:8; 1 Pet. 5:7).
   (c) Praying allows us to communicate with our Father, God and Creator (Heb. 4:16).
   (d) Praying allows the heart to open up and express its desires to God (Rom. 10:1).
2. Prayer should be a daily (and meaningful) part of the Christian's life.
   (a) The Bible gives us examples of men in the Old Testament who prayed every day.
      (1) David said, "Evening and morning and at noon I will pray" (Psa. 55:17).
      (2) Daniel's "custom" was to kneel "down on his knees three times [a] day" (6:10).
      (3) If these men of God needed and wanted to pray every day, shouldn't I?
   (b) The Bible gives us the example of Jesus praying every day (Mark 1:35; Luke 6:12).
   (c) Jesus tells us to pray, "Give us this day our daily bread" (Matt. 6:11).
      (1) We are to pray for "daily bread."
      (2) We are to pray on "this day" for "this day's" bread.
      (3) Jesus tells us that we need to pray every day for physical and spiritual strength.
3. A special bond exists between the pray-er and God, for He will not hear everyone's prayer.
   (a) The foundation of acceptable prayer is a Father-child relationship.
      (1) One must be a child of God to call upon Him as "Father" (Matt. 6:9).
      (2) One must be redeemed by Christ's blood to be His "child" (Eph. 1:7; Gal. 3:26-27).
      (3) One must continue to abide in Him and His Word to sustain that bond (Jn. 15:1-7).
   (b) From Scripture, we learn that God will only hear the prayers of:
      (1) Those who are His children (Matt. 6:9).
      (2) Those who are righteous (1 Pet. 3:12; Jas. 5:16).
      (3) Those who are obedient (1 John 3:22; Prov. 28:9).
   (c) Therefore, we must do all that is necessary to maintain that special bond!
4. The wonderful privilege of prayer needs to consist of these elements to be acceptable:
   (a) Praise and adoration of God, for who He is (Matt. 6:9).
   (b) Thanksgiving to God, for all that He does and gives (Eph. 5:20; 1 Th. 5:18; Phil. 4:6-7).
   (c) Confession of personal struggles and sins (1 John 1:9; Luke 18:13).
   (d) Request for forgiveness of sins (Luke 11:4; Matt. 6:12; Acts 8:22).
   (e) Plea for deliverance from temptations of the devil (Mt. 6:13; 26:41; 1 Cor. 10:13).
   (f) Supplication, petition and request for personal needs (Matt. 7:7-11; Phil. 4:6-7).
   (g) Intercession on behalf of others (1 Tim. 2:1-3; Phil. 1:3-4; Jas. 5:16; 1 John 5:16).
5. God wants us to pray in all situations, about all things and for all people.
   (a) God wants us to pray in all situations.
      (1) "Pray without ceasing" (1 Thess. 5:17; cf. Rom. 12:12; Eph. 6:18).
      (2) "In every situation, by prayer...present your requests to God" (Phil. 4:6, NIV).
      (3) "Continue earnestly in prayer, being vigilant in it with thanksgiving" (Col. 4:2).
      (4) "Men always ought to pray and not lose heart" (Luke 18:1-5).

(5) "These texts do not mean that one can never cease to pray (Lk. 11:1). These texts rather mean that we should never get through praying; also, that we cannot pray too much. These verses also suggest that we should constantly, always, be in a prayerful attitude, and should pray to God regularly" (Winkler, *Toward Spiritual Maturity*, p. 19).
- (b) God wants us to pray about all things.
  - (1) "In everything...let your requests be made known to God" (Phil. 4:6).
  - (2) Pray for the church and its unity (Matt. 6:10; John 17:20-21; Phil. 1:3-4).
  - (3) Pray for physical, material needs (Matt. 6:11; 7:7-11).
  - (4) Pray for forgiveness of sins (Matt. 6:12; 1 John 1:9).
  - (5) Pray for strength in and deliverance from temptation (Matt. 6:13; 26:41).
  - (6) Pray for wisdom and understanding (Jas. 1:5-7).
  - (7) Pray for strength during personal struggles (2 Cor. 12:7-9; Matt. 26:39-44).
  - (8) Pray for laborers to work in the vineyard of God (Matt. 9:38).
  - (9) Pray for God's will to be done (Matt. 6:10; 26:39).
  - (10) Pray for spiritual matters more than for material things (Matt. 6:9-11).
- (c) God wants us to pray for all people.
  - (1) Pray for "all people" (1 Tim. 2:1).
  - (2) Pray for governing officials and rulers of all lands (1 Tim. 2:1-2).
  - (3) Pray for "all the saints" (Eph. 6:18; Phil. 1:9-11).
  - (4) "Pray for one another" (Jas. 5:14-16).
  - (5) Pray for brethren who are facing various hardships (Acts 12:5, 12).
  - (6) Pray for brethren who are struggling with sin (1 John 5:16).
  - (7) Pray for gospel preachers and their work (Col. 4:2-4; Eph. 6:18-19; 2 Th. 3:1-2).
  - (8) Pray for the lost (Rom. 10:1).
  - (9) Pray for our enemies (Matt. 5:44).
  - (10) Pray for peace (Phil. 4:6-7; 1 Tim. 2:1-2).
6. The Bible makes it clear that praying to God has conditions.
   - (a) We must pray to the Father (Mt. 6:9; Eph. 5:20), not someone or something else.
   - (b) We must pray in Jesus' name (John 14:13-14; Col. 3:17; 1 Tim. 2:5; Eph. 5:20).
   - (c) We must pray in faith (Jas. 1:5-7; Matt. 21:22), without doubting (1 Tim. 2:8).
   - (d) We must pray in accordance with God's will (1 John 5:14; Matt. 6:10; 26:39-42).
   - (e) We must pray while abiding in Christ and His Word, and vice versa (John 15:7).
   - (f) We must pray while submitting to God and avoiding sin (Prov. 28:9; Psa. 66:18).
   - (g) We must pray with the right motive and intent (Jas. 4:3; 1 John 3:22).
   - (h) We must pray with a humble heart (Jas. 4:6; Luke 18:9-14).
   - (i) We must pray with a forgiving spirit (Matt. 6:12-15; Jas. 5:15-16).
   - (j) We must pray fervently and sincerely (Jas. 5:16; 1 Th. 3:10; Mt. 7:7-11; Lk. 18:1-14).
7. The Bible makes it clear that praying to God has great rewards.
   - (a) We are promised that "the prayer of a righteous person has great power" (Jas. 5:16).
   - (b) We are permitted direct and bold access to the throne of God (Heb. 4:16; Eph. 2:18).
   - (c) We are assured that the Almighty God "hears us, whatever we ask" (1 Jn. 5:14-15).
   - (d) We are promised that God answers our prayers (Matt. 7:7-11; Psa. 118:5).
     - (1) Sometimes God answers by saying, "Yes" (Mt. 7:7; Jas. 5:17; 1 Sam. 1:1-20).
     - (2) Sometimes God answers by saying, "No" (Mt. 26:39-44; Heb. 5:7; 2 Sam. 12).
     - (3) Sometimes God answers by saying, "Wait" (Jer. 42:4-7; Luke 1:5-25, 57-58).
     - (4) Sometimes God answers by giving us something different (2 Cor. 12:7-9).

                (5) Sometimes God answers by giving us more than we ask (1 Kg. 3:9-13; Ep. 3:20).
                (6) "God really answers prayer!" (Winkler, *Toward Spiritual Maturity,* p. 22).
            (e) We are assured to "obtain mercy and find grace to help in time of need" (Heb. 4:16).
            (f) We are granted a surpassing peace and heavenly protection (Phil. 4:6-7).
            (g) We are given strength and power to withstand the devil (Eph. 6:13-18).
            (h) We are reminded, "You do not have because you do not ask" (Jas. 4:2).
        8. When we pray, we are made to be more like Jesus, who was a man of prayer! Consider some of the occasions when Jesus prayed (emphasized in Luke's account) and contemplate how those same occasions apply to us. Jesus prayed:
            (a) After His baptism (3:21; cf. Matt. 7:7-11; James 1:5-6).
            (b) After a surge in His popularity (5:12-16; cf. Jas. 4:6-10).
            (c) After encounters with harm-wishers (6:1-12; cf. 6:27-28).
            (d) Before making major decisions (6:12-16; cf. Jas. 4:15).
            (e) Before a meal (9:16; 22:17-19; 24:30; cf. 1 Tim. 4:4-5).
            (f) After a long day's work (9:12-18; cf. Matt. 11:28-30).
            (g) When He was alone (9:18; 5:16) – morning (Mk. 1:35) and evening (Mt. 14:23).
            (h) When He was burdened (9:28-31; cf. Phil. 4:6-7).
            (i) When He was overjoyed at the Lord's work (10:17-22; Col. 1:3).
            (j) In front of His friends (11:1-4; John 17:1-16; cf. Mt. 5:16; 1 Tim. 4:12).
            (k) When His friends needed God's help (22:31-34; cf. 1 Tim. 2:1).
            (l) When He agonized over coming events (22:39-46; cf. 1 Pet. 5:7).
            (m) When He was dying (23:34, 36; Matt. 27:46; cf. 1 Thess. 5:17).
        9. Set goals for your prayer life and identify specific steps to reach those goals.
            (a) Set a goal to be in a constant mindset of prayer and communication with God.
            (b) Set a goal to sit down and seriously pray at least once a day.
            (c) Set a goal to maintain a "prayer list" and pray for at least 5-10 minutes every day.
    D. Strong Christian growth comes from assembling with brethren regularly!
        1. One of the greatest joys and privileges of being a Christian, and an essential part of Christian growth, is gathering with brethren to study and to worship God together!
        2. Personal, spiritual growth certainly requires personal and private time in Bible study and prayer. One will not grow as a Christian without purposeful, personal effort.
        3. But, God intended for true personal, spiritual growth to also incorporate brethren.
            (a) A Christian cannot effectively and successfully grow as a Christian on his/her own.
            (b) Have you ever seen a single stalk of wheat or a single blade of grass flourishing?
            (c) The great redwood trees in California are only able to stand and survive because their root systems intertwine with each other and even fuse together.
        4. Thus, God designed the church to assemble together and to worship together.
            (a) The act of worshiping God itself causes Christians to grow in their faith, in their relationship with God and in their determination to serve the Lord faithfully. Being in the presence of God and before His very throne cannot help but build up the worshiper (Isa. 6:1-8).
            (b) Then, the act of worshiping God with brethren (those of "like precious faith," 2 Pet. 1:1) strengthens a Christian even more in his/her walk with the Lord.
        5. One purpose of the worship assembly is to "edify" one another (1 Cor. 14:26).
            (a) In edifying, brethren are building each other up in the faith (1 Thess. 5:11).

- (b) In the assembly, brethren are considering "one another in order to stir up love and good works" and are "exhorting one another," in order to stimulate growth (Heb. 10:24-25).
- (c) God designed the assembly to be a place where brethren are strengthened together.
6. In true worship, true worshipers will naturally grow stronger as a result of:
  - (a) Being in the presence of God and worshiping God (John 4:23-24; Matt. 4:10).
  - (b) Being in the presence of Jesus and worshiping with Him (Heb. 2:12; Matt. 26:29).
  - (c) Being in the presence of brethren and worshiping God with them (1 Cor. 14:1-40).
7. A Christian cannot grow fully or properly without regularly worshiping God!
8. A Christian cannot grow fully or properly without regular interaction with brethren!
9. The importance of assembling with the church cannot be overemphasized in the life and spiritual health of a child of God!
  - (a) God designed for it to have a central place in the life of a Christian.
  - (b) More will be studied about worshiping with the church under V, C on page 395.

E. Strong Christian growth comes from teaching the gospel to others regularly!
  1. One of the greatest joys and privileges of being a Christian, and an essential part of Christian growth, is personally teaching someone the gospel of Jesus Christ!
  2. The growth that takes place in teaching the gospel is mutual growth.
    - (a) The one being taught is able to hear, learn and grow.
    - (b) The one doing the teaching is able to study, learn and grow, and the growth of the teacher is often more than the student.
  3. Christians who are not growing are Christians who are not teaching (Heb. 5:12-14).
    - (a) The Hebrew Christians were censured for not growing as they should have.
      - (1) One evidence of their lack of growth was that they were not "teachers" (5:12).
      - (2) Instead, they themselves needed to be taught "again the first principles" (5:12).
      - (3) They were "unskilled in the word of righteousness" and unable to teach it (5:13).
    - (b) Teachers are constantly studying to be ready to teach. This produces growth.
    - (c) Teachers are constantly asking God for help in teaching. This produces growth.
    - (d) Teachers who regularly feed upon the "solid food" of God's Word become "mature" in their faith," for they "have their powers of discernment trained by constant practice to distinguish good from evil" (5:14, ESV).
    - (e) Spiritual maturity comes not only through learning, but also through teaching!
  4. The more you teach God's Word, the more you'll learn yourself, the more you'll know, the more you'll believe, the more you'll love, the more you'll grow, the more you'll teach!
    - (a) Teaching the Word of God to others can be habit-forming.
      - (1) The more you do it, the better you will get.
      - (2) The more you do it, the more you will enjoy it.
      - (3) The more you do it, the more you will want to do it.
      - (4) Sometimes it is hard and intimidating to think about teaching someone the gospel, but doing it once will motivate you to want to do it more.
    - (b) Teaching the Word of God to others should be contagious.
      - (1) The Lord instructs us, "Entrust these [things] to faithful men who will be able to teach others also" (2 Tim. 2:2).
      - (2) When we teach the gospel to others, it should not stop there.
      - (3) What others learn from us, they will be empowered to turn around and teach to others also.
      - (4) The entire process is waiting on individual Christians to start.

                (c) Teaching the Word of God to others will increase our own faith.
                    (1) True, cedar-like strength of faith develops from teaching and defending truth.
                    (2) If "faith comes by hearing" (Rom. 10:17), what will happen to the faith of the one who is doing the speaking?
                    (3) The more you teach the gospel, the more your own faith will be fortified in:
                        (i) The authority of Christ.
                        (ii) The all-sufficiency of God's Word.
                        (iii) The finality of the revelation of God.
                        (iv) The unique nature of the Lord's church.
                        (v) The beauty and purity of true, New Testament worship.
                        (vi) The essentiality of the church to the eternal plan of God.
                        (vii) The simple and unchangeable plan of salvation revealed by God.
            5. More will be studied about teaching God's Word under IV, J (p. 393) and V, F (p. 398).
    F. Like every loving Father, God wants His children to grow into mature, strong Christians!
        1. Christian growth is not optional or ornamental, it is absolutely essential!
        2. All Christians must give themselves diligently (not casually) to their growth as a Christian!
        3. Your Christian growth and strength is directly proportional to all four ingredients: your Bible study, your prayer life, your assembling with brethren and your teaching frequency.
        4. If you are not growing, examine these four areas. In which area are you falling short?
IV. According to Scripture, the Christian Life Is to Be Characterized By Faithful Stewardship.
    A. Being a Christian steward is a fundamental Bible topic.
        1. First, it helps to define what "stewardship" is.
            (a) The English word means "the conducting, supervising, or managing of something; the careful and responsible management of something entrusted to one's care."
            (b) The Greek word for "steward" is *oikonomos,* which is a compound word of *oikos,* "a house," and *nemo*, "to manage." Literally the word means, "a house manager."
            (c) The emphasis is on responsible management of something that does not belong to you but belongs to someone else.
        2. The Parable of the Talents (Matt. 25:14-30) describes the Biblical emphasis of a steward.
            (a) The owner/master "delivered his goods" to the workers/servants (25:14).
            (b) The "goods" did not belong to the servants but to the master (cf. Luke 16:1).
            (c) Those entrusted with the master's goods were responsible for using them properly, increasing them where applicable, and then returning them to the master.
            (d) The principal amount and the increase all still belonged to the master, not the servant.
            (e) The servants were held accountable for how they managed their owner's goods.
        3. The concept of stewardship is found throughout Scripture, which will be examined in the following points.
    B. A Christian steward recognizes that all things belong to God.
        1. A Christian knows that he does not own anything, but he is only a steward.
        2. ALL THINGS belong to God! There is nothing that is not God's!
            (a) "The Lord made the heavens...the earth...and all that is in them" (Ex. 20:11).
            (b) "The earth is the Lord's, and all its fullness...and those who dwell therein" (Ps. 24:1).
            (c) "'The silver is Mine, and the gold is Mine,' says the Lord of hosts" (Hag. 2:8).
            (d) "For every beast of the forest is Mine, And the cattle on a thousand hills...If I were hungry, I would not tell you; For the world is Mine, and all its fullness" (Ps. 50:10-12).
        3. ALL BODIES belong to God!
            (a) He created all of us, therefore, we belong to Him (Gen. 1:26; 2:7; Jn. 1:3; Acts 17:28)!

                (1) Our very souls are His (Ezek. 18:4)!
                (2) Our very purpose for living is His (Isa. 43:7).
            (b) He bought us, therefore, we belong to Him (1 Cor. 6:19-20; 1 Pet. 1:18-19)!
        4. As hard as it can be to accept and admit, nothing that we have actually belongs to us!
            (a) This principle is the foundation of understanding Biblical stewardship.
            (b) By right of creation and by right of purchase, we belong to God!
    C. A Christian steward recognizes that all he has comes from God.
        1. "Every good gift and every perfect gift is from above…from the Father" (Jas. 1:17).
        2. God gives man wisdom (Jas. 1:5).
        3. God gives man the skills and ability to figure things out (Isa. 28:23-29).
        4. God gives man the power to obtain wealth (Deut. 8:17-18).
        5. God gives man (and all creatures) life and breath (Acts 17:25).
        6. God gives man all things (Acts 17:25).
        7. Paul asks this searching question, "And what do you have that you did not receive?" (1 Cor. 4:7).
    D. A Christian steward recognizes that he might possess, but he does not own.
        1. The early church recognized that what they personally possessed was not actually their own – "…neither did anyone say that any of the things he possessed was his own" (Acts 4:32).
        2. Since we are not the owners, stewards have only temporary control of God's gifts.
            (a) Job said, "Naked I came from my mother's womb, And naked shall I return there. The Lord gave, and the Lord has taken away; Blessed be the name of the Lord" (1:21).
            (b) Paul said, "For we brought nothing into this world, and it is certain we can carry nothing out" (1 Tim. 6:7).
        3. Since I do not own what I possess, I must be an especially diligent and careful steward!
    E. A Christian steward recognizes that he must give an account for his stewardship.
        1. God is looking for and expecting faithfulness in His stewards (1 Cor. 4:1-2; Luke 16:10).
        2. God is going to come and "settle accounts with His servants" one day (Mt. 18:23-24).
        3. Each one of us will "give account of himself to God" (Rom. 14:11).
        4. Each one of us will receive his due, "according to what he has done" (2 Cor. 5:10).
        5. We will be required to give an account for how we've managed His gifts (Mt. 25:14-30).
    F. A Christian steward will carefully manage his life, which belongs to God.
        1. Christians are to "glorify God in your body and in your spirit, which are God's" (1 Cor. 6:20).
        2. Christians are instructed to "present your bodies a living sacrifice…" (Rom. 12:1).
        3. As an example for us today, the Christians in Macedonia "first gave themselves to the Lord" (2 Cor. 8:5). Before they gave any money, they gave their own lives.
        4. In properly managing the body and life that God has given to us, we must be:
            (a) Faithful stewards of our minds (2 Cor. 10:5; Prov. 4:23; Psa. 119:97; Phil. 4:8).
            (b) Faithful stewards of our mouths (Ps. 141:3; 35:28; Pro. 18:21; 21:23; Jas. 1:19; 3:1-12).
            (c) Faithful stewards of our eyes (Job 31:1; Prov. 23:31; John 4:35; Col. 3:1-2; 1 Jn. 2:16).
            (d) Faithful stewards of our ears (Psa. 81:13; Prov. 10:20; 23:22; Mark 4:9; Rev. 2:7, 29).
            (e) Faithful stewards of our hands (Ecc. 9:10; Rom. 12:11; Col. 3:23; Eph. 4:28; Gal. 6:10).
            (f) Faithful stewards of our feet (Prov. 5:8; 4:27; Jer. 35:15; Psa. 119:59; 1 John 1:7).
            (g) Faithful stewards of our hearts (Matt. 22:37; Prov. 23:26; Deut. 10:12).
            (h) Faithful stewards of our influence (Rom. 14:7; 1 Pet. 4:1-5; Matt. 5:16; 1 Tim. 4:12).
            (i) Faithful stewards of our will (Matt. 6:10; Luke 22:42; Rev. 22:17; John 7:17).
        5. Our life belongs to God! Let us use it for Him and His service!

G. A Christian steward will carefully manage his <u>time</u>, which belongs to God.
  1. As with all things, even our time belongs to God. As a gift from Him, we must use it wisely, knowing that we will give an account to Him for how we manage His time.
  2. Time is an ever-passing commodity, which cannot be created or re-created.
     (a) The Bible speaks frequently about the passing of time (Job 14:1-2; 7:6-7; 9:25-26).
        (1) James summarizes it: "For what is your life? It is even a vapor that appears for a little time and then vanishes away" (Jas. 4:14).
     (b) The Bible speaks of using the time we have, for it is all we have (Matt. 6:33-34).
     (c) Time, once it has passed, "cannot be gathered up again" (2 Sam. 14:14).
     (d) We cannot create time, save time, lose time, rush time, slow time, borrow time, purchase time, etc.
     (e) Every person on earth has the same amount of time, which cannot be changed.
  3. Therefore, every bit of time with which we are blessed must be used very wisely.
     (a) The brevity and uncertainty of life/time give added emphasis to its value and our responsibility toward it.
     (b) We must learn to "number our days, that we may gain a heart of wisdom" (Ps. 90:12).
     (c) We must learn to "walk circumspectly...redeeming the time" (Eph. 5:15-16).
     (d) We must learn to see all things in life as "but for a moment" (2 Cor. 4:17).
     (e) We must learn to make use of every "opportunity" we have to "do good" (Gal. 6:10).
  4. Our time belongs to God! Let us use it for Him and His service!
H. A Christian steward will carefully manage his <u>abilities/skills</u>, which belong to God.
  1. As with all things, even our talents, abilities and skills belong to God. As gifts from Him, we must use them wisely, knowing that we will give an account to Him for how we manage them.
  2. All of our abilities and skills come from God.
     (a) We may tend to think that our abilities, talents, skills and jobs belong to us—that we have developed them, honed them and made them what they are (leaving God out of it). But such could not be further from the truth!
     (b) God does "freely give us all things" (Rom. 8:32).
     (c) "...In Him we live and move and have our being" (Acts 17:28).
     (d) The abilities that we have are blessings given to us directly from God.
  3. Therefore, every ability and skill with which we are blessed must be used very wisely.
     (a) "For everyone to whom much is given, from him much will be required" (Lk. 12:48).
     (b) "Whatever you do, do all to the glory of God" (1 Cor. 10:31).
     (c) God asked Moses a question that ought to ring in our ears when considering what we have from the Lord to use for Him, "What is that in your hand?" (Ex. 4:2).
     (d) The Parable of the Talents (Matt. 25:14-30) helps to put it into perspective.
        (1) God has given us gifts, "each according to his own ability" (25:15).
        (2) God expects us to be "faithful over" the things He has given us (25:21, 23).
        (3) God expects us to use them, develop them and increase them...for Him.
        (4) God will come to "settle accounts" with us, to see how we've used His gifts (v. 19).
        (5) Even if we are not the most talented, able and skillful person (like the one-talent man), what we have has still been given to us by God and must be used wisely.
  4. Our abilities, skills and talents belong to God! Let us use them for Him and His service!
I. A Christian steward will carefully manage his <u>money</u>, which belongs to God.
  1. As with all things, even our money belongs to God. As a gift from Him, we must use it wisely, knowing that we will give an account to Him for how we manage His money.

(a) Whenever we talk about money, and especially when we talk about "giving," people get uncomfortable and sometimes even defensive.
(b) Let us remember that even "our" money belongs to God (Psa. 24:1; Hag. 2:8).
(c) Let us remember that Jesus "loved us" and gave "Himself for us, an offering and a sacrifice to God" (Eph. 5:2), so that we could be saved from our sins (Gal. 1:4).
(d) Let us remember that "the love of money is a root of all kinds of evil" (1 Tim. 6:10).
(e) Let us remember that working hard and earning money are expectations of God (2 Thess. 3:10; Eph. 4:28), and that "every gift" in our paycheck is from Him (Jas. 1:17).
(f) Let us realize that the Bible has more to say about giving than nearly any other topic.
2. Proper management of money involves making good choices.
(a) We must make good choices in how we "earn" our money and not engage in unlawful, ungodly, unethical, questionable means of "gaining" money.
(b) We must make good choices in how we "spend" our money and not be wasteful (prodigal), thoughtless and entirely selfish in how we disperse and use our money.
(c) We must make good choices in how we "invest" our money and not "gamble" God's money away in casinos, card games, betting on sports, lotteries, raffles, etc.
3. Proper management of money involves giving back to God what He has given to us.
(a) If we will "first give ourselves to the Lord" (cf. 2 Cor. 8:5), giving money will be easier!
(b) If we will give "our bodies a living sacrifice" (Rom. 12:2), giving money will be easier!
(c) If we will remember how much the Lord gave for us (Gal. 2:20), giving will be easier!
(d) If we will see our giving as a demonstration of our love (2 Cor. 8:8, 24), it will be easier!
4. God has instructed us in the purpose of our giving to Him.
(a) We need to give because He commanded us to do so (1 Cor. 16:1-2; 2 Cor. 9:6-7).
(b) We need to give as "the proof" of the "sincerity" of our love for Him (2 Cor. 8:8, 24).
(c) We need to give because it is God's only means of supporting the needs of His church and the continued work of His kingdom on earth (1 Cor. 16:1-2; 9:14).
(d) The purpose of our giving is not about us! The purpose of our giving is about Him!
5. God has instructed us in the manner of our giving to Him.
(a) A Christian steward is to give to God firstly (Prov. 3:9-10; Matt. 6:33; Mal. 3:7-10).
(1) "Honor the Lord with your possessions, And with the firstfruits of all your increase" (Prov. 3:9).
(2) As someone has so aptly stated it: "God must not get 'what's left'! He must get 'what's right'!" God's portion is the first portion!
(3) Before taxes, rent, cars, food, education, etc. comes God's first-sized portion!
(b) A Christian steward is to give to God regularly (1 Cor. 16:1-2).
(1) "On the first day of every week," one of the avenues of worship (every week) is giving to God.
(2) The frequency of the giving is specified by the occurrence of the first day of the week—every week has a first day.
(3) Therefore, giving must be a priority and done weekly.
(c) A Christian steward is to give to God individually (1 Cor. 16:1-2).
(1) The instruction is, "...let each one of you." This cannot be done by proxy.
(2) Each one is responsible. No one can give to God for you or in your stead.
(3) Each one is to bear/carry part of the load (2 Cor. 8:13-15; cf. Mark 12:41-44).
(d) A Christian steward is to give to God systematically (1 Cor. 16:1-2).
(1) Each Lord's day, Christians are to "put something aside and store it up."
(2) The words here literally carry the idea of "putting into the treasury."

                (3) The local congregation must have a plan/system for giving on the first day.
            (e) A Christian steward is to give to God <u>proportionally</u> (1 Cor. 16:1-2; cf. 2 Cor. 9:12).
                (1) A Christian is to give "as he may prosper" or "in keeping with your income" (NIV).
                    (i) There is not a specific class of members addressed in this passage.
                    (ii) Every person of every class in the church is addressed.
                (2) As God has prospered (given to) each one, let that one give in return to God.
                (3) "…[T]o whom much is given…much will be required" (Luke 12:48). Everyone has been given "much" by God! For that, we will be held accountable.
                (4) The more one makes, the more one must give (incl. raises, bonuses, tips, etc.).
            (f) A Christian steward is to give to God <u>liberally</u> (2 Cor. 8:1-4, 7; 9:6; Prov. 11:24-25).
                (1) God wants Christians to give liberally (Rom. 12:8), abundantly (2 Cor. 8:7) and bountifully (2 Cor. 9:6).
                    (i) After all, He gave (and continues to give) in that exact manner to us!
                    (ii) Do we give with the same spirit that He gave to us?
                (2) Some in the Bible gave even beyond their ability (Mark 12:41-44; 2 Cor. 8:1-3).
                    (i) Do you suppose they suffered as a result?
            (g) A Christian steward is to give to God <u>purposefully</u> (2 Cor. 9:7; 8:10-15).
                (1) A Christian must "decide in his heart" (ESV) how much to give ahead of time.
                (2) There must be a personal plan and commitment in advance regarding our giving.
                (3) Our giving should not be done haphazardly or without proper forethought.
            (h) A Christian steward is to give to God <u>cheerfully</u> (2 Cor. 9:7; 8:12, 3).
                (1) A Christian must not give grudgingly, reluctantly or under compulsion (9:7).
                (2) There should first be a willing mind (8:12), which leads to a joy-filled heart longing (and eager) to express love and thanksgiving to God through giving.
                (3) The Christian should not look at giving as something we "have" to do, but something that we "get" to do because we "want" to do it!
                (4) Imagine if God looked at giving to us grudgingly, reluctantly or under compulsion! Thankfully He gave to us cheerfully, willingly and lovingly!
            (i) A Christian steward is to give to God <u>sacrificially</u> (2 Cor. 8:1-7; Lk. 21:1-4; Rom. 12:1).
                (1) God sacrificed His Son for us!
                (2) Jesus sacrificed Himself for us!
                (3) Do we readily and truly sacrifice in our giving to Him?
                (4) Do we willingly sacrifice, not for our good, but His?
                (5) King David announced that he refused to "offer burnt offerings to the Lord my God with that which costs me nothing" (2 Sam. 24:24).
    6. God has instructed us in the <u>promised blessings</u> of our giving to Him.
        (a) Scripture is full of wonderful promises to those who put the Lord first in their giving:
            (1) "Give, and it will be given to you: good measure, pressed down, shaken together, and running over will be put into your bosom" (Luke 6:38).
            (2) "…All these things shall be added to you" (Matt. 6:33).
            (3) "Whatever a man sows, that he will also reap" (Gal. 6:7).
            (4) "He who sows bountifully will also reap bountifully" (2 Cor. 9:6).
            (5) "God is able to make all grace abound toward you…" (2 Cor. 9:8-12).
            (6) "It is more blessed to give than to receive" (Acts 20:35).
        (b) God bestows great blessings upon those who give freely and lovingly to Him! Read also Proverbs 3:9-10; 11:24-25; Malachi 3:8-10; Luke 18:28-30; 2 Chronicles 31:10-11.
    7. Our money belongs to God! Let us use it for Him and His service!

J. A Christian steward will carefully manage <u>the gospel and men's souls</u>, which belong to God.
   1. Christians are the "earthen vessels" entrusted with the saving gospel of Christ (2 Cor. 4:7).
      (a) As Ruth Carruth penned in a favorite hymn, "Into our hands the gospel is given."
      (b) The gospel has no hands or feet of its own. We are responsible for carrying it into all the world (Mark 16:15).
   2. Christians know the value of the soul and its need for God's salvation (Matt. 10:28).
      (a) Christians recognize the preciousness of each soul to God (John 3:16; Ezek. 18:4).
      (b) Christians recognize the lost condition of every soul around them (Rom. 3:23).
      (c) Christians recognize the personal commission given by Jesus (Matt. 28:18-20).
   3. Christians are responsible for converging these two things under their stewardship:
      (a) The saving message of the gospel of Jesus Christ,
      (b) With the lost souls that surround them every day (Mark 16:15).
   4. Faithful Christian stewards will:
      (a) "See souls" around them every day.
      (b) Seek out (and make) opportunities to share the gospel with them.
      (c) Pray for doors of opportunity to be opened (Col. 4:3).
      (d) Not be ashamed of the gospel of Christ and their responsibility to teach it.
      (e) Not make excuses for failing to carry out the Great Commission.
   5. The gospel and men's souls belong to God! Let us be good stewards of both!
K. All that we have belongs to God and has been entrusted to our care and management!
   1. God expects us to use, develop and increase all that He has bestowed upon us...for Him, for His cause and for His good!
   2. Christians must be faithful stewards of their lives, time, abilities, money and the gospel!
   3. All Christians will give an account to God for how they have used His gifts to them!
   4. The manner in which we use His gifts is a demonstration of our love and devotion to Him!

V. **According to Scripture, the Christian Life Is to Be Characterized By Active Membership.**
   A. Membership in the local church is essential!
      1. The Bible uses the word "church" primarily in two senses (see also pages 88 and 130).
         (a) In a "universal" sense, it refers to all saved persons of all time in all places.
            (1) This is how Jesus used the word when He promised His disciples, "I will build my church" (Matt. 16:18).
            (2) This is how Paul used the word when he affirmed that "Christ is head of the church" (Eph. 5:23), and that there is only "one" (Eph. 4:4+1:22-23).
         (b) In a "local" sense, it refers to a group of Christians in a local community.
            (1) This is how the Bible used the word when Paul visited various congregations or appointed elders in congregations (Acts 13:1; 14:23; 20:17).
            (2) This is how the Bible used the word when Paul wrote letters to specific congregations of the Lord's church (1 Cor. 1:2; 1 Thess. 1:1; Gal. 1:2).
            (3) This is how the Bible used the word when elders were instructed "to shepherd the church of God" (Acts 20:28).
      2. When baptized into Christ, a person is automatically "added" to the church (Ac. 2:41, 47).
         (a) This is the church "universal"—i.e., the body of Christ composed of all the saved.
         (b) One is "baptized into one body" (1 Cor. 12:13), added by God to that body.
         (c) The saved are in the church; and the church is all the saved (Acts 2:47; Eph. 5:23).
         (d) Membership in Christ's universal church is automatic, expected and divinely fulfilled upon one's conversion to Christ.

3. Once converted, every Christian must become associated with a local congregation.
   (a) In the book of Acts, the first converts of a city became an established local church.
   (b) The local church was a group of Christians who were banded together to work and worship together in collectively serving the Lord.
   (c) A Christian being a member of a local congregation was and is not optional.
      (1) The first Christians "were together" (Acts 2:42-46).
         (i) Christians did not remain separate or "members at large."
      (2) When Saul, a Christian, came to Jerusalem, "he tried to join the disciples" (9:26).
         (i) The word "join" comes from the Greek word *kollao*, which means "*cling to, attach to...associate with* on intimate terms, *join*" (BDAG [2000], p. 556).
         (ii) Paul did not move to town and not seek to attach himself to a local church.
      (3) Saul and Barnabas were among those "in the church at Antioch" (13:1; 11:26).
      (4) Phoebe was a "servant of the church in Cenchrea" (Rom. 16:1).
      (5) Onesimus was "one of you" – a member of the church in Colosse (Col. 4:9).
   (d) Paul emphasized that "the body is not one member but many" (1 Cor. 12:14).
      (1) Therefore, where two or more Christians unite in a community, a congregation of the Lord's church is formed.
      (2) The local church is "joined and held together by every joint [member]" (Eph. 4:16).
   (e) Each local church is to be properly organized, with elders from "among" each congregation overseeing and deacons serving (Acts 14:23; 20:28; Phil. 1:1).
      (1) There was no organization in the church higher than the local congregation.
      (2) No elders ever served in any capacity except in and over a local congregation.
      (3) Therefore, this necessitated that:
         (i) The elders must be members of that local congregation (to oversee it).
         (ii) There must be members in that local congregation (to be overseen).
   (f) Each local church assembled as a body to worship (Ac. 2:42; 20:7; 1 Cor. 11:17-23).
   (g) Why would God give specific purposes for the local church and why would He place such emphasis on the local church if membership was an optional matter?
      (1) Why would God emphasize each individual member if it was just optional?
      (2) Why would God organize the local church if it was just optional?
      (3) Why would God expect worshipers to assemble together if it was optional?
4. The local church remains today a group of Christians who are banded together to work and worship together in collectively serving the Lord.
   (a) There is no such thing, in the New Testament, as being a member "at large."
   (b) God expects every Christian to be an active part of a local congregation of His church.
   (c) The local congregation is God's only collective functioning unit to carry out His work.
5. As with any divine organization, membership in the Lord's church has responsibilities!
   (a) One cannot be a member of a local congregation with no responsibilities.
   (b) When one is part of a family, there are responsibilities.
   (c) When one is part of a kingdom, there are responsibilities.
   (d) When one is part of a body, there are responsibilities.
   (e) When one is part of an army, there are responsibilities.

B. Each church member is responsible for being an active member of the local church!
   1. Every Christian needs to "be ready for every good work," be "zealous for good works" and "be careful to maintain good works" (Tit. 2:14, 3:1, 8).
      (a) Every Christian is "created in Christ Jesus for good works" (Eph. 2:10).
      (b) Therefore, every Christian is to be active in serving the Lord.

2. This work is to be done cooperatively and collectively in the church (Eph. 4:16).
   (a) The Bible emphasizes "every joint" and "every part" of the body must be working.
   (b) Every part must be "joined and knit together" to the other parts and do its "share."
   (c) Every part must be involved in "supplying," "working," "doing" and "edifying."
   (d) When every part does the work, it "causes growth" of the whole body.
   (e) This verse alone demands that every Christian be:
      (1) A member of a local congregation.
      (2) An active member of a local congregation
      (3) An interactive member of a local congregation.
   (f) A Christian who seeks to "be a Christian" outside of and separate from a local congregation finds no support (or even existence) in the New Testament.
3. God has a place and a function in His body for every member of the church (1 Cor. 12:12-27; Rom 12:3-8).
   (a) While some "functions" will be different from others, some will seem more significant than others, some will appear less honorable, they are all essential!
   (b) We must each find and utilize our "function" in the local body to the glory of God!
   (c) The health, maturity and growth of the Lord's church (in the local congregation) is dependent upon our personal and active involvement in the work!
   (d) Like Jesus, we "must be about [our] Father's business" (Luke 2:49).
   (e) Like Archippus and Timothy, we must "fulfill" our various responsibilities in the church and not leave them unfulfilled (Col. 4:17; 2 Tim. 4:5).
4. Membership and active involvement in the local church is not optional! It is essential!

C. Each church member is responsible for attending and participating in worship assemblies!
   1. The Lord expects His children to worship Him (Matt. 4:10; John 4:23-24).
   2. The Lord expects His children to worship Him every Sunday (1 Cor. 16:1-2; Acts 20:7).
   3. The Lord expects His children to truly participate in every aspect of worship (Acts 2:42).
   4. The Lord expects His children not to "forsake the assembling together" (Heb. 10:24-26).
   5. There are many reasons why we should attend every service, including:
      (a) To express and prove my love for the Lord (John 14:15).
      (b) To obey the command of God (Heb. 10:25; Acts 20:7).
      (c) To consider my brothers and sisters in Christ (Heb. 10:24).
      (d) To stimulate my brothers and sisters to love and good works (Heb. 10:24).
      (e) To encourage and build up my fellow brethren (Heb. 10:25; Rom. 1:11-12).
      (f) To express and prove my love for my brethren (1 John 4:7-12; John 13:34-35).
      (g) To do my part as a member of the body (1 Cor. 12:12-27; Eph. 4:16).
      (h) To exhibit the priorities that Christ wants me to have (Matt. 6:33).
      (i) To be where Jesus is and to commune with Him (Heb. 2:12; Matt. 26:29; 18:20).
      (j) To be where I should be when Jesus returns (2 Pet. 3:14; Mt. 24:36; 25:13; Lk. 12:43).
      (k) To remember Jesus just like He told me to do (Luke 22:19; 1 Cor. 11:24-25).
      (l) To have an opportunity to praise God as He desires and expects (Jn. 4:24; Mt. 4:10).
      (m) To draw closer to God, which is what I long to do (Jas. 4:7-10; Psa. 122:1).
      (n) To enjoy a foretaste of heaven (Rev. 5:9-14; 14:1-3; 15:1-3; 2:10).
      (o) To guard against falling away (the book of Hebrews; 2 Pet. 2:20-22; 1 Cor. 11:20-33).
      (p) To be the priest God expects me to be (Rev. 1:6; 1 Pet. 2:5; Heb. 13:15).
      (q) To satisfy my hunger and thirst for righteousness (Matt. 5:6; 1 Pet. 2:2-3).
      (r) To show the deep sincerity of my faith—I'm not pretending (1 Pet. 1:7-9; 2 Tim. 1:5).
      (s) To avoid a sin of omission and suffering the consequences (Heb. 10:25-31; Jas. 4:17).

- (t) To focus my heart and mind on what is most important (Matt. 22:37-40).
- (u) To follow the example of the early church (Acts 2:42; 20:7; 1 Cor. 16:1-2; 14:23).
- (v) To benefit from being in the presence of God and from fellowshipping with faithful brethren (Isa. 6:1-8; Acts 2:42).
- (w) To be in subjection to the elders and to show them that I want to make their shepherding a joy (Heb. 13:17).
- (x) To set a good example for others and not give an occasion for stumbling (Matt. 5:16; 1 Cor. 11:1; 1 Tim. 4:12; Matt. 18:6; Rom. 14:13; 15:1-2).
- (y) To strengthen my faith and my resolve and to not deprive myself (2 Pet. 3:18; Rom. 10:17; Psa. 119:9-16; Rev. 2:10; 1 Tim. 4:16; Heb. 5:12-6:1).
- (z) Because Jesus died on the cross for me (Gal. 2:20). Where else would I want to be?
6. We should see worship as something we *get* to do, not something we *have* to do!
   - (a) Worship is not merely about attendance but about wholehearted participation.
   - (b) Our hearts should long to worship God every week with great gladness (Ps. 122:1).
   - (c) When the church assembles, where else would a child of God want to be?
   - (d) We must not look to do *as little as we can*, but long to do *all that we can* for God!
   - (e) Some Christians see "going to church" as the major portion of their Christian responsibilities. However, it is only a part of what God expects of us.
7. Participating regularly in worship assemblies of the church is not optional! It is essential!
8. See Lesson 15 for more details on the avenues of New Testament worship.

D. Each church member is responsible for ministering to the other members of the church!
   1. The Lord says that members of His body are "members of one another" (Rom. 12:4-5).
      - (a) That verse is also translated, "Each member belongs to all the others" (NIV).
      - (b) "One another" is a reciprocal pronoun, which indicates:
         - (1) There is mutual action, interaction and responsibility.
         - (2) The action of any verbs associated with it is a two-way action.
         - (3) As two people mutually carry out an action, they both mutually benefit from the action.
      - (c) There is a reciprocal relationship that exists between the members of Christ's body.
      - (d) We are literally responsible:
         - (1) *To* each other and
         - (2) *For* each other in the sight of God.
   2. We are responsible for exhibiting Christian attitudes toward one another.
      - (a) We are to "love one another" (John 13:34-35; 15:12; 1 Pet. 3:8; 4:8).
      - (b) We are to "give preference to one another" (Rom. 12:10; cf. Phil. 2:3-4; Eph. 5:21).
      - (c) We are to "be kindly affectionate to one another" (Rom. 12:10; Eph. 4:32).
      - (d) We are to have "compassion for one another" (1 Pet. 3:8; Rom. 12:16; 15:5).
      - (e) We are to "consider one another...to stir up love and good works" (Heb. 10:24).
      - (f) We are to "bear with one another" (Eph. 4:2; Col. 3:13).
   3. We are responsible for engaging in Christian actions toward one another.
      - (a) We are to have "fellowship with one another" (1 John 1:7; Rom. 15:7).
      - (b) We are to "be hospitable to one another" (1 Pet. 4:9; Heb. 13:1-2).
      - (c) We are to "edify" and "exhort one another" (1 Thess. 5:11; Heb. 3:13).
      - (d) We are to "comfort" and "encourage one another" (1 Thess. 4:18; Heb. 10:25).
      - (e) We are to "admonish one another" (Rom. 15:14; Col. 3:16).
      - (f) We are to "serve one another" through love (Gal. 5:13; 6:10; 1 Pet. 4:10).
      - (g) We are to "bear one another's burdens" (Gal. 6:2).

(h) We are to "forgive one another" (Eph. 4:32; Matt. 6:14-15).
    (i) We are to "pray for one another" (Jas. 5:16).
   4. There is a mutual responsibility to look out for and "care for one another" (1 Cor. 12:25).
      (a) "If one member suffers, all the members suffer with" him/her (1 Cor. 12:26).
      (b) We "rejoice with those who rejoice, and weep with those who weep" (Rom. 12:15).
      (c) We must "warn the unruly, comfort the fainthearted, uphold the weak" (1 Th. 5:14).
      (d) We must look out for those who are weak and endeavor to restore them (Gal. 6:1), for we could "save a soul from death and cover a multitude of sins" (Jas. 5:19-20).
      (e) "Therefore, as we have opportunity, let us do good to all, especially to those who are of the household of faith" (Gal. 6:10).
   5. Caring for and ministering to other members of the church is not optional! It is essential!
E. Each church member is responsible for preserving the unity and purity of the body!
   1. The Lord desires for His body to be united in doctrine and practice (Eph. 4:1-16).
      (a) His desire is for "brethren to dwell together in unity" (Psa. 133:1).
      (b) His desire is for His people to be "one," as the Father and the Son (John 17:20-21).
      (c) His desire is for His people to be of "one heart and one soul" (Acts 4:32).
      (d) His desire is for His people to be of "one mind" (Phil. 1:27; 2:2; Rom. 12:16).
      (e) His desire is for "no divisions" or "schism" to be in His body (1 Cor. 1:10; 12:25).
      (f) His desire is for His people to all "walk by the same rule" (Phil. 3:16).
      (g) His desire is that we "all speak the same thing" (1 Cor. 1:10; cf. 1 Tim. 1:3).
      (h) His desire is for there to be "the unity of the Spirit in the bond of peace" (Eph. 4:3).
      (i) His desire is that we "put on love, which is the bond of unity" (Col. 3:14, NASB).
   2. The unity of the body of Christ depends on each member (Phil. 1:27-2:11; Rom. 12:18).
      (a) We must be humble in our dealings with each other (Phil. 2:3-11; 1 Pet. 5:5).
      (b) We must set the proper example and influence (Mt. 5:13-14; 1 Tim. 4:12; Ro. 14:13).
      (c) We must be impartial in our treatment of each other (Jas. 2:1-9; 3:17; Ac. 10:34-35).
      (d) We must control our anger (Eph. 4:26-27), our selfishness (Jas. 3:17), our words (Jas. 3:1-12), our urge to talk about others (1 Tim. 5:13; 1 Pet. 4:15), etc.
      (e) We must settle disputes in God's prescribed manner (Matt. 18:15-20; 5:23-24).
   3. Preserving the unity of the body also involves preserving the purity of the body.
      (a) While the Lord wants His church to be united, all unity is not desired or accepted.
         (1) The church must not be united with doctrinal error (Rom. 16:17; 2 Jn. 9-11).
         (2) The church must not be united with the "works of darkness" (Eph. 5:11).
         (3) The church must not be united with "unbelievers" (2 Cor. 6:14-7:1).
         (4) The church must not be united with those who will not repent (Mt. 18:15-20).
      (b) While we all sin, if a member will not repent of sin, his fellow members must act.
         (1) The Lord tells us to not have fellowship with brethren living in sin (1 Cor. 5:1-13).
         (2) The Lord tells us to withdraw from those who walk disorderly (2 Thess. 3:6-15).
         (3) The Lord tells us that we cannot allow sin to persist in the church (1 Cor. 5:1-7).
      (c) Withdrawing fellowship is not done to "kick someone out" or to be unkind.
         (1) It is done as an action of love for the person and his soul (Heb. 12:5-11).
         (2) It is done to help create a sense of shame in his heart and life (2 Thess. 3:14).
         (3) It is done to help him to "be saved in the day of the Lord Jesus" (1 Cor. 5:5).
         (4) It is done to help preserve the purity of the whole church (1 Cor. 5:6-8).
         (5) It is done to help save the world from sin (1 Cor. 5:7-13).
      (d) Even after withdrawing fellowship, we must urge repentance (2 Th. 3:15; Gal. 6:1).
      (e) See Lesson 22 for more details on withdrawing fellowship.

4. When the unity and purity of the body of Christ is preserved:
   (a) Souls of brethren who "wander from the truth" can be saved (Jas. 5:19-10).
   (b) Brethren who have been "overtaken in sin" can be restored (Gal. 6:1).
   (c) "The world" will have an opportunity to "believe" in Jesus (John 17:20-21).
   (d) The Lord describes it this way: "Behold, how good and how pleasant it is for brethren to dwell together in unity!" (Psa. 133:1).
5. Preserving the unity and purity of the body is not optional! It is essential!

F. Each church member is responsible for teaching and defending the truth!
   1. The commission of the Lord to His church is the commission of the Lord to each member.
      (a) Each of us have a personal responsibility to:
         (1) "Preach the gospel" to lost souls around us in the world (Mark 16:15).
         (2) "Teach them to observe all things" that Jesus commanded (Matt. 28:19-29).
         (3) "Bear much fruit," that we may be disciples and God may be glorified (Jn. 15:1-8).
         (4) "Commit" the truth to others "who will be able to teach others also" (2 Tim. 2:2).
      (b) It is not merely the responsibility of the preacher or elders to teach the gospel!
         (1) It is the responsibility of every Christian!
         (2) The early Christians "went everywhere preaching the word" (Acts 8:4).
      (c) We must not be "ashamed of the gospel of Christ" (Rom. 1:16) or of the trials that preaching it may bring into our lives (2 Tim. 1:8, 12).
         (1) We must be willing to teach it in public and in private (Acts 5:42; 20:20).
         (2) We must be willing to teach with boldness and confidence (Acts 19:8; 28:31).
         (3) We must be willing to endure any hardships that come with it (2 Cor. 4:6-11).
   2. The church is commissioned to both teach the truth and defend the truth.
      (a) Each of us have a personal responsibility to:
         (1) Take a stand for "the defense of the gospel" (Phil. 1:16-17).
         (2) "Contend earnestly for the faith" (Jude 3).
         (3) "Strive together for the faith of the gospel (Phil. 1:27).
         (4) "Always be ready to give a defense to everyone who asks…" (1 Pet. 3:15).
         (5) Ensure the church remains "the pillar and ground of the truth" (1 Tim. 3:15).
      (b) Again, this is the responsibility of every member, not just the preacher or elders!
      (c) To effectively defend the gospel:
         (1) We must have a good knowledge of the gospel (Eph. 5:17; 2 Pet. 1:5; 3:18).
         (2) We must have a true faith in the gospel (Rom. 1:16-17; 10:9-17; Heb. 11:6).
         (3) We must have a deep love for the gospel (2 Thess. 2:10; Psa. 119:47, 97, 127).
   3. The gospel of Jesus was precious to us when we obeyed it so that it could save us!
      (a) The gospel of Jesus must remain precious to us, so that we long to teach it!
      (b) The gospel of Jesus must remain precious to us, so that we long to defend it!
   4. Teaching and defending the truth of the gospel is not optional! It is essential!

G. Each church member is responsible for respecting and submitting to the elders!
   1. The Lord Himself is the one who set up and designed His church!
      (a) He set up Christ as the one and only "head of the church" (Eph. 5:23).
      (b) He set up His church to have certain men "oversee" local congregations (Acts 14:23).
      (c) He set up His church to have no organizational structure higher than the local level.
      (d) He set up His church to have every Christian to be a member of a local congregation (see V, A-B beginning on page 393) and for certain men from that local church to "shepherd the flock of God which is among" them (1 Pet. 5:2).

2. The Lord specified the qualifications and work of the men who lead the local church.
   (a) These men must meet the divine qualifications in 1 Timothy 3:1-7 and Titus 1:5-9.
   (b) These men are responsible for:
      (1) "Serving as overseers" of the work of the congregation (Acts 20:28; 1 Pet. 5:2).
      (2) "Shepherd[ing] the church of God" (Acts 20:28; 1 Pet. 5:2).
      (3) Protecting the congregation from "savage wolves" that seek to destroy the local congregation and "draw away the disciples" (Acts 20:29-30).
      (4) Feeding the flock, ensuring they are properly nourished (John 21:15-17).
   (c) These men are responsible to God for the spiritual welfare and eternal destiny of the congregation (Heb. 13:17).
   (d) These men are called bishops, elders, overseers, shepherds and pastors.
   (e) See Lesson 13 for more on the qualifications and responsibilities of the elders.
3. Each member is responsible for humbly following the eldership, as they follow Christ.
   (a) We must respect and honor those men who are elders (1 Thess. 5:12; 1 Tim. 5:17).
   (b) We must respect their God-given authority (Acts 20:28-32; 1 Tim. 3:5; Heb. 13:7, 17).
   (c) We must respect their weighty responsibility as elders (Heb. 13:17).
   (d) We must "esteem them very highly in love for their work's sake" (1 Thess. 5:13).
   (e) We must emulate their faith and follow their godly example (Heb. 13:7; 1 Pet. 5:3).
   (f) We must submit to them and obey them (Heb. 13:17).
   (g) We must make their work a joy and not a grief (Heb. 13:17).
   (h) We must pray for our elders (1 Tim. 2:1-2).
   (i) We must be slow and cautious with criticism and not receive unwarranted or uncorroborated accusations (1 Tim. 5:19).
4. God put elders in place to watch for our souls.
   (a) To respect and submit to our elders is to respect and submit to God!
   (b) To disrespect and rebel against our elders is to disrespect and rebel against God!
   (c) Let us have respect for God, respect for His plan and respect for our elders!
5. Respecting and submitting to elders is not optional! It is essential!

H. Active and responsible membership in the Lord's church is not optional! It is essential!
   1. Every member is needed, so that the body can properly function and grow as designed!
   2. Every Christian must be an active part of a local congregation of the Lord's church!
   3. Every Christian must actively participate in the worship of the church, in the lives of the members, in the unity of the body and in the teaching and defending of the truth!
   4. Every Christian must respect and submit to the elders who shepherd the congregation!

VI. Conclusion
A. The Christian life is the most blessed life on this earth!
   1. Jesus announced, "I have come that they may have life, and that they may have it more abundantly" (John 10:10).
   2. Faithful New Testament Christians are the most blessed people living on earth!
   3. Jesus intended for the Christian life to stand out above all others, as He repeatedly emphasized the word "Blessed" in the Sermon on the Mount (Matt. 5:3-10):
      (a) "Blessed are the poor in spirit, For theirs is the kingdom of heaven."
      (b) "Blessed are those who mourn, For they shall be comforted."
      (c) "Blessed are the meek, For they shall inherit the earth."
      (d) "Blessed are those who hunger and thirst for righteousness, For they shall be filled."
      (e) "Blessed are the merciful, For they shall obtain mercy."
      (f) "Blessed are the pure in heart, For they shall see God."

- (g) "Blessed are the peacemakers, For they shall be called sons of God."
- (h) "Blessed are those who are persecuted for righteousness' sake…"
    4. There is no other life on this earth like the Christian life!
  B. The faithful Christian is promised eternal life with God in heaven!
    1. Faithful Christians are promised "the crown of life" (Rev. 2:10).
    2. Faithful Christians are promised "the crown of righteousness" (2 Tim. 4:8).
    3. Faithful Christians are promised "eternal life" (Matt. 25:46; Rom. 6:23; 1 John 5:11).
    4. Faithful Christians are promised "an eternal house in heaven" (2 Cor. 5:1, NIV).
    5. Faithful Christians are promised "rest from their labors" (Rev. 14:13; Heb. 4:1-11).
    6. Faithful Christians are promised to "always be with the Lord" (1 Thess. 4:17).
  C. With such a blessed life to enjoy in Christ now and the promise of eternal life with Christ:
    1. Let us determine to "be holy" as our Lord is "holy" (1 Pet. 1:15-16)!
    2. Let us determine to unashamedly wear the name of Christ (1 Pet. 4:16)!
    3. Let us determine to "be steadfast" and "faithful unto death" (1 Cor. 15:58; Rev. 2:10)!
    4. Let us determine to be "always abounding in the work of the Lord" (1 Cor. 15:58)!
    5. Let us determine to "set [our] mind on things above" and not "this earth" (Col. 3:2)!
    6. Let us determine to be "transformed" even more into His "image" (2 Cor. 3:18)!
    7. Let us determine to have the "mind" Christ—thinking and acting like Him (Phil. 2:5)!
    8. Let us determine to "grow in the grace and knowledge of our Lord" (2 Pet. 3:18)!
    9. Let us determine to "give all diligence" to increase our faith (2 Pet. 1:5-11)!
    10. Let us determine to "study" and "accurately handle" the Word of God (2 Tim. 2:15)!
    11. Let us determine to "continue steadfastly in prayer" (Rom. 12:12; Col. 4:2)!
    12. Let us determine to "not forsake the assembling of ourselves together" (Heb. 10:25)!
    13. Let us determine to "go into all the world and preach the gospel" (Mark 16:15)!
    14. Let us determine to be "faithful stewards" of all God has entrusted to us (1 Cor. 4:2)!
    15. Let us determine to "work" and do our "share" as part of the body of Christ (Eph. 4:16)!
    16. Let us determine to "serve one another" through *agape* love (Gal. 5:13)!
    17. Let us determine to "do good," especially to our family in Christ (Gal. 6:10)!
    18. Let us determine to "keep the unity of the Spirit in the bond of peace" (Eph. 4:3)!
    19. Let us determine to "contend earnestly for the faith…delivered" to us (Jude 3)!
    20. Let us determine to "respect" and "honor" our elders (1 Thess. 5:12; 1 Tim. 5:17)!
  D. As we contemplate and apply what God's Word teaches us about the Christian life:
    1. Let us examine ourselves—comparing ourselves to the divine standard.
    2. Let us challenge ourselves—urging ourselves to conform even more to His will.
    3. Let us improve ourselves—finding those areas that need our attention the most.
    4. Let us commit ourselves—determining to fix our eyes on Jesus and never look back.
    5. Let us enjoy ourselves—knowing that we are experiencing the abundant life.
  E. How strong is your faith? How fortified is your faith?
    1. God's Word is the source of a fortified faith (Rom. 10:17)! Let's get in it and stay in it!
    2. God's Word is the foundation of a fortified faith (Col. 2:7)! Let's get in it and stay in it!
    3. God's Word is the power for a fortified faith (Acts 20:32)! Let's get in it and stay in it!
    4. Let us determine to be faithful students of His Word (Acts 17:11), faithful stewards of His work (1 Cor. 4:2) and faithful servants in His church (1 Cor. 15:58)!
    5. Let us determine to put the Lord, His church and His will first in our lives (Mt. 6:33; 7:21)!
    6. And, in all things, to God be the glory!

Recommended Resources

<u>Books</u>

Black, V.P. *Lord, Teach Us How to Give.* Chickasaw, AL: V.P. Black, 1971.

---. *My God and My Money.* Chickasaw, AL: V.P. Black, 1969.

---. *Rust As a Witness.* Chickasaw, AL: V.P. Black, 1968.

Brownlow, Leroy. *Some "Do's" and "Don'ts" for the Christian.* Fort Worth: Brownlow Publishing, 1951.

---. *The Christian's Everyday Problems.* Fort Worth: Brownlow Publishing, 1966.

Harris, Mason. *Now That You Are in Christ.* Bowling Green, KY: Guardian of Truth, 1998.

McCay, Quentin. *The Life of a Christian.* Bowling Green, KY: Guardian of Truth, 1998.

Winkler, Wendell. *Heart Diseases and Their Cure.* Tuscaloosa, AL: Winkler Publications, 1972.

---. *The Mission of the Local Church.* Tuscaloosa, AL: Winkler Publications, 1971.

---. *Toward Spiritual Maturity.* Tuscaloosa, AL: Winkler Publications, 1974.

<u>Articles</u>

Black, V.P. "Identifying Marks of a Faithful Steward." *Lord, Teach Us How to Give.* Chickasaw, AL: V.P. Black, 1971. 3-8.

---. "Some Facts About Our Contribution." *Lord, Teach Us How to Give.* Chickasaw, AL: V.P. Black, 1971. 27-32.

Brownlow, Leroy. "Because of Its Teaching and Practice Concerning Prayer." *Why I Am a Member of the Church of Christ.* Fort Worth: Brownlow Publishing, 1973. 124-131.

Cogdill, Roy E. "Church Membership." *New Testament Church.* Fairmount, IN: Truth Magazine Bookstore, 1982. 33-43.

Fulford, Hugh. "Forsake Not the Assembly." *The Spiritual Sword* (Apr. 2000): 8-10.

Jackson, Wayne. "Effective Bible Study – An Urgent Need for Everyone." *ChristianCourier.com* https://www.christiancourier.com/articles/371-effective-bible-study-an-urgent-need-for-everyone

---."What About 'Local' Church Membership?" *ChristianCourier.com* https://www.christiancourier.com/articles/781-what-about-local-church-membership

Jenkins, Ancil. "Pray Without Ceasing." *The Spiritual Sword* (Apr. 2008): 20-23.

Jenkins, Dan. "She Upholds God's Standard for Godly Living." *Introducing the Church of Christ.* Ed. Alvin Jennings. Fort Worth: Star Bible, 1981. 126-130.

Jenkins, Jerry. "If You Do These Things." *The Spiritual Sword* (Apr. 2000): 34-37.

Warnock, Weldon E. "Soul Winners for Jesus." *Bible Basic for Believers.* Bowling Green, KY: Guardian of Truth, 1989. 57-61.

Winkler, Wendell. "Add to Your Faith." *Toward Spiritual Maturity.* Tuscaloosa, AL: Winkler Publications, 1974. 12-18.

---. "Bury Not Thy Talent." *Toward Spiritual Maturity.* Tuscaloosa, AL: Winkler Publications, 1974. 56-61.

---. "Give Attendance to Reading…Meditate…Study." *Toward Spiritual Maturity.* Tuscaloosa, AL: Winkler Publications, 1974. 27-33.

---. "Giving: A Spiritual Barometer." *Worship That Pleases God (South Florida Lectureship).* Ed. David Sproule. Palm Beach Gardens, FL: Palm Beach Lakes church of Christ, 2000. 265-274.

---. "He That Winneth Souls Is Wise." *Toward Spiritual Maturity.* Tuscaloosa, AL: Winkler Publications, 1974. 68-74.

---. "Keep Thy Heart With All Diligence and Watch Your Habits." *Toward Spiritual Maturity.* Tuscaloosa, AL: Winkler Publications, 1974. 34-41.

---. "Keep Your Windows Toward Jerusalem Open." *Toward Spiritual Maturity.* Tuscaloosa, AL: Winkler Publications, 1974. 19-26.

---. "Let Us Go into the House of the Lord and Worship God." *Toward Spiritual Maturity.* Tuscaloosa, AL: Winkler Publications, 1974. 42-48.

---. "The Local Church and I." *The Mission of the Local Church.* Tuscaloosa, AL: Winkler Publications, 1971. 8-15.

---. "Members of One Another." *Toward Spiritual Maturity.* Tuscaloosa, AL: Winkler Publications, 1974. 62-67.

Woodson, William. "Be Set for the Defense of the Gospel." *The Spiritual Sword* (Apr. 2000): 30-33.

---. "Grow in Knowledge." *The Spiritual Sword* (Apr. 2008): 16-19.

Periodicals

The Spiritual Sword. December 1970. "Evangelism."

The Spiritual Sword. July 1971. "Worldliness."

The Spiritual Sword. July 1978. "Christian Ethics."

The Spiritual Sword. January 1981. "Keep on Growing."

The Spiritual Sword. October 1990. "Moral Issues Facing the Christian."

The Spiritual Sword. April 2000. "How to Remain Faithful."

The Spiritual Sword. April 2008. "Daily Christian Living."

The Spiritual Sword. July 2010. "A Handy Guide to Biblical Morality."

Made in United States
Orlando, FL
20 August 2022